ATLAS OF HUMAN PHYSIOLOGY

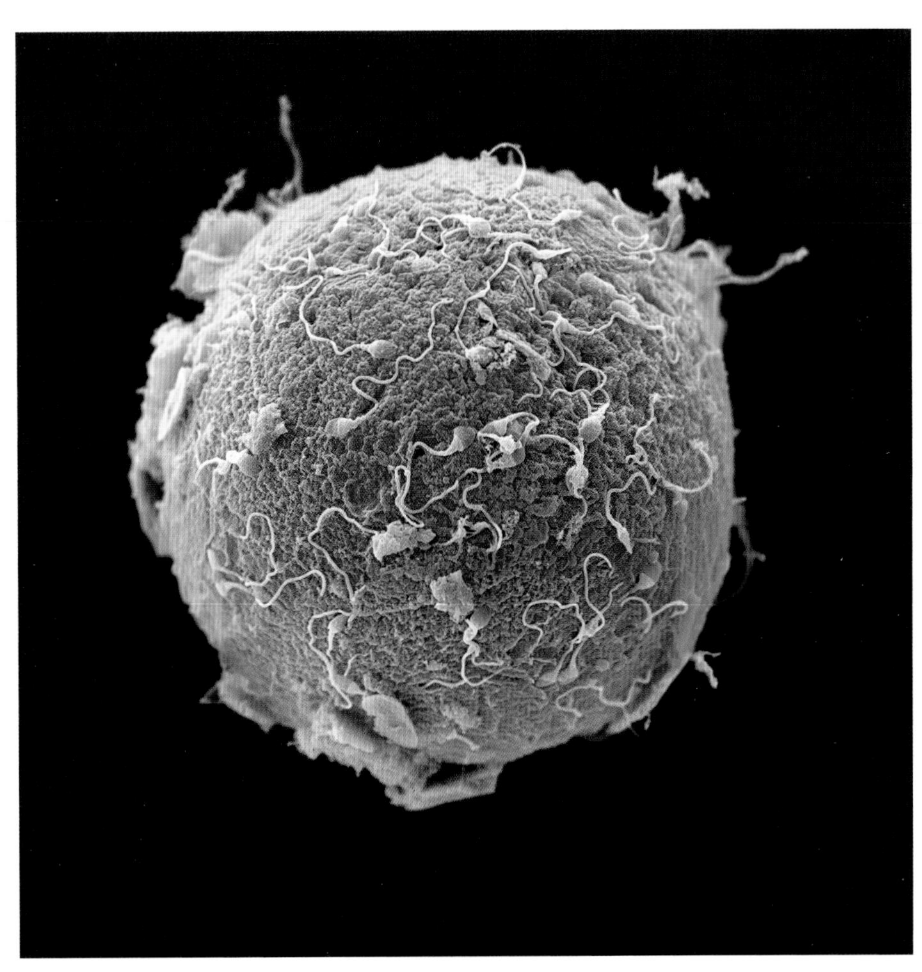

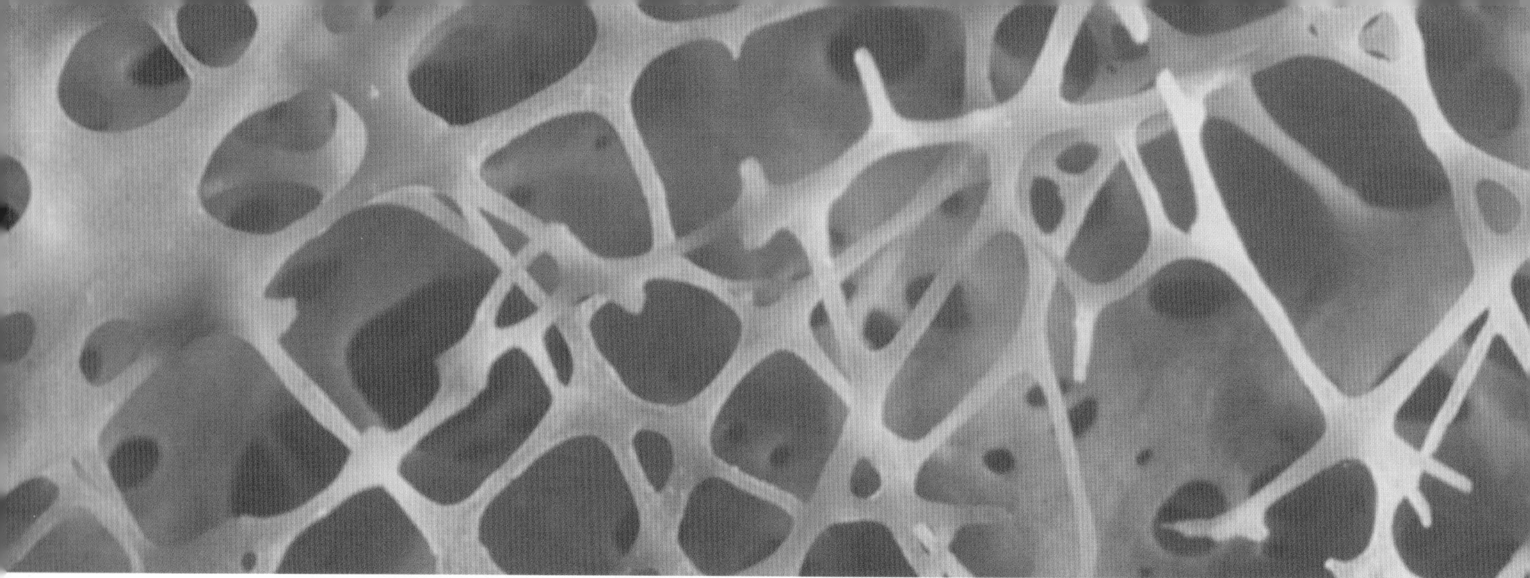

Ichonographic references
Where it is not expressly indicated, the images come from the Giunti Ichonographic Archive.
As for the rights of reproduction, the Editor is fully available to settle any possible fee due for those images whose source it was impossible to retrieve.

Published 2009

TAJ BOOKS INTERNATIONAL LLP
27 Ferndown Gardens
Cobham
Surrey
KT11 2BH

info@tajbooks.com

ISBN: 978-184406-115-0

Originally published by

Via Bolognese 165, 50139 Firenze - Italia
Via Dante 4, 20121 Milano - Italia

www.giunti.it

Printed in China

ATLAS OF HUMAN PHYSIOLOGY

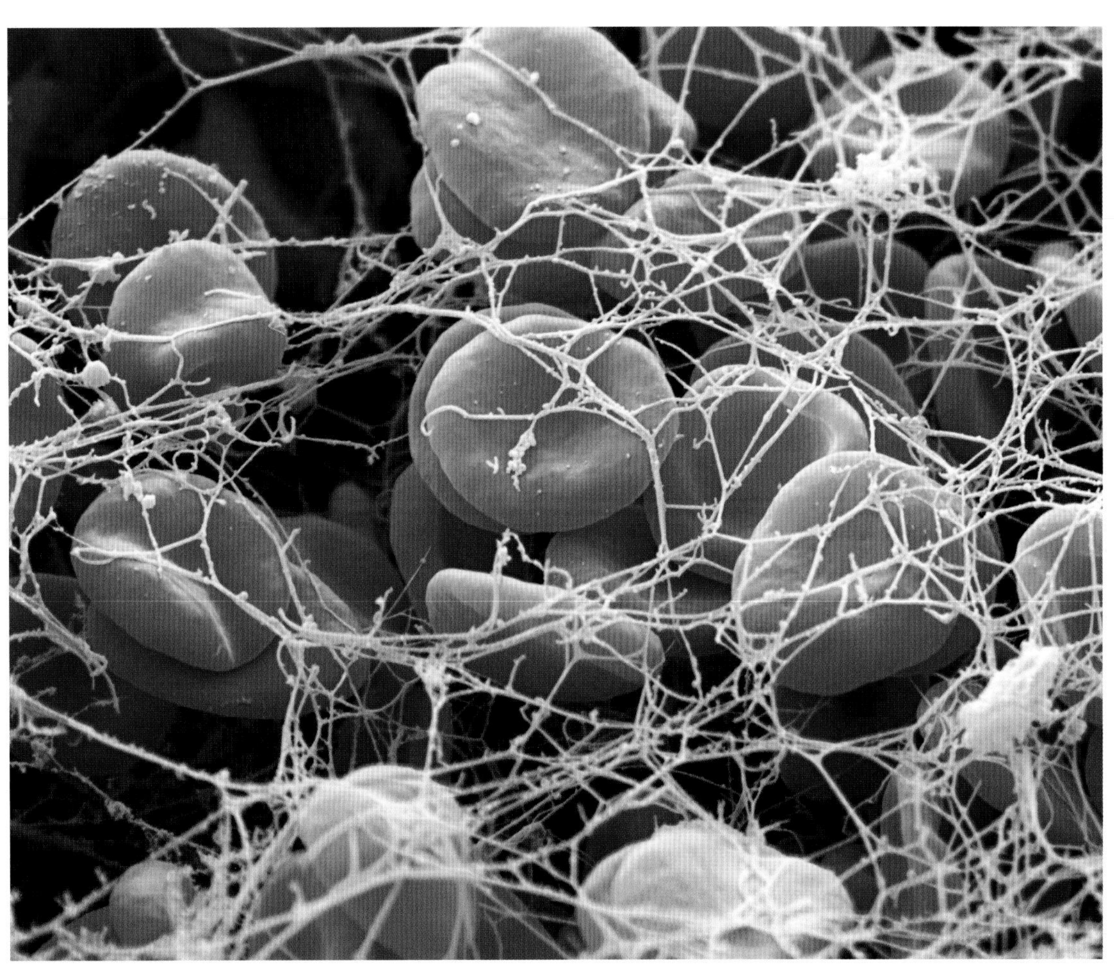

T&J

GENERAL INDEX

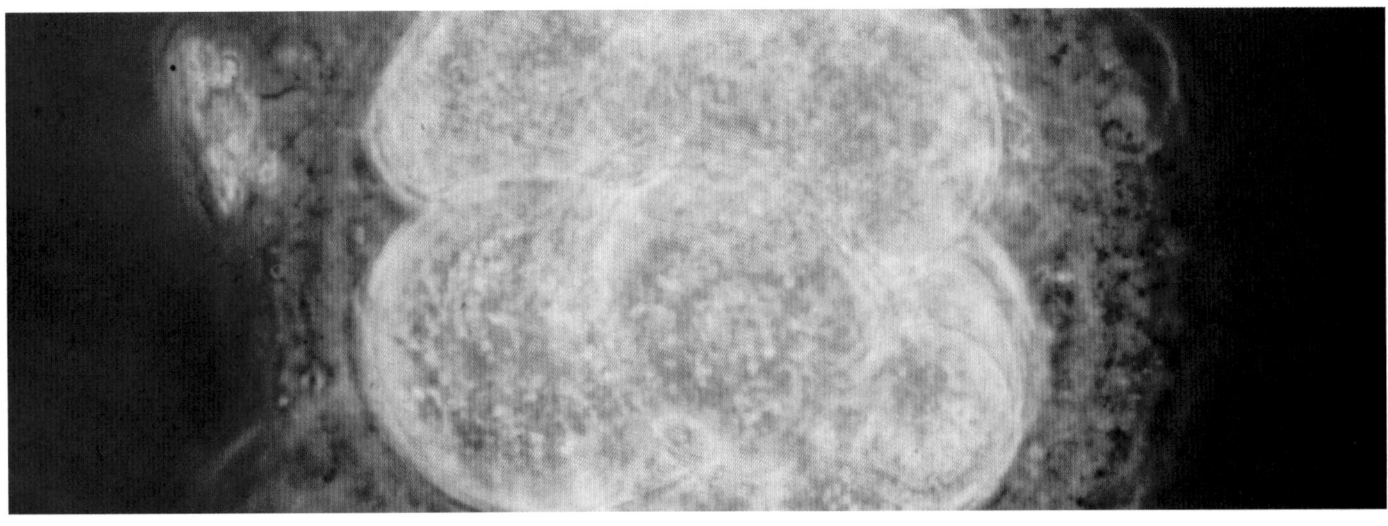

THE BASIC ORGANISATION OF THE BODY

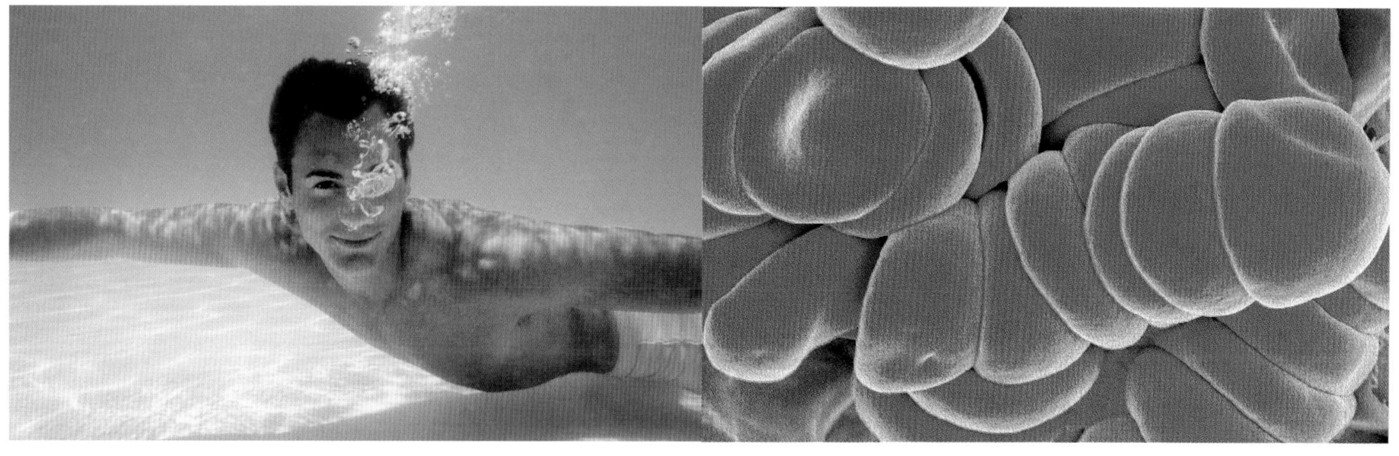

INTERCHANGE BETWEEN THE INTERNAL AND EXTERNAL ENVIRONMENT

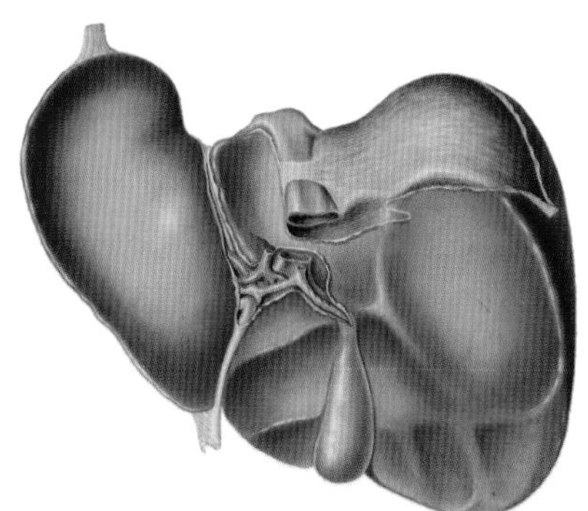

THE INTERNAL ENVIRONMENT

THE CONTROLS OF THE ACTIVITIES OF THE BODY

THE INTERACTION BETWEEN BODY AND ENVIRONMENT

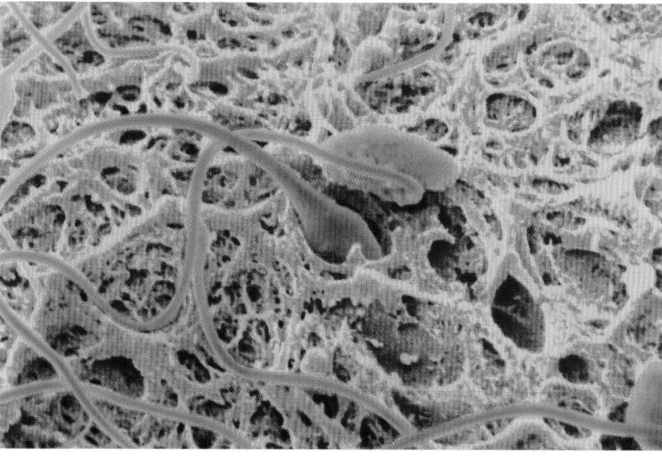

REPRODUCTION

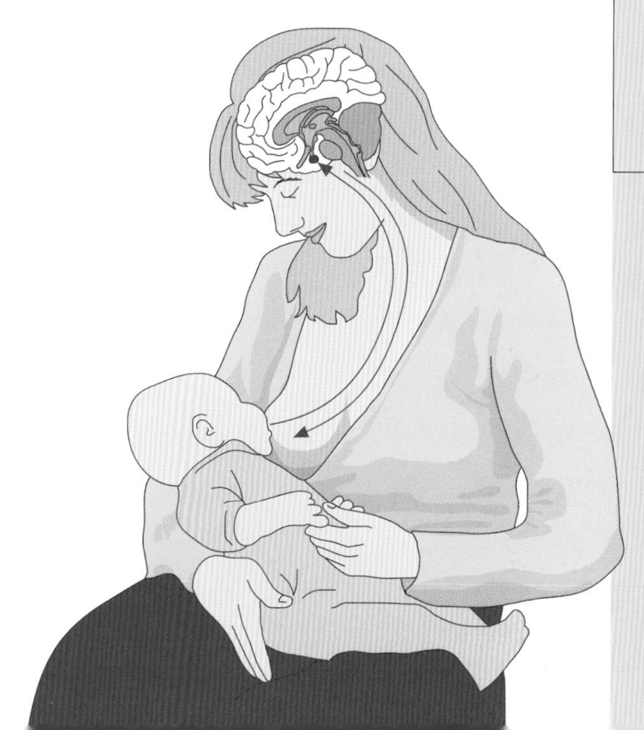

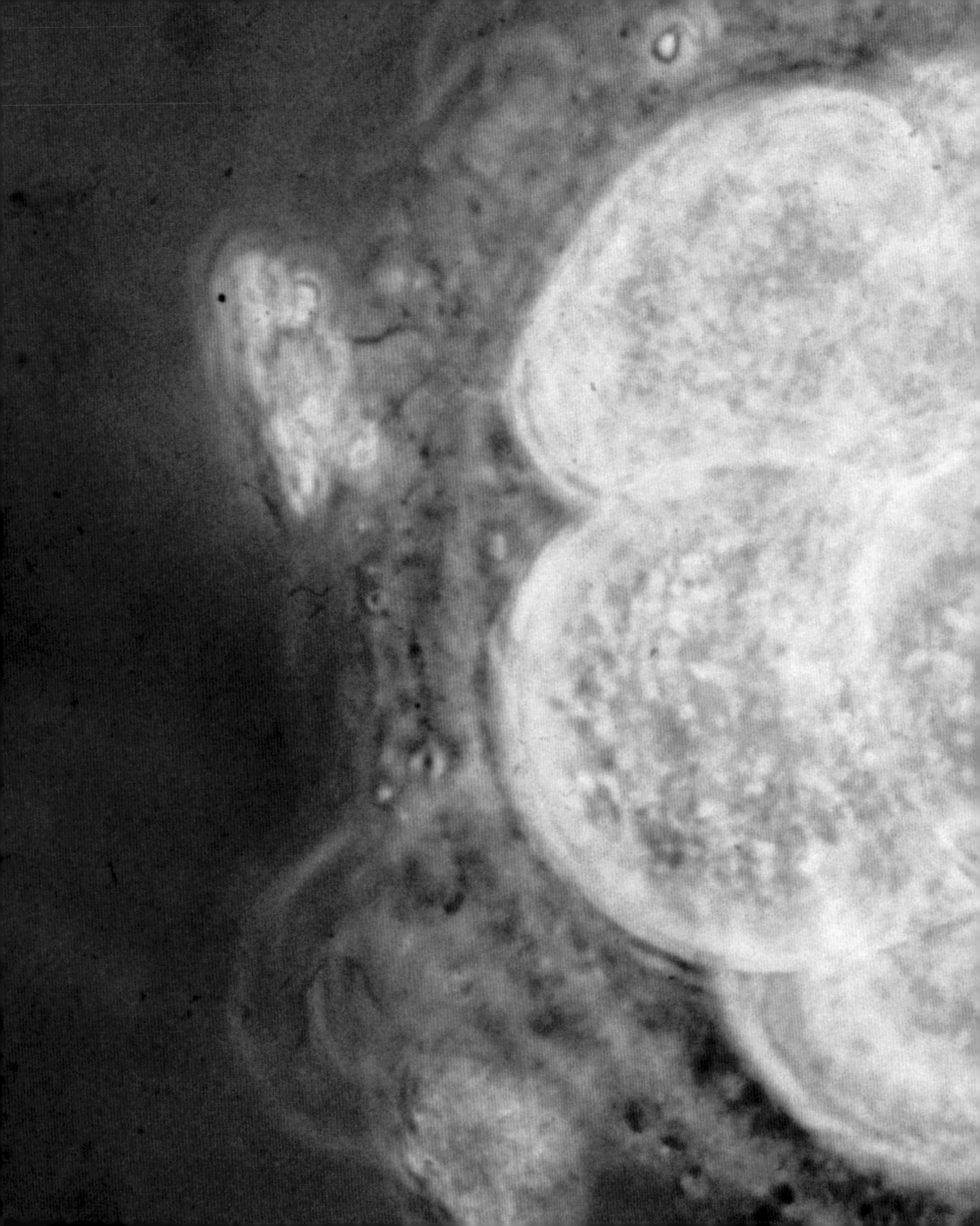

THE BASIC ORGANISATION OF THE BODY

"THERE IS ONLY ONE ROAD TO LIFE, AND A UNIQUE PHYSIOLOGY FOR ALL LIVING BEINGS": THE INTUITION OF CLAUDE BERNARD PROVED TO BE VALID EVEN AFTER THE LATEST DISCOVERIES IN MICROBIOLOGY AND GENETICS.

THE BASIC VITAL AND CELLULAR PROCESSES

The human body, as well as other higher forms of life (that is, those with a more complex physiology), is a super-body formed by vast numbers of cells. Specifically, there are billions of individual cells with precise anatomical structure that, through the processes of evolution, have become well-suited to life on this planet. After many millions of years of natural development there has been a massive diversification of life forms, with those at the higher end of the scale demonstrating the development of cellular systems increasingly based on complex and specialised cells.

A unicellular organism finds what it needs (nutrients, water, gas, etc.) in the environment in which it lives. It is independent in every vital function (it feeds, moves, breathes, reacts to stimuli, reproduces, defends itself, and so on). Within a body, however, every cell specialises in a particular function and does not deal with others, this allows it to carry out its tasks to their maximum effect. For example, while continuing to perform vital basic functions (breathing, processing of nutrients and expulsion of waste), a nerve cell will develop its maximum capacity of response to environmental stimuli, while other cells of the body will have responsibilities to defend it, procure nutrients, maintain the environment, and where appropriate, ensure its survival.

What happens, therefore, is a transfer of functions: every cell has to carry out functions in which it is not specialised. From the functional point of view, then, the organism develops the same vital functions of a cell: it feeds, moves, breathes, reacts to stimuli, it reproduces, defends itself, and so on. At the same time though, it must ensure that all its constituent cells are situated in an ideal environment. This typically means that their physical conditions are kept as constant as possible - this enables them

▼ **FREE CELLS**
These scanning electron microscope images make it possible to see the finest detail in the structure of Escherichia coli bacteria (right) and planktonic algae (left). Each of the cells in these small organisms plays the role of organs in a larger body.

to operate at optimal efficiency, regardless of the physical-chemical fluctuations of the external environment.

Just as a cell has specific "compartments" (organs) within which it performs vital basic functions, the superior body has a number of bodies carrying out those same functions, but at the macroscopic level. For example, each cell is surrounded by a semi-permeable membrane that, in addition to giving it a shape, "protects" and allows exchange of substances with the environment. Almost the same functions are carried out by skin and mucous membranes. These protect the inside of the body from contact with the environment and prevent internal and external physical-chemical changes. At the same time, it allows the exchange of substances (water, oxygen, carbon dioxide, etc.) and active interactions with the world around it.

The cells are therefore essential elements of the body: they provide the necessary mechanisms for the exchange of matter and energy required for life. The following sections present an overview of the components that make up a cell, what functions these play, the major types of cells and their specialised functions in the human body.

CELLULAR STRUCTURES & THEIR FUNCTIONS

Over the hundreds of millions of years that evolution has been underway, many different kinds of cells have developed, and while most have very specialised functions, they typically share a number of common features, such as the nucleus, nucleolus, mitochondria, cytoplasm, and so on.

THE NUCLEUS

The nucleus is an organelle that is contained within a double membrane. This has a series of pores distributed across its surface - these allow ions and macromolecules to pass between the nucleus and the cytoplasm ▸15 which surrounds it. The nucleus is composed of many distinct features, and carries the whole history of the cell and the organism to which it belongs. These include the chromosomes, which encode the genetic information that guides the embryonic development ▸248. They also set out the type of specialisation, the duration of life, and the reproductive capacity of each cell. The information is stored in DNA molecules via a succession of chemical bases. These transmit messages in a similar manner to that of Morse code. The overall sequence determines the features of every cell and therefore exactly how the entire body is constructed.

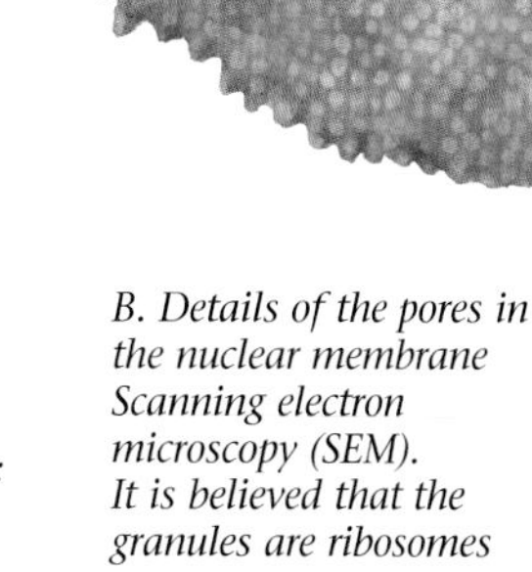

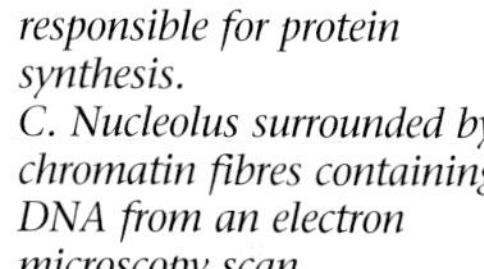

▶ **Principal Structures** *Indicated In this "typical animal cell" are the organelles: ❶ nucleus; ❷ nucleolus; ❸ mitochondria; ❹ smooth endoplasmic reticulum; ❺ Wrinkled endoplasmic reticulum; ❻ the Golgi apparatus; ❼ lisosoma; ❽ membrane.*

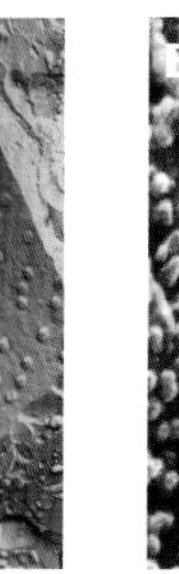

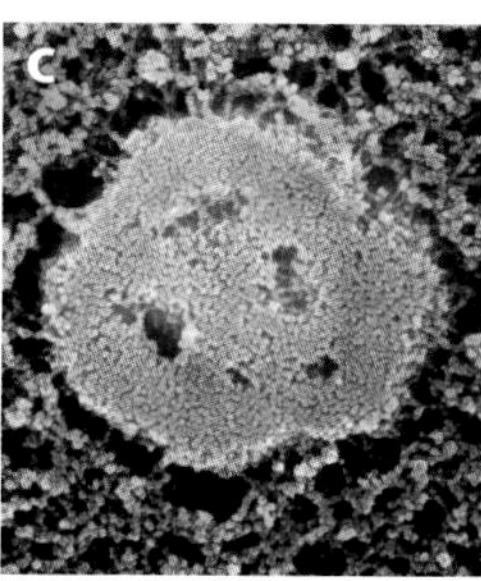

▼ **Nucleus and nucleolus** *Four microphotographs in false color. A. In this high-resolution photo taken with a transmission electron microscope (TEM) the surface of the nuclear membrane appears grainy: in relief you can see the pores. B. Details of the pores in the nuclear membrane Scanning electron microscopy (SEM). It is believed that the granules are ribosomes responsible for protein synthesis. C. Nucleolus surrounded by chromatin fibres containing DNA from an electron microscopy scan.*

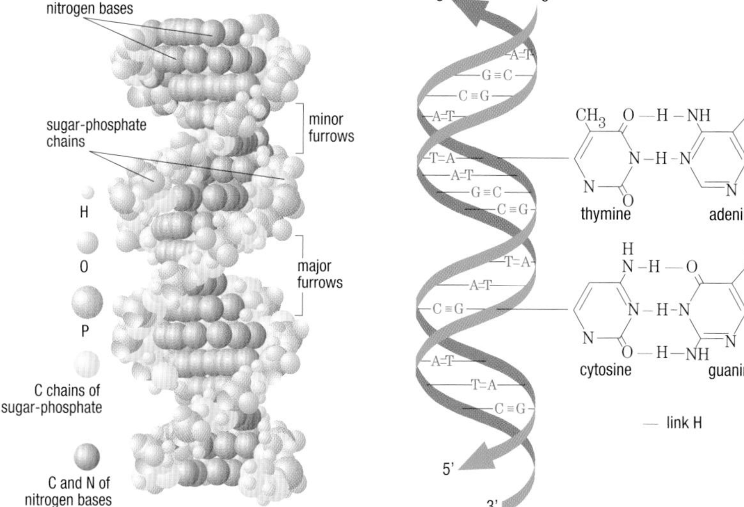

▲ **The double helix** *The first two drawings show the same stretch of DNA: on the left, each constituent atom is reproduced with its "sphere of influence": the greater the size the greater the atomic weight. On the right, however, it is difficult to see how a stretch of DNA is formed by two molecules. Wrapped each other in order to allow the formation of electrostatic hydrogen links (H) between the nitrogen bases.*

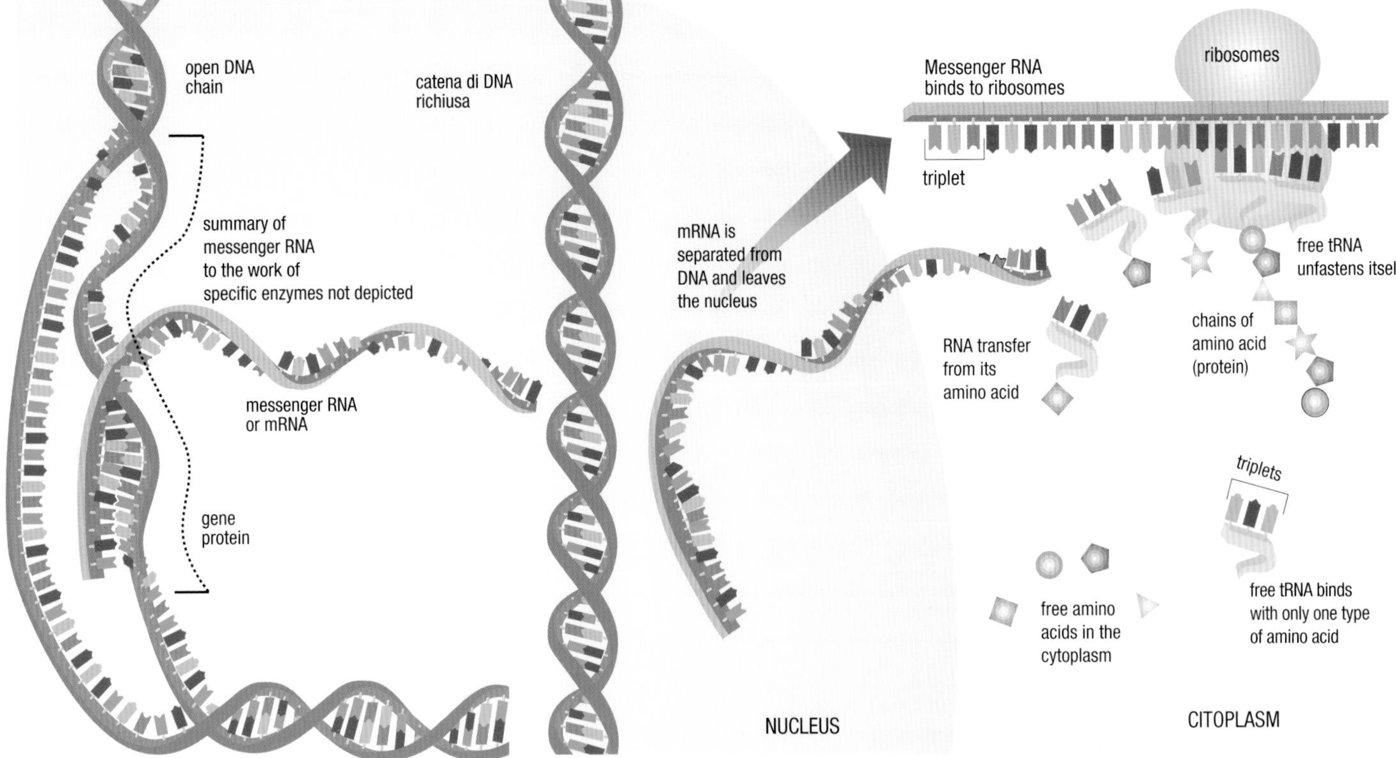

▲ **Protein synthesis**
When used to produce a protein, you need to read the genetic code, that is the order in which the foundations of another gene that encodes the protein. The two molecules of DNA split at the "right", making room for enzymes capable of producing a filament of messenger ribonucleic acid (mRNA). The messenger RNA leaves the nucleus and binds with other nucleic acids: the ribosomal RNA that are added to form ribosomes, that is the functional units that allow the orderly combination of transfer RNA and mRNA. In this way, the amino acid linked to tRNA can polymerise in the correct sequence and shape the protein described in the DNA.

THE NUCLEOLUS

The nucleolus is the most active part of the nucleus, and is the structure that shows up best in histological preparations. It features large numbers of proteins and nucleic acids, together with the enzymes that are needed to interpret the genetic code. It also synthesises the nucleic acids that mediate and promote protein synthesis. Messenger RNA (mRNA) is used to carry information outside the nucleus, ribosomal RNA (rRNA) and transfer RNA (tRNA), once outside the nucleus form ribosomes and reversibly bind to specific amino acids.

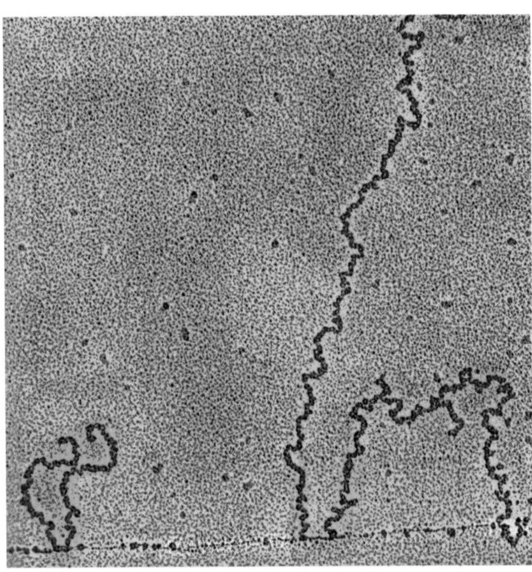

▶ **Transcription of DNA**
In false colors, this photograph from a transmission electron microscopy (TEM) shows the synthesis of four different chains of RNA, starting in the same RNA helix (E. coli).

MITOCHONDRIA

The mitochondria are considered to form the 'engine-room' of the cell as one of their primary roles is to produce adenosine triphosphate (ATP), one of the base units of cellular energy transfer. It is thought that these specialised structures may well have derived from primitive bacteria that began to cohabit with the first nucleated cells of biological history. Mitochondria are contained within a contorted double membrane that features a number of ridges or tubules. Attached to the inner surface of the membrane are various enzymes, and in the interior space is filled with a matrix that contains the substances needed to produce energy. These are sugars and fats which are oxidised through lengthy and complex biochemical chain reactions and reduced to water and carbon dioxide. The most important of these processes is known as the citric acid or Krebs cycle.

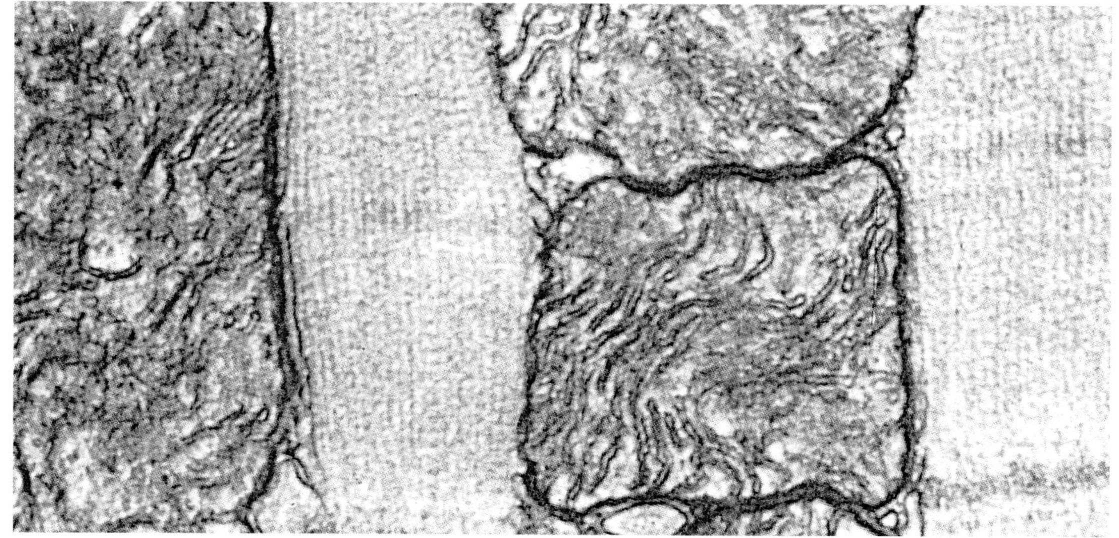

◀ **Muscle cell** *Mitochondria flanked fibres showing contractility: electron microscopy photo of a striated muscle cell.*

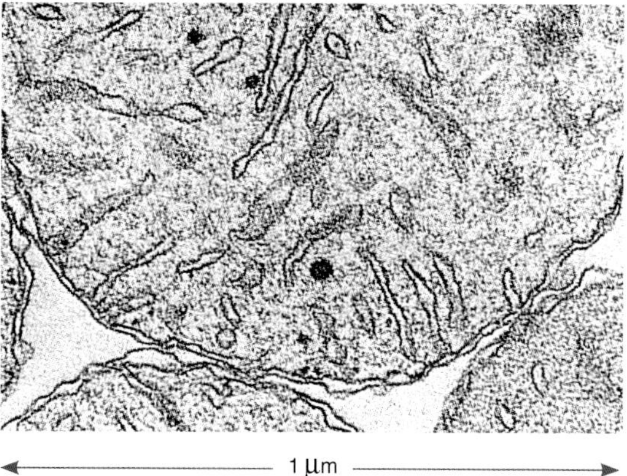

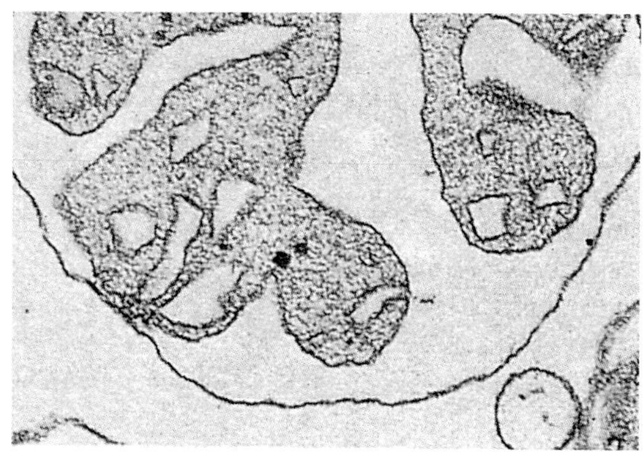

◀ **Mitochondria** *These two mitochondria seem very different. In fact, the profound changes in layout and scale of ridges is due to their state of relative quiet (left) or intense metabolic activity (right). In the latter case, the water and carbon dioxide produced are outside the mitochondria "inflating" the ridges.*

The oxidation and degradation of sugar and fat is an important part of cellular metabolisms, and involves special molecules such as NAD, FAD and ADP which are able to leave the mitochondria and reach those areas of the cell where energy is needed. Once there, they are transformed again as part of the process of making the stored energy available. At the time of cell division, mitochondria are duplicated in all the cells of the body. Cells which need a lot of energy - for example muscle tissues, are particularly rich in mitochondria.

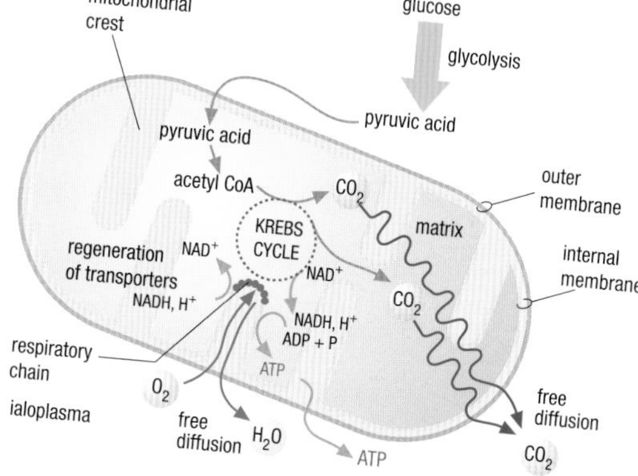

▲ **Functions** *Diagram of metabolic activity that takes place in a mitochondria. On the ridges, are housed the complex enzymes that make possible the oxidation of sugars and fats and production of chemical energy.*

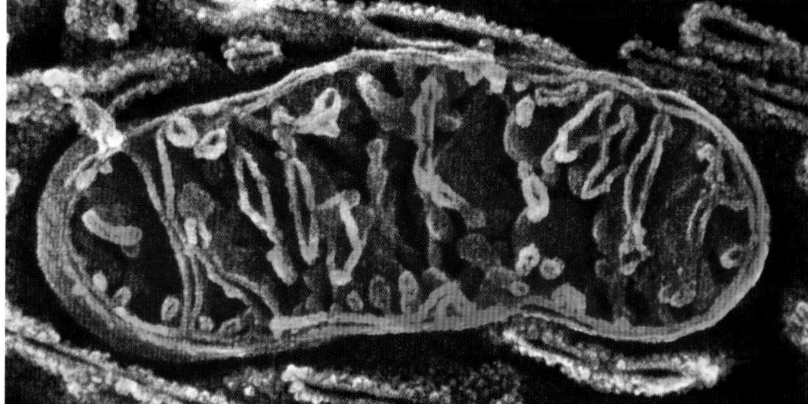

▲ **Mitochondria** *In false colors, this photograph from a scanning electron microscope (SEM) allows you to clearly see a cylindrical mitochondria. While the outer membrane completely surrounds the cell, the inner flexes, expanding the area available for metabolic processes.*

▶ **Lysosomes**
In green, two lysosomes. In particular, in the vacuum on the right it is evident that the membrane is composed of a single layer.

▶▶ **Golgi apparatus**
Colored in fuchsia are the cisternae and the vesicles of the Golgi body. The elements of the Golgi are marked by a single membrane.

▼ **Smooth endoplasmic lattice (RE)**
In fuchsia are coloured membranes of the endoplasmic reticulum, and visible in yellow are some ribosomes. In the box, the micrograph shows the smooth RE, that is devoid of ribosomes.

▼▶ **Rough RE**
In this three-dimensional micrograph, some mitochondria (blue) seem supported a maze of rough membranes: they make up the RE where many ribosomes are actively synthesizing proteins. In the box, the micrograph shows the layout of ribosomes on both sides of the double membranes of the grid.

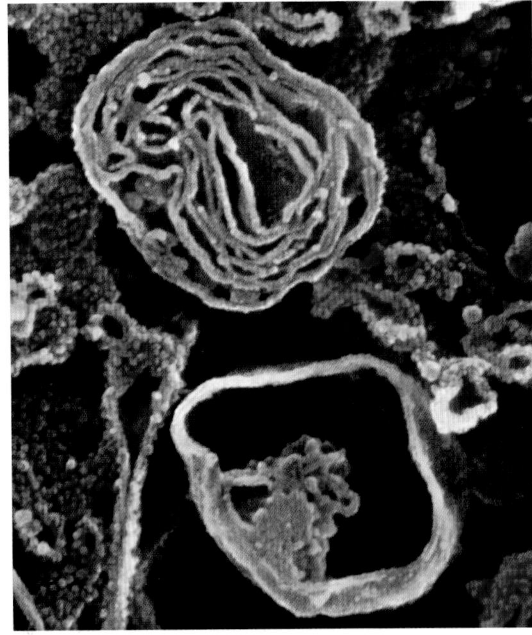

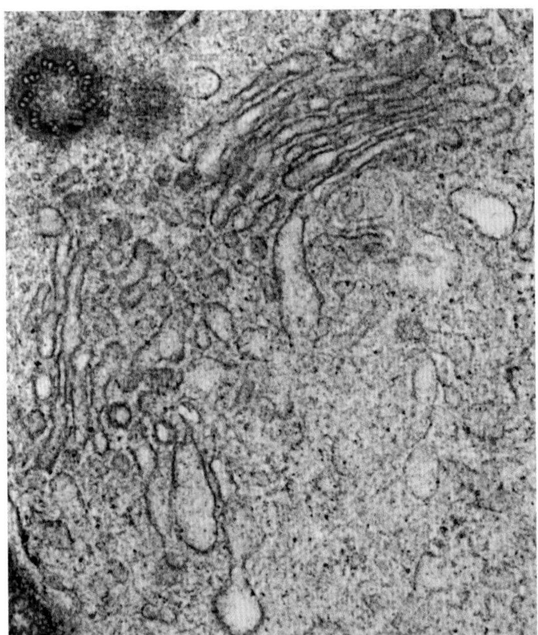

LYSOSOMES

Lysosomes are tiny spheroidal vesicles that are bounded by a single membrane. They contain a high concentration of digestive enzymes - these are used to destroy unwanted organelles that are either in excess or damaged, as well as unusable molecules coming from inside or outside the cell.

THE GOLGI APPARATUS

The Golgi Apparatus is an organelle that was first discovered in 1898 by an Italian doctor called Camillo Golgi. He called the structure a "reticular apparatus" - it is always very recognisable, being comprised of a number of sack-like features called cisternae. These may be present as associated individuals or in groups; in the latter case the members are closely bound to each other and form what are referred to as 'bodies of Golgiani'. The function of the Golgi apparatus is to store or modify various macromolecules until they are used or their expulsion from the cell.

THE ENDOPLASMIC RETICULUM

The Endoplasmic Reticulum is an organelle that is made up from a dense network of double membranes which are folded into various forms (layers, tubules, sacs and flattened vesicles) that crosses the whole cell. Situated on these membranes are combinations of enzymes that take part in specific biochemical reactions such as protein translation and transport or secretion. The endoplasmic reticulum also stores a number of macromolecules such as glycogen.

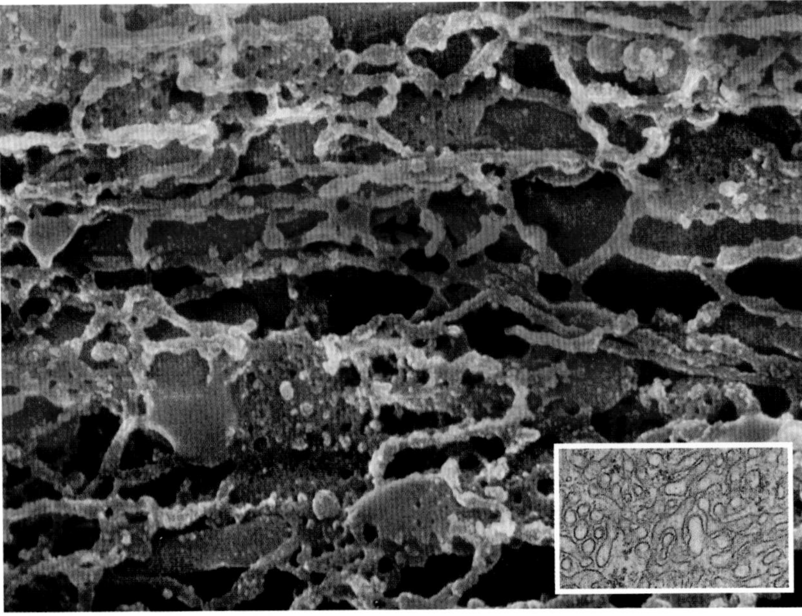

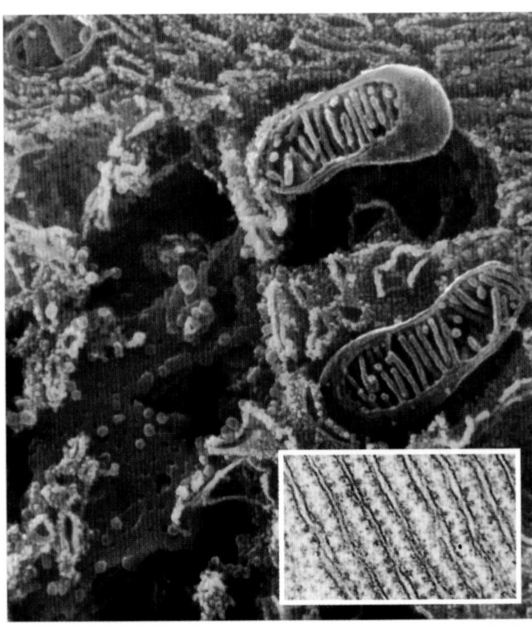

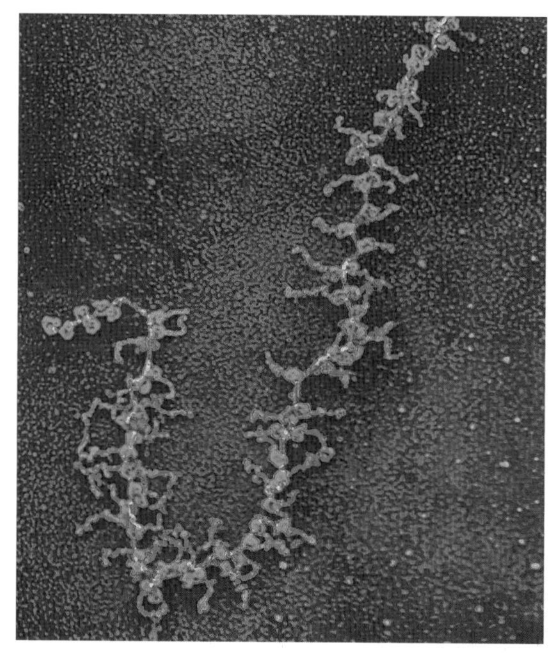

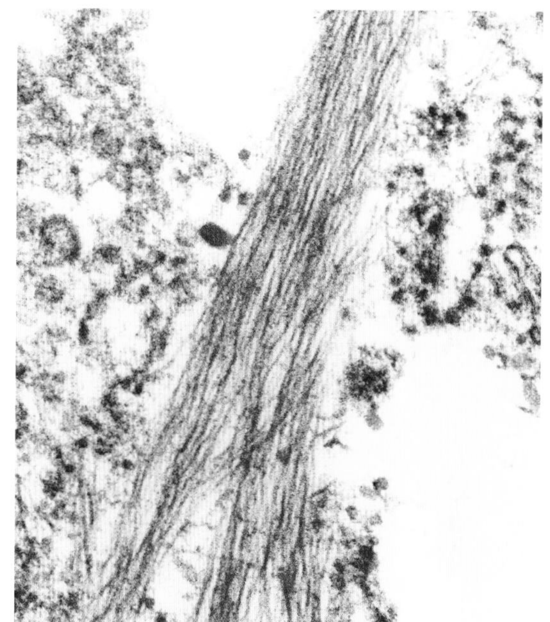

◀◀ **Ribosomes in activity**
In this spectacular transmission electron microscopy (TEM) a series of ribosomes (corpuscles in blue) is linked to a long strand of mRNA (fuchsia) and is synthesizing proteins (green). As ribosomes move along the mRNA strand, the chain of the protein that are synthesizing stretches.

◀ **Cytoskeleton**
In this TEM image, a section through a cell shows clearly the fibrous protein filaments of a cytoskeleton.

THE CYTOPLASM

The cytoplasm is a liquid matrix that is held within a cell's plasma membrane. It contains the organelles as well as other components known as inclusions. It fills all areas of the cell, circulating through the membranes of the endoplasmic reticulum. The cytoplasm comprises about 80% of the total volume of a cell, and consists mainly of water. It has a colloidal consistency due to the high percentage of proteins in solution, including large quantities of enzymes. In the aqueous phase are also dissolved all substances necessary to life: salts, sugars, ions of chemical elements, nucleic acids (most of the various types of RNA), amino acids, nucleotides and many other biomolecules or their constituent parts. It is in the cytoplasm that most of the vital cell activity takes place.

THE CYTOSKELETON

The cytoskeleton is a kind of cellular scaffolding that is made up of a complex network of fibrous proteins that join together to form filaments. This is arranged throughout the cell giving it strength and also determining its overall shape. Typical of eukaryotic cells (i.e. those equipped with a complex core), the cytoskeleton also acts as a guide for the movement of organelles, and is crucial at the time of cell division.

THE PLASMA MEMBRANE

From a metabolic perspective, one of the most important aspects of a cell is its ability to pass messages through the outer membrane. This allows cells to communicate and co-ordinate the supply and removal of various substances, as well as receive environmental stimuli. To carry out all these functions, the plasma membrane has very special characteristics:

- it is deformable but tough, able to adapt to environmental changes, and allows autonomous movements;
- is semi-permeable, which allows the passage of molecules inwards and outwards on a selective basis ►17;
- is structured in such a way as to recognise certain molecules and physical stimuli from the environment (changes in the concentration of salts, alterations in light or temperature, the presence of an electric field, etc.) which may require some form of response.

These characteristics are present in all the membranes that form the cell. It is likely that since it first evolved the plasma membrane has adapted

THE MEMBRANE

Thickness	8 nm
Function	• isolate the environment from internal and external
	• regular exchanges
	• provide structural support to cellular constituents
Principal constituents	
LIPIDS	PHOSPHOLIPIDS: amphipathic
	SPHINGOLIPIDS: amphipathic
	STEROLS: apolar
	GLYCOLIPIDS
PROTEINS	INHERENT OR INTEGRAL: have hydrophobic interactions with the interior
	TRANSPORT • ION CHANNELS
	• CARRIERS OR *CARRIER*
	• MEMBRANE PUMPS
	RECEPTOR
	ENZYME
	EXTRINSIC OR PERIPHERAL: have electrostatic interactions with those inherent
	STRUCTURAL
	• bind membrane cytoskeleton
	• form the joints with adjacent cells
	• connect cells protein matrix
	LIGANDS
	MOLECULES RECOGNITION
CARBOHYDRATES	

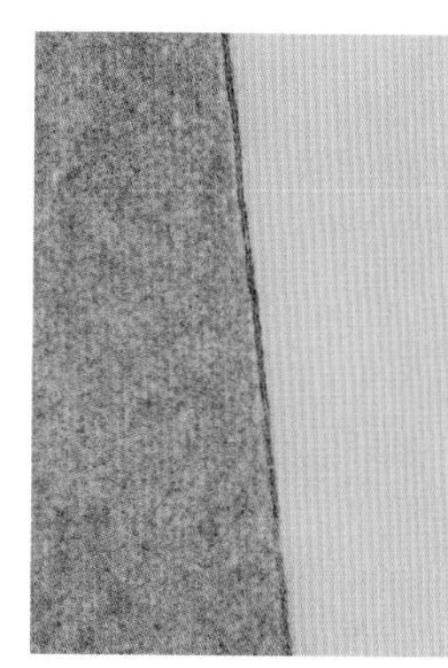

▲ **Double layer**
A TEM micrograph shows clearly how the plasma membrane that surrounds the cell is formed by a double layer of molecules, less "dense" in the middle.

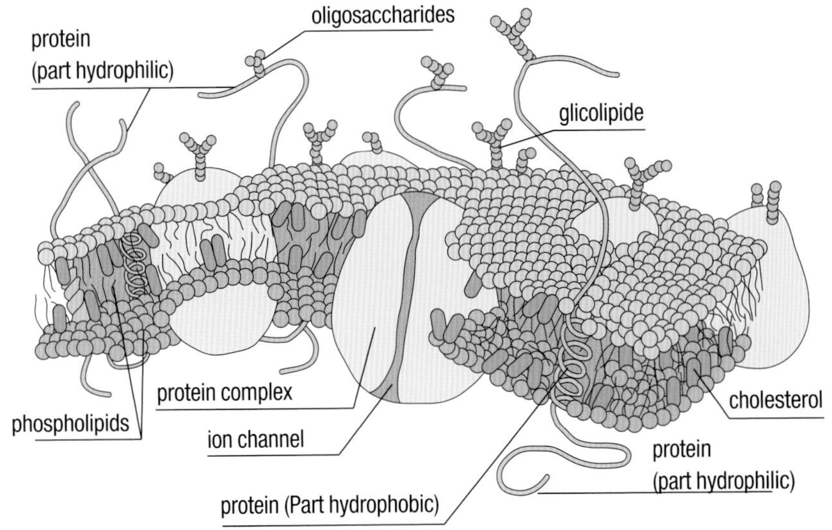

▲ **Model**
"Fluid mosaic" model of the cell membrane. Top is the outside of the cell, down the interior.

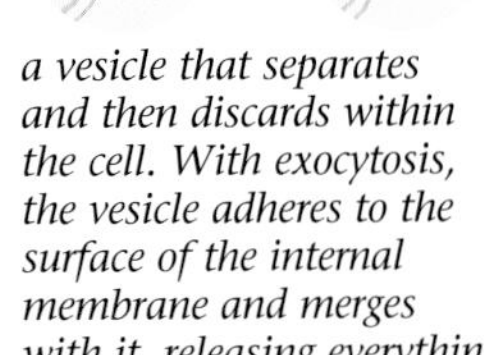

▲ **Endocytosis and exocytosis**
In this diagram, the color blue indicates the outside of the cell and green, the interior. During endocytosis, the particles align themselves with the membrane, which "invaginates" and forms a vesicle that separates and then discards within the cell. With exocytosis, the vesicle adheres to the surface of the internal membrane and merges with it, releasing everything it contains.

▼ **Phospholipids**
Chemistry and three-dimensional structure of a molecule phospholipid.

$$\begin{array}{l} CH_2 - O - \overset{\overset{\large O}{\|}}{C} - R_1 \\ | \\ CH - O - \overset{\overset{\large O}{\|}}{C} - R_2 \\ | \\ CH_2 - O - \overset{\overset{\large O}{\|}}{C} - R_3 \end{array}$$

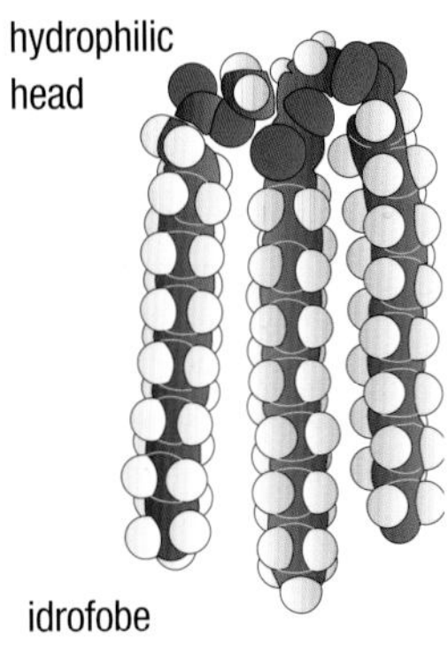

very slowly – this has allowed scientists to perform research work which has provided further proof that all living things derive from a single common ancestor.

The plasma membranes are formed by a double layer of fatty acids (phospholipids) that is typically around 5.5 nm thick. This is crossed by large protein complexes and enhanced by molecules of cholesterol and glycolipids. This structure can be explained if the chemical and physical properties of the main constituents are considered. It can be explained by comparison with the phenomenon of putting a little oil on water and vigorously shaking it to form an emulsion is well known. In this process, the oil is reduced to tiny droplets that remain separate from the water. If these drops are examined at the molecular level, it can be seen that the fats - whose molecules have no electric charge, are evenly distributed. They are polarised – that is, they are arranged so as to isolate the hydrophobic tail that is exposed to the molecules of water. They form a compact double layer of molecules – this is extremely stable and at the same time able to move in a fluid manner.

THE TWO METABOLIC PATHWAYS: CATABOLISM AND ANABOLISM

The term 'metabolism' refers to all the chemical and physical reactions that are essential to life which occur in a cell or organism. Studying the biochemistry involved in cellular metabolism is extremely difficult. To do this properly means that it is necessary to identify all the molecules that are present, as well as the complex series of energetic interactions that they are involved in. To make matters more complicated, a full understanding of all the enzymes that participate is also required. Many metabolic reactions are reversible and their direction is determined by the conditions in which energy is the cell. All of these reactions are regulated by enzymes, and because they are proteins, their manufacture is regulated by the instructions encoded in the organism's DNA. Consequently, all metabolic processes are ultimately controlled by genetic heritage, - this becomes evident in some pathological conditions in the clinic, such as phenylketonuria. This is where the body is unable to synthesise specific enzymes and as a result cannot carry out certain metabolic reactions.

Overall, the human metabolism is much more complex than a single cell, consisting as it does of tens of thousands of biochemical processes. These involve enormous amounts of genetically determined enzymes, but in spite of this the basic processes are very similar.

Moreover, even in the simplest organisms, all the metabolic reactions form extremely complex

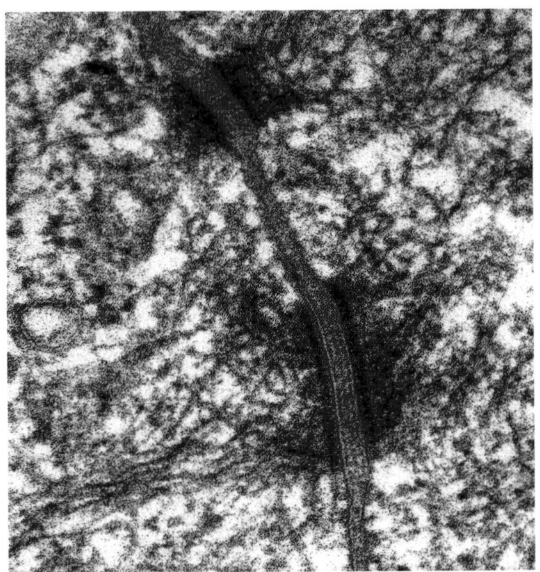

▶ **Desmosoma**
A TEM micrograph that shows clearly how the plasma membrane that surrounds the cell is formed by a double layer of molecules,which in the center are less dense.

OSMOSIS, DISTRIBUTION, TRANSPORT PASSIVE AND ACTIVE TRANSPORT

When the internal and external chemical compositions of a cell are examined, it can be seen that the substances do not have equal distribution on both sides of the bounding membrane.

The ability of molecules to pass through this membrane, in fact, depend on their chemical and physical properties. Some will move based on the laws of free distribution, however, others are helped by various membrane structures as they need the cell to expend some energy before they can cross through. The are several different ways in which a molecule can pass into or out of a cell. The components involved all have to obey the laws of fluid dynamics, however.

The flow or osmosis of solvent through the membrane depends on the specific concentrations of the fluids on either side. The higher the concentration of the molecules and ions of one of the solutions relative to the other, the higher the osmotic pressure. The net flow of solvent tends to even out the concentration on both sides of the membrane. Overall, there is therefore a motion of molecules of solvent from B to A.

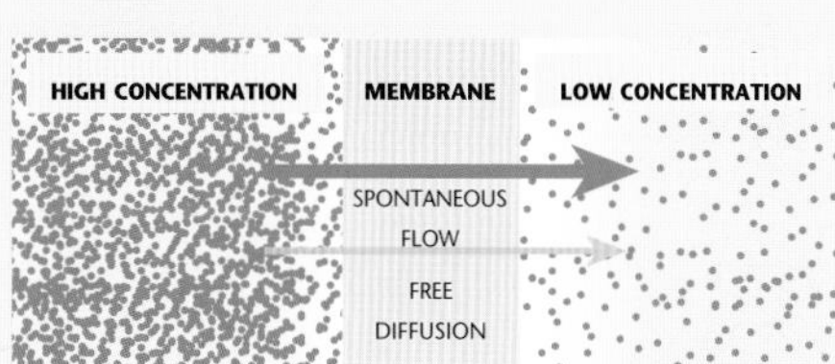

1. In the above illustration, it can be said that the molecules of solvent are distributed through the membrane, which means that their transition is governed solely by the osmotic pressure. In the cell, however, there is passage in both directions not only from water and gas, but also of substances held in solution. This mechanism ensures that if the amount of water inside the cell decreases, it is immediately replaced, ensuring the conservation of optimal endocellular conditions.

HIGHER CONCENTRATION
MEMBRANE
LOWER CONCENTRATION
SPONTANEOUS FLOW
EASY SPREAD

2. The speed at which dissolved substances are distributed through the membrane is governed by the concentration gradient - moving from highest to lowest. The rate of transfer does not remain the same, however - at first there is an initial acceleration, until a certain concentration is reached within the cell. From then the movement slows down until equilibrium is achieved, when it stops altogether. It only resumes when the internal concentration decreases again. This type of dissemination is typical of substances such as sugar, a common source of cell energy.

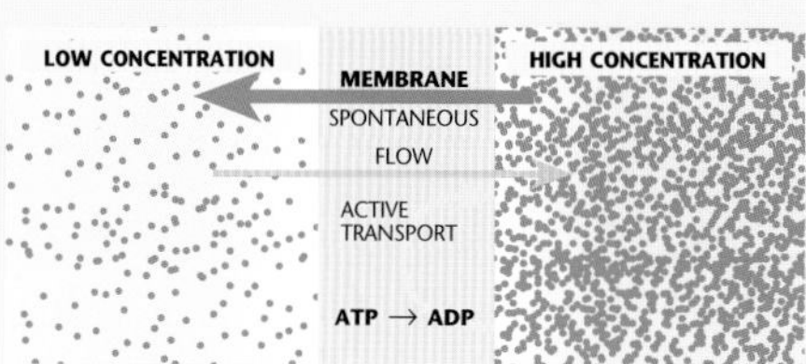

3. In some cases - for example with some ions, the cell needs concentrations much higher than those which surround it. In these cases, the movement of molecules through the membrane is directed against the gradient of concentration. For this to happen, the cell has to expend energy - this process is referred to as active transport. As an example, many cells continuously expel sodium ions (Na +). To do this requires a series of functional changes in the three-dimensional structure of the membrane. This is something that can only be achieved with an input of energy, however - this is produced from the processing of ATP into ADP.

There are flows of other substances which, while going against a gradient of concentration, have no need for energy produced by the cell. This is what happens when an unwanted negative ion is exchanged for another one that is needed. Again, the molecules that form the membrane actively take part in the transport, but as there is no waste of energy the phenomenon is referred to as passive transport.

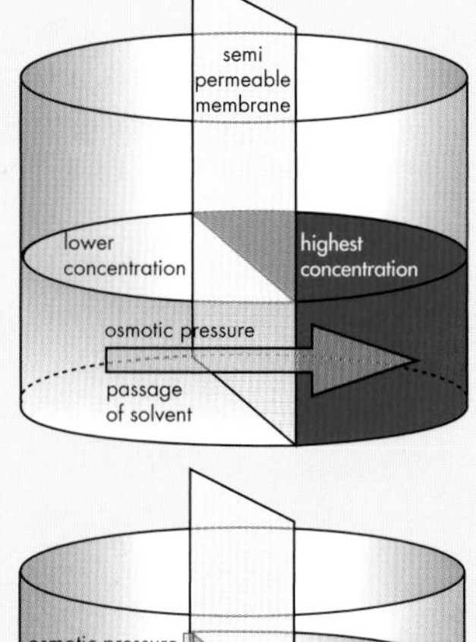

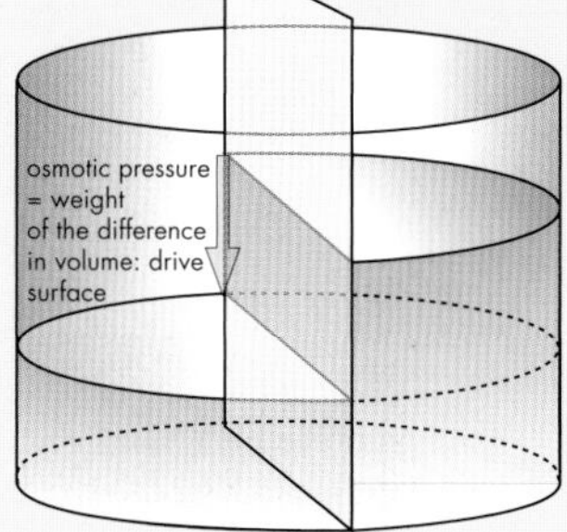

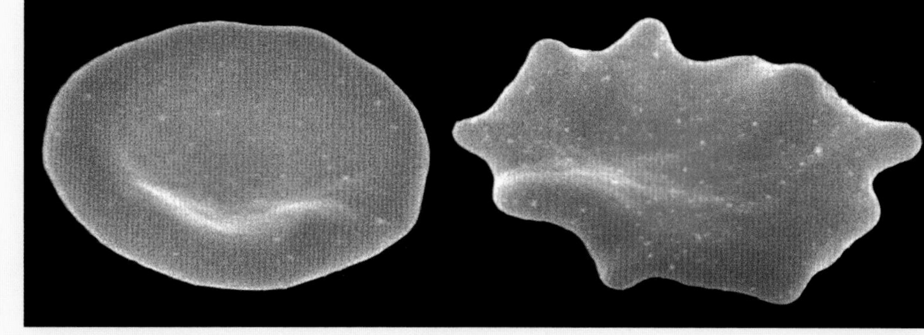

▲ **OSMOSIS**
This physico-chemical phenomenon occurs when a semi-membrane separates two solutions with different concentrations. As the system tends to equilibrium, the solvent tends to cross the membrane until the concentration of solutes on both sides is not equal, that is flowing towards the more concentrated solution, and increases the volume. Thus, the osmotic pressure decreases until the weight exerted on the surface of separation causes an "excess" as "compensation".

▲ **RED CELLS**
The red blood cells (or erythrocytes) have normally a rounded and flattened shape. However, if you find them in an environment too rich in salts (hypertonic) they lose a lot of water which controls the form - like the one on the right - very abnormal compared to the one on the left.

Enzymes and cofactors

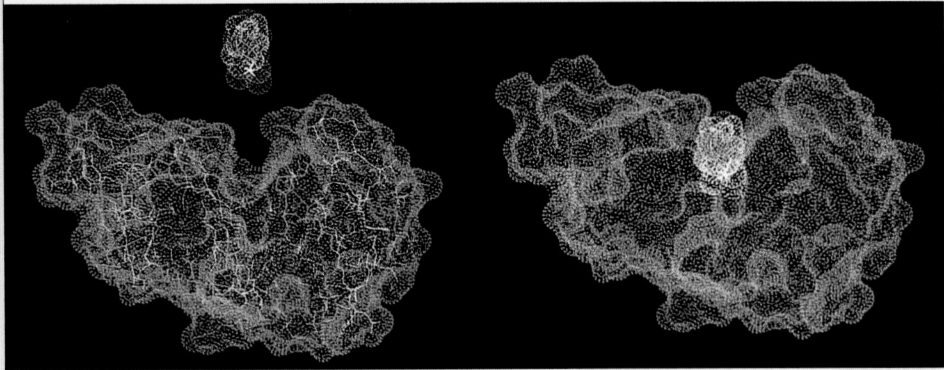

Enzymes are special proteins that speed up certain processes. Their name derives from the Greek word for "yeast", because the first examples were discovered in such cells. Each plays a vital role in catalysing specific biochemical reactions.

A catalyst is a substance that is not directly involved in a chemical reaction, but which is able to directly influence the speed at which it takes place. Without the presence of the correct catalyst, many of these reactions would be so slow as to have negligible effect.

Unlike inorganic catalysts, however, enzymes are extremely specific, and typically only work with one particular reaction. In a few instances they will work with a very limited set of similar chemicals, but this is unusual. Their effect can be dramatic, making the relevant process take place much more quickly - anything from a hundred to over a thousand times faster!

The substance that interacts with an enzyme and is transformed is called a substrate. The area of the enzyme molecule that comes into contact with it is known as the active site. The fit between the two has to be so close that any small differences in conformation will stop any catalytic effect. One analogy is that the enzyme is like a key that fits in a lock - even a small mismatch will prevent it turning.

Enzymes are characterised by precise three-dimensional shapes that are determined by particular chemical structures. They often require the presence of special non-protein molecules that help to bind them to the active site - these chemicals are known as cofactors, and can be divided into prosthetic and coenzyme groups. The first (many are metal ions) are tied closely to the enzyme, and almost always on a permanent basis. The second (especially vitamins) bind weakly and the same molecule may later detach and join with different enzymes. Some enzymes need to have several cofactors present before they can function. Many coenzymes also allow the transfer of small molecules from one chemical to another.

Some enzymes are allosteric - this means that they have a specific location where an effector molecule can lock itself on. Some effectors help speed a reaction up - these are referred to as 'allosteric activators'. Others act to slow a process down - these are called 'allosteric inhibitors'. Most cells contain numerous copies of about 3000 different types of enzymes, usually in very low concentrations when compared to those of the substrates. Their ability to influence a particular chemical reaction can be expressed using a measurement referred to as an 'enzyme unit'. This specifies the quantity of the enzyme that is required to convert 1 micro-mole of the substrate in one minute. Like most chemical processes, however, the functionality of enzymes is influenced by external factors, such as temperature, pH and the presence of other substances that can alter the behaviour of the enzyme molecule.

Carbonic anhydrase is an example of an enzyme with a very high level of catalytic ability. It is involved in the conversion of carbon dioxide to bicarbonate and protons. On its own, the process is very slow, but when carbonic anhydrase is present the reaction is extremely fast.

Some chemicals that are structurally similar to the substrates are able to bind to an enzyme's active site - this inhibits the reaction, completely blocking the catalysis. For example, several heavy metals - including mercury and lead, are toxic because their ions bind to the cysteine residues present in the molecules of many enzymes. As a result of this, they are rendered inactive, and the life processes that depend on them are unable to function, causing death or disability.

▲ Relations between enzyme and substrate
Computer simulation of the interaction between enzyme and substrate. On the left the enzyme active site with the space, on the right the substrate in place in the active site of the enzyme.

▼ Reactions to confrontation
Representation of the same reaction in the absence of a catalyst (above) and in the presence (below). The diagram on the right summarizes the changes in energy potential of two reactions: It is obvious that in the first case (red line) the activation of energy is much higher than the second (blue line). The presence of the enzyme, thus facilitates the reaction, which in future will need a lesser amount of energy compared to the other. With the same amount energy of available, therefore, can take place more reactions.

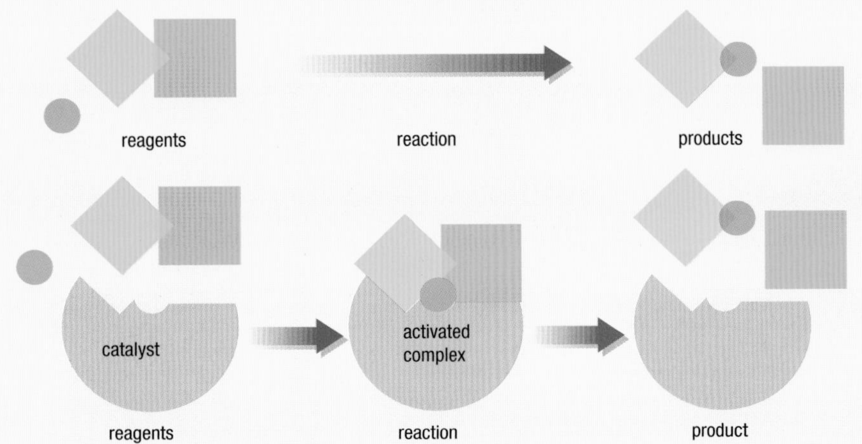

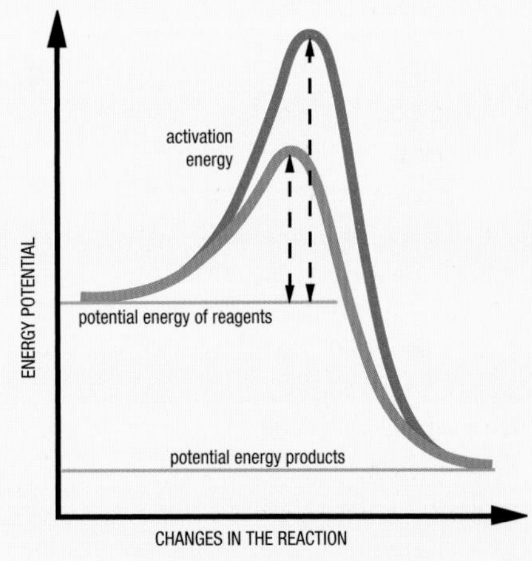

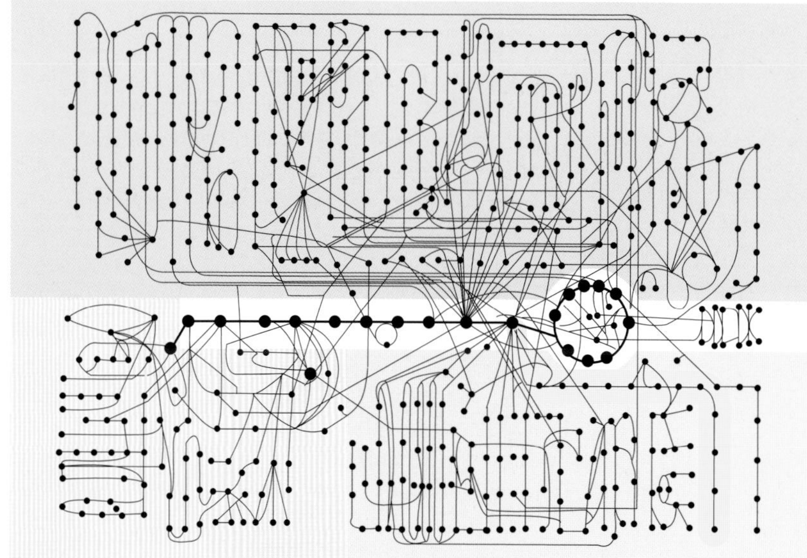

▶ **THE METABOLISM** *The tangle of lines of this figure gives a concrete idea, but still very approximate complexity of the physical-chemical reactions that make up the cellular metabolism. The scheme, in fact, shows all the different metabolic pathways and their intersections. The dots indicate the major metabolites, ie substances that participate in metabolic reactions, the lines suggest the sequences of reactions of the metabolites which are, from time to time, reagents or products. The background colors indicate the major metabolic pathways:*

- ☐ *by glycolysis and Krebs cycle;*
- ☐ *carbohydrate metabolic pathways;*
- ☐ *Lipid metabolic pathways;*
- ☐ *metabolic pathways of amino acids;*
- ☐ *metabolic pathway that leads by acetilysis to cholesterol.*

network that can be sub-divided into metabolic chains and metabolic cycles. Some of the pathways involved are short, whereas others are long. Some are reversible and others are not. In many of the cycles, however, the substances concerned are regenerated over and over again as they are repeatedly transformed back and forth from one chemical form to another.

To simplify the study and understanding of the metabolic processes involved, they have been divided into two major groups:

- the **anabolic** processes, together with any endergonic reactions (those which absorb energy from their surroundings); these lead to the synthesis of complex molecules from simpler molecules;

- the **catabolic** processes, together with any exergonic reactions (those which release energy in the form of work); these lead to the production of complex molecules from simple ones.

THE ANABOLISM

Most of the biological molecules needed to build and keep alive a cell are unable to pass through the cell's outer membrane. Consequently, they must be produced inside the cell. For example, proteins are synthesised from amino acids; membranes are assembled with lipids (phosphorylated or linked to sugar molecules), and so forth. All of these reactions are anabolic - they are not spontaneous reactions, but can only take place with an injection of energy. That is why they are coupled with other reactions that produce the energy needed, especially in the form of two coenzymes: ATP and NADH. These molecules are produced by catabolic reactions: they bind reversibly with the ion phosphate (PO3-) and the hydrogen ion (H-). Under cytoplasmic conditions, the ATP reacts very easily with water (H2O) and hydrolyses according to the reaction:

$$ATP + H_2O \rightarrow ADP + P$$

This frees up to 54.4 kJ / M (~ 13 kcal / M) of energy. It is the availability of ATP that makes it possible for the synthesis of biomolecules, the active transport of substances in the membrane, the contraction of muscle tissues, and many other processes vital for life.

ATP is a form of chemical energy that is instantly usable by the cell, and is therefore constantly being consumed and produced. It is the energy currency that allows vital cell processes to take place. While NADH is mainly present to reduce and oxidise the molecules, the ATP is phosphorylated by enzymes called kinases. These transfer the groups to the phosphate molecules that require energy to react.

THE CATABOLISM

While anabolic reactions are used to build new molecules, catabolic reactions have the double purpose of deconstructing the nutrients in order to reduce them to molecules that are useful to the anabolic processes. At the same time, they also store chemical energy, which is then liberated in the form of ATP. The proteins, lipids and polysaccharides - that is, the substances that make up the majority of foods, are divided into their fundamental units in the digestive system. There they are reduced to relatively small molecules, but these are then reduced further when they are used as fuel for the catabolic reactions. These are almost all catabolic oxidation events that develop energy thanks to the formation of strong links between the carbon and hydrogen atoms that are contained in the nutrients.

▲ **NADH AND ATP** *Chemical Structure of the main energy molecules produced during the reactions cataboliche: NADH (nicotinamide-adenin-dinucleotide reduced) el'ATP (adenosin-triphosphate).*

Oxidative catabolism, therefore is a process that, from a chemical perspective, is analogous to combustion. Like a fire burning, glucose that is combined with oxygen turns completely into carbon dioxide (CO2). Catabolic reactions take place almost exclusively in mitochondria. The only significant catabolic reaction that occurs in the cytoplasm is the transformation of mono-pyruvic acid in what is known as glycolysis. This, together with the Krebs cycle, plays a crucial role in cellular activity, and is an anaerobic process that does not require the presence of oxygen. It is thought that this came about at a time when the primordial Earth's atmosphere of was devoid of oxygen. It may well therefore represent one of the oldest mechanisms in nature that was developed by cells to exploit the chemical energy of sugar.

In the process of glycolysis, pyruvic acid is transformed into an acetyl group (CH3COS-) which is then used to build the acetyl-coenzyme A (acetyl-CoA), a biological molecule of great importance that is produced in large quantities during the degradation of fatty acids. The last act of chemical deconstruction takes place entirely within mitochondria. There, it is the decomposition of the acetyl-CoA acetyl group in carbon dioxide and water, that produces most of the ATP in the cell.

The reaction that leads to the production of ATP is disadvantaged from the energetic point of view because it, in turn, needs energy to occur. It therefore only becomes possible if the relevant reactions take place to provide the necessary elements. The reaction itself is very efficient - approximately 50% of the theoretically available energy is obtained from the combustion of carbohydrates and fats. This efficiency is remarkable compared to the fact that the very best energy performance that can be extracted from the very best internal combustion engines is only around 20%. The remaining energy – as with a car engine, is lost as heat. The further reduction of nutrients to carbon dioxide and water then occurs through a series of aerobic reactions (which require oxygen). The efficient and orderly removal of energy from these molecules begins with the citric acid or Krebs cycle (named in honour of its discoverer) and ends with the oxidative phosphorylation.

The Krebs cycle is carried out by a series of enzymes that are a constitutive part of the structure of mitochondria. This process is crucial for the cellular metabolism, and is where the oxidation of the acetyl group acetyl-CoA takes place. The carbon atoms from this are transformed into carbon dioxide, and for each acetyl group, three molecules of NADH are produced. The oxidative phosphorylation involves the transfer of hydrogen from NADH and FADH2 into molecular oxygen which then spreads within the cell. Simultaneously, a series of enzymes and molecules of the so-called respiratory chain (which are also an integral part of the inner membrane of mitochondria) as the result of the transport of electrons force the expulsion of H+ ions. In the matrix, the free hydrogen binds to oxygen so that, for every atom of oxygen that is transformed into water, 3 molecules of ATP are produced. The presence of oxygen, therefore, is essential both to complete the Krebs cycle, and to allow the normal transport of electrons; its absence leads to early cell death.

Complete oxidation of 1 mole (R) of glucose (180 g) develops 2870 kJ (about 686 kcal), 1159 of which are stored in 38 M ATP. In theoretical terms, therefore, the energetic return of the catabolism of glucose is 40.4%. The cell, however, still manages to increase this by exploiting various conditions under which the metabolic reactions take place.

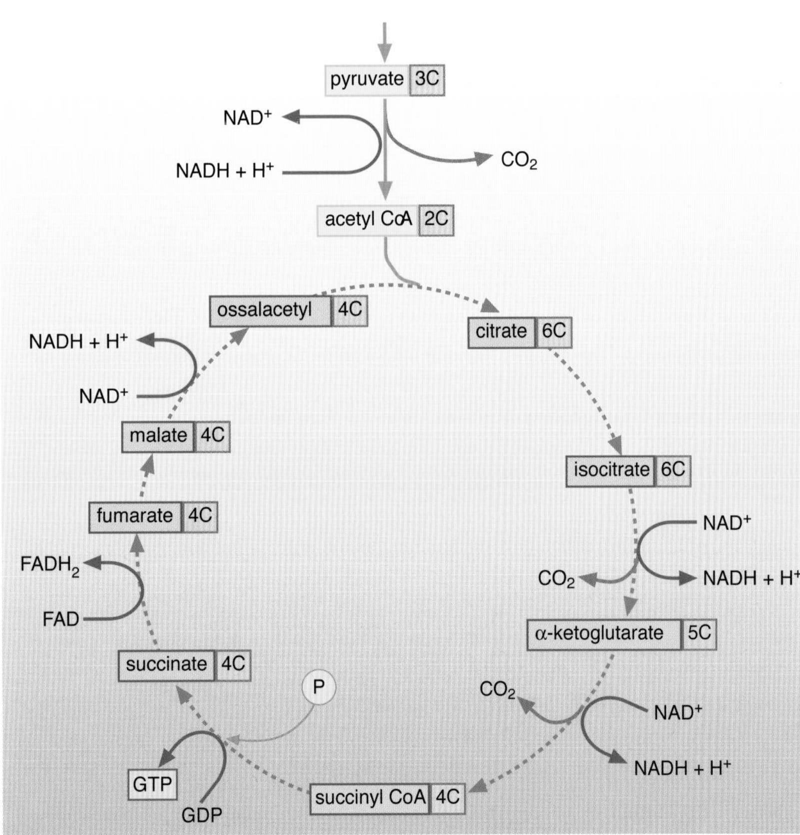

▼ **Krebs cycle**
Outline of the reactions forming this fundamental metabolic pathway. His understanding, which has yielded Hans A. Krebs the Nobel Prize, has made it possible to make considerable progress in understanding the cellular biochemistry.

FROM THE CELL BODY: BASIC METABOLISM

Since the reactions that are vital to life are conducted at the cellular level, any physiological activity that concerns structures like tissues and organs relies entirely on the cells performing their roles correctly. To eat and breathe, for example, requires the maintenance of cellular metabolic reactions that take in a constant flow of substances that cells are not able to produce themselves (energy-rich sugars, cofactors such as vitamins and minerals, but also water and oxygen). For

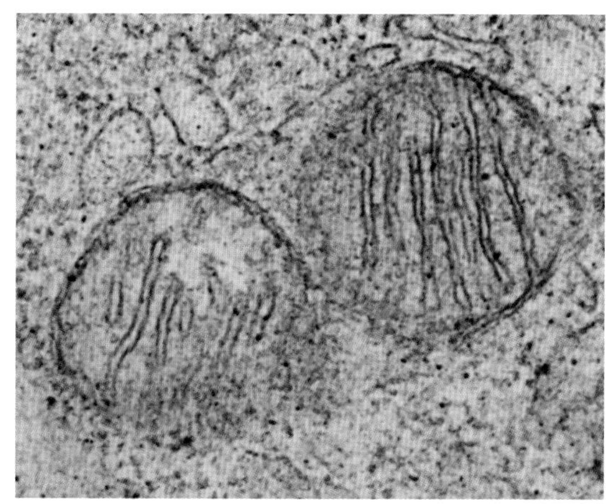

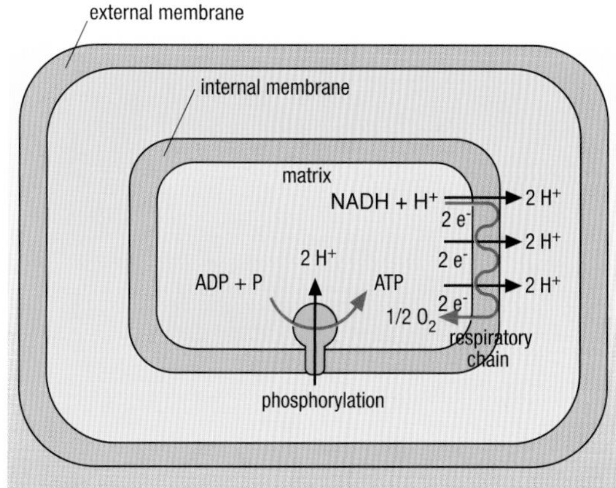

◀◀ **Central energy**
Micrograph of mitochondria (green, in section).

◀ **Respiration**
Schematic of a mitochondria and the events leading to the synthesis of ATP. The ridges are located inside the system of enzymes and electron carriers of the respiratory chain. These are sorted according to the reduction potential. At the end of the chain there is oxygen, with the highest potential, "greedy" for electrons. The energy released from the transfer of electrons is used to pump H + ions out of the inner membrane and synthesize ATP.
The components of the chain are: flavinmononucleotide (FMN); ubichinone or coenzyme Q, cytochrome (cit)

the body's activities to function smoothly, all the processes have to be well co-ordinated. Thus it is necessary for all the physical-chemical conditions to remain constant. This includes such factors as the chemical composition of all the internal components, as well as their internal temperatures, and so on, as well as higher level matters such as cardiac function, respiration, etc. The minimum amount of energy that is needed to maintain active processes and still survive in a state of absolute rest is called the basal metabolism. This corresponds to the intensity of the overall cellular respiration and is linked to the consumption of oxygen. This can be quantified with the use of indirect calorimetry, a technique that allows you to measure in vivo and in a non-invasive manner the heat of oxidation of energy substrates. The calculations used take into account age, sex, weight and body surface area, all variables that may interfere with the metabolism baseline as well as some substances (amphetamines or thyroid hormones). The amount of oxygen consumed can be traced back to the energy needs of an individual per unit of time.

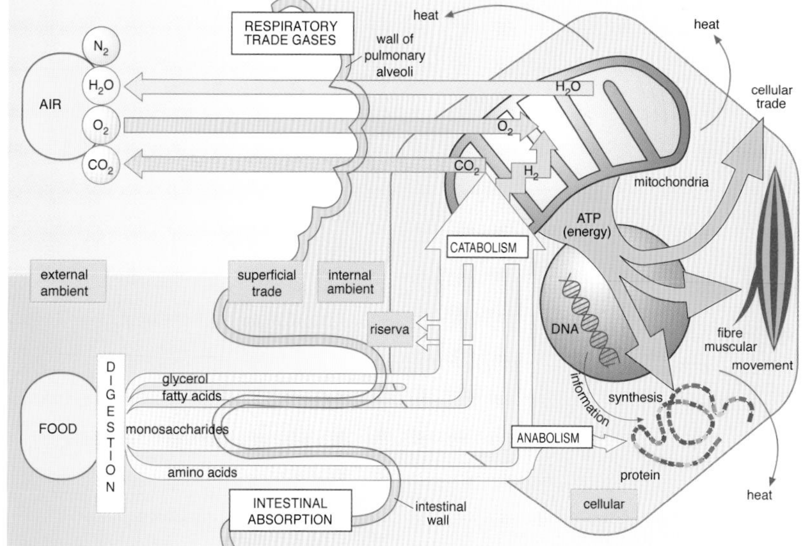

▲ **From the body to the cell and back**
The chemical energy absorbed from the outside in the form of food is transformed into another type of chemical energy by cellular respiration: the synthesis of ATP is necessary in order to more easily create energy for other changes.
In addition to simple nutrients (amino acids, lipids carbohydrates) the cell receives oxygen necessary to complete reactions of oxidative catabolism.
Conversely, the cell succumbs to ambient heat, carbon dioxide, water vapor and other molecules waste.

THE BASIC STRUCTURES AND PROCESSES OF LIFE REMAIN THE SAME IN EVERY CELL DURING EMBRYONIC DEVELOPMENT OF THE BODY.
THERE ARE MANY DIFFERENT TYPES OF SPECIALIZED CELLS, EACH PERFORMING A PARTICULAR FUNCTION.

TYPES OF CELLS

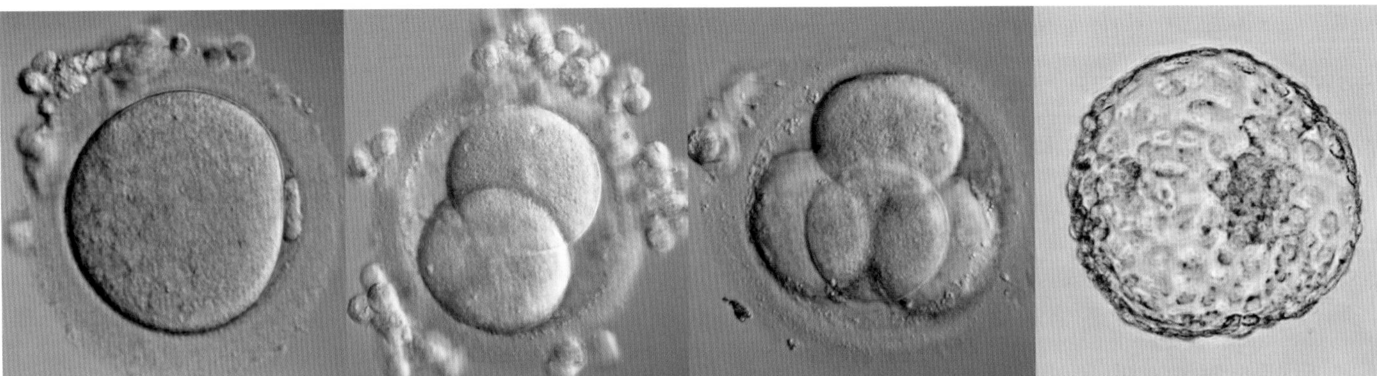

▲ **EMBRYONIC DEVELOPMENT**
Some stages of human embryonic development: from left to right a zygote, an embryo in the 2 cell stage; an embryo in the 4-cells stage and in the Blastocyst stage.

▼ **CELLS IN DIVISION**
An image showing the mitotic spindles. In flourescent are the cell structures that separate the duplicating chromosones that form two new nuclei.

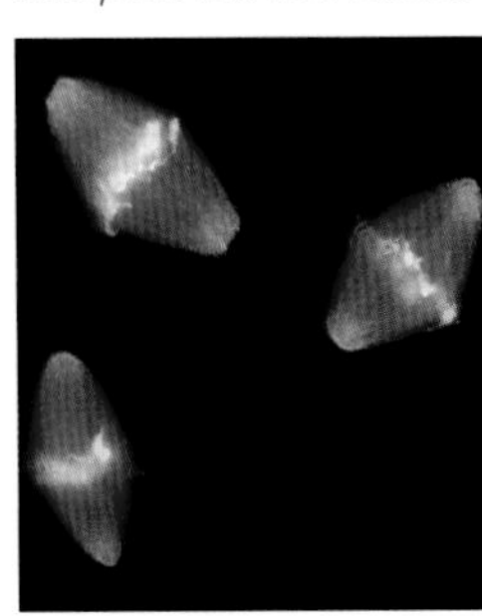

Every cell in the body has all the characteristics of a living organism its own right, however, each is just one of many components that go together to create biological tissues. These, in turn, then combine to form more complex structures. The same organisation of tissues, organs and systems is the result of chemical and physical messages that are closely linked with other cells. The structural and functional specialisation of cells and their organisation in complex networks of relationships, therefore, is crucial for the development of an body evolved organisation in complex networks of relationships, therefore, is crucial for the development of an body.

THE DIFFERENTIATION

All cells within a body are born equal, in that they are all created from stem cells that arose from the same fertilised egg or zygote ►248. A short time after fertilisation, when a few divisions have occurred but before the embryo has been implanted ►248, the cells begin to diversify more and more until, at birth, all are recognisable as cells of different tissues. In many cases they have also lost some functional capacity, such as that of replication.

GENES AND CHEMICAL SIGNALS

Underlying the processes of cell differentiation are the differential expressions of genes that lead totipotent stem cells - which form the embryo and have unlimited opportunities to replicate and transform themselves, to gradually lose the ability to express some specific parts of their genetic heritage.
As the divisions take place, only a portion of the DNA remains in each of the daughter cells, and many of the internal structures that form become specific to each type of cell. In fact, while retaining full genetic potential, much of the DNA in differentiated cells becomes redundant. This modulation of cellular genetics depends on a number of regulator factors which act on the transcription of genes or molecules that control the expression. According to recent theories, in fact, genes are not autonomous and independent entities that control protein synthesis, but are controlled in turn by proteins that are already present in the cell. While specialised cells remain, therefore, regulator factors must continue to be present. In other words, genes that produce them must always be active while other regions of DNA can be blocked permanently. Regulator factors are usually substances that are produced by each cell which then co-operate as a network.

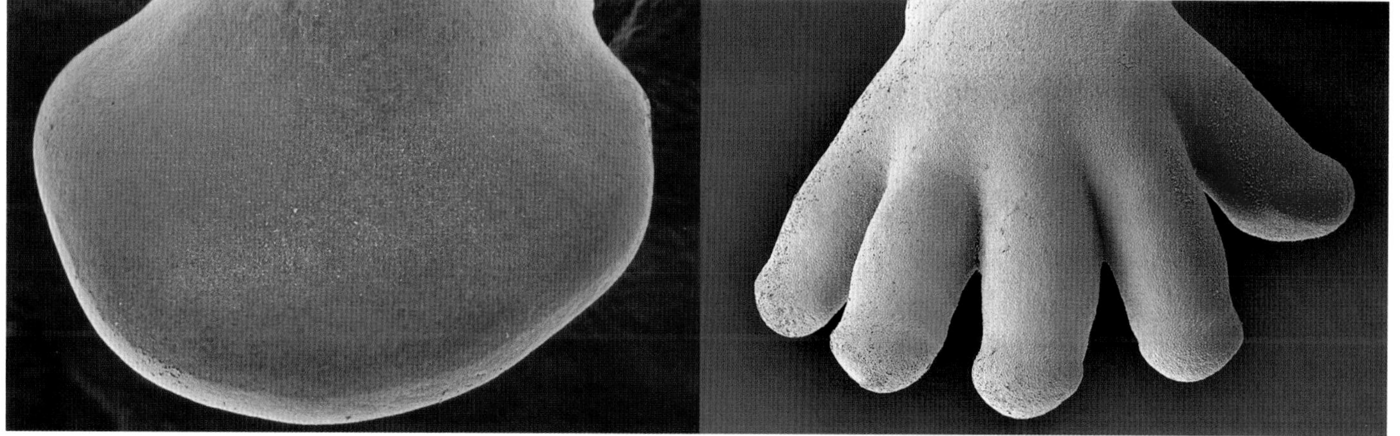

GROWTH FACTORS, RECEPTORS AND PROGRAMMED DEATH

The growth factors are soluble and pass through the membranes of cells that produce them, spreading in the extracellular matrix and also reaching the cells that are differentiating (cell-cell signals). The ones that are attached to the membrane and have specific receptors that bind chemically to growth factors are the only ones that are sensitive to these factors. This begins a chain of biochemical events that lead to differentiation. Often this cascade of reactions is driven by different signals that stimulate differentiated cells to produce their signals - these then contribute to drive the entire embryo into a coherent development. Each cell, therefore, checks and stimulates the differentiation of others. The growth factors play multiple functions:

- they make it possible for the cell to survive;
- they stimulate proliferation, namely cell division;
- they induce differentiation by blocking the expression of certain genes.

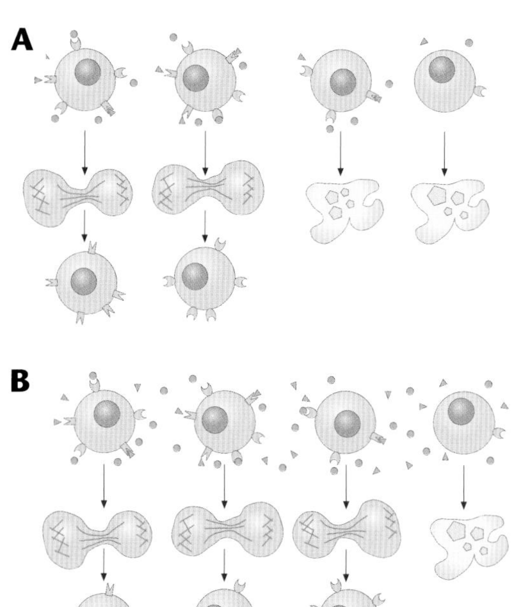

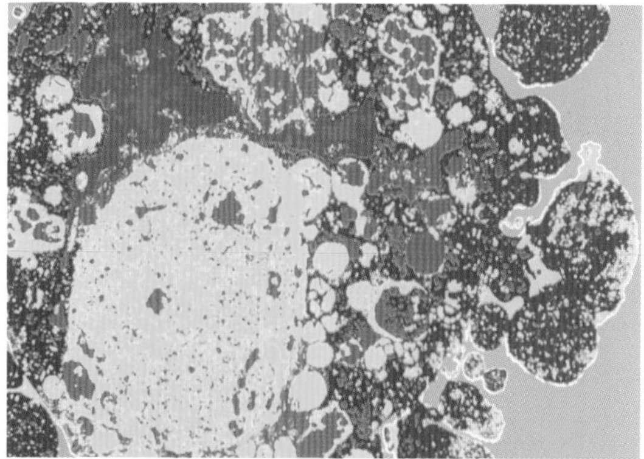

But things are not always so simple - at different times of differentiation the same factor can play a variety of different roles. In different cells they can produce receptors that recognise other factors.

Further to this, the growth factors are not available in unlimited quantities - any stem cells that are unable to acquire enough will die. This creates a constant competition for survival. In terms of balanced development, a part of the stem cell is destined to die. The term for this is 'apoptosis', and is a process of death led by intercellular signals; this helps to shape the new body.

Embryonic differentiation ►248 is a very complex process of actions and reactions, with cells destined to form an entire region of the body gradually acquiring the necessary specialisation. The genetic and molecular mechanisms lead to the production of different cell types. These are used to build tissues and, finally, the construction of the new body. The construction of a precise biological architecture is determined by a specific chain of events which differs from tissue to tissue. Each being tailored to the needs of each cell in a specific time and at a specific location. Such activities have their own identities that are co-ordinated in a manner consistent with other cells, and are capable of performing all the functions necessary for survival

▲ **Embryonic hand**
The development of fingers from the embryonic skeleton (left) is a typical example in which apoptosis contributes to shaping the body.

◄ **Apoptosis**
During death by apoptosis, a series of processes leading to instability of the membrane releases "drops" of cytoplasm.

◄ **Competition**
The link to growth factors may determine the survival of the cell. Stem cells in relation to the availability of growth factors, die of apoptosis (a). If you need to create a larger number of stem cells, the body produces greater amounts of growth factors (b).

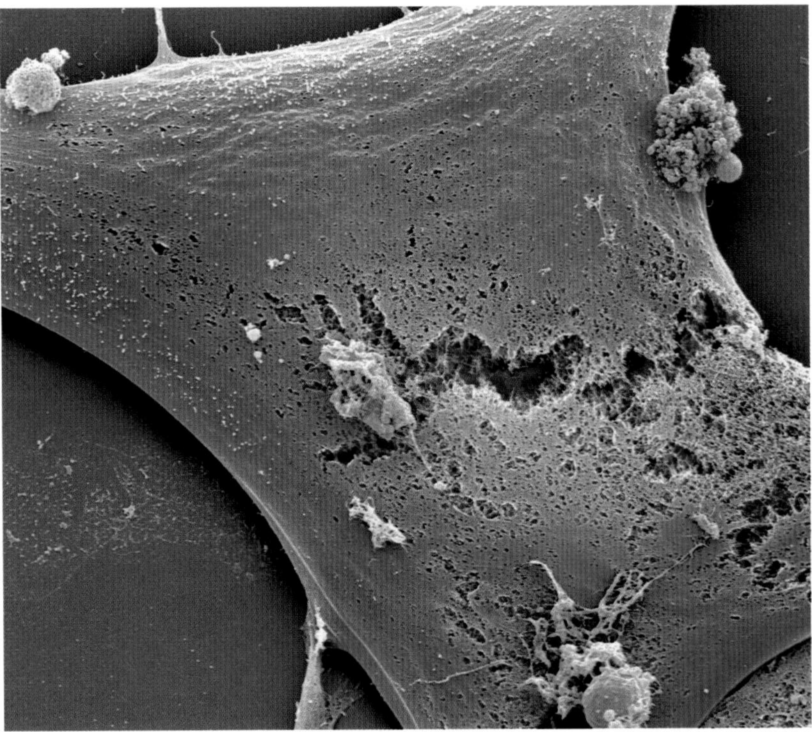

▲ **Cellular nutrition**
A scanning electron microscopy (SEM) micrograph in false colors showing a fibroblast (big and orange). This type of cell is typical of connective tissue: they are able to produce collagen, reticular and elastic fibers and glycoproteins that are found in the extracellular field. Fibroblasts that are treated so as not to split are used to keep a culture of embryonic stem cells (green dots) and they in fact, "adorn" the petri disks with a fund of culture from which the embryonic cells act as biochemical signals that block differentiation, but take active division.

in the body.

THE IMPORTANT THING IS TO COMMUNICATE

It is clear that communication between cells is essential for the correct functioning of a body. The ways of evolution that have produced so many different forms of increasingly complex life are also based on forms of intercellular communication that are increasingly articulated and varied.

Normally, the cells in the body continuously receive and interpret signals that come from such things as the variations in light, temperature, pressure, availability of water or concentrations of particular molecules. This communication either leads to cell division and cell differentiation, or the maintenance of uniform tissues. There are three basic channels:

- adherence involves a continuous passage of information between cells that are in contact with each other;
- the production of substances (hormones, neurotransmitters, cytokines, etc.), in which cells have specific membrane receptors that allow cells to communicate with one another even though they may be located far apart;
- the ability to change the permeability of the cell membrane allows excitable cells to produce and transmit electrochemical signals that involve large numbers of cells throughout the body.

ADHERENCE TO COMMUNICATE

In the body cells often inextricably align themselves with each other. Remaining neighbours to each other, they co-ordinate with regard to specific functions or biological actions through a close network of internal and external chemical messages. The accession takes place thanks to particular molecules in the cell membrane: they recognise each other and bind to one another. In each cell, this close interaction can be associated with internal reporting systems that are activated when they first bond.

The first accession molecules were discovered in immune cells ▸108, however, we now know that every cell of the body owns and uses these molecules or chemical structures in a similar manner. That is why, in recent years, cell membership has increasingly been regarded as a genuine form of intercellular communication. In particular, it is involved in complicated processes such as proliferation and cell differentiation, embryonic development and growth, the genesis of organs and the operation of complex organic systems.

As research in this field progresses, we discover that there is an increasing number of membrane receptors. These are constituents of the cell membrane that are identified by their ability to bind to specific molecules. This communication network has an even more important function for the immune system ▸100. This is where the cells exploit the rich assortment of accession molecules that move through the cells of other tissues and reach areas of the body subjected to an attack. This is both to prevent an immune response to individual subgroups of specialised cells. In particular, dendrites 193 and macrophages 131 are linked to one another by an extensive network of tiny tubules (nanotubules) of variable length and a diameter of between 35 and 200 nm. Each cell can have up to 75 of these minuscule tubes, and uses them to send high-speed signals to other cells that may be some way away. This discovery explains the incredible speed of immune response: in addition to neurons, other cells are able to communicate directly, by contact, with cells over long distances.

CHEMICAL MESSAGES AND MEMBRANE RECEPTORS

A cell is able to receive a chemical signal only if it has specific receptors in the membrane for that signal. The receptors activate specific endocellular mediators inducing the reaction. The receptors, therefore, function as molecular antennae that capture external messages. These are then transmitted inside the cell through a complex chain of biochemical events.

A receptor is a protein that is able to chemically bind to a extracellular molecule. It normally works as an ion channel: the union with the external molecule (the "chemical message") will change the shape and its chemical characteristics. This allows the flow of certain ions into the cell - the ionic current then triggers a series of reactions that cascade and usually lead to the phosphorylation of a protein that plays an essential role in a particular biological cell process.

As often happens in biological reactions, however, this cascade of events is subject to numerous feedbacks: the excess or lack of substances involved in the chain of reactions can slow the transmission of the message enough to block it completely; conversely, they can make it work extremely quickly.

The phosphorylation of proteins is a chemical process that takes place only thanks to a special cellular enzyme - this is the protein kinase. Their work is regulated by molecules like adenosin-3 ', 5'-cyclic phosphate (better known as AMPc), guanosin-cyclic monophosphate (or GMPc), the calcium ion ($Ca2 +$), the inositol triphosphate ($IP3$). Some diglycerides are known as second messengers - these spring into operation at the moment that a link is established between the receptor and an external messenger.

The substances that can bind to receptors membrane are:

- hormones ►200, endocrine substances that are released from other cells that are often far from the source of the chemical message. These reach the receptors through blood circulation and target the cells that modulate the metabolism and / or the activities of cells within tissues and organs;
- cytokines, proteins similar to hormones (paracrine ►201) and histamine ►95, which are produced by a wide range of cells, including those in the immune system. They reach the target cells by spreading through the intercellular mass, and control the survival, growth and cell differentiation;
- the neurotransmitters and neuromodulators ►28, neurocrine substances that are produced by the nervous system and released from neurons which act in the immediate vicinity of the cell that produced them (synapses). They mediate the transmission of signals to excitable cells and interact with receptors in the membrane of nearby cells.

Sometimes, as well as triggering a cascade of biochemical events, the signalling and receptor systems merge into a single structure that penetrates

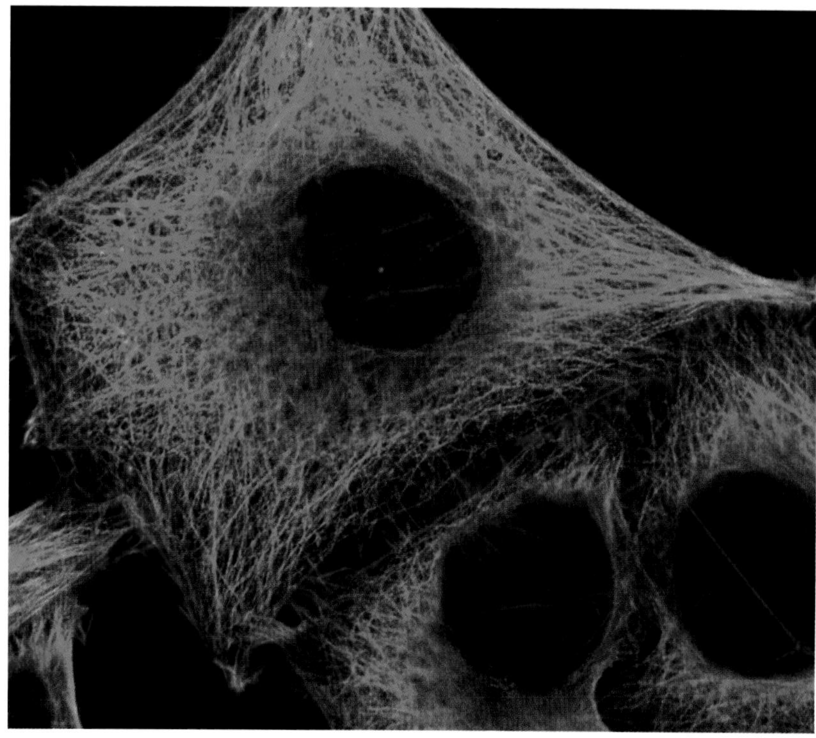

▲ **Nanotubules**
Co-focal optical microscope view of a cell culture. Fluorescent dyes were used to show the details of the red actin molecules (elastic) and green microtubulina that form the cytoskeleton. The microtubules - biological hollow fiber - were already known to be important elements in cell reproduction and formation of cilia and flagella. Today we know that they may also represent an important part of communication between cells.

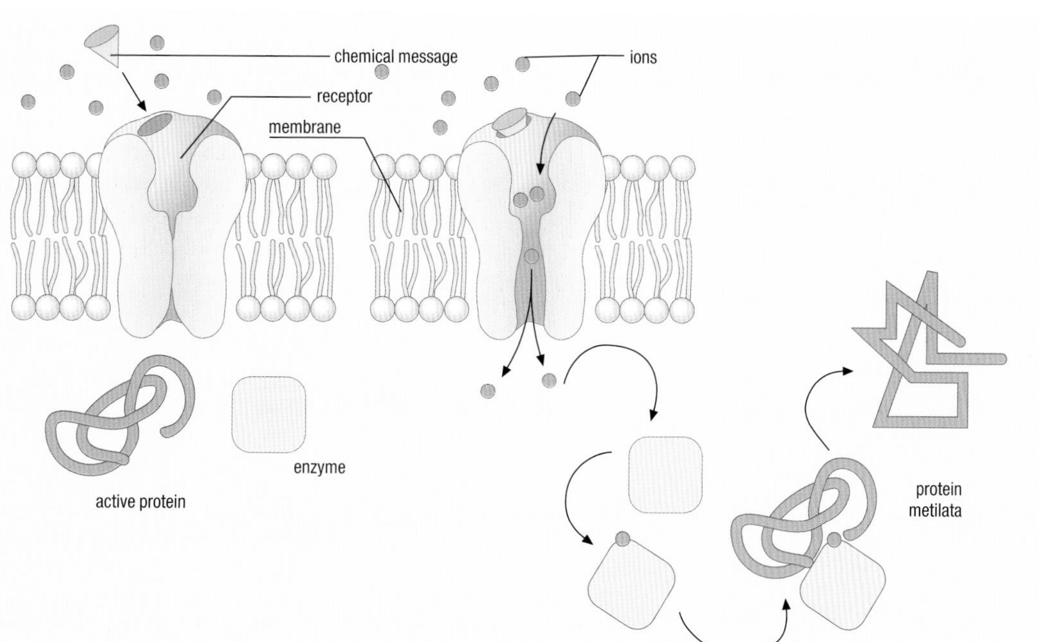

◄ **Chemical messages**
By binding to a membrane receptor, a "chemical message" alters their function, for example by allowing an influx into the cell of specific ions. Often these are cofactors of enzymes inside the cell, altering a particular protein (eg methylation) and they influence in this way the entire cellular metabolism.

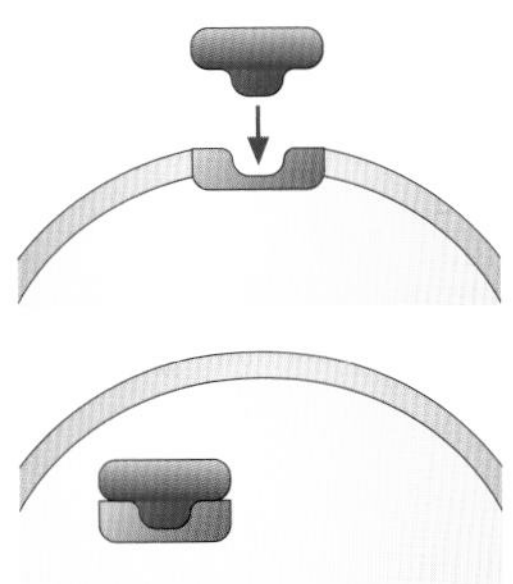

▲ **Hormonal stimulation**
Some hormones form with their receptors a unique chemical structure that sinks in, triggering specific cell biochemical processes.

into the cell and triggers specific processes. This is what happens, for example, with certain hormones. In order for this to be possible, the plasma membrane is fluid (rich in unsaturated fats) making it easy for hormones to act on the cell. This also applies to hormones such as insulin or thyroid hormones and steroids, which enter directly into the cell in order to bind onto receptors or the cytoplasmic membrane of the nucleus.

THE EXCITABLE CELLS

Some of the body's cells specialise in the collection and transmission of signals. These are the so-called excitable cells which are found in both nerve and muscle tissues. They are able to react quickly to any stimulus by changing its electric charge. Both of these types of cells have specific characteristics which are described in greater detail below.

THE POTENTIAL FOR MEMBRANE:

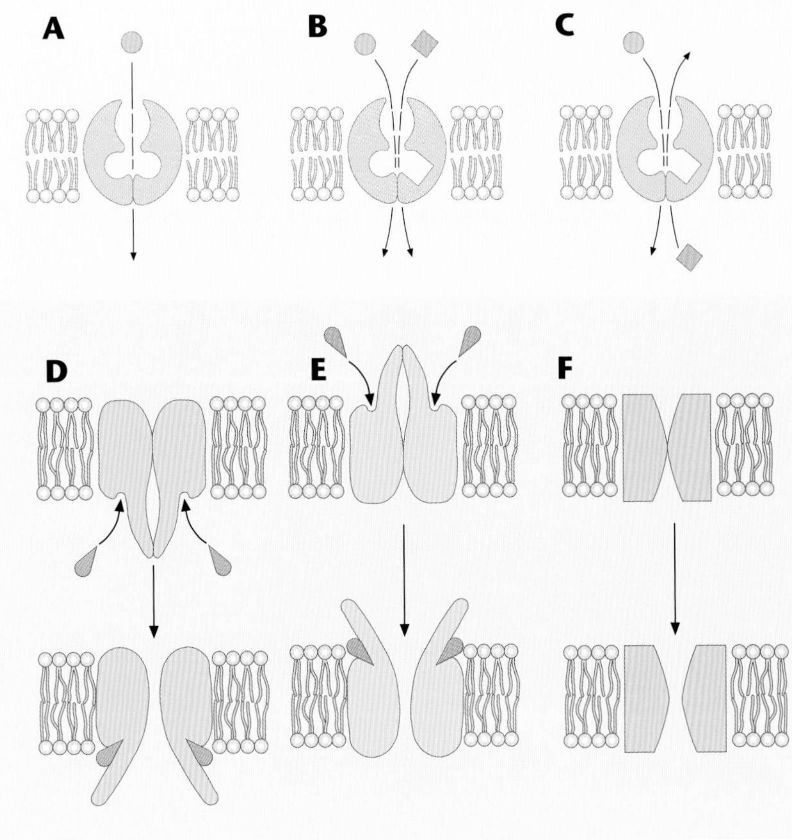

▲ **Ionic channels**
The images show different types of ion channels: **A**. *a protein carrier of a specific molecule (uniporto);* **B**. *a channel that allows the simultaneous transmission of a specific molecule and an ion (simporto);* **C**. *a channel that allows the exchange of contemporary molecule and ion (Antiporta);* **D**. *and* **E**. *channels that open and close in the presence of specific molecules (chemo-dependent) and extracellular endocellulari respectively;*
F. *channel that opens and closes according to the cellular electrical charge (voltage-dependent channel).*

ION CHANNELS, PUMPS AND VOLTAGE

The fundamental difference between the excitable cells and others is in their membranes.

All of the body's cell membrane channels have proteins that permit communication with the cytoplasm. These mainly allow the passive transport ▸17 of inorganic ions and therefore create an efficient pathway from one side of the membrane to the other. In addition, the large protein structures which form the pores or ion channels are highly selective. They are able to recognise specific ions, and in so doing only allow the correct ones to pass through the membrane. Over 100 different types have been identified, and various types can be found in the same cell.

The selectivity of an ion channel depends on the size of the ion (for example, the radius of the potassium ion K + is 0133 nm, that of the sodium ion Na + is 0095 nm), its electrical charge (positive or negative) and from the hydrating energy. In order to bind the respective ions together, the polarised proteins that are located in the membrane's channel must be partially dehydrated. The higher the energy of hydration, the harder it is for the bond to form - this is a disadvantage as far as the passage of ion through the membrane is concerned. Ions, however, remain bound in the channel for less than a thousandth of a second. They are pushed through by an electrochemical gradient membrane and rehydrated as soon as they arrive in the cytoplasm. These channels are 1000 times faster than proteins can be transported. The ion channels can be closed (inactive), open (active), or temporarily inactivated for the duration of the transport.

They respond to specific cell signals:

- As membrane ion concentration increases, their passive flow through the specific channels increases, but this can only happen up to the maximum speed at which the flow becomes saturated.
- The passive influx of ions through ion channels is constantly being countered by the active expulsion of specific ions ▸17 through ionic pumps that are controlled by the cell. The number of positive electric charges inputs is, in fact, balanced by the expulsion of an equal number of electric charges. This is the explanation, for example, of the pumping of sodium (Na +-K +-ATP) through a set of molecular membranes that exploit the energy released from the hydrolysation of ATP in ADP + P. This pushes 3 molecules of Na + out of the cell and simultaneously pulls inside 2 molecules of K +, restoring the original ion gradient.
- There can be an unequal distribution of ions on both sides of the cell membrane. This is because of the difference between the ion concentrations inside and outside the cell, and is equivalent to

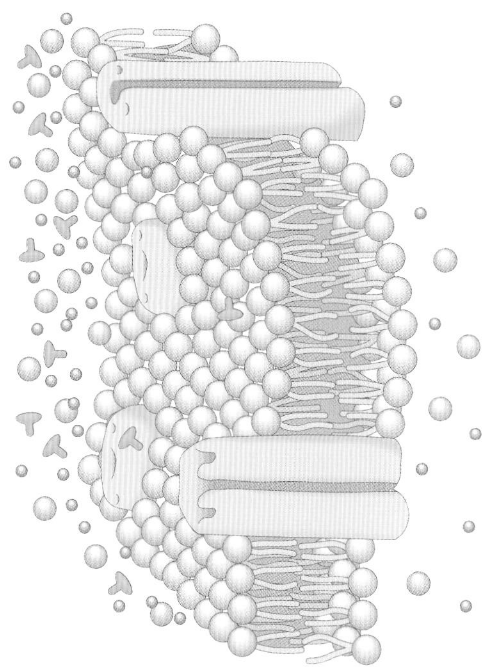

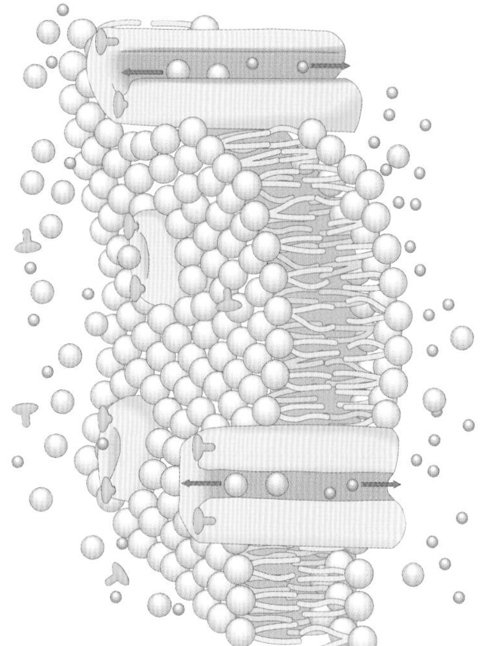

◀ **The passage of ions**
In this model of a membrane, a group of substances in solution (ions, sugars, amino acids) are found in different concentrations to the outside and inside the cell: **A**. *the outside, left, has a higher concentration.* **B**. *By binding to specific sites of ion channels, some molecules (orange tacks) activate the pump for the exchange of sodium and potassium: Na + ions (blue balls) are actively pumped out of the cell while simultaneously potassium ions K + (green balls) are pumped the into the cell.*

a difference in measurable electric charge which is called membrane potential. In particular, in animal cells it depends on the ion channels that continually take in K +, and the ionic pumps which actively draw this ion from the environment. The membrane potential, therefore, is the manifestation of electrical power which tends to enter K + ions in the cell, and its value can be calculated based on the intensity of the concentration gradient of K + ions.

The balance that occurs in cells is due to the fact that in the cytoplasm, there are proteins in solution that have a negative electrical charge (protein anions) that cannot cross the membrane. The interior of the cell, therefore, tends to always remains negative. So the influx of ions with the same negative electrical charge (such as with the ion chlorine, Cl-) is more difficult.

In terms of creating a balance - within the membrane there is less of a concentration of diffusible anions than outside it. On the outside you have a greater concentration of diffusible ions of opposite sign (cations). For the same reason, to maintain the electrochemical balance, the passage of each ion (K + or Cl-) from one side of the membrane to the other must be correctly offset. This can be done either by the passage in the opposite direction of an equal ion (since concentrations on the two sides must remain constant), or by an ion with opposite charge passing in the same direction and at the same time.

Like any other difference in electrical potential - including that of the cell membrane, is measured in volts, but these are minor differences, the unit of measurement used is the millivolt (mV). If we consider that a membrane potential can be -90 mV, we can see that potential equilibrium theory for K + ions (-102 mV) and Na + (+45 mV) are far from this value. The high membrane permeability of the K + ion is about 10 times greater than that of Na + ions. This avoids the rapid decay of the membrane potential that could occur with the massive input if it was not balanced by positive charges. This creates a situation of electrical balance but not a chemical one. The membrane potential remains constant until the ATP-dependent pump starts to operate. This situation occurs in all cells of the body.

POTENTIAL FOR STORING AND POTENTIAL ACTION

In excitable cells the membrane potential can change rapidly as a result of changes in the chemical or electrochemical state. This is what happens in response to environmental stimuli in nerve fibres and those muscle, as well as the glandular cells. In these types of cells, the potential remains stable if the separation of charges on both sides of the membrane remains constant. It may happen, however, that in a circumscribed area of the

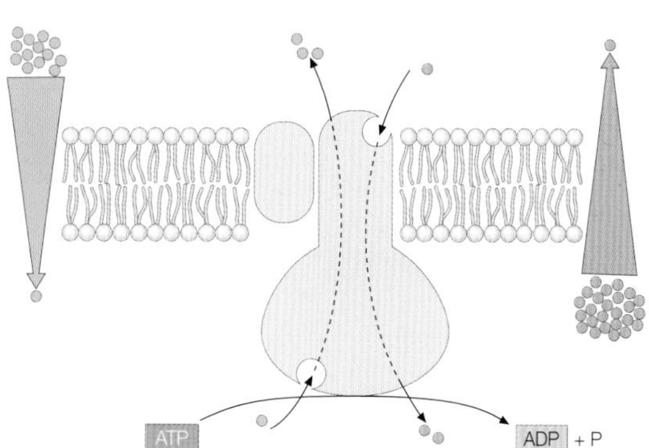

◀ **Na^{+}-ATP dependant onic pump**
The activity of ion channels of this kind (like the calcium ion channel or potassium ion), together with that of transport through the membrane, leading to the construction of a transmembrane electric potential, vital to cellular trade, both for the activity of excitable cells (muscle and nerve fibers).

membrane the following circumstances occur:

- membrane proteins specific to the transport of ions create a different ion concentration on the two sides of the cell membrane;
- an electrochemical gradient develops which becomes a source of potential energy;
- ion channels open which allow the flow of different ions according to their concentration gradients.

In this way, if it exceeds a specified threshold membrane depolarisation, it creates (according to a process of "all or nothing") rapid and transitional change in the rest potential, which is called potential action. This modification spreads fast (even 120 m / s) across the membrane of the cell: in this way the stimulus turns into an electrical signal, creating a transitional modification of the membrane potential. This makes it possible for signals to be transmitted across substantial distances from the point of the original stimulation. The potential for this to happen, however, becomes weaker with increasing distance. It is why it is necessary to expend energy on amplifying the signal if considerable distances are involved. In the body there are neurons of both types: ones which amplify the signal and ones that do not.

COMMUNICATION BETWEEN NERVE CELLS

The communication between nerve cells occurs through electrical signals or chemicals. The point where the messages pass from one nerve cell to another is called a synapse, and the cell that transmits the electrical signal is said to be 'presynaptic'. In a similar manner, the cell that receives the message referred to as 'postsynaptic'. The synapses may be of two types:

- an electrical synapse is a point where two excitable cells are so closely positioned that ions and other molecules (e.g. sucrose, AMPc and small peptides) can be exchanged between them. This therefore comprises a mechanism for transmitting information and electrical stimuli. When examined under electron microscopy, it can be seen that the membranes between such adjoining cells are merged. In fact, the two cells are connected by protein channels that cross the space that separates the synapse. This kind of synapse is typical of the links between neurons, and is an exceptionally quick communication route that allows the synchronisation of activity between many nearby cells. It is often found in tissues where it is necessary to co-ordinate cellular activity both effectively and quickly, for example, in cardiac muscles or the tissues in various smooth muscles.
- the chemical synapses are more numerous and also mediate communications between nerve cells and muscle cells or between nerve cells and glandular cells. In the vicinity of synapses, the cell produces specific presynaptic substances called neurotransmitters or chemical mediators (such as acetylcholine). When the location where the substances are accumulated is depolarised by the arrival of a potential action, they are released at the synapse where they bind to specific receptors on the postsynaptic cell membrane.

The chemical synapses may have contradictory effects:

- excitatory synapses in the neurotransmitter work to depolarise the postsynaptic cell - this causes the changes required to produce a new potential for action in the membrane. If the postsynaptic cell is another neuron, it develops a potential action identical to the previous one. This then quickly propagates to the nucleus of the postsynaptic cell; if this is a muscle fibre, for example, the receipt of the signal will produce a contraction. If it is part of a gland, it will cause a secretion.
- inhibitory synapses in the neurotransmitter bind to the membrane of the postsynaptic cell increasing the potential for rest. This causes inhibition in the postsynaptic cell, and opposes any excitatory signal in the cell and helps neutralise it. In this

▼ **Nerve fibers**
A nerve fiber through an optical microscope. These cells are excitable: there are very different types that are, sensitive to light or auditory stimuli, pain, differences in pressure or temperature, and so on. All stimuli triggering an act in some way, a potential action.

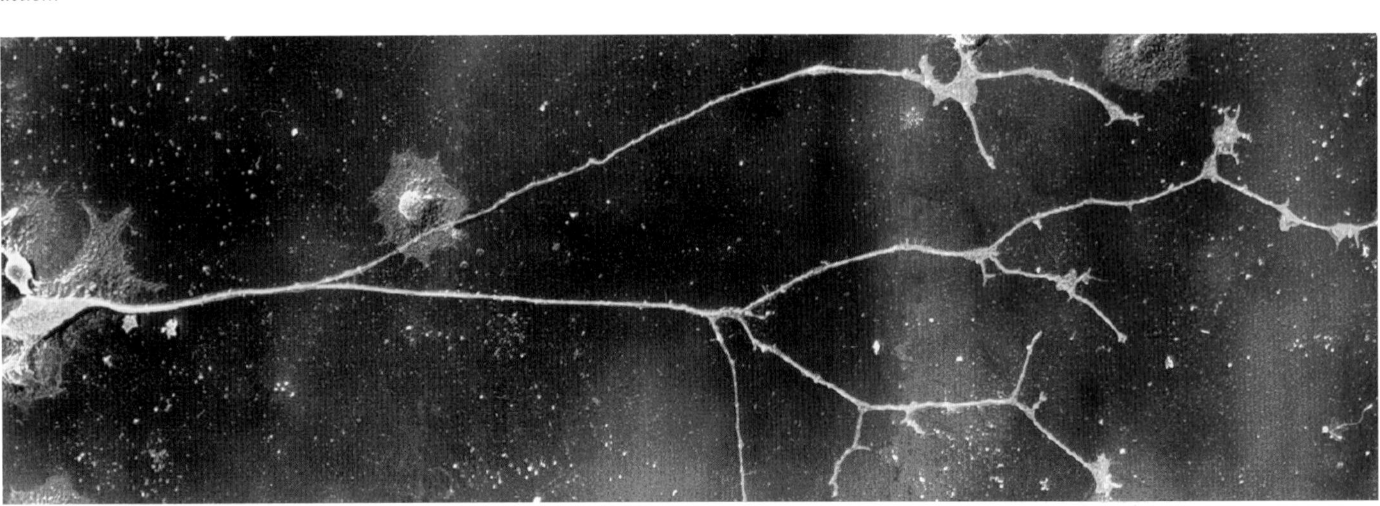

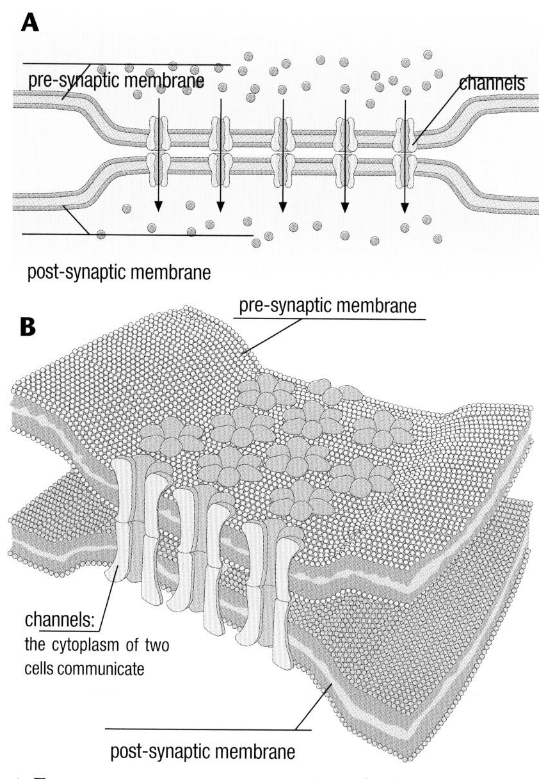

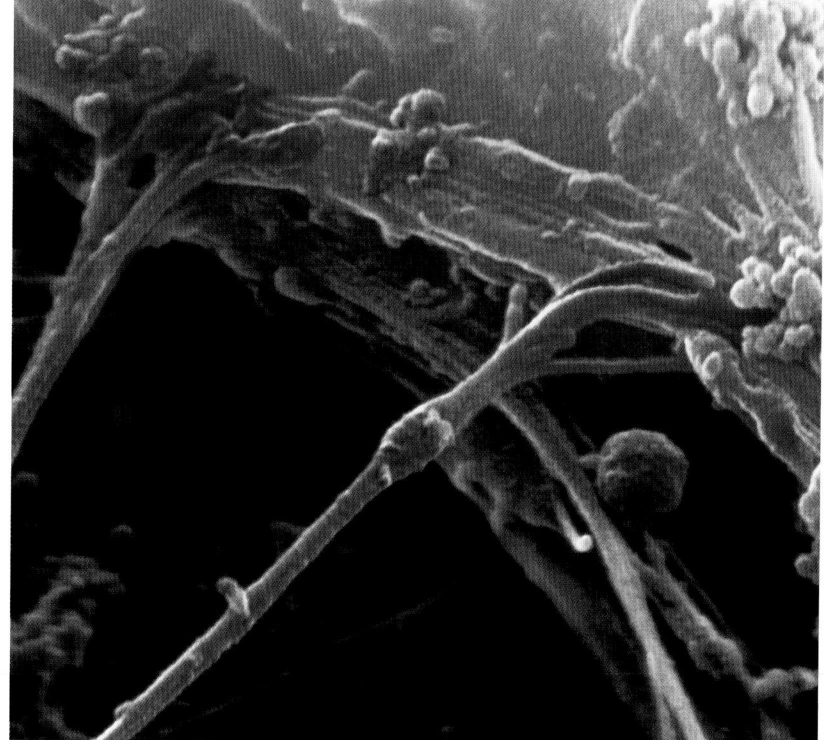

▲ **Electrical synapses**
*Section (**A**) and three-dimensional reconstruction (**B**) of an electrical synapse. The membranes of both excitable cells are in direct connection and through the protein channel (the connection) you can exchange ions and molecular information, coordinating with efficiency and speed of their physiological action. SEM Photography in false colors shows that the contact points between two nerve fibers (one in purple, the other in yellow). Pulses are transmitted through the viola come inside the body from cell-mediated synapses, which appear as slight swellings. The shift in the cell of various types of substances determines - in the second cell - the emergence of a potential action away from the nucleus is spread along the membrane.*

case, if the postsynaptic cell is another neuron, it will be inhibited and not send any other electrical signal. If it is a muscle fibre it will be relaxed or prevented from contracting again. If the cell is glandular, its action will be inhibited for a certain period, or secretion will be prevented.

In a similar manner to the stimulatory effects, the inhibitors only work temporarily. But what happens in an excitable cell when it is stimulated? Take for example a neuron at rest - that is, one which is not excited. It does not transmit electrical signals, and its conditions are equivalent to those of other cells of the body, with the interior electrically negative compared to externally. Its membrane potential is about -70 mV, determined mainly by the gradient of concentration of K + ions. In a neuron at rest, then, most of the K + ions are internal (their concentration is about 20 times higher than externally) while most of the Na + ions are external (their concentration is approximately 10 times that of the internal).

When a point on a neuron's membrane receives a stimulus - be this mechanical (such as sound,

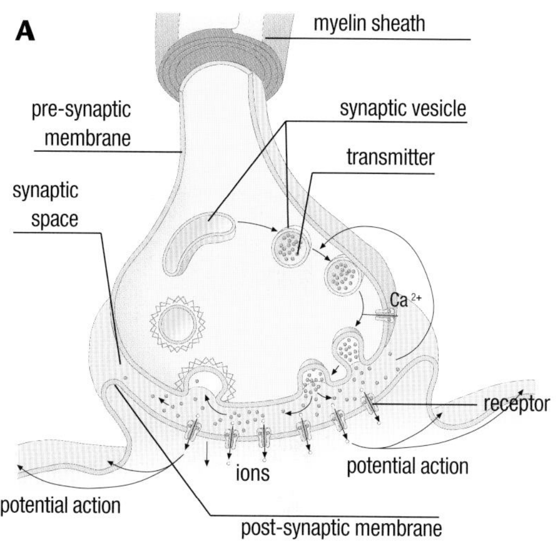

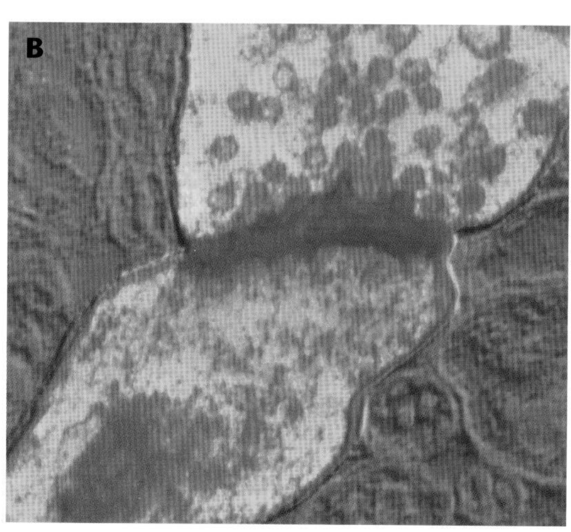

◀ **Chemical synapse**
A. *Section of a chemical synapses, mediated by neurotransmitters.*
B. *MET Photography of a chemical synapses. The cell presynaptics (top) is rich in vesicles where there are granules of neurotransmitter which will be released intersynaptic in the space (red).*

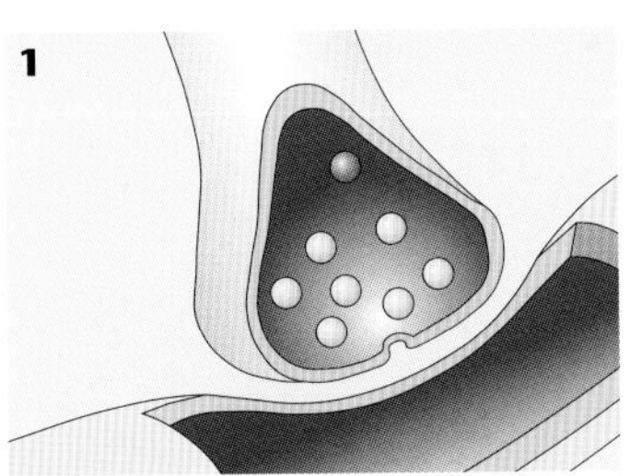

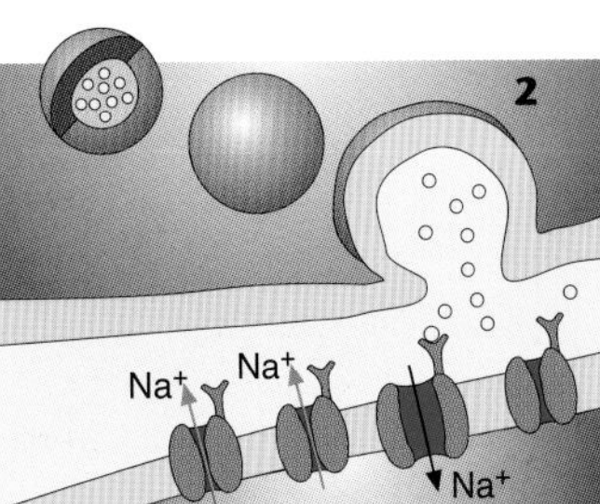

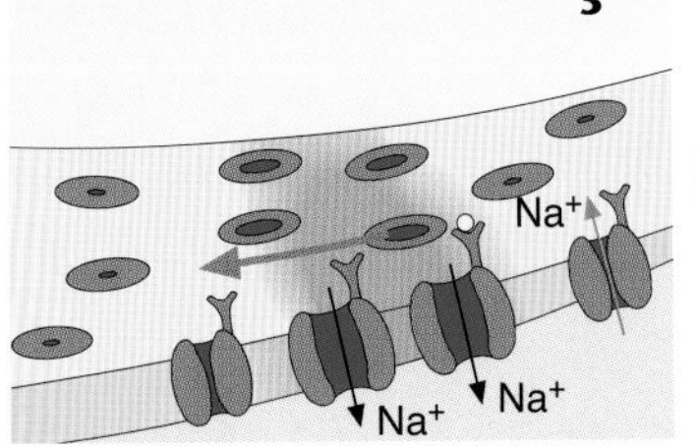

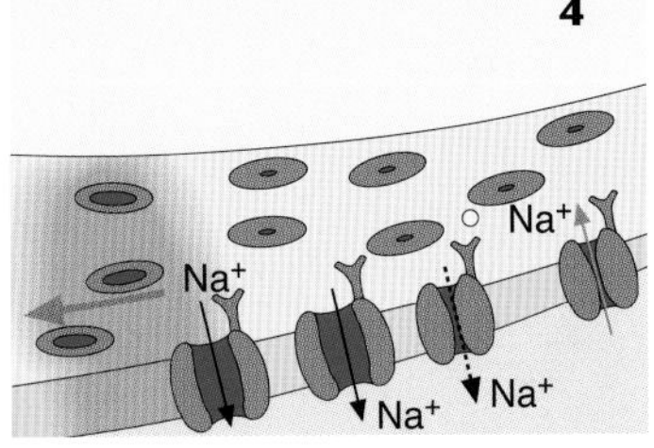

▲ **Nerve transmission**
Stages of chemically mediated nervosa transmission.
1. *The potential for action is approaching vesicles neurotransmitter of the membrane of a pre-synaptic neuron and melds with it: it was the release of chemical mediators.*
2. *The molecules of mediators bind to specific membrane receptors of the postsynaptic neuron and change the flow of sodium ions (Na +).*
3. *When the number of receptors modified reaches the threshold value, it triggers the potential action that propagates along the membrane while 4. the point of departure returns the pumps to push out the Na + ions.*

pressure, pain, etc.), chemical, electrical or light - it experiences a rapid series of events:

A. the stimulus opens some channels for sodium;

B. as Na + ions flow into the neuron, changes in the membrane increase until the potential reaches the threshold of activation. The difference of potential between external and internal membrane increases to +50 mV.;

C. a few milliseconds later channels are opened to voltage-dependent potassium, which leaves the cell as it follows the gradient of concentration;

D. the release of positive charges block the sodium channels and stops the potential rising - after this it soon begins decreasing;

E. at the end of the action the amount of K + ions leaving is greatest with respect to the ones that are positive, and the membrane becomes "hyperpolarised";

F. the channels for sodium inactivation and the passage of potassium are hampered by the growing re-polarisation of the membrane while the sodium pump rapidly restores the difference in original potential. The membrane reverts back to the initial conditions;

G. the reversal of charge and its immediate restoration spreads as a wave throughout the nerve cell and away from the cell nucleus, increasing in intensity as they proceed.

During and after each potential action, every area of membrane stays inactive to stimuli for a very short time: this reduced excitability ensures that any two pulses remain distinct, so that they can propagate separately. It also makes it possible to ensure that the transmission of each pulse can only go in one direction: an electrical signal should always proceed along the neuron without being able to turn back on itself.

When a neuron is stimulated by a series of pulses that are below the threshold, it can modify the level at which it triggers: it can raise or lower the excitement threshold. In other words, it can reset itself so that it is necessary for any stimulus to be of a greater intensity than normal. This is, however, a transient condition that can be changed back at any time.

▶ **Transmission of potential action**
Suppose that a stimulus has come on the nerve cell on the side: it propagates along the membrane in the direction opposite to that of the cell nucleus, as a wave of depolarization.

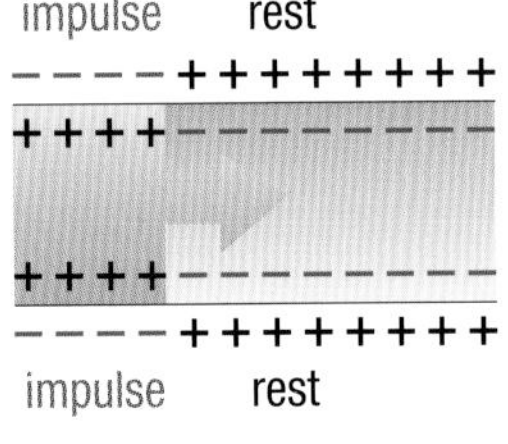

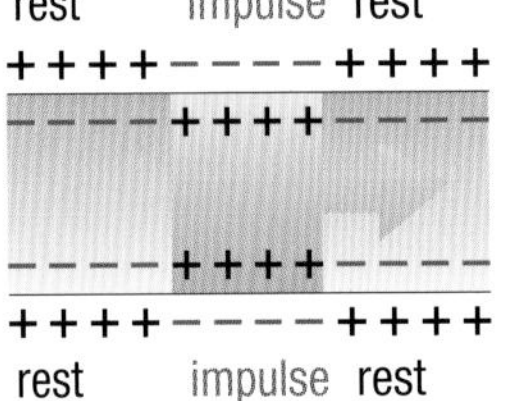

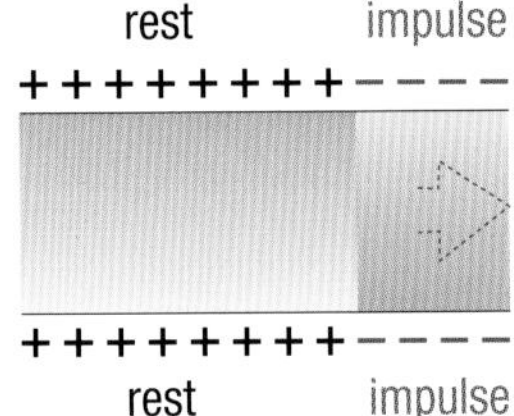

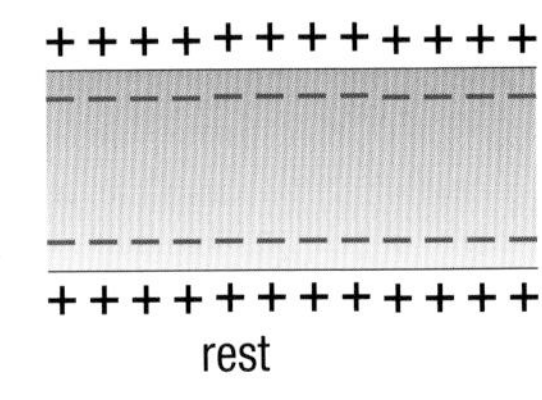

Ion transmissions

Ion channels are special proteins that are used to control the small electrical charges that develop on cell membranes. These molecules act as conduits for ion transmission, and those for sodium, potassium and calcium show surprising structural similarities that underline the fundamental role of evolution. The sequences of amino acids of the various sub-units of proteins that form these channels suggest an evolutionary link. One of these has a structure that is almost unchanged in all the ion channels regulated by the voltage. It is made up of amino acids with positive charges that are regularly distributed in space - its role is to sensor voltage. None of these chains, however, is the pore protein that physically allows the passage of the ions. The chains are represented by a single stretch of twenty amino acids in a polypeptide chain that extends through the membrane, and other functional regions. It is thought that the amino acids at the end of each sub-unit probably acts in the manner of a ball that is attached to a flexible arm. As such, it has the role of physically opening and closing the opening in the cytoplasmic pore.

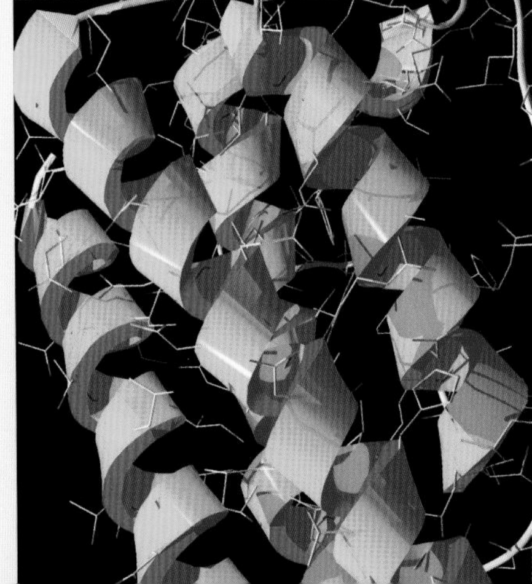

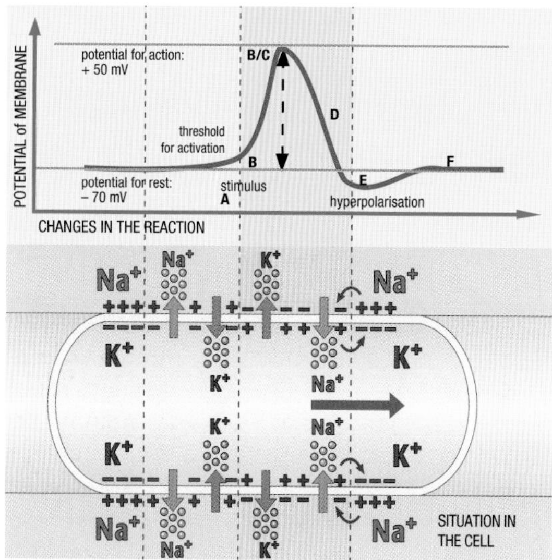

The transmission of stimuli along the nerve fibres that form the nerves ▸156 follows a different dynamic. These neurons, which connect areas of the body that are far from one another have a branch that is much longer than the others (the axon) that is surrounded by a myelin sheath. This sort of insulation coverage is created in the membranes of Schwann cells which curl around the axons forming a kind of blanket that envelops the neuron and prevents ions from crossing the membrane. The layers grow but are separated from one another: the myelin sheath is interrupted at regular intervals (known as Ranvier rings) where the membrane of the neuron remains free. In these areas, where the concentration of sodium pumps is high, action potential is developed: the nervous impulse spreads, jumping from one ring to another along the axon. It does this even faster than if it were doing so along the length of the membrane. The presence of the myelin sheath therefore increases both the speed of propagation and efficiency of the potential action.

COMMUNICATION BETWEEN NERVE CELLS AND MUSCLE CELLS

The point where a nerve cell and a cell or myocellular muscle communicate is called a neuromuscular synapse or a neuromuscular junction. Here the electrical signal that results from the nerve stimulates the myocellular muscle to shrink or relax. Each synapse terminates in a single muscle fibre, but because every synaptic junction can have an independent (excitatory or inhibitory) state, the fibre reacts to the sum of all the stimuli received.

The contraction of a muscle fibre can be explained thus:

A **1.** The action potential spreads along the motor axon to reach every synaptic junction. Here, in response to depolarisation of the membrane, calcium ion channels open allowing a mass influx of ions Ca2 +.

2. The rapid increase of calcium in the junction causes migration to the presynaptic membrane of vesicles containing acetylcholine (ACh), a neurotransmitter. They make contact with the vesicle membranes and merge with it in accordance with a process of exocytosis ▸16 and release their contents into the intersynaptic space.

B **1.** The ACh molecules move through the intersynaptic space until they meet the postsynaptic membrane, where they bind to specific receptors. In so doing, they cause the opening of the sodium ion channels, which pour Na + ions into the muscle fibre. The ACh has a direct impact making the cell membranes permeable to Ca2 + ions; it then acts at various levels. Firstly, it works on the membrane of the plaque and then the sarcoplasmic reticulum "275 as well as the membranes which surround the myofibril bundles. Freed Ca2 + ions then become vital catalysts for the many chemical

◀◀ Graph
Development of potential in a membrane eccitabile, represented in the figure below and described in the text.

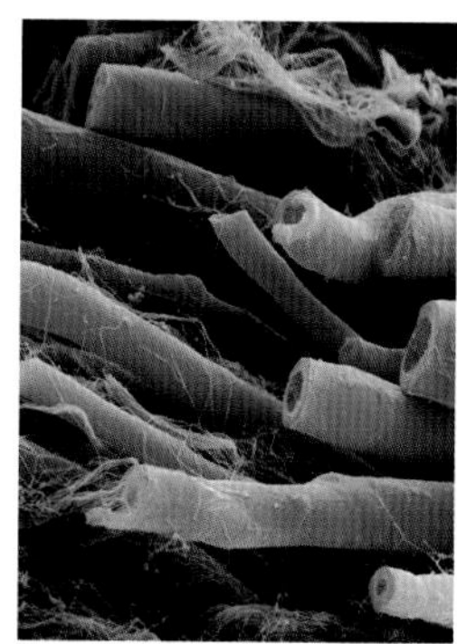

▲ Nerve fiber
SEM Micrograph of a bundle of neurons covered with a thick myelin sheath.

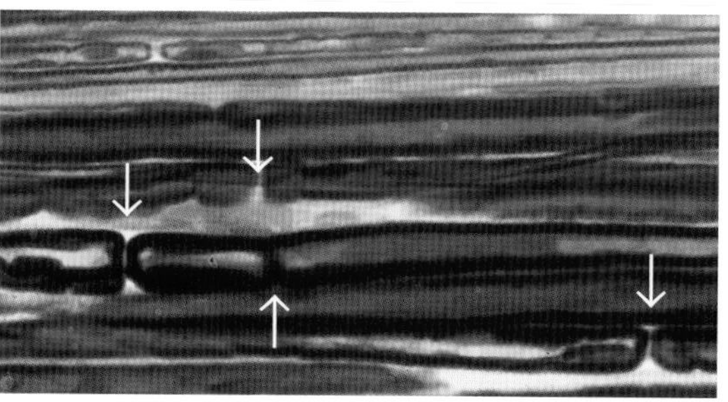

◀ Rings of Ranvier
In this optical microphotograph arrows indicate the disruption of myelin sheath in many neurons of a nerve bundle.

▼ Neurons and nerves
A. *Core elements of a (cell) nerve fiber,* **B**. *Structure of a nerve.*

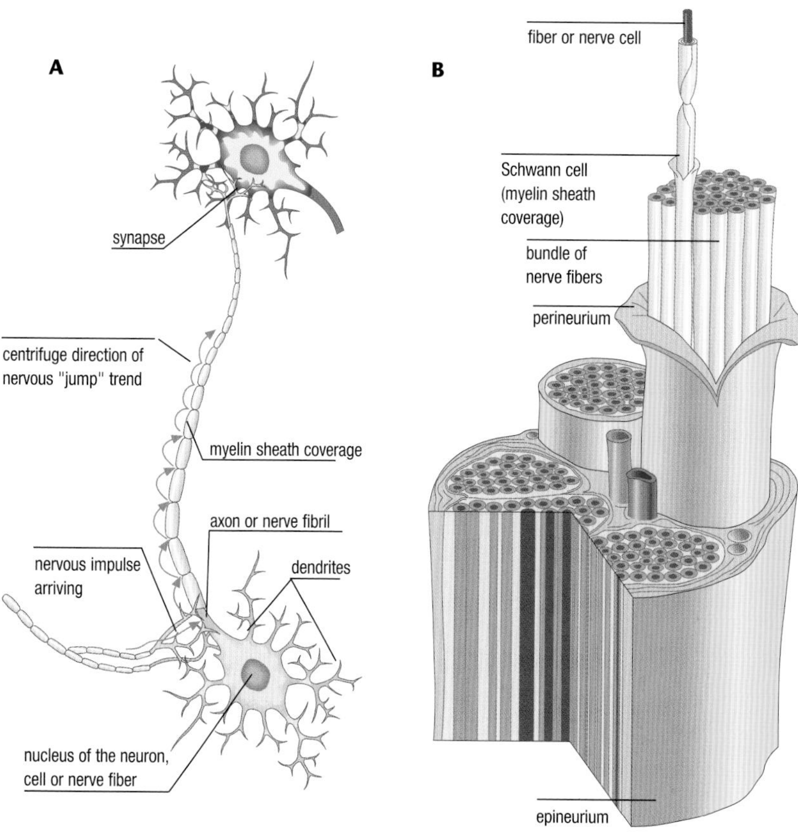

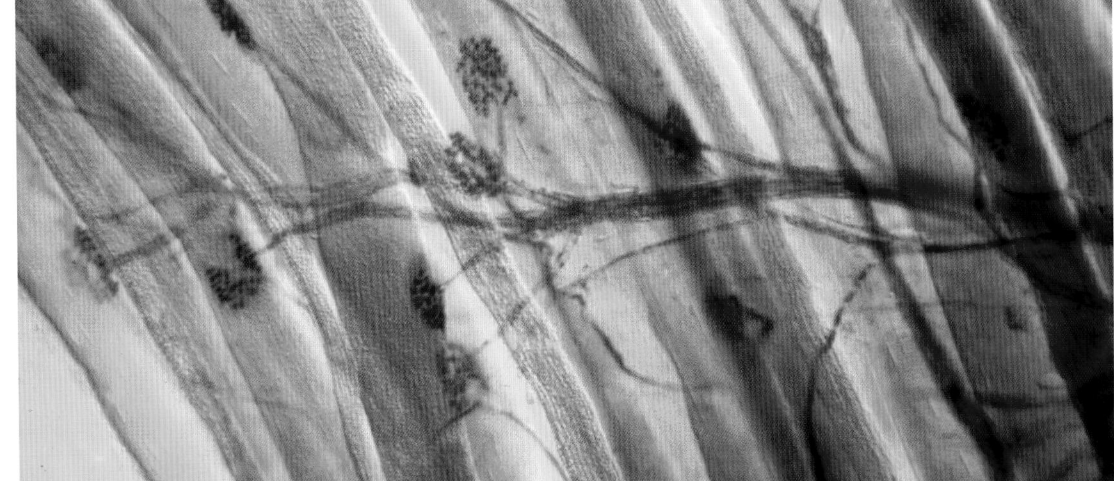

▶ **Synaptic snap**
In this optical microphotograph are clearly visible the ends of a motorneural fiber on a striated muscle. In this type, the synapses are distinguished by 3 elements:
- The synaptic button, a swelling at the ends of each branch of the terminal motor axons, often incorporated into a groove of the muscle cell membrane;
- Space or wall that separates synaptic cells;
- Plaque engine takes part in the postsynaptic membrane of the cell. Here synaptic buttons are dark, they stick to the yellow-orange muscle fibers.

reactions necessary for muscle contraction.

2. The rest potential in muscle cell membrane is about -80 mV: the mass influx of Na + ions and the simultaneous increase in permeability of K + ions ensures a move towards a value of about -15 mV, the so-called plaque potential.

3. This drastic depolarisation, although graduated and limited, is always sufficient to induce a potential action in the myocellular muscle. It translates into local currents which flow along the myocellular membrane.

4. At the same time, the mitochondria produce myocellular ATP which spreads in the cytoplasm. The dephosphorylation of ADP + P frees the energy needed to change the stereochemistry of the molecules that lead to the contraction of the sarcomere fibres ▶239.

C 1. While the myocellular muscle contracts, the molecules of ACh still present in the intersynaptic space are divided (hydrolysed) into their components (acetate and choline) and the enzyme acetylcholinesterase. This puts an end to their activities: choline is absorbed by the membrane of the neuron and used for the creation of new molecules ACh.

2. The ion channels of the myofibrils are closed; the vesicle membranes which had merged with the synaptic junctions are recycled to form new vesicles. Once the muscle has reached a state of relaxation, the procedure is reversed.

After the myofibril has contracted and relaxation occurred, a latent phase follows in which there is no response to stimuli.

A muscle's tone is not derived from a gradual contraction but by the number of muscle fibres in action. In muscles that need to work with great precision, the fibres are innervated by lots of nerves. Conversely, those which only have to generate power are typically innervated by single nerves.

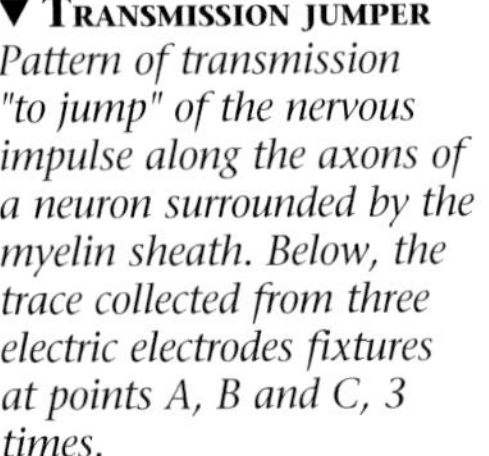

▼ **Transmission jumper**
Pattern of transmission "to jump" of the nervous impulse along the axons of a neuron surrounded by the myelin sheath. Below, the trace collected from three electric electrodes fixtures at points A, B and C, 3 times.

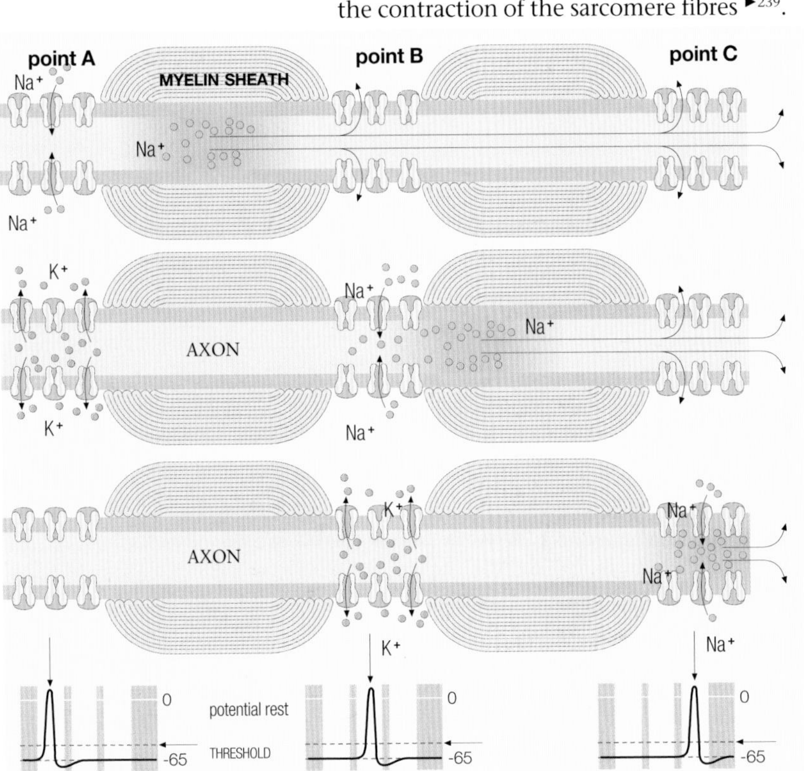

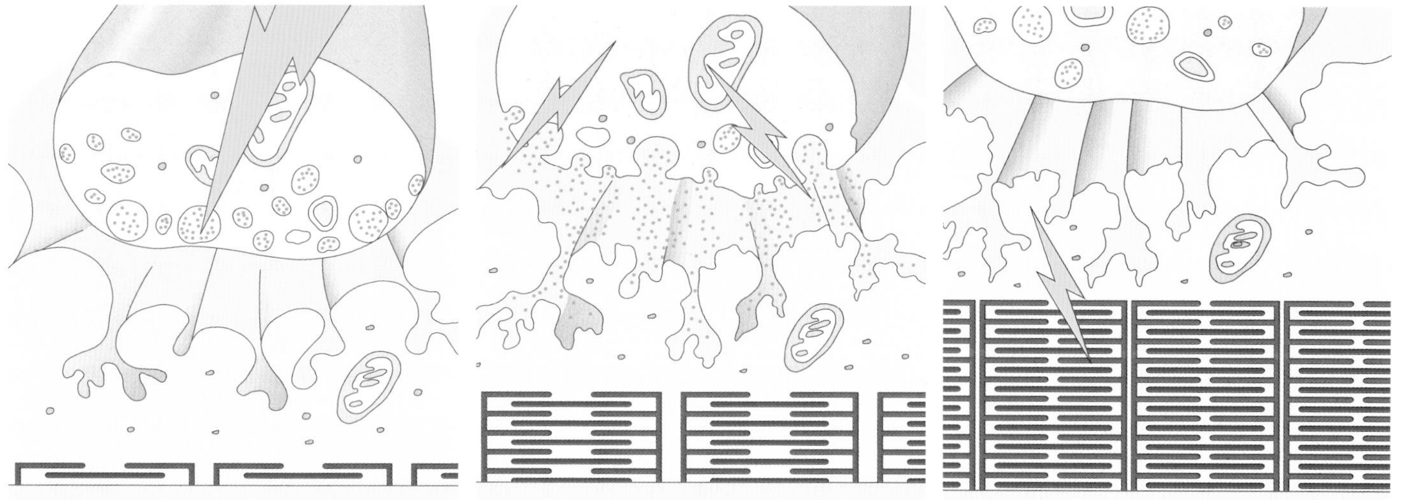

▲ **Neuromuscular communication**
Events during the passage of a stimulus to a motor myofibrillar.

▼ **Framework of skeletal muscle and miofibrilla** ►274
On the right: structural elements of a muscle and a miofibra (cell or muscle fiber).
Right: **A**. *a sarcomero relaxed. The bonds between molecules of actin and myosin are few, and the Z lines are spaced.* **B**. *sarcomere contract: the bonds increases by sliding a Z lines to the other.*

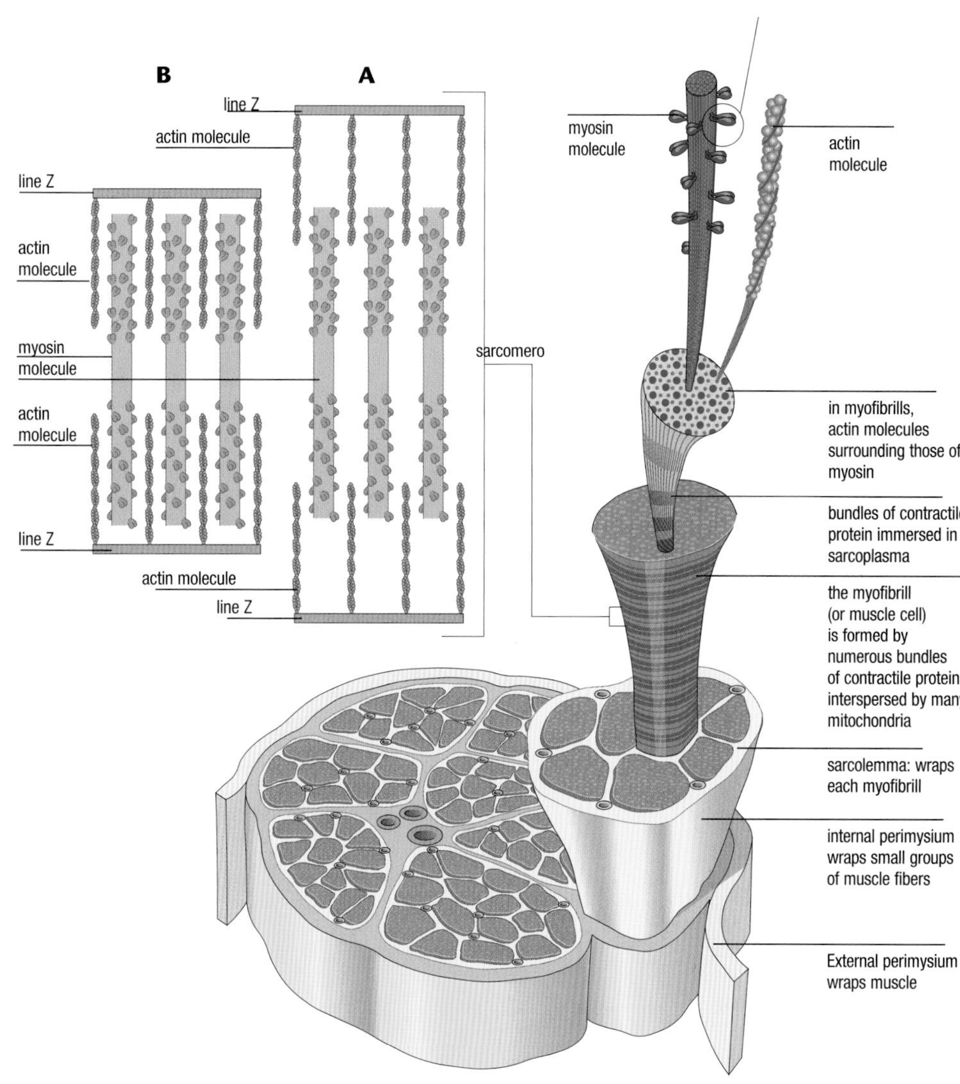

DIFFERENT TYPES OF CELLS COOPERATE WITH EACH OTHER AND CELLS WITH UNIFORM CHARACTERISTICS FORMING TISSUES. IN TURN, DIFFERENT TISSUES COOPERATE SHAPING ORGANS AND SYSTEMS: ALL ARE INTERDEPENDENT.

TISSUES, ORGANS, & PHYSICAL STRUCTURES

These days modern physiology is more focused on gaining an understanding of the low level detail of bodily functions rather than just the organisation of particular anatomical structures. This inevitably leads to the study of cellular dynamics rather than those of specific groups of cells. With the sophisticated techniques provided by the latest microscopic and biochemical procedures, it is now much easier to study cellular activities than it has ever been before, and this has led to big advances in our knowledge of how cells function and interact with those around them. The body is not just the sum of cells of which it is composed, however, but is something that is much more structured and complex. It acts as a environment for wide array of cells and must be able to provide all the necessary conditions to keep them alive. In order to do this, it must:

- must be able to maintain a continuous supply of oxygen and nutrients;
- must undertake the collection and disposal of waste substances produced by cells;
- must be able to maintain the right internal conditions required for cellular life to be possible - usually this has to be within very tight physicochemical constraints;
- must be able to interact with the external environment to source the necessary raw materials (nutrients, water), for a cell to reproduce and defend itself. In other words, the body must consistently find a balance between the need to be isolated and distinct from the surrounding environment and the need to remain continually in touch and in contact with it;
- must always co-ordinate the cellular activities;
- must be able to store and recognise chemicals and objects, deal with specific situations and be able to interpret communications signals and exploit them efficiently.

▼ **HUMAN TISSUE**
From left, microfotografie: **A**. *connective fat tissue: detail of adipocytes;* **B**. *epithelial tissue: detail hair emerging from the epidermis,* **C**. *striated muscle tissue;* **D**. *reproductive tissue: detail of an ovum surrounded by many sperm;* **E**. *glandular tissue: pancreas endogenous (clear cells, producing insulin) and exogenous (dark cells);* **F**. *nervous tissue: neuron.*

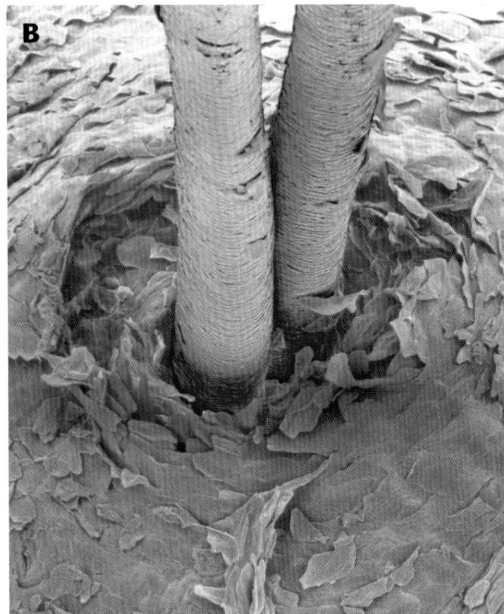

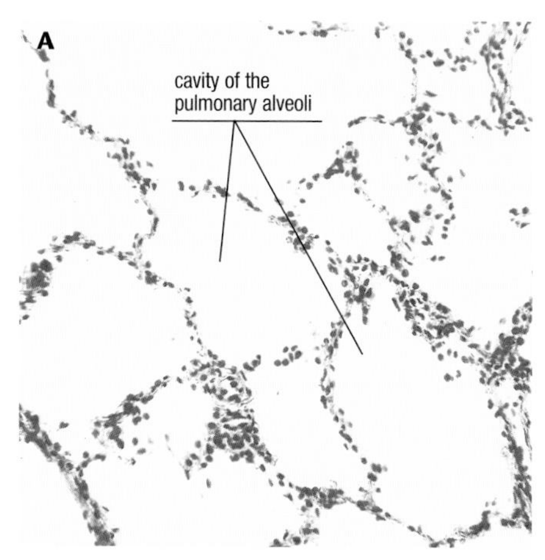

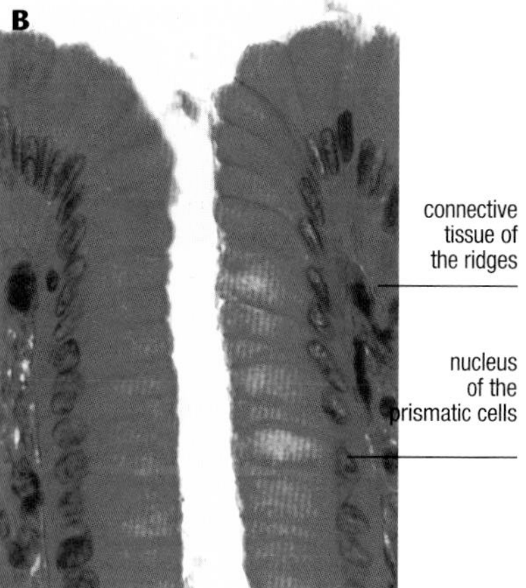

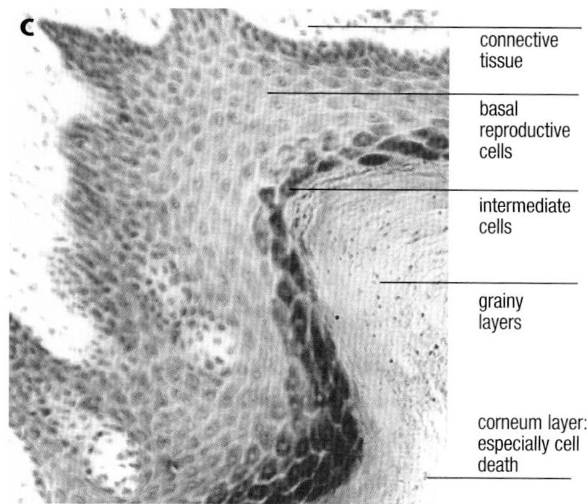

▲◀ **Epithelial**
A. *Squamous epithelium: section of a human adult lung, fuchsia, the cell nuclei.*
B. *Simple columnar epithelium: section of a ridge of gastric mucosa, fuchsia, the cytoplasm, in blue the cell nuclei.*
C. *Stratified squamous epithelium: section from a foot, the violet epithelial cells are alive.*

All these functions, which go well beyond those undertaken by each cell, occur thanks to super-organisation in tissues, organs and specialist anatomical systems.

BODY TISSUES

A tissue is a collection of cells that essentially undertake similar functions - these often have structural similarities, and typically share a common embryonic derivation. All tissue types are composed of the same basic elements - these are cells, intercellular substances, and liquid substrates. They also stem from only one of three embryonic sources ▸248 these are referred to as the ectoderm, mesoderm and endoderm. The main types of tissue are epithelial, muscular, nervous and connective. Each of these is further characterised by role, as discussed here.

EPITHELIAL TISSUE: this is made up of cells that have regular, almost geometric shapes, and where the members are closely arranged with one another, with little free intercellular room. Since the tissue is not interspersed by blood vessels, the cells receive their nourishment by distribution from cell to cell. They are also characterised by a high potential for proliferation.
The epithelial tissue is found in the whole body, both externally (epidermis, dermis), and internally (mucous membranes); it forms all the glands, especially those structures that secrete substances inside (endocrine glands) and outside (exocrine glands) the body. It also produces some other special parts (hair, teeth, nails, the eye lens...).
Examples of epithelial tissues include the following structures:
- **epithelial coating**: this is the interface between the internal and external parts of the body and has different characteristics in accordance with the area or bodies that it covers;

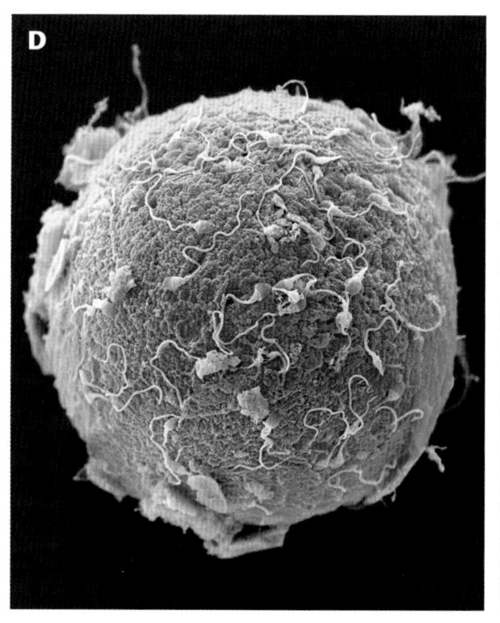

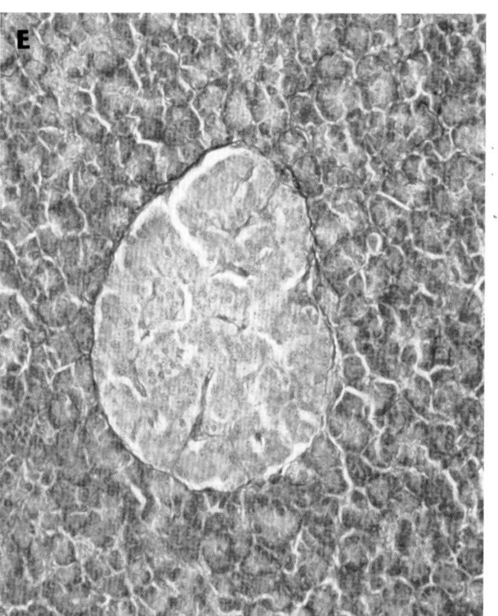

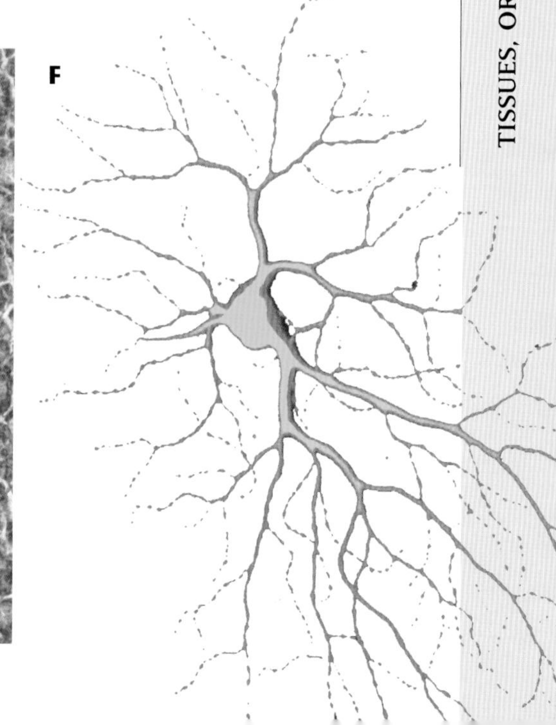

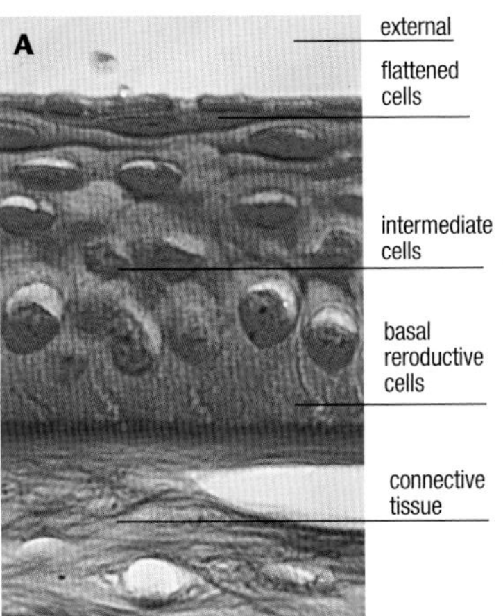

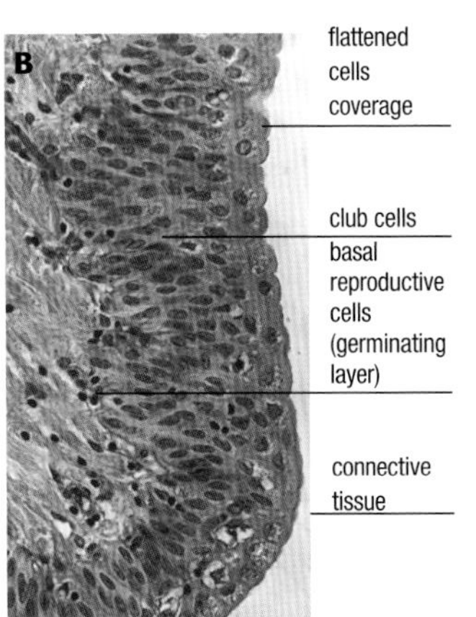

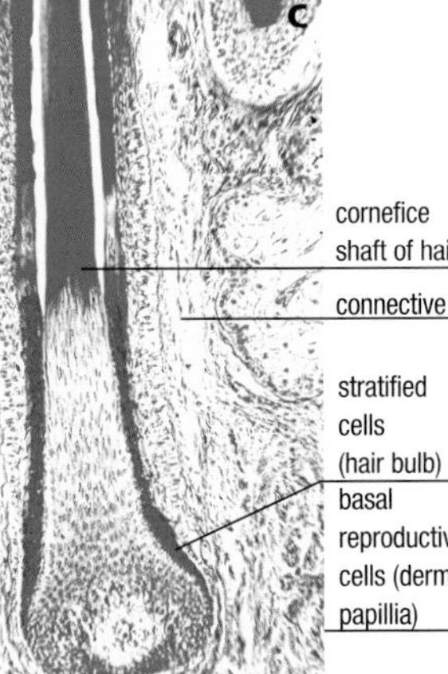

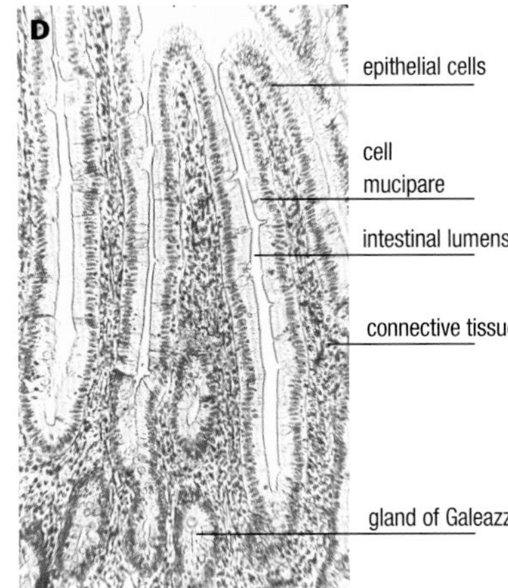

▲ **Epithelium**
A. *Paved epithelium: stratified section of the cornea, in fuchsia epithelial and in blue, connective cells.*
B. *Epithelium transition lumen of ureter.*
C. *Differentiated epithelium: Section of skin with hair.*
D. *Glandular epithelium exocrine: simple ghiadole alveolar (of Galeazzi).*

▼ **Epithelium**
A. *Glandular exocrine epithelium; alveolar gland simple section of the eyelid with the gland Meibomio; the alveoli to open clusters in a common duct.*
B. *Glandular exocrine epithelium, tubular gland simple maze: section of a gland sudoripara; fuchsia in the cell nuclei.*
C. *Glandular epithelium endocrine section of the thyroid with the typical structure follicles full of colloid, in red, follicles at rest, in blue active follicles, in pink epithelial cell nuclei.*
D. *Glandular epithelium endocrine section of adenoipofisi; fuchsia in the cell nuclei.*

- **simple squamous epithelial tissue**: this is formed from basal laminar cells and is found in places where passive diffusion takes place, such as the pulmonary alveoli ▸47;
- **simple cubiodal epithelial tissue**: this is formed of cube-shaped cells that are both aligned and compact. They can be found in a variety of places including the foetal lung;
- **simple columnar epithelial tissue**: this is formed by prismatic cells and can be found in places such as the gastric mucosa ▸64;
- **pseudostratified epithelial tissue**: this is formed by cells of varying height and shape, all of which are planted on a connective baseline so that they seem to lie on multiple layers. An example includes the mucous membrane that covers the trachea ▸48-49;
- **stratified squamous epithelial tissue**: here the cells grow in layers from the connective baseline. The deeper layer, which is composed of rounded cells that continuously reproduce, follows an intermediate layer of cells that are slightly flattened. Finally, there is a layer of surface cells that are completely flattened. This is the typical structure of the cornea, while the surface of structures like the oesophagus are much more numerous and varied;
- **transitional epithelium**: this is part-way between a stratified epithelium and a differentiated epithelium, and is typical of the tissues found in the urinary tract;
- **differentiated epithelium**: this has a number of forms which differ greatly from each other: it is found in the hair, nails, teeth, the lens of the eye etc. ▸220.
- **sensory epithelium**: this is made up of cells that react to stimuli; sensory structures ▸234 of epithelial origin are located in the skin, in the tongue and in the nose. Their characteristics are very different in accordance with their location;
- **exocrine glandular epithelium**: these are glands that produce and secrete their products outside the body or in cavities that are connected to the exterior of the body (exocrine glands).
  • **Simple cellular glands**: these include the glands that are known as the 'Crypts of Lieberkühn', structures that produce lubricating mucus in the small intestine and colon. Unlike mucosal cells, these glands are formed by several cell types. An example of this type is the sebaceous gland which secretes an oily substance onto the scalp;
  • **Tubular branched glands**: one example is the Brunner's gland in the intestines; this gland has a structure very similar to that of simple tubular glands;
  • **Simple tubular glands**: these have bulky and rounded cells that secrete products into a common duct, surrounded by parietal cells; examples of this type include the stomach glands ▸64;

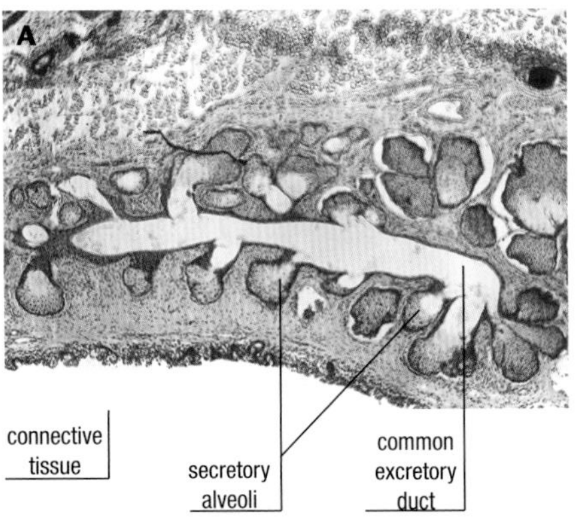

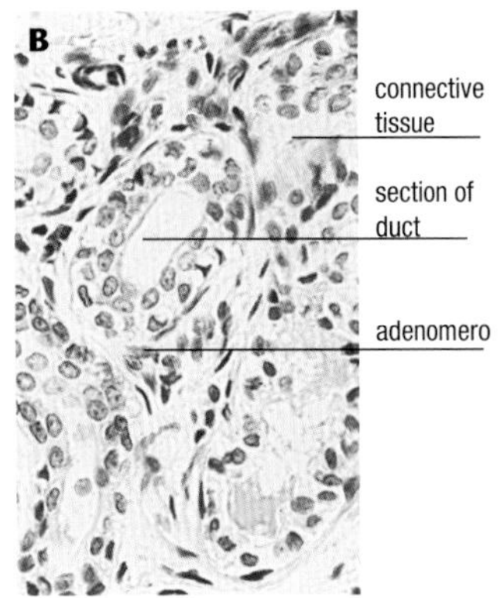

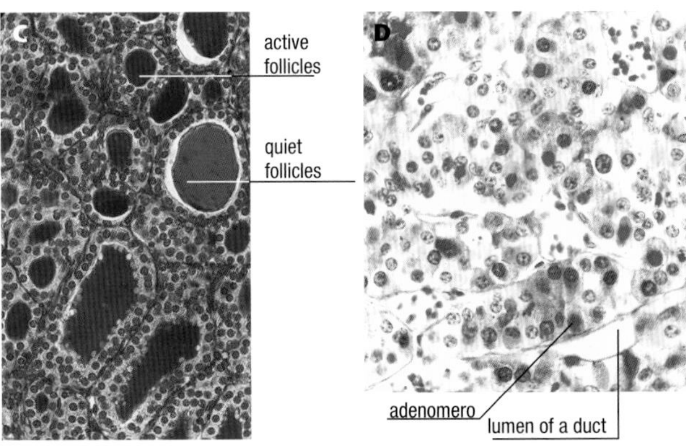

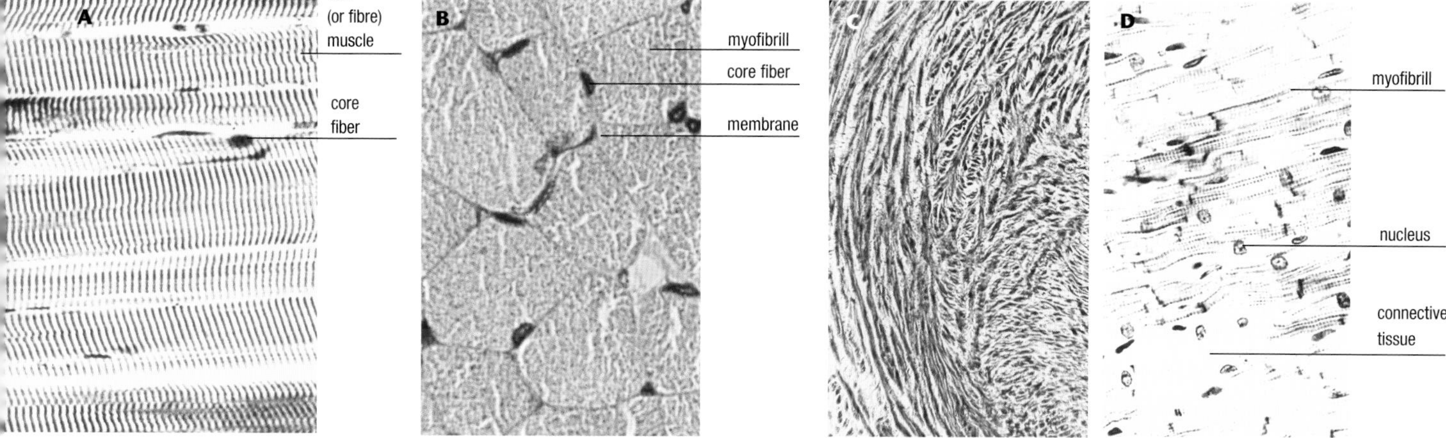

• **Tubular ball straight glands**: these have many functional units called adenomeres which are delimited by a double layer of cubic cells; sweat glands are examples of this type ▸140;
• **Acinose glands (or cellular)**: the parotid gland is an example of this type; the adenomeres (the functional units of the glandular epithelium bounded by a double layer of cubic cells) are very extensive. Examples of this type include the submandibular gland ▸61, the sublingual gland ▸61, the mammary glands ▸249 and the tear glands;

MUSCLE TISSUE: this is made up of specialised cells called contractile tissue and carries out the function of movement and support. It is everywhere: bundles of muscle tissue surround the digestive cavity and blood vessels, it binds to bone, is interwoven in the dermis, is used to moving the hair and so on. There are three main types of muscle tissue, each of which presides over a particular movement:

– **Striated Muscle Tissue**: this owes its name to the typical striped appearance when observed under the microscope. It is responsible for voluntary movements, that is, those which are intentionally made by the brain. In striated muscle, the myofibrils in each cell are compact, and the overall structure is highly regimented.
– **Smooth Muscle Tissue**: this is called so because when samples are viewed under a microscope it can be seen that the muscle fibres are surrounded by abundant connective material. It is responsible for involuntary movements, namely the movements that the body performs spontaneously without conscious thought (e.g. the movements of the intestines).
– **Heart Muscle Tissue**: this is typical of the heart ▸114, and although it is very similar to striped tissue, it is, in fact, involuntary.

NERVOUS TISSUE: this is made up of specialised cells that are used to recognise and transmit signals and impulses from nerve cells and to support nourishment. The brain is formed from nervous tissue ▸178, as is the spinal cord and the whole network of nerves ▸190 and nerve endings throughout the body. The cells have different forms in different parts of the nervous system: in the spinal cord they are star-shaped, whereas in the dorsal root ganglia they are round. They may have sensory function (sensory neurons) or motor (motor), but all have a number of short extensions branched (dendrites) which make contact with other nerve cells, muscle (by adjusting the movement) and glands (by adjusting the secretory activity). If they are extended they are referred to as neurons, or axons and may be covered by one or two sheaths: the Schwann and

▲ **Muscular Tissue**
A. *Striated muscle tissue: the long muscle cells (one for each core, visible as a dark stain) are tied in bundles cross the strips side by side (Z lines) to give each cell a striated appearance.*
B. *Striated muscle tissue in a cross-section of a muscle: each cell contains miofibrille (pink) and is bounded by a membrane (fuchsia thread). The nucleus is dark pink crushed on one side.*
C. *Smooth muscle tissue: a section of wall of muscular artery. The fibers have a concentric pattern to the jar.*
D. *Cardiac muscle tissue: the cell contractility are very separated from their nuclei and may also occupy a central area.*

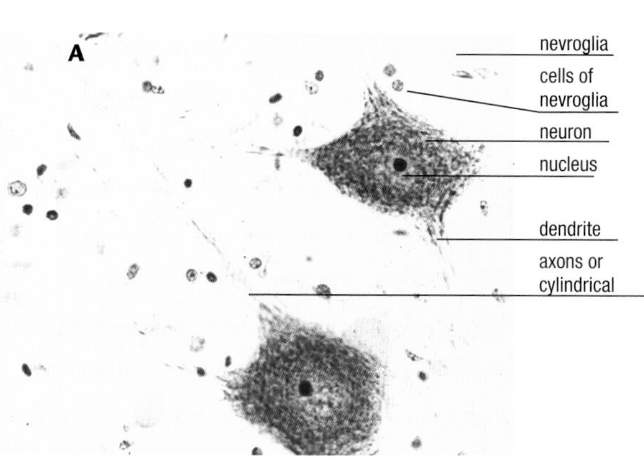

◀ **Nervous tissues**
A. *Individual nerve cells (purple) embedded in connective tissue typical of the nervous system (nevroglia). Identify some supporting cells (glial, viola), the dendrites, threads that bring the neuron into contact with other cells, axons, and much longer dendrites of others.*
B. *Cross section of a nerve, in which many fibers are distinguished: the purple dots are the axons of each neuron, surrounded by myelin (white). The fibers are separated by a connective tissue called neurilemma (purple fibers) and the outer, form a connective sheath around the nerve (perineurium).*

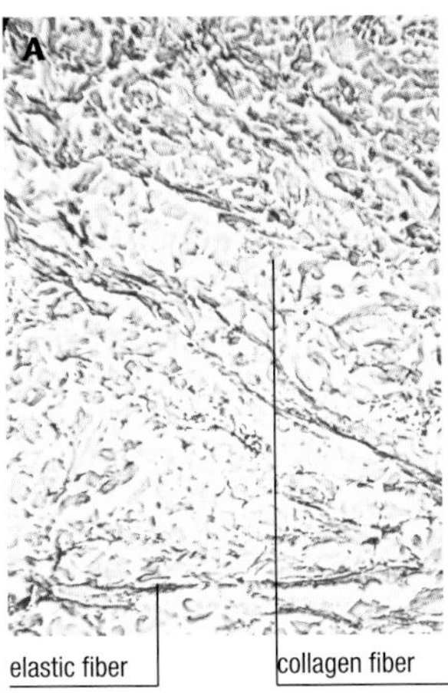

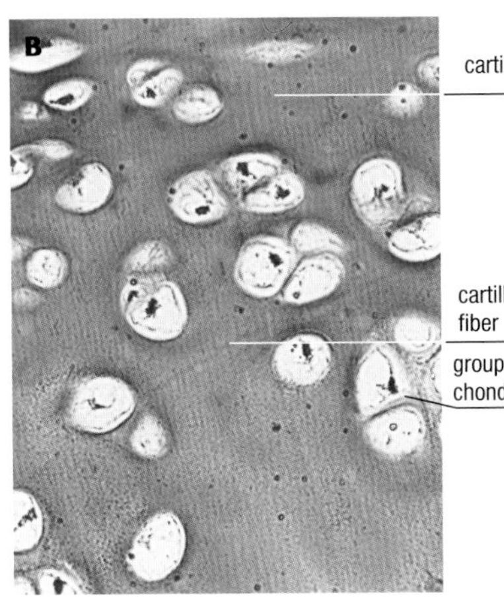

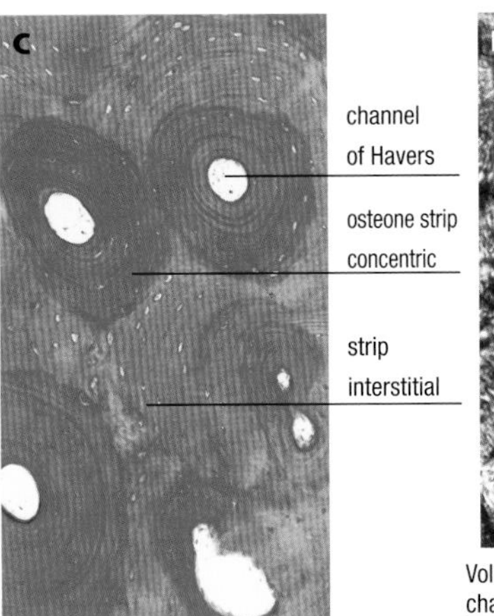

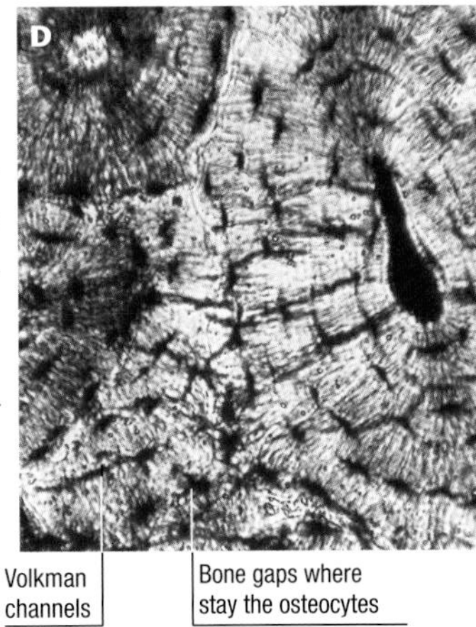

▲ **Connective**
A. *Dermis, sectional, with elastic cells in fuchsia and fibers of collagen purple, a protein which is rich a amorphous substance of the connective tissue.*
B. *Ialina cartilage of the trachea: in violation of the cartilage, the white gap in which there are cells (condrocites) that were cartilage. In each gap condrocites are derived from the same osteocite.*
C. Compact bone tissue in a cross-section of bone: we recognize the typical structures of concentric lamellae osteons.
D. Bone in cross section. The coloring highlights the system of Volkman channels (transverse) and Havers (concentric to osteon).

myelinic or spinal cord.

- **Collagen protein filaments** are made up of cylindrical triple helix bundles that are around 0.1 μm thick and not branched;
- **Reticulate**, composed of thin filaments that are interwoven in a three-dimensional grid;
- **Elastic**, made up of cylindrical fibres similar to those of collagen fibres or tape.

There are various types of connective tissue: those with well-characterised tissue are often considered in isolation or even as organs.

- **Fibrous Connective Tissue**: this is largely composed of a tough protein known as collagen. Dense forms can be found in structures that require significant strength, such as tendons and ligaments.
- **Elastic Connective Tissue** is made up predominantly of elastic fibres such as those which are found in the walls of large arteries.
- **Reticular Connective Tissue**: this consists primarily of fibres that bind reticular cells together in many organs (generally in glands) and wrap the bundles of muscle fibres or blood capillaries in the form of sheaths ▸91.
- **Endothelial Tissue**: this is made up primarily of epithelial cells that are very flattened and with a polygonal shape. It is found in the surfaces of organs and cavities that do not communicate with the outside world, such as the surface of the heart. The endothelium forms a thin sheet of mesodermic origin that covers blood vessels, and may be continuous or fenestrated.
- **Cartilaginous Tissue**: is regarded as an elastic connective structure that is mostly composed of collagen fibres. This tissue is the embryonic state of bone tissue: with growth, in fact, most of the cartilage becomes rich in minerals and turns into bone. Cartilage remains only in very limited areas including the outer ear, nose, trachea and bronchi.
- **Bone**: this derives directly from cartilage tissue and some regard it as a particular type of connective tissue where the collagen fibres have become calcified. They are largely comprised of special cells called osteocytes. Bones are used to provide both support and for the protection of some internal organs. Several of the longer bones feature a space called a medullary cavity - this houses the bone marrow, used for the production of blood cells.
- **Blood And Lymphatic Tissue**: these are tissues where clear fluids can be found - in the former this is known as plasma, and in the latter as lymph. Both have similar characteristics, being made of

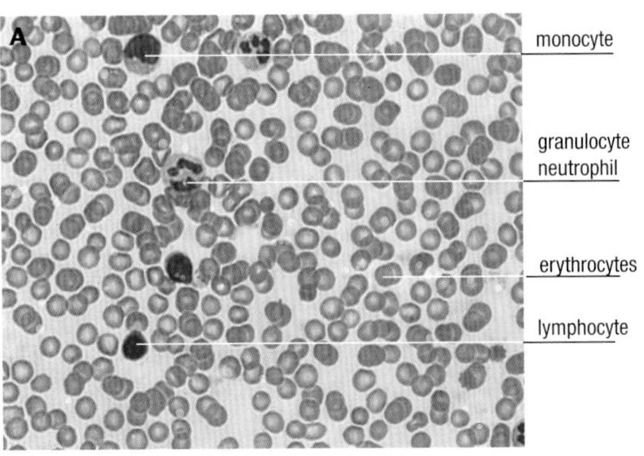

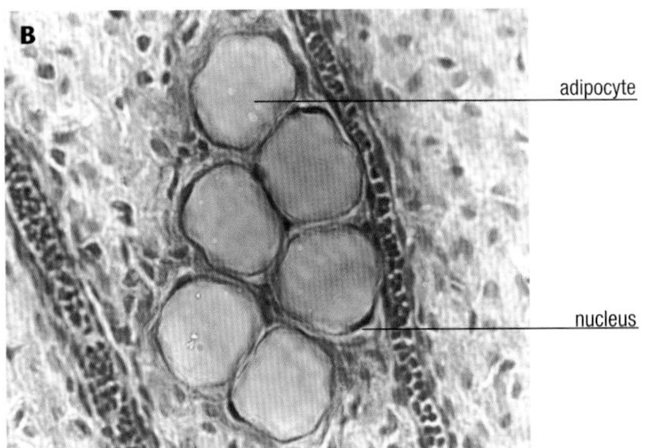

▶ **Connective**
A. *Blood tissue: there are some cellular components common to both the blood and the lymph. The neutrophil granulocytes (lymphocytes and monocytes) or white blood cells. In pink, numerous red blood cells.*
B. *Adipose tissue: a group of adipocyte fat swollen, pink in the cell cytoplasm, darker nuclei.*

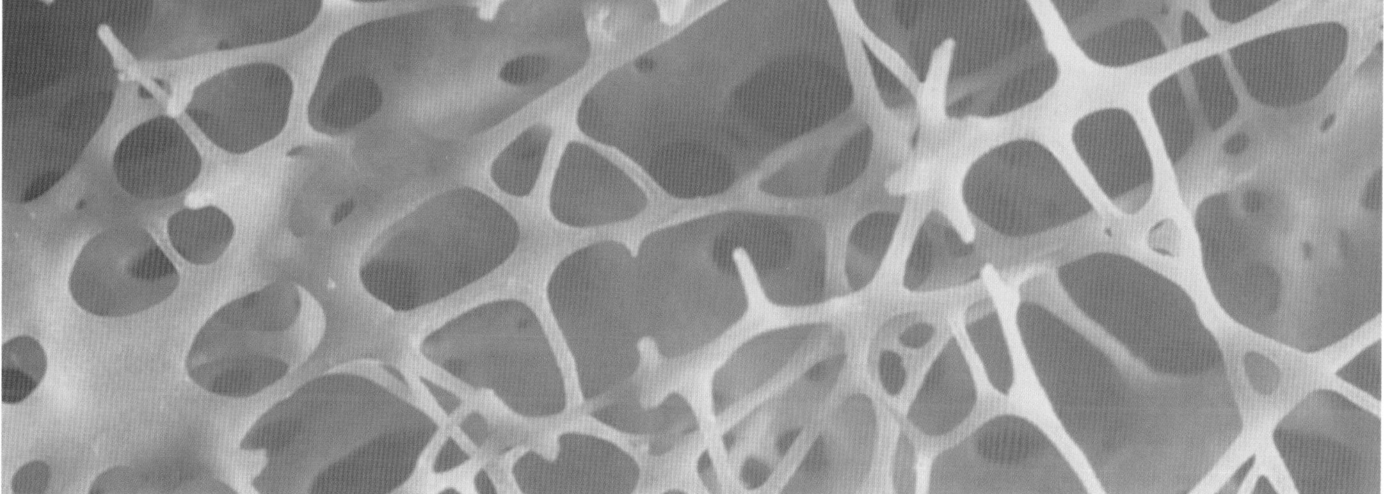

many cells. Blood cells are produced in the bone marrow, while lymphatic tissues first arise from lymph sacs in about the fifth week of embryonic life.

- **Fat Tissue**: this is made up of cells called adipocytes that accumulate fat: these are usually large globular structures that are crushed laterally. They may be present singly or gathered in groups that are immersed in the connective tissue. Fatty tissues play important roles in thermal insulation and the body's structural mechanics. 45% of all fat tissue is typically located inside in the abdominal cavity and about 5% in muscles where it has a prominent role in the storage of energy.

▲ **Spongy bone tissue**
In this SEM micrograph, you can see good disposition in a chaotic strip of bone. In living bone, the spaces are "filled" from bone marrow.

▼ **Blood tissue**
This three-dimensional image by scanning electron microscopy (SEM) shows some blood cells: red blood cells (normal and echinocyte) surround a white globule (lymphocyte).

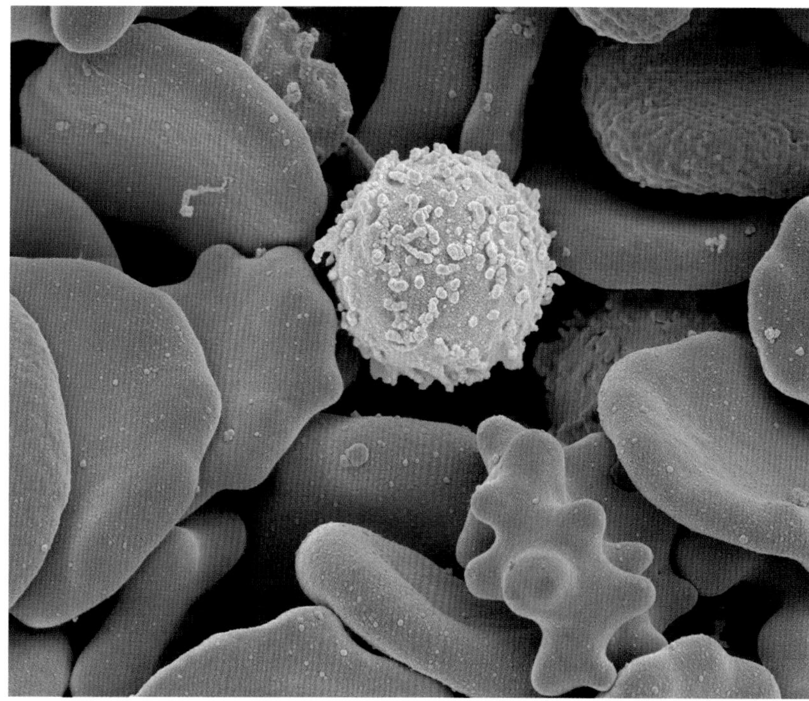

skeletal system

THE ORGANISATION OF THE BODY

The specific needs of different organisms are genetically determined: they are the result of a slow evolution during which tissues and organs have developed into increasingly complex structures. Since the body's life processes occur at the cellular level, the body plays - macroscopically - the same functions necessary for the survival of a cell. The skeletal system has developed to give support and protection to various organs, and - in close collaboration with the muscular system, allow various kinds of movement.

The circulatory system is necessary to distribute capillary nutrients and energy, as well as to deliver vital substances and collect waste products and then transport them to the relevant disposal sites. Further to this, it also provides a complex communication system via the distribution of chemical messages to distant cells.

The digestive system provides the body with the means to turn nutritional substances into chemical energy, and allows the body to acquire the elements that are necessary for life. It also functions as an excretory system that expels the bulk of the waste products.

The respiratory system provides the means for gaseous exchanges between the circulatory system and the environment - this allows oxygen to be taken in and carbon dioxide to be discharged.

All these activities are controlled through a complicated network of chemical and electrical signals from the nervous and endocrine systems, which by necessity are very closely synchronised.

From a functional point of view we can bring together the body's various systems in order to understand their activities more clearly:

– Systems which carry out the exchange of substances between the internal and external environments: these include the digestive, respiratory and excretory systems.

Such schemes are constructed with the same logic - they are all linked to the exterior by tubular structures that are covered with mucous, and take part in the exchange of substances between the internal and external environments:

▲ System
Any system in the body which subdivides is made up of living cells that work together. Above the skeletal system, here, from left to right: skeletal system, muscular, circulatory and lymphatic system.

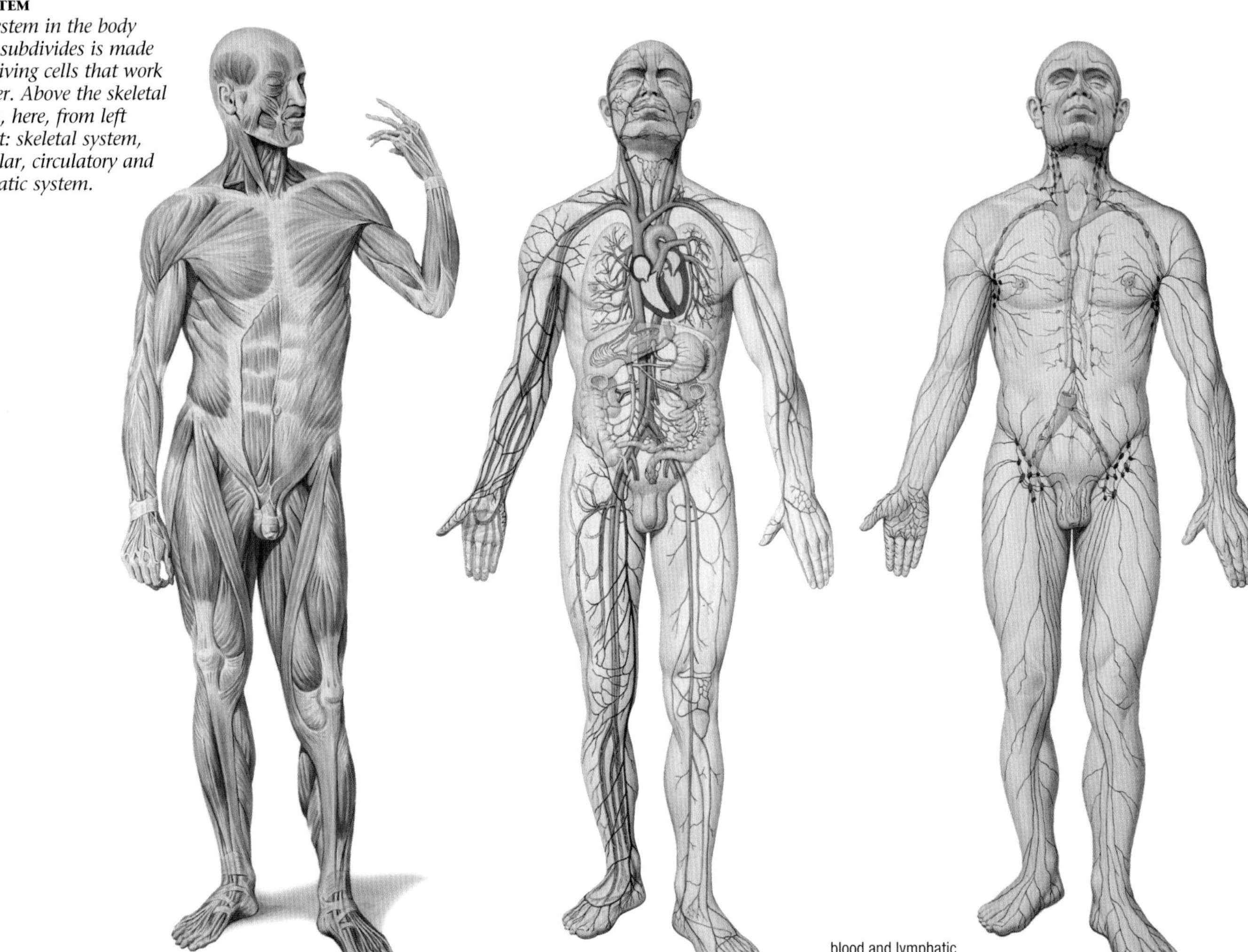

muscular system

blood and lymphatic circulatory system

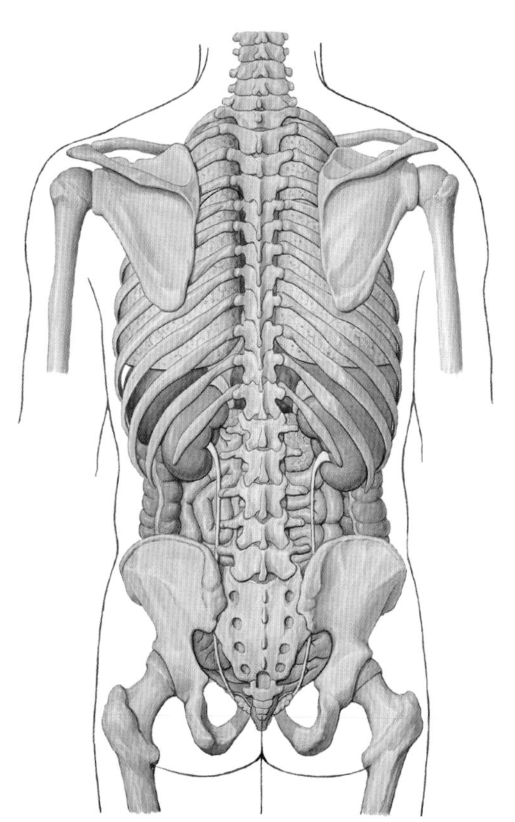

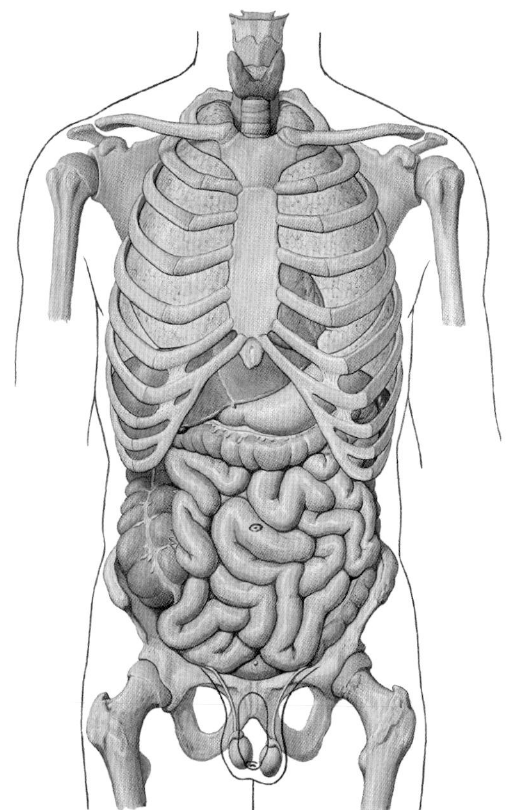

◀ **Organs**
View from behind and in front, the abdominal organs make up the digestive, respiratory and excretory systems, systems that trade matter and energy between the internal and external environment.

In addition, they are all made up of elements in which the surface of contact with the outside world - albeit hidden inside the body - is greatly expanded;

- Systems that maintain the internal environment so that cells are always kept in the best physiochemical conditions. These include the circulatory system, the immune system (which monitors the physical integrity of the internal environment any watches for invasion by alien cells), and the excretory and endocrine systems.
- Control systems: the entire operation of the body is co-ordinated by the nervous system using specific electrochemical messages. Using this mechanism it adjusts the action of muscles and directly modulates the activity of things like the endocrine glands and the production of pituitary hormones and neurotransmitters;
- Sensory systems: these gather stimuli from the outside world and internal organs and use this information to help process and develop an appropriate response. The interaction between body and environment is mediated by the nervous system, and takes place via the sense organs (skin, eyes, nose, mouth, ears), as well as the motor nerves, and the parts of the muscular and skeletal systems that are needed for movement.

◀ **Nervous system**
It's more complicated: it plays a general control on the activity of each organ, a role of coordination of the movement, processing and storage of information, stimulation and suppression of the various functions of the body as well as the endocrine control and balance.

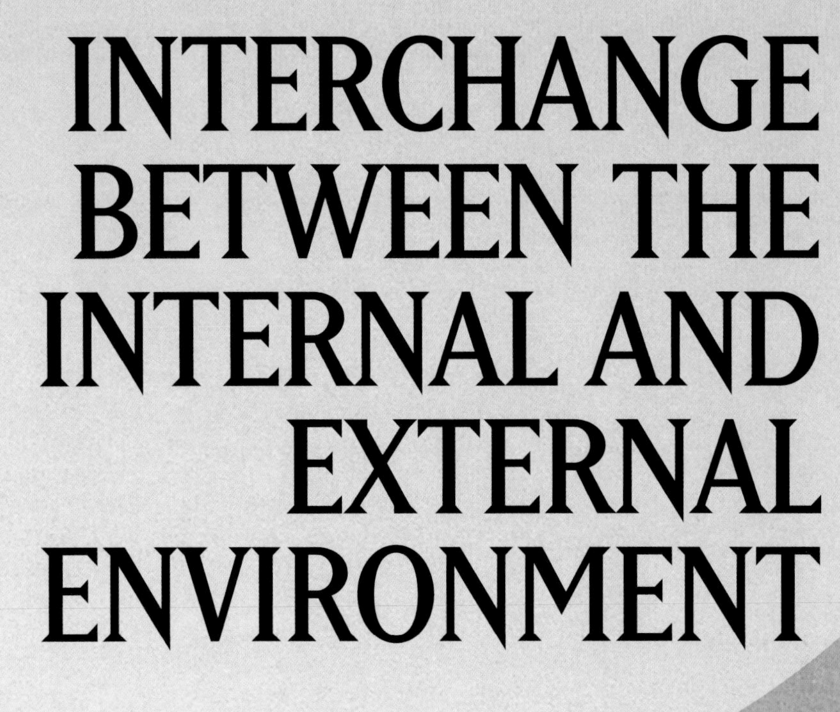

INTERCHANGE BETWEEN THE INTERNAL AND EXTERNAL ENVIRONMENT

THE BODY IS A CONSTANTLY EVOLVING DYNAMIC: EXCHANGES CONTINUALLY GAS, SUBSTANCES AND ENERGY WITH THE ENVIRONMENT AROUND HIM, SO AS TO MAINTAIN ALL VITAL PARAMETERS IN BALANCE, WITHIN CLEAR LIMITS.

GAS INTERCHANGE

All of the body's cells need oxygen in abundance in order to carry out respiration and other oxidative processes. At the same time, these all produce carbon dioxide as a metabolic waste gas that, if it were not quickly removed from the body, would cause lethal poisoning. Ensuring the continued replacement of gas - that is, the inflow of oxygen and removal of carbon dioxide - is a task for the respiratory system. This collaborates with the circulatory and muscular-skeletal systems under the control of the 'automatic' involuntary nervous system.

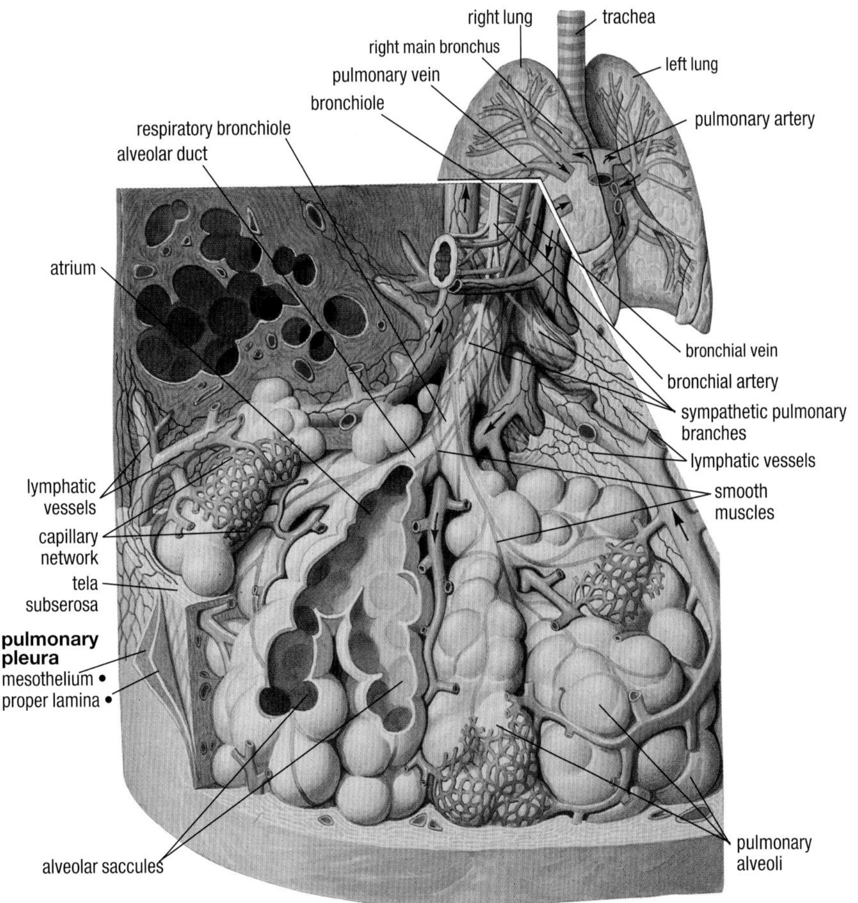

▼ **ACINO PULMONARY**
Anatomical, structural and circulatory elements that make up the lungs.

RESPIRATORY SYSTEM AND BREATHING

The respiratory system is made up of organs that form the airways and lungs:

- The respiratory tract (nose-mouth, pharynx-larynx, trachea-bronchi-bronchioles) which are passive transport routes that let the air pass through, both in the incoming and outgoing directions. They also have an active task in modifying the physical-chemical conditions such as humidity, temperature and purity, including limiting any pollution that reaches the lungs.
- The lungs, and in particular the alveoli, are where the gaseous exchanges take place between the body and the external environment. The connective tissues involved are very elastic. This permits them to follow the increase in volume produced in the chest by the contraction of muscles and thoracic diaphragm. It also allows them to return to their original positions when the muscles and diaphragm relax. In this way the abdominal muscular-skeletal structure and chest works as a pump that allows air to reach into the depths of the lungs. Here, thanks to 300 million alveoli, the lungs have exposed to the air an area of exchange of about 100 m2 that is protected from the exterior and kept in ideal conditions of temperature and humidity for the exchange of gases.

Breathing can be distinguished by the various processes, and, from time to time, the different parts of the body that are involved. These processes, which are kept under control by the autonomic nervous system, go through repeated cycles:

1. with ventilation, air is drawn through the airways until they reach the pulmonary alveoli, this is done by the chest muscles and diaphragm, while the lungs dilate passively;
2. dissemination takes place in the alveoli, the oxygen ($O2$) passes from the air in the alveoli through their membranes and into the blood where it binds to the haemoglobin in the red

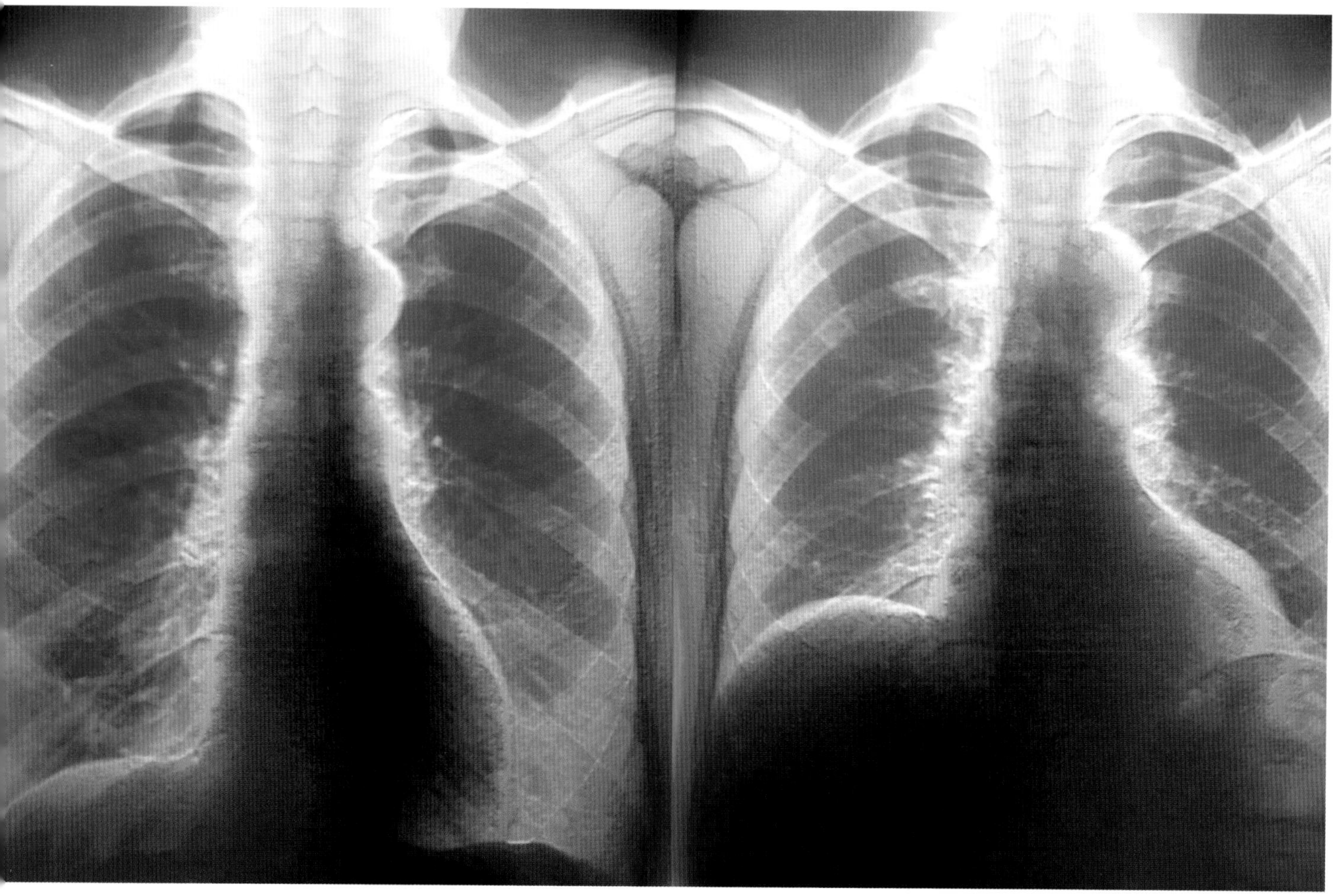

blood cells ▸83 - this is a spontaneous process;

3. the transport of oxygen and its distribution throughout the body processes are carried out by the circulation of the blood ▸82, which is kept in constant movement by cardiac pulses ▸160;
4. once the oxygen has been distributed around the body, it passes spontaneously from blood cells into various tissues;
5. the use of oxygen and the production of carbon dioxide (CO_2) are the two contemporary processes which take place in each cell of the body ▸19;
6. the waste CO_2 that has been produced by the cells then binds to the haemoglobin in the red blood cells in a second spontaneous process;
7. the transport of CO_2 from the lung cells is also carried out by the blood, and is again driven by the cardiac pulse;
8. the distribution that occurs when the red blood cells pass through the capillaries of the pulmonary alveoli allows the CO_2 to spontaneously pass from the blood to the air;
9. with ventilation, the thoracic muscles and diaphragm relax; accordingly lung tissue, which is elastic, expels the air from the alveoli to outside the body.

The respiratory cycle then recurs. It should be noted that the two moments of ventilation (1 and 9) take place in rapid succession, while the phenomena of dissemination (2, 4, 6 and 8) are concurrent.

VENTILATION

Every minute, without even thinking about it, a typical person makes 10-15 respiratory acts. In a day, on average, this means they move about 13,500 litres of air through their lungs! This may, however, vary a great deal with physical activity, age, sex and overall health. An infant, for example, breathes very quickly, having about 60 - 70 respiratory acts per minute. In stark contrast, a normal adult male has about 16/min, whereas the rate for women and obese people is a little less. The rate increases significantly for people who have well developed muscular systems, such as athletes and manual labourers.

Even the inhaled volume can vary - the amount of air drawn in and exhaled in a normal breathing cycle, for example, is about 500 cm3. With forced inhalation this can increase by about 2000 - 3000 cm3 over and above the normal amount - this is referred to as the reserve inhalation volume. Likewise, forced exhalation can expel around 1000 cm3 more than usual. This is known as the

▲▼ INSPIRATION AND EXPIRATION
The X-ray photos show false colors in the expansion (left) and constriction (right) of the lungs during respiration (opposite view). The diagram below shows the same conditions seen in a chest from the right side.

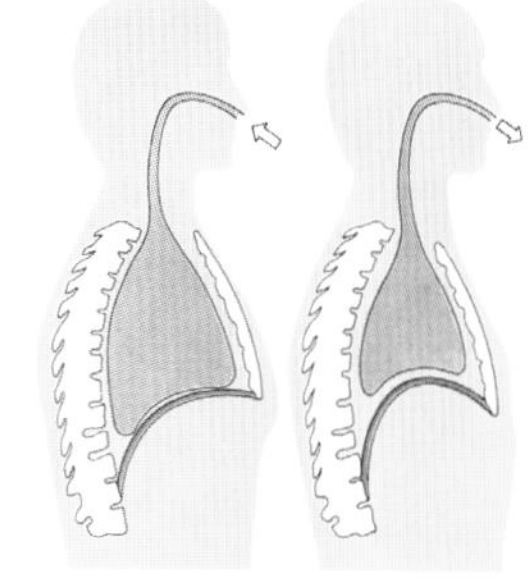

▶ **Respiratory rythm**
The diagram describes the pattern of breathing before and after resection of the vagus nerve. Before the operation, the breaths are more frequent and superficial, and after are less frequent but more profound.

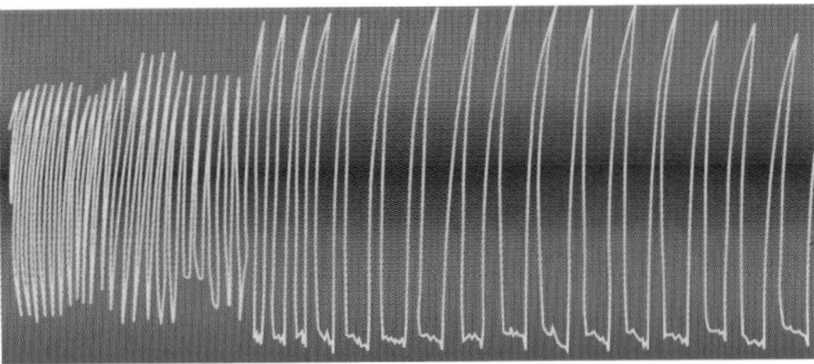

▶ **Quantity of air**
The diagram describes the amount of air expelled and placed in a series of breaths during a normal inspiration and a forced exhalation. The residual air that remains is to "inflate" the lungs after all the air possible has expired.

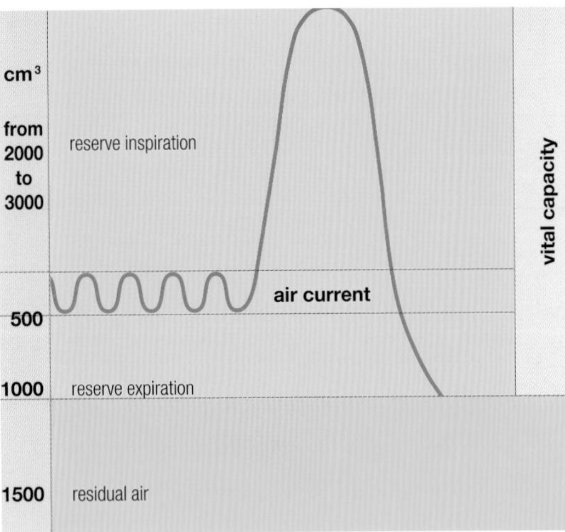

reserve exhalation volume. On average, the sum of the current and reserve volumes of inhalation and exhalation equals 4000 - 4500 cm3, and is called the 'vital capacity'.

The changes in rhythm and breathing capacity are the direct consequence of any changes of activity, and are undertaken by the involuntary ventilation muscles. In turn, this is under the control of the specific respiratory centres that are in the encephalic bulb. The brain changes the respiratory pace according to the needs of the body, from moment to moment. This is in order to maintain a constant and appropriate intake of oxygen and low concentrations carbon dioxide in the blood. The body is particularly sensitive to the concentration of CO2 in the blood, in fact, the neurons in the respiratory centre are activated as soon as the partial pressure of CO2 (pCO2) exceeds a certain threshold. The higher the levels of carbon dioxide in the blood, the more oxygen is drawn in. This is due to the neurons sending impulses to the motor controls that are located in the front of the spinal cord - these then make the inhalation muscles contract.

When the diaphragm contracts, it lowers the external intercostal muscles, while the scalene muscles and the sternocleidomastoid muscle contract. This raises the sternum, causing an increase in the chest's volume and a decrease in the intrapleural pressure. This refers to the pressure that is measured in the pleural space that separates the two thin sheets of serous pleural membranes. Normally, the pressure of this cavity is lower than that of the external environment by about 0.4 - 0.7 kPa (3-5 mmHg). The difference in pressure allows the pleura to balance out any forces to which the chest is subjected as the result of the breathing movements. These are caused by the elastic forces that are generated by the lungs pulling towards the inside of the chest, and the compressive forces from the chest that are directed outwards.

When the levels of carbon dioxide have been brought back below the threshold, the activity of the respiratory centre slows, the signals to the motor controls cease, and the muscles relax. This: occurs as part of the exhalation process. The neurons in the respiratory centres are also encouraged or incapacitated by the signals that flow from the vagus nerve ▶176 which provide information about the state of relaxation or contraction of the lungs. During the exhalation phase, the contraction of the lungs stimulates certain muscle fibre receptors that are sensitive to stretch. These send impulses to stimulate the respiratory centre which then sends a fresh set of commands that trigger a new inspiration cycle.

As the movement of inspiration proceeds, the process happens again, but instead the pulmonary fibre receptors - which are sensitive to compression, produce impulses that slow down the stimulation of the respiratory centre. This causes it to pause, limiting the expansion of the lungs. The neurons in the respirator centre are also indirectly stimulated by any reductions in the levels of oxygen in the blood through receptors that are sensitive to blood concentrations of this gas.

Any changes in rhythm and breathing rate, therefore, can act as alarm signals that need to be taken into careful consideration as they may well be the expression of anatomical damage to the functional respiratory centres.

The regulation of breath is not entirely under autonomous control - it is possible, for instance, to voluntarily hyperventilate the lungs. This can be done by accelerating the respiratory pace, forcing the exhalations with active movements of the thoracic muscles and the diaphragm. It is also possible to stop breathing altogether, a state that is called apnoea.

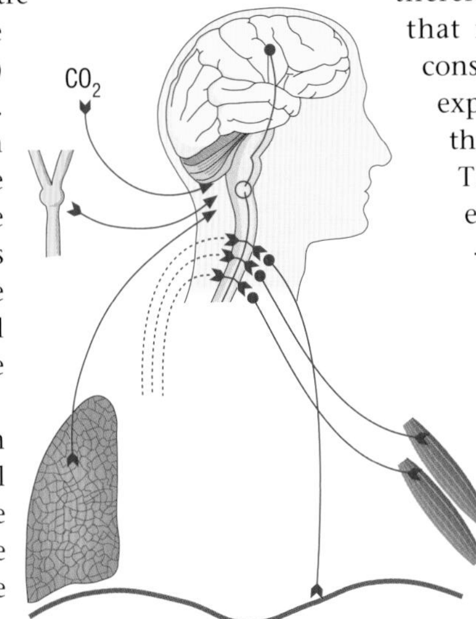

▶ **Respiratory system**
The diagram shows the ties that bind the bulbar neural centers for breath, sensitive to the concentration of CO2 and the signals from the nerve receptors in the vagus and lungs, chest muscles and diaphragm.

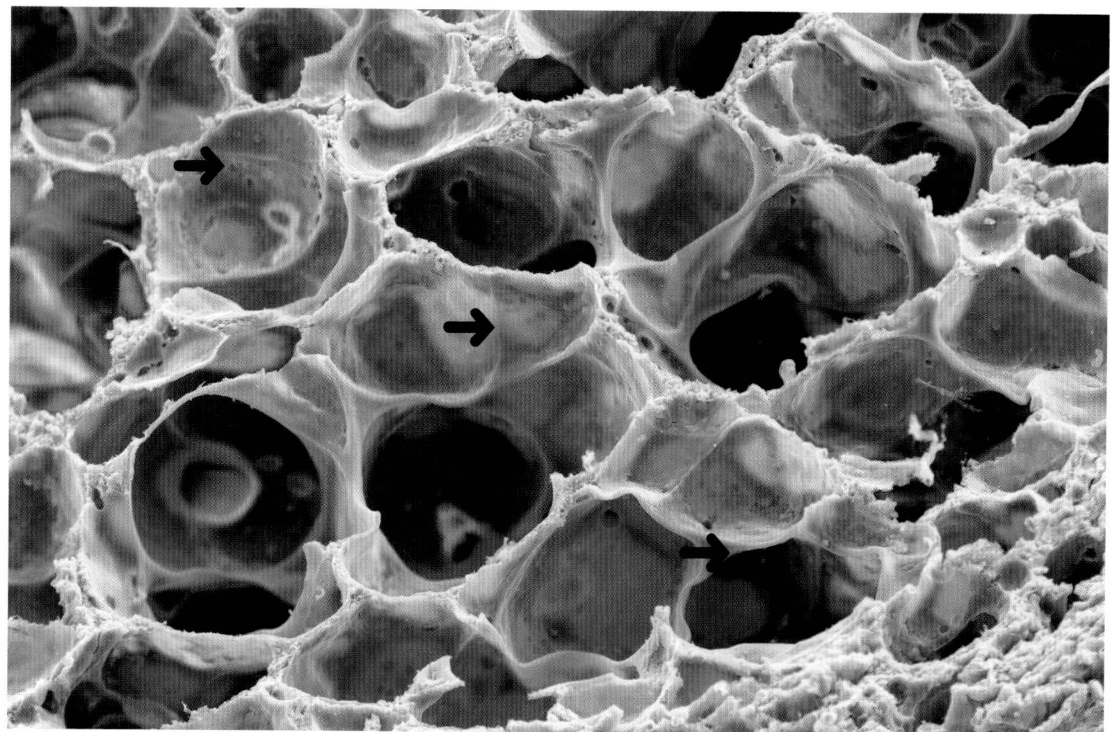

◀ **Pulmonary alveoli**
False-color SEM photograph of some alveoli. The red blood cells flowing in the capillaries surrounding the alveoli differ in transparency through the alveolar wall (→) which is only 0.2 mm thick. The appearance of iridescent aleveoli, like soap bubbles, is given by the mucus, rich in surfactant, which covers the lung tissue by facilitating the exchange gas.

These voluntarily respiration actions cannot be undertaken for very long though. For example, it is only possible to remain in apnoea for a few minutes before active breathing starts again spontaneously. The length of this period depends on the expansion capacity of the lungs, the speed with which our body consumes oxygen (that is, by age, sex and especially physical activity) and therefore the amount of carbon dioxide that accumulates in the blood. In particular, when the pCO2 in the blood exceeds the threshold value of 0.8 kPa (6 mm Hg), the mechanism of automatic breathing takes over, irrespective of any will on the part of the individual. This is because the brain requires the body to breathe.

THE WALLS OF THE ALVEOLI

The wall of foam that separates the air from the blood that is flowing in the capillaries, is formed by several layers. The alveolar epithelium is, in turn, comprised of three types of cells:

- Type I pneumocytes, these are very large thin squamous epithelial cells, through which the gaseous exchange occurs; they cover about 95% of the alveolar surface.
- Type II pneumocytes, these are glandular cells that are much smaller and thicker than those of Type I. They have microvilli that produce a special surfactant - this is a mixture of phospholipids and lipoproteins that decreases the surface tension of the alveolar liquid making it easier for gaseous solution in air;
- Macrophages ▸95 - these are immune cells that are able to make amoeboid movements, and are distributed throughout the epithelium. They play a defensive role, and help the phagocytes clean away debris and destroy any microbes or foreign substances that were not captured in the mucus or blocked by the fine hairs that line the mucous membranes of the respiratory tract;

The endothelium contains large numbers of very thin pulmonary capillaries - these have a diameter of 5-6 μ m, which is only wide enough to take one red corpuscle at a time. The endothelium which demarcates this region is continuous, without pores or fenestrations, and is wrapped in elastic fibres and collagen as well as connective cells that form a thin layer. The capillaries originate

▼ **Ciglia**
Detail in a scanning electron microscope (SEM) of the surface of a bronco cillia.

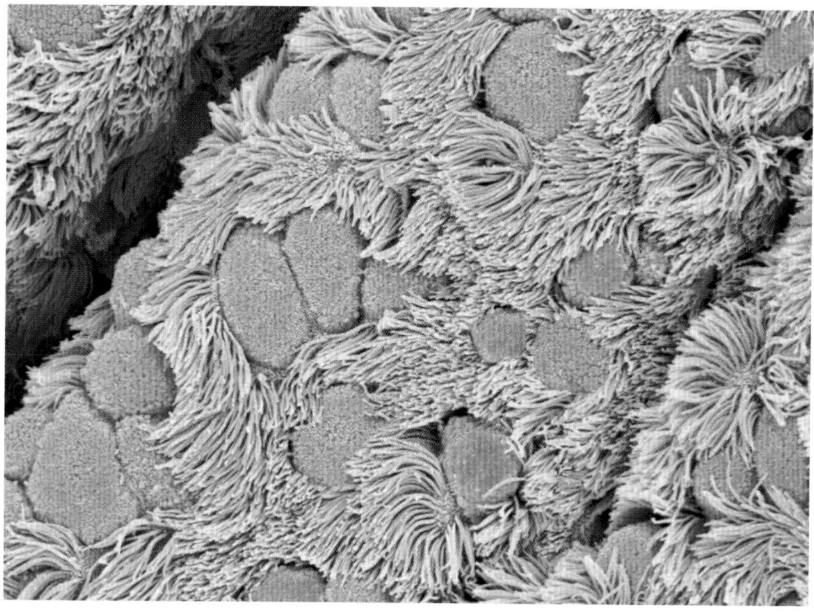

THE RESPIRATORY SYSTEM

The respiratory system, which is composed of a set of organs, cavities (mouth and nose, pharynx and larynx, lungs) and channels (trachea, bronchi, bronchiole) where circulating air, is composed of the following features:

- **Respiratory airways**: these are the parts of the nasal cavity and paranasal sinuses, mouth, pharynx, larynx, trachea and bronchial pathways (bronchi and bronchiole) that connect to the lungs. All of these structures have a skeleton that is composed of bone or cartilage which guarantees its structural integrity. The mucosa that lines the walls performs several functions. It is richly vascularised and so heats the air during inspiration. The mucus, which is produced by numerous glands, humidifies the inspired air and filters it, capturing any dust that has been drawn in - this is then pushed outside or toward the throat by the continuous movement of ciliary cells;

- **Lungs**: these have a spongy appearance because they are constructed from many small cavities called the pulmonary or respiratory cells. This is where the air that has been drawn into the lungs comes into closest contact with the blood. The wall of foam, in fact, is thin, like that of the blood capillaries that surround them: this facilitates the dissemination of the respiratory gases. The lungs are very elastic organs, and are able to expand and contract. Each is wrapped in a pleura, a two layer serous membrane - the space between the layers is filled with a thin layer of pleural liquid. This lubricates the linings, making it possible for the two to slide past each other during the respiratory movements. It also ensures that there is no adhesion between the pleural sheets or between the lung, chest and diaphragm. If for any reason, air penetrates into the pleural space (pneumothorax), the elasticity of the lung tissue causes it to collapse and the lung volume is severely reduced, with an almost total loss of respiratory capacity.

THE AIR PASSAGES

The air should preferably be inhaled from the nose: the nostrils, which can expand and shrink for voluntary action and reflexes, have hairs that block the nasal inhalation of harmful particles. Moreover, it is precisely in the nasal cavity that the respiratory mucosa, which is rich in blood vessels, has the highest population of mucous glands - this allows it to purify the air better. Indeed, the mucosa is very efficient at removing the dust and air pollution that gets trapped in the mucous.

▶ **RESPIRATORY SYSTEM**
In the picture are the main elements of the anatomical respiratory system of an adult.

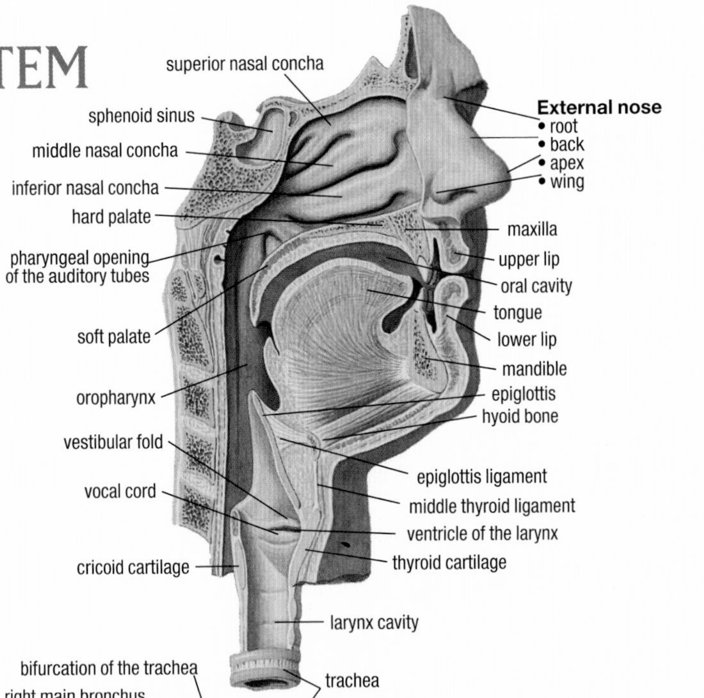

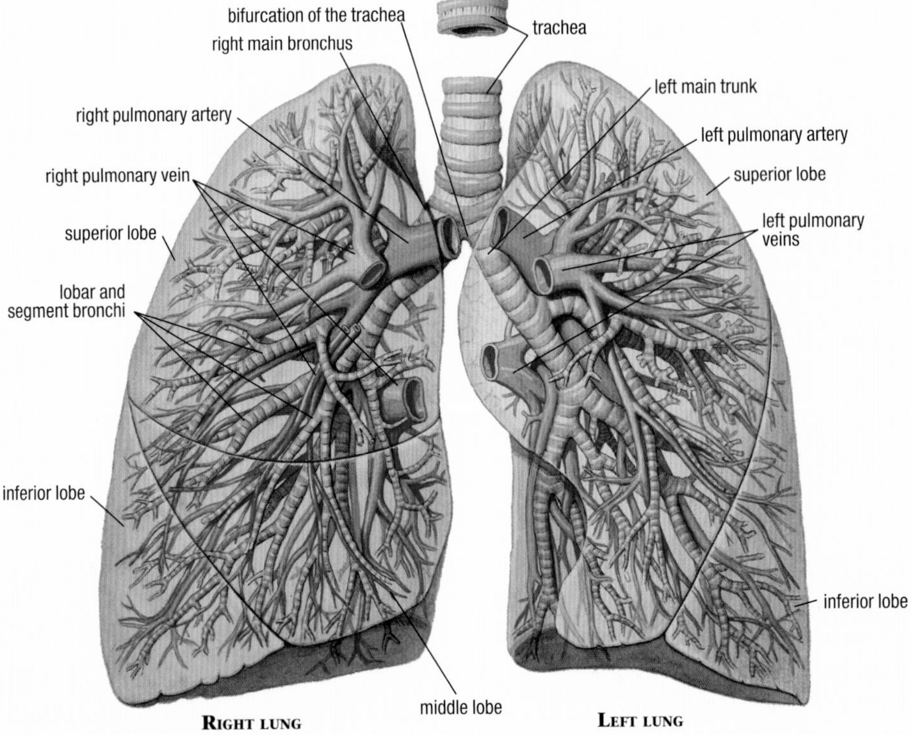

▼ **PULMONARY PLEURA**
The position of the two pleural membranes in the thoracic cage.
1 Section from above
2 front view;
3 Right lateral artificial pneumothorax.

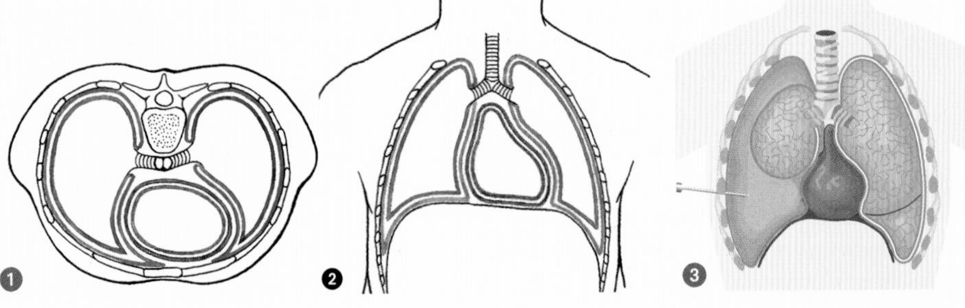

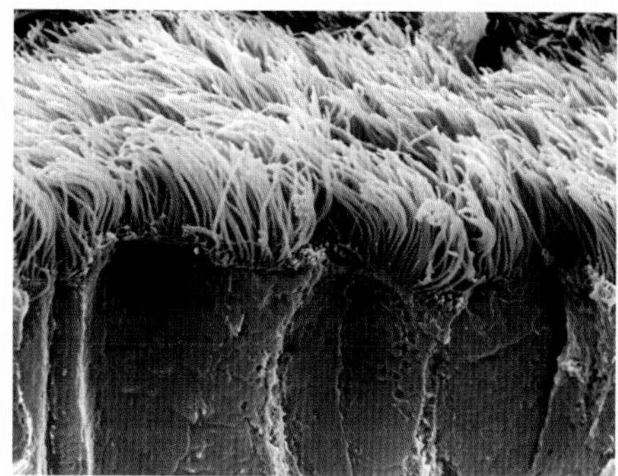

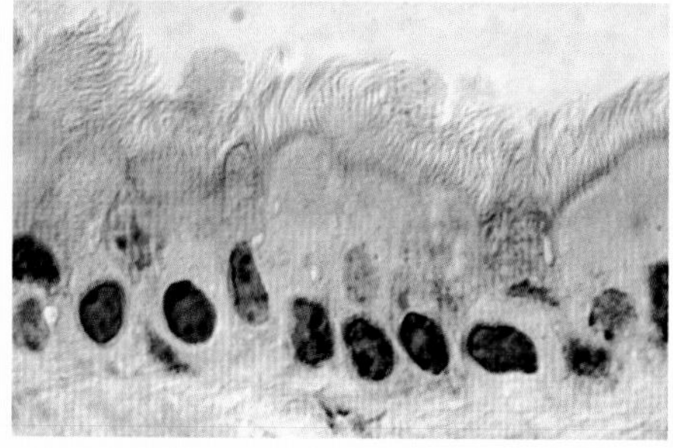

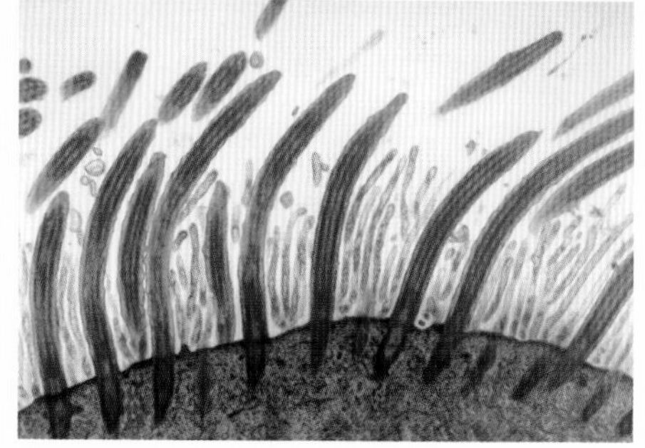

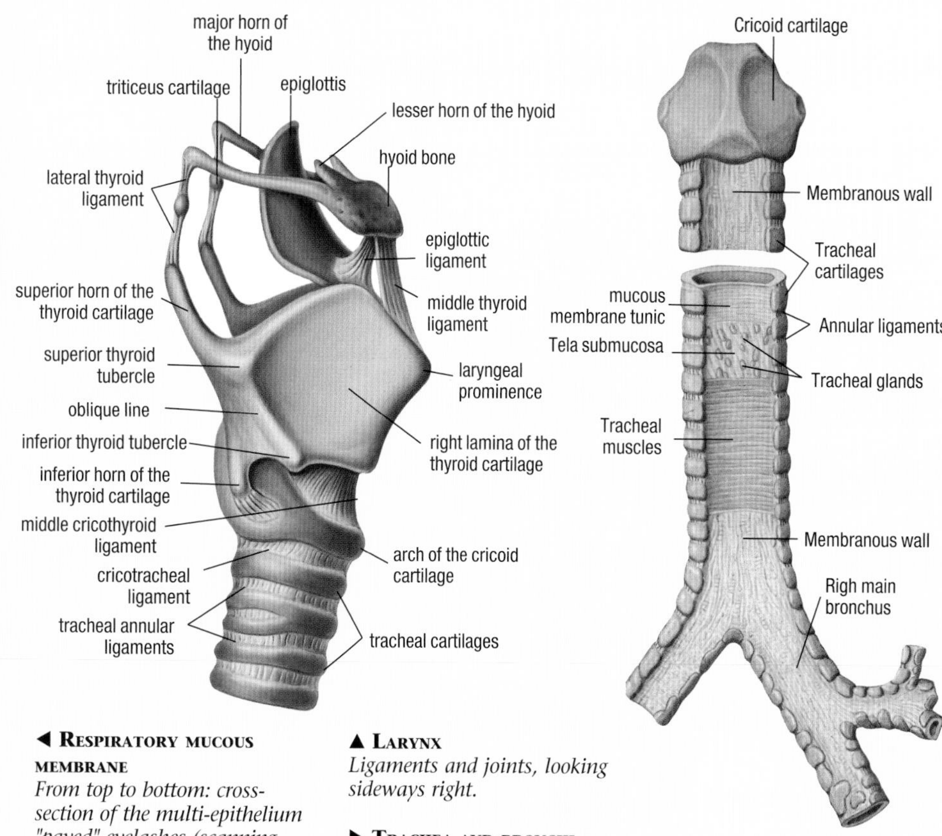

◀ **Respiratory mucous membrane**
From top to bottom: cross-section of the multi-epithelium "paved" eyelashes (scanning electron microscope, SEM), the section of respiratory mucosa: the hair cells are clearly visible, with the dark nucleus (light microscopy)

▲ **Larynx**
Ligaments and joints, looking sideways right.

▶ **Trachea and bronchi**
Structure of the trachea and bronchi the first parts of the main front view.

Air from the nose is purified, humidified and heated to body temperature. It then passes through the choana in the pharynx. From there it leads into the larynx - this is the body which opens to both the oesophagus - the first part of the digestive tract, and the trachea - the passage that continues to the lungs. The larynx, made up of a series of cartilage segments and ligaments, is made so that it can make the whole series of necessary movements. It not only has to be able to cope with the flexure needed for breathing and speech, but it also has to permit swallowing, as well as the extension and flexion of the neck. After the larynx, the air passes through the trachea - this is a 10-12 cm long tube with a diameter of 16-18 mm, that is lined by ciliate epithelial tissue. In this there is a succession of 16-20 cartilaginous tracheal rings; these are interspersed by annular ligaments that provide both structural integrity and flexibility. The trachea divides into two large main bronchi that have a structure which is reinforced by similar cartilaginous rings. The main bronchi connect to the lungs through passageways that subdivide many times into smaller and smaller diameter tubes, with an overall structure much like that of a branched tree. As it shrinks in diameter, the bronchi lose their cartilaginous support. In the intra-pulmonary bronchi, it is already much reduced, while in the bronchi with a diameter less than a millimetre, it is totally absent. By this stage, the air has reached the depths of the alveoli.

▲ **Trachea**
Epithelium that carpets the trachea. From a scanning electron microscope (SEM).

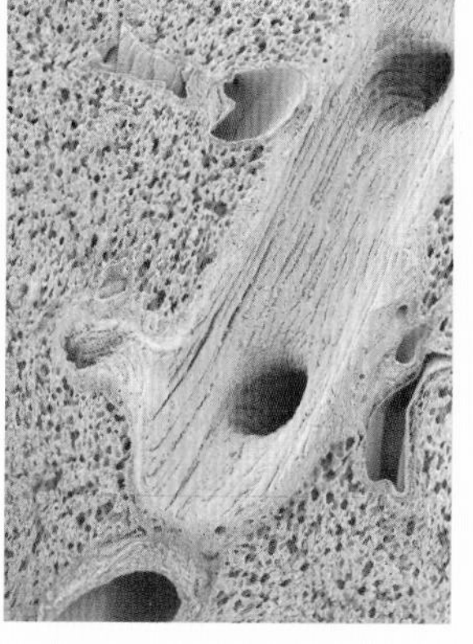

▲ **Bronchiolo**
Section of a bronchiole (electron microscope Scanning SEM).

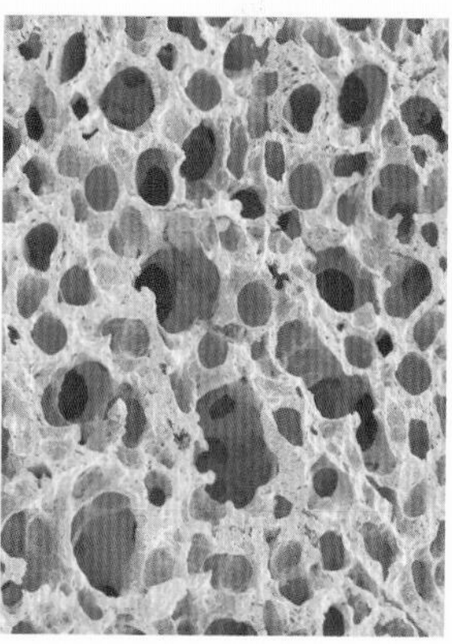

▲ **Alveoli**
Pulmonary alveoli seen through a scanning electron microscope (SEM).

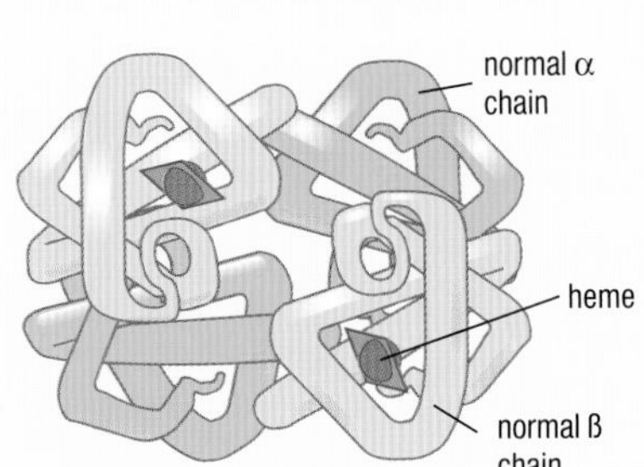

◀ **Haemoglobin**
Three-dimensional pattern of a molecule of hemoglobin. Notice the two chains, alpha (α) chains and two beta (β) that form.

Each of them is bound to a prosthetic group (ie non-protein) in the center containing one atom of iron: this is what binds with the gas transported to the hemoglobin.

▼ **Circulation**
A diagram showing the circulation of air around the alveoli.

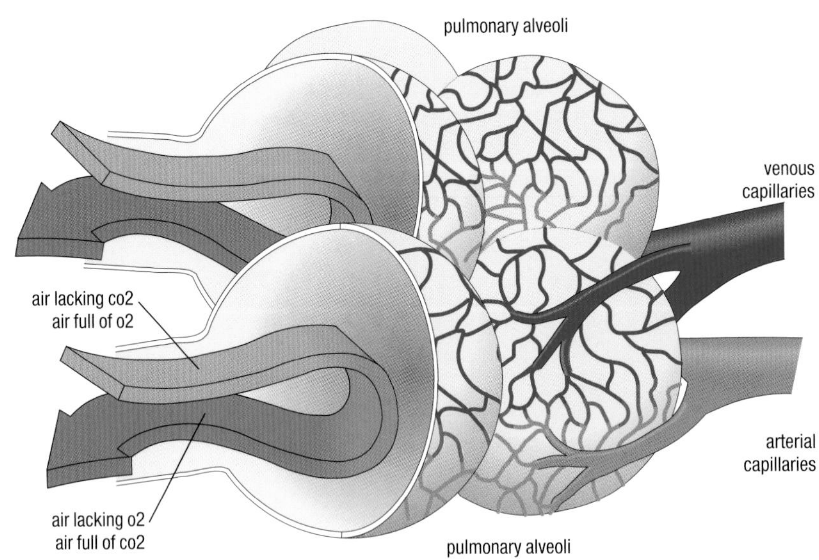

▲ **Heme**
Chemical structure of the prosthetic group of hemoglobin. The physico-chemical properties of the heme are linked mainly to the ferrous ion which is located at the center, as well as some amino acids of the protein chain to which it is attached.

from branches in the pulmonary arteries that carry oxygen-poor blood and are rich in carbon dioxide. These end in venous vessels that convey oxygenated blood in the pulmonary veins. The total thickness of the alveolar wall varies from 0.2 to 0.7 mm.

THE EXCHANGE OF GASES

The passage of a gas through a biological membrane depends on the permeability of the membrane to the gas and the partial pressure that the gas exerts on its two sides. In breathing, the factor that varies and is crucial for gaseous exchange is not just the permeability of the membranes. The permeabilities of both the alveolar epithelia and the endothelial capillaries are high enough not to be limiting factors to the passage of air. It is the partial pressures, especially those of oxygen (pO2) and carbon dioxide (pCO2) that really matter.

PARTIAL RESPIRATORY GAS PRESSURES

Gas	Atmospheric air		Alveolar		Blood	
					Venous	Arterial
	%	**kPa**	**%**	**kPa**	**kPa**	**kPa**
O_2	20.94	21.3	14.2	13.3	5.3	13.3
CO_2	0.04	0.04	5.5	5.3	6.1	5.3
N_2	79.02	80.0	80.3	76.4	76.4	76.4
Total	**100.00**	**101.3**	**100.0**	**95.0**	**87.8**	**95.0**

PARTIAL PRESSURES IN THE AIR & THE ALVEOLI

Under normal conditions, air that is external to the body has an atmospheric pressure of about 101.5 kPa at 37 ° C, and the partial pressure of oxygen (pO2) is 21.3 kPa (160 mm Hg). When it is inhaled, however, it is rapidly drawn into the lungs where it mixes with the oxygen-deprived air that is already present in the airways. The partial pressure in the alveoli is 13.3 kPa (100 mm Hg). At the same time and under normal conditions, the partial pressure of carbon dioxide (pCO2) in the exterior air is 0.04 kPa (0.3 mm Hg). This value is insignificant when contrasted with the figure in the alveoli, where it is 5.32 kPa (40 mmHg).

PARTIAL PRESSURES IN THE BLOOD

In capillaries, on the other side of the alveolar membranes, venous blood flows which has lost oxygen and is loaded with carbon dioxide. The partial pressures of pO2 and pCO2 in this blood varies according to the metabolic activity of the cells. For example, there is more carbon dioxide when the body is in active and less when it is at rest. On average, the pO2 value is 5.32 kPa (40 mm Hg) and for pCO2 it is 6.1 kPa (46 mmHg). When it is released by the alveoli, the blood flowing in arterial capillaries has values of pO2 is 13.3 kPa (100 mm Hg) and pCO2 is 5.32 kPa (40 mmHg). These are also the characteristics of blood that is circulating in the body.

THE ALVEOLI

The partial pressure differences between the two sides of the double membrane are not huge, but they are sufficient to ensure the passage of oxygen and carbon dioxide to and from the blood in the alveoli in the required directions. The 3rd law of gases, in fact, means that the gases move spontaneously from a high pressure towards an area of low pressure. This means that the oxygen follows the pO2 partial pressure gradient ranging from outside the body at 13.3 kPa to inside the blood at 5.32 kPa. Likewise, the carbon dioxide follows the pCO2 gradient that goes from inside (6.1 kPa) to outside (5.32 kPa). The balance is not fixed - while the oxygenated blood is continuously replaced by new oxygen-poor blood, the breathing activity constantly changes the gaseous composition in the alveoli. In this way, the partial pressure gradients of the gases stay in favour of continuous exchange.

THE BLOOD & HAEMOGLOBIN

The amount of oxygen that can be transported from a given volume of blood is 100 times higher than what would be expected if the gas were simply dissolved in plasma. The quantity of gas that can dissolve in a liquid is, in fact, constrained by the 4th law of gases. This is determined by the partial pressure of the gas and its solubility in the liquid. In the case of oxygen and plasma, these are not high. In fact, the amount of oxygen present in solution in the blood would always be too low to support all the metabolic needs of the body. The big difference in measured values is due to the ability of oxygen molecules (O2) to bind to haemoglobin (Hb), a large and complex protein which is present in the blood ▸83. It is haemoglobin that gives the red colour to blood - it is a dark red when it is rich in carbon dioxide, but a bright red when rich in oxygen.

The haemoglobin molecule is made up of four globular protein chains, each of which has a group called embedded haem, at the centre of which is a ferrous ion (Fe2 +). This is a cofactor that binds more or less reversibly with molecules of different substances (O2, CO2, CO or carbon monoxide, etc.).

When blood passes through the alveoli, oxygen flows into the red blood cells and binds weakly to atoms of iron. The percentage of haemoglobin that is saturated with O2 (known as oxyhaemoglobin, or HbO2) depends on the partial pressure of oxygen in the blood. The function that binds the pO2 and saturation of Hb is not linear: its graphic representation is a sigmoid curve. This is because the bond of a haem with oxygen amends

▼ **Structure**
Structure in detail a group of pulmonary alveoli.

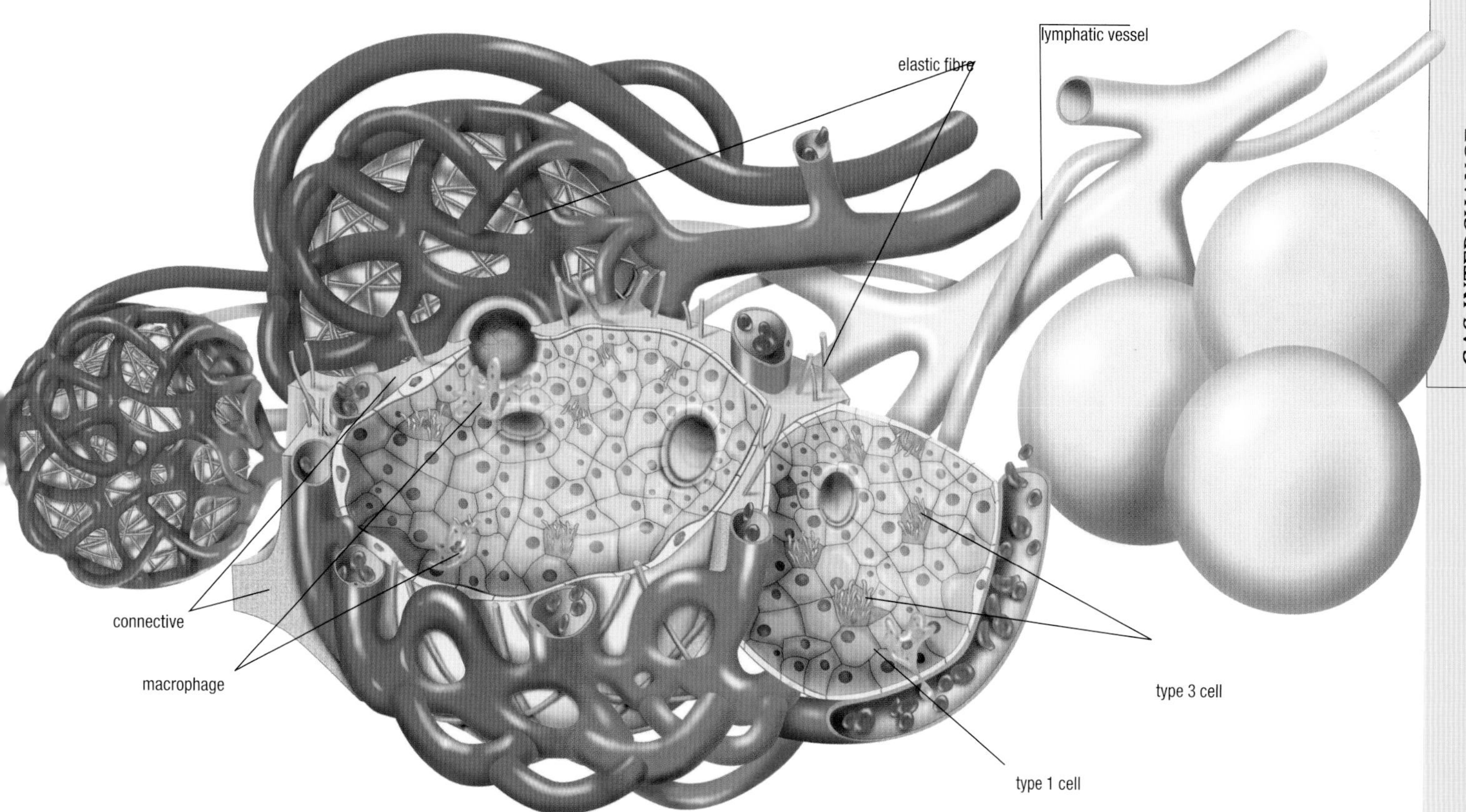

▶ **Curves of hemoglobin**
Sigmoid trend of saturation of blood during a change of partial pressure of oxygen. If the hemoglobin does not take an active part in the process, the curve is a straight line, conforming to the law of Henry. In tissue (left) the high partial pressure of carbon dioxide, which competes for binding with the hemoglobin causes the release of a 5% more oxygen. Conversely, in aleveoli (right) is the high partial pressure of oxygen which causes the release of carbon dioxide bound to hemoglobin. The affinity of hemoglobin for carbon dioxide is slightly lower than that for oxygen, but if the first gas is present, the curve moves to right. Since the quantity in the lungs is different from that in tissues, none of the curves reproduce the physiological conditions in the presence of carbon dioxide, however, the curve changes from A to B, and occurs in the tissues increased supply of oxygen.

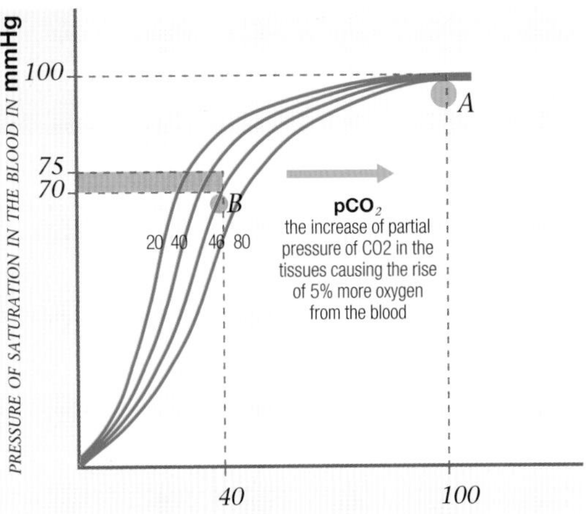

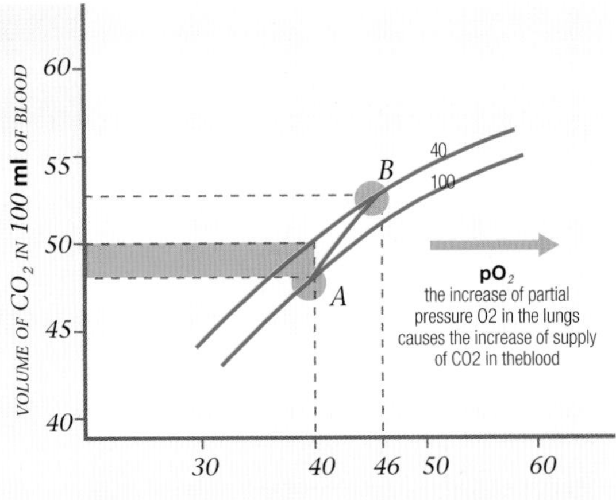

the stereochemistry of Hb, so as to make it easier for other groups to link with this gas. The events follow this sequence: oxygen gas enters into solution, and then binds to Hb as shown in this formula:

$$O_{2(g)} \rightarrow O_{2(sol)} \rightarrow Hb{+}O_2 \rightarrow HbO_2$$

As long as there is free haemoglobin, this reaction tends towards right side of the equation, namely towards the formation of oxyhaemoglobin. Since 100 ml of human blood contains, on average, 15 grams of haemoglobin, and as every gram of Hb binds with 1.34 mg of O2, 100 ml of blood can carry up to 20.1 mg of oxygen. When this happens, it is said that the blood is saturated with oxygen, or that its percentage saturation is 100.
The conditions where the blood reaches a full saturation of oxygen occur in its passage through the alveoli, where pO2 blood rises to 13.3 kPa and beyond. Under these conditions, the haemoglobin becomes oxyhaemoglobin.
The haemoglobin may also bind to carbon dioxide to form carboxyhaemoglobin (HbCO2); this bond, however, is less favoured than that for oxyhaemoglobin. This is because the affinity of Hb for carbon dioxide is slightly lower than that for oxygen. When the pCO2 increases it decreases the pO2 , however, the decoupling of HbO2 accelerates in parallel to form HbCO2. This happens when the blood has reached the peripheral tissues, where the partial pressure of oxygen drops rapidly and that of carbon dioxide grows. Under these conditions, oxygen is separated from the ferrous ions leaving their sites on the Hb molecule free for carbon dioxide. The presence of this gas also helps to reduce the affinity between haem and oxygen, and causes a change in pH, which favours the uptake of carbon dioxide by the Hb. In this way it is transported away from the plasma. The CO2, which is the main waste product of many metabolic processes such as the Krebs cycle ▶20, dissolves in plasma to form carbonic acid. It is thanks to this spontaneous process, in which every molecule of carbon dioxide combines with a molecule water to form carbonic acid, that gas in solution cannot form blood clots. The carbonic acid is dissociated into ions according to the equation:

$$CO_2 + H_2O \rightleftarrows H_2CO_3 \rightleftarrows HCO_3^- + H^+$$

Where the symbol x indicates a balance (these

The law of Henry

Henry's Law describes the solubility of gases in a liquid; discovered by William Henry in 1803. It states:

'At a constant temperature, the amount of a given gas dissolved in a given type and volume of liquid is directly proportional to the partial pressure of that gas in equilibrium with that liquid'.

In simplified terms, it can be written thus:

$$P = kC$$

where P is the external pressure of gas, C is its concentration in the liquid k is a constant characteristic of each gas. The constants k vary from gas to gas, solvent solvent and the second temperature. When drawing up the balance, because, overall, gas in solution does not increase more, the liquid is defined saturated with the gas to that pressure.
Until the external pressure gas remains the same, the situation remains in constant balance, if decreases, the liquid will sovrasaturo and gas release again until find a new point of equilibrium, if increases, however, may enter into other solution gas until the pressure will again be balanced.
The speed with which a gas enters into solution in a liquid (or go free) varies with the difference of external and internal pressures means the process, therefore, is faster when there are conditions far from equilibrium. It also depends on the molecular composition of gases and the nature of the liquid.
Finally, any gas enters solution (or free return) so independent of what they do other gases present.

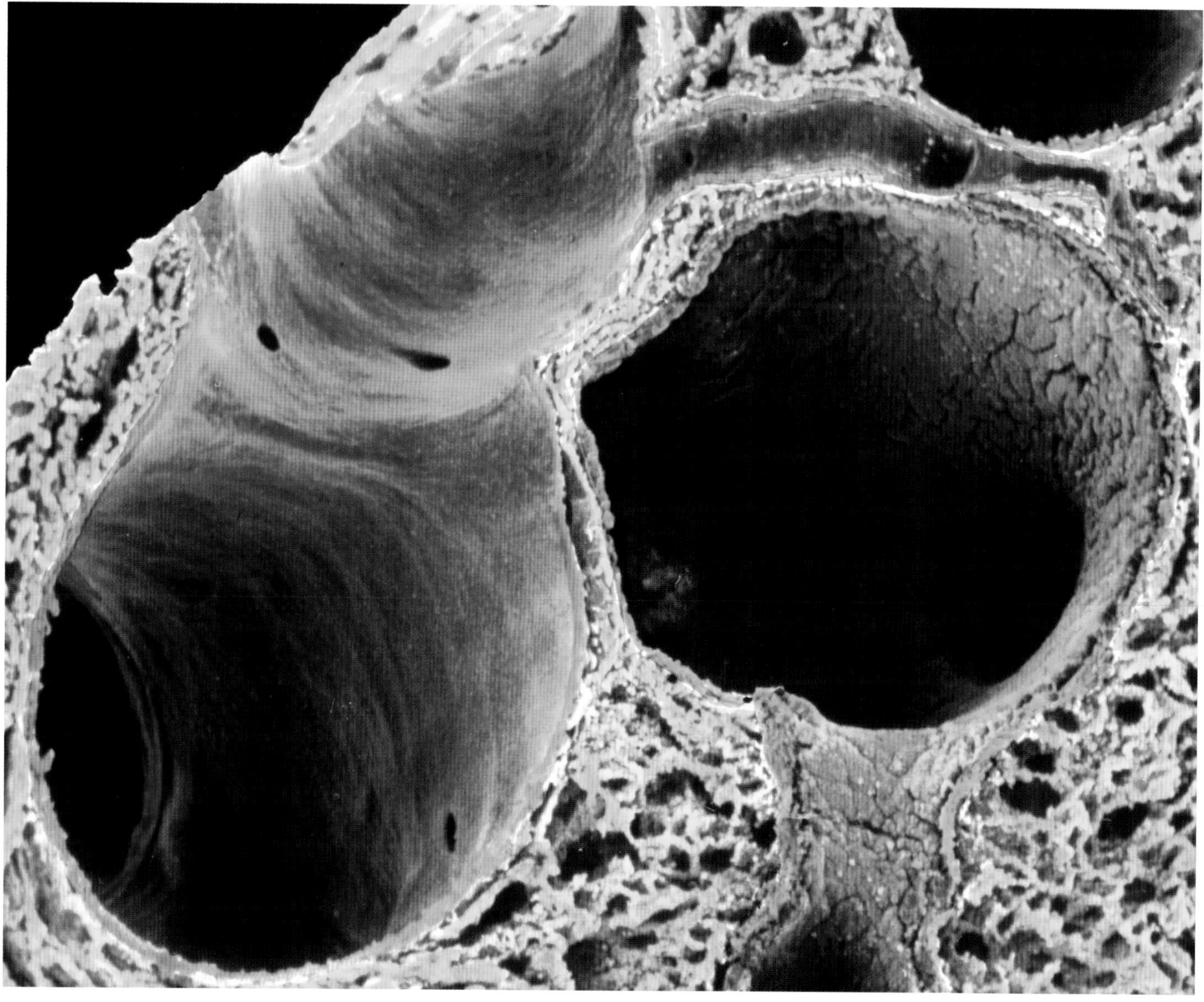

reactions are reversible). When one of the final products ($HCO3^-$ or H^+) is removed from equilibrium, the law of mass action causes the balance to be lost and, in an attempt to restore a greater amount of carbon dioxide, it turns into carbonic acid.

Conversely, when one of the final products becomes free, the carbon dioxide excess returns to its gaseous form. On its own, however, the reaction is too slow to be of any use to the body, and so there is a special enzyme accelerator called carbonic anhydrase - this is found in red blood cells.

Where the pCO_2 is high, namely in the peripheral tissues, carbonate ions ($HCO3^-$) are stored, while free hydrogen ions (H^+), passing in plasma are captured by buffer substances present in the blood. Conversely, when the pCO_2 is lower - as is the case in the alveoli, the red blood cells release the carbonate ions. Once back in solution, these then bind to hydrogen ions, and in this way the chemistry favours the ejection of carbon dioxide gas from the blood. This, together with the other reactions that take place in gaseous exchange, are essential factors in the control of the average pH of blood, which fluctuates constantly around a value of 7.2.

▲ **Bronchiole and the alveoli**
This false color scanning electron microscope (SEM) photograph shows a detail of lung tissue (yellow) with cavities (dark niches), bronchioles (blue) and blood vessels (red). The difference between the endothelium of blood vessel which are smooth and the rough of the bronchioles are evident even at this magnification.

Speech

▼ **Comparative Anatomy**
The different position ot the larynx in the neck of a monkey ①, of a newborn ② and an adult ③ determine the different possibilities of vocals

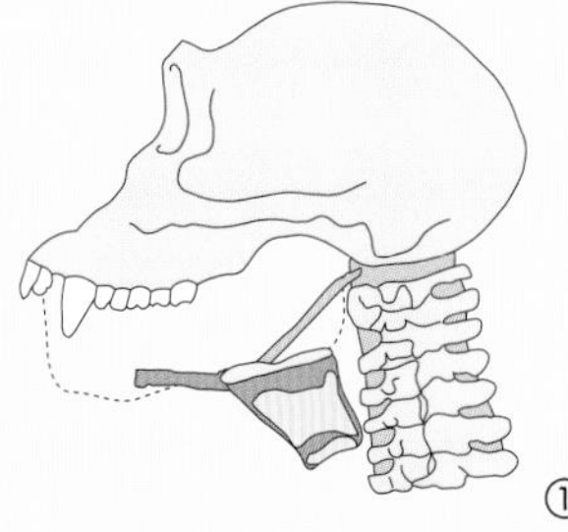

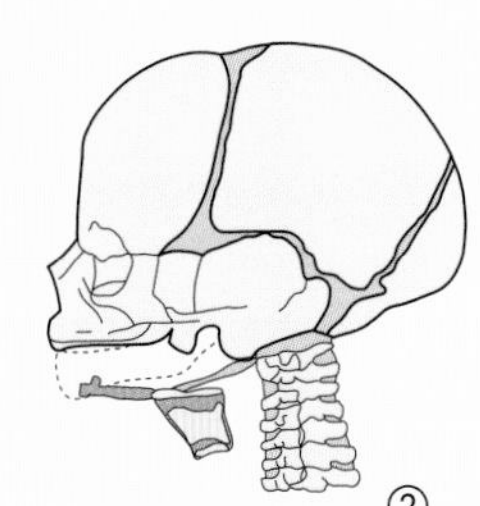

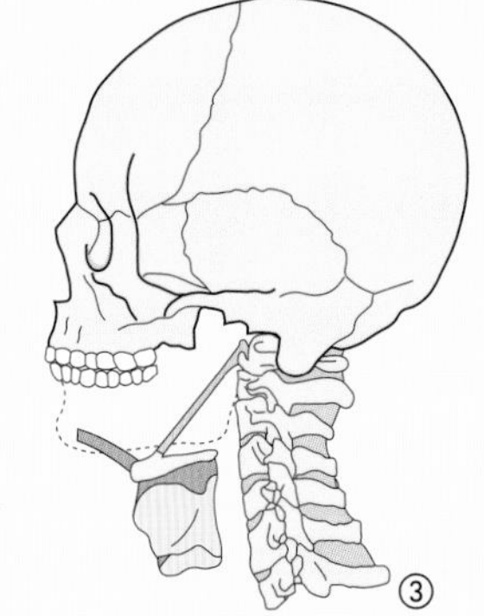

The respiratory system also carries out functions related to speech, namely all the articulations of sounds and words. The larynx - also known as the voice-box, in fact, plays a central role both in producing the sounds, and in modulating the pharynx, which acts as a sounding board. The internal cavity of the larynx is bounded by cartilage, ligaments and muscles, and is very small compared to its outer circumference. It is divided into three segments:

- the upper segment or vestibule, this delimited at the rear by the epiglottis and works in conjunction with the pharynx;
- the medial segment, this includes the folds: within which are vocal folds and the rima glottidis. The size and shape of the rima glottidis varies with sex, the individual, the phases of breathing and the type of speech;
- the lower segment, this continues downwards taking a cylindrical shape.

The length, thickness and the tension of the vocal cords - that is, the extent of rima glottidis - determine the quality and timbre of any sounds that the individual makes. The pressure of the air current produced by the lungs modulates the intensity of the sound, while the individual characteristics are almost exclusively due to the internal shapes of the air passages. The larynx, tongue, soft palate and lips are essential to the correct articulation of the language. The position of the larynx in the neck, however, also affects the way in which a person breathes and swallows.

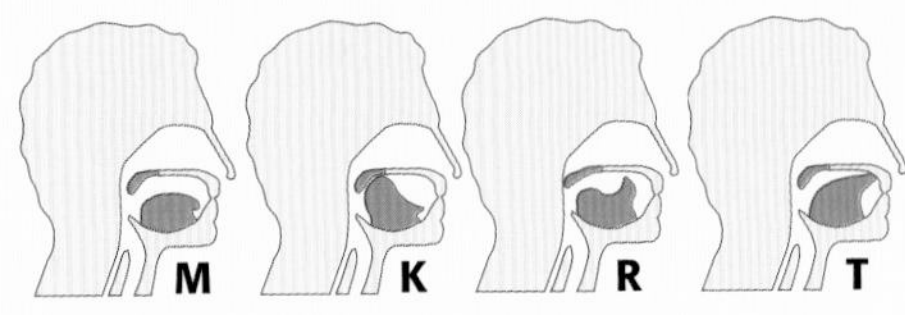

▲ **Language and palate**
The positions of the tongue and palate modulate the sounds of consonants: from left to right, M sound, CH or K, R sound, sound T.

In a monkey or newborn baby, it is so high in the neck that it blocks the nose-throat allowing the individual to drink and breathe at the same time. However, having the larynx located so high up reduces the capacity of the pharyngeal sounding board, making it impossible to articulate different sounds, therefore making speech impossible. This is why both monkeys and babies use their lips and mouth more than adult humans do. With growth, however, the infant larynx moves downwards - within two years its form changes radically, significantly altering the actions of swallowing and breathing; this makes speech possible.

The process of speech is still mysterious though - besides the larynx and pharynx it also involves other vital structures. The spoken language is so essential to the human species that when we talk it also affects the respiratory frequency. The carbon dioxide in our breath is expelled at a different pace from normal. In fact, if a person was to breath in and out that quickly without speaking, they would soon be in hyper-ventilation. Yet even though breathing varies the rhythm of speech, this is unnoticeable in everyday use.

Talking is actually a function that is closely linked to the development of the human brain. From an anatomical point of view, there are two main centres of language control - one is Broca's area ▸194 in the left frontal lobe (in the vast majority of people), the other is Wernicke's area, in the left temporal lobe. The former presides over the functions of language and controls the oral muscles, tongue and pharynx. Wernicke's area has a very different role - it is the "design centre" of language. It is where organised meanings, phrases and speeches are developed. It undertakes

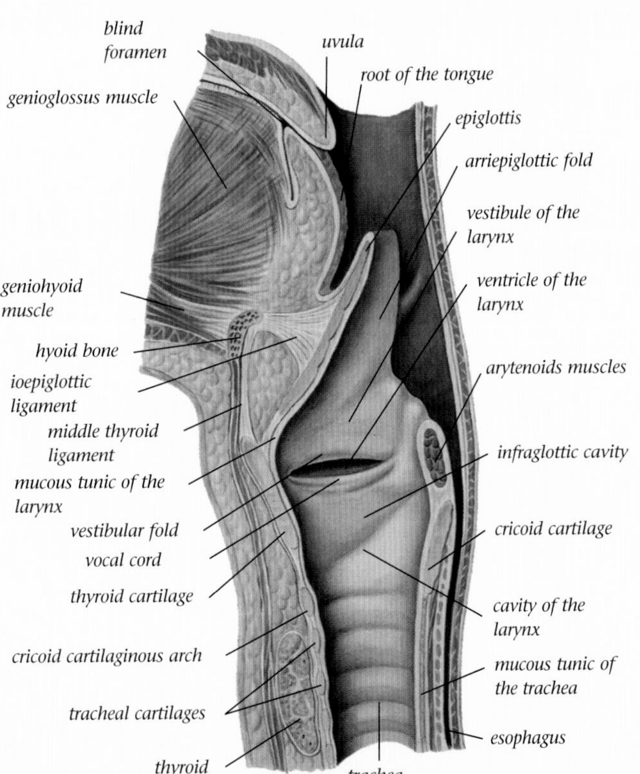

◀ **Larynx**
Elements of anatomical section right side.

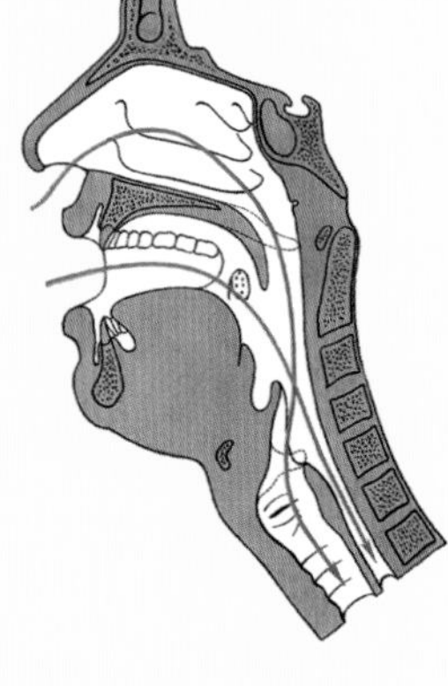

▲ **Alternative Routes**
While the food moves through the pharynx in the direction of the esophagus (red line), the air comes mainly from the nose and continues to the trachea (blue line). To close the access to food of the trachea, there is the epiglottis.

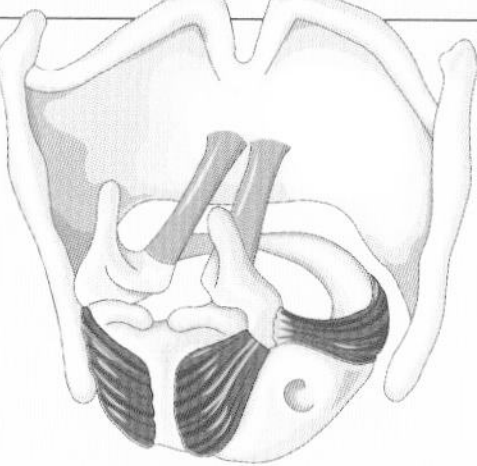

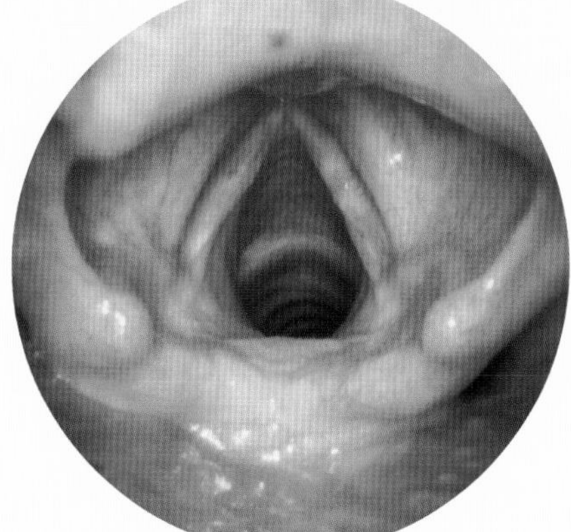

▶ **Breathing**
The vocal cords are separated when you breathe.

▼▶ **Voice elements**
The anatomical larynx involved in spoken language are few:
❶ *thyroid cartilage;*
❷ *rhyme glottis;*
❸ *process voice;*
❹ *aritenoidea cartilage;*
❺ *Cricoid* ligament rear;
❻ *Cricoid cartilage;*
❼ *cone elastic;*
❽ *vocal ligament.*

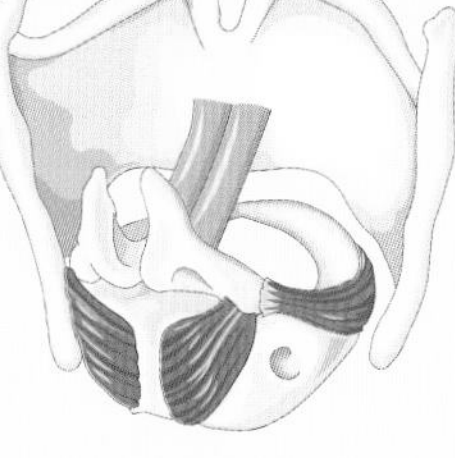

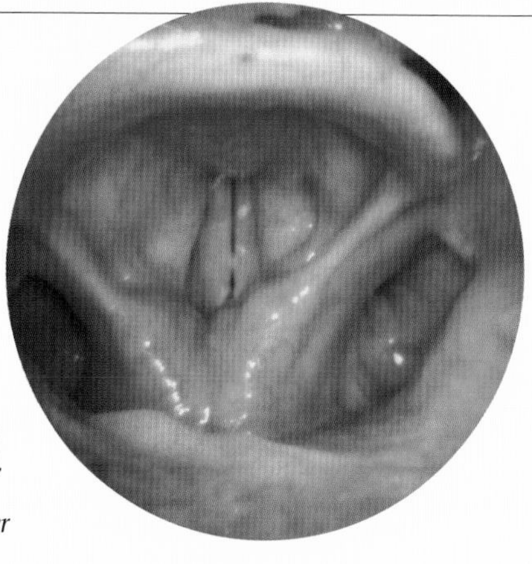

▶ **Talking**
When it comes to the vocal cords are close: their voltage changes with the inclination of cartilage which are linked, based on voluntary muscles. The more strained, the higher the sound.

the processing required for the translation of sounds and words heard - this information is then passed to Broca's area where it is subsequently transformed into nerve signals.

But the production of the language requires the involvement of many more nerve centres, where the flow of blood is kept both constant and high. These include the thalamus, auditory cortex ▸264, and primary motor ▸226 which formulate and co-ordinate speech, hearing, and perceptive muscle movements.

In close collaboration with the cerebellum ▸218, there are the structures that are responsible for the rhythm and grammar of speech. These receive information from a wide range of sensory regions in the cortex and then transmit the necessary information to a number of motor areas. It is clear that knowing how to speak requires the co-operation of many encephalic areas. When a word is heard, the primary auditory cortex receives a sensation that is collected by the ears. It is not actually understood, however, until Wernicke's area has interpreted the sound and recognised it. Conversely, when we want to say a word, Wernicke's area transmits a signal to Broca's area. This then initiates a second a detailed programme of articulation, from which specific stimuli are produced for that word. These are sent in direct succession to the motor cortex, which passes the information on as signals that are suitable for the muscles of the lips, tongue and larynx. Even when we read a word, the interpretation still falls on the brain. The sight of the word is registered by the primary visual cortex, and this is then processed so that a visual representation can be correlated in Wernicke's area with the corresponding aural representation.

Researchers have successfully used PET scans of different brain regions to identify the areas where the neurones are individually enabled by the various aspects of spoken language. Each of them is able to recognise the phonetic aspects (the pronunciation of sounds, syllables and words), the structure of the sentence, the chain of phrases and the consistency of the logical-semantics of the phrases in a sentence. Therefore, the processing and understanding of languages - which are inherently articulated and complex, requires significant mental activity.

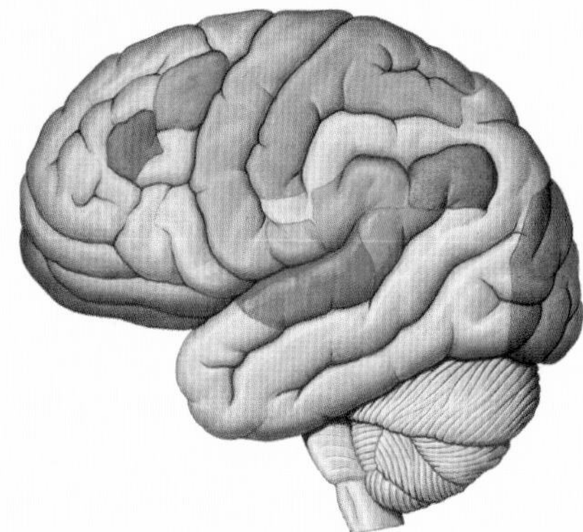

▲ **Areas of sound**
The different colors indicate areas of the cerebral cortex involved in the language:
occipital pole (visual area);
precentral gyrus (auditory area);
front internal gyrus (language area);
superior parietal lobule
super marginal gyrus
superior temple gyrus.

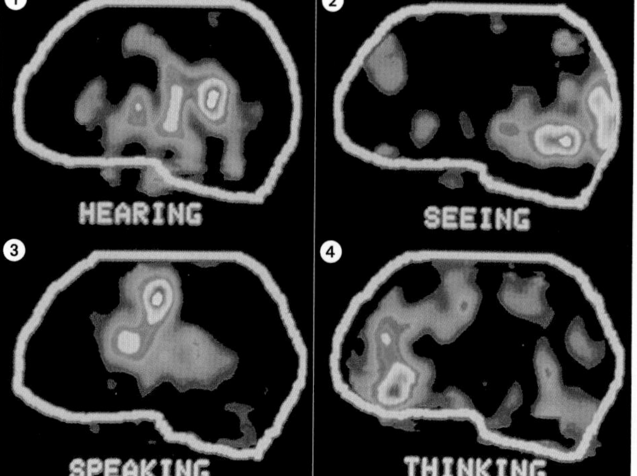

▲ **Brain cortex activity**
Computed tomography positron emission (PET) is a radiation technique that, locates radioactive glucose administered to the subject of investigation, it allows you to view areas of the active brain. They are, in fact, particularly "greedy" for energy (sugar). In these images, you can recognize areas of the cortex activated by specific cognitive functions: ❶ *Hearing,* ❷ *seeing,* ❸ *speech,* ❹ *abstract thinking.*

THE CONTINUOUS INJECTION OF NEW "CONSTRUCTION MATERIALS" AND ENERGY IN THE FORM OF BIOCHEMICAL MOLECULES IS VITAL FOR EVERY BODY. BUT TO BECOME ACCESSIBLE TO CELLS, FOOD MUST UNDERGO MANY CHANGES.

MATERIAL INTERCHANGE

All the body's cells have to obtain various substances in order to perform their manifold metabolic functions. These include a variety of construction materials that are used to produce new structural and functional molecules. In addition, the body also needs to continually build new cells to replace those that are damaged or destroyed or to make new ones as part of growth and development. A vital part of all this is to provide sufficient energy for the functioning of the organs and to maintain constant levels of the substances that make up the internal environment. Both the construction materials (amino acids, fats, minerals, water etc.) and the energy (in the form of complex biomolecules such as sugars or fat), are contained in abundance in a normal diet. In order to be accessible to the cells, however, these substances have to be profoundly changed. They have to be reduced in size and made fit for transport in the blood, which involves making them soluble in water. The necessary conversions are undertaken by the organs that make up the digestive system, and these perform all the necessary mechanical, physical and chemical actions that transform food into nutrients for the body. This is a process that follows a precise sequence of events:

1. The ingestion of food or nutrition;

2. The processing of food and useful substances in keeping with the needs of the body, or digestion. The actual process is regulated by the exocrine glands ▸36, with the relevant control substances being secreted into the digestive tract;

3. The transport - either passive or active, of the nutrients from the digestive tract through the mucous membranes and the walls of the capillaries to the blood and lymph, or via assimilation;

4. The expulsion of waste materials.

▶ **Component nutrients**
A man who weighs 75 kg, includes: approximately 42 kg water, approx 25 kg protein and reserves fat, approximately 8 kg glycogen, minerals other substances such as nucleic acids. Each component of the body must be continually renewed, and becomes a nutrient that must be present in the daily diet.

THE DIGESTIVE SYSTEM

It is also called the digestive tract because of its shape - a long channel through which are distributed various digestive glands. From the mouth to the anus - the two openings through which it communicates with the outside world - the digestive tract has constant characteristics in spite of being differentiated in the areas that have

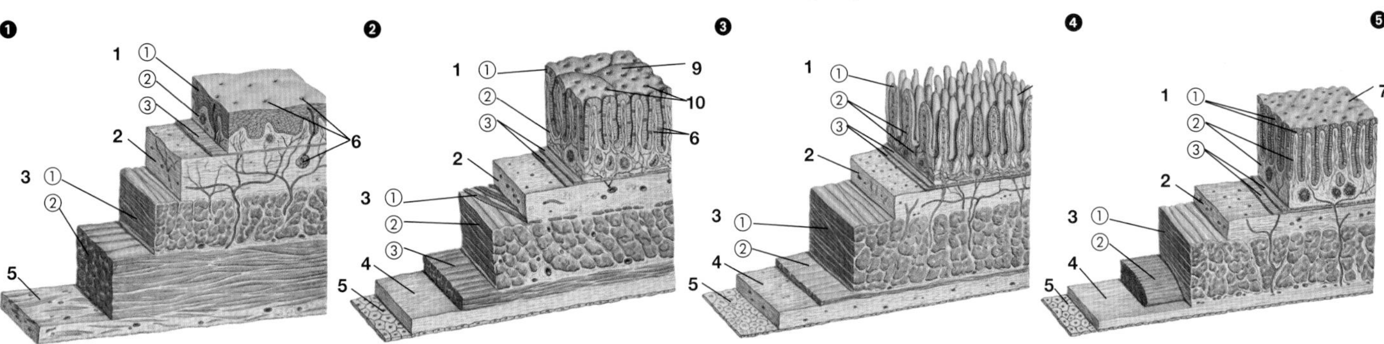

▲ **Digestive tube**
Differences and similarities in anatomical structural elements of the various sections of the digestive tract: ❶ *oesophagus,* ❷ *stomach,* ❸ *small intestine* ❹ *rectum.*

1. *MUCOUS TUNIC:* ① *epithelium;* ② *lamina propria;* ③ *lamina muscle;*
2. *CANVAS SUBMUCOSA;*
3. *TUNIC MUSCLE:* ① *Circular layer circolare;* ② *layer longitudinal;* ③ *oblique layer;*
4. *SUBMUSCULAR CANVAS;*
5. *SEROUS TUNIC in the esophagus that is a adventitial tunic. Specific anatomical tunic elements of different mucous:*
6. *oesophageal and gastric glands;*
7. *intestinal crypts*
8. *intestinal villous*
9. *gastric areas*
10. *gastric dimple*

different functions:

- a mucous membrane that is exposed within the lumen through which the food passes. It is where glands of various kinds can be found, as well as villous tissue;
- a submucosa tissue that separates the mucosa from the underlying smooth muscle;
- smooth muscle that is formed from involuntary muscle fibres and controlled by the autonomic nervous system ▸176;
- a sub-serous tissue separating the muscles from the serous tissue;
- serous tissue that envelops and surrounds the entire digestive tract.

While some of the bodies that form the digestive system only have a transient function (oesophagus, rectum, anus), most of them perform precise actions on the digestive food. Digestion is, in fact, a continuous process of the simplification of the food's chemistry which is performed by digestive enzymes. These are protein molecules that are produced by special digestive glands, and they catalyse specific chemical reactions, making them fast and efficient. Most of the digestive enzymes bind to a specific nutritional molecule and support its breakdown. They retain their ability to repeat the operation over and over again until they are eventually degraded, regardless of activity. Each enzyme digester, therefore, has a limited scope - for example, the pepsin of gastric juice divides only proteins; rennet only divides milk casein; maltase divides only maltose and so forth. In this way, the digestive enzymes transform the large molecules of organic food into nutritional units, namely small organic molecules, which can then be assimilated through the intestinal epithelium.

THE MOUTH: THE CHEWING & DIGESTION OF CARBOHYDRATES

The digestion of food solid starts with chewing, that is with the mechanical fragmentation of food by the teeth. Each tooth consists of a set of tissues with different structures and consistency, but with the same physiological function. There are three main parts:

- The crown, which is formed by the tooth that emerges from gum;
- The collar, which is located at the edge of gum;
- The root, which is the hidden part of the tooth, and is fixed into the bone of the dental alveolus.

The outer layer is formed by the enamel - this has a shiny appearance, and is the hardest tissue of the human body. It is made up of 96% limestone and 4% organic materials, and covers the entire outer surface of the tooth down as far as the collar. The thickness of the layer differs depending on the part of a tooth. Beneath the enamel the tooth is composed of ivory or dentin - this is a particular type of bone that is calcified and contains a high percentage of minerals (fluoride, iron, potassium and hydroxylapatite crystals). It represents the main part of the tooth. While the outer surface of the dentin is covered by enamel, the area in contact with the bone of the dental alveolus is covered with cement. This is made up of connective tissue that has become calcified, which is composed of around 65% of hydroxylapatite crystals. The cement envelops the root of a tooth providing it with a firm anchor, and thus guaranteeing the stability of the teeth. The mineralised dentine is completely permeated by small canals that branch from the enamel or cement, reaching the

◀ **Digestive system**
Anatomical elements:
❶ parotid salivary glands; ❷ mouth; ❸ submaxillary salivary glands; ❹ lingual salivary glands; esophagus ❺; ❻ stomach, liver ❼; ❽ gall bladder or bile sacks; ❾ pancreas; ❿ small intestine: ① duodenum ② jejunum; ③ ileum; ⓫ large intestine ④ blind, ⑤ and colon; ⓬ Appendix ⓭ rectum; ⓮ anus.

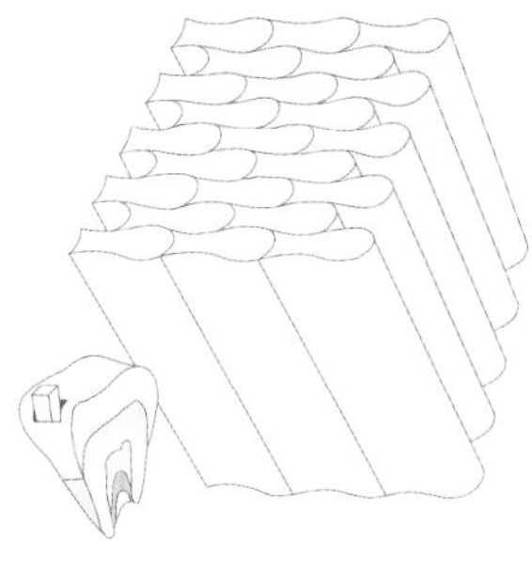

▼ **Enamel**
The enamel that covers the crown is a similar supply to the fabric: a section trasverale here shows its structure of crystals of calcium phosphate in the form of prisms or rod inserted in a cradle.

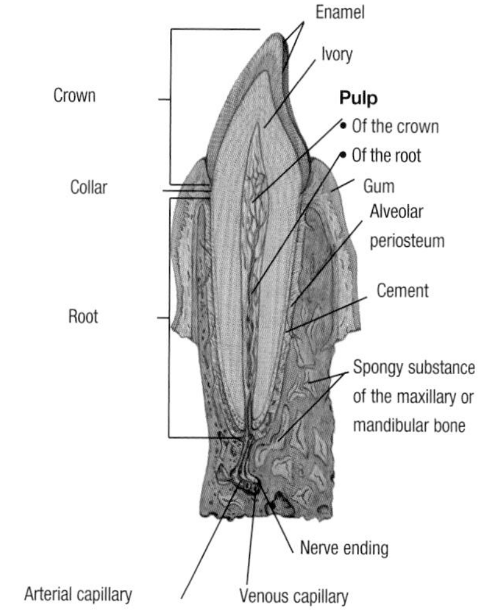

◀ **Tooth**
Anatomical elements.

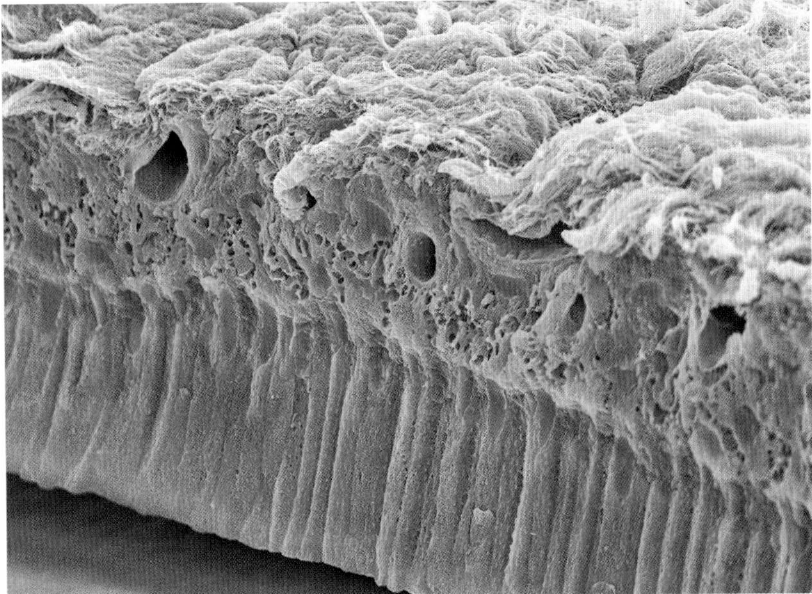

▲ **Section of a tooth**
In false color SEM photo of a section of a tooth: in green, the layer of cells that produce enamel. This epithelium consists of columnar cells called ameloblasts. The plane of the section through the glazed surface (orange, bottom left): the layer of cells appears detached from the tooth where it is normally located. At other end, the ameloblasts produce tissue inside the tooth (in brown, top).

▲ **Denture**
Methods differ for specific functions: ❶ incisors: cut; ❷ canine: rip; ❸ premolars: breaking, chipping; ❹ molars: grind.

▶ **Movements of chewing**
Are produced mostly from 5 pairs of muscles: ❶ the buccinator, which are relaxed and in the cheeks, the internal pterygoid ❷: lateral movement in the mandible, ❸ external pterygoid that open and close your mouth and move the jaw forward and back; ❹ masseter that raise the lower jaw, giving the power to bite, ❺ the temporal muscles close the teeth cooperating with the masseter.

inner dental pulp. This is in the centre of the tooth, and is made up of connective tissues that are rich in the blood capillaries which sustain the living tissues. The teeth have nerve endings (branches of the facial and trigeminal nerves ▸216) that give them a tactile sensitivity, as well as to heat and pain. The tactile sensitivity is the most important part of this, and is essential to calibrate the chewing actions. The thermal sensitivity, however, is especially developed in the pulp and dentin. The surface layer of cells in the pulp is made up of odontoblasts, which are the cells that produce dentin.
To carry out the masticatory functions, the dentition is composed of teeth that have different functions, and are characterised by specific sizes and forms of crown and root:

- the 8 incisors (4 upper and lower 4) and 4 canine (2 upper and lower 2), are housed in the front of the jaw and jaw and are used to cut and tear food;
- the 8 premolars (4 upper and lower 4) and 12 molars (6 upper and lower 6), are housed in the middle and rear of the jaw and jaw. They are used to crush fine food, exerting a pressure of about 85 kg/cm2. They also help to mix the crushed matter with saliva.

The chewing process is composed of a succession of complex actions that involve tearing and crushing by the teeth, as well as movements of the tongue and cheeks to stir the food. This muscular activity is directed by the cortex and the olfactory bulb via the trigeminal and facial nerves which control the muscles of the skull, and co-ordinate the articulations of the jaw.

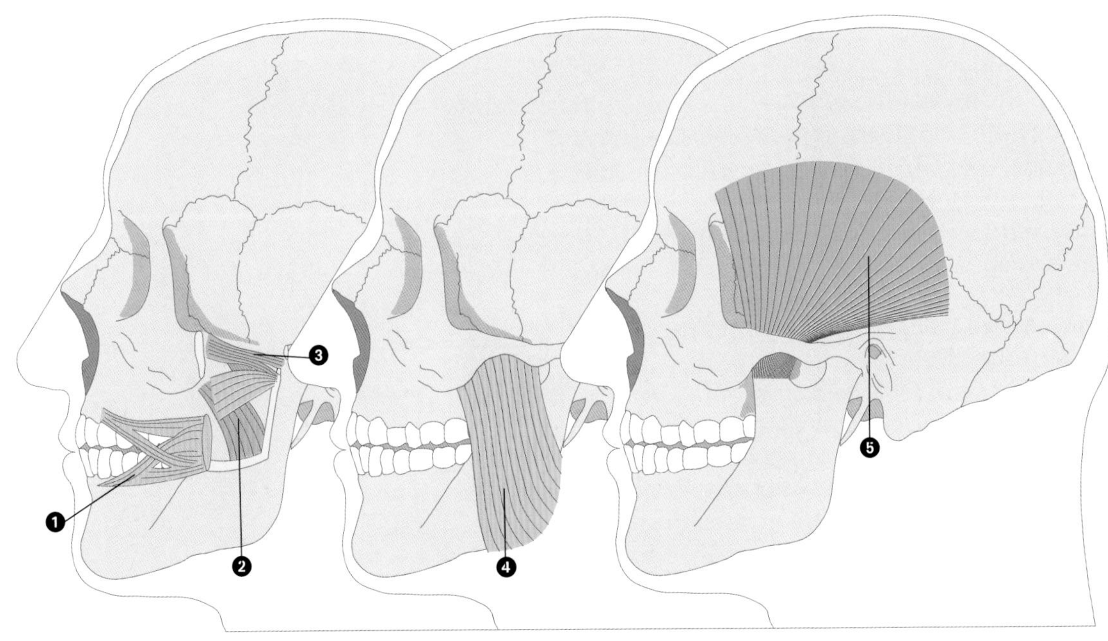

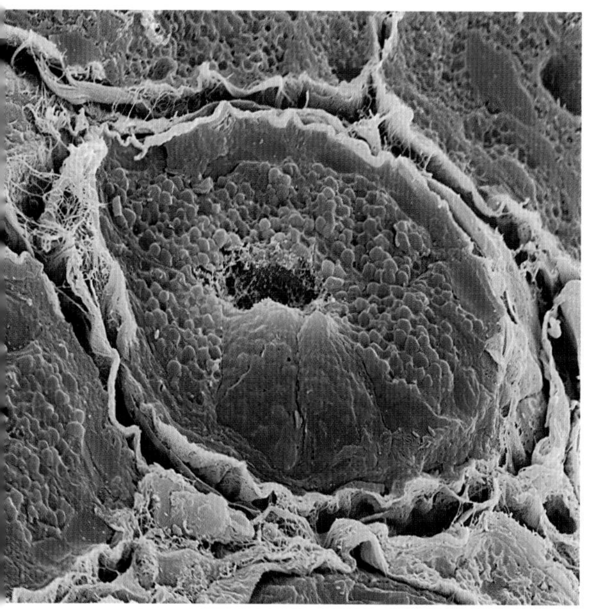

◀ **Acinus to salivary gland**
False-color SEM photograph of a section of salivary gland and acinus. They consist of a concentric group of cells that eject their products in a central duct (dark) which converges in a larger duct. These acinus, in particular, produce granules of mucus fluid, lubricating saliva. Each acinus is surrounded by a layer of connective tissue (pink).

A key role in chewing is played by the saliva - in the mouth there are numerous salivary glands including the parotid, sublingual and the submaxillary. All have the appearance of grapes and secrete saliva, a liquid that does not always have the same composition. The saliva that is produced by the parotid gland is very fluid and contains ptyalin or salivary amylase, an enzyme that is active in the demolition of starch. That secreted by the sublingual gland is viscous and very rich in mucins but low in ptyalin. That from the submaxillary is mixed and contains ptyalin and mucins. These differences, however, are very limited: saliva, is formed of around 98.7% by weight of water, organic substances (mucins and amylase, namely enzymes that dismantle starch) only represent 0.5%. The remaining 0.8% is made up of minerals such as bicarbonates, phosphates and especially chlorides, which are essential for activating amylase and for keeping the saliva's pH close to neutral.

The mouth, therefore, prepares food for enzyme activity: the amylase breaks starch down into sugar, and the resulting glucose is used to provide the body with energy. The enzyme activity breaks the bonds that hold the glucose molecules together, and the process may continue until only dextrin or maltose remains. These molecules are relatively small, and as the enzyme cannot break them down any further, it ceases to be active.

The action of the enzyme amylase, and in particular that of ptyalin, may be interrupted by changes in pH, for example, when it mixes with hydrochloric acid in the stomach. They are only able to remain active where the pH is close to neutral. In addition, the amylase is more effective on starch that has been cooked, when the grains are no longer protected by their hard cellulose coatings.

The salivary glands secrete their products in different areas of the oral cavity. The parotid gland, for instance, does so close to the second upper molar. The sublingual glands, on the other hand, are formed by a group of 15-30 glands, each with a duct of their own - these are located under the tongue. The submaxillary gland secretes is products either side of the lingual frenulum. All the salivary glands are involved with chewing, but are not limited to it. Saliva is produced continuously in order to keep the oral region moist, and the quantities which are produced vary depending on whether there is food in the mouth, and the type of food involved. It is also produced when there are relevant visual or olfactory sensations or memories associated with food. The salivary glands are innervated by fibres of the autonomic, parasympathetic, and sympathetic

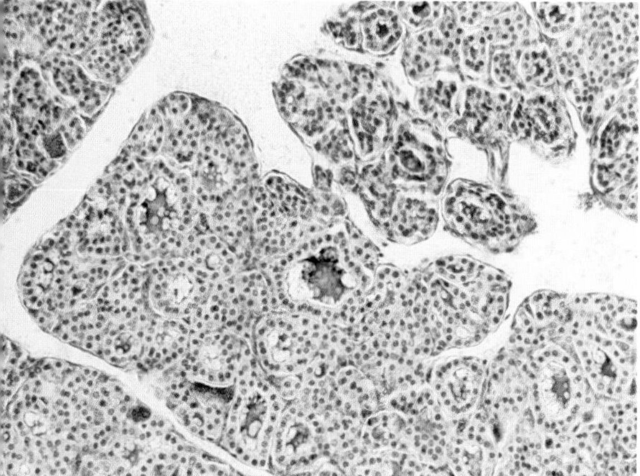

▲ **Parotid gland**
Optical microphotography of a section of parotid gland. The acinus are organized into lobes (groups of blue cells) separated by connective clear tissue. The cells produce serum (dark) which is visibly concentrated in products with internal lobes.

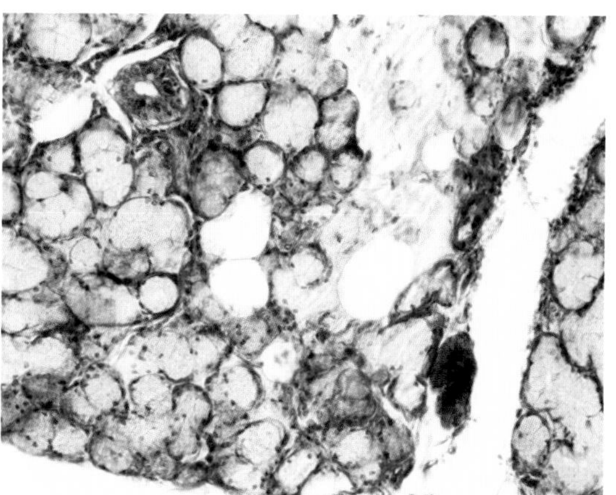

▲ **Submandibular**
Optical microphotography of a section of one of the salivary glands that are located under the base of the tongue. The lobes are surrounded by connective (clear space at the bottom and right) while the upper-left to recognize the section of a duct excretory (fuchsia ring cells).

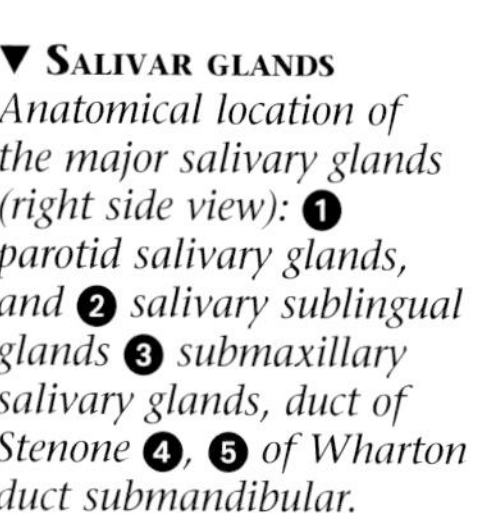

▼ **Salivar glands**
Anatomical location of the major salivary glands (right side view): ❶ parotid salivary glands, and ❷ salivary sublingual glands ❸ submaxillary salivary glands, duct of Stenone ❹, ❺ of Wharton duct submandibular.

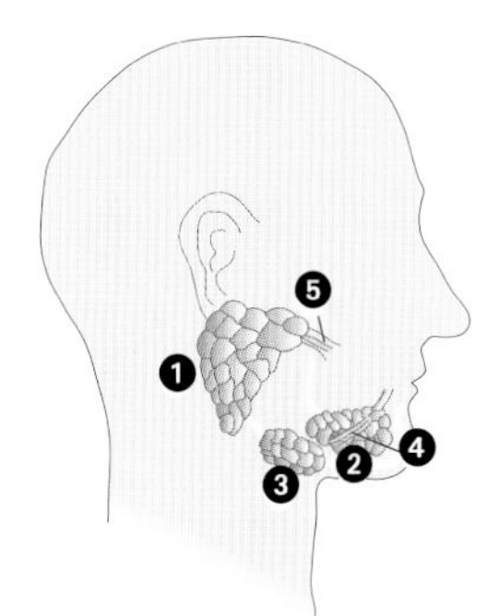

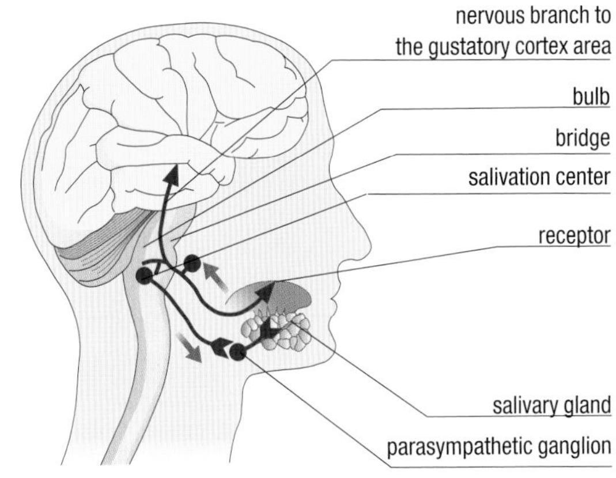

▶▶ **Controls**
Diagram showing control of nervous salivation.

nervous systems, which interact with each other in regulating the secretions.
Under normal conditions, saliva is produced in large quantities when the mechanical stimuli that are related to chewing and the chemical stimuli of the taste buds trigger a reflex nervous mechanism. The nerve impulses are produced by receptors from the olfactory bulb where there are centres of salivation: In turn, these send impulses to the salivary glands via the parasympathetic nervous system. In addition to having a digestive function, saliva promotes both chewing, and the creation of a food bolus - that is, an almost uniform of mix of crushed foods that can be swallowed, which thanks to the presence of mucins, even lubricates the oesophagus as it passes through. It even encourages the digestive process as it helps to dissolve the molecules, and also plays protective action on the teeth as the lysozyme it contains acts as an antibacterial enzyme.

SWALLOWING

In the mouth the food is chewed and salivated until, with swallowing, it passes through the pharynx. From this moment onwards, it moves throughout the entire digestive system where it stimulates a series of reflex acts that are governed by the olfactory bulb. When the food bolus arrives in the pharynx, the soft palate rises and closes the postnasal cavity, preventing any food getting into the nasal passages. At the same time, there is an involuntary contraction of the pharyngeal muscles which makes the hyoid bone rise. In turn this movement causes the epiglottis to fall. This is a strip of elastic cartilage that temporarily blocks the trachea, blocking the access of food and liquids to the larynx. Breathing, of course, stops (apnoea through swallowing) while the bolus passes through to the oesophagus.
There, it is pushed forward by the contractions of the muscular sheath that wraps around the oesophagus; this action is controlled by autonomic nervous system. Once started, the complex series of movements – both contractions and relaxations of the sheath muscles, spreads to the rest of the digestive tract - this is movement is referred to as peristalsis. The contractions propagate as slow waves that travel away from the mouth, while the muscles

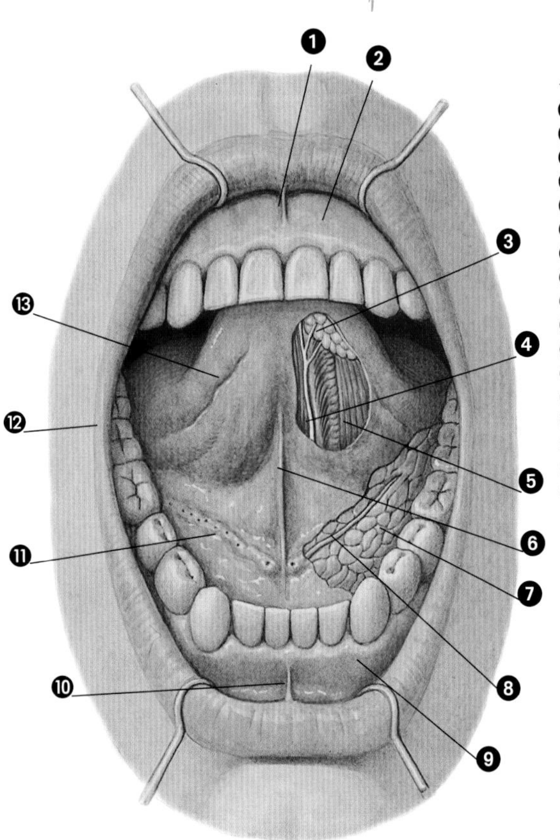

◀ **The mouth**
1 *Frenulum of the upper lip.*
2 *Superior gum*
3 *Anterior lingual gland*
4 *Margin of the tongue*
5 *Lingual nerve*
6 *Inferior longitudinal muscle*
7 *Frenulum of the tongue*
8 *Sublingual salivary gland*
9 *Submandibular duct*
10 *Inferior gum.*
11 *Frenulum of the inferior lip.*
12 *Sublingual caruncle*
13 *Sublingual fold*
14 *Inferior surface of the tongue*
15 *Commisure of the lips*
16 *Fimbriated fold*
17 *Back of the tongue*

▶ **Structure of throat**
The throat is the meeting point between oral and nasal cavity, trachea and esophagus. The swallowing, managed by the autonomic nervous system, must ensure that food and liquids are never diverted down the wrong route, but always go towards the esophagus, which is the first part of the digestive tract.

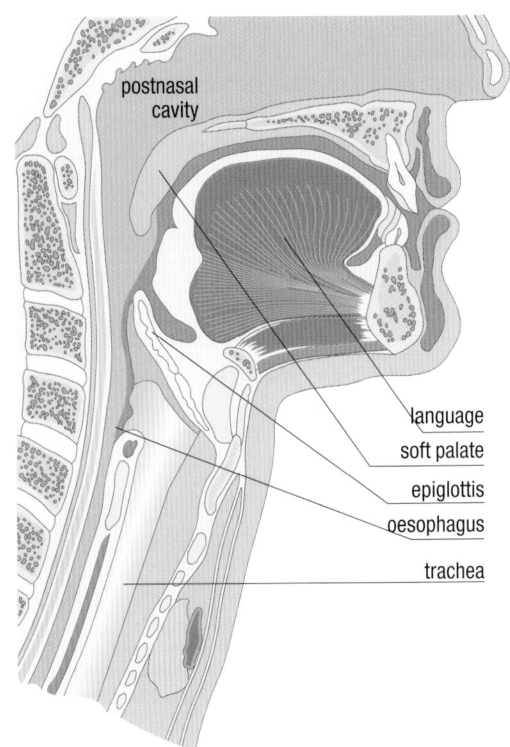

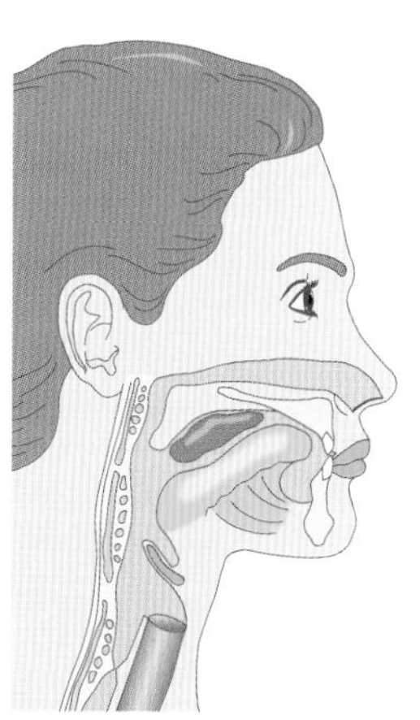
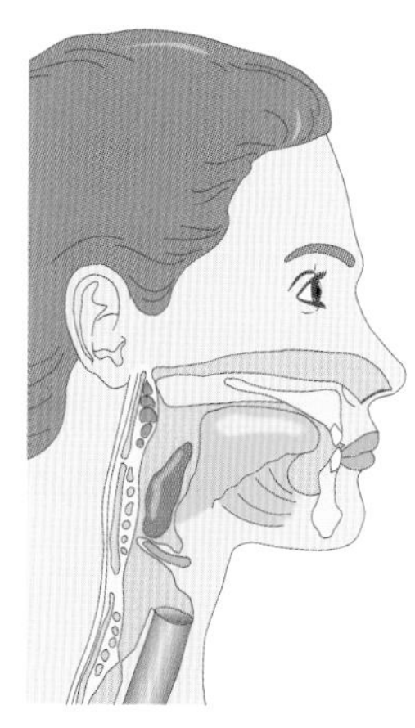
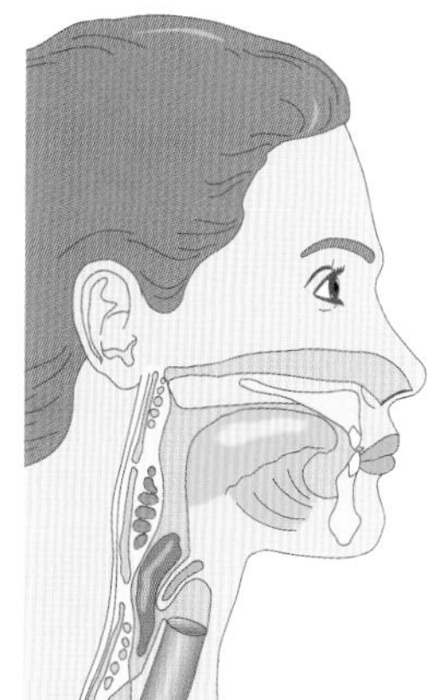
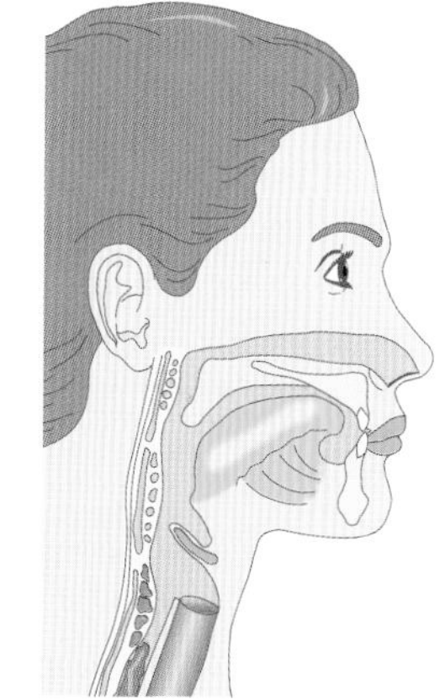

◀ **Swallow**
Succession of events on swallowing.

▼ **Peristalsis**
When the bolus enters the esophagus, the hollow fibers will be reduced "upstream" with respect to it, while relaxing "downstream." Longitudinal fibers, outer, produce undulatory movements in the same direction opposite to the mouth.

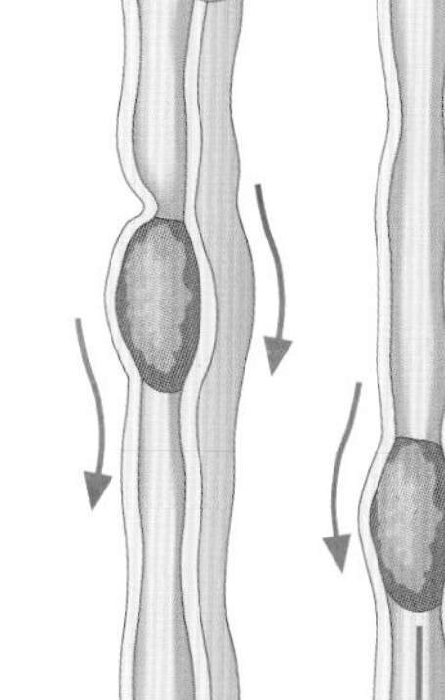

that are upstream of the bolus contract, the muscles on the opposite side remain relaxed thereby only allowing the bolus to pass in one direction.
When the bolus reaches the end the oesophagus, the wave of contractions and relaxations causes the opening of the cardia. This a sphincter that is formed almost exclusively from circular muscle fibres. When these contract, they close the tract, and when they relax they open it up again. This separates the oesophagus from the stomach. In this way the bolus arrives in the stomach: it is thanks to this system of automatic muscle movements that it is possible to swallow both liquids and solids, even with the head down - although it is an uncomfortable position.

THE STOMACH & DIGESTION OF PROTEINS

The stomach has a shape that has been compared to that of a bagpipe. It is the widest part of the digestive tract and its volume can vary according to the degree of filling. The walls throughout the digestive tract, including those of the stomach, are formed by a series of overlapping sheaths. In particular, the muscular sheath consists of three layers of fibres The outermost one has the fibres oriented in a longitudinal manner, whereas those of the intermediate and inner layers are both annular and oblique.
The lively muscle gastric contractions ensure that two main things happen. The first is the mixing of the food with the digestive juices that are produced by the mucous layer that lines the inside of the stomach. The second is the opening of the pyloric sphincter that connects the stomach and the intestine, and, as the result of this, the emptying of the stomach. It is still possible to have very intense contractions even when the stomach is empty. This is due to the feelings of hunger that are produced by the brain.
The movements of the muscle fibres of the stomach – as with the rest of the digestive tract, are regulated by chains of nerve impulses that come and go through the complex neural networks of the autonomous system. The rhythmic alternation of signals from the sympathetic and para sympathetic nervous systems produce the succession of contractions and distension required for the peristaltic movements as well as those of the stomach.
The mucous membrane, which is richly folded (gastric folds) is crossed by many furrows that divide it into sectors with clear geometric shapes (gastric areas). In the centre of each of them, in a hollow area (gastric dimple), is a gastric excretory duct. The mucous membrane of the stomach, in fact, is home to millions of tubular glands (either straight or branched) which secrete their products into the gastric cavity through many pores. The cells

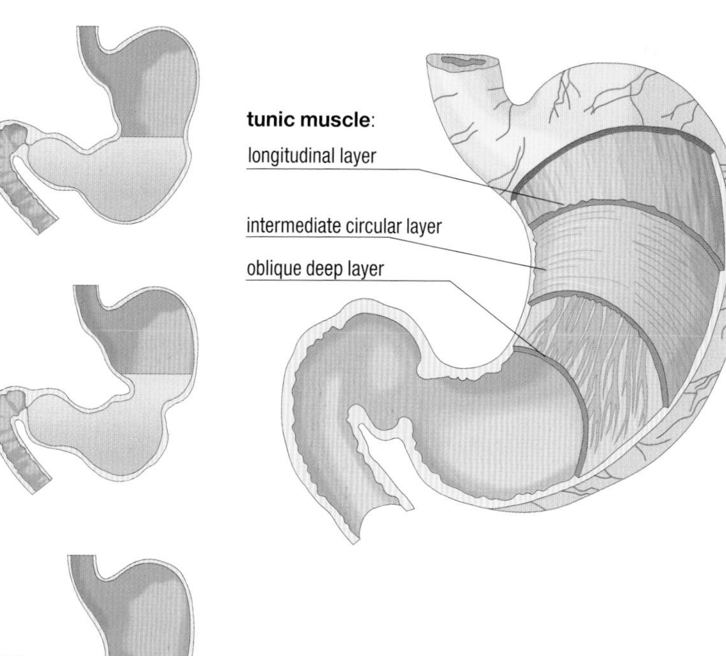

▲ **Stomach**
Tunic stomach muscle and its movements

MATERIAL INTERCHANGE

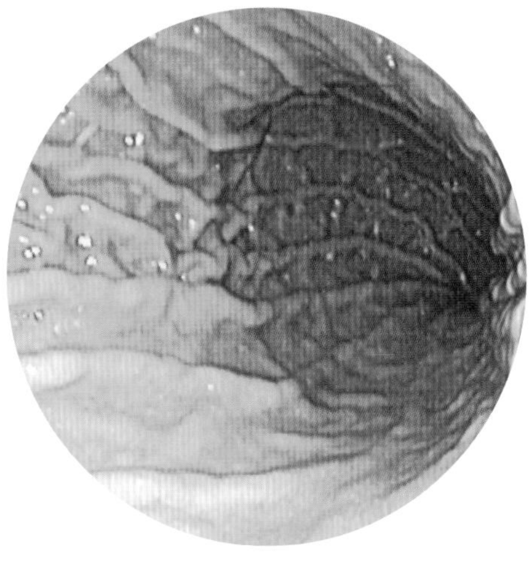

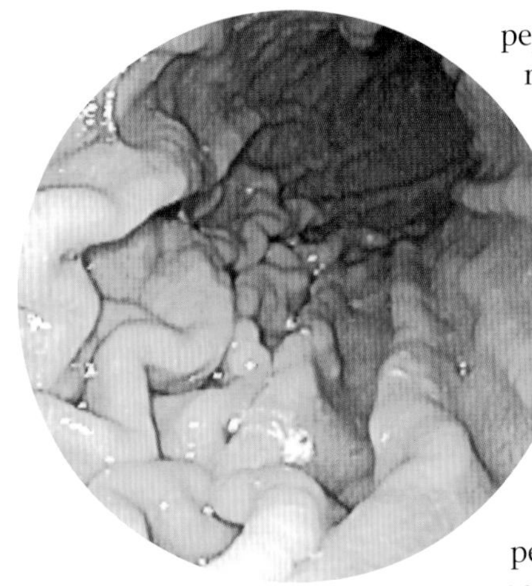

▲ **Contraction**
Stomach relaxed (left) and contracted (right) seen in endoscopy. The gastric folds are more evident when the stomach is contracted.

that form these glands are of three types, which can be distinguished from the characteristics of their exocrine production as well as their placement along the glandular duct:

- Parietal cells or oxyntic cells, which produce hydrochloric acid, are distributed irregularly along the gland;
- The main cells, which producing pepsinogen, a pro-enzyme that remains inactive until it's activated by hydrochloric or pepsin, are grouped together in the deepest part of the gland.

The pepsinogen arriving in the gastric cavity becomes pepsin, the enzyme that breaks down large protein molecules into peptone, which are smaller and soluble. The enzyme pepsin is very efficient: in one hour and under natural conditions (37°C and pH 1.5), it can hydrolyse the peptide bonds that link the aromatic amino acids of each protein, and can digest a quantity of protein equal to 1000 times its weight.

The hydrochloric acid plays a number of important functions. For a start, it is essential for the transformation of molecules of pepsinogen into pepsin - that, once formed, are then able to activate more molecules of pepsinogen. It also makes the stomach sufficiently acid to denature proteins. In addition, it keeps the pH of gastric juice within the optimal limits for the enzyme pepsin and makes the gastric juice antiseptic, eliminating most of the pathogens that could be mixed in with the food.

The gastric juice also contains other substances. In the aqueous solutions of hydrochloric acid, in fact, there are dissolved in varying proportions the secretions of mucous cells and other enzymes, such as rennin or chymosin that cause the clotting of milk. This is particularly important in infants, where it makes the milk proteins form clots. This causes them to remain in the stomach for much longer, and in so doing exposes them to the action

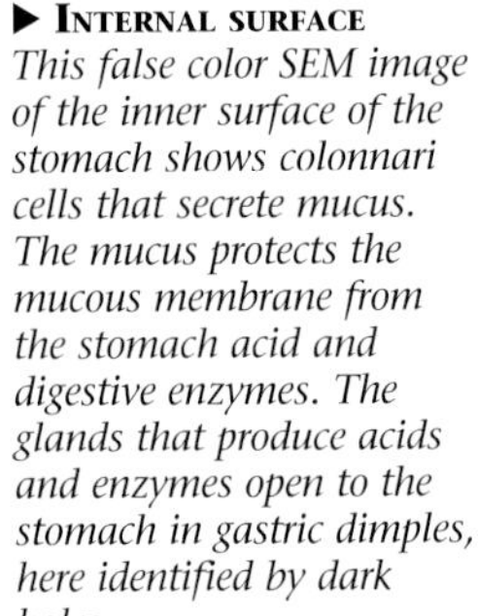

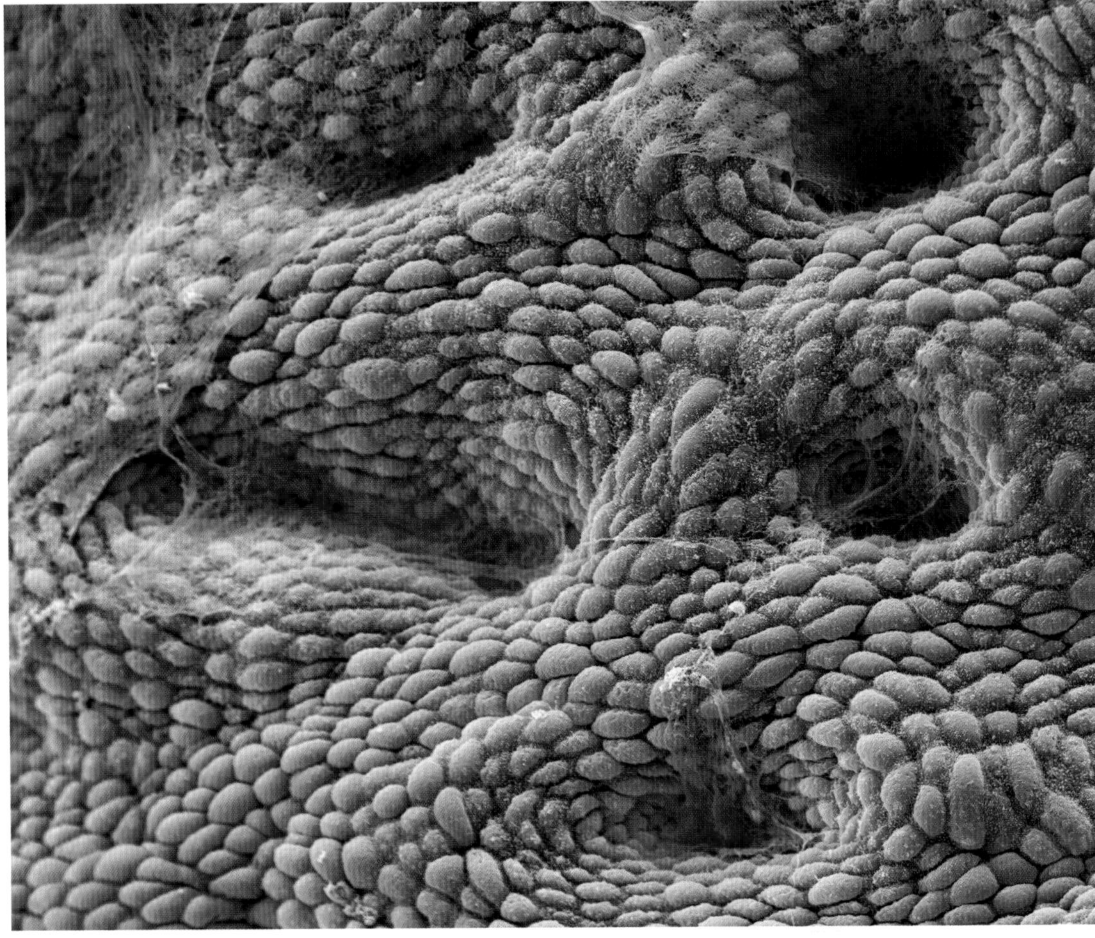

▶ **Internal surface**
This false color SEM image of the inner surface of the stomach shows colonnari cells that secrete mucus. The mucus protects the mucous membrane from the stomach acid and digestive enzymes. The glands that produce acids and enzymes open to the stomach in gastric dimples, here identified by dark holes.

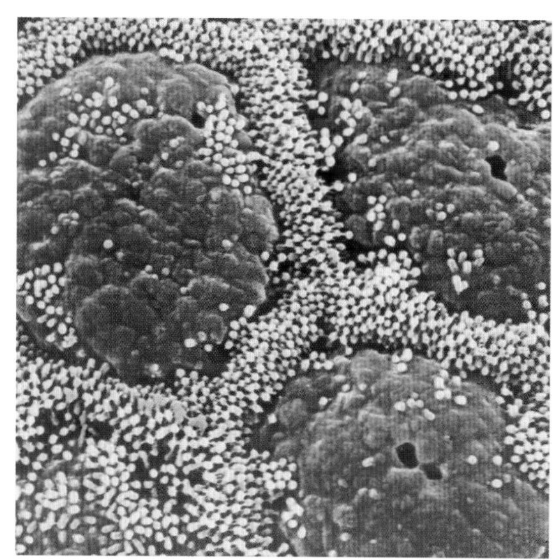

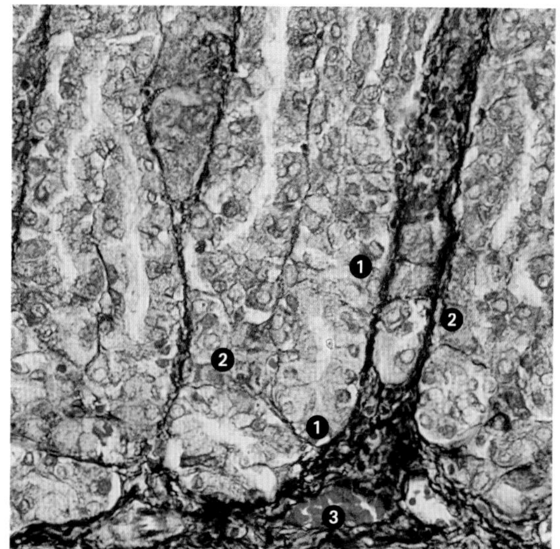

◄◄ Cells and mucous
In this photograph, in false colors of the gastric mucosa scanning electron microscope, the epithelial cells (brown-orange color) with the centre of the outlet duct glandular are surrounded by drops of mucus (yellow), a viscous protective fluid.

◄ Mucous membrane in section
This optical microscope photo shows a section of gastric mucosa. It distinguishes the deepest part of gastric fossette, which leads to glands that produce and secrete gastric juices. They are formed by digestive enzymes in a solution of water and hydrochloric acid. In gastric glands you can distinguish three different types of cells: ❶ those that produce mucus that cover the outer surface of fossette; those that produce hydrochloric acid ❷ are in the middle of the gland, while underlying cells are grouped ❸ producing pepsinogen.

of pepsin. Finally, in gastric juices there is also lipase, an enzyme that breaks down fats and mucins, this is a protein that not only acts as a lubricant, but also protects the cells from gastric self-digestion.

As in the case of saliva, the production of gastric juice is not constant, and increases with the intake of food. It is initially activated by stimuli from the vagus nerve. This may be from the sight, smell or flavour of flood, or simply by the appetite for it - whatever the cause, it triggers secretion by the gastric glands. When the food bolus arrives in the stomach, the secretion is stimulated by more nervous reflexes. Later, when the chyme (the pulp and whitish fluid resulting from the digestion of food) reaches the lower part of the stomach and is in contact with mucous pyloric, this secretes gastrin, a hormone that stimulates further production of gastric juice.

The bolus becomes fully transformed into chyme in a period of time that varies depending on the quality and quantity of food. For example, the presence of fat delays the secretion of hydrochloric acid and thus gastric emptying. When the bolus has turned into chyme, a more intense peristalsis of the pyloric hollow causes the pyloric sphincter to dilate. This remained closed throughout the gastric digestion, but with the arrival of each peristaltic wave, it opens allowing the release of chyme from the stomach. When it passes into the duodenum, however, the chyme encourages a nervous reflex that closes the sphincter: the emptying of the stomach therefore happens in an intermittent manner.

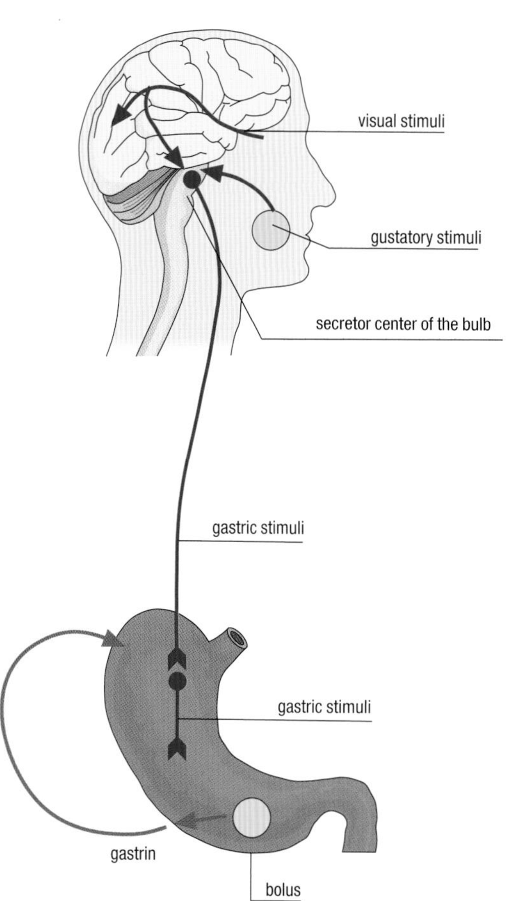

◄ Gastric stimulus
The pressures that begins the proccess of secretion of gastric juice are generally odoriferous, visual and gustatory: they activate the secretory center bulb through the brain and vagus nerve endings, this stimulate movements and gastric secretion, which is further intensified after the food enters the stomach. Once it has reached the pyloric, then, it is the same food that stimulates the production of gastric juices: the pyloric mucosa, in fact secretes the gastrin, a hormone that maintains the active glands of the stomach.

THE DUODENUM: THE END OF DIGESTION & BEGINNING OF ABSORPTION

The duodenum is the part of the small intestine immediately after the opening of the pyloric sphincter from the stomach. The inner surface of the small intestine has a very particular aspect: in addition to cross-folds, it shows many villi, these become more concentrated as one moves along its length. The maximum density of villi per unit of intestinal area is achieved around the ileum, the last stretch of the small intestine. Here there may be up to 1000 villi per square centimetre. Each villus is a protrusion of intestinal mucosa It forms a network of internal tissue which contains smooth muscle fibres, blood and lymphatic vessels and nerve fibres. It is covered with a layer of epithelial cells (enterocytes). These surface cells form a kind of

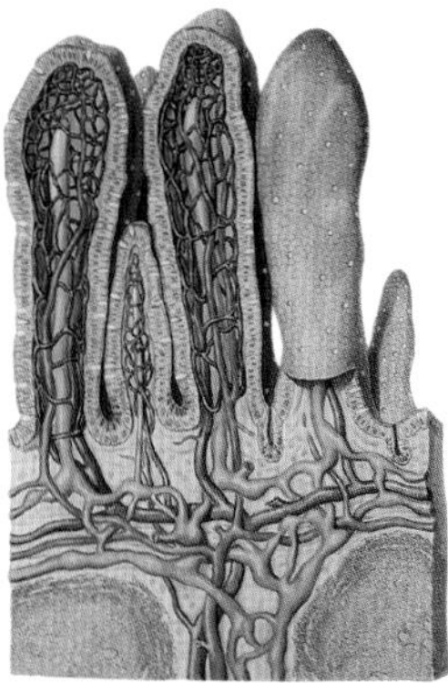

▲ **Structure of villi**
The villi are evaginations of the internal mucosa. They flow between arterial and venous capillaries as well as lymphatic capillaries.

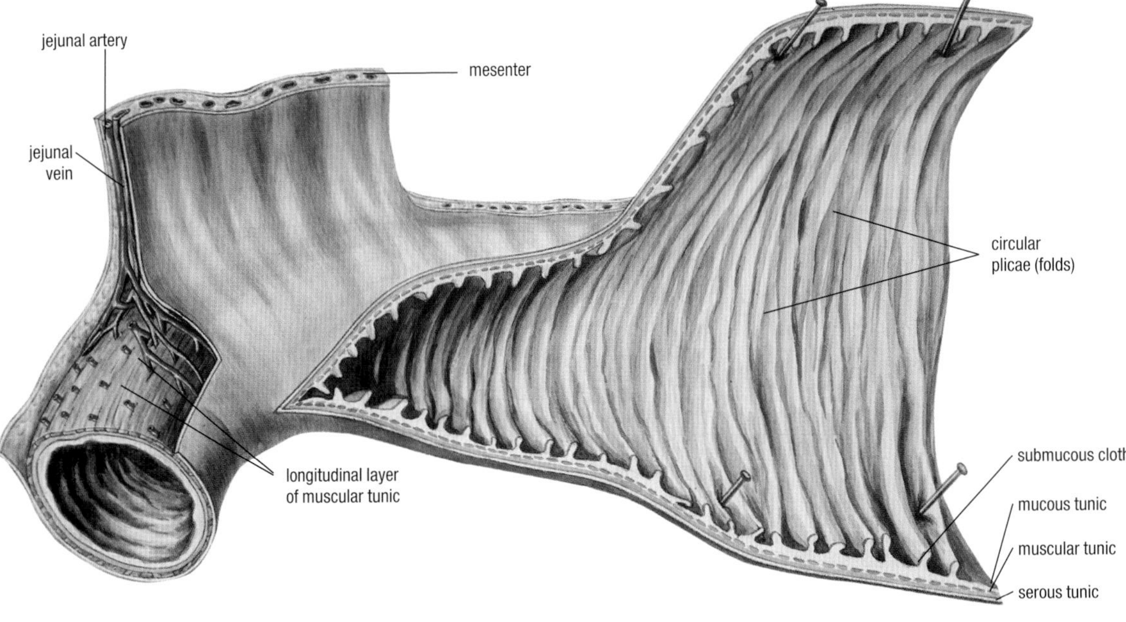

▶ **Structure of the small intestine**
Anatomical elements of the duodenum and small intestine. Are clearly visible in the transverse folds. The mesentery is a membrane that takes hold the intestine, linked to the abdominal cavity.

dense intestinal hair that is made up of microscopic cytoplasmic eversions. Referred to as microvilli, these increase the surface area that is available for material exchange. In the surface membranes of the villus cells, there are many complex enzymes that split disaccharides. Lactose, for example, is converted into glucose and galactose, maltose into two molecules of glucose, and sucrose into glucose and fructose. Many complex enzymes are released when cells detach from the mucosa, and continue to collaborate with other substances produced by the intestinal mucosa to complete the food's decomposition.

There are two large ducts that lead into the short duodenum - these are digestive glands from the liver and pancreas. The duodenal mucosa also features numerous Brunner's glands which produce alkaline mucus that mainly serves to protect the intestinal mucosa from the stomach acids, as well as the crypts of Lieberkühn that secrete various enteric juices. This liquid, which is characterised by a near neutral pH, consists essentially of water, mucus and electrolytes. That is, substances which, in solution, break down into the ions that are essential in the process of adjusting the balance of the saline solution and maintaining a constant pH. It also

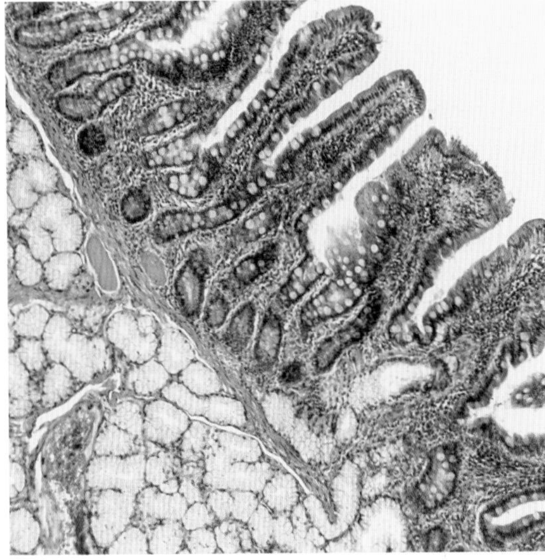

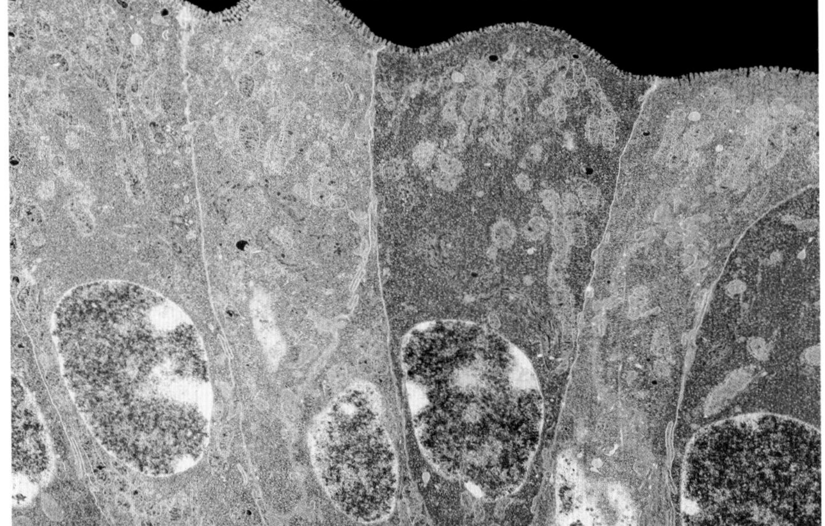

▲ **Duodenum**
Optical microphotography of a section of duodenal mucosa. You notice the villi (dark purple) that increase the surface contact with food. Below is the muscular tunic (in fuchsia) and still

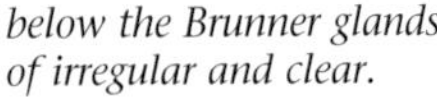
below the Brunner glands of irregular and clear.

▲ **Duodenal secretin cells**
False color photos using transmission electron microscopy (TEM) showing a section of duodenal mucosa. The layer of columnar cells, each of which features a rounded nucleus (violet) and mitochondria (blue) shows the surface of the intestinal lumen (top) a faint green line: the microvilli. These cells produce digestive enzymes and alkaline fluids that neutralize stomach acids.

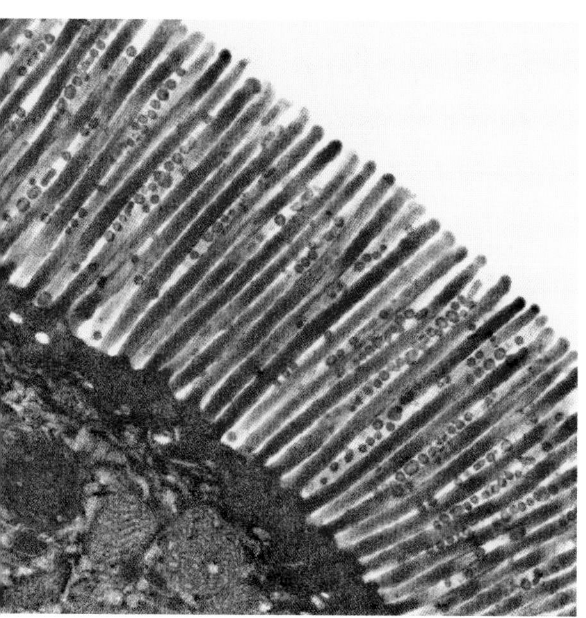

◀ **Microvilli**
TEM photograph in false colors of microvilli (green) from a cell of the columnar epithelium of the intestinal surface. Each contains 40-50 microvilli microfilamenti crossing throughout the cytoplasm, they contain actin, the contractility protein also present in muscles. This suggests that the microvilli are of primitive mobility.

▼ **Hormonal secretion**
When the Chimo passes into the duodenum, the duodenal mucosa produce secretin, a hormone that stimulates the production of gastric juices of the pancreas and liver: on pancreatic juice and bile. The secretin has been one of the first hormones to be discovered.

contains enterokinase, an enzyme that activates the trypsinogen that is produced by the pancreas ▸68 transforming it into trypsin.

In the presence of chyme, the duodenal mucosa also produces some hormones, of which two are particularly important:

- secretin, which stimulates the excretion of water and bicarbonates by the pancreas and blocks the secretion of gastrin by the stomach;
- cholecystokinin-cholecystokinin (previously called pancreozymin-cholecystokinin), which stimulates the production of enzymes from the pancreas and gallbladder (which also secretes bile).

If the stomach prepares food for the first stages of absorption, it is in the duodenum that the digestion is actually completed. It is only here that the products of the main digestive glands are secreted. In addition, it is where all the enzymes which act on the different substances are able to bring about the division of the protein molecules in peptone, and the reduction of soluble fat.

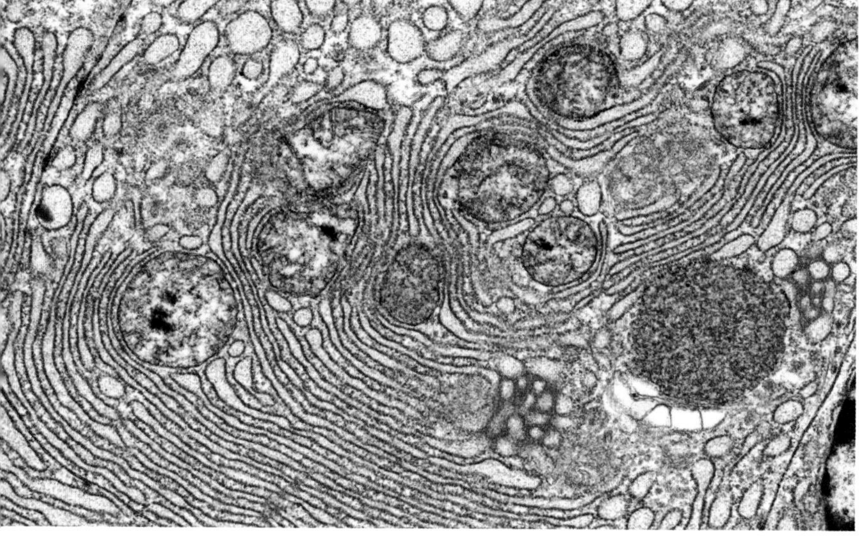

▲ **Esocrine cells**
TEM microphotography in false colors of a of pancreatic acinus cell (esocrina). Numerous mitochondria (blue) are in the midst of the endoplasmic reticulum (dark yellow lines) that controls the secretion of zymogenics, inactive precursors of digestive enzymes. They are excreted in the form of vesicles (zymogenic granules) and activated by specific intestinal enzymes to help digestion of carbohydrates, fats and proteins.

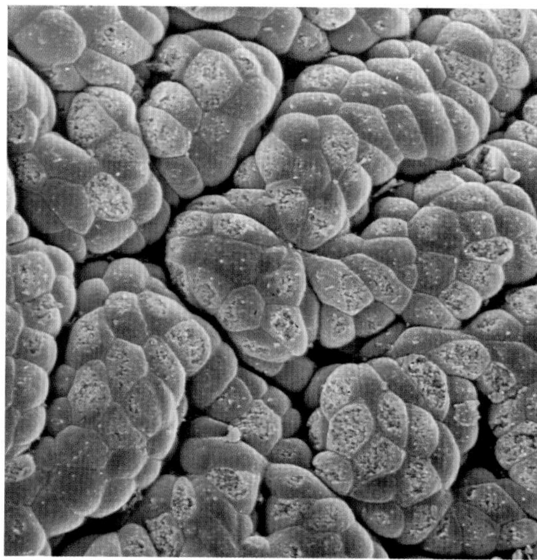

▲ **Pancreatic acid**
SEM false color microphotography of cells from a pancreatic acinus that shows the available external "cluster". The red-stained cells are those that actively produce more secretions. Their products arrive at the main pancreatic duct leading to the duodenum through a much branched tree of secondary ducts.

The pancreas

The pancreas is a gland organ that is long and flat with a domed top, and is located just below the stomach near the start of the duodenum. From the anatomical perspective, it has a number of distinctive features:

- It has a voluminous head that is in contact with the duodenal loop, but is separated from the body of the pancreas by an isthmus, an area that is delimited by two fissures;
- The largest part of the pancreas is the body, and is located below the stomach.
- It has a tail that is in contact with the spleen, and is covered by the parietal peritoneum.

The pancreas is a complex gland with a number of different functions in the exocrine (digestive) and endocrine (control of sugar metabolism) systems. The region known as the islands of Langerhans, for instance is an area that produces the endocrine hormones insulin and glucagon. When released into the bloodstream, these regulate the body's sugar levels. The islands of Langerhans have no connection with the excretory products produced by the pancreatic cells, as there is no excretory duct leading to the blood capillaries. Instead, their products are passed along a network of small channels that convey them to two main channels:

- the main duct of Wirsung, which crosses the pancreas throughout its length and ends in the greater papilla of the duodenum or papilla of Vater, which are joined distally to the common bile duct;
- the duct of Santorini, which ends in the minor duodenal papilla.

inferior vena cava
aorta
spleen
celiac trunk
lineal artery
portal vein
superior part of the duodenum
superior margin
superior duodenal curve
pancreatic tail
gastrolienal ligament
anterior surface
anterior margin
inferior margin
descending part of the duodenum
jejunum
ascending part of the duodenum
mesenteric root
head of the pancreas
inferior curve of the duodenum
left common iliac artery
horizontal (inferior) part of the duodenum
left common iliac vein

minor papilla of the duodenum
accessory pancreatic duct
pancreatic duct
major papilla of the duodenum

▲ **Frontal view**
Main anatomical elements of the pancreas and bowel.

▲ **Front view duct**
Pancreatic ducts and their main outlets in the duodenum.

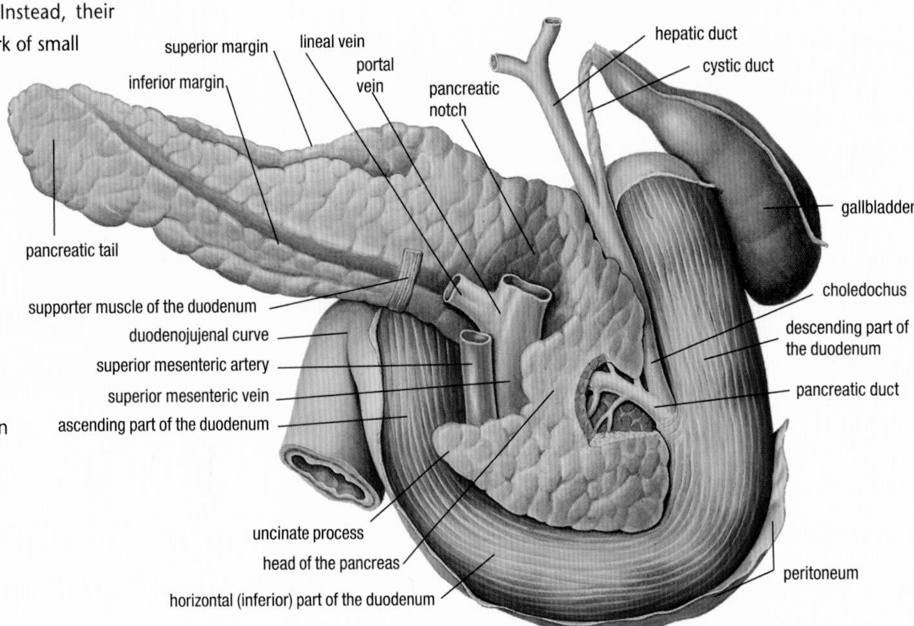

▼ **Dorsal view**
Main anatomical elements of the pancreas, bowel and gallbladder.

THE PANCREAS DIGESTER

The chyme becomes mixed with the enteric juices and arrives in the duodenum through the pyloric sphincter. The secretion of exocrine pancreatic digestive enzymes is regulated by a stimulating nerve from the celiac plexus, and especially by the two hormones - secretin and cholecystokinin-cholecystokinin which are produced by the duodenal mucosa, and reach the pancreas through the blood.

In a similar manner to the events that take place in the stomach, the production by the pancreas gland is continuous but not constant. There is a minimum baseline secretion, but this increases by a large amount after a meal has been consumed. Since the pancreatic juices do not accumulate in a tank, the production of a substantial digestive secretion involves specific regulatory mechanisms. These are both nervous and hormonal, and cause emptying of the exocrine cells. They expel granules of zymogen that blend together, and in a short time accumulate behind the sphincter of the duodenal papilla and into the main pancreatic duct (this is also referred to as the duct of Wirsung). The duct then quickly empties into the duodenum. The pancreatic juice is composed of:

- proteolytic enzymes, namely those which promote the digestion of proteins. They differ from exopeptidase (like carboxypeptidase) which acts on the chemical bonds between amino acids, and endopeptidase (as chymotrypsin and trypsin) which dismantles proteins by splitting the chemical bonds between the amino acids;
- glycolytic enzymes, namely promoting the digestion of carbohydrates or sugars, such amylase;
- lipolytic enzymes, namely those which promote the digestion of lipids, or fats, such lipase;
- enzymes that promote the digestion of nucleic acids, such as nuclease (ribonuclease and deoxyribonuclease).

Let us briefly examine the enzymatic action of the most important examples:

- Carboxypeptidase: this hydrolyses the peptide bonds of the amino acid COOH-terminal. Unlike trypsin and chymotrypsin, this enzyme continues to digest the protein detaching one amino acid terminal after another.
- Chymotrypsin: this hydrolyses the peptide bonds that bind phenylalanine, tyrosine or tryptophan to the other amino acids. The higher the number of these amino acids in a protein, the greater the resulting fragmentation.
- Trypsin: this hydrolyses the peptide bonds that bind lysine or arginine to the other amino acids: Again, the higher the number of amino acids in the protein structure, the greater the degree of fragmentation of the protein. This enzyme comes from trypsinogen that is activated by intestinal enterokinase, in turn, the trypsin activates other pancreatic proenzymes.
- Amylase: this hydrolyses the α bonds throughout the amylose chain. In other words, it transforms all carbohydrates and starches that have not been attacked by ptyalin that reach the duodenum into a mixture of elementary sugar (glucose and maltose) so that they are able to easily cross the intestinal mucosa and enter into the blood.
- Lipase: this hydrolyses fats, turning them into free fatty acids and glycerol, which is easily assimilated by the cells. It also divides neutral fats or triglycerides into their components: fatty acids and glycerine. Its action is favoured by the presence of bile salts and lecithin, substances that are part of bile and that emulsify lipids, which reduces them to micro-droplets diameter of 1 μ m or so. In this way, it greatly increases the surface contact of the pancreatic lipase which, being soluble in water, cannot get to the bigger drops of fat. When the production of bile is reduced or missing, the drops of fat remain large and their digestion by the lipase becomes much more slow and difficult.
- Ribonucleic and deoxyribonucleic: these are two types of enzymes (α and β) that dismantle ribonucleic acids (RNA) and deoxyribonucleic acids (DNA).

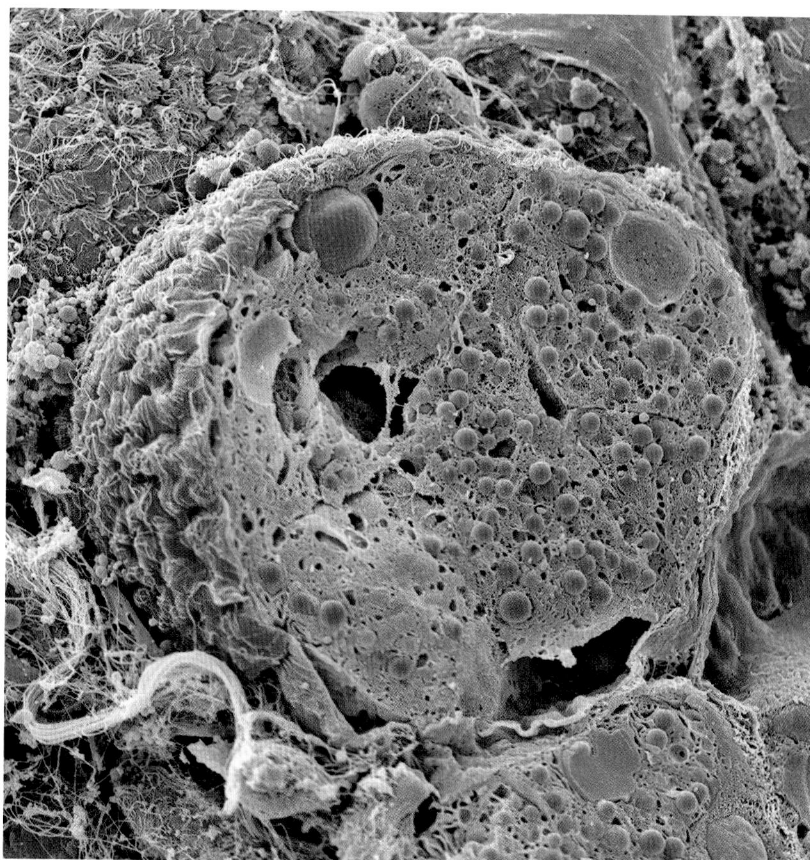

▲ **Pancreatic esocrine cells**
This false-color photograph taken with a scanning electron microscope (SEM) shows that there is a good unit with a acinus pancreatic vesicles in preparation for zimogeno (orange balls).

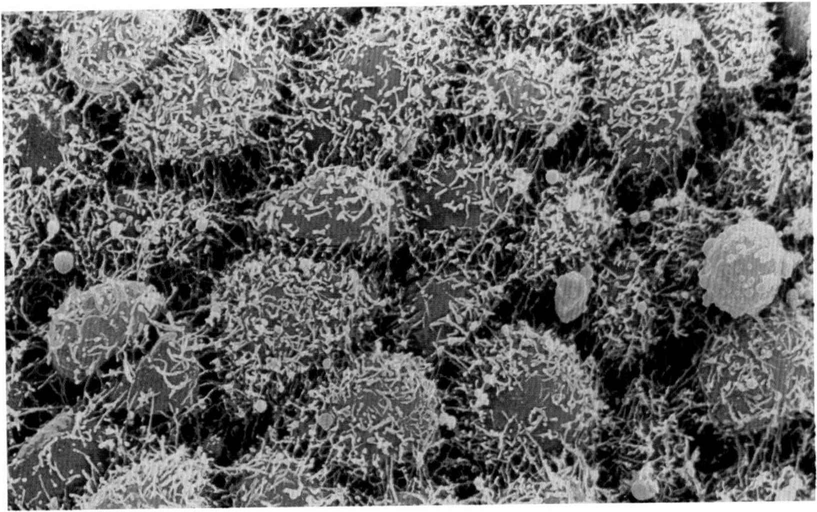

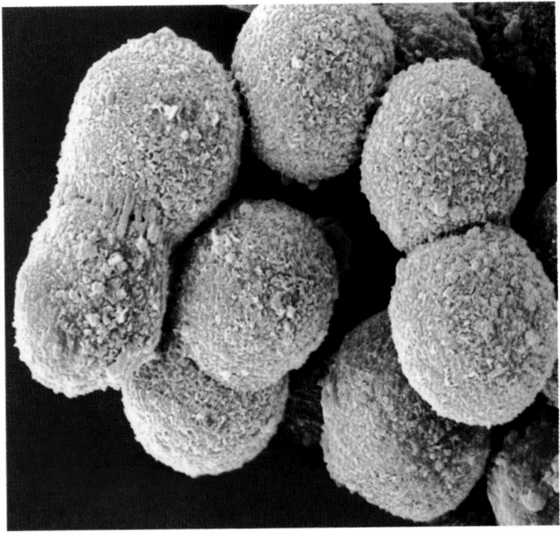

▲ **PERITONEO**
SEM microphotography in false colors showing a layer of peritoneal cells that surrounds the liver. Flattened, perhaps rich in microvilli capillaries, these cells produce a fluid derived from blood serum that enables the liver to move slightly in the abdomen.

▲▶ **LIVER CELLS**
SEM microphotograph in false colors of a group of hepatocytes, some of them in division. These specialized epithelial cells constitute about 80% of liver mass and are "crammed" in lobules, the functional units of the liver.

▶ **BILE DUCT**
SEM Microphotograph in false colors of a group of hepatocytes (red-brown) along the bile duct (green). The bile secreted by hepatocytes in the liver is drained by a dense network of biliary canals.

▼▶ **BLOOD VESSEL**
Optical microphotography of a section of liver with hepatocytes around a blood vessel (blue). Acknowledging the large nuclei of hepatocytes, round and red. The branches of the hepatic artery and portal vein through the entire liver can be found along the efferent tubules of bile along each edge of the lobules which are irregular polyhedral.

LIVER & BILE

Bile, which is produced by the liver, is crucial for the completion of the digestion in the small intestine. The liver is a large abdominal organ, which, with an average weight of 1.5kg, is essential for survival. The nutrients that have been absorbed by the intestines are then transported by the bloodstream to the liver where they are further processed. In addition to this, all the waste products from the body's metabolism activities are neutralised and transformed into substances that can be excreted. The functions of the liver are therefore extremely diverse - it promotes:

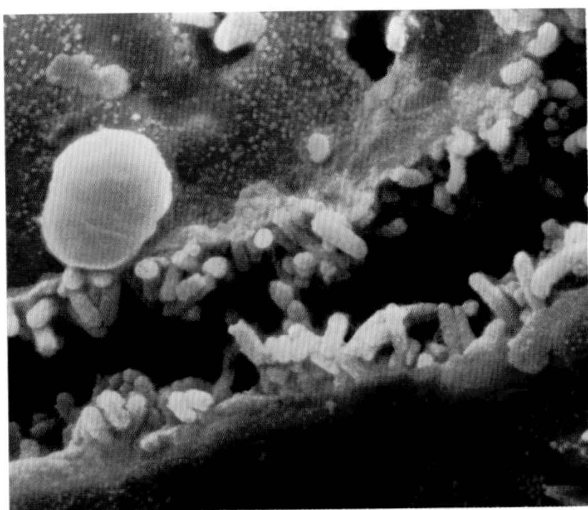

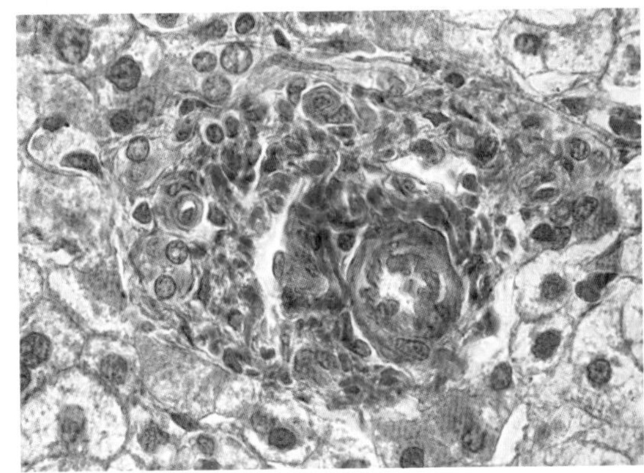

- the synthesis of glucose from amino acids, lipids and carbohydrates,
- the synthesis of glycogen from the glucose which is in circulation;
- the synthesis of cholesterol, from which bile acids and salts are then produced;
- the production of bilirubin;
- the production of amino acids for the synthesis of proteins;
- the production of key plasma proteins ▸82 (lipoprotein, albumin, globulin, fibrinogen) and other coagulation factors ▸85;
- the oxidative demolition of fatty acids:
- the destruction or inactivation of toxic substances that are either externally derived or produced by the body (medicines, toxins, hormones);
- the phosphorylation of triglycerides for the synthesis of phospholipids;
- the deamination of amino acids, with the consequent formation of ammonia which is then converted into urea;
- the storage of several metabolites (such as glycogen, iron, vitamins etc.).
- the formation of some immune defences ▸100.

Bile is a liquid with a yellow-green colour that is produced on an ongoing basis by liver cells (hepatocytes), and stored in the gallbladder from where it is secreted into the duodenum when it is needed. The gallbladder, however, is not just a simple container; its interior walls, in fact, are rich in cells that secrete mucins and are able to absorb water and carbonate ions (HCO3-).

The bile duct, namely the tube that connects the gallbladder to the duodenum, is kept closed by the sphincter of Oddi that can resist pressures of about 1.2 kPa. The liver produces about 1 litre of bile every 24 hours. Only the contraction of the gallbladder, which is regulated by hormonal factors produced by the duodenum and stimulated by the vagus nerve - can cause it to open. This raises the internal pressure to about 2.0 kPa, and leads to the release of bile in

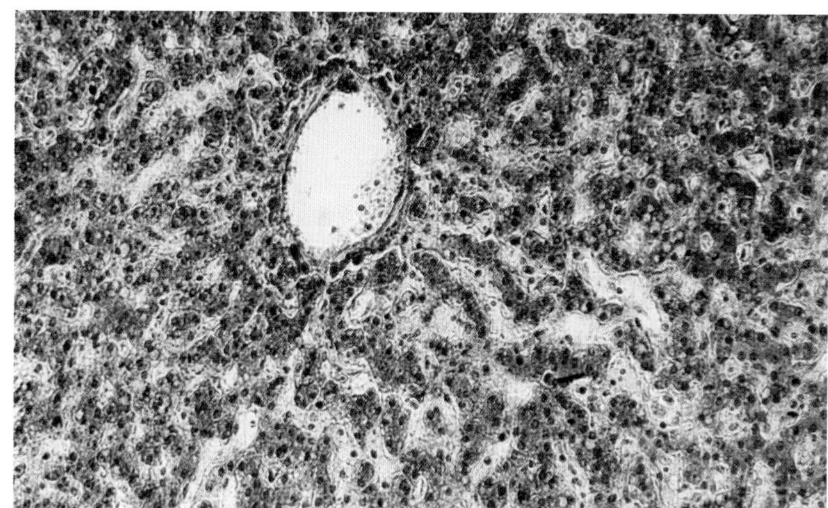

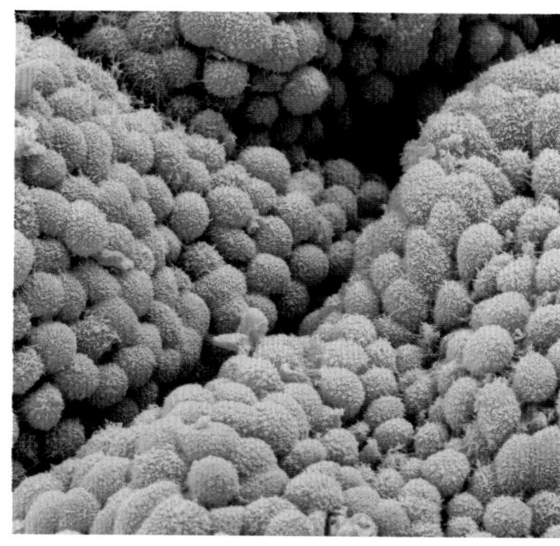

the duodenum. The secretion of bile is stimulated by cholecystokinin-cholecystokinin, the hormone that is produced by the duodenum as soon as it is in contact with the incoming chyme from the stomach. The bile is alkaline, and so neutralises the hydrochloric acid in the chyme, bringing the pH to around 6. This helps to prevent damage to the intestinal mucosa. In addition, it activates the pancreatic lipase making the action of the digestive pancreatic juices more effective. It also stimulates the intestinal peristalsis and promotes the antiseptic action. In addition, it prevents intestinal flora from giving rise to the processes of putrefaction. The main role of bile, however, is to facilitate the development and absorption of fats. Its action as an emulsifier is due to the way that bile salts strongly lower the surface tension of water. In this way, ingested fats are reduced to micro-droplets that react more efficiently with the lipase.

▲ **Liver Cells**
Optical microphotography of a section of liver showing the center of a lobule in blue with a double layer of endothelial central vein. The hepatocytes are arranged so that the blood can easily switch between them. Cells regulate the level of blood substances, and render harmless the toxic substances and produce proteins and digestive compounds (bile).

▲ **Biliary mucous membrane**
A SEM false-color photo of the internal mucosa of the gallbladder. Columnar epithelial cells are rounded to the surface and wrapped in a muscular tunic. Each cell has numerous microvilli which increase the inner surface of the body, facilitating the absorption of water and salts. The function of bile is to emulsify fats.

▼ **Biliary duct**
A SEM false-color photo of a section of a bile duct: This type of duct transports the bile produced by hepatocytes to the gallbladder. The inner lining consists of columnar epithelium cells (yellow) surrounded by the lamina propria (in brown below), a highly vascularised connective tissue.

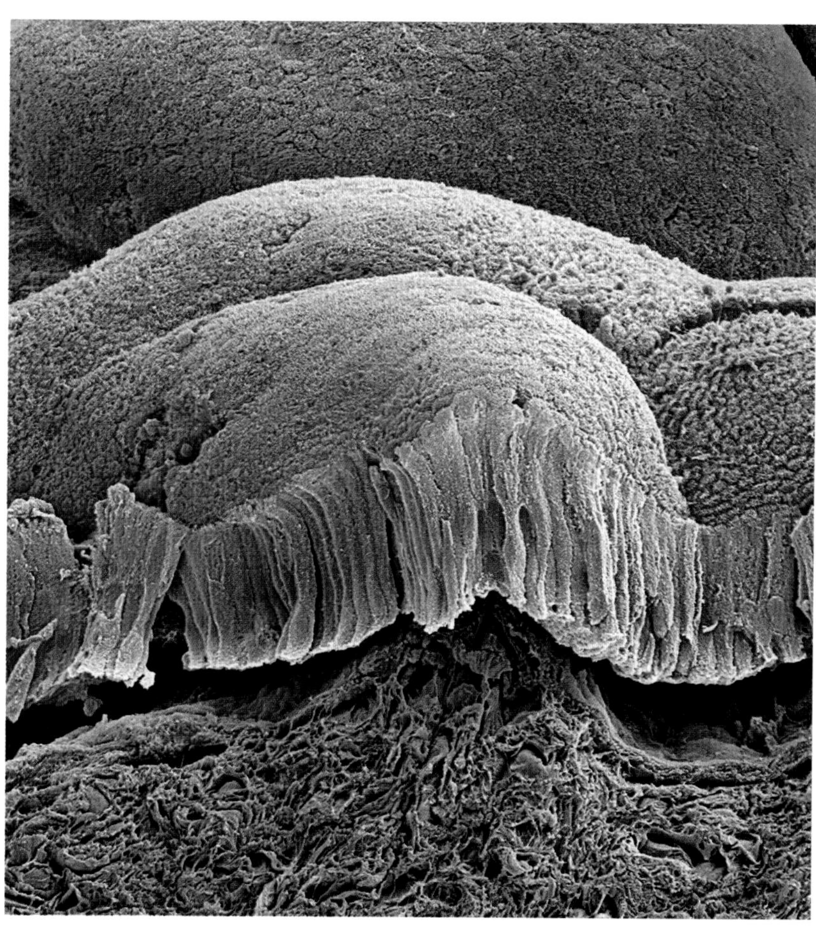

THE INTESTINES: THE ABSORPTION & EXPULSION OF WASTE

The action of the enzymes are facilitated by the movements of the small intestine, thus by the rhythmic contractions of the circular muscles there is a continuous mixing action. The bowel secretes a substantial quantity of water that makes the chyme more fluid and more vulnerable to enzymes. The chyme is a milky liquid that is composed of relatively small soluble molecules, and so is readily absorbed.

Absorption is the second important role played by bowel: it consists of a series of events that are governed by the laws of physics and chemistry. The absorption of fat, sugars and proteins begins in the duodenum and is completed within the first section. The absorption of other nutrients and water continues further down the ileum where the intestinal villi reach their maximum density. Usually, however, the absorption of all nutrients is already complete within the first half of the small

THE LIVER

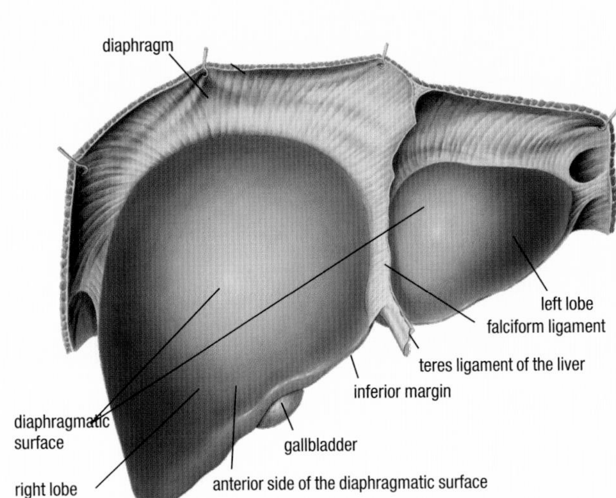

▼ **FRONTAL VIEW**
Principal elements of the anatomy of the liver.

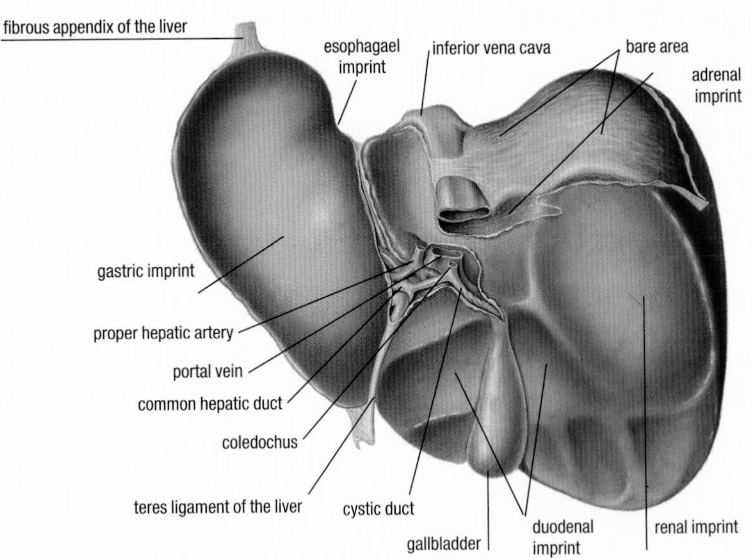

▼ **DORSAL VIEW**
Principal elements of the anatomy of the liver.

The liver is the largest of all the body's glands - typically weighing around 1.5 kg, and is the largest internal organ. It is a red-brown colour and is located in the upper part of the abdominal cavity, below the diaphragm on the right. It is in close proximity to and surrounded by the kidneys, adrenal glands, duodenum, stomach and colon. It has a rich vascular system, and is connected to the duodenum by the common bile duct.

In addition to being the main organ which controls the levels of carbohydrates, fats and proteins, its functions include the neutralisation of toxic waste, the recycling of old red blood cells and the excretion of bile. It is also responsible for the synthesis of the blood clotting agents fibrinogen and prothrombin, as well as the production of vitamin A. The internal structure of the liver is based on four lobules - these are the left and right anatomical lobes, the caudate lobe and the quadrate lobe.

The edges of each lobule are identifiable from the positions of the common hepatic artery and the hepatic portal vein. These supply the sinusoids with a rich supply of blood which is then screened for any unwanted materials such as bacteria which are then destroyed. Where the lobules meet is a region known as the portal triad or portal area. This is composed of four structures - the hepatic artery, hepatic portal vein, common bile duct and lymphatic vessels. About 75% of the liver's cytoplasmic mass is composed of hepatocytes, these are its primary functional units. They have a number of functions, including the synthesis and storage of various proteins, the conversion of carbohydrates into fatty acids and the production of important materials such as bile, cholesterol and phospholipids. The hepatocytes also play a vital role

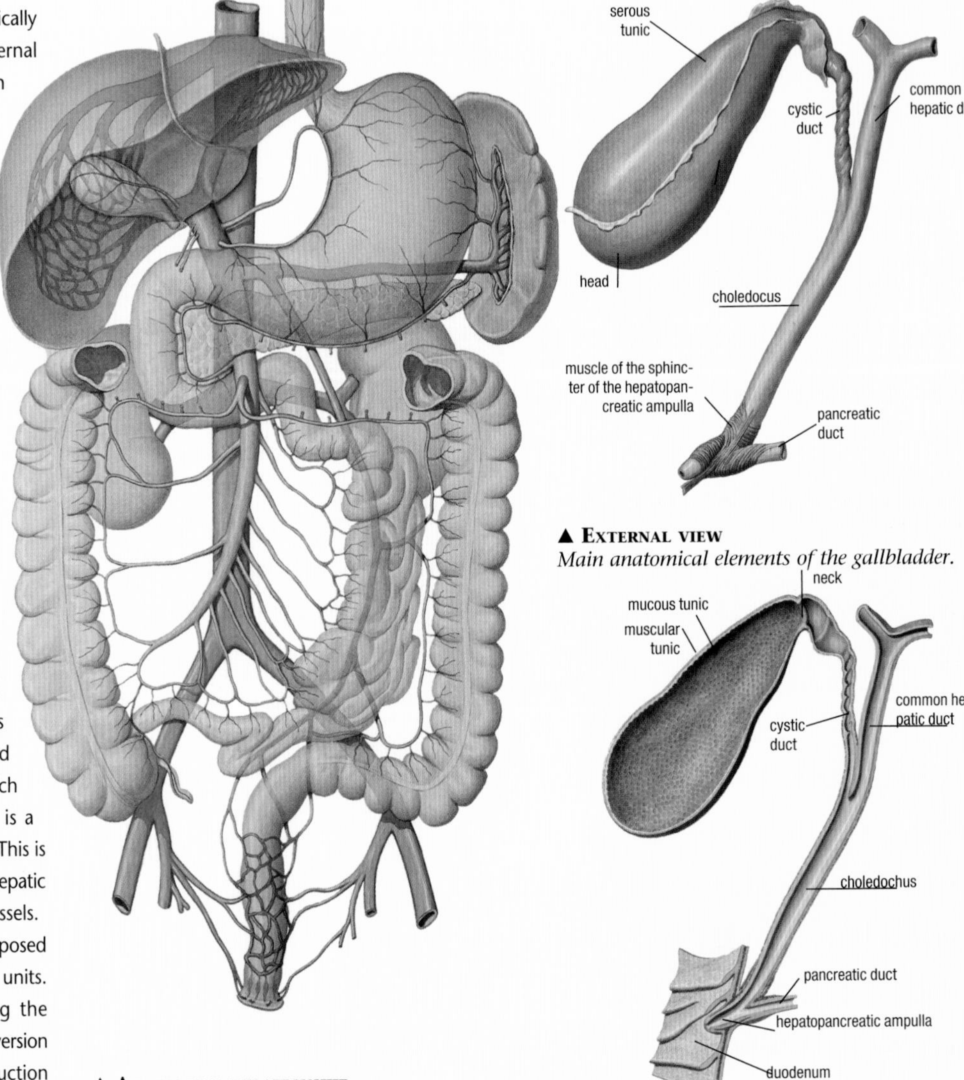

▲ **ANATOMICAL RELATIONSHIP**
Portal vein system (pink) with links between the liver and digestive organs.

▲ **EXTERNAL VIEW**
Main anatomical elements of the gallbladder.

▲ **SECTIONAL VIEW**
Main anatomical elements of the gallbladder.

in the detoxification and excretion of substances that would otherwise be harmful. Examples of such chemicals include such things as the residues of pharmaceutical drugs and any environmental pollutants that may have been ingested. Sometimes, however, these are too toxic and if present in sufficient quantities can result in significant liver damage.

Once bile has been produced it drains down through any one of many bile ducts and into the common hepatic duct and into the gallbladder where it is stored until it is needed. It is a strongly alkaline liquid with a vivid coloration - it may be yellow, green or blue. It is then secreted into the duodenum where it is used for a number of purposes including the decomposition of lipids, the neutralisation of acids, and the destruction of microbes such as bacteria.

The liver performs many other functions too, such as the storage of a number of important substances, including glycogen, the vitamins A, D and B12, as well as iron and copper. It also produces hormones that are used in the control of blood pressure, and converts ammonia to urea.

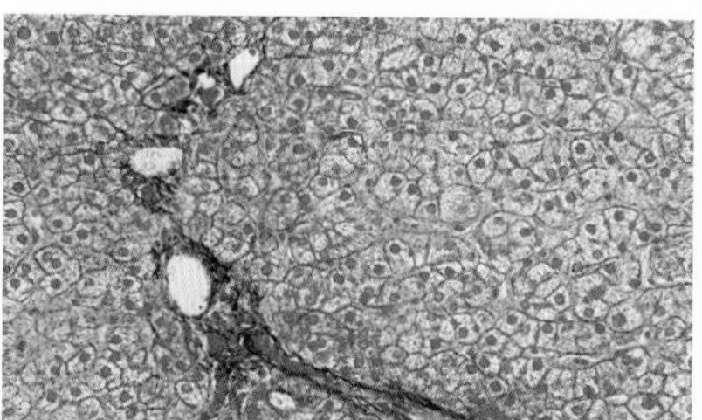

◀ **Parenchima**
This optical microphotograph shows the disposition of hepatocytes from large nuclei (red spots, parenchymal fabric) in a lobule. The hepatocytes process the lipids and accumulate glycogen, metabolized by this excess glucose in the blood.

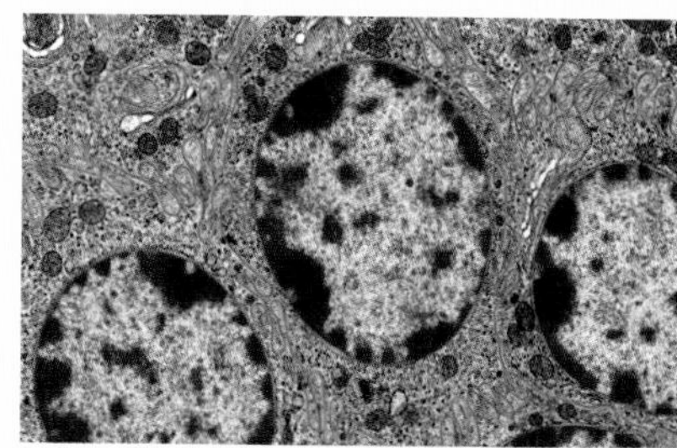

◀ **Liver Cells**
SEM microphotography in false colors that shows the sinusiod that surround the hepatocytes, evident in the red blood cells. The liver cells receive from the portal vein sinusoid nutrients, and those of the hepatic artery oxygen to live.

❶

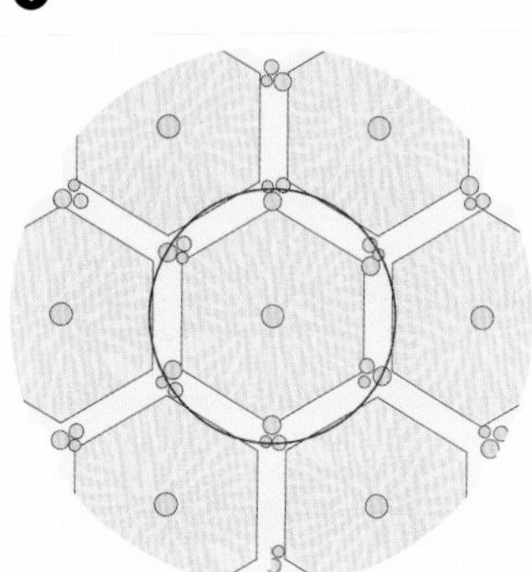

❷

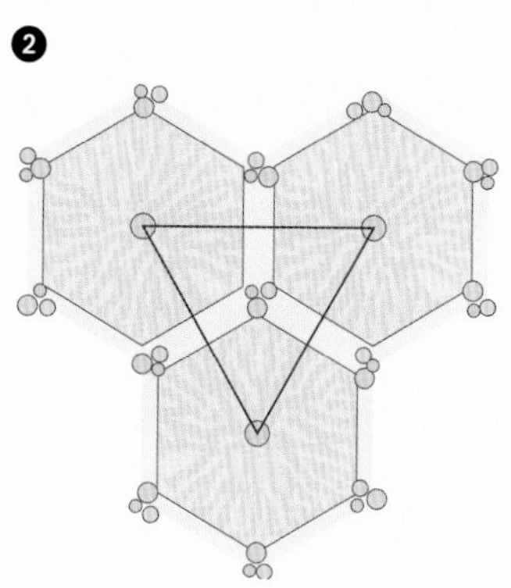

❸

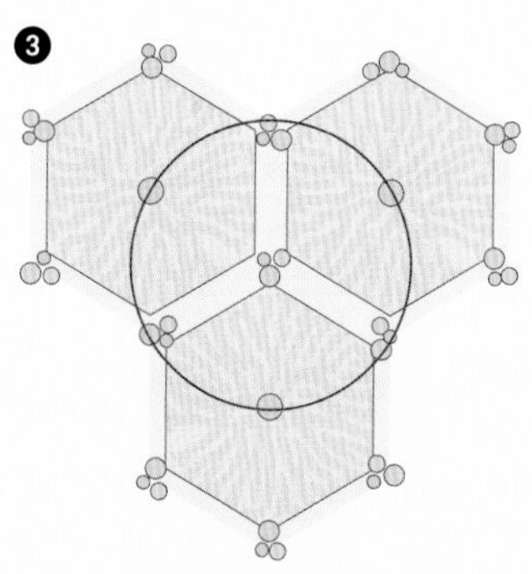

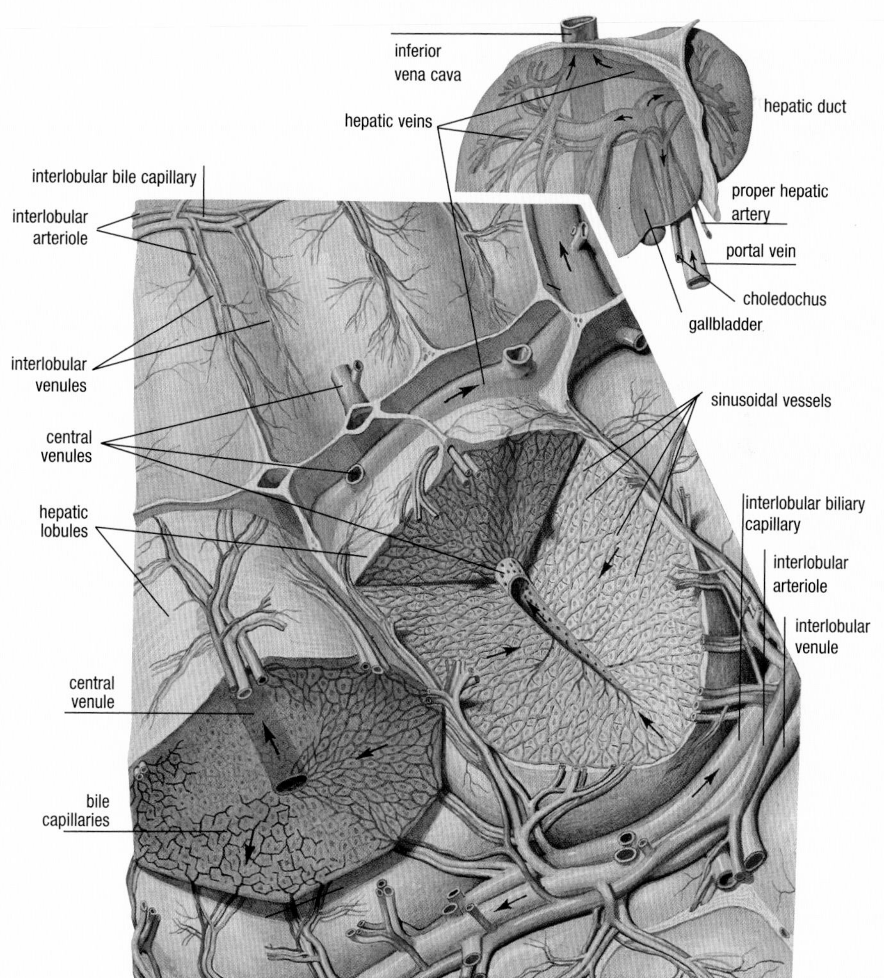

◀ **Hepatic lobules**
Depending on the function being considered, the liver lobules can be: ❶ classic, ❷ billiary or ❸ of Rappaport.

▲ **Lobular structure**
Microanatomy of a classic lobule: in green bile ducts; venous in blue, pink interlobular pockets, arterial in red.

Large and small problems of the liver

There are many different conditions which can affect the liver. These include various diseases and dysfunctions. The most common being the one that leads to the formation of gallstones: it afflicts about 25% of women and 12% of men under 60 years of age. These form as the result of an accumulation of cholesterol or bile salts, and can occur either spontaneously or as a response to an infection which has caused an imbalance in the bile composition. The slow and gradual formation of crystals in the gallbladder is often asymptomatic, but they can eventually grow to a size where they begin to block the cystic duct or the sphincter of the common bile duct, preventing the passage of bile and pancreatic juice to the duodenum. One way of treating gallstones is to use a procedure known as 'lithotripsy' - this is where an external ultrasound probe is used to create fractures in the stones. If the treatment is successful, they gradually begin to break up into small pieces that can be passed out of the body in the urine.

The diseases that can afflict the liver include:

- jaundice; this is due to imbalances in the levels of bilirubin
- hepatic steatosis; this is the most common liver disease and is treated with aggressive drugs
- hepatitis; this an inflammation characterised by necrosis - namely the death of liver cells, and may be due to infections (from viruses or parasites) or poisoning (from abuse of alcohol or drugs)
- cirrhosis, this is an alteration of normal liver structure in which nodules are formed that are surrounded by a fibrous tissue. It causes a gradual deterioration of liver function
- hepatomegaly, this is an increase in the volume of the liver - it indicates that there is a disorder of some kind, although there are many possible causes
- glycogen imbalances - these are characterised by the build-up of glycogen in the liver and muscles

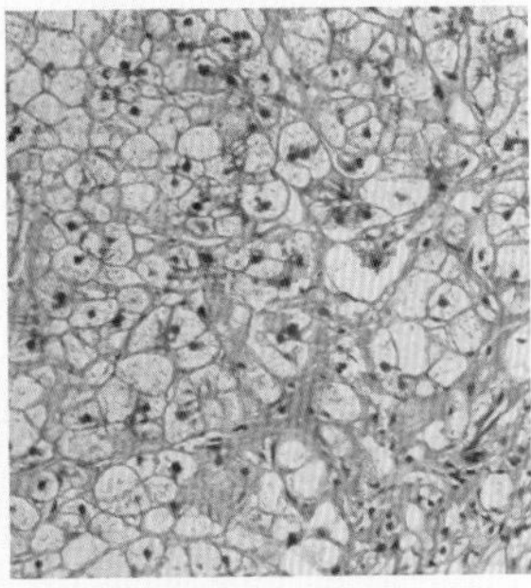

▲ **Liver affected by Glycogen**
Optical microphotography of a section of liver affected by glycogen storage disease. The glycogen is a polymer of glucose and serves as the basis of energy: in this type of genetic disorder, it accumulates in hepatocytes taking this irregular shape.

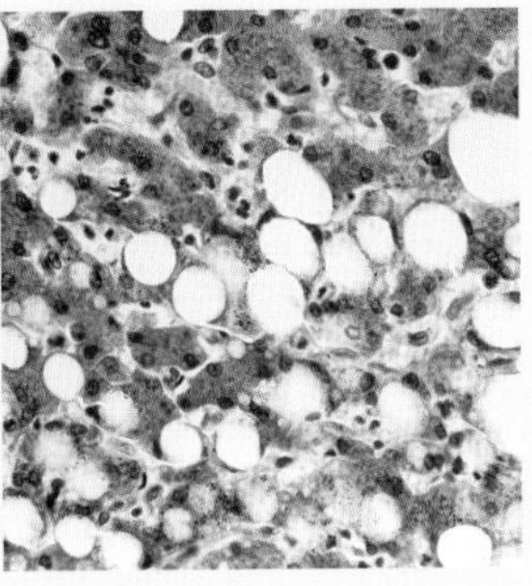

▲ **Liver "Fat"**
Optical microphotography of a section of liver affected by hepatic steatosis, thus by the abnormal accumulation of fat that deforms the hepatocytes (purple, with dark nuclei, with deposits in clear). The "fat liver" occurs frequently in big drinkers, in cases of hypoxia, intoxication or diabetes mellitus, but is more common than you might think and provides a serious liver disorder.

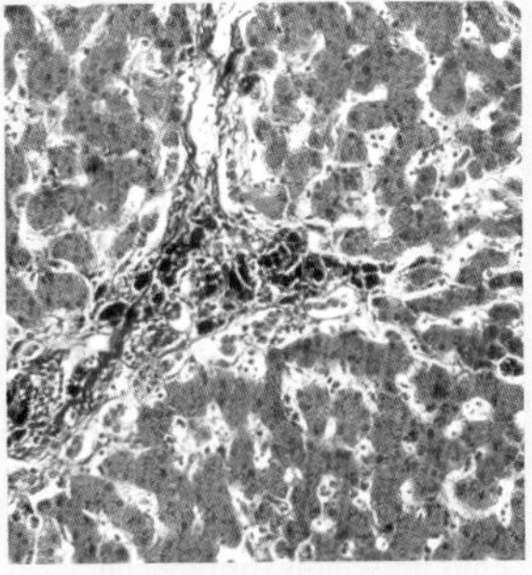

▲ **Cirrhosis**
Optical microphotography of a section of liver showing the classic signs of cirrhosis. The bands represent the dark fiber disintegration of the structure around the livers healthy hepatocytes (pink). Cirrhosis is a disease of chronic liver damage, often produced by alcohol, hepatitis (inflammation), heart problems, and can lead to death.

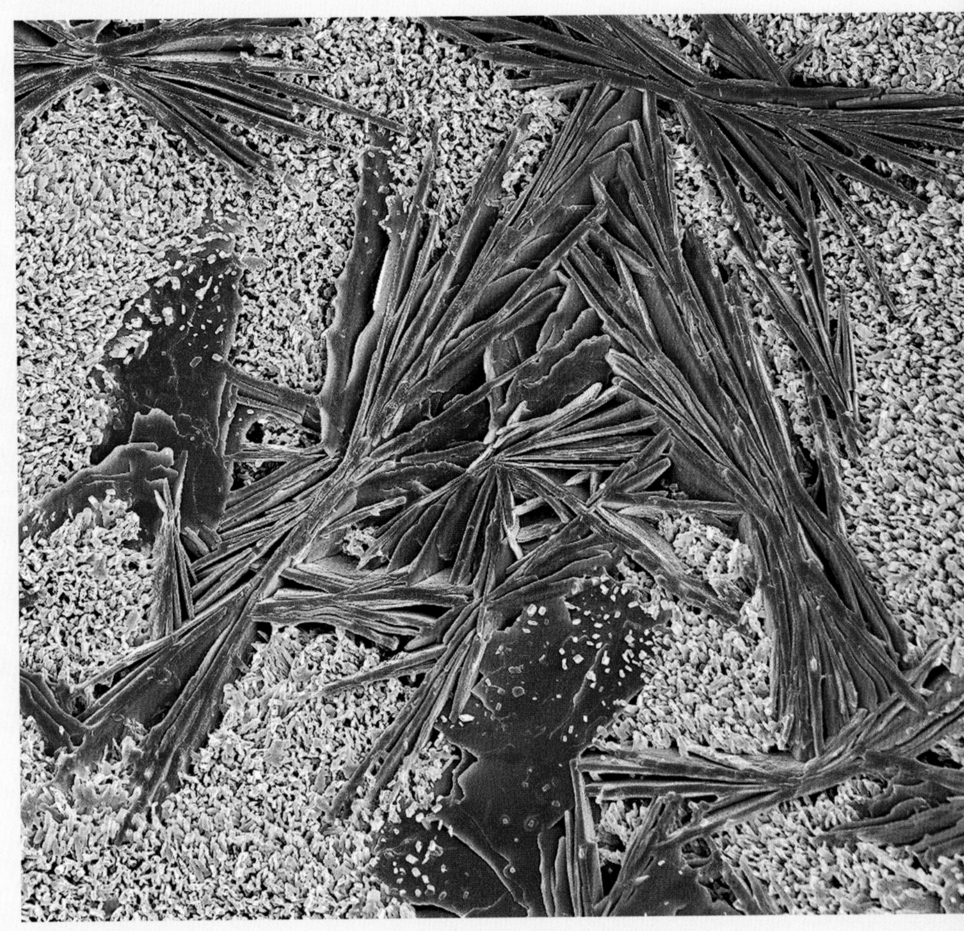

▶ **Biliary crystals**
False color SEM Photography of gallstones which reveals the fractured internal crystal. The gallstones are formed when the chemical composition of bile is unbalanced: in this case cholesterol, which may precipitate bile pigments in the form of crystals that, over time, enlarge to become sufficient to block the choledochus.

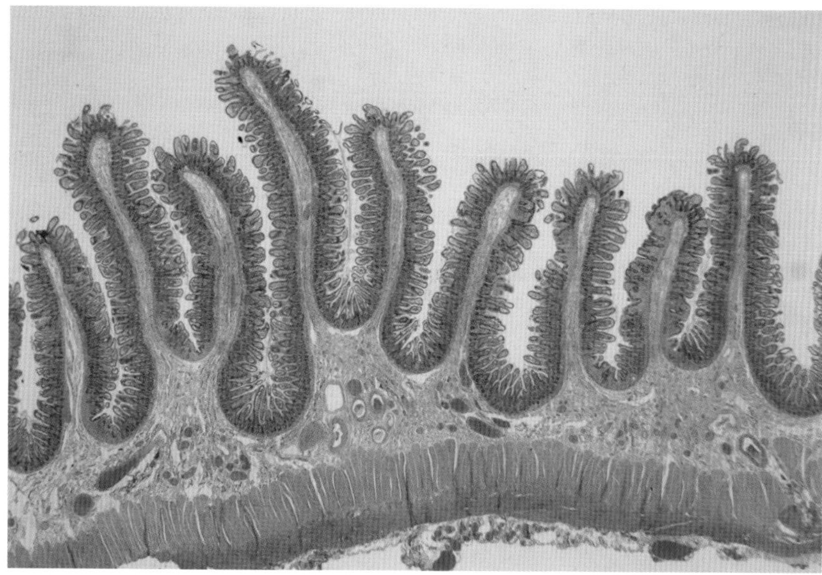

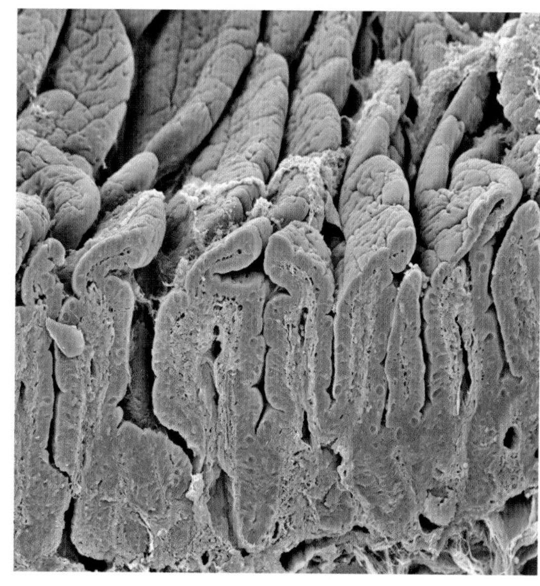

intestine, and it is unlikely that in the material that proceeds towards the ileum and colon there is still much left to absorb. This must have been a point of evolutionary favour, given that the digestive system produces a bilio-pancreatic secretion that is capable of digesting a meal that is ten times larger than the maximum imaginable. In the past, this must have made it possible to absorb the largest possible quantity of nutrients before the available food went bad.

The absorption of nutrients is a complicated process involving absorbent intestinal cell membranes both for the transport ▸17 of particular nutrients, as well as the various osmotic factors ▸17. The membrane of the epithelial cells of the villi is rich in microvilli, more than a billion and half per square centimetre. In an intestinal path of just 6-8 metres and a diameter of about 3 cm (the extent of the entire bowel) there is an absorption area of over 300 m2. This is approximately 200 times the area of the skin. Just visible to the naked eye (they are about 1 mm high), and with a relatively short life (with a turnover of 3-4 days), the intestinal villi have a structure that facilitates the immediate passage in the bloodstream and lymphatic system of nutrients absorbed by the epithelium. All the hydrophilic substances - these include amino acids, monosaccharides such as glucose, glycerine and water-soluble vitamins as well as water and minerals, pass directly into the blood capillaries, and so reach the mesenteric veins, then the liver, and eventually the rest of body.

Most of fatty acids, fat-soluble vitamins and glycerol, however, are absorbed by the epithelial cells in the form of micelles and transformed into chylomicron. These are columns of spherical triglycerides with a diameter of 1μm and a low density, that are covered with phospholipids, cholesterol and proteins.

As the absorption proceeds, the intestinal contents become more consistent. Under the influence of

▲ **Fasting**
Optical microphotography of a section of the wall of jejunum: the mucosa (purple) is folded into circular folds or Kerckring covered with villi. Beneath the mucosa is the submucosa canvas (pink, in the folds) of the connective and, at the base, the smooth muscle tunic (pink, bottom).

▲ **Duodenum**
SEM microphotography in false colors of the duodenal surface (green). The plan shows the deep rift folds of the mucous membrane: a layer of epithelial cells with microvilli (blue) supported by a connective tissue (brown).

▼ **Ileum**
SEM False-color photograph of villi (brown) on the surface of intestinal ileus. In the epithelium of each villa there are many enterocytes that actively absorb nutrients, and globular cells, which secrete mucus.

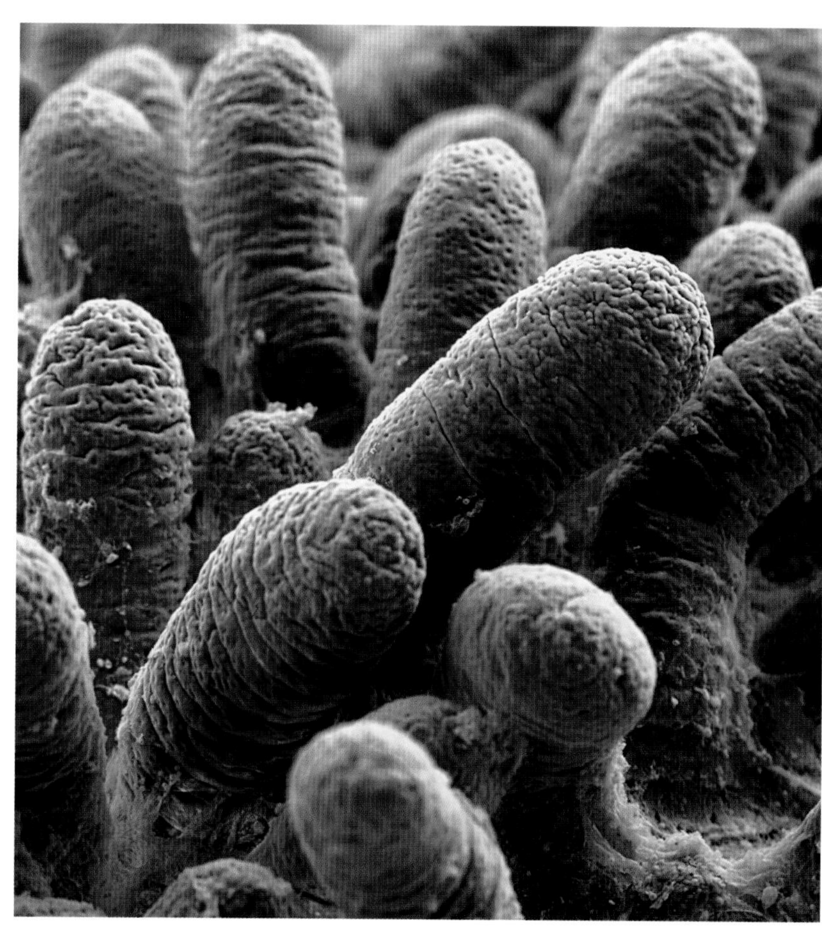

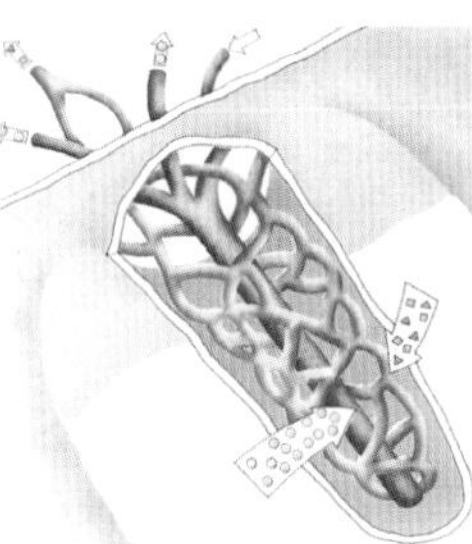

▲ **Structure of a villus**
Below the epithelium absorbent, each villus is crossed by a network of blood vessels (derived from the vein and mesenteric artery) in addition to a lymphatic vessel or chyliferous.

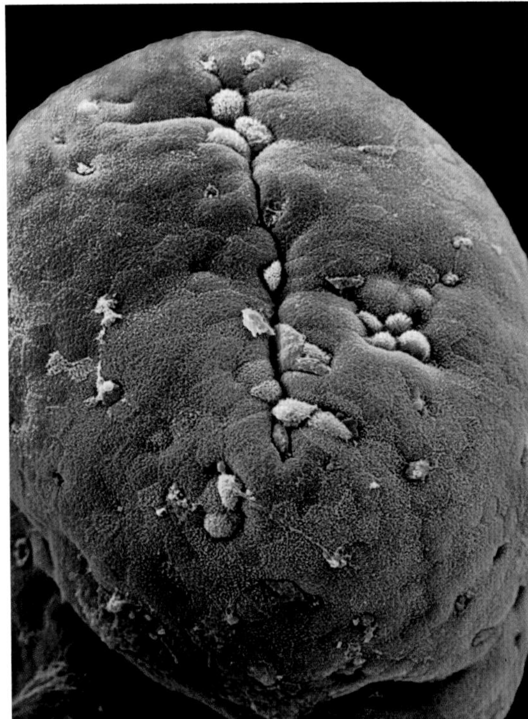

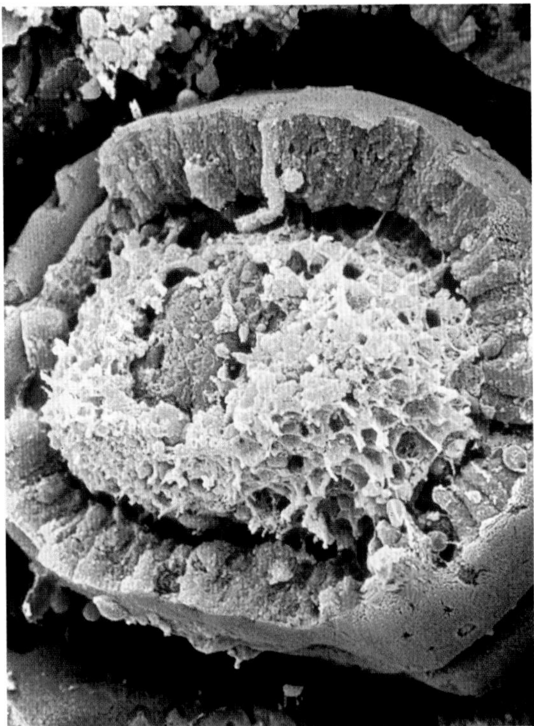

▶ **Villus**
SEM False-color photograph of a villus. The epithelium of the intestinal mucosa consists of globular cells (pink) that produce mucus, which facilitates the flow of food along the intestine, and absorptive cells (green). On the right, the section of the villus shows better conformation of the palisade of mucosal epithelium, cells with green and pink, while the center of the lamina propria villa (in white and light green) contains the blood and lymphatic vessels where they are channeled the nutrients absorbed.

the peristaltic pulses, the remaining food progresses along the large intestine where there are no villi. By this stage, the mucosa no longer produces any enzymes and digestion effectively stops, however, the vitamins produced by bacteria, water and mineral salts continue to be absorbed.

The contents are increasingly dehydrated, and the substances that are left are not digestible. It gets increasingly dense and starts to become faeces. After about another two metres, the faeces begin to accumulate in the rectum. When this relaxes, it gives rise to the need to defecate. If the sympathetic control system does not prevent it, there is a reflex that is co-ordinated by the parasympathetic nervous system. This relaxes the anal sphincter, while the diaphragm, the abdominal muscles, and the anus muscles contract. This forces the expulsion of the faeces, which not only empties the rectum, but most of the large bowel too.

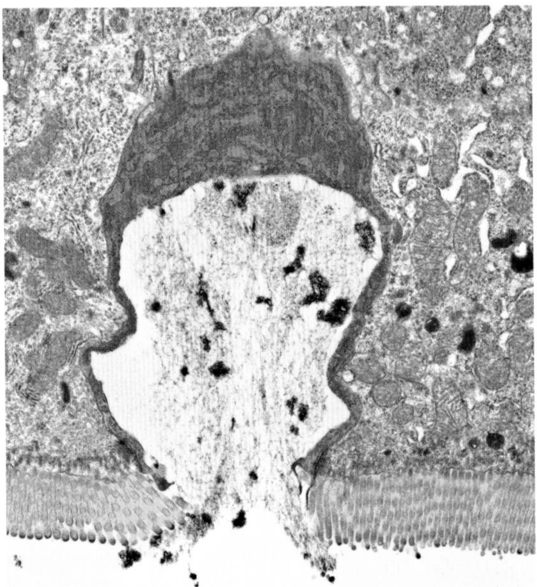

▲ **Globular cell**
Transmission electron microscope (TEM) false-color photograph of the section of a mucosal intestinal digestive globular cell. Most of the mucus produced (Brown) has already been released in the intestinal lumen, protecting the mucosa and facilitating the progress of food through the digestive tract.

THE CONTROL OF GASTROINTESTINAL DIGESTION

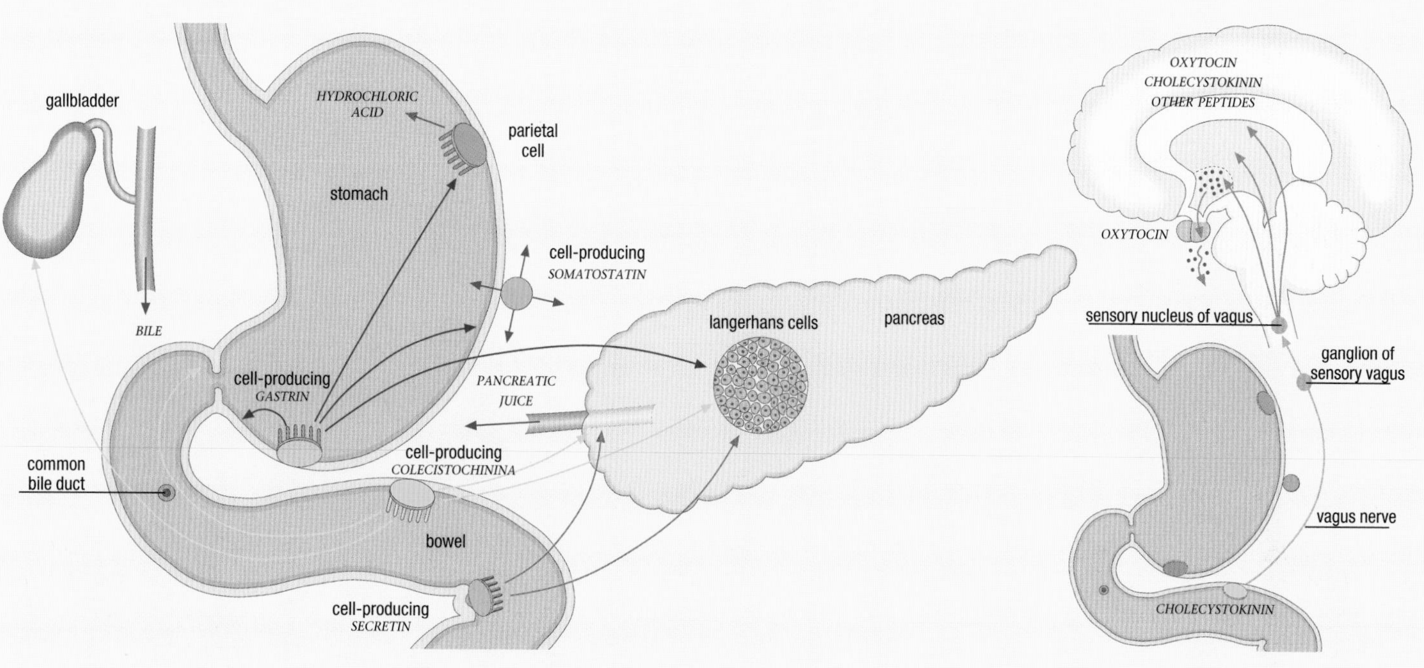

The functioning of the gastrointestinal organs is regulated by a combination of the hormonal and nervous systems. Special cells that are located in the endocrine gastric mucosa and the small intestine react to the arrival of food by producing certain hormones - these include gastrin, cholecystokinin and secretin.

These hormones trigger the production of insulin in the pancreas - once it has entered the blood circulation, it also stimulates many other processes:

- the secretin stimulates the production of alkaline substances that make the pancreatic juices;
- the gastrin stimulates the release of gastric acid (hydrochloric acid) by the parietal cells, the growth of epithelial cells that form the digestive mucous, and helps with the digestive movements.
- the cholecystokinin slows gastric emptying, stimulates the release of bile from the gallbladder and the secretion of pancreatic digestive enzymes. It also generates nerve impulses via the vagus nerve - when these reach the brain they promote the development of a sense of satiety and induce sleepiness.

In turn, the activities of the vagus and splanchnic nerves directly affect the production of the hormonal endocrine cells in the digestive tract. For example, the nerve fibres stimulate or inhibit the vagus nerve, and the consequent hormone excretions stimulate or block the processes that are involved, such as the production of insulin in the pancreas. At the same time, the signals from the splanchnic nerves have an opposite effect. In this way, any imbalances are held to a minimum as the result of the delicate balancing of the various physical-chemical stimuli which together precisely modulate the complicated digestive processes.

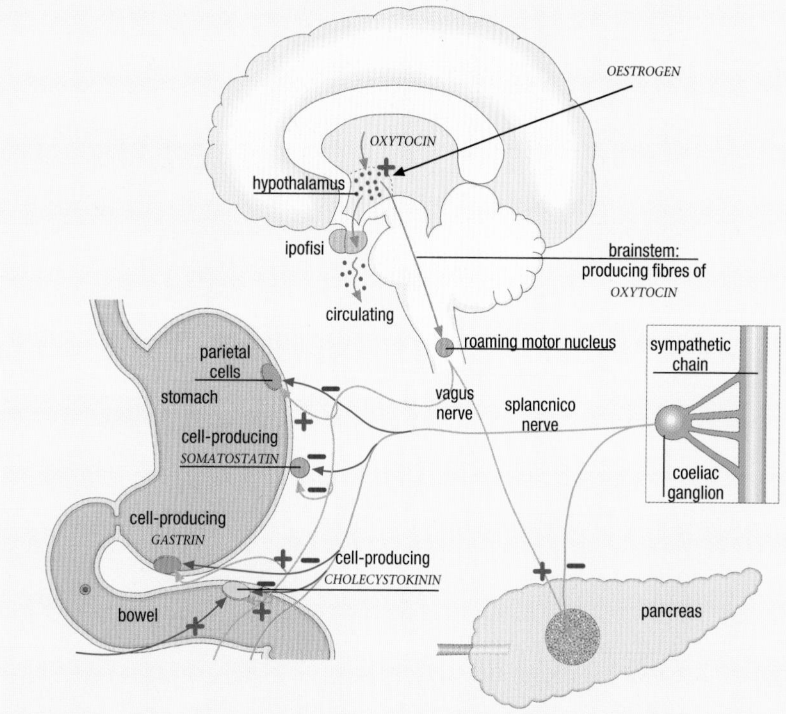

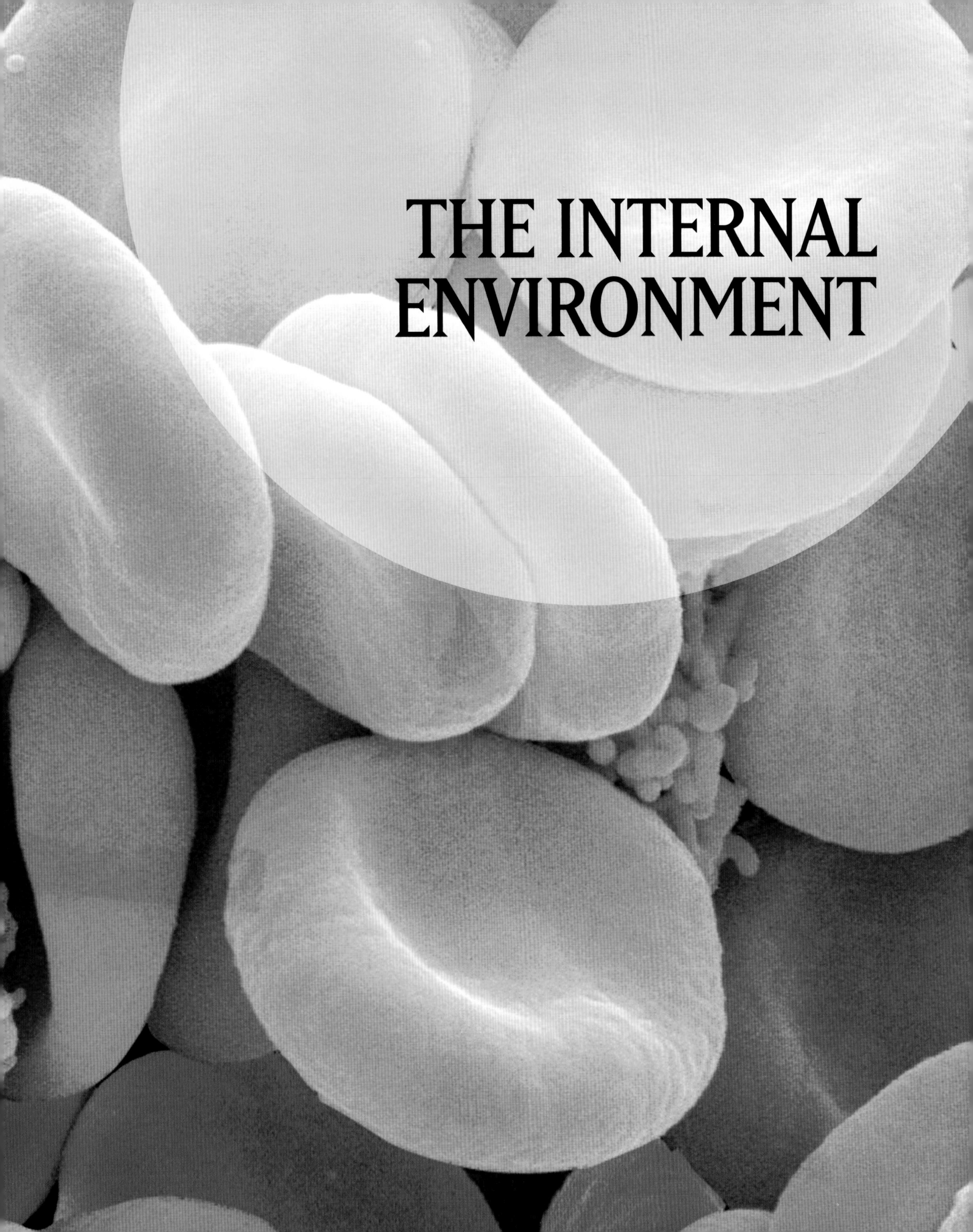

THE INTERNAL ENVIRONMENT

The internal environment that surrounds every cell of our body, must have consistent and balanced characteristics, such as to facilitate the maximum life of each living element. First, there must always be the right concentration of nutrients and oxygen, and metabolic waste must be cleaned up.

COLLECTION AND DISTRIBUTION

At the macroscopic level, one of the problems that concerns the collection and distribution of substances such as nutrients and waste matter is that of how to get them safely in and out of the body. This is resolved by ensuring that their entry and exit can only be undertaken through protected orifices that connect with the relevant specialised internal cavities. At the microscopic level, however, this is not good enough. Every one of the billions of cells that form the body has to have available everything that it needs for survival.

For this to happen, it is necessary that the useful substances reach the environment in which each cell is situated, this consisting of the delicate film of liquid that surrounds it. Further to this, the vital processes take place at a fast and continuous pace. In order for the cell to survive therefore, it has to receive regular replacements of the liquids that it needs, and well as the continuous removal of waste products and the maintenance of the optimal environmental characteristics. There are many nervous receptors which continuously collect information on both the inner and external environments - this information is then sent to the encephalon where it is compared with stored data. Once processed, the output signals co-ordinate the activities of all the body's various systems, including the nervous, muscular, respiratory, excretory and circulatory. This makes it possible for the body to

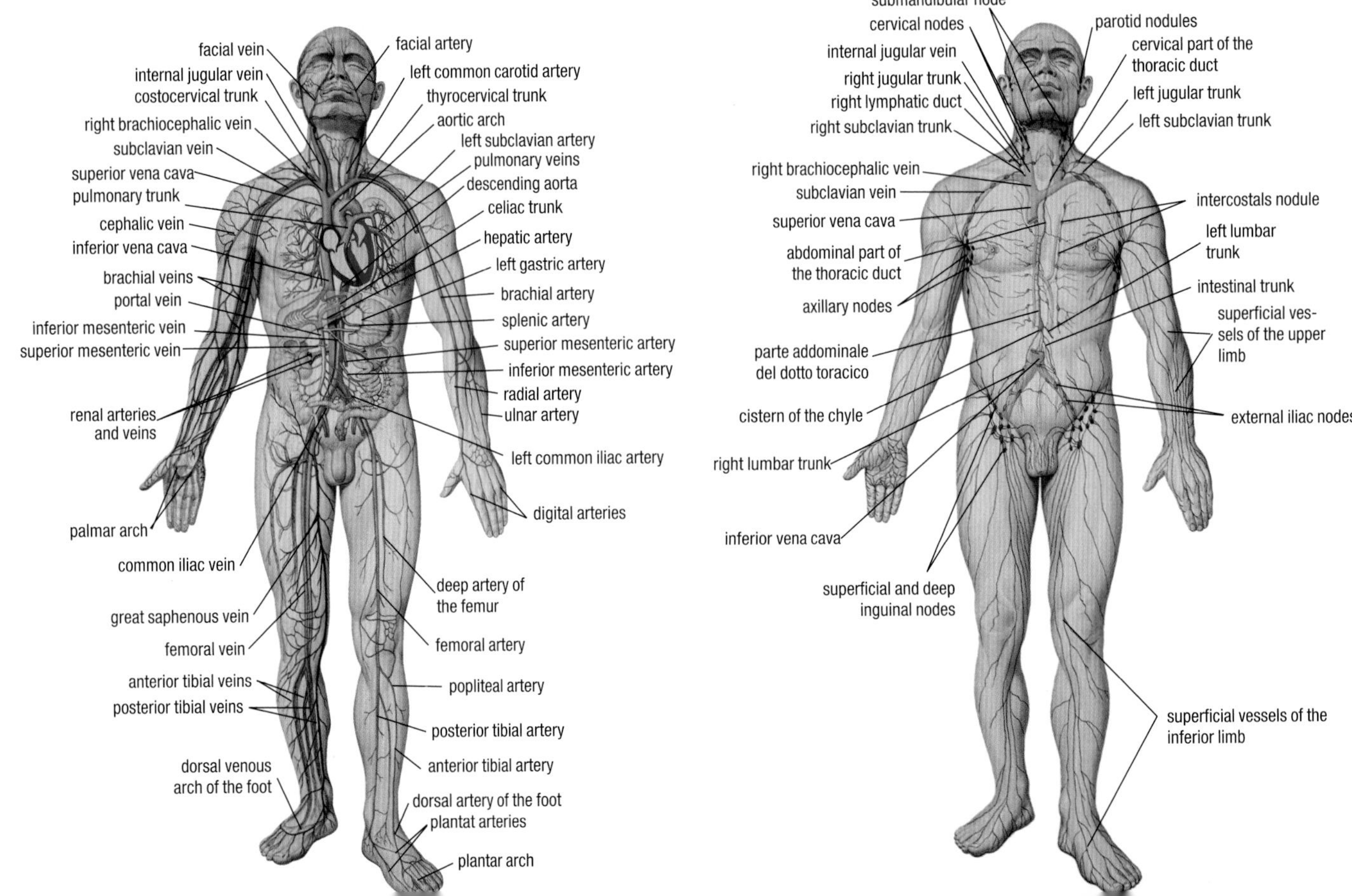

▼ **Collection schemes and distribution**
Main anatomical elements of the circulatory system and arterial venous (left) and lymphatic (right).

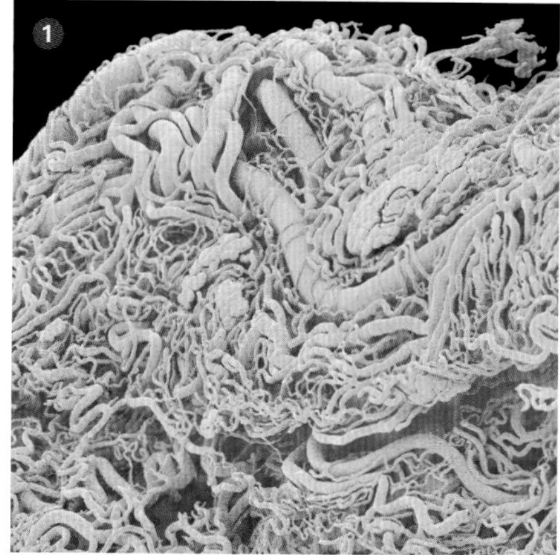

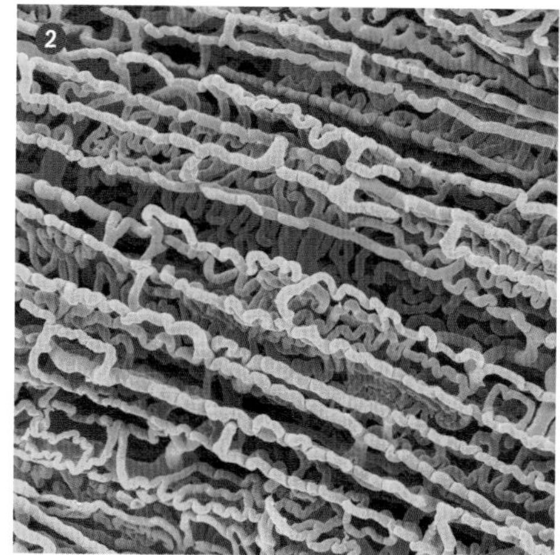

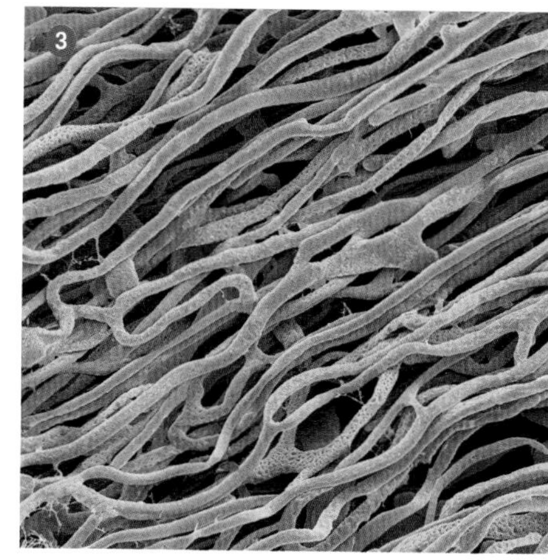

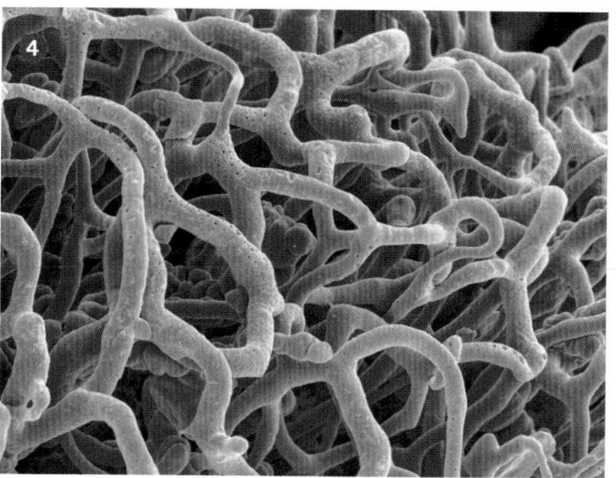

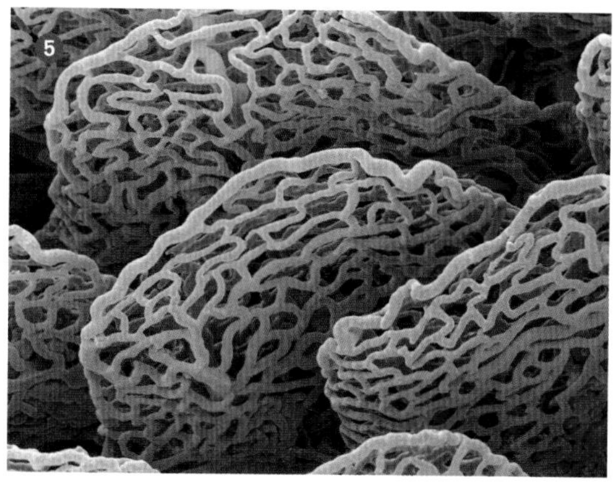

◄▲ **CIRCULATORY NETWORK**
Networks of blood vessels through different tissues of the body, seen in false color images taken with a scanning electron microscope (SEM). While the vessels were made by injecting a resin, the surrounding tissues were removed chemically. ❶ Connective tissue coverage of a skeletal muscle, ❷ skeletal muscle, ❸ cardiac muscle , ❹ wall of the stomach, ❺ intestinal villi.

maintain a balance in its internal conditions. The circulatory system has the function of collecting all the substances – be they useful or discarded, from the exchange mechanisms and taking them to their destination. That is, the cells that need them, or to the secreting bodies that eject them.

The blood and lymph - both tissue fluids that are in continuous movement, always remain in contact with the exchange mechanisms. Although they have similar characteristics and flow in vessels that drain one another, blood and lymph follow different paths and have different functions.

- The blood: this is pumped around the body by the heart, and circulates in a closed system of impermeable vessels (arteries and veins) as well as permeable capillaries that reach all the cells. It transports oxygen collected from the lungs, as well as nutrients and water absorbed by the intestines, together with hormones and chemical messages from various glands and internal cells, and distributes them to every cell in the body. At the same time, it collects carbon dioxide and water-soluble wastes from the interstitial regions and distributes them to the structures that acts as filters, such as the lungs and kidneys, from where they are expelled.
- The lymph: this moves passively in an open system of permeable vessels, and carries various substances that have been specifically absorbed by the intestines and carries them to the bloodstream. It also plays a key role in defence of the body.

The circulatory apparatus also has a homeostatic function, helping to preserve the balances between different parts of the body. For example, it maintains a uniform overall temperature, although the heat levels are not the same everywhere. It also modulates the distribution of substances to the organs while adapting them to the specific operational requirements. This control is possible thanks to the capabilities of both the heart to change its rate and of the blood vessels to change their tone, thus directing a greater flow of blood to the most active organs.

◄ **CIRCULATION**
The movement differs depending on the type of tissue in circulating blood and lymph; blood circulation also is divided into ***circulatory lung****, which originates on the left side of the heart, and great movement, which originates on the right side. Poorly oxygenated blood is in* **blue** *and in* **red** *the blood is oxygenated. Where the system brings the blood in* **lilac**, **yellow** *are the lymphatic ducts.*
❶ Vessels that lead and take blood from the head, by the upper limbs and the chest, ❷ lungs; chest lymphatic duct ❸, ❹ liver, stomach ❺, ❻ spleen, kidney ❼; intestine ❽, ❾ intestinal lymphatic ducts; ❿ vessels that lead and take blood from the lower limbs and the abdomen.

The fluids circulating within the bloodstream and lymphatic system have similar characteristics, suitable for carrying out many functions in our body.

BLOOD AND LYMPH: FUNCTION AND COMPOSITION

▼ Plasma
By using a centrifuge the whole blood is easily split into its numerous cellular elements suspended in the solvent fluid. The isolated plasma may have numerous therapeutic uses.

Let us examine in more detail the main chemical and physical characteristics of circulatory tissue (blood and lymph), their similarities and their differences, and briefly review their main physiological functions.

THE BLOOD

The blood is a connective tissue that is formed by cells of various kinds ►90, including macrophages ►95, red blood cells ►83 and platelets ►85 - these are dispersed in a yellowish fluid called the blood plasma.

According to its oxygenation characteristics, blood is said to be arterial (rich in oxygen and coloured bright red) or venous (poor in oxygen and a dark red colour). Pumped from the heart ►114 through the blood vessels ►126, it runs continuously in a cycle. If for some reason it escapes from the vessels through a cut or other problem, it spontaneously sets into a semisolid clot that blocks the injury ►88. The pale yellow transparent liquid that remains after the blood has clotted is called serum. It has a chemical composition that is similar to plasma, but is devoid of fibrinogen and most of the clotting factors ►85 and, therefore, can not coagulate further.

On average, the total volume of blood circulating in an adult male is approximately 5 litres, and corresponds to almost 6% of his body weight. However, this average value varies from individual to individual, and with age and sex - in the elderly and women, for example, the figure is slightly lower.

THE BLOOD PLASMA

The blood plasma is an aqueous solution of proteins, salts and other inorganic substances in small concentrations (by volume, water represents 92%; proteins the 5.5-8%; minerals 0.8%; lipids 0.6%; glucose 0.1%; metabolite cells less than 0.1%; there are also trace amounts of gas and hormones). Produced for the most part by the liver (except immunoglobulins, hormones ►102 and some enzymes ►200), proteins are separated according to their molecular weight and other physical and chemical characteristics into albumin, globulin and clotting factors.

Albumin (3.5 - 5 g/100 ml of blood) is the most abundant protein fraction - it constitutes 60% of the serum protein and can bind to water, bilirubin, $Ca2+$ and $Na+$ ions, fatty acids, hormones and drugs, that are transported in blood circulation. Moreover, it is the main regulator of osmotic pressure ►17 because water affects the exchanges that take place between plasma and the tissues at the level of the capillaries.

Globulin is distinguished into four main groups indicated by letters from the Greek alphabet - these are: $\alpha 1$, α 2, β and γ. Their physical and chemical properties have a significant bearing on the viscosity of the blood, which helps to modulate the capillary movement.

The $\alpha 1$ globulins include mucoprotein as $\alpha 1$-antitrypsin and acid glycoprotein; among the α 2 globulins are haptoglobin (50-300 mg/100 ml) and antithrombin III (22-40 mg/100 ml) which are

involved in the clotting of blood.
Among the β globulins are fibrinogen (200-400 mg/100 ml), which plays an important role in blood clotting ▸121 and transferrin (200-320 mg/100 ml), which is essential in transporting iron to all the intestinal tissues as well as those in the bone marrow, where the most important production of red blood cells and haemoglobin takes place.
The γ -globulin, or immunoglobulin (Ig) as these antibodies are commonly called ▸102 are molecules that are involved in the immune reactions that protect the body from attack by foreign substances and organisms.
The most important inorganic salts in the plasma are sodium chloride and sodium carbonate, but - in smaller quantities, there are also potassium chloride, calcium and magnesium. For the maintenance of the constant functioning of cells, it is not so much the absolute quantity of these substances, but rather the balance between their relative proportions. To ensure that this balance is preserved, there are numerous integrated regulatory mechanisms which modulate the possible variations of concentration very accurately ▸139. In the plasma there are also many other substances. Among them are included: urea and nitrogen compounds which are the waste products of cell metabolism ▸19; glucose, amino acids and lipids, which are vital nutrients, as well as vitamins and hormones, metabolic factors and chemical messages.

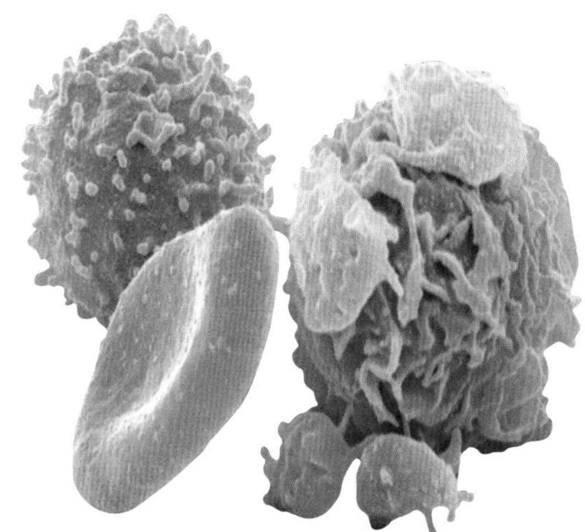
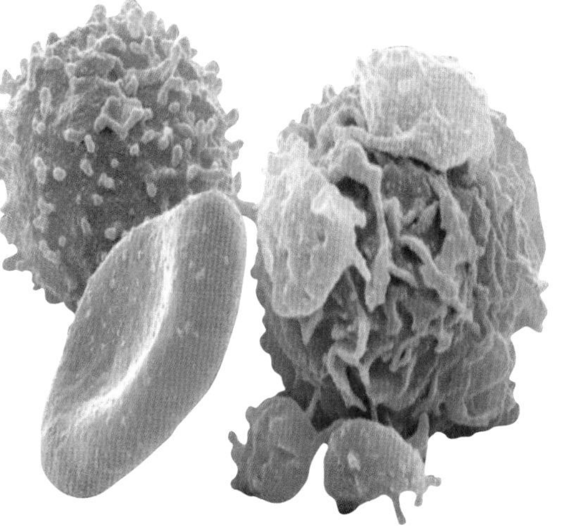

◂ **Cells or not**
In blood, carried away by a current, there are numerous corpuscles: some cells are whole such as the white blood cells, others are just what remains of cells: red cells, no nucleus, and platelets, cells produced by "breaking up". In the SEM pictures there are four yellow platelets, an erythrocyte in red, a lymphocyte in blue and a leukocyte neutrophil in purple.

ERYTHROCYTES OR RED BLOOD CELLS

Cells are the elements that give the colour to blood. Under normal conditions, in the body of an adult there are about 5,400,000 erythrocytes/mm3 blood, although this number varies from individual to individual and depends on functional conditions as well as sex. In women, for example, there are on average less than 4,800,000 erythrocytes/ mm3 blood. Without a core, endoplasmic reticulum or mitochondria, 97% of their volume is haemoglobin. They have a diameter of 7.5 µm and a biconcave disc form which makes the area ratio / volume particularly favourable to trade with the environment that surrounds them.

▾ **Creeping blood**
A film of blood on a slide under a microscope, shows the most frequent cell, recognizable by their characteristic shape and color. Here, among numerous erythrocytes, there are two lymphocytes, almost completely occupied by a blue nucleus; mielocytes with a large nucleus and two heart-granulocytes, their nucleus elongated and lumpy.

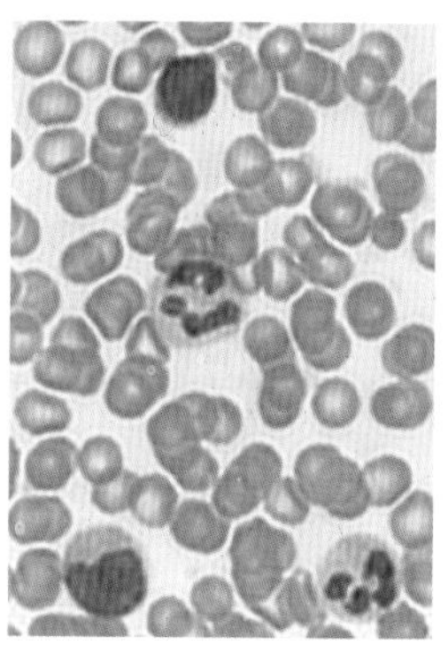

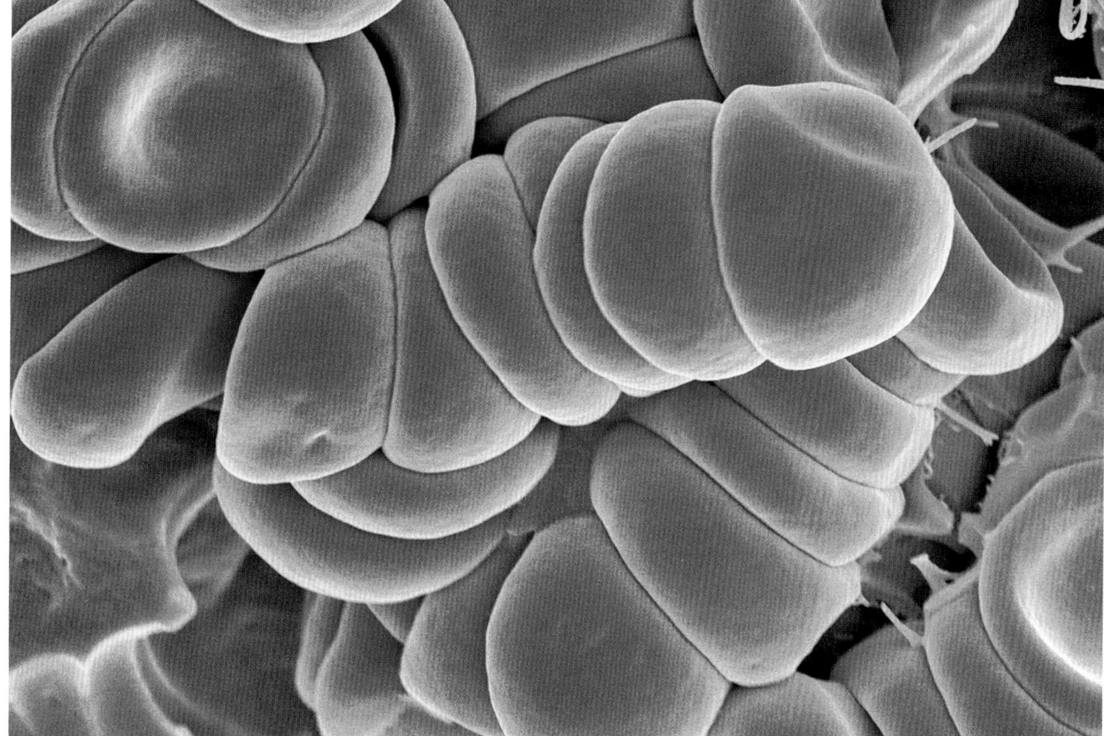

◂ **Red cells "stack of coins"**
Often, especially in passing capillaries, the red blood cells overlap one another.

In the adult they are produced by bone marrow that is located in the long and flat bones ►[86]. They arise from nucleated cells and undifferentiated (erythroblasts), and pass through complex stages (erythropoiesis) and finally end up as erythrocytes which, before entering the bloodstream, expel the nucleus. With the loss of the nucleus - and thus of genetic material, they lose their ability to carry out their cellular activities. This is an important functional advantage, as it prevents them from consuming the oxygen they are carrying. The lack of a nucleus also allows them to change shape, overlap, to occupy less space, and to conform to the capillaries, which may have a diameter less than theirs. These are all important features which allow them to always maintain their integrity even when the speed of blood flow decreases or when they are crowded in the capillaries.

Essentially, then, the red blood cells are bags of haemoglobin which only play the role of transporting gas ►[51]. In the four haem molecules that form each haemoglobin molecule ►[52] there are atoms of iron that can bind reversibly with various gases. In the presence of a high partial pressure of oxygen, oxyhaemoglobin is formed - this has a rich red colour. When there is a high partial pressure of carbon dioxide, carboxyhaemoglobin is formed; this has a dark red colour. Other gases - like carbon monoxide, can form bonds that are much stronger, and this blocks the transport activity of blood, which for the haemoglobin is crucial. Even the structure of the protein chains that form haemoglobin has an important physiological function. Their conformation space is genetically determined ►[89], and can promote or hinder the bonds between gas and iron. In normal physiological conditions, the red blood cells circulate in the body for about 120 days. Those which are damaged or grow old are destroyed by the spleen and the liver that, respectively, recycle the iron and transform most of haemoglobin pigment..

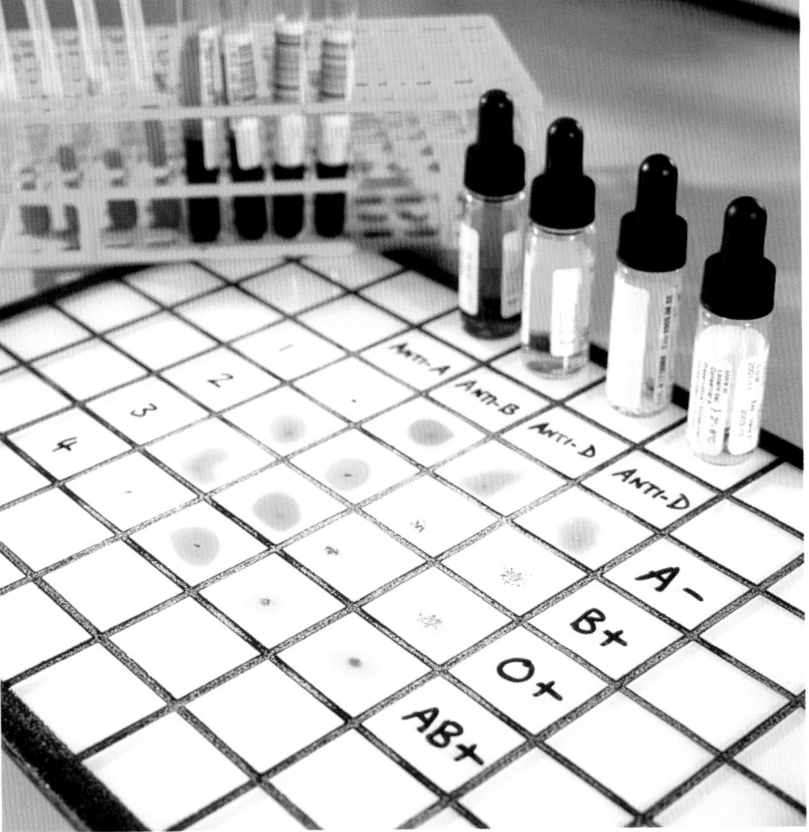

▼ **Blood groups**
A test showing the reactions between different types of blood (lines) with their serums (columns). Each blood type reacts differently to the same serum for the presence of different antigens on the surface of erythrocytes. The reaction with the antibodies produces agglutination of red blood cells that form a red focused spot. "Anti-D" is the antiserum used to recognize the Rh + type of blood.

THE BLOOD GROUPS

In the membrane of red blood cells are - among others, certain proteins that, from individual to individual, differ in a hereditary manner. Their presence may hinder transfusions. The immune system of an individual that is transfused with a blood that does not have the same characteristics, recognises the red blood cells as foreign and attacks and destroys them. In this case it is said that the recipient is not compatible with the blood transfusion. In its plasma are specific antibodies or haemagglutinin that, by binding to the transfused red blood cells, results in agglutination. In other words, antibodies bind to the transfused red blood cells and form clusters that obstruct the vessels and are attacked and destroyed by the white blood cells ►[90] and macrophages ►[95].

The different kinds of blood can be grouped using the AB0 system, which classifies the types of blood into four groups:

- **Group A** which has erythrocytes with A antigens;

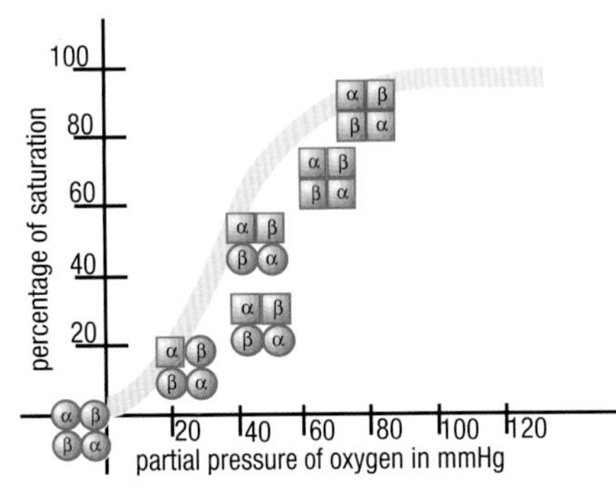

► **Diagram**
The curve shows the evolution of the saturation of hemoglobin to increase the partial pressure of oxygen: it is a similar behavior to that of regulatory enzymes, and shows that the binding of a molecule of oxygen strengthens the bonds later.

BLOOD GROUP (donor)	ANTIGENS PRESENT IN RED BLOOD CELLS	CAN PRODUCE ANTIBODIES	BLOOD GROUP (receiver)			
			A	B	A B	0
A	A	anti-B	○	–	○	–
B	B	anti-A	–	○	○	–
A B	A, B		–	–	○	–
0	none	anti-A anti-B	○	○	○	○

○ : no immunization — : reaction to immunization

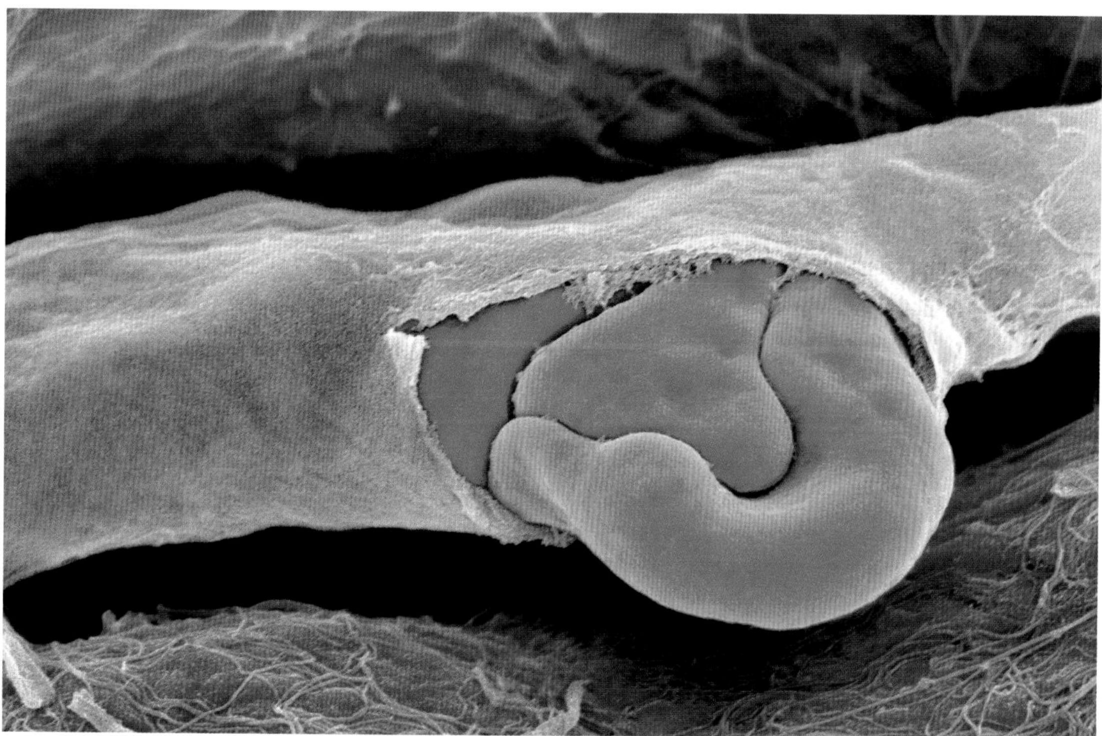

◀ **Lesion**
Scanning electron microscope image (SEM) of a damaged capillary: Primary hemostasis occurs to stem the outflow of blood

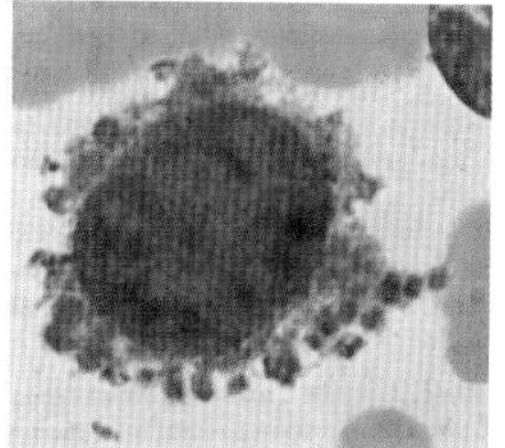

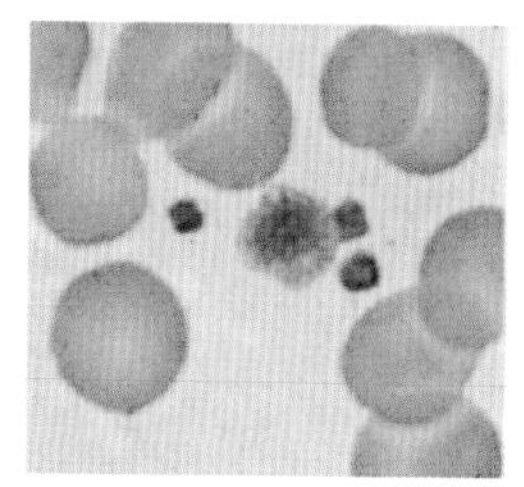

▲ **Platelets**
A megakaryocyte results in many piatrine while below, one can see platelets released in two dimensions.

- **Group B** which has erythrocytes that have B antigens;
- **0 group**, which has erythrocytes without antigens;
- **AB group**, which has red blood cells that have both the A antigen and the B antigen.

Since the body does not normally produce antibodies that are directed to attack substances already present in it, the four groups have different types of plasma; calling the α antibody 'anti-A' (antigen A) and the β antibody 'anti-B' (antigen B); they are characterised thus:

- **Group A**, plasma with antibodies α;
- **Group B**, plasma with antibodies β;
- **0 Group**, has plasma with antibodies α and β;
- **AB group**, has plasma without antibodies.

The presence of antibodies determines the compatibility between the types of blood. In a transfusion, the blood of the donor should not be recognised by the antibodies of the recipient, that is, it must have the same antigens or have none at all (as in the case of group 0 Rh-). To determine the blood group of a sample of blood, the red cells are diluted and divided into two parts which are then mixed, respectively, with serums containing antibodies known as α or β:

Agglutinated blood deduces the presence of antigens A or B, or their absence. Only the blood of group O does not agglutinate, and only that of AB is agglutinated in both cases.

In addition to the ABO system, there are many other antigenic blood systems. The Rh system, for instance, is used to denote the presence or absence of the rhesus antigen. Where it is present, the blood is labelled Rh+, and where it is absent it is marked Rh-. It is named after the species of monkey in whose blood it was first identified. It is particularly relevant in pregnancy - an Rh incompatibility is caused by foetal erythroblasts launching an immunological attack if the foetus is Rh+ and the mother is Rh-.

PLATELETS OR THROMBOCYTES

In an adult there are usually from 130,000 to 400,000 platelets/mm3 blood. They are irregular fragments of cytoplasm that are about 2 µm long, and that detach from megakaryocytes. These are large polyploid cells (which are characterised by a higher than usual number of chromosomes) that are found in the bone marrow ▸86. Platelets have a transparent exterior and a centre that is rich in granules that contain, among other things, thrombosthenin, a protein that can shrink, which is important for the formation of blood clots ▸88. Once produced, they rapidly enter the bloodstream where they live on average for ten days. A third of them, however, stay in the spleen as a sort of reserve

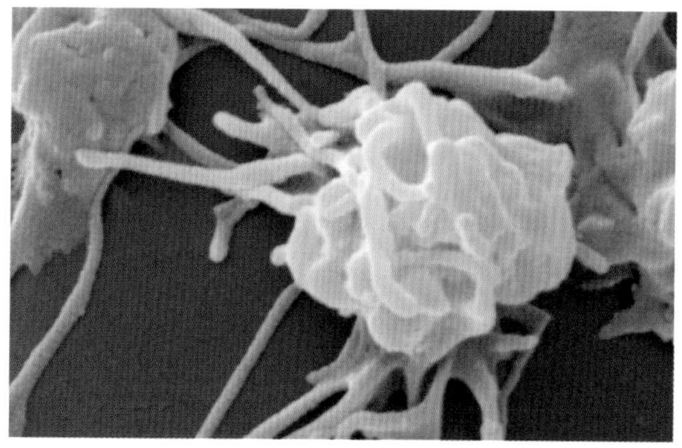

◀ **Platelets activated**
Scanning electron microscopy photograph of activated platelets: you can see the threadlike contractility extensions that will be retracting clot.

Formation of blood cells

In the adult human, all of the blood and lymph cells and their cellular elements are produced in a process called erythropoiesis. This takes place in the red bone marrow, which is found within the larger bones, such as the vertebrae, sternum, pelvis, skull, femur and humerus. These bodies, together with the liver, foetal spleen, and other types of bone marrow are called "haemopoietic" (from the Greek = producers of blood), and the process in which they specialise is referred to as 'haematopoiesis'.

The production of blood cells involves a number of stages. In the early foetus, it starts with the mesodermal cells in the yolk sac, but as development progresses, it later moves to the liver and spleen. It is essential that the body has a continuous supply of all types of blood cells as they only have a short life cycle. Usually the immature cells remain localised in the bone marrow and are only released into the blood stream when they have matured. If an analysis of the blood that is in circulation shows the presence of immature cells, it is an indication that there is a serious blood disease.

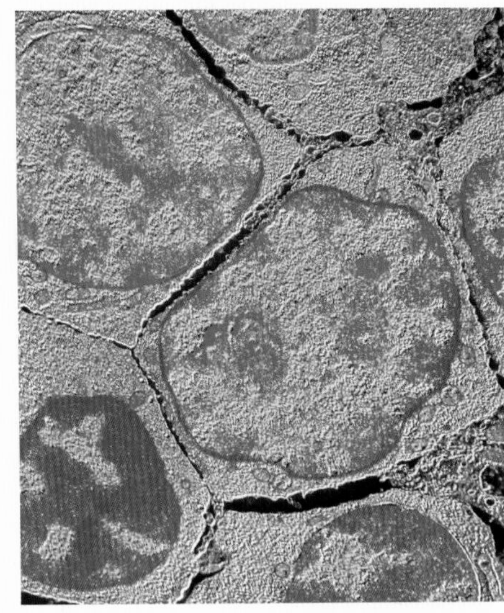

▲ **Erythroblast**
Primitive red cells photographed in the bone marrow: still have the nucleus.

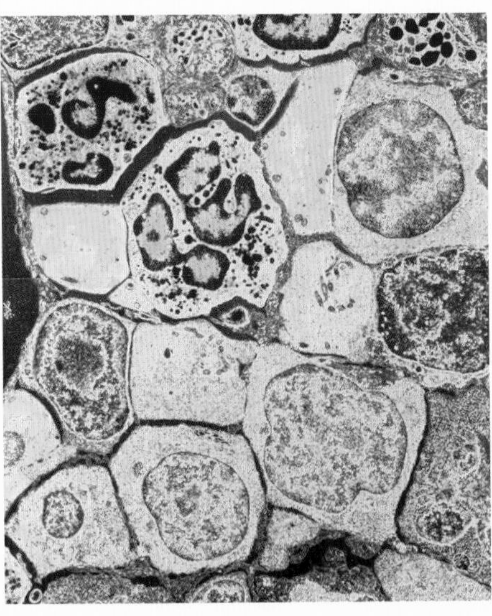

▲ **Bone Marrow Bone**
TEM Photography showing bone marrow with different precursors of blood elements.

▼ **Erythropoiesis**
Outline of development of both hematopoietic lines.

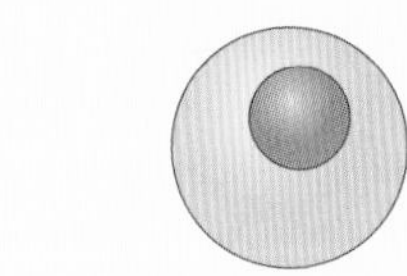

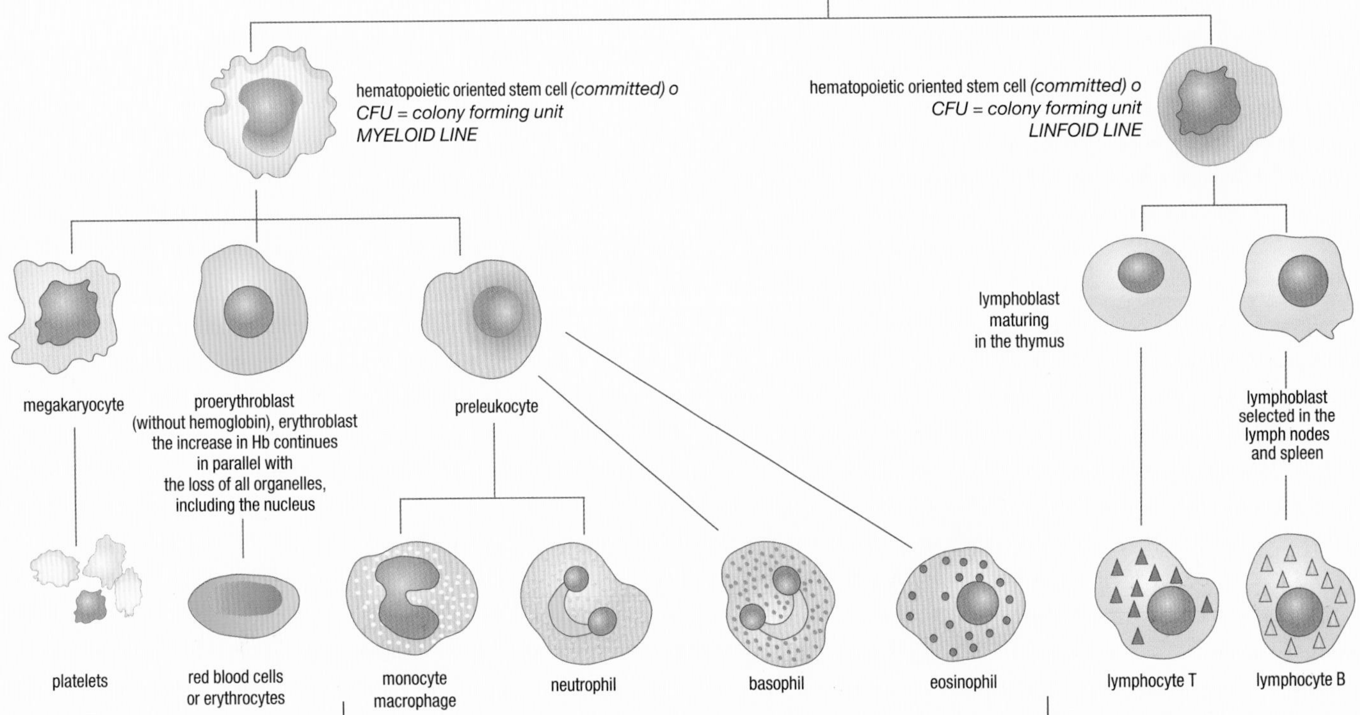

in order to intervene rapidly and extensively in the first stages of clotting blood.

BLOOD CLOTTING OR HAEMOSTASIS

Blood clotting is the process that blocks the loss of blood from a blood vessel. This is performed by a cascade of cellular and chemical reactions, and which is triggered by a stimulus such as the leakage of blood from a vessel, or a trauma in the wall of a vessel and the surrounding tissue. Alternatively, it may due to contact between blood or damaged endothelial cells and other elements of tissue that are normally outside the vascular wall. In this chain of reactions, each blood factor is characterised by a specific enzyme activity. It proceeds according to a mechanism called haemostasis which can either work in two different ways or in both simultaneously:

Extrinsic tissue factor pathway – this is where the clotting originates in the blood due to factors that are present in the blood plasma (these are XII, XI, IX and VIII, especially anti-haemophilia) and an essential factor not derived from platelets. These components come into action if the blood comes into contact with an anomalous surface;

Intrinsic contact activation pathway – this is where the coagulation starts from an injury that releases the tissue factor. The main elements involved in this process are: vessels and platelets, as well the cascade enzyme coagulation and fibrinolytic systems. This type of haemostasis, therefore, can be divided into four phases:

Vascular Phase – This is where the walls of a vessel are damaged – it exposes sub-endothelial connective tissue under the endothelium.

Platelet Activation Phase - Within a few seconds of the injury occurring, some platelets adhere to the collagen fibrils of the connective tissue in the sub-endothelial vessels. This accession process, as well as that of platelet aggregation, takes place thanks to the presence - on the surface of the platelets, of integrins. These are proteins that are triggered by specific receptors for collagen. Since the injury has exposed the blood to collagen, they will bind (if the endothelium is intact, however, the platelets continue to flow). The accession process, however, is not sufficient to bind the platelets at the site of the lesion. This requires the intervention of GPIb, a complex glycoprotein that is also present on the surface of platelets, which has the ability to bind to the von Willebrand factor (a glycoprotein adhesive normally present in plasma) that is produced by the endothelial cells. In this way, the link between the platelet receptors and the endothelium of the fibrils stabilises the adhesion of the platelets to the wall of the vessel. It then hardens, preventing the blood flow from dragging them away. Platelets are activated by important clotting factors such as serotonin, the key factor IV and V. These substances attract other platelets that bind to the first, forming the so-called primary platelet cap. This phase is sufficient to repair minor injuries, and is fulfilled in a few minutes. When considered with the vascular phase it is called primary haemostasis.

Coagulation Phase – This takes place only if the lesion is important and exposed to the action of factor III or TF (Tissue Factor). This molecule is the only element of the coagulation cascade that is linked to a membrane. Typical of extra-vascular tissue, TF also abounds in the cell membranes of adventitious blood vessels where it triggers the correct response to injury. Besides being a potent inducer of coagulation, it also acts as a cell signaller. If it comes into contact with blood, it binds to factor VII and, in the presence of calcium, the activity forms the complex thrombus-plastin TF-factor VII-Ca2+, active factor IX, and X factor.

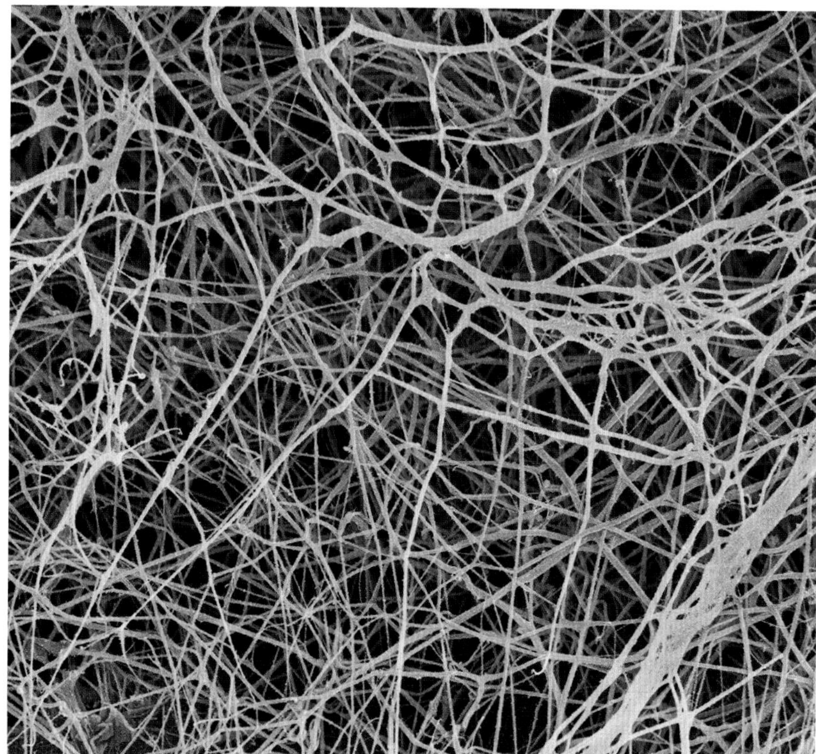

▲ **CLOT LATTICE**
Fibre weave of fibrin seen through a scanning electron microscope.

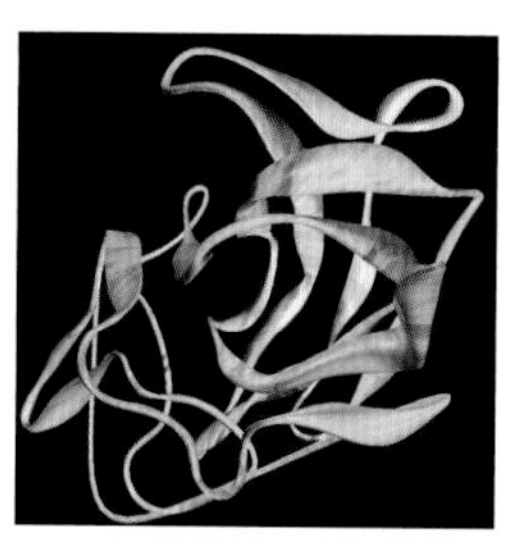

▼ **FACTOR VIII**
Computer model of factor VIII or antiemophilia globulin, normally present in inactive form in the plasma: its lack causes haemophilia.

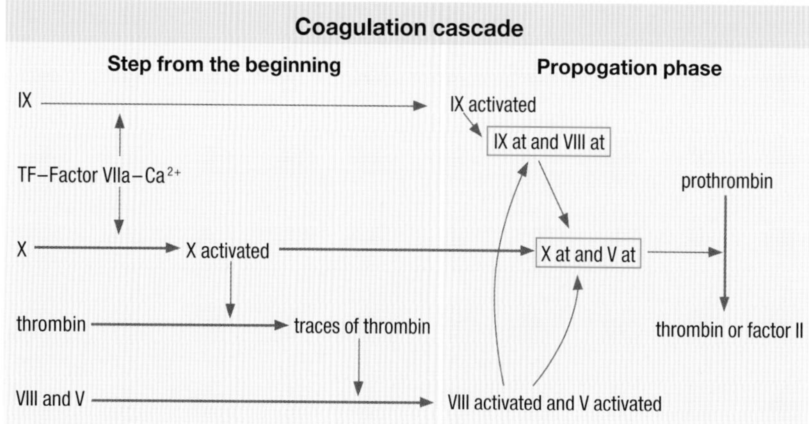

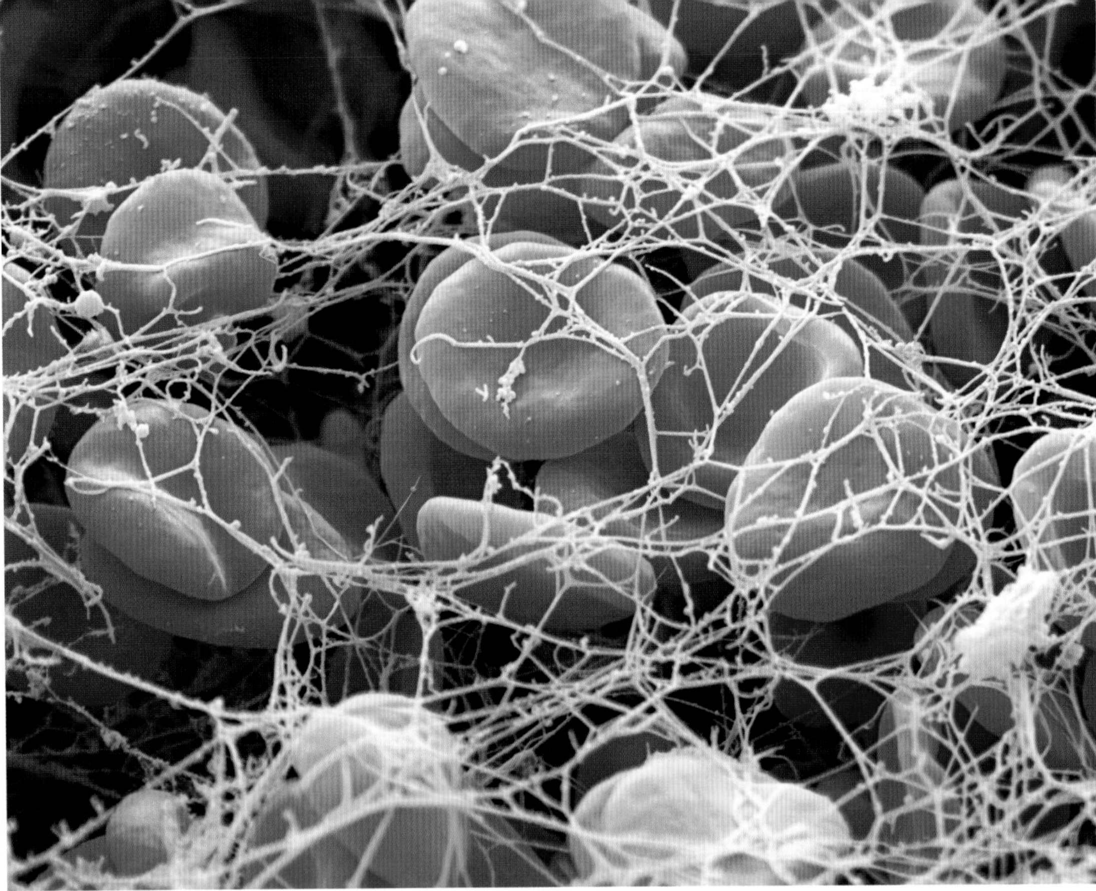

▼▶ **Blood clot**
Two different magnifications of a clot under a scanning electron microscope. Below, there are numerous platelets linked to one another with fibers that form the fibrin lattice of the clot, on the right: red blood cells trapped by fibrin strands.

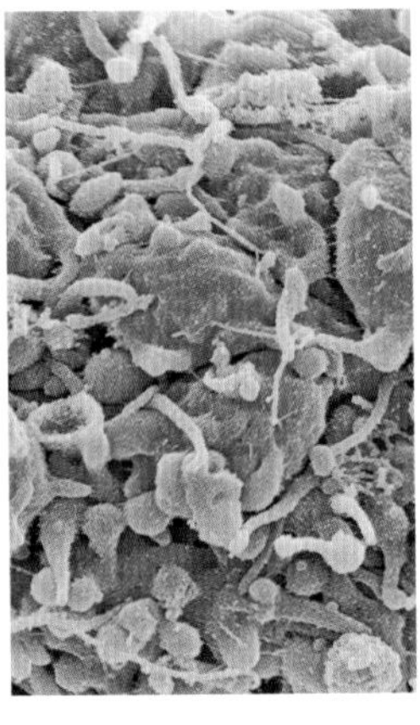

In turn, the X factor begins to produce thrombin, but a new tissue factor (TFPI, Tissue Factor Pathway Inhibitor) quickly blocks it. The traces of thrombin produced, however, are sufficient to stimulate the production of factors V and VIII that, together with the activated factor IX, amplify the clotting action. This phase of propagation is crucial: indeed, it allows the massive transformation of prothrombin - a γ2-globulin synthesised by the liver and normally present in plasma - into thrombin or factor II. Thrombin is a protein enzyme that processes fibrinogen (a glycoprotein synthesised in the liver by hepatocytes and megakaryocytes) and turns it into fibrin-monomers. These polymerise spontaneously into fibrin and form a stable clot thanks to factor XIII (plasma transglutaminase). Activated by thrombin, it stimulates the formation of covalent bonds between the adjacent molecules of fibrin. The fibrin also binds the plasminogen and forms a network of protein (lattice clot) where the blocked platelets remain, together with red and white blood cells.

With the production of the thrombus or platelet stopper that stops the bleeding at the site of the lesion, it closes the process of secondary haemostasis. The mechanism that regulates this second phase of haemostasis tends to limit the clot so that the chain of clotting reactions does not extend to any undamaged areas.

Fibrinolytic Phase - In reality this phase is not part of haemostasis, but is the series of events that restore normal physiological conditions in the injured area as well as normal blood flow. Once the lesion is repaired, the clot must be destroyed: this is what happens with fibrinolysis. It is a process that is regulated by mechanisms that ensure that everything takes place rapidly and only in the area of the injury. The removal of fibrin is vital to keep the clot intact while it is needed to stop the bleeding and, at the same time, to prevent the spontaneous formation of intra-vascular thrombi in other areas of the body. This is why fibrinolysis is governed by a complex control system.

It starts with the production and release by the endothelial cells of plasminogen activators: the most important is the tissue plasminogen activator (tPA) of urokinase. These substances are produced in response to cell damage or thrombin. Following various stimuli such as venous occlusion, physical effort, hypoglycaemia, hypovolemic shock, stress, or a reduction of mass of blood, they are released into the bloodstream. When this happens, they break the bonds between fibrin and plasminogen, and in doing so form plasmin. This is a proteolytic enzyme that degrades fibrin, fibrinogen and factors V and VIII. The uncontrolled release of plasmin would have devastating effects in the bloodstream if there were its inhibitors, which is why there are substances that can neutralise it quickly.

In a healthy body, the haemostasis system is always active. Even in normal physiological conditions, the body must deal with spontaneous micro-lesions or

Genetic diseases of the blood

Genes are segments of hereditary material (DNA) with specific functions: Since DNA can be modified, it may happen that a gene becomes altered for some reason. The result of this is a mutation - most of these have little or no consequence for the health of the individual. Some, however, can cause harmful effects and diseases that are transmitted in families according to the laws of hereditary.

The modified gene may well be part of a sex chromosome or on an autosome. Since there are two copies of each autosomal chromosome, we also have two copies of each gene. If the disease still occurs even when only a single gene has mutated, it is referred to as being autosomally dominant. On the other hand, if the disease only occurs when both copies of the gene have changed in the same way, it is known as an autosomally recessive disease. The same goes for mutations of genes on the X chromosome. The disease will always manifest itself in males (who have a single X chromosome), while in females (where there are two) diseases will only occur in autosomally dominant cases.

If the parents of a child are healthy carriers of an autosomally recessive disorder - that is, each of them is heterozygous for that disease, (therefore having one of two copies of the gene changed and the other normal) - every child has a 25% probability of inheriting the mutated gene. When the genes of both the father and the mother are homozygous there is a 50% probability of their offspring developing the disease. Among the autosomal recessive disorders, haemoglobinopathy - namely genetic diseases that alter the structure of haemoglobin - are among the most common worldwide. While heterozygous individuals may be healthy and may not even know they are carriers, those who are homozygous often suffer from severe health problems. Some of these conditions may require continuous transfusion or bone marrow transplants.

Haemoglobinopathy: The most common diseases are those which have undergone positive selection in malarious areas. Those individuals who are healthy carriers of α-o-β thalassemia or haemoglobin S (sickle-cell anaemia) are, in fact, able to prevent - within certain limits, infection by plasmodia (the parasitic protozoa which cause malaria). A comparison of the spread of these genetic alterations in the world's populations demonstrates just how much evolutionary pressure there is for such malarial resistance.

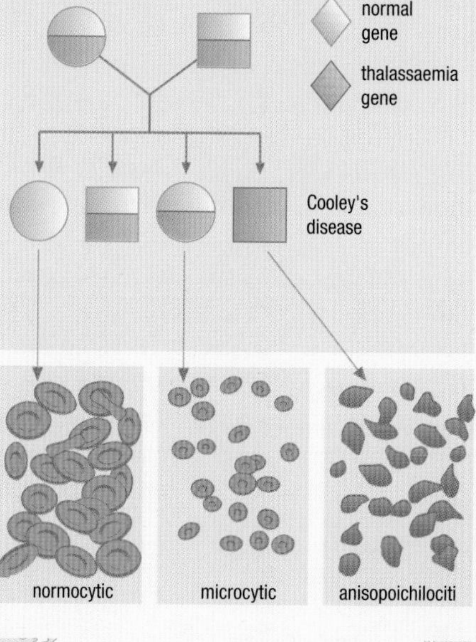

► **Inheritance**
Transmission of the thalassemia gene and its effects on blood. Heterozygotes in red blood cells are smaller than normal and the poorest have effects on hemoglobin (about 15% less) and 20% of heterozygotes have a slightly enlarged spleen. In most, however, production of red blood cells and hemoglobin is more than enough for a normal life. In the homozygote, however, the development of Cooley's disease, a severe anemia with reduced red blood cells, are deformed and contain hemoglobin in insufficient quantities. The homozygous therefore are forced to blood transfusions every 15-20 days, for life. In addition, the iron accumulation in major organs (heart, endocrine glands, liver) compromises the functions if nothing is done with appropriate medications.

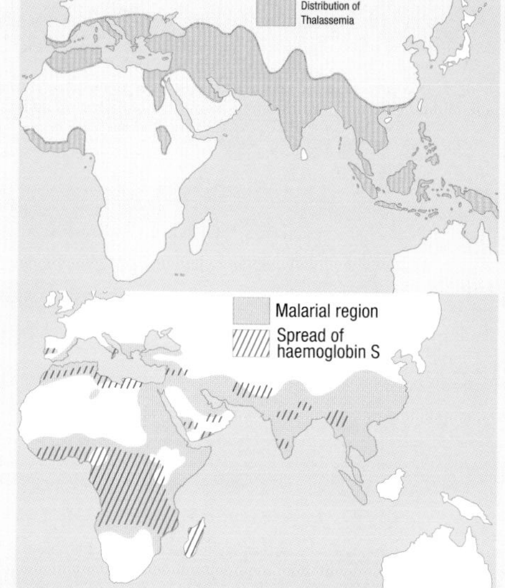

► **Planisphere**
Dissemination of genetic blood diseases worldwide and distribution areas of malaria.
The match is likely to constitute evidence in support of natural selection of positive hemoglobinopathy.

▲ **Anemia falciform**
Red cells containing hemoglobin S are deforming in the classical sickle shape of the same name for this type of anemia. When the hemoglobin S - consisting of 2 α chains from normal and abnormal β 2 chains - is exposed to a low partial pressure of oxygen they irreversibly polymerize. The deformation of red blood cells prevents the physiological functions and can block the blood vessels.

▲ **Consequences**
The transformation of red blood cells in falciform causes clogging of the circulatory vessels and necrosis from infarction in the "downstream" of the block. The spleen, which removes the inactive red cells thickens.

▶ **Abnormal clot**
Deterioration of balance can cause the formation of a thrombus endovasal.

▶▶ **Basophil**
Section of basophils in false color taken by transmission electron microscope (TEM).

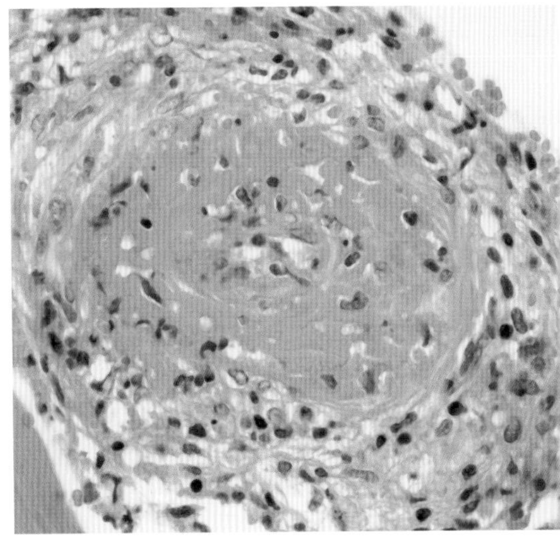

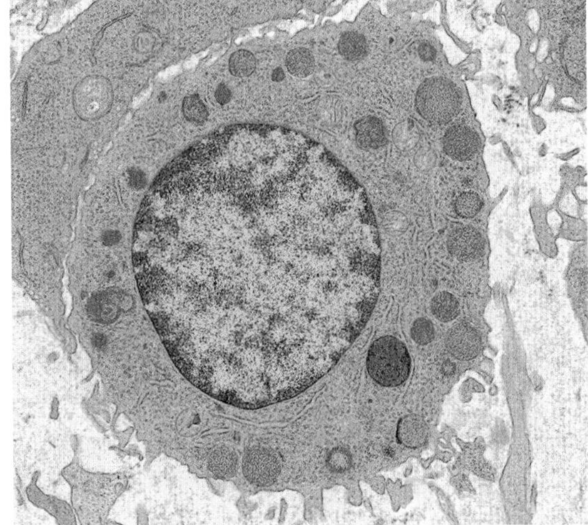

those derived from microtraumas, and a part of fibrinogen is continuously transformed into fibrin and then eliminated by fibrinolysis. If this state of balance alters, pathological conditions arise. If the balance shifts towards a decrease in haemostasis, the individual will develop haemorrhagic diseases. Conversely, thrombotic diseases arise if there is an uncontrolled activation of haemostasis. In both cases, health problems can be very serious. For example, individuals suffering from haemophilia - a genetic disease that is characterised by a lack of production of the plasma coagulation factors, risk fatal bleeding even from minor injuries. More common, but no less serious are the problems due to excessive clotting that occur within vessels rather than lesions. The production of TF as well as a decrease in the anticoagulant factors present in the blood, can begin to form pathological clotting (thrombosis). If it persists, this hampers the flow of blood in tissues such as heart or brain, and can soon lead to death.

In poor health, the delicate balances are kept under control by various physiological systems that prevent these conditions:

1. the Tissue Factor Pathway Inhibitor (TFPI); this is produced mainly by the endothelial cells of the capillaries, and is an enzyme that directly inhibits the factor X and the complex TF-factor VII, and is a key component for maintaining the normal haemostasis balance;

2. the antithrombin (AT), is an enzyme that is produced by the liver and is normally present in plasma. It is a serine protease that blocks the action of thrombin and factor VII, IX, X, XI and XII. Every molecule binds to inactivated clotting factors and forms a complex that is removed from the lattice-endothelial system;

3. protein C is another enzyme that is produced by the liver and enters the bloodstream in an inactive state. This vitamin K-dependent protease is activated by binding to the complex format thrombomodulin (TM, an endothelial membrane protein). This is facilitated by the presence on the surface of the Endothelial Protein C Receptor (EPCR). This is another protein membrane that has the effect of increasing the concentration of protein C around the TM;

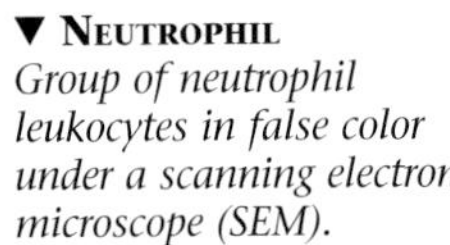

▼ **Neutrophil**
Group of neutrophil leukocytes in false color under a scanning electron microscope (SEM).

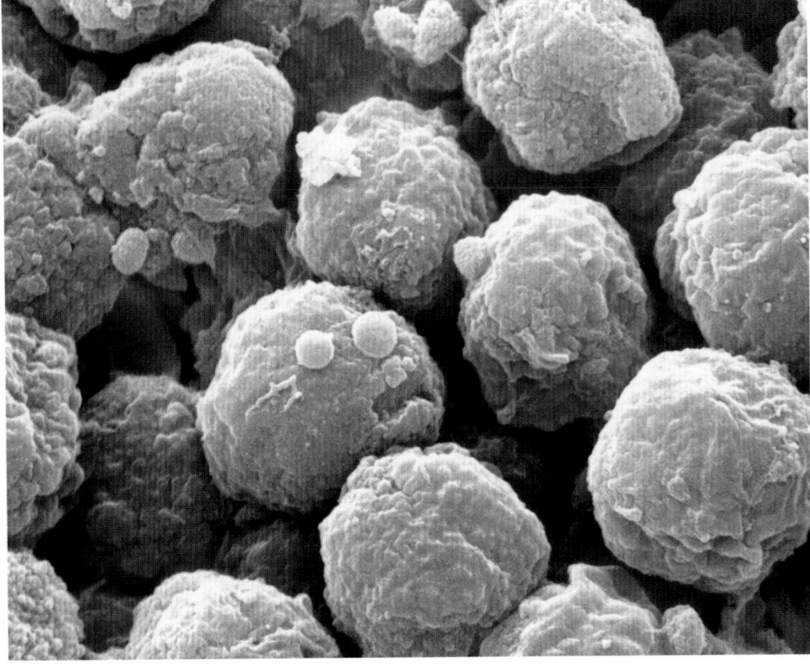

LEUKOCYTES OR WHITE BLOOD CELLS

Leukocytes are colourless blood cells that occur in fewer numbers than those of red blood cells. They have some very important functional properties, including motility. Besides being transported passively by the circulatory flow, they are also capable of amoeboid movements thanks to some of their cytoskeleton proteins. They are extremely deformable, and can pass through the vessel walls and move about in the intracellular areas (diapedesis). Leukocytes only leave the blood vessels, however, when it is actually necessary for them to

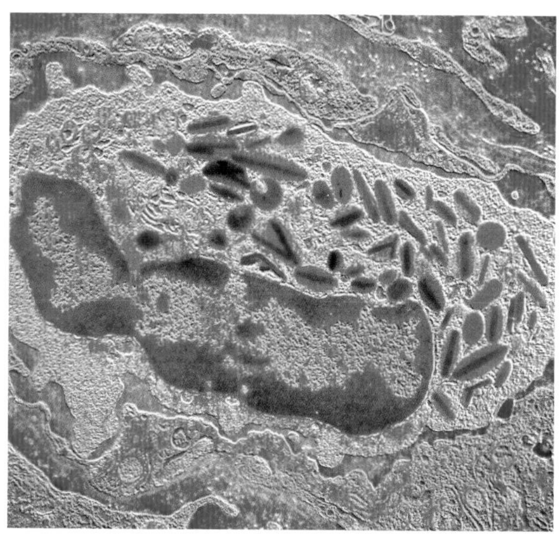

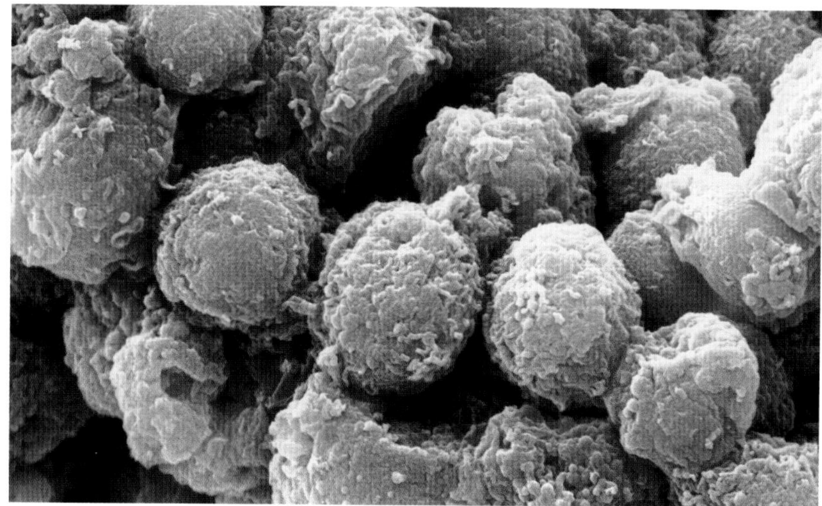

do so. This is stimulated by various chemical signals including cytokines and chemokines. They are produced by haematopoietic stem cells in the bone marrow. In general, the main function carried out by white blood cells is to defend the integrity of the body. They are used as defence mechanisms against aggressor organisms such as viruses, bacteria, fungi and parasites, as well as against foreign objects or substances. The term white blood cells, however, is generic - it includes cell populations that are structurally and behaviourally different. These are:

• Polymorphonuclear leukocytes; (PMN) are sometimes also called 'granulocytes' due to the typical graininess of their cytoplasm. They have a nucleus that is often lobed and are part of the myeloid line, the cells that are derived from the myeloblasts of red bone marrow ►86. They are divided into three groups, according to their affinity to certain histological dyes:

- Neutrophil leukocytes; these cells, together with monocytes ►92 and macrophages ►95 form the group that is collectively known as 'phagocytes'. These are aggressive cells that attack foreign organisms or particles, incorporating and then digesting them. They are capable of active movements, and migrate via chemotaxis. This means that they follow chemical stimuli such as the traces of bacterial, viral, complement or cytokine molecules ►102. During inflammation ►107 they become 'sticky' and adhere to the endothelia of vascular cells that, following the same chemotactic stimuli, have produced and exposed their membrane receptors. In essence, neutrophil leukocytes migrate from the blood vessels to the tissues that surround them, where they kill and digest infectious micro-organisms. The neutrophil leukocytes represent the first line of non-specific defence cells ►102 against infection. When they degenerate they liberate elastase and collagenase, enzymes that produce factors that attract more chemotactic monocytes. Their secretory ability is also an important part of the body's regulatory functions.
- Basophil leukocytes; these are relatively rare in the bloodstream (less than 1%), and have a diameter of 9-10 μm with a cytoplasm that is full of granular substances containing anticoagulants and vasodilators such as histamine and serotonin. Like the other leukocytes, they are also attracted by the substances that are produced by lymphocytes, and are also able to migrate out of blood vessels into the surrounding areas. They also react to complement receptors that have linked to foreign cells. Their presence stimulates the basophils to adhere to the cells and perform phagocytosis. This phagocytic ability is not the main function of basophils, however. Their primary role is to secrete substances that are needed to develop hypersensitivity reactions. They are particularly important when acute inflammation occurs ►107, which is the major component of the chronic injuries produced by immune reactions. When they degrade, they release histamine and serotonin that has significant effects on the permeability of the local blood vessels.
- Eosinophil leukocytes; these have an average life cycle of 6-12 hours, and are derived from the same progenitor cells as monocytes ►92, macrophages ►96, neutrophils and basophils. It is believed that their production is regulated by T-cells ►94, mainly through the secretion of interleukin-5 as well as other growth factors. These are used to stimulate the colonies of leukocytes and macrophages. The normal number of eosinophils in the blood stream is greater than 350/ml, although this varies during the day with a peak in the night and a minimum in the morning. Most reside in the tissues, but their roles there are not yet fully understood. They provide defences against intracellular bacteria, and although their phagocytic activities are less efficient than that of neutrophils. It is thought

▲ **Leukocytes**
Examples of leukocytes seen in false colors taken with a scanning electron microscope (SEM) and by transmission electron microscopy (TEM): on the left a section of eosinophils seen in the TEM, on the right a group of monocytes seen by SEM.

▼ **Amoeba movement**
The movement of chemotactic leukocytes occurs through contact points on fixed endothelial cells (receptors for adhesion) and the presence of cytoskeletal proteins migrating, polymerizing and making contract repeatedly.

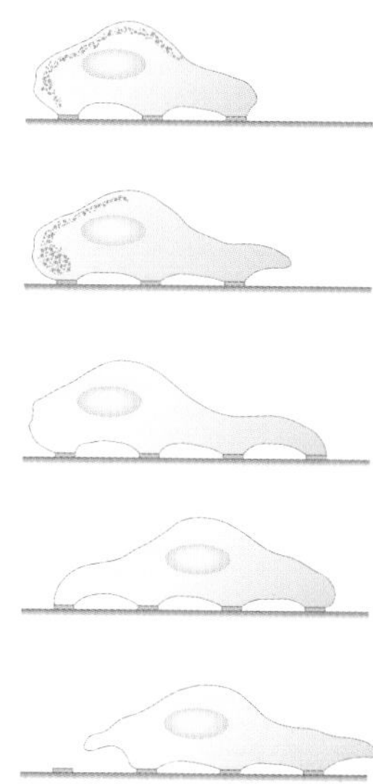

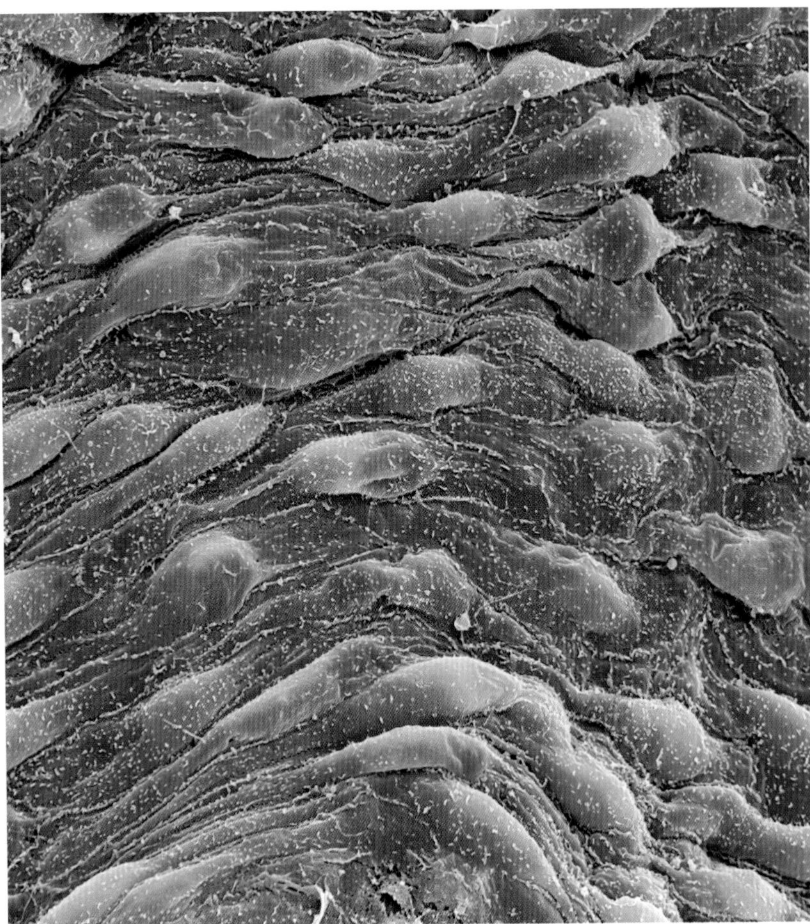

▲ **Vascular endothelium**
Endothelial cells in false color from a scanning electron microscope (SEM), viewed from inside of a blood vessel. The coverage of these individual cells, which are flat and thin (the swelling is produced by the cell nuclei) is not continuous: Here and there they are separated by pores, and between one and the other can become immune cells.

that that they may be toxic to helminths (parasitic worms), although this yet to be proven 'in vivo'. It is known, however, that the granules of their cytoplasm contain proteins that are toxic to various parasites. It is likely that they also have roles in the modulation of hypersensitivity reactions as well as in degrading inactivated mediators such as histamine, lysophospholipids or heparin that have been released by mast cells ►95. The proteins of their granules, in fact, bind to heparin and neutralise the anticoagulant activity.

- The agranulocytes or lymphoid cells; these are characterised by the absence of cytoplasmic granules. It is divided into:
  - Monocytes; these have a horseshoe nucleus and are the immature form of macrophages ►95. They are produced by the haematopoietic stem cells in the bone marrow ►86. Together with several other elements (macrophages, endothelial cells), they are an important part of the immune system ►138. Together with the leukocytes that are involved in the non-specific defence mechanisms ►102, they are able to perform phagocytic activities on foreign substances, bacteria and viruses which they digest with enzymes. They survive in the circulatory system for several months.
  - Lymphocytes, these are typical of lymph. Under normal circumstances, there are between 5000 and 10,000 leucocytes/mm3 blood in the average adult. The duration of their lives varies from a few hours to several years, depending on the type of cell. The proportions of the different populations vary - in adults, and in normal physiological conditions, there are typically 10,000 white blood cells present in every 1mm3 of blood. Of these, 49 – 78% are neutrophils, lymphocytes are 16-45%; 4-10% are monocytes, eosinophils are 0-7% and 0-2% are basophils.

THE INTERSTITIAL FLUID

The interstitial fluid is so-named as it is found in the areas between the cells. It is formed from blood plasma that filters through from the capillaries. Almost all of it is made up of serum, and the surplus quantities - that is, the liquids that are not absorbed into the venous blood vessels, gather in the vessels of the lymphatic system. It occurs in amounts that range from 2 to 4 litres per day. In a similar manner to that of blood, it consists of part fluid, part plasma and part corpuscles. Among these, the lymphocyte cells are the most abundant.

THE LYMPH

The lymph, which is a clear liquid that is incapable of clotting, is similar to blood plasma but has a greater proportion of water and lipids, and a lower content of mineral salts and proteins. These typically comprise around 0.5 - 5% by volume, and include many functional proteins, hormones and enzymes (as lipase, maltase and amylase). The lymph that is produced in the small intestine during digestion is referred to as 'chyle' - this is a pale coloured fluid that is rich in fatty acids.

LYMPHOCYTES

White blood cells are also present in the blood, but only reach a high percentage in the lymph. With a diameter of 7-15 µm, they have a round nucleus and a relatively low cytoplasm content. They are produced in the bone marrow ►86. Once they have matured, they enter the bloodstream and can also be found in the spleen and the lymph tissue that forms the ganglia or lymph nodes ►98.

There are three basic types of lymphocytes:

- B lymphocytes; these are named after the word 'bursa', a structure that was first discovered in birds by Hieronymus Fabricius in 1621. They are found in the tonsils, bone marrow, liver, appendix, Peyer's patch and other lymphoid tissues such as those associated with the digestive tract. None of these, however, have the necessary characteristics of the primary lymphoid organs. Some recent studies into comparative anatomy and immunology suggest that the structural and functional equivalent of the bursa in man is the coccygeal glomus (or coccygeal gland). This is always present from foetus to adult, and has a diameter of 2-3 mm. It is composed of irregular nodules, each of which is covered with connective tissue and is surrounded by glandular cells.

- T lymphocytes, or stem T-cells, are so-named because they mature in the thymus. During foetal development, the bone marrow produces stem cells T;
- Natural killer lymphocytes (NK); these play a very important role in the immune system. This is due to the presence of specific membrane receptors which identify foreign substances. This is achieved by the detection of particular groups or chemical sequences of amino acids – antigens, which they react to in a specific way. They are named after the fact that in order to perform their roles, they do not have to be activated.

The main differences between the lymphocytes are:

The B lymphocytes - these are the custodians of the body's immunological memory, and produce antibodies ▸102 which are released into the bloodstream ensuring humoral immunity ▸102.

The T lymphocytes – which are divided into various groups according to their functions:

- T Killer or TK lymphocytes; these recognise foreign micro-organisms and infected cells in the body and kill them. The process is mediated by the presence on the surface of the target of Major Histocompatibility Complex (MHC) molecules. These are complex polymorphic proteins which have a large inter-individual variability. In organ transplants they represent the main reason for donor rejection, as they are attacked by the recipient's cytotoxic T lymphocytes. This is why, in order to reduce cases of rejection, donors are so closely screened for MHC compatibility.

When cells have been infected by foreign matter, they are recognised by TK lymphocytes through protein fragments that are linked with the protein MCH. As a result of contact, the lymphocytes release perforin, a protein that is also secreted by

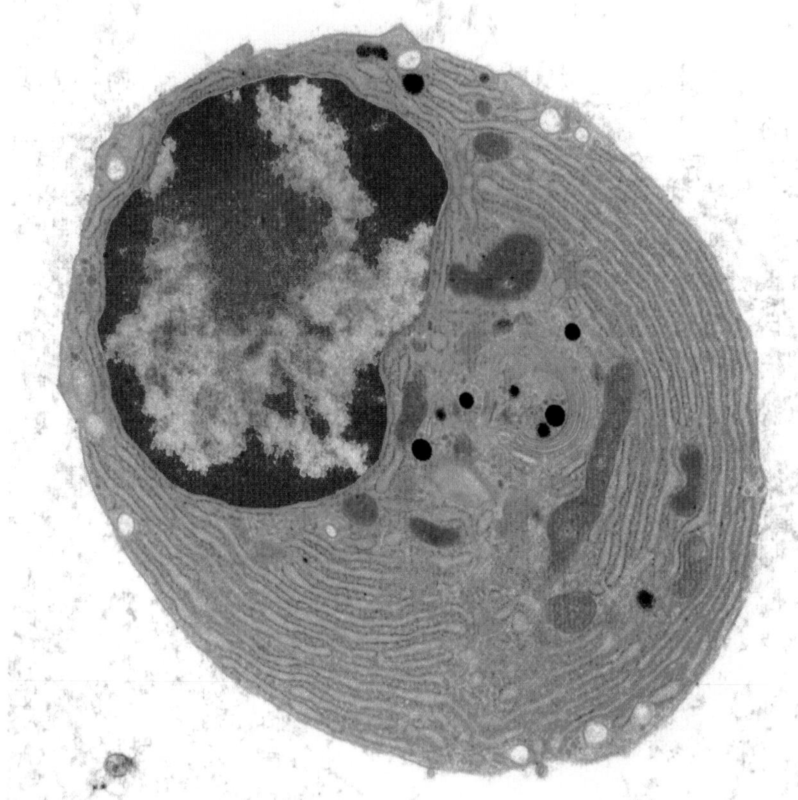

▲ **Lymphocyte**
Plasmacellular sectional view in false colors taken with a transmission electron microscopy (TEM): This is a mature B lymphocyte passing in a lymphatic circle.

◀ **Formation of lymph**
While red blood cells and other cellular elements remain in blood vessels, blood pressure pushes the plasma outside the capillaries.
*The water (**A**) passes freely through the endothelium, other substances (**B**, **C**) such as proteins, switch from pores of different diameter that interrupt the endothelium, but all follow the gradient of pressure. The plasma occupies the interstitial spaces surrounding tissue and the excess is absorbed where the pressure in the vessels decreases, or is being drained by lymphatic vessels.*
❶ wall of the capillary; ❷ surrounding tissue; ❸ erythrocytes; ❹ leukocytes; ❺ pores; ❻ lymphatic vessel.

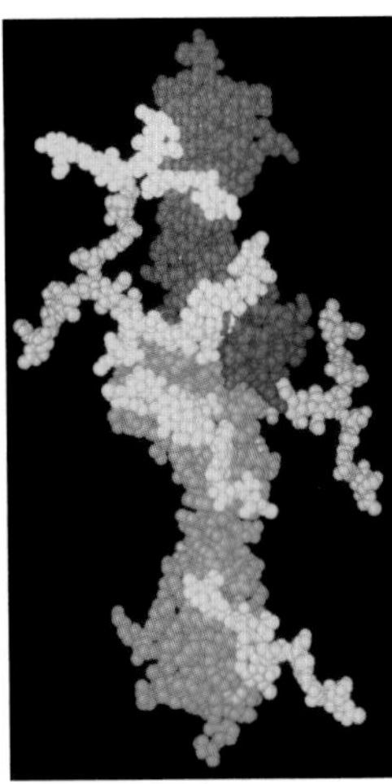

▲ **Adhesive molecule**
Reconstruction of a sticky CD2 molecule (red) linked to another CD2 molecule (green) and a structure of oligosaccharides (yellow). This type of molecule membrane of T cells allows them to adhere to other cells (infected or foreign): these were the first of the adhesion molecules, which have been given chemical structure.

▼ **T killer**
Action of a cytotoxic T lymphocyte

▼▶ **Natural killer**
An NK in false colors from a scanning electron microscope (SEM).

natural killer cells. In the presence of calcium, each molecule of perforin is able to cross the target cell's membrane, where they polymerise and form a pore. This forms a gateway into the target cell, which then allows the enzymes that trigger the cell apoptosis to enter. They then initiate a process that causes the destruction of the cell by exploiting the electrolytic gradient to induce osmotic lysis ▶104;

– T Helper lymphocytes or TH cells – these support the action of other immune cells coming into contact with them through the MHC molecules and producing lymphokines, substances that modulate the immune response. In turn, this lymphocytes are divided into two groups:
  • Type 1 Helper or TH1 cells – these secrete three different types of signalling molecules (cytokines) that have actions targeted at activating macrophages ▶95 and lymphocytes:
  – Interleukin 2 or IL2; this activates the TK and other TH cells;
  – Gamma interferon activates the TK and stimulates the answers antivirals;
  – the tumour necrosis factor beta or (TNF-β) is able to induce cell death;
  • Type 2 Helper or TH2 cells – these secrete three types of cytokines and other protein messengers that stimulate lymphocytes:
  – Interleukin 4 and interleukin 5 cause the proliferation and activation of B lymphocytes;
  – Interleukin 6 stimulates the production of antibodies in B lymphocytes;

– T Suppresser or TS lymphocytes modulate the immune response, either slowing it down or blocking it completely.

The Natural Killer lymphocytes (NK) – these were originally considered to be T lymphocytes, but it has been found that they are quite distinct from both T and B lymphocytes. This is despite the fact that they all originate from bone marrow precursors common to other lymphocytes ▶92. The NK lymphocytes are larger and have a richer cytoplasm as well as a granular form (and so are related to Large Granular Lymphocytes). The 10-15% of lymphocytes that are in the spleen or blood circulation are of this type, but their percentage is much lower in other lymphoid organs. They are named after the fact that in vitro they can kill many types of cells without having any activation or immune stimulation. It seems that their main function is to contain viral infections, pending the specific responses that are mediated by the T-cells ▶93. The natural killers, in fact, are able to directly kill cells infected by viruses other than those of cancer. Unlike what happens in other lymphocytes, they activate without any clonal expansion or cell differentiation. This is triggered when a signal is received that is opposed produced by two types of receptors:

– receptor-acting activators; these include both receptors that recognise a wide variety of molecules of carbohydrates present on many cells, and the receptors that are responsible for the cytotoxicity that is mediated by antibodies ▶108;
– receptor-acting inhibitors; these are part of the group of immunoglobulins, and recognise proteins HLA-B, HLA-C and HLA-E (MHC-1 and 1b) and prevent the killing of normal cells.

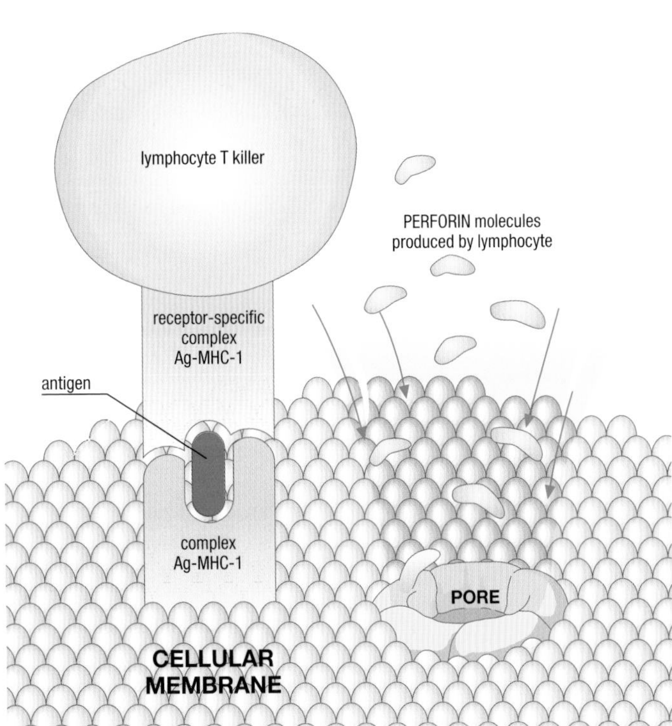

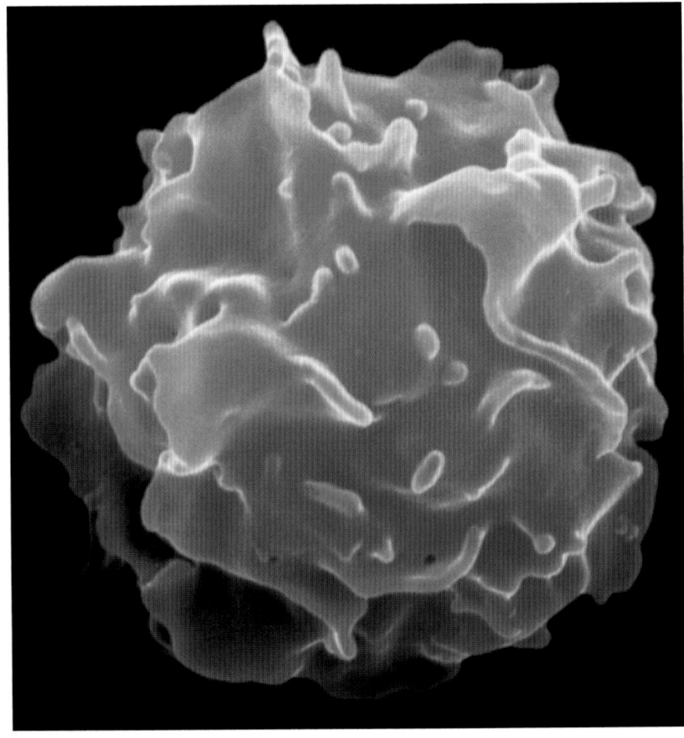

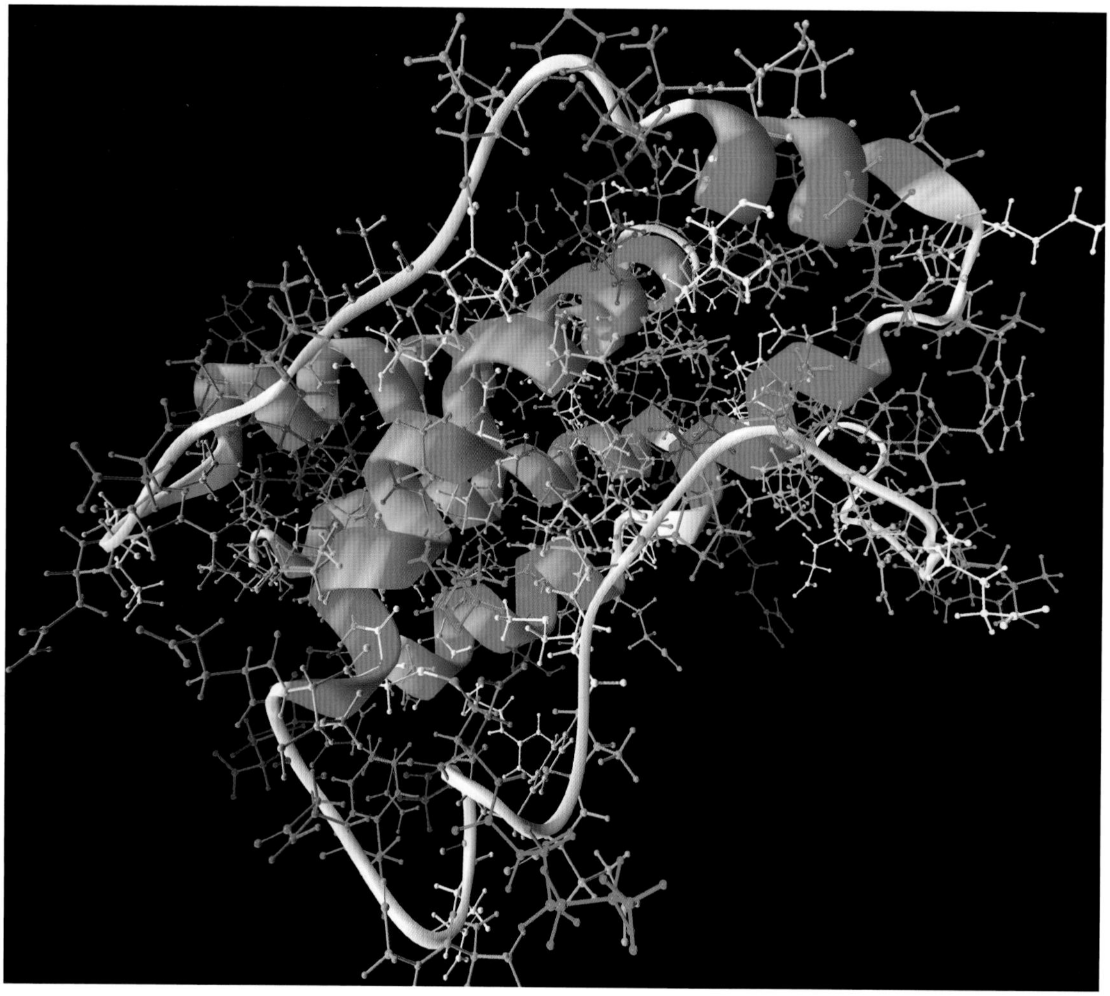

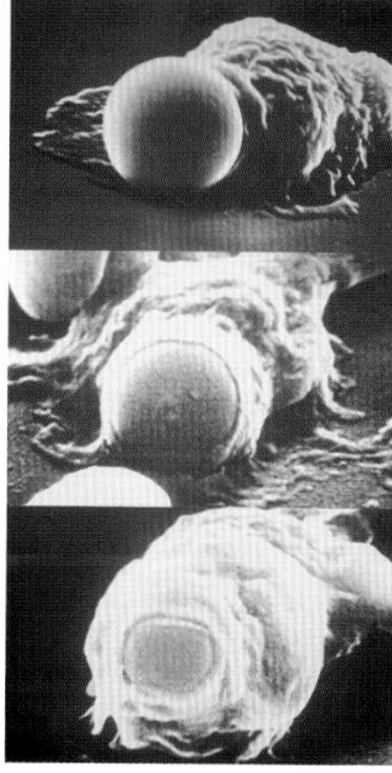

▲◄ **INTERLEUKIN 6**
biochemical Structure of interleukin 6 produced by TH2.

▲ **IN ACTION**
A macrophage absorbs a mature erythrocyte.

▼ **MACROPHAGE**
A section of a macrophage seen in false color by a transmission electron microscopy (TEM).

MACROPHAGES & HISTIOCYTES

Macrophages and histiocytes are forms of monocytes ►92 and both are important parts of the immune system. They are divided into:

- fixed tissue macrophages, these are cells with long survival times that are distributed in various tissues of the body and derived from circulating monocytes; their precise physiological role is not well understood;
- histiocytes, these are cells that are capable of active movements, such as the neutrophil leukocytes ►91 and monocytes. Following an infection ►100 or inflammation ►107 they migrate outside the circulatory system and lymphatic vessels to follow chemical stimuli via chemotaxis. They have the ability to incorporate and destroy foreign bodies, such as micro-organisms, foreign proteins, and infected or decomposing cells). The macrophages may have different levels of activation and are able to produce and secrete numerous inflammatory mediators.

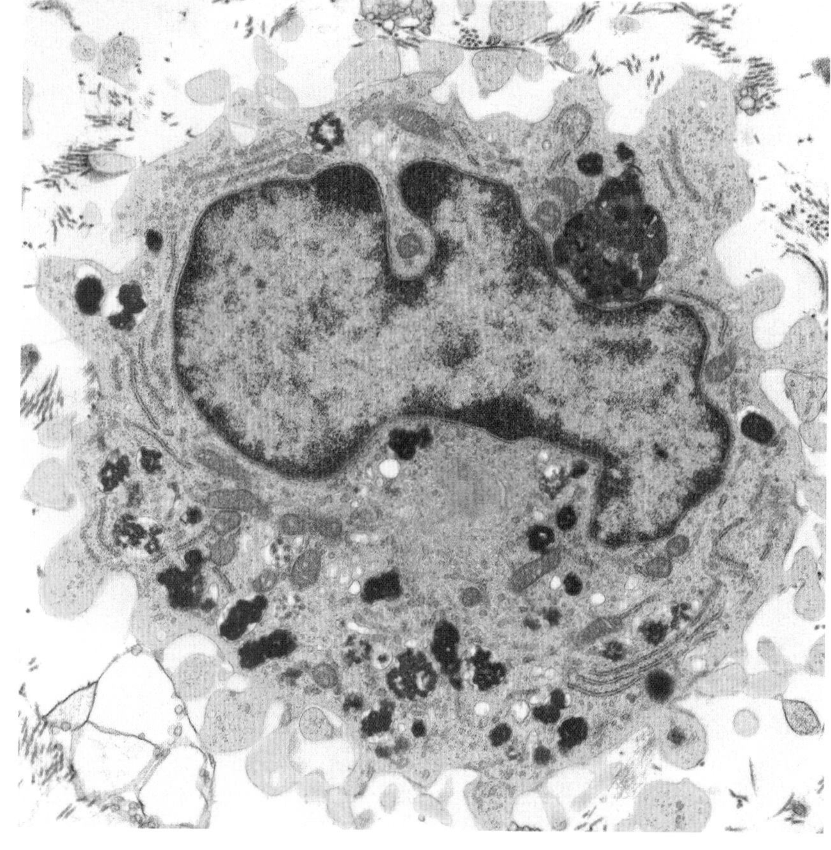

THE MASTOCYTES, PRODUCERS OF HISTAMINE

The mastocyte cells are cells of the immune system that are produced by the bone marrow ►86 which, in undifferentiated form, pass into the blood

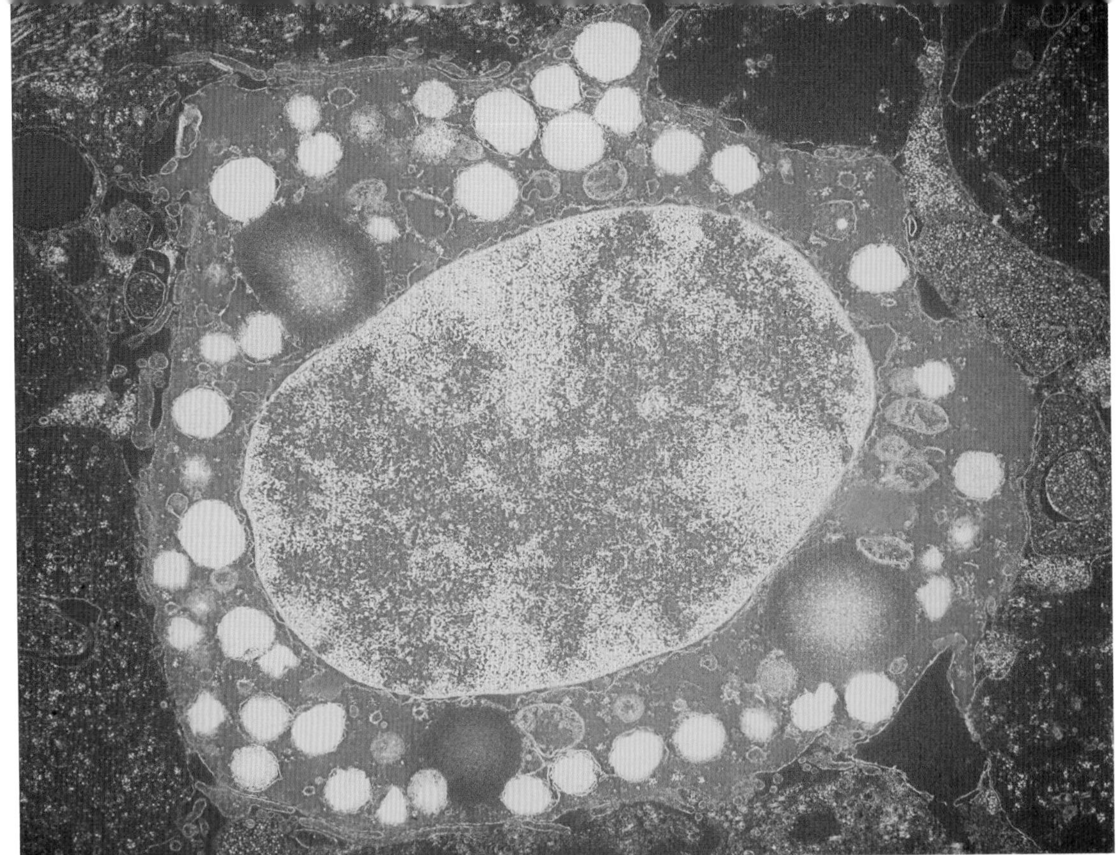

► **Mastocyte**
Section of a connective tissue of mastocyte cells, in false color transmission electron microscopy (TEM). You can see the nucleus (bright) and the cytoplasm (dark green) and granules (pink). In response to environmental stimuli they release their contents to the outside.

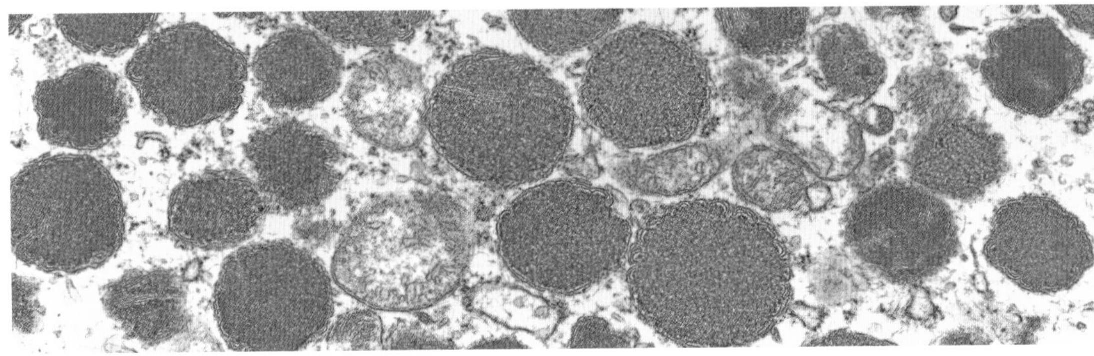

► **Granules**
Details of the granules of a mastocyte. They contain mainly heparin (anticoagulant), histamine (hormone that increases vascular permeability) and serotonin (a neurotransmitter).

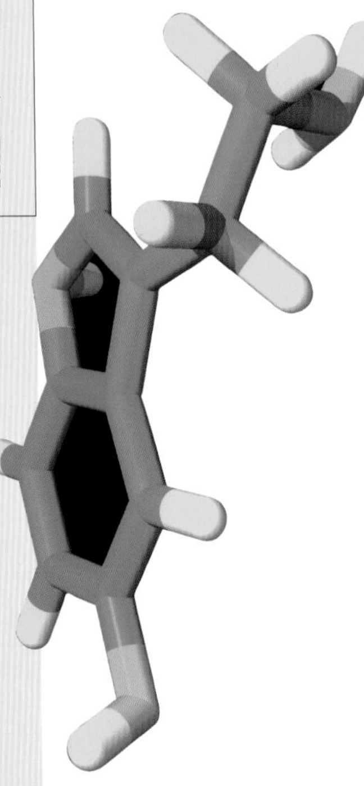

▼ **Serotons**
Molecular structure.

stream and then into specific tissues. They disperse throughout the connective tissues ►38 of the entire body, focusing mainly around the veins, skin and mucous membranes. Once this has happened, they complete their differentiation in response to the release of certain micro-environmental factors. The largest of these is the SCF (Stem Cell Factor), a substance that is produced by different types of cells, such as the mesenchymal, keratinocytes and neurons, which bind to the receptor membrane of the mastocyte.

The mastocyte cells are a heterogeneous group of cells that are characterised by a cytoplasm which is rich in granules. These contain mainly histamine, but also enzymes, heparin and other substances. When the immunoglobulin E (IgE) ►102, which is located on the membrane surface of mastocyte cells, recognises specific foreign bodies (allergens), the granules release their contents into the environment.

The mastocyte cells have a function in monitoring the immunological system, and act so as to amplify the defensive reaction against bacteria and parasites. The speed of their action, and the magnitude of their effects can often cause circulatory collapse and anaphylactic shock. In addition to intervening in allergies, anaphylactic reactions and hypersensitivity, mastocytes stimulate the vascular system playing an important role in several inflammatory conditions such as parasitism and inflammation of the nervous system.

In addition, they provide a vital protective function when sepsis occurs - a severe bacterial infection of potentially lethal blood, occurs. They are also capable of destroying endothelin-1, a substance that the body produces in large amounts and causes extreme constriction in the veins. As a result, the mastocyte cells help to mediate the effects of some of the most serious symptoms of diseases that could otherwise cause death.

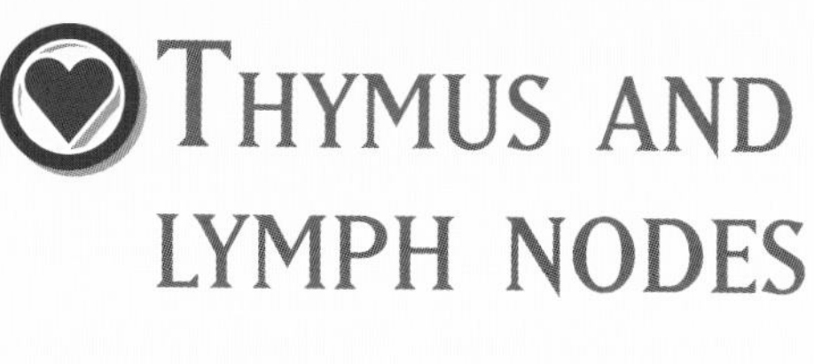

THYMUS AND LYMPH NODES

The thymus and lymph nodes are the bodies which govern the specialisation of the lymphocytes. While the thymus "teaches" the various types of T cells to distinguish between foreign cells and the body's own cells, the lymph nodes stimulate B lymphocytes to develop into specialised immune response cells.

The Thymus

The thymus is a lympho-epithelial body that consists of a large quantity of lobules each of which is divided into a cortical area and bone marrow. It is characterised by three types of cells:

The epithelial reticular cells which contain secretory granules that release thymic hormones occur in six different forms.

The thymic or Hassall's corpuscles are located in the thymic medulla, however, their actual role is poorly understood other than the fact that they produce certain cytokines.

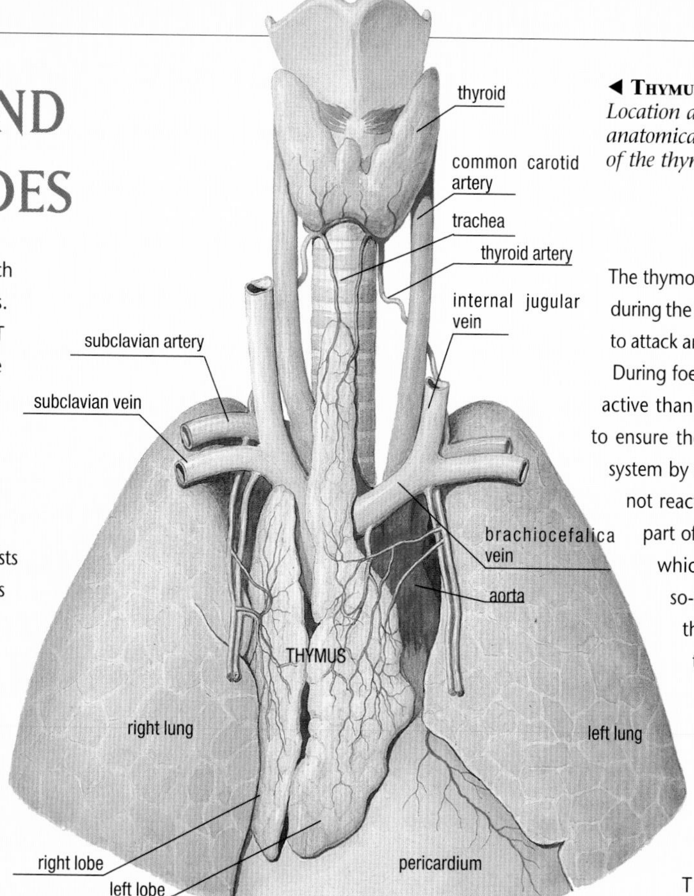

◀ **Thymus**
Location and main anatomical elements of the thymus.

The thymocytes (T cells) are especially significant during the foetal period, and are used by the body to attack and neutralise pathogens.

During foetal growth, the thymus is much more active than it is during adult life. Its function is to ensure the proper maturation of the immune system by selecting only lymphocytes which do not react against the body's own cells. A key part of this process is undertaken by T cells, which are special lymphocytes that are so-called because they are derived from the thymus. Negative selection is used to quickly eliminate those T cells that attack the wrong cells. In this way, the only ones that survive are those that do not attack the body. They can proliferate, mature and migrate into tissues where they take part in cytotoxic action, or act as helper T cells. The cellular and molecular mechanisms that underlie this selection

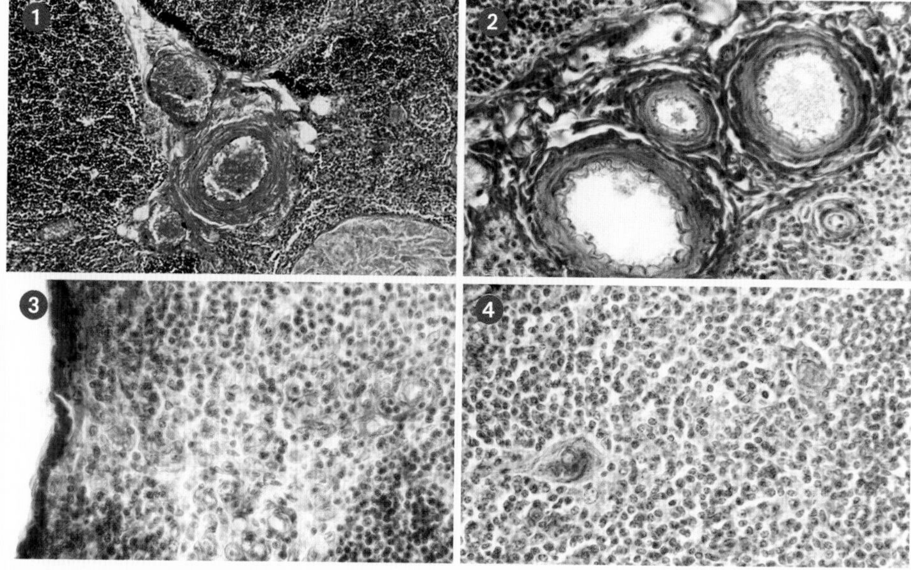

▲ **Microscopic structure of the thymus**
❶ Section of thymus through an optical microscope: divided into lobules by septa of connective tissue (white space) the thymus is traversed by blood vessels (center and right). In this body there are two very different parts in function and in structure: the cortex, the more superficial (in blue) and the marrow inside. The circular areas and the pink inside of the marrow of Hassal corpuscles. ❷ Centered on some blood vessels (white) surrounded by a fibrous capsule (blue), this photo shows the upper left of the cortex, densely populated, and the lower right the marrow, where the T cells migrate before returning. Section ❸ of the cortex under the optical microscope. In blue on the left, the T lymphocytes that are here are in active proliferation and, when mature, migrate to the marrow below. Section ❹ of the marrow through the optical microscope. Top, purple and oval, has a Hassal corpuscle. Aging T lymphocytes are colored red.

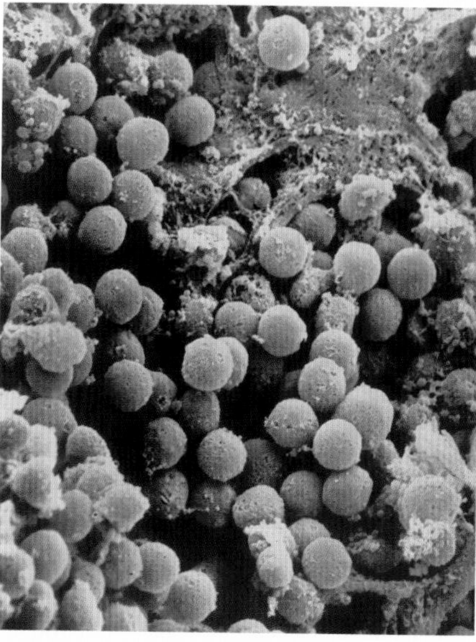

▲ **Lymphocytes T**
SEM Photograph in false colors of the thymus cortex: green beads are T lymphocytes.

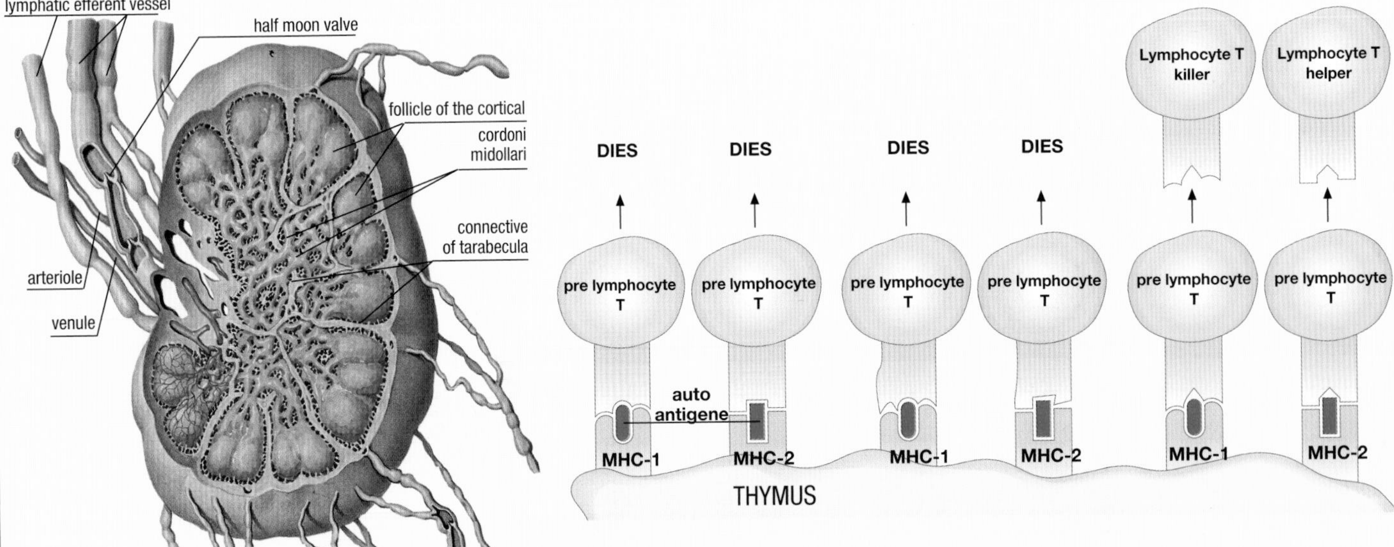

▲ **Lymph node**
Anatomical Structure

▲ **Selction of T lymphocytes**
Thymus cells exhibiting MHC proteins bound to their antigens: lymphocytes that do not recognize the MHC proteins or react to the complex, are eliminated. Lymphocytes that can recognize the MHC proteins but not autoantigenic, breed and mature in TK and TH.

process are not yet fully understood. In addition, recent research has emphasised the crucial role of the Autoimmune Regulator (abbreviated AIRE) which is located in the thymus. It is known to be involved in the reactions of some kinds of autoimmune diseases, and ensures the development of immunological tolerance, namely the ability of T cells to recognise cells of the body without destroying them. In the absence of AIRE, the T-cells attack the body's cells, rendering it incapable of defending itself against infectious agents. The population of lymphocytes also changes according to the roles that they play: while the membranes of the T cells have both the CD4 and the CD8 protein receptors, the mature lymphocytes only have one or the other. After birth, the passage of time reduces the size of the thymus and, simultaneously, decreases its function. The immune system, therefore, tends to weaken. It decreases until, in adulthood, it is almost indistinguishable from the surrounding connective tissues, with some minor differences according to sex. Several studies have shown, in fact, that in women the thymus remains active for longer. It is possible that this is why the average female's life is longer than that of males. At the same age, women have a greater number of T cells, and it may be that this keeps the immune system more responsive, and thus better able to cope with infection.

The Lymph Nodes

The lymph nodes are 600-700 organelles consisting of a small ovoid globular mass of magnitudes varying from that of a pinhead to that of a hazelnut. They are spread throughout the body or grouped into long cords, and are in direct contact with the network of lymphatic vessels. They take their name from the area of the body from which the lymph drains (e.g. inguinal lymph nodes). They are enclosed by a capsule

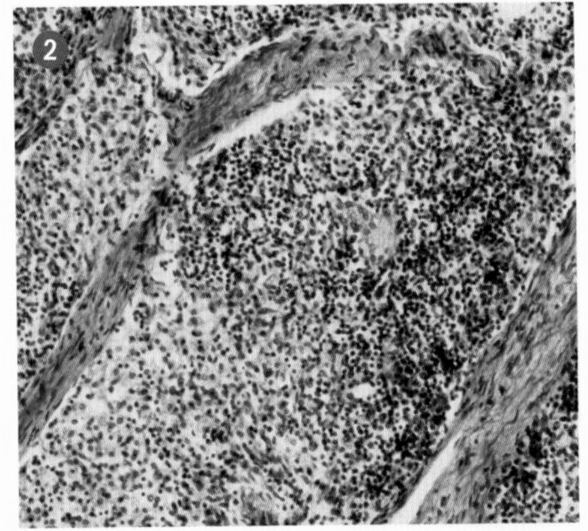

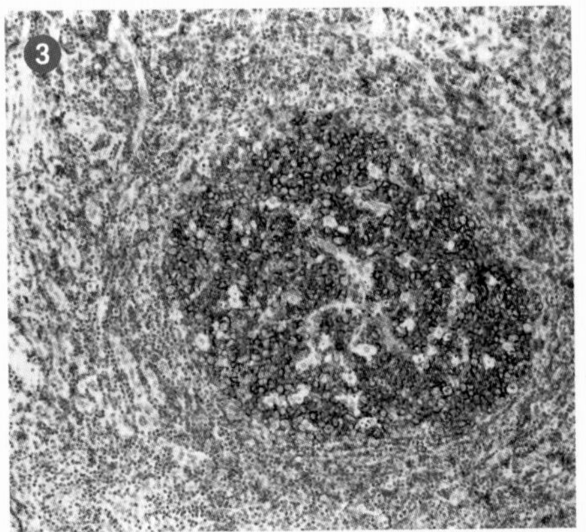

▲ **Microscopic structure of a lymph node**
❶ A section of the outer zone of a lymph node under an optical microscope: below the fibrous capsule (blue, top right), is the subcapsular (white) which extends the use of trabecular connective tissue (blue filaments) which separate the follicles. Purple macrophages (follicular dendrites) that the internal sinuses use to filter the lymph fluid, collecting and processing antigens that "present" to B lymphocytes, identified by the dark color of their nuclei, and stored in the follicles. ❷ Each node consists of follicles separated by connective tissue (blue). In this picture there are a mass of lymphocytes (purple). ❸ Detail of a follicle seen under the optical microscope. Germinating in the center (brown) are the B lymphocytes and the immune specialized cells (follicular inside). Thus, B lymphocytes begin to divide (more clearly in the middle).

▼ Movement of lymphocytes
Produced by bone marrow, lymphocytes reach the blood by circulating through all the other lymphoid organs (primary and secondary). But there are still not fixed to a particular place: all mature lymphocytes are present in the body in continuous flow through all the bodies involved. For example, "filtering" through the arterioles of a lymph node, they can establish themselves within it, but if they are not stimulated by an antigenic reaction, after varying periods they continue to move through the lymphatic vessels and again reach the bloodstream through the thoracic duct. This continuous flow of defensive cells through the body helps to trigger an immediate reaction in case of need.

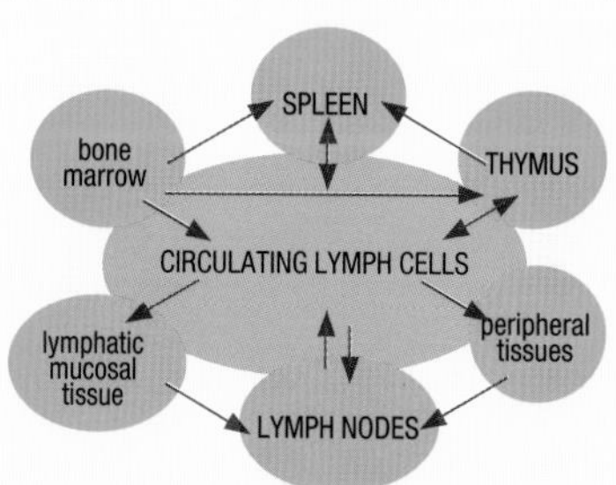

▶ Cells in a lymph node
False-color electron microscope photograph of a section of lymph node showing a medullary cord area. We can distinguish the fine reticular cells that form connective tissue (dark red), lymphocytes (pink), erythrocytes (red) and macrophages or follicular dentre (light brown).

of connective tissue, and inside, the cortical area is formed by numerous lymphatic follicles.

The lymph nodes contain a number of structures that are destined for the interception of foreign objects or substances. These are the monocytes, macrophages, dendritic cells and follicular dendrites, all of which are cells with phagocytic capacity. That is, to remove extraneous agents and trap on their surfaces proteins and the parts of microbes that have been destroyed, as well as to help to concentrate the antigens and to mark target structures as being suitable for lymphocyte action and to stimulate the production of B lymphocytes. When this happens, every follicle lymph node becomes a germinative centre where, thanks to the production of specific B and T lymphocytes, a complex set of cell interactions takes place. These are between dendritic cells and T lymphocytes, including follicular dendritic cells and B lymphocytes, including T-cells and B lymphocytes - which ends with the differentiation of B lymphocytes. Contact with the complex antigen-MHC proteins, in fact, encourages them to become plasma cells that begin intensive production of large quantities of antibodies. At the same time, some B lymphocytes become plasmocytes or "memory cells" that can trigger the same immune reaction in case of a second infection.

Sometimes the reaction that takes place in the lymph nodes, and which is characterised by a remarkable proliferation of the plasma cells that produce antibodies, is so fast and intense that they swell considerably. This can often be distinguished by the naked eye as well as by touch, and normally occurs in the lymph nodes closest to the point where it started, or where infection / inflammation is developing. Their reaction, in fact, is designed to limit the immune reaction to the affected area, preventing infection from spreading to other areas of the body.

▶ Lymphatic system
The lymphatic system consists of about 1 kg of lymphatic tissue, including the primary lymphoid organs (bone marrow, fetal liver and spleen, thymus) and secondary or peripheral lymphoid organs (lymph nodes, spleen, plaques of Peyer and gastrointestinal tissues). In total about 1000 billion cells that run incessantly throughout the body, monitoring the integrity, of which 10 million are replaced by new cells every minute.

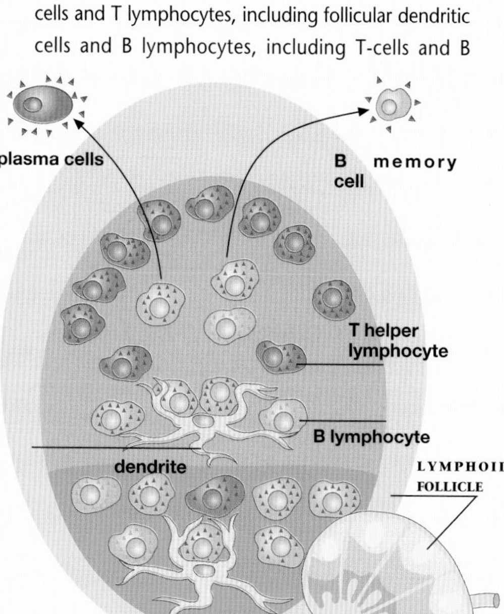

◀ Functions of a lymph node
Because among the millions of immunocompetent cells to have the "right" to meet the antigen which is specific when it enters the body, it is necessary that the meeting is made possible. In addition to an intense lymphocyte movement, therefore, the process involves lymph nodes: continuously filtering the sap circulating through follicular dendrites activate lymphocytes that differentiate into plasma cells and memory cells.

CELLULAR ELEMENTS OF BLOOD AND LYMPH ARE ALSO ENTRUSTED WITH THE IMPORTANT FUNCTION OF PRESERVING THE INTERNAL ENVIRONMENT FROM THE INVASION OF FOREIGN PARTICLES AND TOXIC SUBSTANCES THAT COULD DAMAGE IT.

THE BODY'S DEFENSES

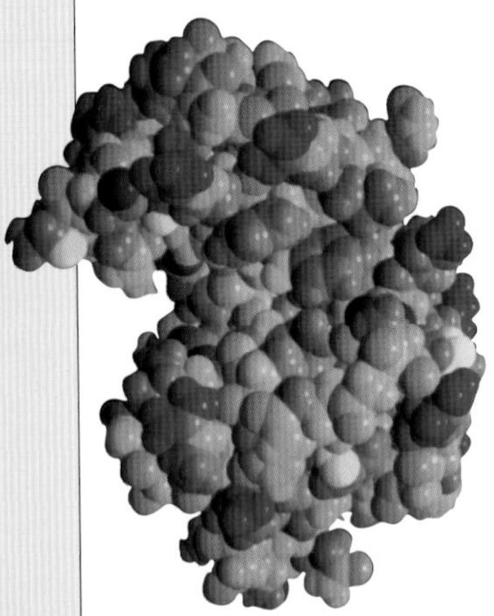

▲ **LYSOZYME**
Structure of a lysozyme molecule created on a computer. Its stereochemistry is crucial so that this enzyme can play its antibacterial action.

Like that of all living beings, even the human body is part of the Earth's ecosystem, meaning that it is part of the food chains as well as in the endless networks of relationships that bind all living beings together. Many of the creatures that invade the body are aggressive micro-organisms such as simple protozoa, bacteria and viruses, but they also include multicellular creatures such as worms, fungi and other parasites are constantly trying to gain a foothold.

DIFFERENT LEVELS OF DEFENCE

To counter the attacks from foreign bodies or harmful substances, the body has several different levels of defense. The first barrier consists of a series of physical and chemical obstacles, and after this there is a subsequent defence composed of non-specific macrophages, granulocytes and mastocytes. The third defence system is a specific one that is produced by the complex mechanisms of the immune system.

PHYSIOCHEMICAL BARRIERS

All areas of the body in contact with the external environment are protected from it by epithelial tissue ▸35. Exposed to trauma and physical aggressions of various kinds, the **skin**, with its many layers of dead cells, is a first physical protective barrier. It is extremely effective in this role, and very few bacteria are able to cross it.

The internal **mucous** membranes provide a more refined means of defence in order to prevent pathogens growing. They are often, for example, equipped with mucous glands and ciliary hairs - these trap and expel micro-organisms. Sometimes they also produce substances like bactericides - for instance, as lysozymes in the mouth, hydrochloric acid in the stomach, urine in the genitourinary apparatus, the tears in the eye, and so forth.

Even symbiotic **bacteria**, which are harmless inhabitants that populate our digestive system, provide an extra defensive system. This is because they compete directly with pathogenic organisms for the available resources but, unlike the latter, do not have to fight the body's resistance. They therefore develop faster and make life very difficult for their competitors.

ANTIGENS & ANTIBODIES

Before discussing the body's non-specific defences, it is good idea to clarify the meaning of certain terms that are used. The substances that bind to specific antibodies and stimulate the immune system to attack unwanted organisms that enter the body, are called antibody generators or antigens and are marked

▶ **DEFENSE**
The main routes of access for pathogenic microorganisms are the wounds, respiration and ingestion. Here are the main defenses gathered throughout the body:

- *skin and mucous membranes: physical barrier and chemistry;*
- *tonsils and adenoids work against viruses and bacteria;*
- *lachrymal glandswith bactericidal substances;*
- *salivary glands with bactericidal substances;*
- *lymphatic nodules with lymphocytes and antibodies;*
- *lymphatic system: transporting the bacteria to nodules where they are destroyed and used to produce antibodies;*
- *liver: produces protein coagulation;*
- *stomach: The acid kills bacteria;*
- *spleen, produces lymphocytes and purifies the blood;*
- *bowel, usually sterile;*
- *large intestine protected by harmless bacterial flora.*

▶ **DEFENSIVE ORGANS**
*The tonsils (**a**) and adenoids (**b**) are lymphoid tissue glands that absorb inhaled micro-organisms from the mouth and nose. White blood cells come to fight the invaders and the glands swell.*

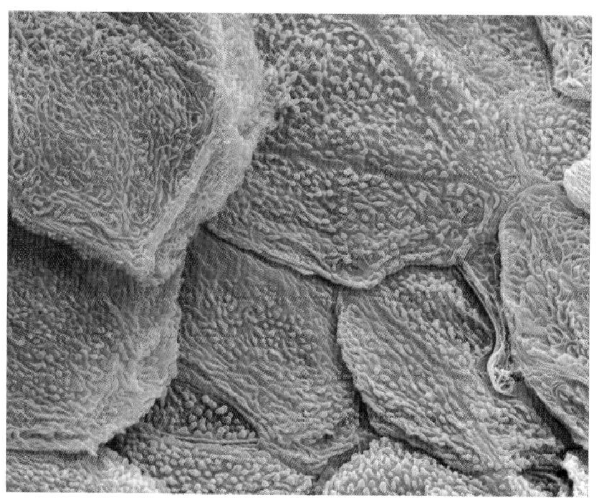

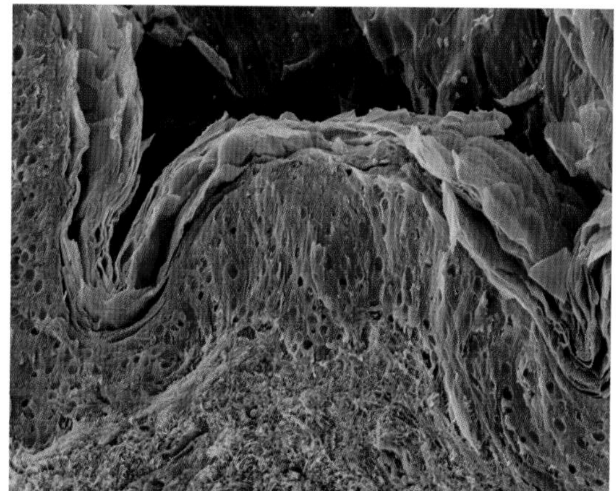

◀ **Skin**
Surface and section of human skin in false colors from a scanning electron microscope (SEM): the barrier that opposes the infection is very effective.

with the symbol Ag. As soon as an antigen comes in contact with particular cells of the body - B lymphocytes ▸92 - they start to produce specific antibodies (marked with Ab, from English antibody), that is, proteins that bind only to antigens that lock into and facilitate the elimination. The plasma ▸94 may continue to produce antibodies even when the antigen that has stimulated the production has disappeared from the body. So antibodies continue to be present in plasma, and, together with a protein complement ▸102, forms the first, and most immediate specific humoral response.

The antibodies have to have a precise form to be perfectly complementary to the antigens that neutralise them. After incorporating a foreign molecule, the B lymphocytes direct the production of the antibody on its conformation stereochemistry, as though the antigen was a mould on which to impress the antibody. The antibody molecule has a "Y" shape, is about 240 Å long, and made up of four subunits of polypeptide proteins that are linked by disulphide bridges. In these antibodies, two of the chains are longer (H chains) and two of them are shorter (L chains), and each is divided into two regions with different functions. Antibodies or immunoglobulins are distinguished into five classes according to the antigenic characteristics of their heavy globular plasma proteins:

- **IgA**: these are found in secretions (sweat, saliva, tears, semen, milk, in the genitourinary and gastrointestinal tracts), serum and mucous membranes, where they stimulate the activation

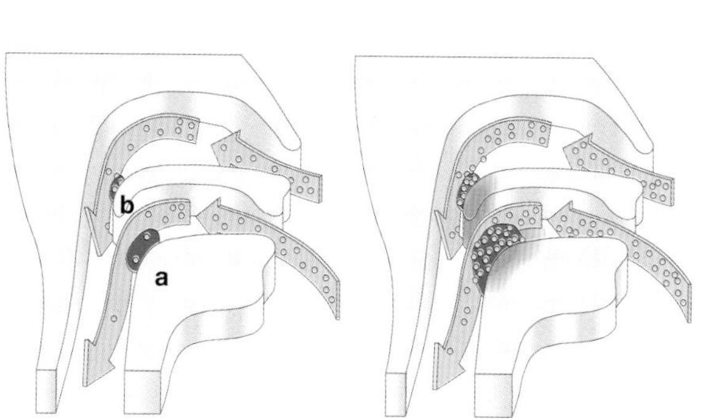

▶ **Antibody**
Structure of an antibody. The chains are green H, L, are yellow. The ends of red chains H and L share the antibody variables designed to specifically recognize the antigen, by binding to it (binding site).

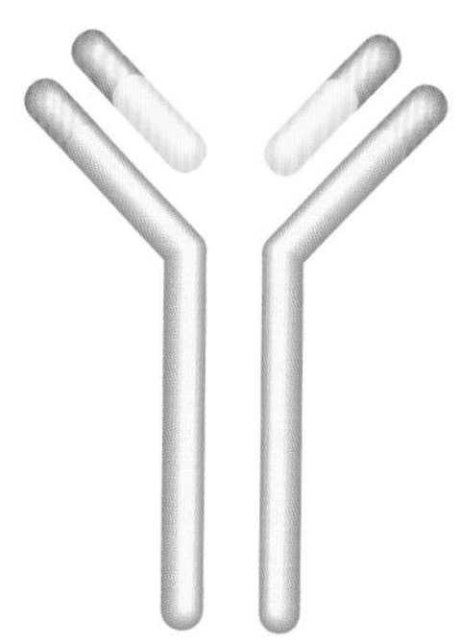

▲ **Defence systems**
Epithelium of the trachea in false color from a scanning electron microscope (SEM). The long cilia are many so as to hide the surface of the mucosal cells from which they emerge. The pale blue balls we have behind them are cells that produce mucus.

▶ **Immunoglobuline type G**
MET Image of two molecules of the type IgG antibody: their form "Y" is obvious.

▶▶ **Classes of immunoglobulins**
Drawings of the structures that characterize the different classes of antibodies.

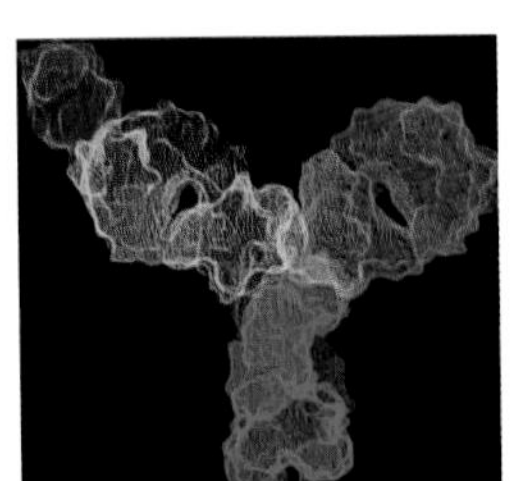

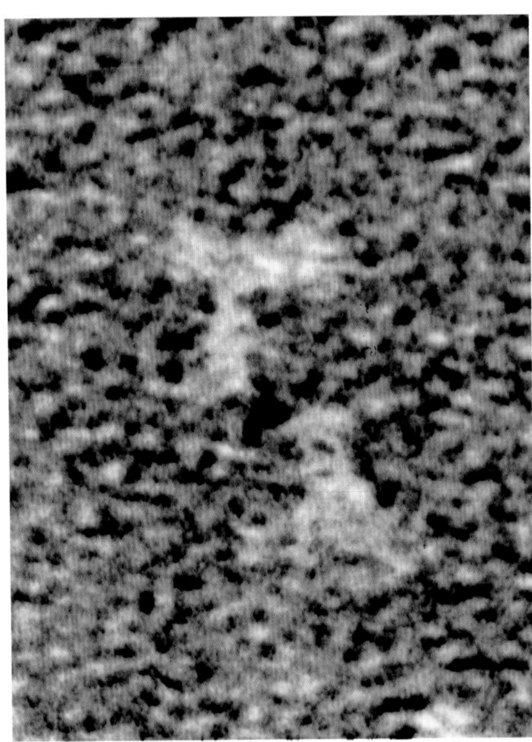

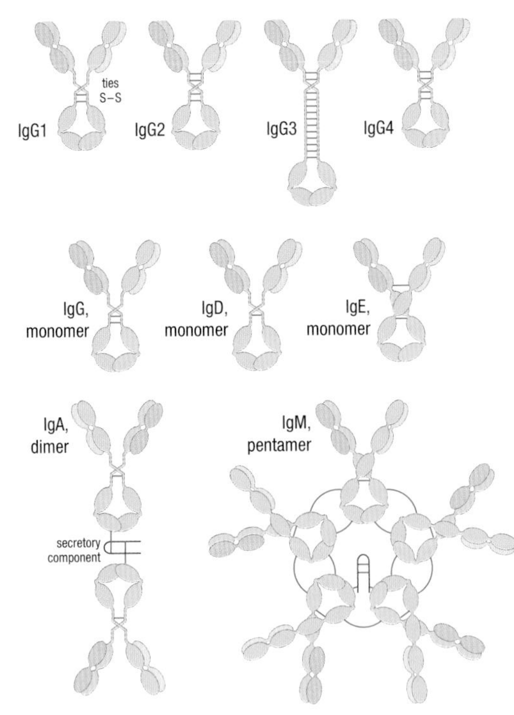

▲ **Rebuilding a computer**
A molecule of IgG with the antigen linked to an arm.

of complement. The serum IgA monomers are similar to IgG; IgA secretory are dimers of serum IgA linked to one another by a β-globulin secretory component.

- **IgD**: these constitute only 1% of all human serum immunoglobulin, which it took a long time to determine their specific functions. Bivalent monomers are present on the surface of B lymphocytes where, as cellular receptors, they bind to the antigen for which they are specific. In this way, they stimulate the cell to proliferate, to mature, to become plasma cells, and to produce antibodies that recognise the same antigens but are in soluble form.
- **IgE**: these are circulating and are responsible for the response to parasites, as well as some hypersensitivity reactions or allergies in certain individuals with allergic conditions, where they reach much higher concentrations than in non-allergic people. Even these antibodies are bivalent dimers - one to bind to leukocytes (eosinophil ▸91, basophile ▸91 or mastocyte ▸95) and one directing the action towards the antigen.
- **IgG**: these antibodies are found in the blood and stimulate the complement reaction. They constitute over 80% of all immunoglobulins in normal human serum, and, during pregnancy, they can pass from mother to child guaranteeing the initial coverage against infection. The IgG monomers are bivalent in four distinct subclasses (IgG1, IgG2, IgG3, IgG4) according to their different structures and abilities to activate the complement.
- **IgM**: these are only found in the circulatory system, and stimulate the complement reaction. They are the first antibodies to act at the time of infection.

THE HUMORAL DEFENSE SPECIFICATION

There are some defences that do not involve specific cells (lymphocytes) but instead incorporate a set of humoral factors. These are specific macromolecules that are produced by the immune system and are not normally present in the blood circulation. This is the primary defense system against infection. The most important humoral factors are organised by the complement system, a group of over 34 serum proteins. The main ones are called C1, C2, C3, C4, C5, C6, C7, C8, C9, C10, C11 - these interact with one another in a cascade of reactions similar to that of clotting. In this way, they are able to mediate various immune reactions such as cell lysis, the neutralisation of bacterial toxins and the chemotaxis of immune cells, anaphylaxis. 90% of the materials that make up the proteins C3, C6, C8 are synthesised by the liver and all the remaining ones are also produced by circulating monocytes ▸92 and macrophages ▸95, and it is likely that even lymphocytes ▸92 and the epithelial cells can do this as well.

The complement proteins are very important: they bind to invading germs to make them recognisable to phagocytes, facilitating their elimination, as well as participating in the pro-inflammatory function. Fragments of these substances, called anaphylotoxins, trigger mast ▸95, released mediators, increase vascular permeability and the chemotaxis of leukocytes to the inflamed area.

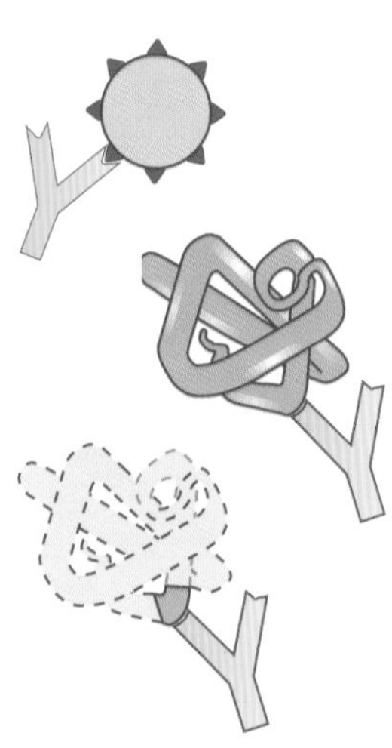

▲ **Antibodies**
Ability of an antibody to recognize an entire micro organism, a protein or a fragment of protein straight away.

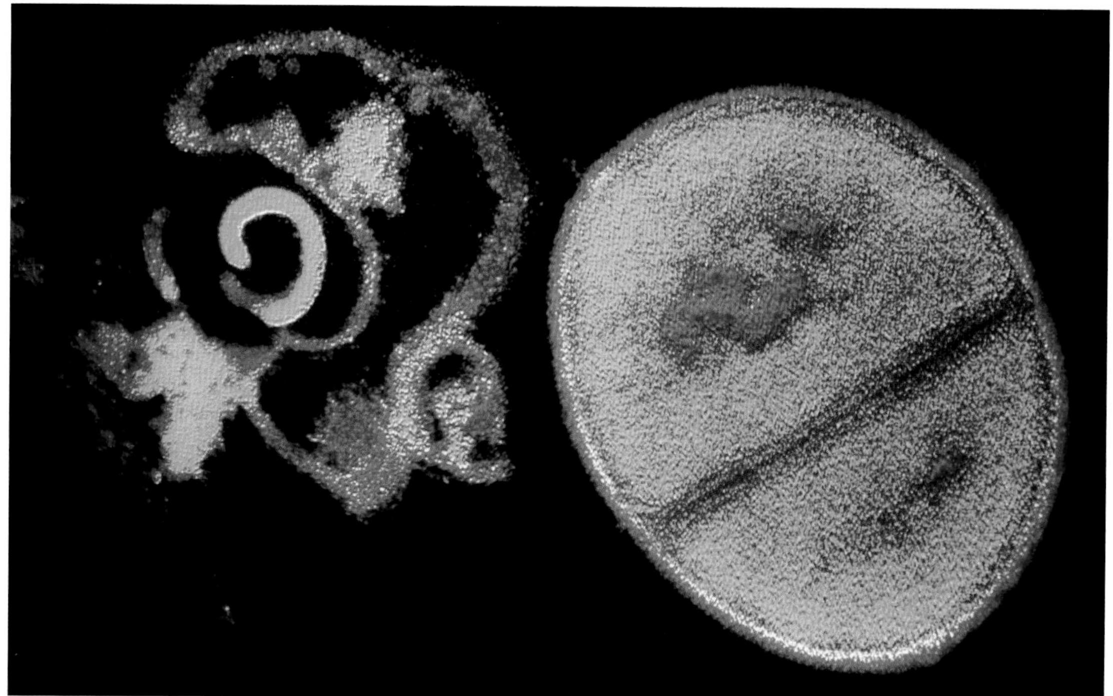

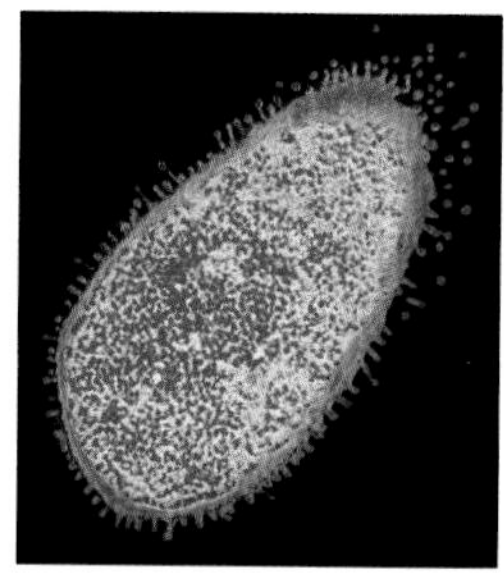

◄▲ **Bacterial lysis**
In these SEM pictures there are two subsequent cell lysis. Above, a Salmonella bacterium begins to lose cytoplasmic contents through the pores that pass the wall and membranes side to side. On the left, two Staphylococcus bacteria aureus, while the second is still intact, the former is now completely lysed: what remains is a small part of the cell wall (blue), while the cytoplasm (yellow) was almost completely digested by the enzymes

• **The complement cascade** - In the first phase of an infection, complement proteins, which circulate in the blood in an inactive form, activate each other in a cascade process. The activation is triggered by proteins from the alien cell. This process can follow the classic path, in which the complement adheres to a complex antibody-antigen, or via an alternative, where the complement adheres directly to the cell wall of the bacteria's carbohydrates. It is important that the complement is activated in this way, as it means that the activity of the body's defensive molecules remains confined to the relevant area and not in the plasma or on the surface of its own cells.

– **The classic way** - This is where the complement is activated by binding to an antibody-antigen complex. Before this can happen though, a complex antibody-antigen must be built, and this requires that antibodies are present in the body so that they can bind to the outside of the cell.

Subsequently, the C1, which remains a macromolecule integrates only in the presence of Ca2+ ions, binds to the antibody that form the complex. However, to take action, the C1 must belong with at least two of its sites: if the antibody is an IgG, therefore, there must be at least two that are related to the antigen, and they should be at the right distance. If the complex was formed by a IgM, however, and the antibody is appropriately located, only one molecule of IgM is needed to activate the cascade reaction.

When the C1 binds to the antibody, it changes and acquires an enzyme capacity (C1 esterase) becoming capable of causing a C4 molecule to divide into two fragments. One of them (the C4b) can be transformed from an inactive substance, or it can bind to proteins or a carbohydrate's membrane. In this case, it becomes able to bind to a C2 molecule, which can in turn be fragmented by the same molecule of C1. It thus forms two fragments of C2, and the C2b remains linked to the C4b.

Also, the C4b-C2b complex, which is linked to the membrane of the pathogen, has an enzymatic activity (the classic complement 3). This hydrolyses the C3 into two subunits, one of which (the C3a) is an anaphylotoxin which enters into solution and gives rise to a local inflammatory response, while the other (the C3b) is inactivated to 90% water.

The 10% which resists decomposition, binds to the membrane near the complex that it has produced. They form a new complex (C4b-C2b-C3b) to enzymatic activity: the C5 classic complement hydrolyses the C5 into two fragments which begin the formation of attack complexes on the membrane (MAC, Membrane Attack Complex). The fragment of C5b may bind to the C6 forming the complex C5b-C6 which may then subsequently anchor the C7. Closely linked, the molecule of c7 changes conformation in a way that exposes a hydrophobic stretch. It is this part of the molecule that fits in the double layer of the lipid membrane, opening a first breakthrough.

Thus linked to the membrane, the complex C5b-C6-C7 can bind, in turn, to the C8 forming the complex C5b-C6-C7-C8. Even this factor changes in a similar way to the C7, and fits in the membrane. This leads to the formation of a passage of 30 Å in diameter, which begins the cell lysis.

Initially slow and not very effective, the lysis becomes effective when the complex also binds to

▶ **The three-way**
Summary of the main reactions that form the "complement cascade" according to the three ways: classic, alternative and MB-Lectin. All three lead to the lysis of cells infected or estrene.

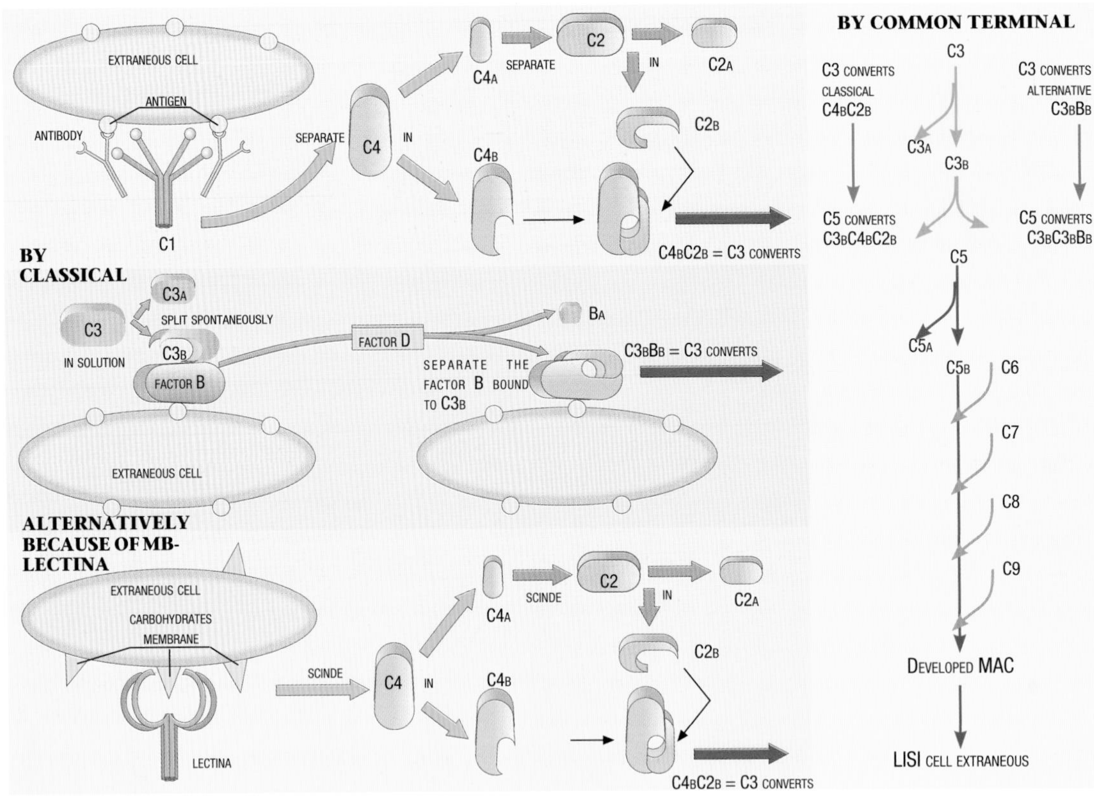

▼ **The MAC**
The complex attack on the membrane (MAC = Membrane Attack Complex) is formed by the union that occurs after the various complementary molecules, sink into the membrane of the cell outside, form a pore leading to lysis.

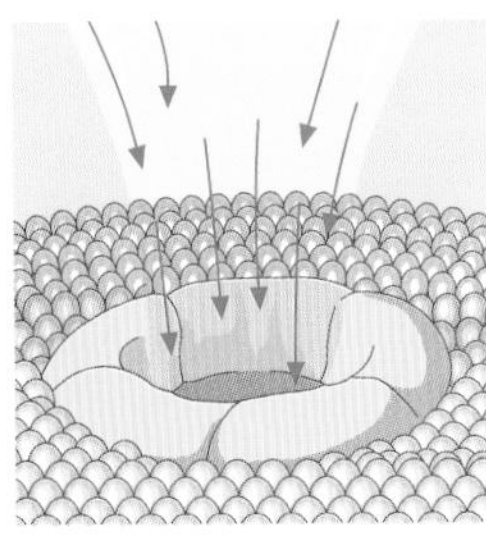

the C9. After having linked to the phospholipids of the membrane, in fact, up to 18 molecules of C9 form a polymerised "doughnut", which defines a channel with a diameter of about 100 Å. The MAC therefore becomes a permeable pore, which spans across the whole membrane. It has a hydrophobic external face and hydrophilic internal one. This creates a channel that allows the passage of ions and water. The cell lysis becomes rapid and devastating: the alterations in the osmotic balance of the cell that are produced by the MAC inflate it so much that it finally bursts. The damage is so severe that it results in certain death. However, this kind of direct attack on foreign cells is not particularly effective: it seems that the formation of the MAC is only useful in the fight against specific types of micro-organisms.

– **The alternative route**: the complement is activated by different types of substances, such as, for example, those that form the cellular walls of yeast and bacteria, endotoxins, or the factors in cobra venom, along with the IgA aggregate. This process, therefore, represents a form of non-specific immune response, that does not depend on an earlier awareness. In other words, it is not part of the classic immune response: this is why it is considered to have the oldest evolutionary development. This is confirmed by the fact that it is present in all vertebrates, and that the proteins involved in this process have a very similar chemical structure. The alternative route, however, remains limited to microbial surfaces and, without involving the molecules of C1, C4 and C2, leads to the production of an active C3 complement component that activates the molecules of C3.

The C3 is the most abundant protein of the entire complement system. It has a cyclical structure that is thought to be constantly and slowly hydrolysed according to a little known process. This determines a continued presence of small amounts of activated C3 in the bloodstream, which can trigger a cascade of enzymatic activity via the alternative route. In the presence of magnesium ions, the fragment of C3b adheres to the exterior surface and binds to factor B, a molecule that is similar to C2 and with enzymatic capacity. It thus forms the complex C3b-B. Once linked to C3b, the factor B can be fragmented by the factor D, an enzyme that is normally present in the active form in the bloodstream, albeit in small concentrations. The factor D detaches a part of the factor B, leaving a fragment (Bb) linked to the complex. The complex C3b-B thus becomes C3b-Bb, and as this is highly unstable, it decomposes spontaneously. In order to delay the decomposition, however, the properdin or factor P intervenes which binds to many areas of pathogenic cells. This fragment becomes available in abundance to form new complexes or to bind to the surface of pathogens and make them recognisable to the immune cells.

To prevent the activation from also occurring in plasma - that is, without the presence of pathogenic surfaces - there is a wide range of control mechanisms. The regulatory proteins present in the circulatory system have a dual task - on the one hand they prevent the activation of the complement component, and on the other to stimulate the rapid decomposition. Thus, for example, factor H - a protein present in the membranes of vertebrates, called Decay Accelerating Factor (DAF or CD55) - competes with factor B for the link with the C3b or replaces the Bb in the C3b-Bb complex, leading to the degradation of C3 complement component that has already formed. On the surface of micro-organisms, however, the regulating proteins are missing: the C3 complement component can be formed and may remain active. In fact, the activation becomes effective only in the presence of the surface of a micro-organism: even cells with a nucleus of pathogenic organisms can stimulate this primitive defensive reaction.

– The way of MB-LECTIN (Mannose-Binding Lectin, or lectin that binds mannose) is a "third way" of activating the complement. It has many similarities with the classic way, with the main difference being that in this case the complement directly recognises extraneous carbohydrates. This is due to the presence of MB-lectin, a protein that is produced by the liver which is often present in normal plasma and increases in concentration in the acute phase of an immune response. The MB-lectin is structurally similar to the active part of C1: as the name implies, it binds specifically to mannose (but also to other sugars that contain the same chemical residues), which means that they can join the bacterial cell wall by activating a direct infection response. As the C1, the MB-lectin activates the complement cascade forming an enzyme activity that - as in the classic way, fragments C4 and C2 and allows the formation of a C3 complement component.

THE CELLULAR DEFENCES SPECIFICATION

The formation of the C3 complement component is the point that unites the three-way activation of the complement (classical, alternative and MB-lectin). The different molecules produced have the same activities and begin the same cascade of events. The most significant is that in the vicinity of each molecule of C3 complement component more than 1000 molecules of C3b can be bound. The accumulation of similar quantities of proteins on the surface of the pathogens is the primary role of complements as this allows phagocytes to recognise, capture and destroy the micro-organisms and infected cells.

- **Phagocytosis** ▸16: This process occurs because phagocytes have surface receptors of the complement (CR), these are molecules that bind in a specific manner with those on the pathogens. Thus far, five types of CR have been identified: The best known is the CR1, which is specific to the C3b. It is located on granulocytes and macrophages, but also on red blood cells. Here it binds the immune complexes that are transported in the blood until the spleen and liver eliminate them. Because it activates phagocytosis, however, it is not enough to just form a link between CR1 and C3b, but it must also occur under other conditions. For example, macrophages must be activated from small fragments of C5a that bind to another type of receptor membrane, or by proteins similar to fibronectin, which is associated with the extracellular matrix.

Three other complement receptors (CR2, CR3 and CR4) recognise the inactive fragments of C3b that remain fixed on the surface of the micro-organism. The CR2, in particular, triggers the phagocytosis by cells that have the CR1, especially in B lymphocytes. These cells produce immune complexes and transport them to the germinative centres of the lymph nodes where they stimulate the activity of the cells that produce antibodies. In this way, the activation of the complement also helps to produce a specific immune response.

– **Interferon**: in addition to phagocytosis being mediated by complements, infection also produces other non-specific cellular reactions. In particular, in the event of an infection by viruses, the infected leukocytes and connective cells produce and release interferon, a signalling substance that stimulates the defences of other cells of the body. The action of interferon drastically reduces the synthesis of proteins: in this way - albeit temporarily, it freezes the multiplication of the virus.

Finally, the non-specific reaction can determine:

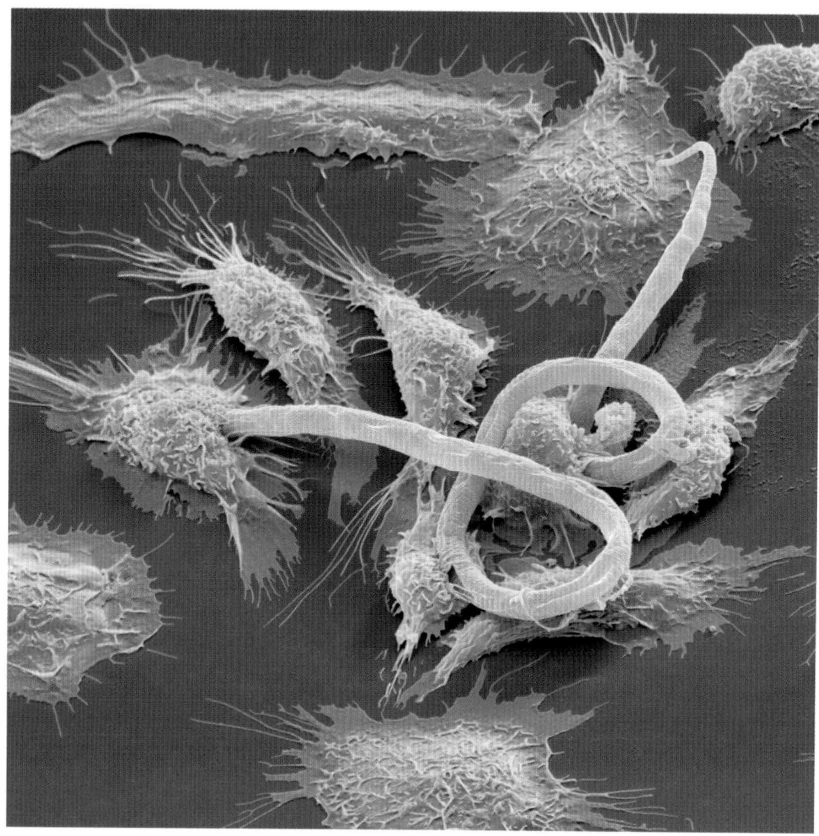

▲ **Battle**
SEM photograph of a worm parasite (elminta) being attacked by many macrophages. This type of attack is part of specific cellular defenses of our body.

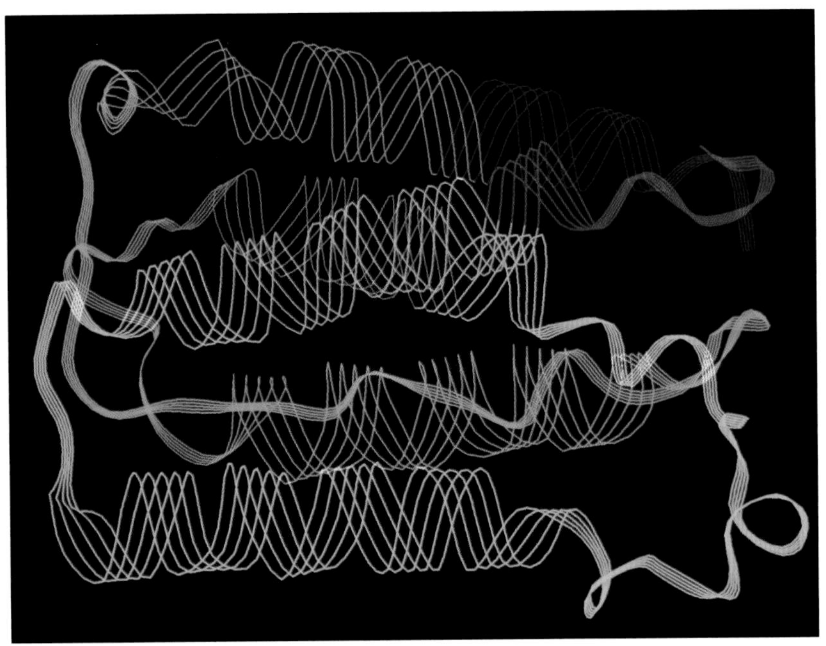

– **Inflammation** is a normal defensive response that is triggered when a tissue is damaged. The damage that leads to this reaction, aside from an infection, can also be caused by an injury or from contact with harmful substances. The inflammatory reaction is triggered by the release of chemical mediators from the damaged tissues and by a massive migration of cells. The body reacts to the signals of suffering tissue by trying to remove the irritants (which can also be produced by micro-organisms or by cell death), and by inactivating or destroying any invaders and by preparing the tissue repair.

The chemical mediators that activate the inflammatory reaction are different (they include histamine ▸96, prostaglandins ▸109, interleukin-1, and others), but the fundamental ones are those that arise from the activation of complement. The small fragments of C3a, C4a and C5a, in fact, can bind to specific receptors on the membrane of many cells.

▲ **Interferon**
Computer rendering of the structure a molecule of interferon α2B, a protein released by white blood cells in response to a viral infection. It plays a role in cytokine that stimulates the response of other leukocytes, and blocks infected cells surrounding the production of the virus.

▶ **Bacterial Infections**
1a. *The bacteria attacks the tissue and white blood cells rush to engulf and destroy them.*
1b. *Some bacteria can reproduce in the interior of a white blood cell: in short, they break the cell and infect other white blood cells.*
1c. *In an effort to combat the infection that is spreading, the body sends more white blood cells.*

2a. *The bacteria that infects the tissue is protected by a capsule that prevents white blood cells attempting to engulf and destroy them.*
2b. *The bacteria rapidly take over.*
2c. *To stem the infection, the body can produce the specific antibodies that attach to the bacteria, they are attacked by white blood cells.*

3a. *The bacteria attack the tissue and white blood cells flock to the scene.*
3b. *The bacteria produce toxins that may have a local or systemic action, in this case the toxins can enter the bloodstream.*
3c. *White blood cells rush to destroy them before damage will occur if a tissue is infected.*

4a. *The bacteria attacks the tissue and white blood cells rush to engulf and destroy them.*
4b. *The bacteria proliferate more quickly than they can be eliminated by the white blood cells.*
4c. *Many bacteria are killed by releasing substances into the containing tissue (endotoxins). White blood cells remove as many toxins and bacteria as they can, to avoid damage to the tissue.*

white blood cell
bacterium
encapsulated bacterium
dead bacterium
bacterium that produces toxin
bacterium that reproduces
antibody

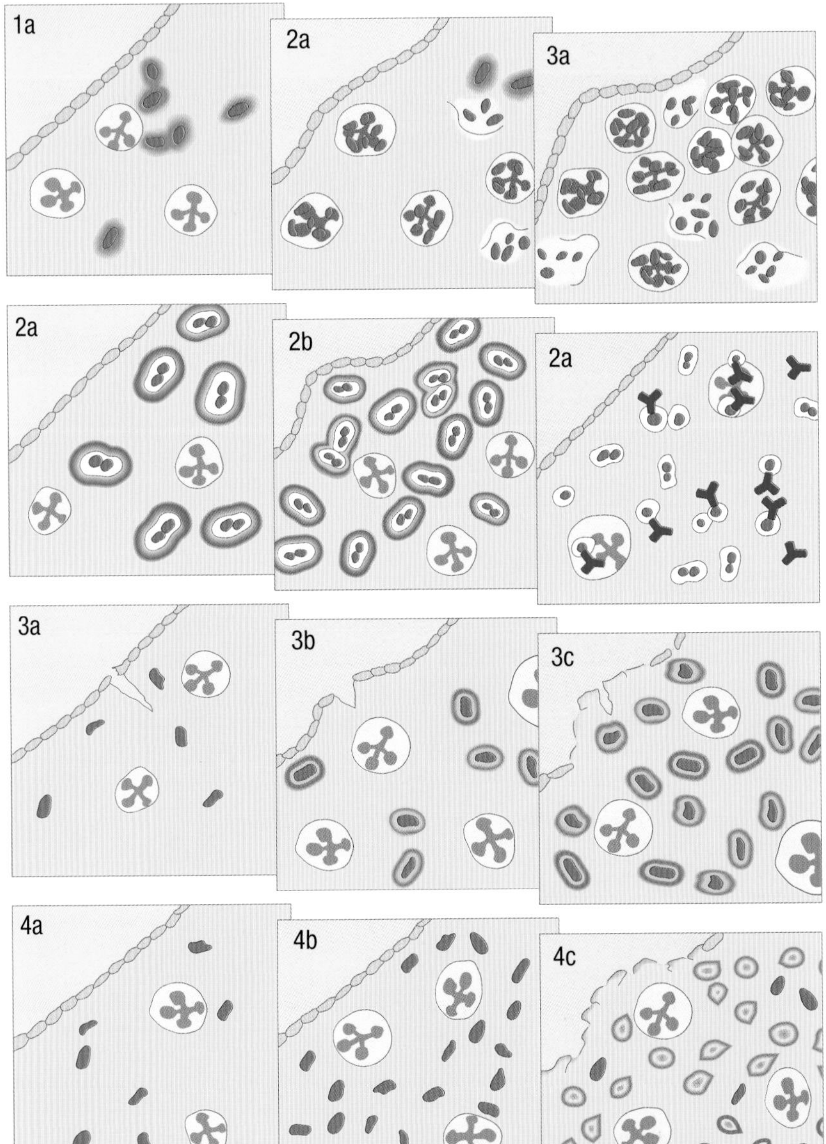

This includes mast cells, the neutrophil, basophils, eosinophils, monocytes and endothelial cells, and stimulates their activity.
In particular, the mast cells cause the release of substances from vasodilation action. In neutrophils it stimulates chemotaxis and adherence to endothelial cells, whereas in endothelial cells it cause changes that lead to increased vascular permeability. The increase in blood flow and, consequently, the contribution of complements and large numbers of phagocyte cells - and in particular, cells from the lymph nodes near the site of inflammation - is very effective in stimulating the production of specific antibodies for the humoral adaptive response ▸108.
The fragments of complement also stimulate numerous types of cells in the submucosa to produce mediators that are similar to histamine, catechin and TNFα (Tumour Necrosis Factor). These are important cytokines that are involved in the acute phases of inflammatory and allergic responses. If these substances are produced in large quantities, it can lead to a reaction that is similar to anaphylactic shock and caused by a systemic allergy that is mediated by IgE. This can include vasodilation, increased permeability of blood vessels, and a massive influx in the area of immunocompetence cells. In some cases, the defence reactions are so vigorous that they cause progressive damage to the tissues. This happens in particular when the inflammation is triggered by an allergic or autoimmune response.
The TNFα, in particular, produces a wide range of effects on many different bodies. These include the stimulation of the hypothalamic-pituitary-adrenal axis (HPA or HTPA axis), which is an active producer of the Corticotropin Release Hormone (CRH). In addition, TNFα stimulates the liver because it produces proteins of the complement and chemical mediators. It also stimulates the recall of neutrophils to the site of the inflammation, allowing them to adhere to endothelial cells and migrate into adjacent vessel tissues. Furthermore, it stimulates macrophages to begin phagocytosis and the production of oxidants, lipids and inflammatory prostaglandin E2 (PGE2).

◀ **Tumor Necrosis Factor α**
Usually the TNFα of a molecule is a trimer, that is made up of 3 sub-identical parts similar to that reproduced here in this computer simulation. This substance is produced predominantly by macrophages during the inflammatory and immune responses as a result of wounds or endotoxins. One of its functions is to kill tumor cells (hence the name) but is involved in many other types of inflammation from rheumatoid arthritis to psoriasis and Crohn's disease.

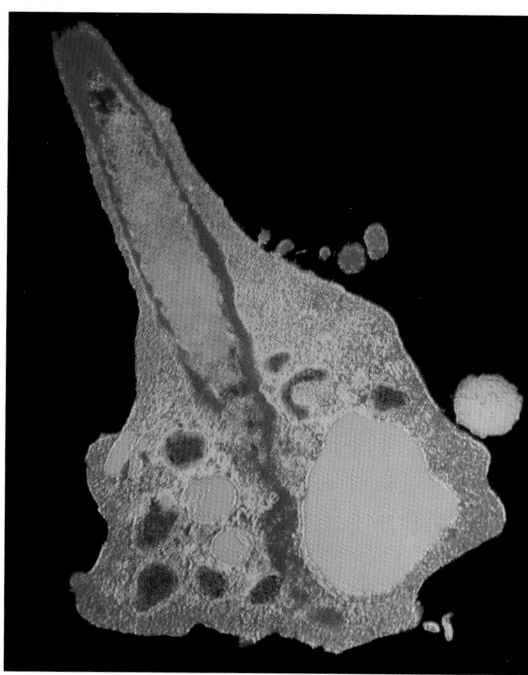

◀ **Phagocytes**
TEM photograph of a polymorphonuclear leukocyte as it absorbs a bacterium of the Selenomonas species (green). At the bottom of the leukocyte notice the round cellular organelles picked out in pale blue in the bulk core. To the outside, in yellow, another bacterium.

THE CELLULAR DEFENCES SPECIFICATIONS: IMMUNITY ACQUIRED OR TAKEN

Immunity is said to be acquired or adopted when an unknown foreign body or substance is recognised by a specific antibody in the blood plasma or on the surface of a lymphatic cell. Those responsible for this complex defence reaction are the T cells ▸93, which are intended for a direct attack or cytotoxic function (NK or natural killers), and B lymphocytes ▸92, which can turn into large plasma cells ▸94 that produce large quantities of specific antibodies. The production of antibodies depends on many complex interactions between cells. The first stimulus comes from the complement system ▸102 that, in addition to activating non-specific defences, intervenes directly to stimulate B lymphocytes. The fragment of C3b interacts with the CR2, a lymphocyte membrane receptor and triggers the humoral response, namely the production of antibodies.
However, B lymphocytes can also be stimulated by helper T-cells. These cells, therefore, must be suitably stimulated. Given that, unlike what happens to B lymphocytes, the T-cells do not recognise an antigen in solution, it must recognise this when it is linked to a membrane, and so they must be

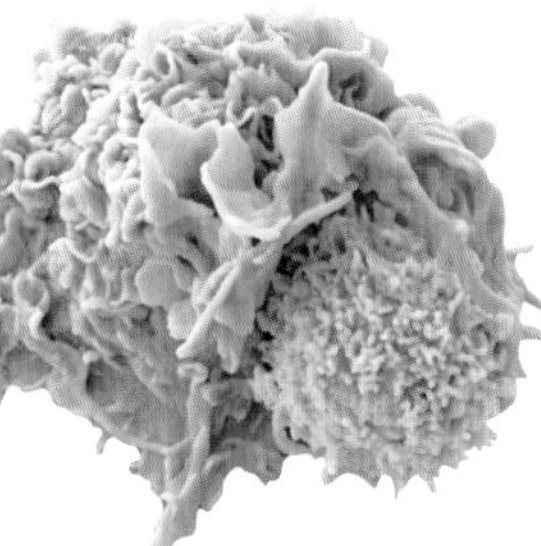

▶ **Direct Stimulus**
A dentritic cell (Pale blue), and a T lymphocyte (yellow or lilac) interact (false color scanning electron microscope, SEM photo). These two types of leukocytes (white blood cells) may recognize antigens: the dendrites that link them to its surface "tells" the T lymphocyte that it is activated. The molecules of the membrane involved in adhesion play a key role in this kind of communication.

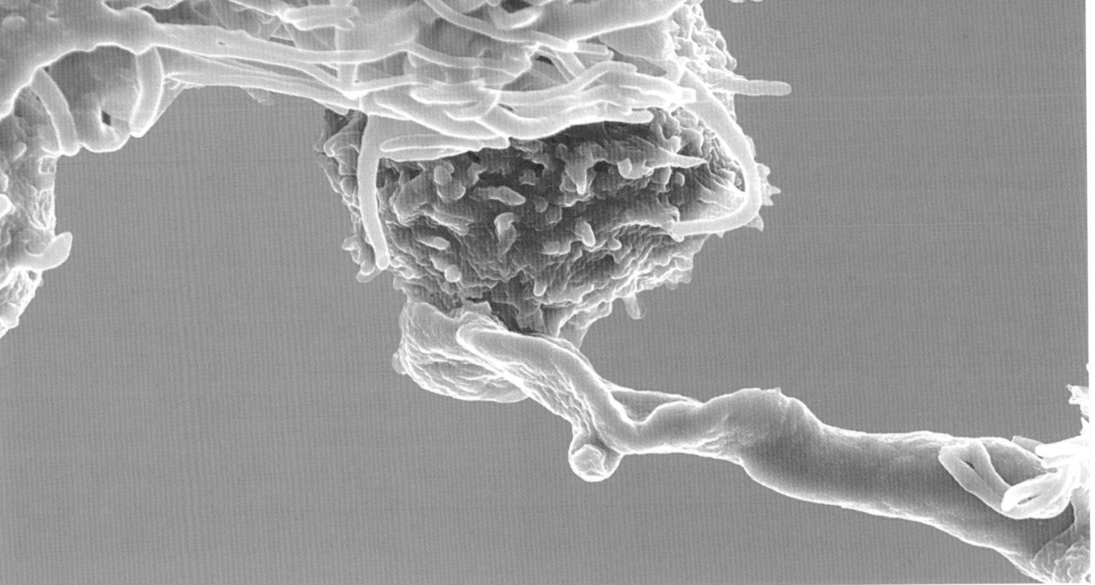

correctly presented.
The peptides (i.e. the pieces of proteins) or the small fragments that are found on a membrane, are associated with the proteins of system MHC P130. If a peptide does not bind to a protein MHC, the T cells do not recognise it, and therefore do not activate. We have already found these important cell surface proteins; let us now examine their functions in the immunological response:

- **The role of MHC**: this system of membrane proteins is regulated by a complex set of 11 co-dominant genes, i.e. genes that are always expressed, whatever their range, and produce numerous variants of molecules. In this way each individual possesses a wealth of MHC proteins each of which has a specific ability to bind certain antigens and present them to immune cells.

There are two classes of MHC molecules with different structures and roles:

- the **MHC-1**, this is directly involved in the phenomenon of transplant rejection. Its synthesis is induced by interferon that is released by cells that have been affected by viral infection. This causes the viral antigens to be exposed to the action of killer T-cells and their consequent death. The red blood cells, which have no nucleus, cannot produce MHC-1. That is why, if they are infected - for example, by the malaria plasmodium, they do not present any surface antigens that show that they are infected with intracellular agents; this hinders the body's defences;
- the **MHC-2**, this is necessary for co-operation in the field of cellular immune response, and is expressed by many cells. These include monocytes, macrophages, dendritic cells, B lymphocytes and only partly in T lymphocytes and is intended to present the antigen in an appropriate way to activate other cells .

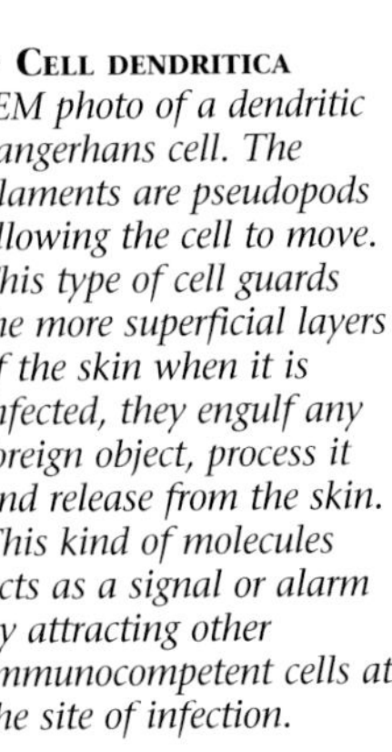

▶ **Cell dendritica**
SEM photo of a dendritic Langerhans cell. The filaments are pseudopods allowing the cell to move. This type of cell guards the more superficial layers of the skin when it is infected, they engulf any foreign object, process it and release from the skin. This kind of molecules acts as a signal or alarm by attracting other immunocompetent cells at the site of infection.

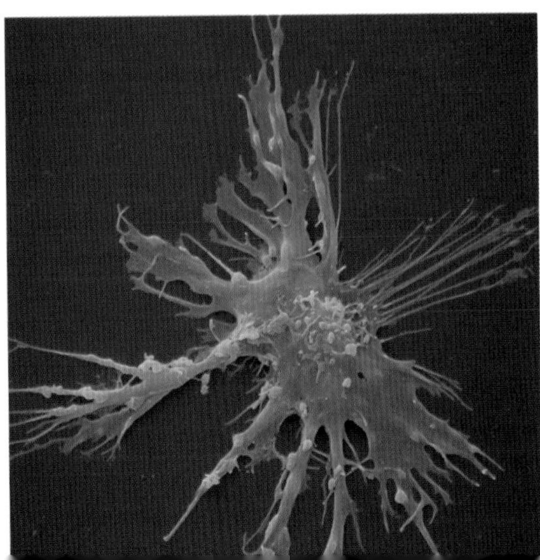

"STRATEGIES" OF DEFENSE IN CASE OF ATTACK

THE FIRST LINE OF DEFENSE

If some germs can overcome the body's physical and chemical barriers, the white blood cells that are in the threat zone receive chemical messages from the cells that have been attacked. When this happens, they mobilise and adhere to the vessel walls, where they distort, stretch and shrink until they are able to pass between the spaces that separate the endothelial cells of the of blood vessel. Once outside, they migrate through the connective tissue heading towards the source of the signals (chemotaxis). The white blood cells can generate tentacles of cytoplasm (pseudopods ▶91) with which they surround the foreign substances or germs, pulling them in and destroying them (phagocytosis).
For their part, the germs do not remain passive to the counterattacks - each different species has its own way of defending itself. Some generate a capsule and then hide inside it, whereas others emit substances that keep the leukocytes away, or produce toxins

THE PROSTAGLANDINS

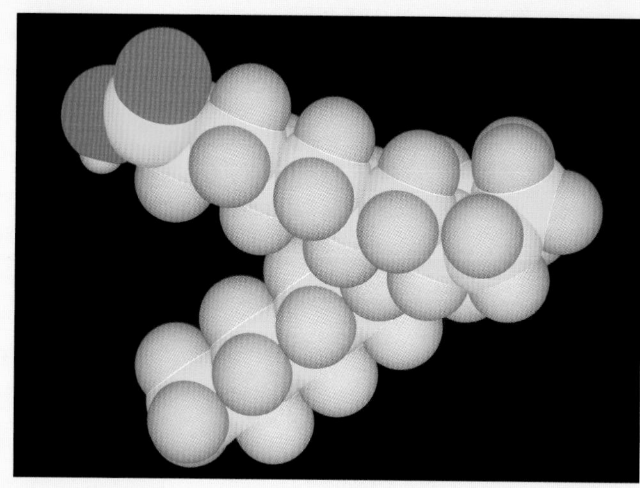

▶ **Immune reactions**
Prostaglandin molecule reproduced in a computer model: here the carbon is yellow, the hydrogen is blue and oxygen is red.

Prostaglandins (PG) were isolated for the first time in 1930 in prostate sheep, and were therefore named after them. They are one of the main families of eicosanoids or super-hormones, substances that perform a number of important psychological roles in the body, including the regulation of the endocrine system. They are derived from unsaturated fatty acids such as linoleic acid, and are produced in very small quantities by nearly all mammalian body tissues from the enzyme cyclooxygenase.

There are more than 30 different types of prostaglandin, each of which is denoted by the initials PG followed by letters ranging from A to I (PGA, PGD, PGE, etc..). These are then sub-divided into 3 main groups, with those in the PG1 and PG3 groups being considered beneficial, while those in the PG2 being deemed harmful.

Arachidonic acid and α-linoleic acid (omega-3) are precursors to the class PG3, whereas linolenic acid (omega-6) is the precursor of classes PG1 and PG2: the relationship between the different groups of prostaglandins produced is closely linked to diet, and in some cases it may be the basis for an increased risk of disease. In general, all these molecules act locally and are then rapidly metabolised and processed into inactive products. Unlike the hormones, therefore, they do not circulate in the blood in significant concentrations.

Prostaglandins can, nevertheless, modulate a wide range of physiological functions: from the aggregation or disaggregation of platelets and the regulation of calcium transport in the body to the control of cell growth. They are also involved in the processes of vasoconstriction and vasodilation, as well as controlling the extent and duration of any inflammatory reactions and the synthesis of hormones.

Many of the actions carried out by these substances are mediated by membrane receptors to which they bind triggering the cell, a process of activating or blocking adenylate cyclase (the enzyme involved in the production of cyclic AMP, a source of cell energy. In internal tissues, the prostaglandins act as chemical signals in the regulation of specific types of cells.

In this way, PG1 and PG3 prostaglandins carry out the following functions:

- they lower blood pressure by the induced contraction of smooth muscle and through vasodilatation.
- they control vascular permeability which influences the formation of exudates, and regulate the chemotaxis (i.e. the movement following a chemical gradient) of macrophages ▶95 and leukocytes ▶90.
- they lower the percentage of cholesterol LDL and increase that of HDL.
- they prevent unjustified platelet aggregation, hindering the formation of thrombi and reducing the risk of strokes.
- they inhibit the inflammatory response (anti-inflammatory action).
- they improve the functioning of intracellular insulin ▶206 helping to maintain constant blood sugar levels.
- they regulate the movement of calcium.
- they improve the functioning of the nervous and immune systems.

PG2 prostaglandins, however, have the opposite effects, notably:

- they cause an increase in blood pressure and water retention.
- they facilitate the aggregation of platelets.
- they promote inflammation.

The presence of PG2 prostaglandins is especially prevalent in some inflammatory diseases such as arthritis. By blocking the enzyme that promotes the processes of synthesis of prostaglandins and reducing the quantity produced, it is possible to reduce the symptomatic manifestations of the disease: pain, swelling, inflammation and fever.

Many of the non-steroidal anti-drugs (NSAIDs) are prevent the synthesis of these substances.

▶ **Unsaturated fats**
*Molecules of linoleic acid (**A**), linonlenic acid (**B**) and arachidonic acid (**C**) reproduced in a computer model. In **A** and **B** the carbon atoms are blue, those in yellow are hydrogen and oxygen in red. In **C** carbon atoms are yellow, blue is hydrogen and oxygen red. The linoleic acid, and linolenic acid and arachidonic acid are ω-6.*

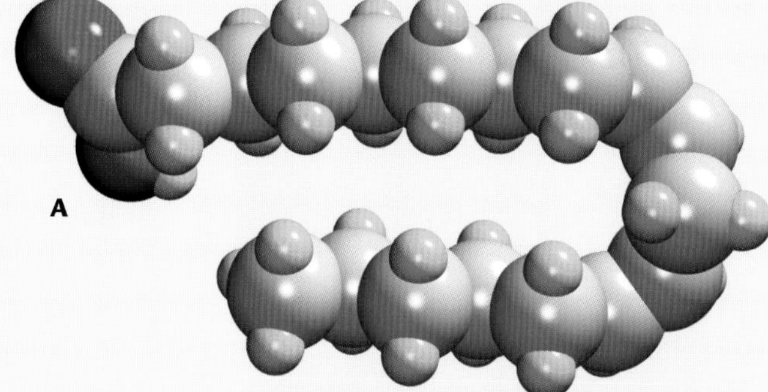

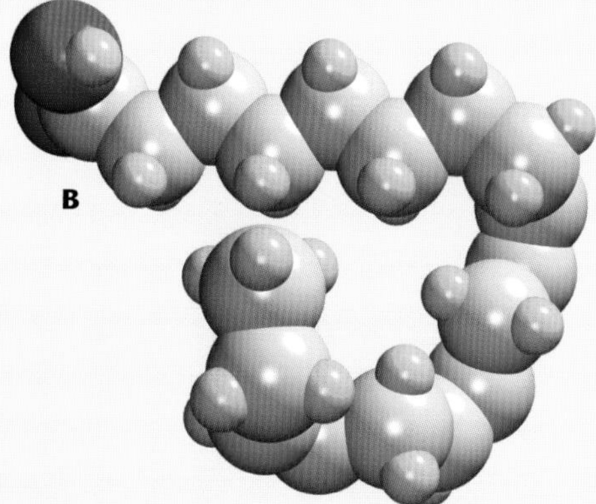

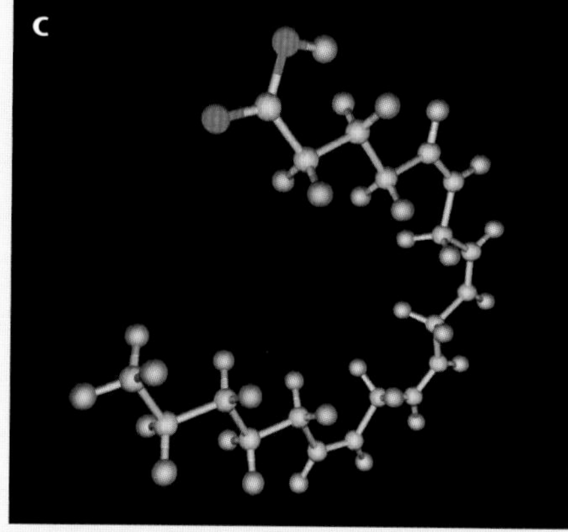

▼ **Activation of lymphocyte B**
The pre-TH cells recognize antigens coupled to exposed MHC proteins on healthy cell membranes (phagocytes). This will activate them , and then cause them to multiply, acknowledging in a similar way, the B lymphocytes that have bound the to the soluble antigen. They are then stimulated to produce interleukins. These substances stimulate the B lymphocytes to divide and develop into plasma cells that release antibodies of specific antigen in the active solution.

▶ **Activation of TK**
The pre-TK lymphocytes recognize antigens coupled to MHC proteins that are present on membranes of abnormal or foreign cells. They activate, multiply and bind to the cell, bringing death to the cell by secreting perforin.

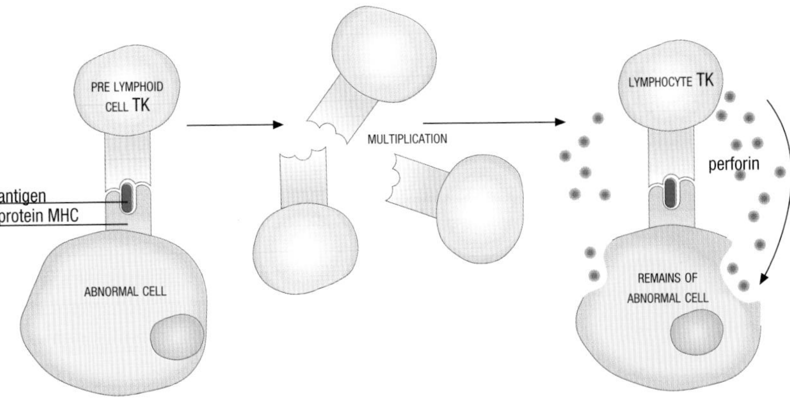

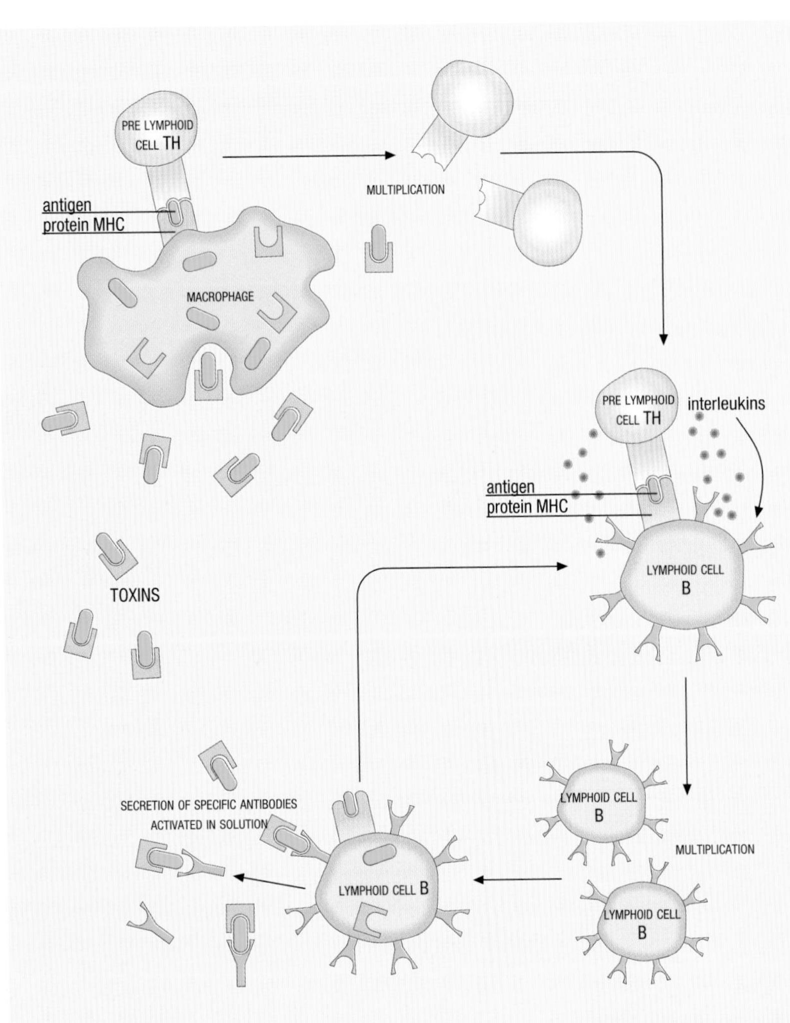

that kill them. The situation often turns into a battle whose outcome depends on the number of invaders killed, their violence, their capacity for proliferation, and the effectiveness of their defences. The most important factor is therefore the speed and efficiency of the body's defences. Moreover, the phagocytes are not always able to completely protect the body. For example, they are not able to neutralise the toxins that poison the body, but only weaken them. For their complete elimination, specific antibodies are needed.

Within a few hours of the intervention of the leukocytes, together with the support of macrophages, most bacteria and extracellular micro-organisms are eliminated. In fact, while phagocytosis is usually a sufficient reaction, it is also essential as it enables the production of antibodies. Most germs camouflage themselves as a protection against antigens, and so avoid being recognised by the B lymphocytes. The phagocytosis and partial digestion of the germs greatly increases the chances of the lymphocytes finding and destroying them.

IF THE ATTACK COMES FROM A VIRUS

If the pathogenic micro-organisms are viruses or other endocellular parasites, that is they enter into the body's cells to reproduce, it involves a variety of different defence systems. If a cell is infected it produces interferon ▸106 which temporarily blocks protein synthesis in nearby cells. In this way it forms an exclusion buffer layer around it in which the micro-organism, for a certain time, cannot find

▶ **Model of protein CD4**
It is a glycoprotein of about 450 amino acids which is typical of the surface of TH lymphocytes: by binding to membrane proteins of other cells or microorganisms, this allows TH to recognize antigens and start the immune response. CD4 binds to HIV: it is due to this that the virus can infect and kill TH, thus compromising the immune system.

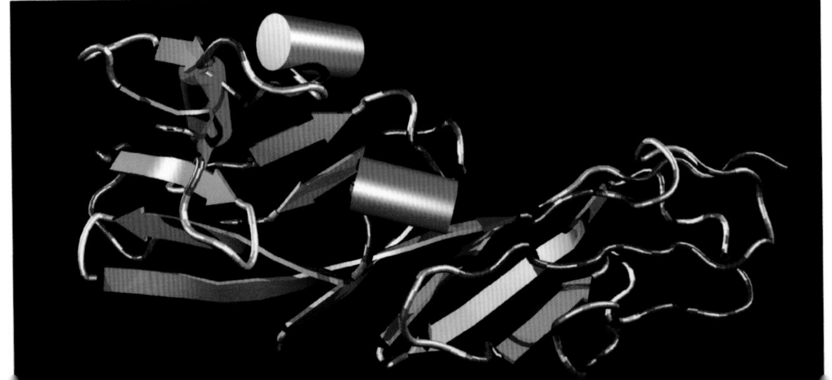

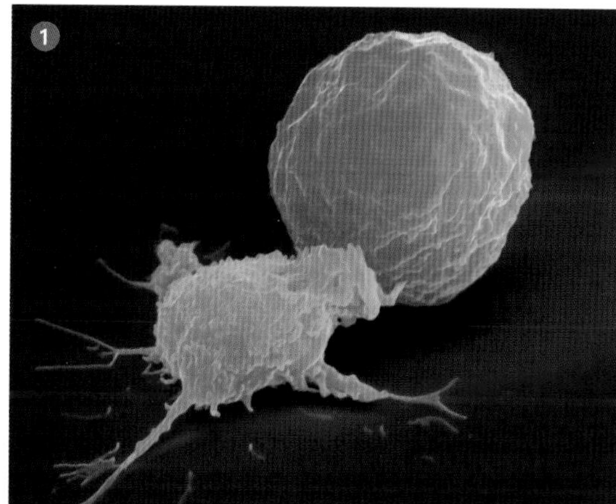

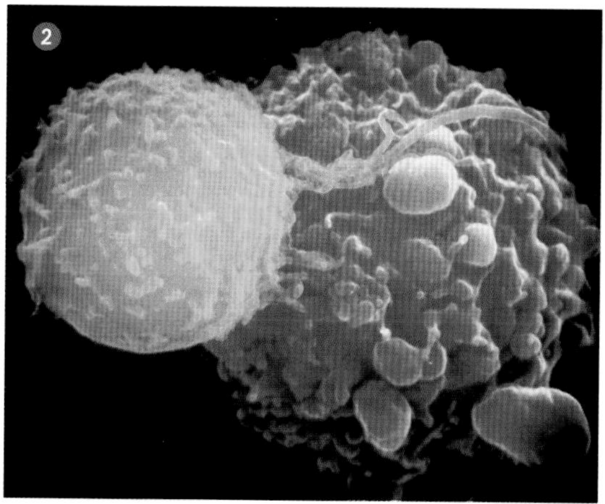

the necessary conditions to reproduce. At the same time, the infected cells display on their complex membrane antigen-MHC-1, which then activates the cytotoxic response ▸94 of killer T-cells and natural killers. These cells which are always present in the circulatory system not only kill the infected cells, but also produce substances that can eliminate the pests that are within them. In addition, these lymphocytes produce special chemical messages (cytokines, etc. interferon) which help to intensify the defensive responses of the body.

WHEN THE FIRST LINES OF DEFENCE ARE NOT ENOUGH

The process of phagocytosis and cytotoxic reaction can last hours or even days. If the germs are not destroyed or they reach the blood, the immune reaction increases and involves the entire body, which then falls ill. At this point the antibodies come into action, unless they are already present because the body has already been infected previously by the same micro-organisms. The reaction that triggers the different types of lymphocytes involved in the production of antibodies, in fact, takes some time and, because it requires the dissemination of large quantities of antibodies in the bloodstream, it is necessary that B lymphocytes multiply, however, it is a process that cannot be done straight away.

In a very general way, it can be said that once micro-organisms have reached the blood, they are intended to pass through the spleen where they come into contact with T cells and B lymphocytes which are present in the germinative centres. Alternatively, they can enter the lymphatic circuit: in this case they are filtered from the lymph nodes ▸98 where there are also germinative centres for the B lymphocytes. In both cases, the expansion of the clonal B lymphocytes that are produced - each with an antibody that is specific to an antigen stranger leads rapidly to the production of sufficient amounts of antibodies to block an infection. The antibodies that are released into the circulatory system, in fact, bind to their respective antigens.

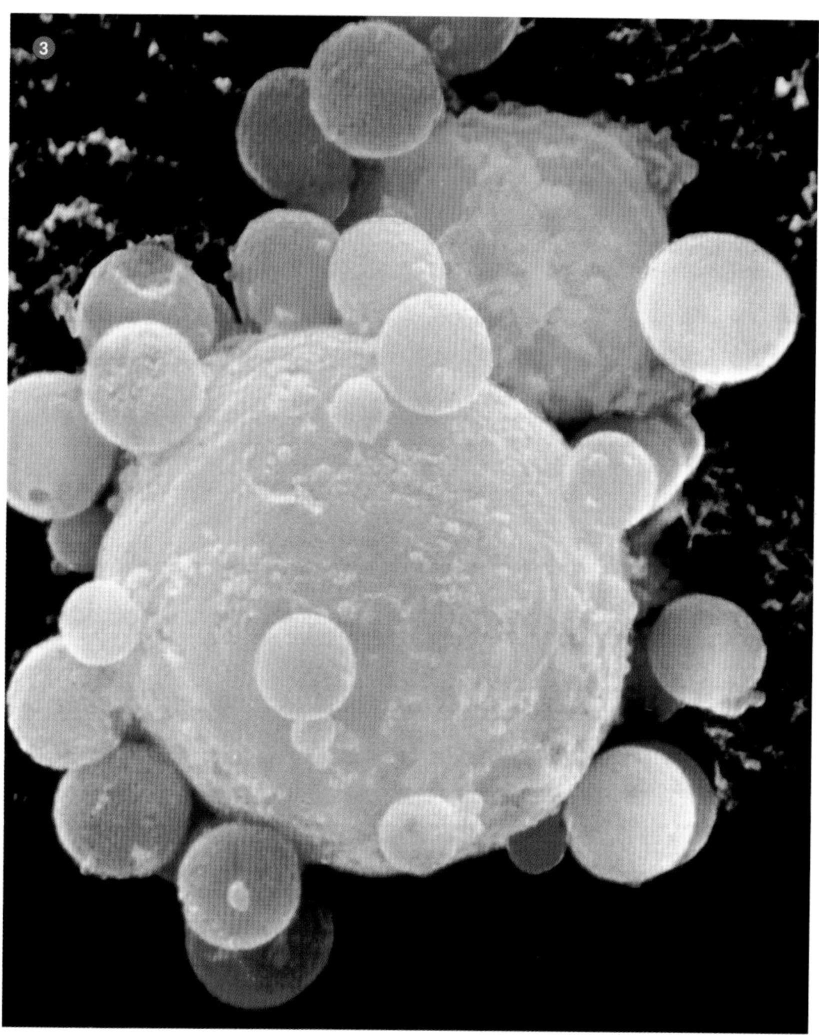

▲ **Cytotoxic reaction**
A cancerous cell is attacked by a TK and brought to death by apoptosis. This sequence of photographs was taken to scanning electron microscope.
❶ *The lymphocyte (green-yellow) adheres to the damaged cell with numerous filaments. Recognizing the complex MHC-antigen, it activates and produces perforin.*
❷ *The unhealthy cell (purple) has already started to give signs of failure in the membrane, due to change of electrolytic concentration.*
❸ *The tumor cells apoptosis is now well advanced: the cell is losing matter in abundance and is destined to rapid death.*

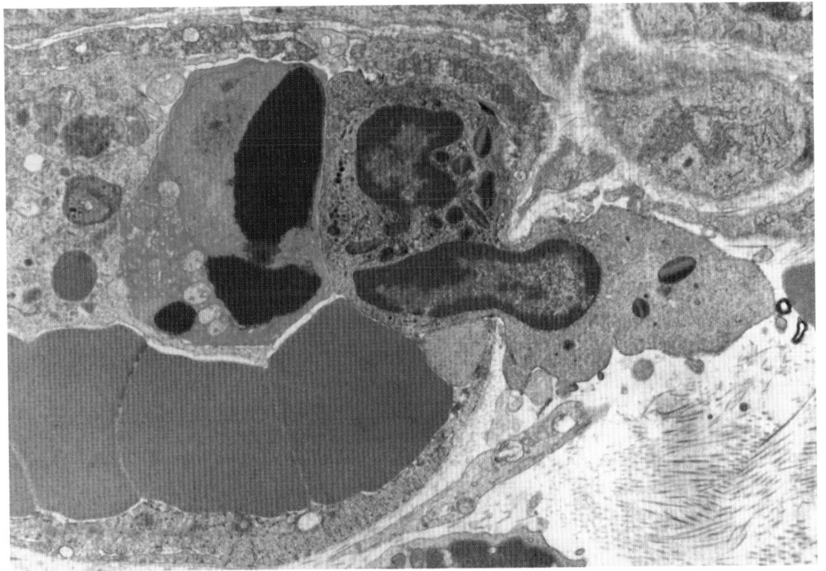

▲ **A white blood cell attacks**
TEM Photograph in false color, showing a white blood cell nucleus (center, in green and brown) that makes its way laboriously through a pore in a blood vessel. The lumen of the vessel forms the light green area on the left, while a row of red blood cells mass below.

These may be toxins or micro-organisms - either in whole or in part. Clusters are recognised by complements that, by binding to them, promotes their removal by the phagocytes, or if this happens and aggregates reach sufficient quantity and size, deposited on vessel walls. In this case it develops a localised inflammatory reaction ▸107.

IMMUNISATION

The end result of this complex battle, in a healthy body, is the defeat of any infectious micro-organisms. But the battle always leaves a track behind it - this involves the cells of the immune memory. Most are B lymphocytes which continue to express the genes that led to the synthesis of the antibodies that were specific to that particular infectious micro-organism, or that particular toxin. By reproducing these cells, it ensures that this immunological memory remains unchanged. There are also memory T cells and helper T killers which continue to produce specific receptors linked to the antigen - these are referred to respectively as MHC-2 and MHC-1.

Thanks to this 'memory cell' an individual who has had a particular disease will, even if it was only present in small quantities, have antibodies against the micro-organism. The cells that manufacture these antibodies, are therefore direct descendants of those B lymphocytes that first produced them. In a similar manner, those which are necessary to activate the production are descendants of the original T helpers. In other words, the individual concerned has developed an immunity to that particular disease. In the case of a new infection, it already has specific weapons ready to neutralise the invaders. The resulting immunisation can be permanent or partial, that is limited in time. In the latter case, the lineage of memory cells ceases to exist sooner or later.

INFECTION IN AN IMMUNISED BODY

The infectious agents that begin the invasion of a body follow the same strategies, whether it is immunised or not. In the first case, however, the invaders are soon under siege - this can be recognised by the presence of free antibodies, which begin the complement cascade ▸103, or by the presence of immune memory cells that were generated during the primary response and then remained dormant.
A cell of memory B, for example, is able to recognise any antigens that are present in solution thanks to the specific antibodies which has on its membrane. Once linked to the antigen, it incorporates and develops on the membrane. Here the antigen is also recognised by the helper T cells. Adhering to the cell of memory B, it starts to secrete cytokines that stimulate the proliferation of cell B and its transformation into plasmocytes that produce antibodies.
Besides the memory B cells having the antibody specific membrane, they also carry CD4 proteins: which can recognise the antigen. This contact stimulates the lymphocyte production and the

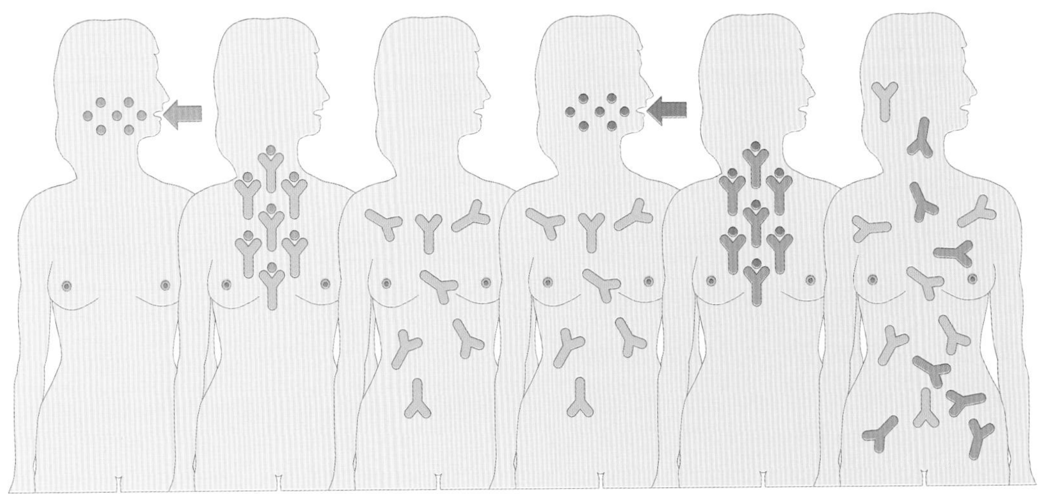

▶ **Double infection**
Outline of the production of antibodies in the immune reactions to two different antigens.
1° antigen
2° antigen
1° antibody
2° antibody

release of cytokines that attract lymphocytes and other phagocytes. This includes interferon-γ which facilitates the exit from vessels by acting on the endothelial cells which increases the production of accession molecules. Not only that: along with interleukin 2, interferon-γ stimulates the proliferation and differentiation of other lymphatic clones and the activation of macrophages.
The immune response in the event of a second infection, therefore, develops a much more rapidly and effectively than for the first time. The primary response was primarily mediated by IgM, as well as less specific antibodies and the activation of the useful complement ▶102. The secondary response, however, is mediated by IgG specifications for a specific antigen. As the cells are able to precisely identify the antigen, their response is much faster and, consequently, also increases the speed with which they proliferate and produce antibodies. Unlike that for the primary response, in which there is always a latency period that can take a few days, the secondary development of antibodies is usually already effective in a matter of hours.

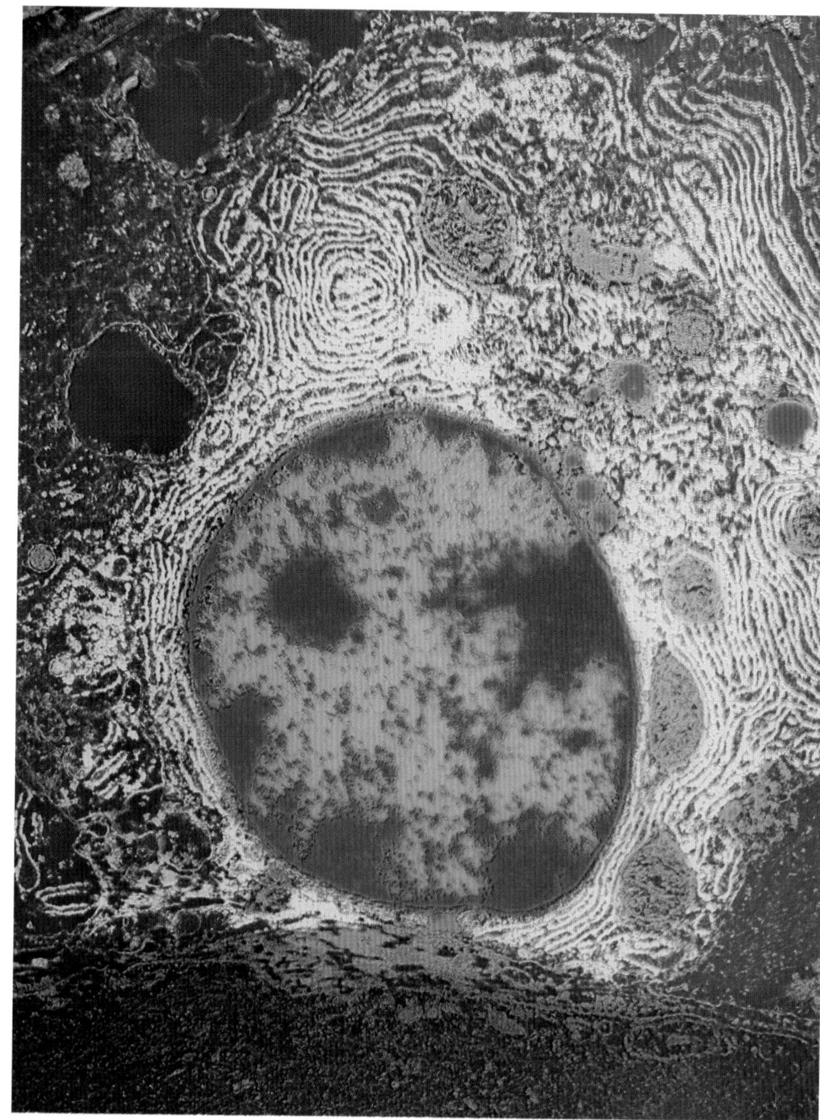

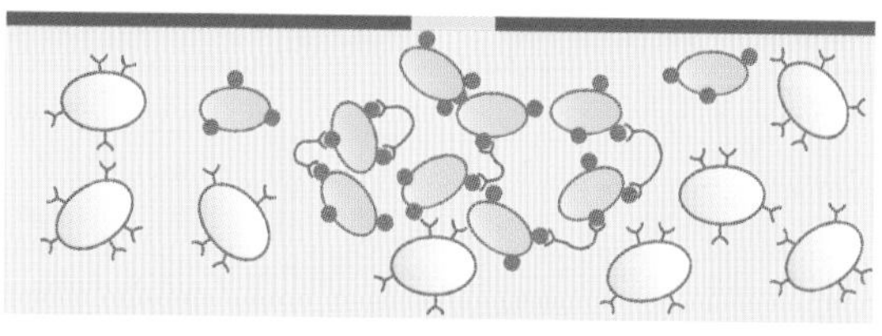

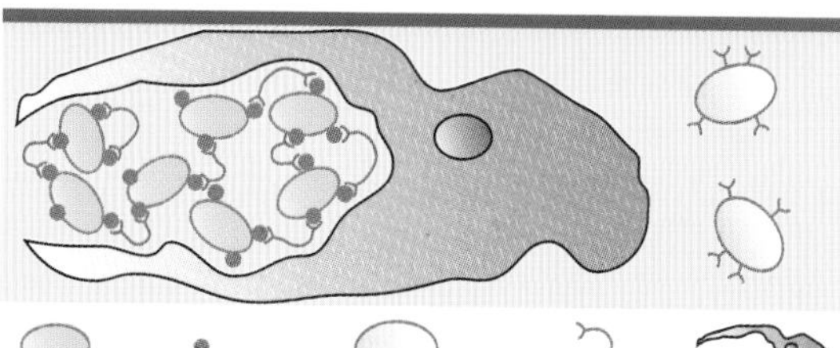

◀ **Phagocytosic reaction**
Diagram which summarizes phagocytosis reaction, mediated by specific antibodies.

▲ **Plasma cells**
transmission electron microscope (TEM) photograph in false colors of active plasma. Antibodies are "fabricated" on the inner surface of the "rough" endoplasmic reticulum, which is covered with ribosomes and distinguished and finely folded, in the yellow zone. At the center you can see the cell nucleus (blue-red) in which genetic material is arranged in typical clusters.

A PARTICULAR MUSCLE, A PUMP THAT DRIVES THE CIRCULATION CONTINUOUSLY, PROVIDING FOOD, OXYGEN AND CLEANSING TO EVERY CELL IN THE BODY: THE HEART, ONCE SEAT OF THE SOUL, AN IRREPLACEABLE ORGAN IS HERE STUDIED IN DETAIL

THE HEART: STRUCTURE AND FUNCTIONS

▶ **ANATOMICAL LOCATION**
The heart occupies the central part of the chest, protected by the rib cage and vertebral column, surrounded by the lungs and "cushioned" by the diaphragm and viscera.

The heart is an organ that is made essentially of muscle tissue that has unique properties. It is a striped muscle fibre typical of skeletal muscles, however, it forms a network more typical of smooth muscles. This structure gives the heart muscles very special characteristics. The heart, in fact, plays a key role in propelling the blood circulation. It acts as a double pump, on the right hand side it draws in blood that is low in oxygen from the body and pushes it into the lungs. On the left side it draws in blood from the lungs and pumps it throughout the body. By alternating the phases of relaxation (diastole) and the phases of contraction (systole), it is always in motion: an adult at rest, performs an average of 70 contractions every minute, for life.

GENETICS TRANSMISSIONS

The optical microscope photographs presented here show a longitudinal section of heart muscle (above) and a cross section of a papilla heart muscle (below). The myocardial fibres clearly show their features. Like the cells of skeletal muscles, they have striae interlayers (A) that are about 50-60 μm long and 20 μm thick. These are produced by the presence of ordered molecules of actin and myosin. Unlike typical skeletal muscle cells, however, the cytoplasm is widespread and branched, giving the tissue an appearance of continuity and that the cells are actually closely connected. The joints in this type of cellular network are called interlayer discs or scalariform striae (B). The electrical resistance of this tissue is low, and allows a rapid and effective dissemination of electrical signals.

Each cell has one or more elongated nuclei (C), these are distributed in length and have a central cell. There are many mitochondria which provide chemical energy continuously, developing large number of glycogen granules - these are dispersed in the cytoplasm (pink). The network of muscle cells is also crossed by connective tissue (D) which is full of blood capillaries (E). These provide the cells with a reliable supply of oxygen and nutrients as well as disposing of various metabolic waste products.

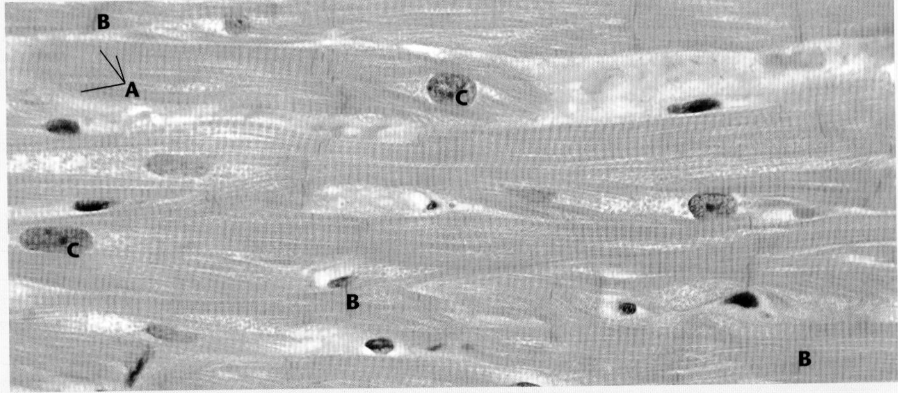

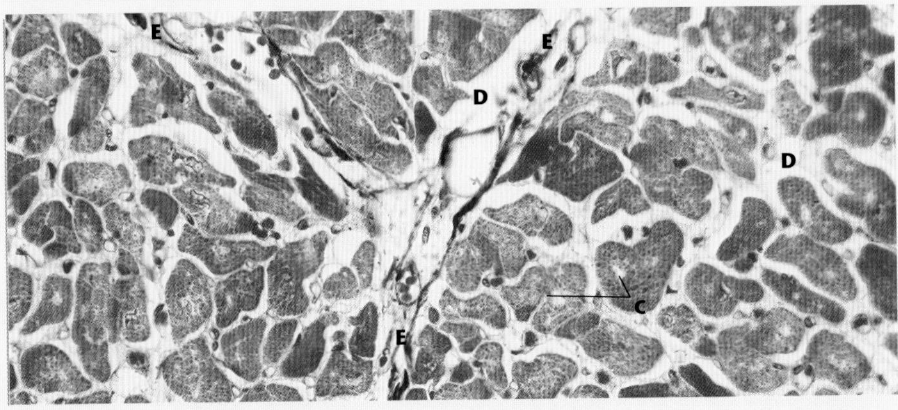

ANATOMY OF THE HEART

The heart has a cone shape with the side walls slightly squashed inwards and is divided into two sections by the interventricular septum. These are then further split into upper and lower chambers - the four structures are thus the left and right atria and the left and right ventricles. Blood that is low in oxygen and high in carbon dioxide is pumped through the heart to the lungs from the right atrium and the right ventricle. At the same time, blood that has been oxygenated by the lungs is pumped to the various parts of the body through the left atrium and the left ventricle. The heart also has a number of external features:

- the left side is more or less triangular and is crossed by two furrows filled with fatty tissue.
  – the coronary furrow or ventricular atrium is horizontal and corresponds to the boundaries between the atria and the ventricles. This is where the left coronary artery begins; beyond it are the right and left auricles;
  – the left interventricular furrow is longitudinal and corresponds to the interventricular septum that separates the ventricles. Along this path runs the descendant branch of the left coronary artery and the bottom of the great cardiac vein;
- the right face is also triangular in shape, and is marked by a coronary furrow, a septum furrow and an interventricular furrow;
- the front or cranial margin corresponds to the wall that delimits the right ventricular auricle and is a convex shape;
- the rear or caudal margin corresponds to the left ventricle and starts as a convex shape before becoming straight;

The heart is divided into four chambers separated by two sections:

- the right atrium or right auricle - this is a roughly cube-shaped cavity with four walls (the cranial, caudal, lateral and medial), an arch and a floor. It has thin, muscular walls, and the superior and inferior vena cavae enter it from the rear side.
- the interatrial septum - this is formed by a section of muscle and a membrane, and is separated from the right atrium by:
- the left atrium or left auricle - although this is smaller than the right atrium, it also has a roughly cubic shape. It is entered by the four pulmonary veins, and features almost entirely smooth interior walls that are muscular and thicker than those of the right side;
- the right ventricle - this is the biggest of the four chambers and has a pyramidal form. It has thick muscular walls and is separated from the right atrium by a circular structure called the tricuspid valve. This prevents any blood that has left the auricle from returning to the ventricle, and instead forces it into the pulmonary artery. This also features special one-way flow restrictors called the semi-lunar valves. These are so-called because they are composed of half-moon shaped folds of tissue. The pulmonary artery itself has a similar diameter to that of the aorta, but it has thinner walls.

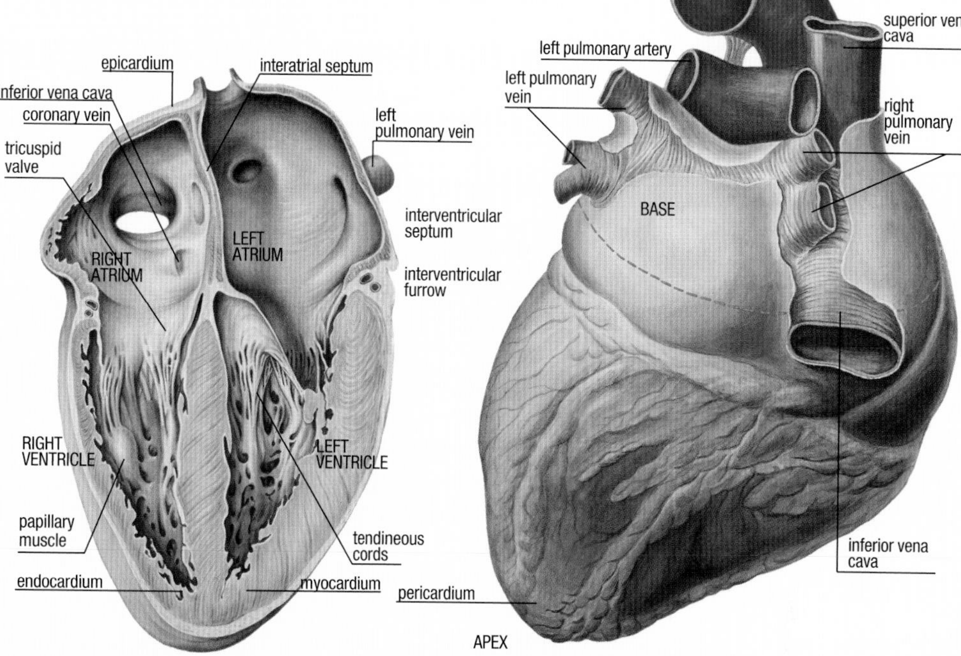

▲ **The heart in section**
left frontal view.

▲ **The hearts surface**
Frontal view.

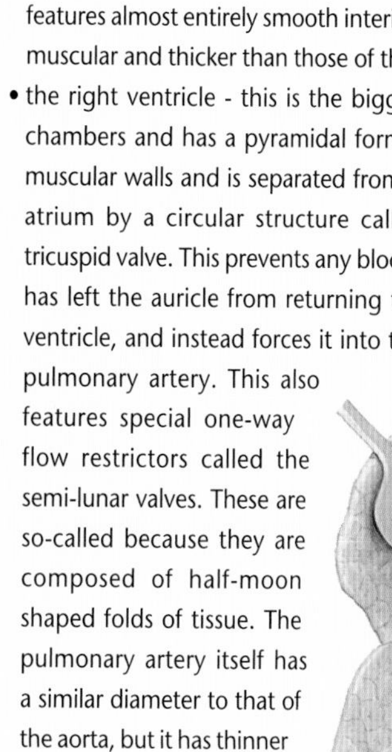

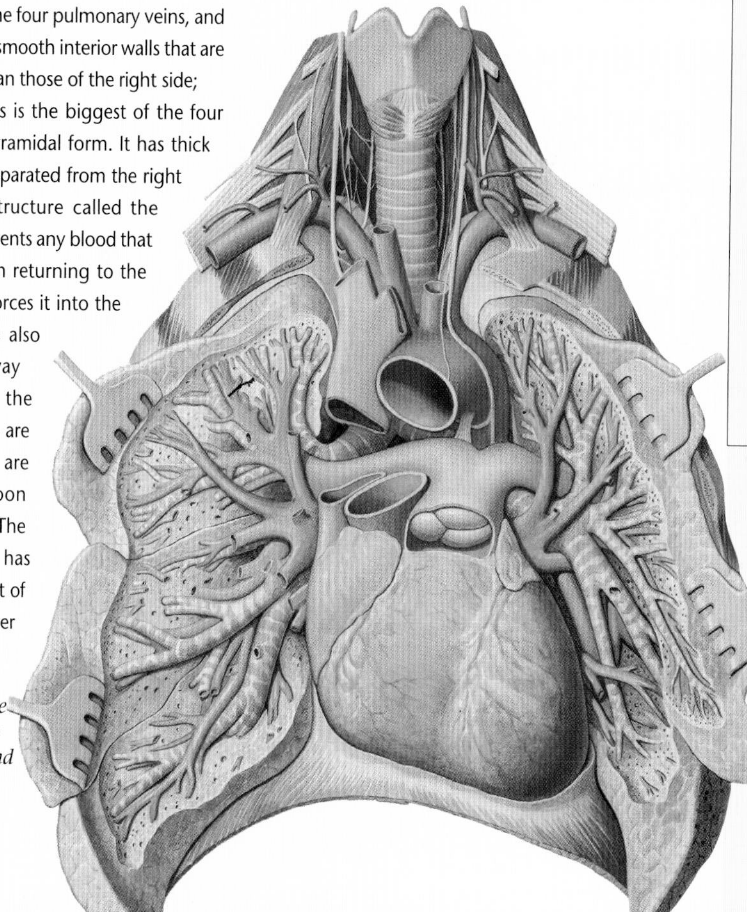

► **Anatomical location**
The heart, in the pericardial sack, borders directly with the lungs and is kept separate from the viscera from the abdominal muscle of the diaphragm. The cardiac base is in contact with the trachea, esophagus and tracheobronchial lymph nodes, while the apex is located between the 5th and 6th costal cartilage. The body remains in this position due to major blood vessels that you post and the connection of the pericardium with the pulmonary pleura, the diaphragm and the sternum.

- the interventricular septum - this is a thick layer of muscle that prevents oxygenated and deoxygenated blood from mixing. Near the origin of the aorta, the structure of the septum changes from muscle into connective tissue;
- the left ventricle - this is more developed than the right ventricle, and is made up from more powerful muscles; it is conical, and forms the apex of the heart. The valve action is performed by the bicuspid or mitral valve, which is so-named because it is composed of two disproportionately sized flaps of tissue. When the ventricle contracts, these are forced against the muscle wall, preventing the blood from flowing anywhere but into the aorta. Delimited before the interventricular septum, the left ventricle has walls with characteristics similar to those of the right one.

The right atrium and right ventricle are not in direct communication with the left atrium and left ventricle. This is because the right side of the heart solely circulates deoxygenated blood that has returned to it from the tissues of the body. The left side, however, only pumps oxygenated blood from the lungs.

The Heart In Detail

A section through the heart reveals four overlapping layers of tissue:

- the endocardium, which consists of endothelial tissue forms the innermost of the four layers.
- the myocardium is composed of muscle tissue: it is made up of a complex network of contractile fibres and bundles that allows independence of movement from area to area. This ensures that the heart is able to move in the manner required for it to beat. The myocardium has significant structural differences in accordance with the part of the heart where it occurs. In the lobules, for example, it is thin, whereas in the in the ventricles it is much thicker and more complex;
- the epicardium is a protective membrane that surrounds the heart and is formed by very smooth, thin, flattened cells;
- the pericardium is a twin-walled serous tissue sac that envelops the heart and the beginning of the great vessels. It is designed to link the heart to the central portion of the chest and sternum. To facilitate the movements of the heart, it does not adhere to the epicardium, and the space that separates them (pericardial cavity) contains a small amount of lubricating liquid (liquor pericardial).

The Coronary

The heart needs a lot of energy to keep moving, as well as a continuous drain of metabolic wastes in order to avoid poisoning. It therefore needs a constant and rich supply of blood - for this reason, there is a dense network of capillaries that belong to the cardiac vessels, commonly known as the coronary arteries. These - known as the left and right coronary arteries, connect to the aorta and carry oxygen and nutrients to every area of the heart - it is therefore the first organ to be supplied with newly oxygenated blood. The coronary veins, instead, collect blood from the heart and convey it directly back into the right side, from where it is then pumped to the lungs through the pulmonary artery.

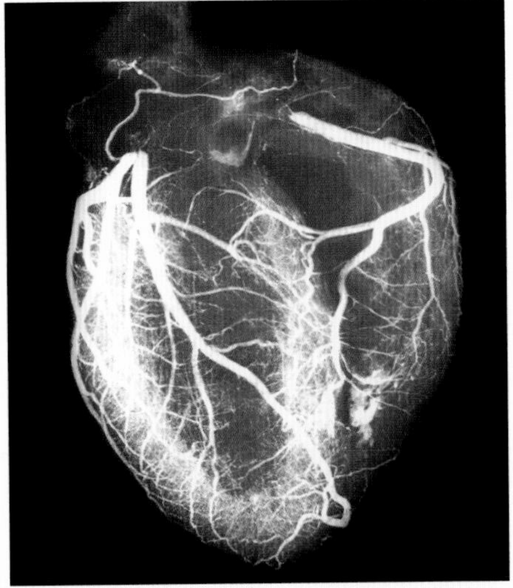

▲ **Arteries and veins**
An angiogram (X-ray arteriography) in false colors shows in detail the coronary arteries.

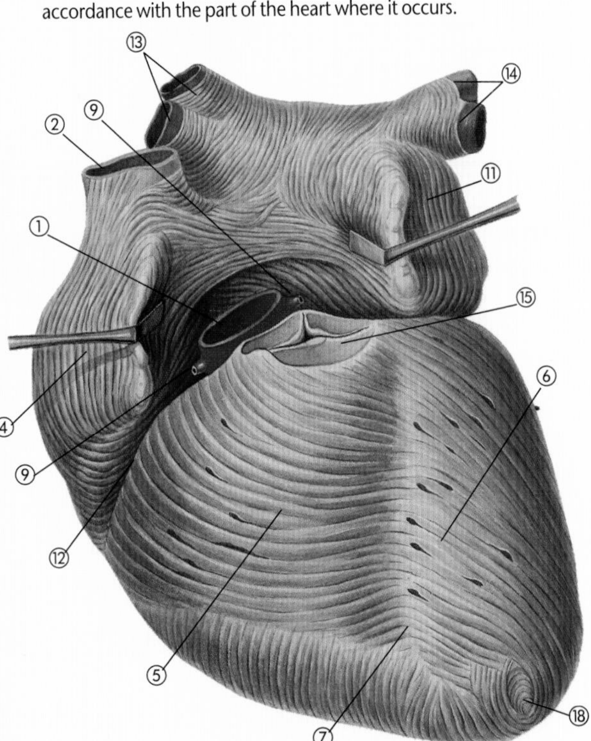

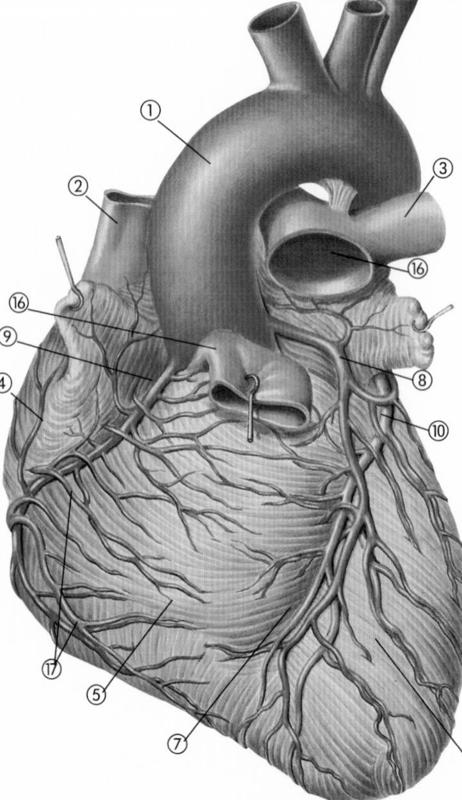

◀ **Muscles and circulation of the heart**
Frontal view.
① *aorta*
② *superior vena cava*
③ *right pulmonary artery*
④ *right atrium*
⑤ *right ventricle*
⑥ *left ventricle*
⑦ *interventricular furrow*
⑨ *right coronary artery*
⑧ *left coronary artery*
⑩ *left coronary vein or great vein of the heart*
⑪ *right atrium*
⑫ *coronary furrow*
⑬ *right pulmonary vein*
⑭ *left pulmonary vein*
⑮ *semi lunar valve of the pulmonary trunk*
⑯ *pulmonary trunk*
⑰ *anterior veins of the heart*
⑱ *vortex*

THE CARDIAC CYCLE

The term "cardiac cycle" means a full movement of the heart, which is where blood from the body passes to the lungs and returns again after re-oxygenation. While the process of pumping blood is outwardly simple, there are, in fact, many elements involved, and these can be studied from several different perspectives.

THE DYNAMICS OF THE CARDIAC CYCLE

A heart at rest beats on average 70 times a minute. This process involves the opening and closing of the atrioventricular valves in a specific order while powerful muscular contractions generate pressure in the blood, which is then forced through the heart's chambers and into the circulatory system. The heart also relaxes, on average, 70 times a minute. This is when the atria and ventricles return to their initial volumes, and in so doing draw in blood through the open valves.

The five main phases of the cardiac cycle are:

Late diastole - this is where the semilunar valves close, the heart relaxes, and the atrioventricular valves open.

Atrial systole - the atria contracts as the atrioventricular valves open, and blood is pumped from the atrium to the ventricle.

Isovolumic ventricular contraction - this is where the atrioventricular and semilunar valves begin closing and the ventricles start contracting.

Ventricular ejection - in this phase the ventricles continue contracting and the semilunar valves remain open.

Isovolumic ventricular relaxation - in this phase the pressure falls, contraction of the ventricles finishes, relaxation begins and the semilunar valves are closed.

This is just a brief outline, however. There is much more to what really happens in the heart to ensure that it is able to function with such great precision, day in, day out, year after year - for life.

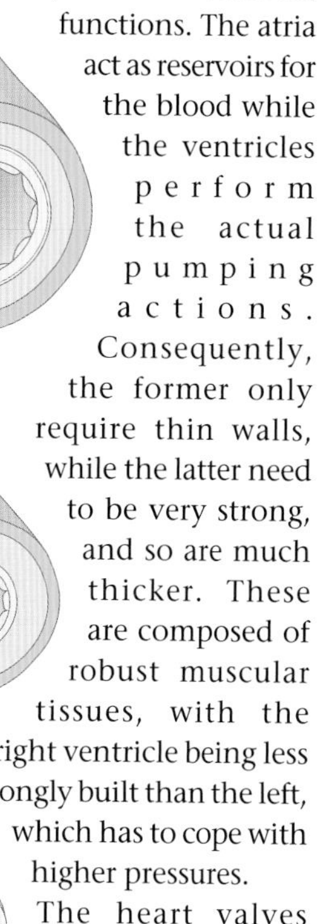

THE CARDIAC MUSCLES

As we have seen, the heart functions as a pump that is divided into two sections, these in turn also consist of two parts, each with different functions. The atria act as reservoirs for the blood while the ventricles perform the actual pumping actions. Consequently, the former only require thin walls, while the latter need to be very strong, and so are much thicker. These are composed of robust muscular tissues, with the right ventricle being less strongly built than the left, which has to cope with higher pressures.

The heart valves play an important function: they ensure that blood flow in a single direction is possible. From the functional point of

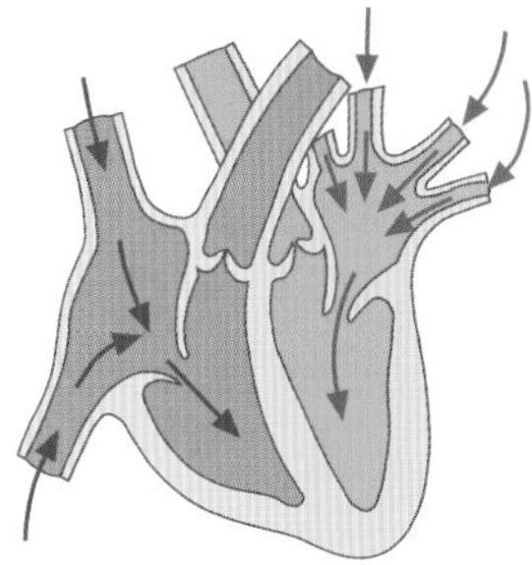

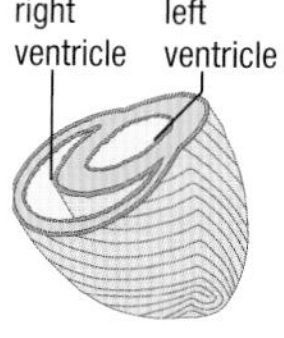

▲ **DIASTOLE**
The heart relaxes: atria and ventricles dilate and fill with blood.

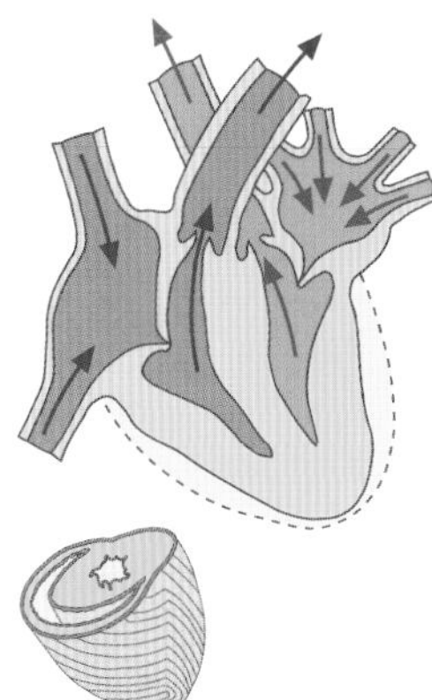

▲ **SISTOLE**
The heart contracts: atria and ventricles shrink and the blood vessels pump.

▼ **CARDIAC CYCLE**
Succession of cardiac cycle events as described in the text.

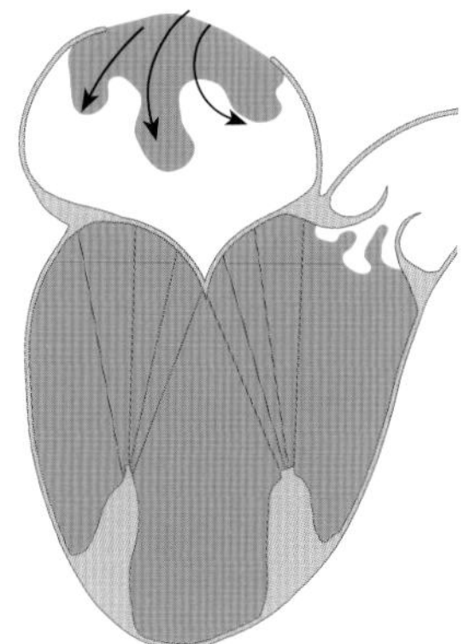

atrial diastole

atrial sistole

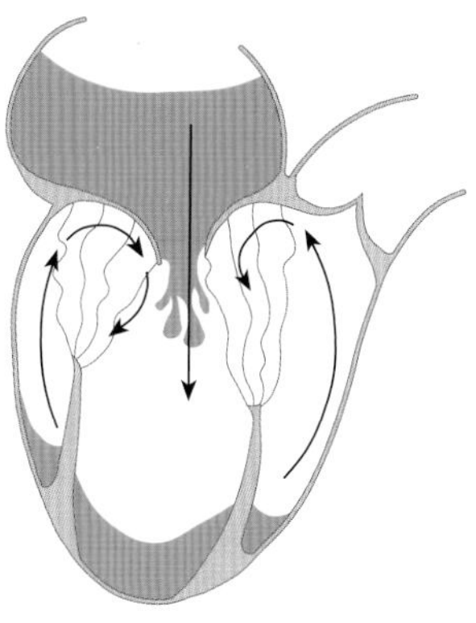

ventrical diastole

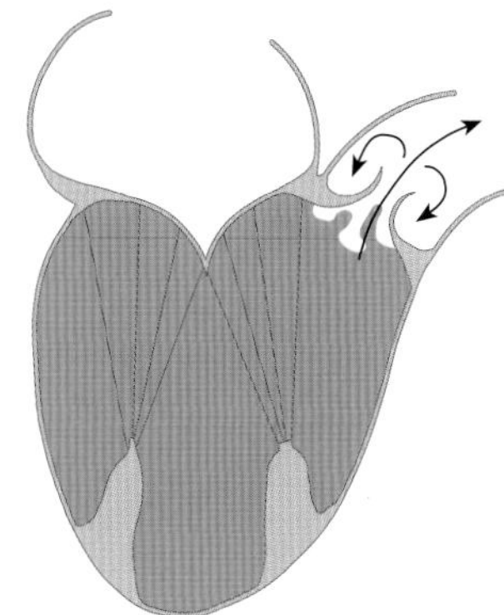

ventrical sistole

view, the heart is an autonomous organ with its own structures that enable it to maintain the momentum that alternates between muscle excitement (contraction) and relaxation (distension) ▸236.

Each cardiac cycle starts in the core of the heart, where there are clusters of cells capable of both autoexcitation and triggering the other nearby cells. When the excitation threshold is exceeded ▸28, the stimulation takes place in an 'all or nothing' manner. The contraction of all the cells that are involved is almost simultaneous, as though they were all wired together. The signal junctions, in fact, have a very low resistance and therefore a high conductance of electrical signals. As in the case with other muscles ▸236, the heart responds to nerve impulses with a precise sequence of events:

- an initial phase during which stimuli are blocked due to the sodium ion channels being inactivated. This prevents the generation of potential actions, and it remains like this until the membrane potential reaches -55mV.
- a plateau period in which the charges necessary for an action potential are built up by the exchange of calcium and potassium ions;
- a rapid repolarisation phase during which the calcium ion channels close but those for potassium ions remain open. This causes a rapid repolarisation of the membrane, which makes it possible for the action potential to be triggered by a lower intensity stimulus;

The contraction starts at the apex of the heart and spreads across it, reducing its overall diameter - this generates the necessary pressure in the blood. Due to the difference in thicknesses, the ventricles develop different pressures.

THE ORIGIN & TRANSMISSION OF THE CONTRACTION

The actual stimulus for the cardiac contraction comes from a group of myocardial cells, that is referred to as the sinoatrial node. It is the structure that is sometimes supplanted by an artificial prosthesis in patients with heart problems. Such devices help reduce cardiac imbalances by stimulating the heart with extra electrical impulses. The cells of the sinoatrial node are located in the wall of the atrium, near the mouth of the superior vena cava - the structure has an ovoid shape, and is made up of muscle cells which have contact with many amyelinic nerve fibres ▸158 and ganglia cells that belong to the sympathetic nervous system ▸176. The cells of the sinoatrial node generate signals that cause the heart to contract rhythmically. As a consequence of each contraction, an impulse

▸ **Valves**
Pictures from inside of the heart: **a**. *mitral valve taken by scanning electron microscope, in false colors;* **b**. *Details of the tendinous cords that bind the ends of a valve in the muscles of the ventricle;* **c**. *photo of a pulmonary valve open and* **d**. *closed. A semilunare valve is formed by 2 or 3 movable flaps (cusps) that can bend in one direction.*

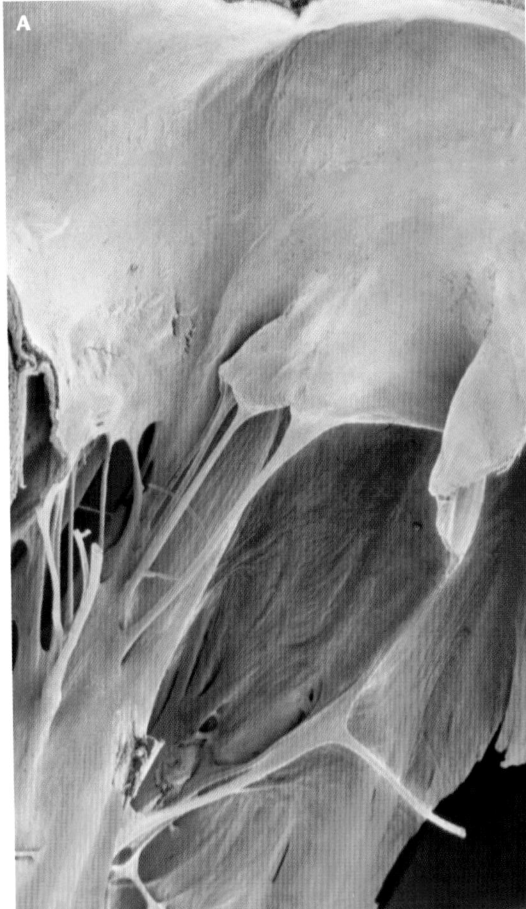

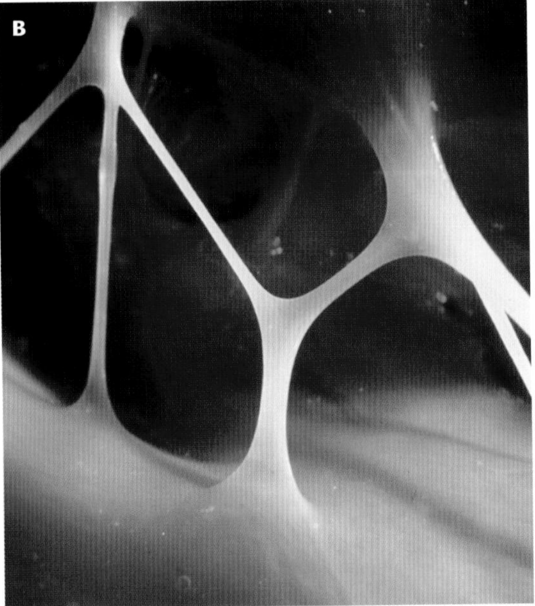

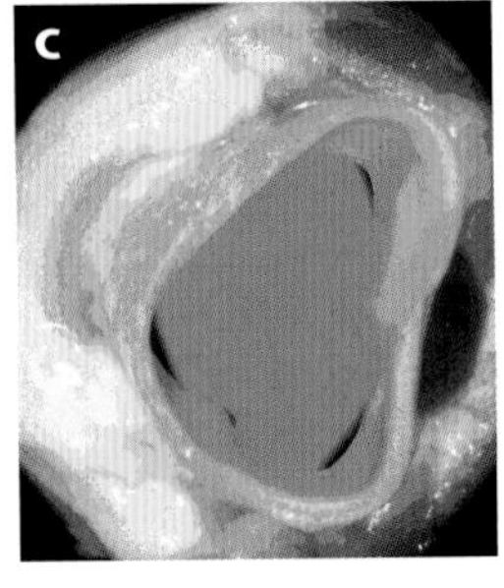

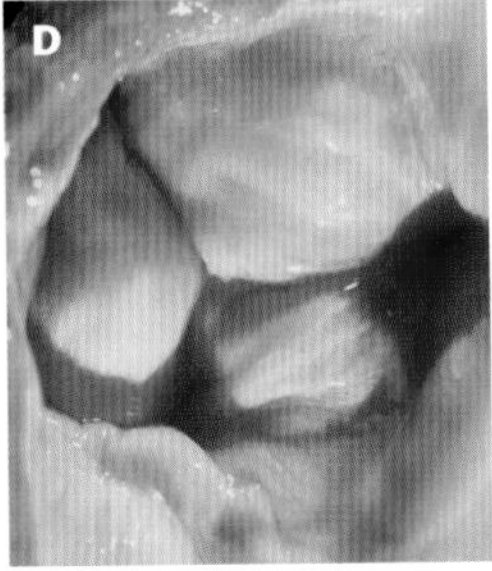

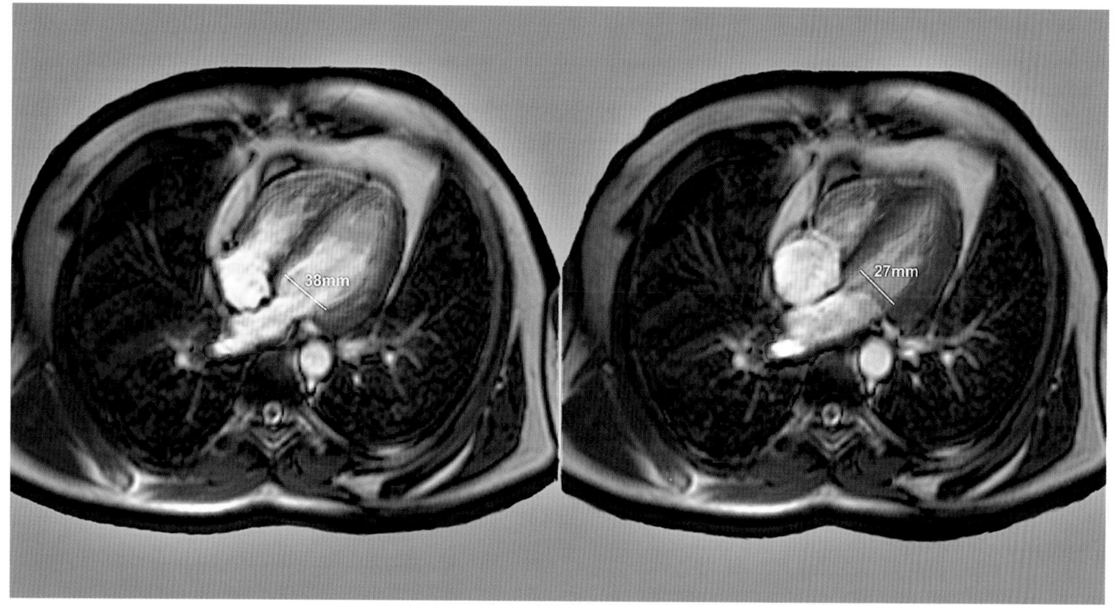

◀ **Heartbeat**
Magnetic Resonance in false colors of a cross section of a chest in which a healthy heart beats, with a marked measurement of the width of the left ventricle. The wall of the heart muscle is picked out in violet, while the areas in which the blood flows (atria and ventricles) are red-yellow, the brighter the color, the higher the content of blood. On the left the heart is in a state of diastole: the ventricles are filled. On the right, the systole: particularly noticeable contraction of the left ventricle, which pushes the blood into the aorta.

spreads through the cavity cardiac via the numerous bundles of Purkinje cells that branch throughout the atrial walls.

The atrial and ventricular chambers are electrically connected to one another via the atrioventricular node. This is sometimes referred to as the Aschoff-Tawara node, and is located in the right side of the interatrial septum, and has an ovoid shape. It is formed by a plexus of fibrous cells and a connective bundle that branches off in the interventricular septum (atrioventricular bundle, or 'bundle of His'). This is made of specially-modified heart fibres that are capable of conducting electrical impulses at a speed greater than that of the atrioventricular node. Thus, the wave of contraction spreads rapidly throughout the bundle of nerve fibres, which are divided into two branches which are initially directed towards the apex of the heart, they then open out and continuing to form a subendocardial network of Purkinje fibres that are distributed

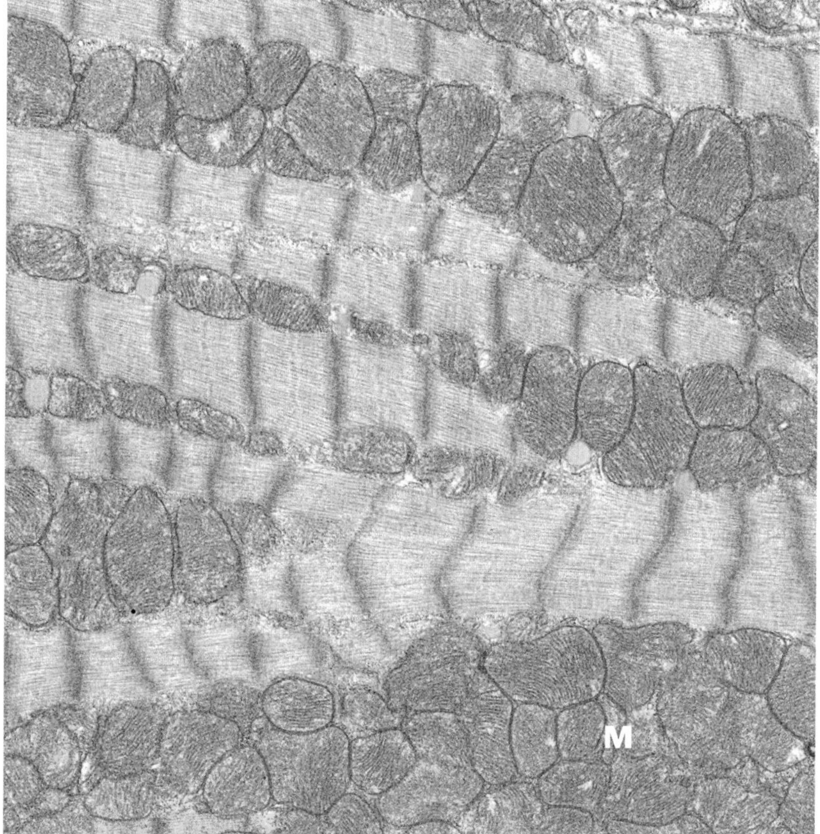

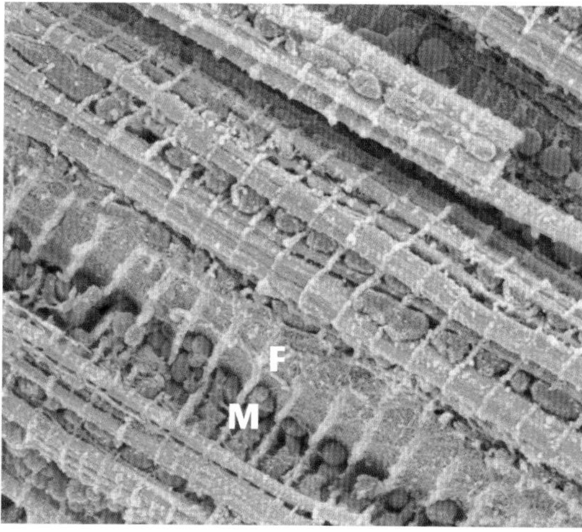

◀▲ **Muscular fibres**
In cardiac cells, unlike what happens in skeletal muscles, there are numerous mitochondria (M) because, unlike skeletal cells, which may go into "oxygen debt" to recover and then be fully operational during the subsequent period of rest, heart muscle can not be short of energy, and can not stop to retrieve energy! The large number of mitochondria, therefore, is necessary to continue the synthesis of energetic materials. Above, a false color SEM photo shows the cardiac fibers (F) in yellow and red of the mitochondria. Left, a TEM photograph of the allows to distinguish the provision of internal cardiac syncytial tissue.

▶ **Contractile system**
A system that allows an electrical impulse from the node to spread to the atrial sinus (blue).

throughout the walls of the ventricles. In this way, the impulse that triggers the cardiac contraction reaches all parts of the heart. The speed at which the signal is generated, however, remains under the control of the sinoatrial node.

ELECTRICAL CONTROL OF THE HEART

The stimulus that causes the contraction of heart muscle is caused by electrical currents, which are generated by the flows of ions which alter the electrical potential ▸[28] of each myocardial region ▸[238]. These signals are then transmitted from one cell to another, involving the entire structure of the heart.
As is the case with other excitable cells ▸[26], the myocardial electrical potential depends on the concentration of ions on both sides of the membrane. Under conditions of rest, there is a mirror situation: the interior of the cell has concentrations of potassium and sodium ions that are in the regions of K+ = 130 meq and Na+ = 5-10 meq/l. Conversely, the exterior of the cell has ion concentrations of K+ = 5 meq/l and Na+ = 130 meq/l. The term 'meq/l' stands for milliequivalents per litre, and indicates the concentration of ions in a given solution. The 'meq' is the thousandth part of the atomic weight in grams of the ion under consideration, divided by the number of electric charges present in the same ion. This measure, therefore, makes it possible to compare the different ions in a solution, since 1 meq always contains the same number of ions regardless of the substances to which they belong.
This ionic condition corresponds to a rest potential ▸[28] of between -70 and -90 mV. The excitation by the myocardial action potential is depolarised, releasing calcium ions (Ca2+). The membrane potential varies very quickly from -90 to + 20 mV, and the cell activates the process of contraction (phase 0), this is followed by a short duration repolarisation, during which the membrane potential returns to a level equal to 0 mV (Phase 1). It then settles for a relatively long time (Phase 2), and then the polarisation takes over and completes (Phase 3) until the -90 mV rest potential is reached again (Phase 4).
The duration of the process of depolarisation and repolarisation varies from one area of the heart to another, and depends on when the excitement signal arrives from the sinoatrial node. The first cells to start this process are those of the node, and from these a "wave of depolarisation" followed by a rapid repolarisation spreads to the cells of the atrial walls. It is this event that generates the electric waves seen by the electrocardiogram P. In this manner the depolarisation passes to the left side of the interatrial

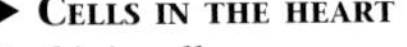

▶ **Cells in the heart**
Purkinje cells, photographed by a scanning electron microscope on the surface of some cardiac muscle cells. Purkinje cells are modified cardiac muscle fibers, which originate from the atrioventricular node and propagate inside the ventricles. They transmit the electrical impulse from the atrioventricular node to the ventricles, ensuring an almost simultaneous contraction. This electric transmission is extremely rapid: 1 to 4 m/s.

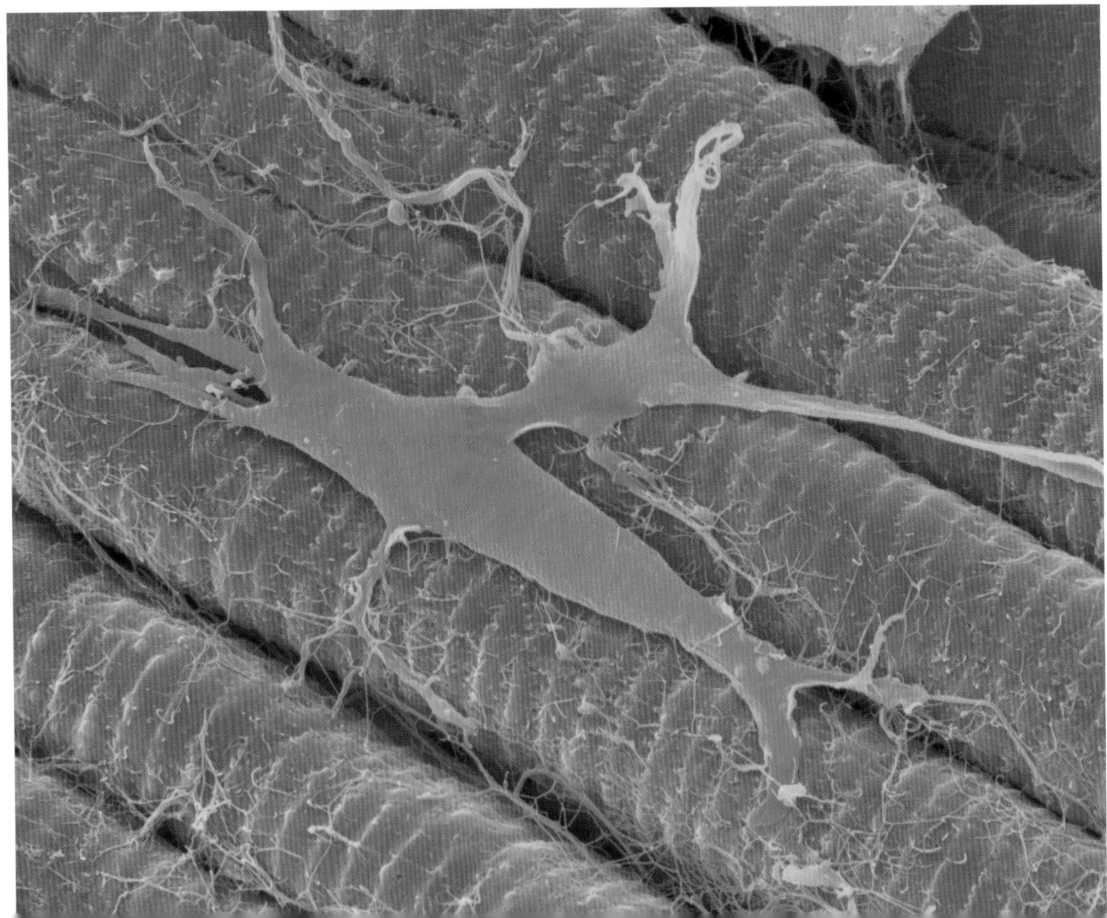

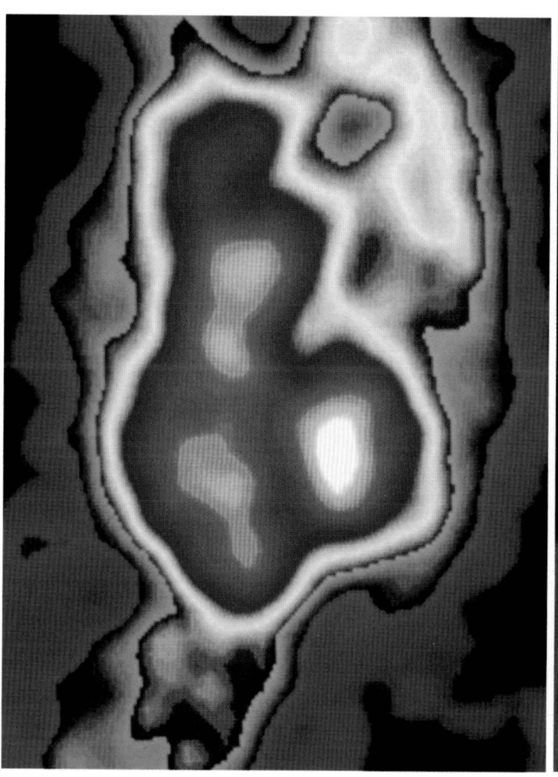

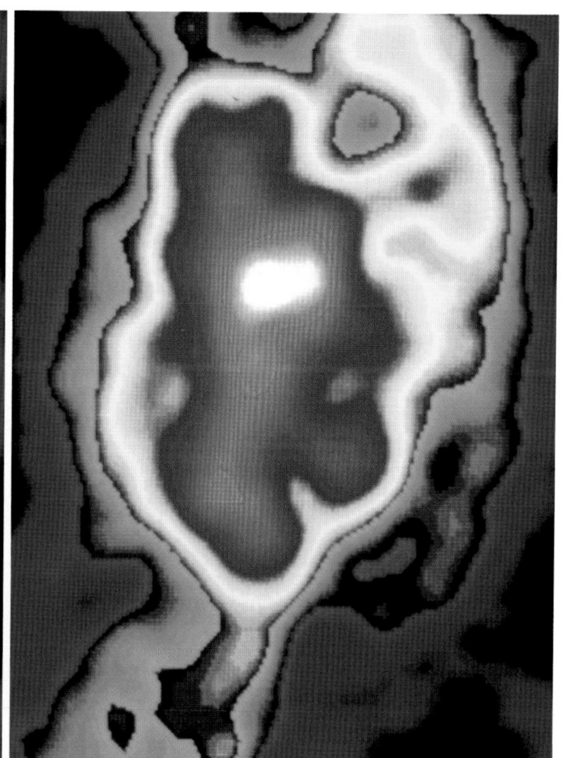

◀◀ Diastole
Scintigraphy in false color of a heart in diastole (when the cardiac chambers are filling with blood). The heart is in the center of the image. The red, pink and white areas indicate the position of the left ventricle filled with blood. The colors were chosen to indicate the amount of gamma radiation emitted from the technetium-labeled blood subsequently recorded by the instrument.

◀ Sistole
Scintigraphy in false color of a heart in systole (when the blood is pumped out of the ventricles). The left ventricle, which was once contracted is the small red area, which is more or less circular in the lower right. The pink and white areas are those in which blood flow has increased.

A

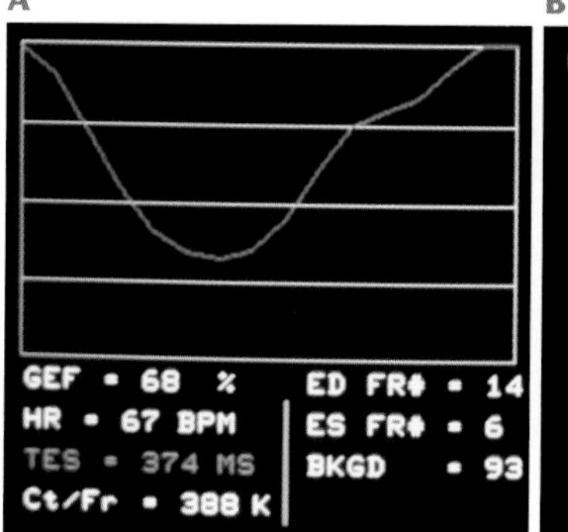

B

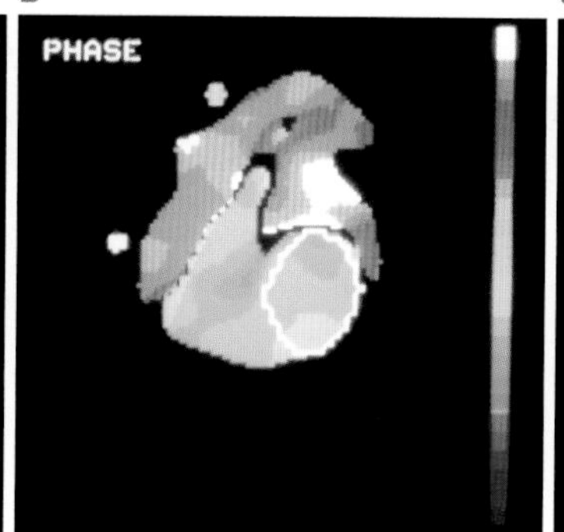

C

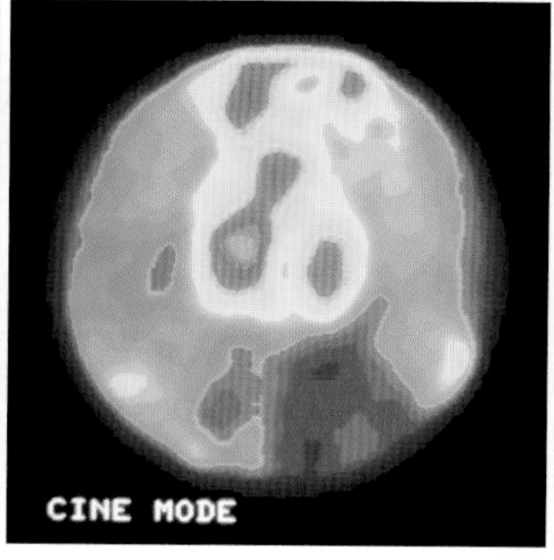

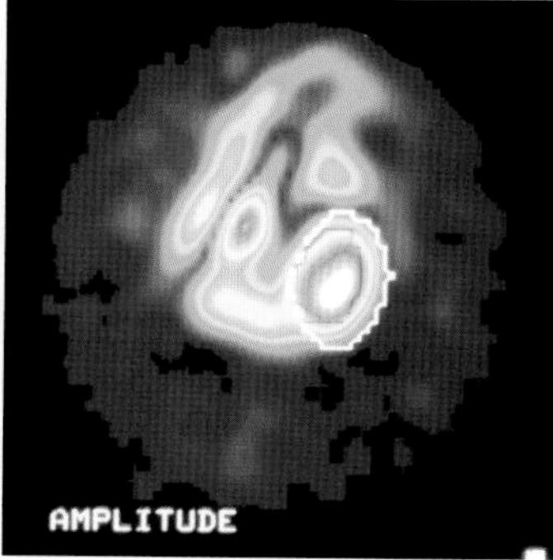

▲ Blood flow
Computed Tomography (SPECT, Single Photon Emission Computed Tomography) in false colors of a healthy heart. The examination is performed by injecting into a vein a radioactive tracer (technetium) and recording the range of emissions from the site of interest (the heart).
A. *The diagram shows the amount of tracer expelled from the heart with each contraction.*
B. *Front section of the heart: the speed of blood flow is indicated by the scale of colors (white faster, blue slower).*
C. *two cross sections show the blood ejected from the ventricles, the white line in the picture demarcates the area of interest.*

septum and then propagates to the right side: This event causes the wave Q. The depolarisation then starts which triggers the contraction of the ventricles; this begins with the immediate depolarisation of the right ventricle (beginning of wave R) and then the left (which transforms the R wave in a clear peak). The period of ventricle depolarisation is identified by the wave S. After this there is a level period in which the ventricles are completely depolarised. Finally, there is the repolarisation, when the wave T indicates the recovery of negative charge that is the prelude to a new impetus.

REGULATORY MECHANISMS & CARDIAC INNERVATION

The mechanisms that regulate heart activity, adapting it from moment to moment to the needs of the body, are primarily carried out by the sympathetic ▸176 and parasympathetic nervous systems ▸177, and mediated by the cardiovascular centre in the brain ▸123.

The heart, while being autonomous from the functional point of view, must always have adequate energy supplies to meet the demands of the body, which are continuously changing. Adapting the cardiac function to the needs of the body quickly is a task which is entrusted to the nervous system and, in particular, to a complex network of components. In the shortest time possible, sensitive receptors and passageways must communicate with the central nervous system via the spinal cord. Together they co-operate to collect information signals from the different parts of the body - these are then processed and appropriate impulses are sent to the heart's regulatory mechanism. The signals include information on the partial pressures of oxygen and carbon dioxide in the blood, along with its volume, blood pressure and, above all, the state of the peripheral vessels. These are sensitive to the stress conditions and the action of hormones such as adrenaline.

The electrocardiogram

The cardiac contractions which make mammalian life possible are triggered by electrochemical events. Each cardiac pulse is preceded by changes in the electrical state of the cardiac cells - these go from rest, to 'ON' and then return to rest. The changes are accompanied by flows of electrical charge that can be measured on the surface of the body.

The body (especially the skin) has a high electrical resistance, and therefore makes the passage of electrical currents - including those generated by the heart, very difficult. Modern instruments are, however, sensitive enough to able to detect the tiny amounts as measurable signals. The device that is used for this is called an electrocardiograph. The first primitive version was invented in 1903 by Dutch scientist W. Einthoven. By linking this tool to the skin on the chest with some electrodes, it is possible to capture the impulses and direct them to an amplifier which turns them into video images or records them on a moving strip of paper.

The result record is called an electrocardiogram: it shows differences in the heart signal down to a thousandth of a volt and, according to the placement of electrodes can be used to provide different kinds of information.

The most commonly used are:

- the three classic Einthoven or bipolar limb derivations: 1st. Right-arm left arm; 2nd. right arm-left leg; 3rd. left arm-left leg.
- precordial or thoracic derivations. Any differences in heartbeat movement can be monitored and usually the cause of any malfunctions identified. In a normal track there are three waves - the positive (P, R and T), and two negative waves (Q and S).
- the P wave or atrial complex is derived from the atrial region.
- the Q, R and D waves or the complex ventricular movements are produced by the ventricular region.
- the T wave is produced at the end of the ventricular cycle.

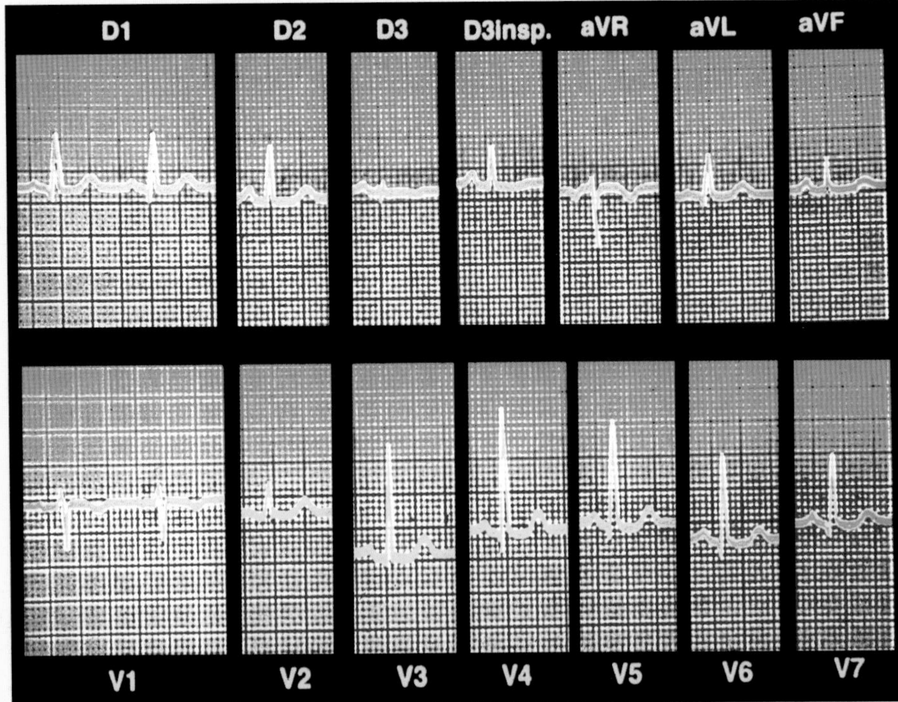

An electrocardiograph may also register so-called noise or tones produced by cardiac valves and the vibration of the walls of the heart and large vessels.

▲▶ Electrocardiogram
The various tracks of this normal electrocardiogram (above) show the heartbeat in the heart cavity measured with 14 different external electrodes (D1-D3, D3insp, aVR, aVL, aVF and V1-V6) and registered as electrical waves (pale blue) for each electrode. The highest peak (for example in the track V4) indicates ventricular contraction, the smaller waves preceding it indicate contraction of the atria. In the diagram on the right, the electrocardiogram can give important indications for the diagnosis of heart problems, revealing the location and nature of many disorders.

normal track (70 beats/min)

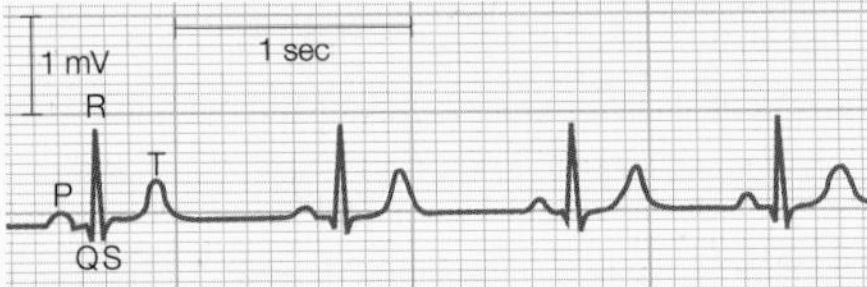

sinusal tachycardia

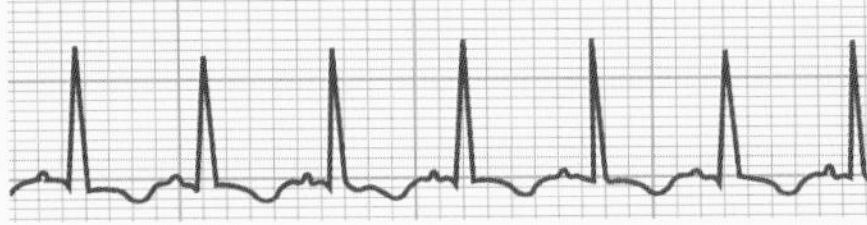

sinusal brachycardia

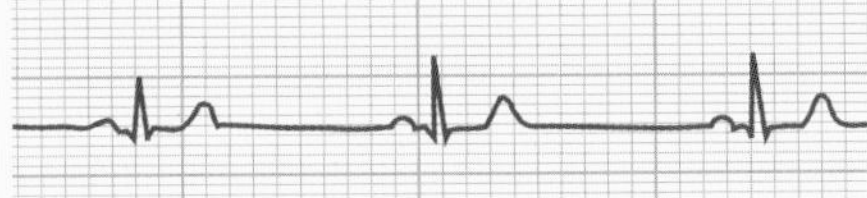

over ventricular extrasystole

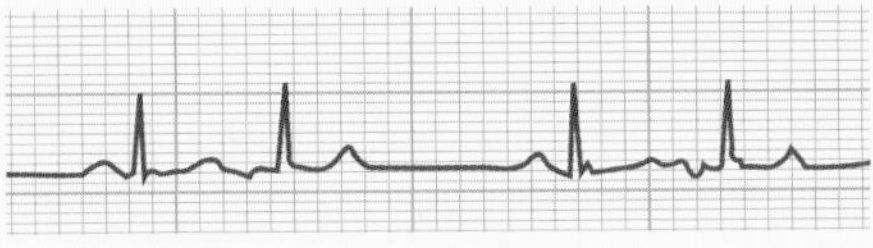

ventricular fibrillation

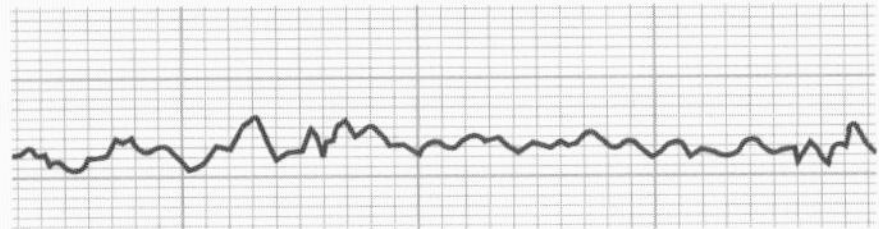

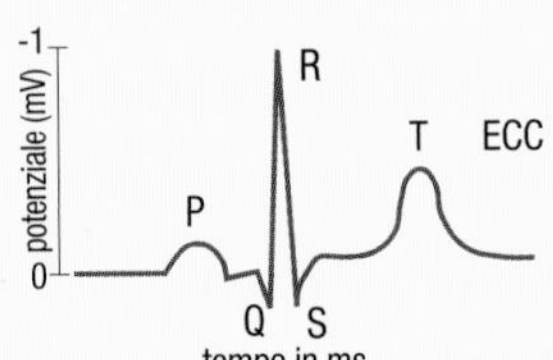

◀ ECG signs of strain
This type of test shows signs of strain serves to highlight cases of angina or to monitor conditions after a heart attack.

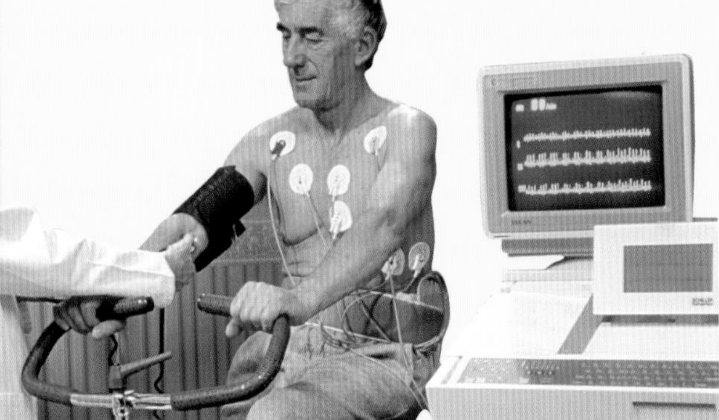

• Receptors are nerve endings that are sensitive to various changes in the immediate environment. These include pressure (baroreceptors), the concentrations of specific chemical substances in the blood (chemoreceptors), or mechanical changes (mechanoreceptors). Precise areas of the circulatory system (heart, arteries, veins) transmit stimuli to the control centres in order that immediate changes can be made to the heart's contractile frequency as well as the sizes of the relevant vessels, and the pace and depth of breathing. In particular these actions involve:

- cardiac receptors; these are mechanoreceptors which are internal to the heart wall;
- aortic receptors and carotid baroreceptors, which are housed in the walls of the great arteries;
- receptors on the carotid body (which is also known as the carotid glomus or glomus caroticum) and the aortic arch ▸200 which are chemoreceptor structures in the vascular system, and characterised by abundant blood circulation. They are sensitive to the partial pressures of oxygen and carbon dioxide as well as the pH of the blood. They send signals to the cardiovascular centre in the brain which also stimulates the respiratory tract.

• Nerves: the frequency of the cardiac cycle, the strength of myocardial contraction, and the output of the heart, are all regulated through extrinsic innervation which acts on the whole myocardial system. The nerves involved are the vagus nerve, which has an inhibitory action, and the branches of the sympathetic and parasympathetic nervous systems. These are excitatory and originate in the cervical region. Together, they form the cardiac plexus, an intricate network of neurons which are intimately interconnected, from which spread out nerve fibres that reach the nodes and bundles of the heart, the coronary vessels and the entire heart muscle. The cardiac plexus produces three cranial nerves (the upper, middle and bottom) that each descend from a cervical ganglion, as well as fibres from the first four thoracic ganglia and the three branches of the cardiac vagus nerve. In particular:

- the vagus nerve has a direct action on the atria. Stimuli from its terminations result in a decrease in heart rate, the timing of the atrial contractions as well as the durations of the resting period and the atrial systole;
- the sympathetic and parasympathetic systems determine any increases in heart rate, the contractions of the atria and ventricles, the speed of conduction, and the myocardial excitability.

• Cardiac centres: nerve signals reach the heart from particular areas of the central nervous system and process the stimuli that result from them ▸164. The information that describes the heart pulses is collected by the following receptors:

- the cardio-acceleratory spinal centre, which is located in the spinal cord, branched off from these ganglia are various autosympathetic nerve fibres;
- the bulbar-cardio acceleratory centres and cardio-inhibitory centres are in the cardiovascular centre of the brain, and are triggered by impulses from the peripheral and central nerve systems. These are activated in response to such stimuli as complex emotions, pain, anger or sudden changes in temperature.

▼ **Involuntary nerves**
Anatomical image that shows the main involuntary nerves that affect the heart:
① sympathetic trunk
② thoracic cardiac branches
③ left anterior plexus
④ right anterior plexus
⑤ plexus of Atri
⑥ laryngeal nerve recurring
⑦ vagus nerve
⑧ subclavian loop
⑨ Cervicothoracic ganglion (stellate)
⑩ middle cervical cardiac nerve

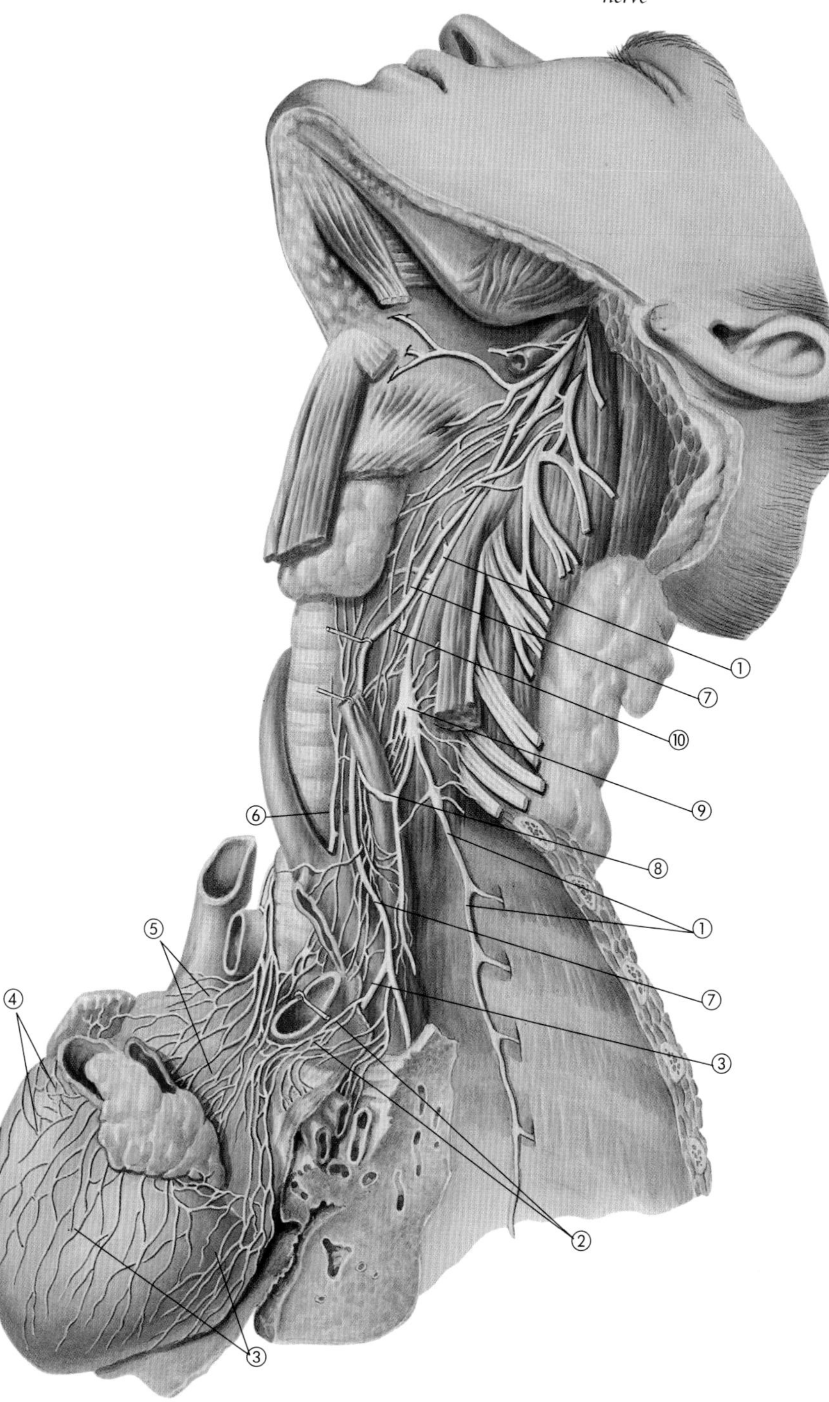

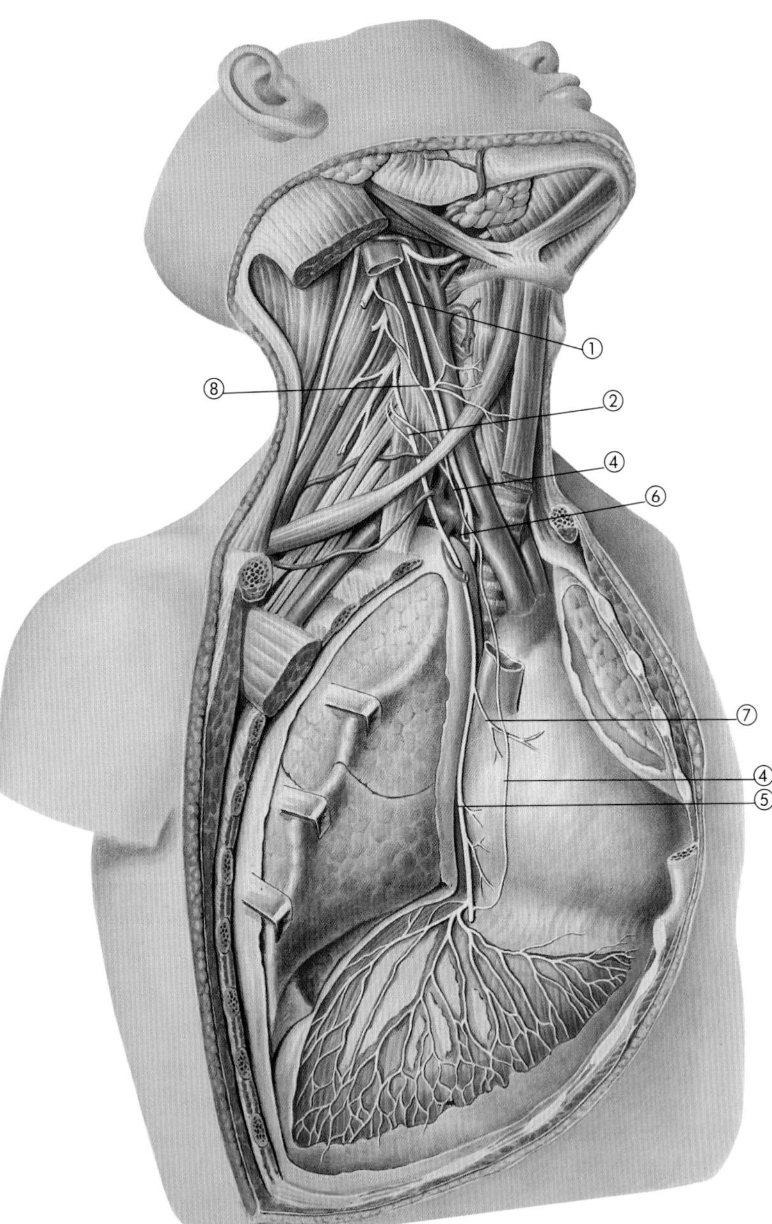

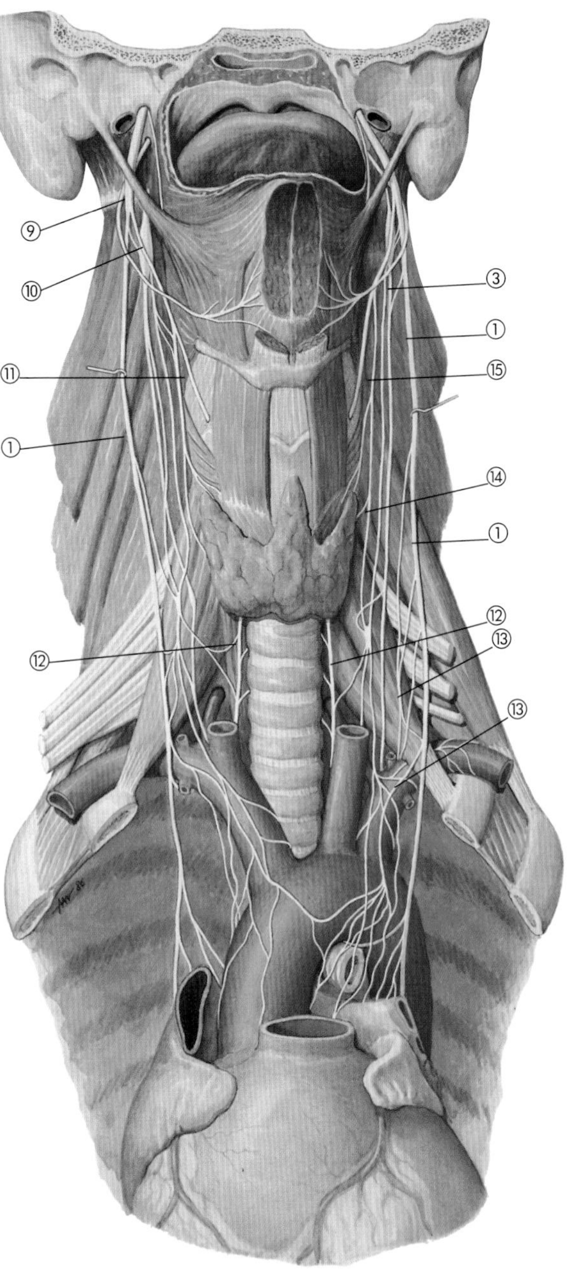

▲ **Middle thoracic abdominal nerves**
Anatomical images that show the main thoracic abdominal involuntary nerves involved in controlling heart:
① *vagus nerve*
② *Phrenic nerve*
③ *sympathetic trunk*
④ *accessory phrenic nerve*
⑤ *abdominal phrenic branch*
⑥ *recurrent nerve*
⑦ *pericardium branch of the phrenic nerve*
⑧ *cervical groove*
⑨ *caudal ganglion of the vagus nerve*
⑩ *superior cervical ganglion*
⑪ *superior laryngeal nerve*
⑫ *recurrent laryngeal nerve*
⑬ *inferior cardiac branch*
⑭ *superior cardiac branch*
⑮ *superior cervical cardiac nerve*

TONES & HEARTBEAT

The physical processes that create the heart beat produce distinct sounds that can be easily heard through a stethoscope. These are due to a number of distinct stages. The systole results in an increase in pressure inside the left atrium and ventricle, and in particular, at the start of ventricular contraction. This is produced by the increase in tension of the muscle fibres, and it forces the closure of the atrioventricular and semilunar valves. At the same time, the atrium relaxes (atrial diastole) and the fall in pressure opens the semilunar valves allowing blood to pour into the atrium from the veins.

When the intra-ventricular pressure exceeds that of the aorta and pulmonary arteries (these are respectively 10.7 and 1.3 kPa) the valves are opened and the ventricle can continue to contract strongly. The first sounds that can be heard correspond to the closure of the mitral valve and vibration from the expulsion of blood and its passage into the arteries.

The blood is driven into the arteries (the ejection phase) until the end of ventricular systole, even if the ventricle is not entirely empty. This happens when the endoventricular pressure drops to a value lower than that of the arteries. This closes the valves and produces the second sound. The time that passes between the first and second sounds is denoted by a short quiet period. After the second sound there is a much longer quiet phase.

The amount of blood that is expelled is called the ejection fraction, and is typically 50-70% of the amount of blood that is present in the heart at the end of diastole. The blood that remains in the ventricles is a functional reserve that can be pumped out when required. The closure of the valves also lowers the blood pressure ▸134, but this happens smoothly due to the elasticity of the arterial walls ▸126.

This begins the stage of ventricular relaxation, during which the pressure drops quickly to values lower than that of atrial region. This causes the opening of the atrioventricular valves which makes it possible for the blood to pass from atrium to the ventricle. It is a phase of rapid filling, in which the atrium and ventricle are completely relaxed (diastole), this drop in pressure determines the closure of semilunar valves which then prevents the flow of blood.

This can be heard as the third sound, and is produced by the vibration of blood on the walls of the fast filling ventricle. It follows a phase of slow filling when the ventricular pressure increases slowly as it is filled with blood. The diastole lasts about 0.4 seconds, which is sufficient time for the ventricles to fill almost completely. At the end of the ventricular diastole, the cycle begins again: the fourth sound corresponds to the completion of the atrial systole.

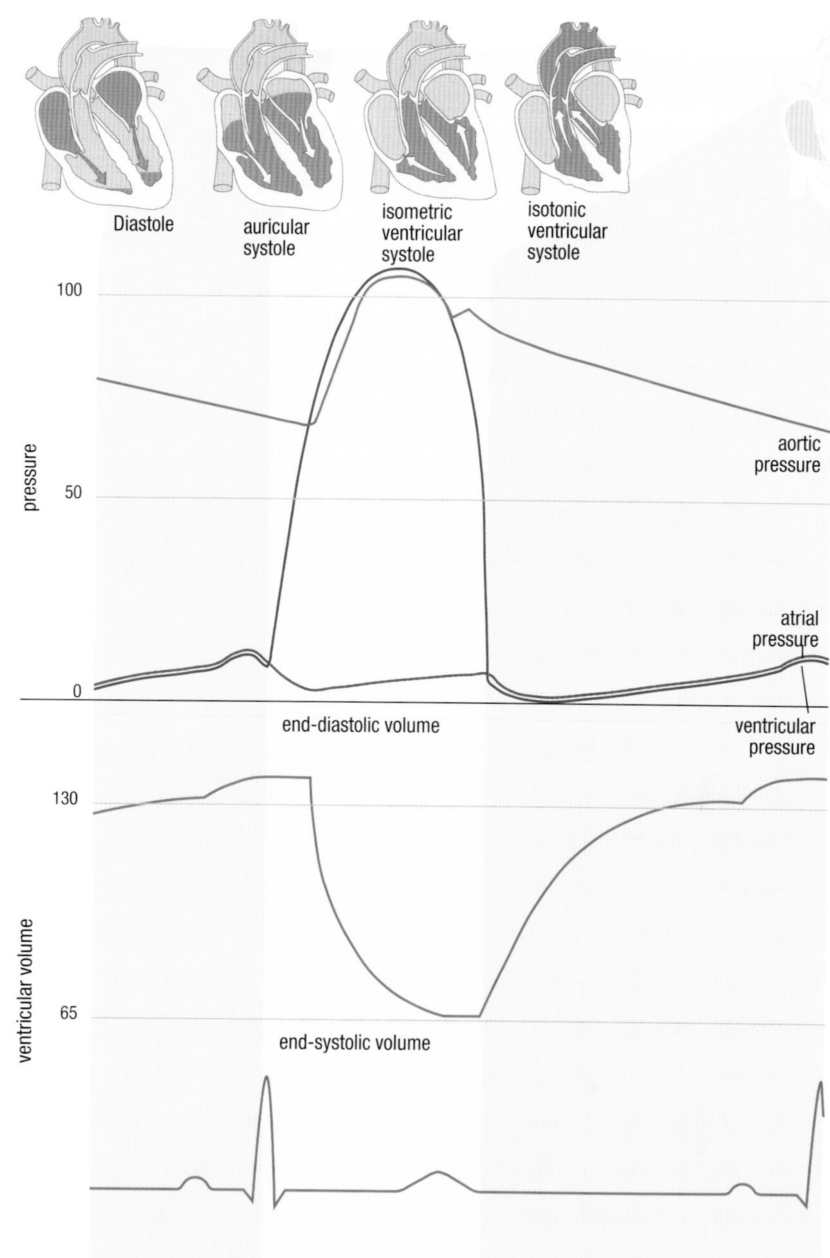

▲ **Cycle of cardiac events and volumetric-pressure**

The diagram shows the changes in volume and pressure occurring in the heart during the cardiac cycle. For several of these events the facts are matched to their corresponding electrical events (ECG track).

RANGE & FREQUENCY HEART

The term 'cardiac output' or 'cardiac scope' refers to the volume of blood that is ejected from a ventricle in 1 minute. It is the pulse range (volume expelled each beat) multiplied by the heart rate (F, number of beats per minute, bpm). The average frequency of an adult male human is 72 bpm: if it is between 60 and 100 bpm is considered physiological, but if it is less than 60 bpm it is referred to as bradycardia. If it is in excess of 100 bpm, however, it is called tachycardia. These conditions are not always pathological though - for example, tachycardia is considered to be a normal physiological state during physical activity or foetal development (where it is typically around 120 bpm).

The range changes according to the physiological needs: in sleep it is usually around 5 l / min, but during moderate physical activity it can be twice that, and heavy physical activity can result in figures of as much as 20 l / min.

Even the vessels in which flowing fluids circulate - veins, arteries and capillaries that carry blood, as well as vessels and capillaries that carry lymph - have similar characteristics peculiar but essential for the physiological functions that they involve.

THE VEINS: FEATURES AND FUNCTIONS

The circulation of blood in the body is undertaken through a complex and sophisticated network of vessels with different properties in accordance with the main function they play. Let us see first of all their features and functions, and then move on to analyse how the movements involved are accomplished, and what parameters are important for their characterisation.

THE ARTERIES & THE TRANSPORT OF BLOOD

GENERAL CHARACTERISTICS

The arteries are the vessels that originate from the heart and lead blood to the organs of the body. As they move away from the heart, the main vessels are cylindrical in shape and mostly straight, and are recognisable for their pink colour and elastic consistency. As they progress, they divide into branches. The arteries often run side by side with one or more veins that exploit the movements of the arteries to help drive the blood inside them. These are known as satellite veins, and if they and the arteries are also accompanied by one or more nerves, they are said to form vascular bundles. Each artery wall has three characteristic layers. The tunica intima is the innermost layer, and is composed of a layer of endothelial cells, a subendothelial layer, and an elastic layer. The middle layer is called the tunica media, and is made up of smooth muscle fibres arranged circularly and elastic tissues. The external layer is referred to as the tunica externa, and is largely comprised of fibres of collagen and elastic fibres that are arranged lengthwise. The composition of the various layers, however, is not constant. The proportion of muscle fibres, for example, increases significantly where the arteries have to assist the circulation due to the cardiac impulses being insufficient. Alternatively, the amount of elastic components rises where the ability to dilate is more important.

The arteries can therefore be divided into two groups, according to their structures:

– Muscular Arteries. These are the arteries that have diameters that make it hard for blood to flow through them without extra assistance. As a result, they are capable of contractile muscular movements that serve to advance the blood. In these arteries the tunica intima consists of a thin endothelium that is stratified with a delicate connective tissue with a small layer of elastic fibres that separates it from the tunic media. Formed by smooth muscle cells in concentric relation to the vessel, the tunica media is very thick, enriched with fibres of collagen and elastic fibres. The external elastic lamina, which is most prominent in arteries of medium size, separates the layer from the outer sheath. This has a thickness equal to 50-75% of that of tunica media, and is made up of fibrous connective tissue

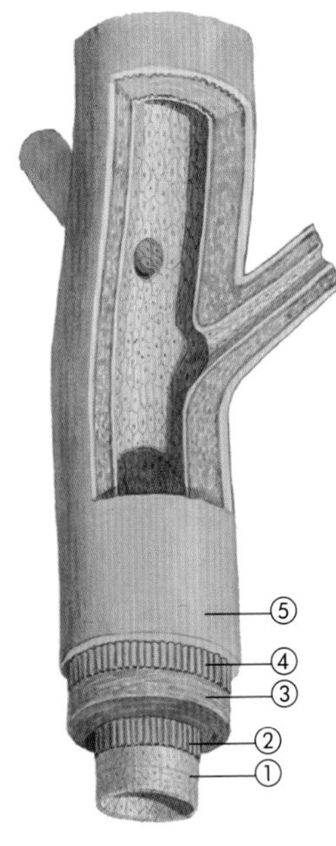

▲ **Structure of the walls of arteries**
Elements of the wall of a typical artery:
① *intimate tunic*
② *internal elastic lamina*
③ *tunic media or muscle*
④ *external elastic lamina*
⑤ *outer or adventitious*

▶ **Principal Arteries**
Branch of the main arteries in the body.

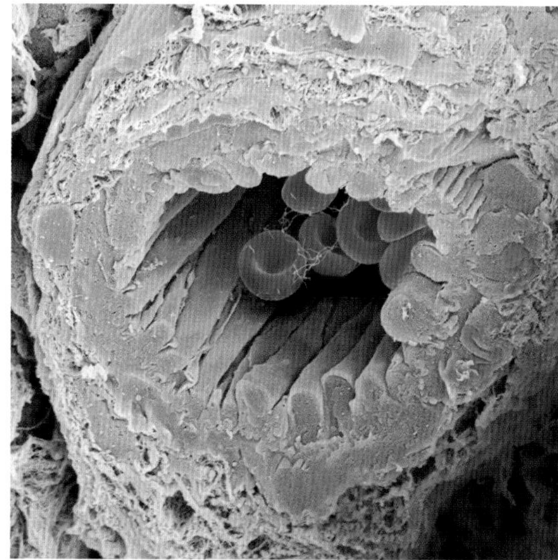

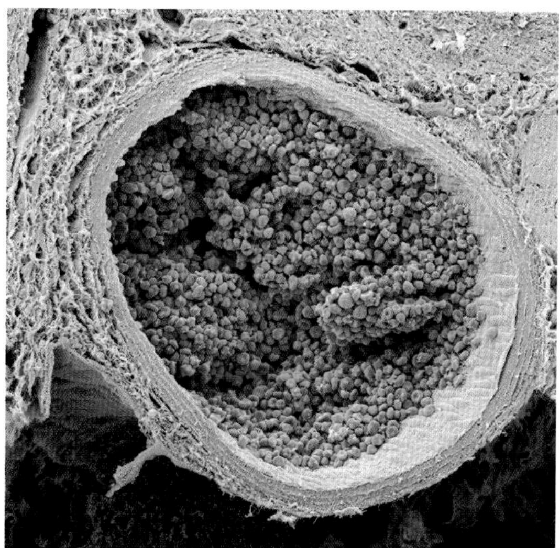

◀◀ Arteriola, typical muscular artery
SEM photo of a section through an arteriole. In addition to red blood cells and certain proteins, it has the tunica intima (yellow), thin and folded, and a tunica media (pink) thick and almost completely made up of muscle cells. The outer tunica adventitia is merged with the surrounding connective tissue.

◀ Fetal aorta
Sectional view through the fetal aorta by a scanning electron microscope (SEM). The aorta is the largest artery of the body and standing out here is the tunica intima, fused with the endothelial layer (yellow) that wraps around the inside of the vessel which is filled with red blood cells. Around the outside, in pink, is the tunica media, rich in elastic fiber while the tunica adventitia there is a off-white thin layer, just before the connective brown tissue.

and elastic fibres and, in larger vessels, features a network of small blood capillaries called the vasa vasorum;

- Elastic Arteries. These are the arteries that are closest to the heart, and have internal diameters greater than 7-8 mm. They are flexible enough to expand with every new pulse of blood. While they are similar to the muscular arteries, the tunica intima has more elastic fibres while the tunica media is made up of layers of elastic fibre plates that are arranged circularly around the vessel. In the smaller arteries, the plates are separated by spaces between them in which muscle cells are smooth. The external layer is thin and less obvious - it is elastic and formed from connective tissue fibres and hosts the vasa vasorum as well as the nerve endings.

PROPERTY AND FUNCTIONS

The characteristics of arteries vary such that they are able to better play the physiological functions for which they are intended. These are the most important ones:

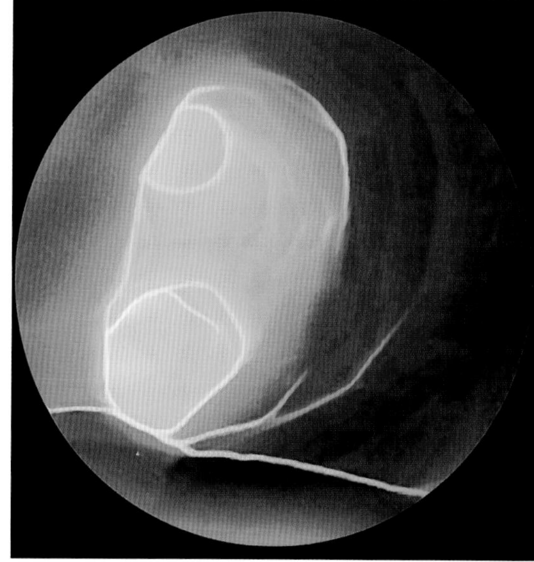

▲ Carotid artery
Three-dimensional tomography in false colors of the interior of a common carotid artery, one of two large vessels that, from the aortic arch passing along the neck, carry blood to the head and brain. In particular, the photos show the point where the artery has branches in the internal carotid artery and external carotid artery, indicated by yellow clearer spaces below and above, on the right.

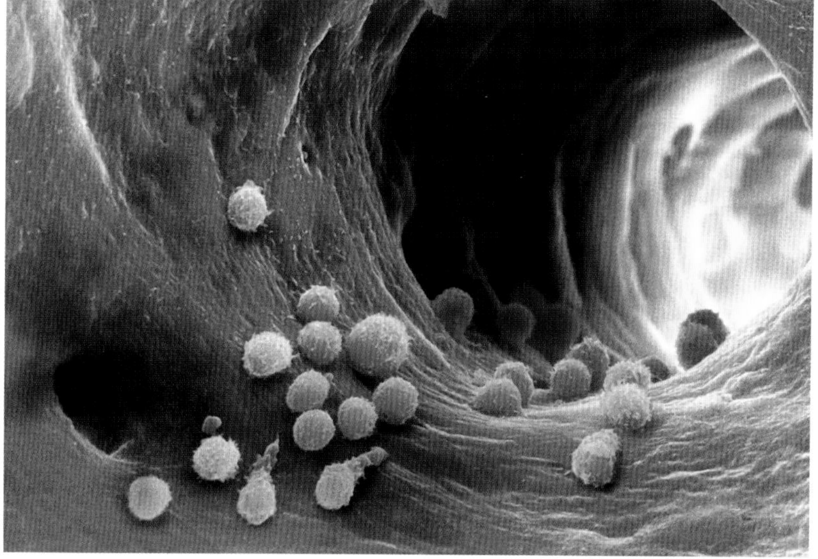

▲ Hepatic artery
Scanning electron microscope photograph in false colors of the interior of a hepatic artery. The cells that are in the lumen are lymphocytes that adhere to the wall of the artery: the liver vessels are rich, because the liver is constantly exposed to antigens that come directly from the intestine, transported by the portal vein.

▼ **Capillary**
Transmission electron microscope (TEM) photograph of a section of a capillary in an ovary. The dark stain in the middle is a red blood cell in the lumen of the vessel surrounded by endothelial cells (green) and large nuclei in rose. The outer tunic of capillaries is formed by smooth muscle cells (orange) and from the elongated nuclei (also pink). Currently in a relaxed state, they regulate the opening and closing of the capillary lumen.

▼▶ **Red blood cell emerging from a capillary**
Photograph (SEM) showing a section of a capillary. The wall of these vessels is thin and permeable, so as to allow gas and nutrient solution to diffuse through the tissues. At the same time, following gradients of concentration, allowing metabolic waste spread across the capillary walls to disperse.

1. inextensibility; this is typical of large and medium size arteries with walls that are rich in elastic fibres. It is a property that allows them to help push the cardiac blood. With the passing of time, although offset by a progressive increase in diameter, the inextensibility of the arterial wall is reduced because of the increased proportion of collagen fibres in the tunica media. The loss of inextensibility determines the physiological increase in blood pressure;
2. resistance to flow; this is typical, although in different ways, of arterioles with walls that are full of smooth muscle fibres. It is a property that interacts with the inextensibility that is so instrumental in maintaining the blood's pressure. In particular, the interaction between the inextensibility of the aorta and the major arteries, and the resistance to flow exerted by the arterioles, makes sure that the pulse range ▶125 does not pass immediately across the capillaries, but remains partly in large arteries. In this way, the blood that comes from the aorta - the exit from heart ventricle, which is intermittent, is evened out. The result of this is that at the level of capillaries it becomes continuous, ensuring a constant influx of oxygen and nutrients to the peripheral tissues and the continued removal of metabolic waste, without sudden changes in pressure or speed;
3. pressure: because of their structure, all the arteries can withstand constant pressure and pulses that are much higher than that borne by the capillaries and veins. This property makes it possible for the accumulation of blood in the arteries;
4. flow speed: by virtue of their properties, arteries can maintain a high rate of blood flow, it is always higher than that measured in the capillaries and veins, ensuring consistent pressure;
5.Section total area and capacity: while the total area of the section of the arteries is less than that of capillaries and veins, the capacity is higher than that of capillaries and lower than that of the venous system. This property ensures that there is a consistent supply of blood to the tissues.

CAPILLARIES AND EXCHANGES BETWEEN BLOOD AND TISSUES

GENERAL CHARACTERISTICS

The capillaries are the final branches which divide the arterioles and represent the roots of the bloodstream. They merge with each other repeatedly and form the first vessels of the venous system. The capillaries are so-called because of their reduced size: their diameters vary from 5 μm in the pulmonary capillaries to 20 μm in the capillaries of the bone marrow. It is estimated that there are about three and a half billion capillaries in the human body. Their walls are formed from a single layer of endothelial cells, which allows the passage of all the elements of the blood plasma and interstitial fluids, with the exception of large protein molecules.
Unlike other vessels, in fact, the capillaries are permeable: they provide the means for gaseous exchange, as well as the transfer of nutrients and metabolic wastes between the tissues and the blood. Exceptions to this include the epithelial coating, as well as the cornea, lens and cartilage.
According to the structures of their walls, there are three different types of capillaries:

- **Continous capillaries**. These are the most common, and are characterised by flat endothelium cells that are intimately linked with each other;
- **Fenestrated capillaries**. These are typical of the renal glomerulus ▶148 and are characterised by an

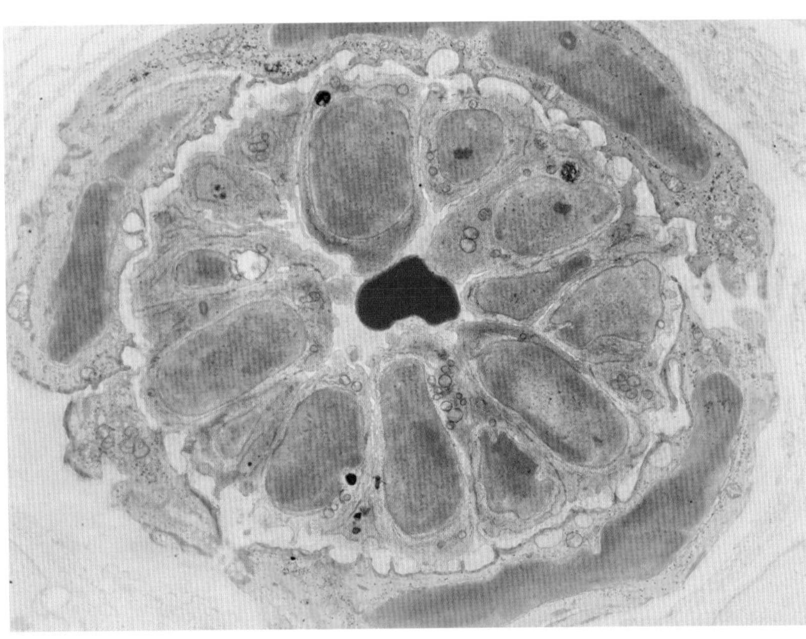

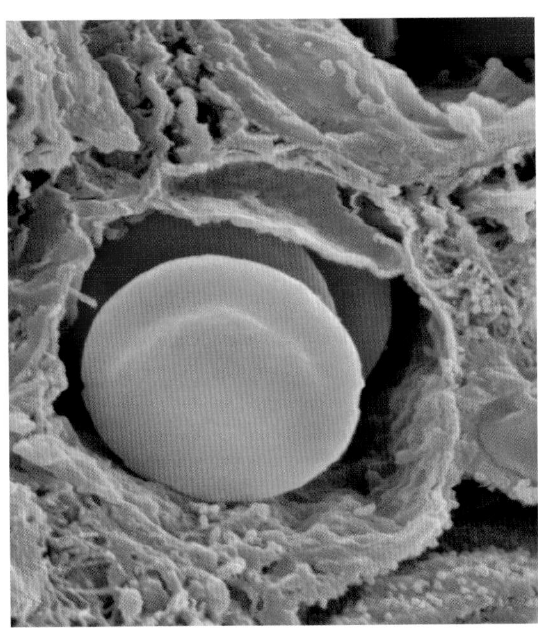

endothelium that is interrupted by pores with a diameter of between 200 and 1200 Å;
- **Sinusoidal capillaries**. These are typically found in glands (liver ►72 glands, pituitary glands ►197) where they form a complex network (plexus), and are characterised by an endothelium which is sometimes fenestrated.

The sectional area of the capillaries is greater than that the other blood vessels. This causes a reduction in pressure and a considerable slowdown in the speed of the bloodstream. The flow of blood in a capillary, in fact, depends on its pressure in the arterioles, as well as the downstream pressure and the state of the capillary sphincters. These are rings of muscle fibres that can contract when necessary. For example, when they work as a vasoconstriction device under the control of a hormone such as adrenaline. When stimulated to do so, they can shut down the movement of blood in a area covered by the network. The pressure of the blood when it arrives in the capillaries varies from 4.7 to 5.3 kPa, while the output can be reduced down to 2,0-2,7 kPa. In the capillaries, therefore, the blood flow slows down considerably, with speeds in the region of 1 mm per second - this makes the exchange of substances easier.

EXCHANGE BETWEEN CAPILLARIES & TISSUES

The passage of gas and nutrients from the blood to the tissues, or waste from the tissues to the blood is carried out according to a purely physical process, which is determined by the hydrostatic and osmotic pressures involved ►17. It can take occur in two ways:
- by diffusion, following the gradient of concentration; substances in solution pass from the side of a capillary membrane where they are most concentrated, to the other side;

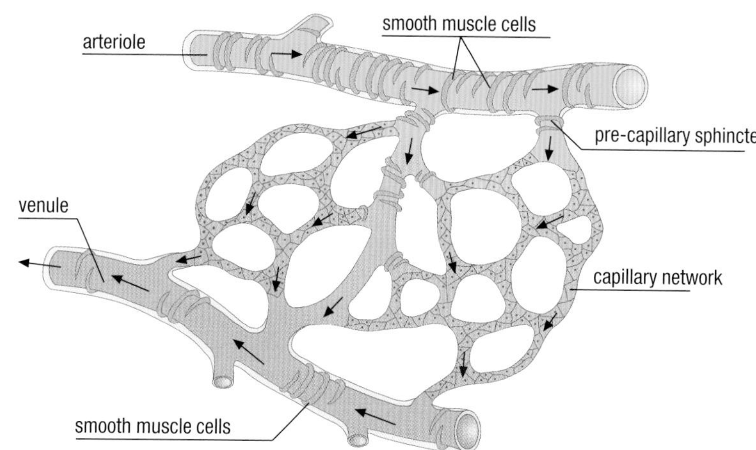

- filter or ultrafiltration: water and any substances dissolved in it passes from one side of a capillary to the other because of the difference in hydrostatic pressures between the inside and the outside of the capillary wall.

The speed of dissemination and filtration depends on a number of factors, including the exchange surfaces and the permeability of the various molecules through the capillary membrane. All those which are fat-soluble pass through the epithelial surface, whereas those which are water-soluble pass through the pores. The speed of deployment and its direction is also based on the equilibrium between the pressure of blood in the capillaries and the pressure of the liquid in the surrounding tissues. The endocapillary pressure (that which is exerted outwards from the middle) varies greatly from the point where the capillaries branch out from the arterioles (approximately 5.3 kPa) to the location where they blend into the venules (2.3 kPa). In addition, there is a capillary osmotic pressure of 3.5 kPa due to plasma proteins that are not removed. This prevents the leakage of liquids and substances from inside the vessel.

▲ **From the arteries to the veins**
The capillaries through every tissue of the body forming a permeable network that connects the waterproof network and venous blood, .

▼◄ **Adrenaline**
Computer reconstruction of a molecule of adrenaline or epinephrine (C9 H13NO3: carbon atoms are yellow, oxygen red, nitrogen blue and white for hydrogen). It is a Chemical mediator of the sympathetic transmission nervous system, and acts as vasoconstrictor on capillaries.

▼ **Muscle**
This SEM photograph in false colors shows the capillary of a muscle (brown fibers). The capillary (pink) is so thin that only one red blood cell can pass at a time.

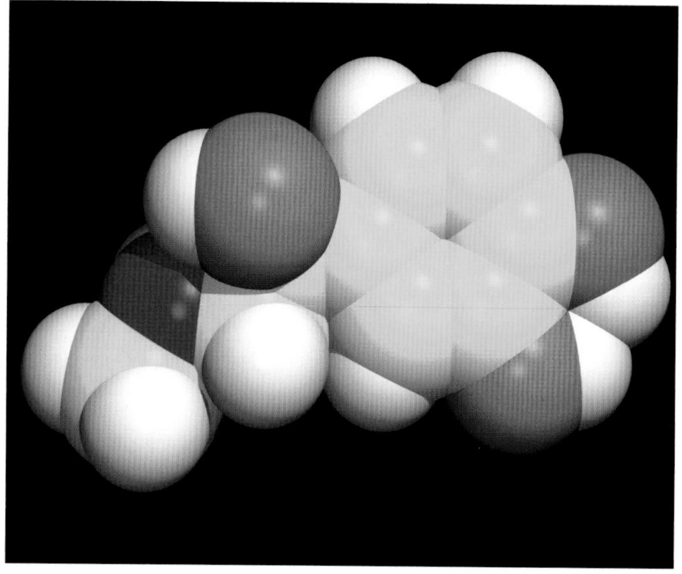

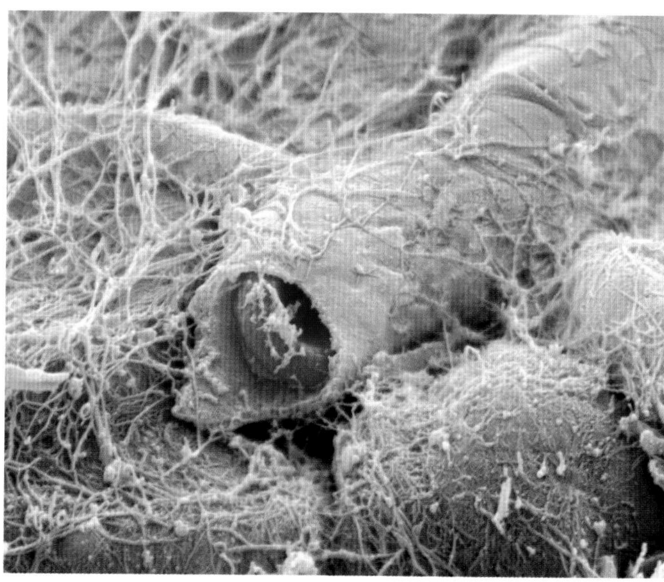

▶ EXCHANGES
Through the wall of capillaries, which are formed by a single layer of flattened endothelial cells and interspersed from pores, occur exchanges necessary for the survival of cells of tissues. While the water and substances in the solution pass through the pores, the fat-soluble substances, such as respiratory gases follow the gradient of concentration across the membrane.

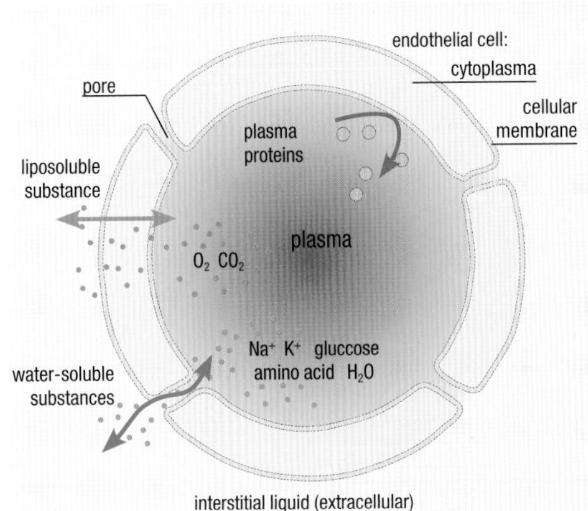

If the differences in pressure recorded in the bloodstream are kept constant by the continuous renewal of internal solution to the capillary vessels, the osmotic pressure of the liquid in the tissue is constant at about 0.7 kPa. It also is partially countered by the presence of proteins that produce a constant negative pressure of about 0.1 kPa. The net filtration pressure in capillaries - that is, the force with which the substances move from the capillaries to the tissue spaces, therefore, varies from the beginning to the end of each capillary by a maximum value of:

$$(5.3 - 0.7) - (3.5 - 0.1) = 4.6 - 3.4 = 1.2 \text{ kPa}$$

to a minimum value of:

$$(2.3 - 0.7) - (3.5 - 0.1) = 1.6 - 3.4 = -4 \text{ kPa}$$

The negative sign of the minimum value indicates that substances can be pushed into the capillaries with a force of about 4 kPa, instead of being drawn out of them. All this means the permeability of the capillary walls is not constant, but is sensitive to the actions of many substances. If it increases sufficiently, proteins can also pass through the endothelial membrane, which alters the dynamics of the balance of exchange.

DRAINAGE: THE LYMPHATIC SYSTEM & LYMPHATIC VESSELS

The main function of the lymphatic system is to remove from the tissue spaces any excess proteins and liquids. Under normal conditions the quantity of interstitial liquids is low, but under certain conditions – for example, when the permeability of the capillaries changes the amount may increase significantly. In this situation, the extra fluids are disposed of by the blood system.

This system consists of a vast network of lymphatic capillaries. These are characterised by thin wall endothelial cells that are located on a very thin membrane. They form three-dimensional networks in and around the internal organs. The flow in lymphatic vessels is characterised by collections of crescent valves that are similar to those found in certain vessels that prevent venous reflux. Since there is no 'lymphatic heart' to pump the fluids, their movement is primarily achieved by the activity of the contractile sheath muscles of the lymphatic vessels. These contract rhythmically to cause the interstitial fluid to be aspired even when the pressure in the tissues becomes negative.

There are lymphatic vessels that are near the surface of the tissues as well as others that are deep within. They all make it possible for fluids to flow into the

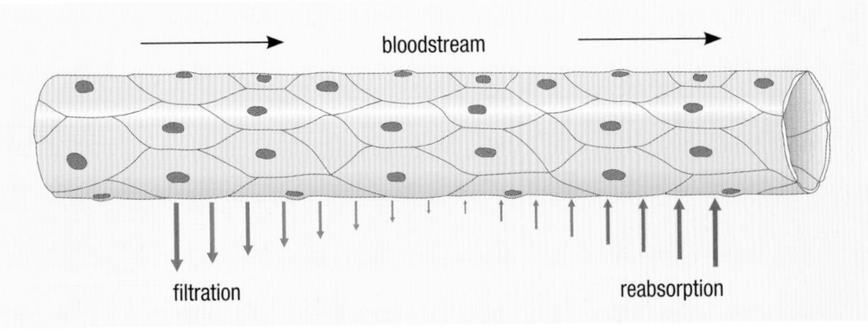

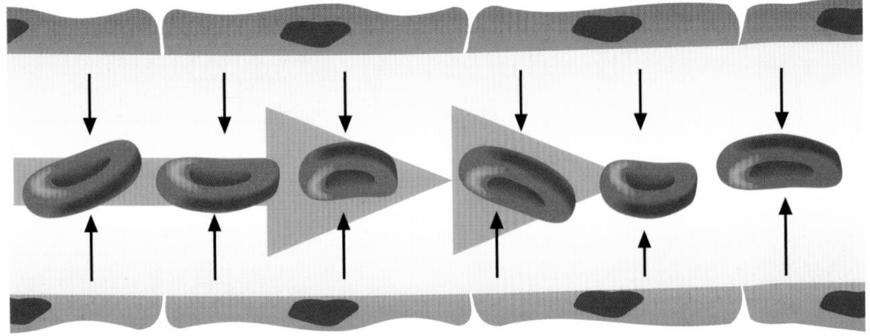

◀ FROM THE ARTERIES TO VEINS
At the beginning (arterial side) the capillary contains a plasma rich in water. Since the interstitial fluid through is poor, the hydrostatic pressure in this section is greater than the osmotic. This causes the clear passage of substances and water from the capillary to the tissues. As the equlibrium moves to the external concentration, the direction of the switch is reversed: the liquid is overcome with metabolic waste that the capillary contains.

◀▼ RED BLOOD CELLS
Although often the diameter of capillaries is almost identical to that of red blood cells and other cellular components of blood travelling through it, the flow through the vessel walls is not without friction. This is because the friction increases as you get closer to the walls: the velocity of the blood is greater at the center which is not close to the walls. For a simple physical law of fluid dynamics, the peripheral pressure becomes greater than that at the heart and blood will thicken along the axis of the vessel that it travels.

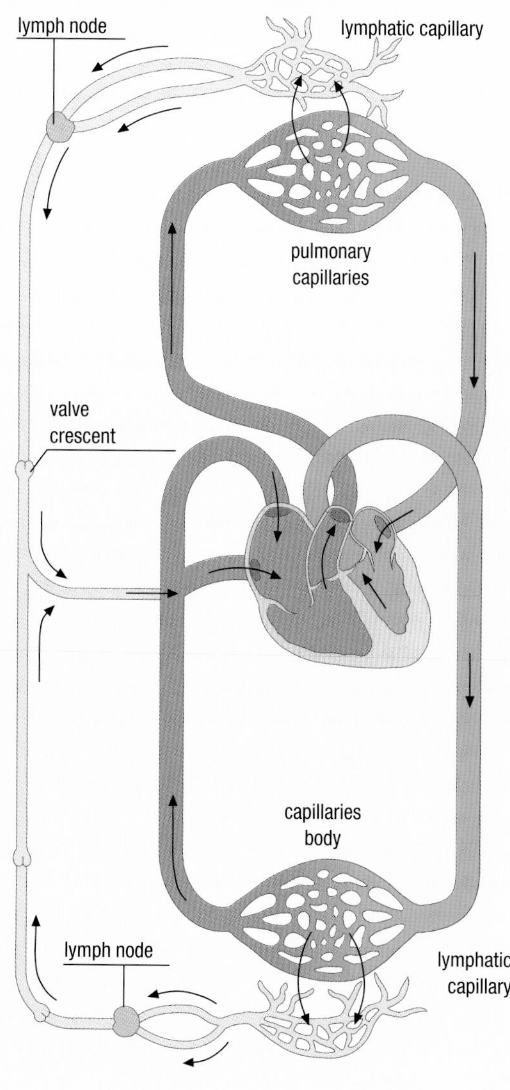

THE VEINS & BLOOD TRANSPORT

GENERAL CHARACTERISTICS

The veins are vessels which grow in diameter as they progress towards the heart. They have a cylindrical cross section, with relatively thin walls and a structure that is similar to that of lymphatic vessels. The content of muscle fibres in the tunica media also varies according to the different blood pressures. Their diameter is always greater than that of the arteries that are in the same area of the body. Like the lymphatic vessels collectors, they differ:

- superficial veins, these are more developed in the arms and in the neck. They are subcutaneous, have no direct relations with the arteries and have thin walls. Often, these veins are anastomosed forming a venous plexus similar to those of arteries;
- deep veins: these are more numerous in the arms and the inter-muscular and visceral areas. They run parallel to the arteries, and because the blood exerts a gravitational pressure, they take on a driving force: their tunica media have well-developed semilunar valves that prevent the reflux of blood.

The veins can be categorised according to their diameters:

- venules or postcapillary veins; these are of small diameter, and the thinner ones feature endothelium fenestrations, while those above 1 mm in diameter become continuous. They have a prevalence of networked collagen fibres, with some smooth muscle fibres and a thin tunica adventitia of connective tissue;

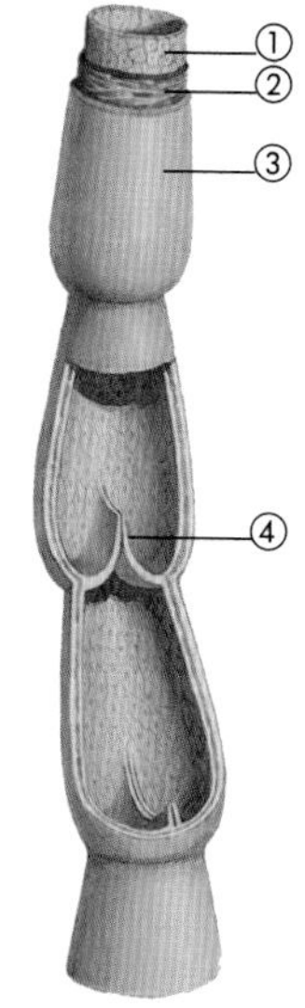

▲ **Lymphatic vessel**
Structure of the wall of lymphatic collector vessels:
① intimate tunic
② medium muscular tunic
③ outer or tunica adventitia
④ half-moon valve

◀ **Entwined systems**
The lymphatic system and bloodstream that are parallel and confluent: the lymphatic drains liquid and excess extracellular protein and conveys blood into the system. At the same time it monitors and provides protection from infection.

lymphatic trunks, and are characterised by a wide diameter. The fluids then enter special drainage ducts (tracheal, celiac, intestinal lumbar...). The deep lymphatic vessels which run parallel to the veins and arteries, drain more efficiently than those near the surface thanks to the contribution of the skeletal muscles.

The lymphatic trunks run from the lower limbs, pelvis, and abdomen (which meet in the thoracic duct), the left side of the chest, upper limbs and left half of the neck and head into the chest. Here they discharge into the blood system at the dividing line between the left subclavian vein and the jugular vein. The lymphatic system also includes some other lymphoid organs - these are the lymph nodes, the spleen and the thymus. The spleen is also an important body for the blood system as it destroys any red blood cells that have become aged or damaged, and is where the platelets are stored until they are needed.

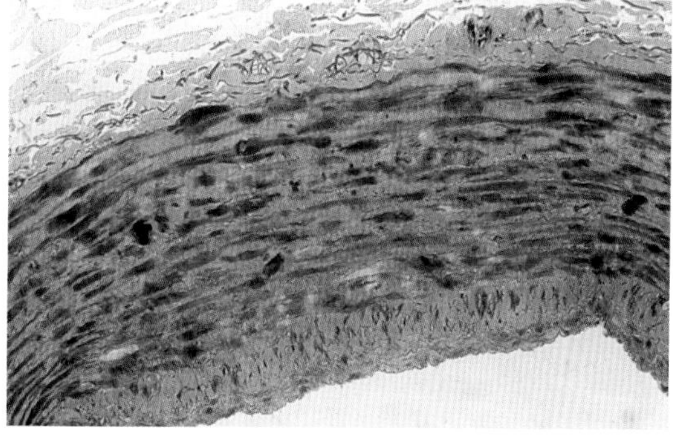

▲ **Saphena**
Section under an optical microscope of a saphenous vein, one of the most important in the lower limbs. The wall is full of muscle fibers (purple) in concentric layers by the light vein (white, below). The muscle motions and action of valves contrasts the action of gravity on blood.

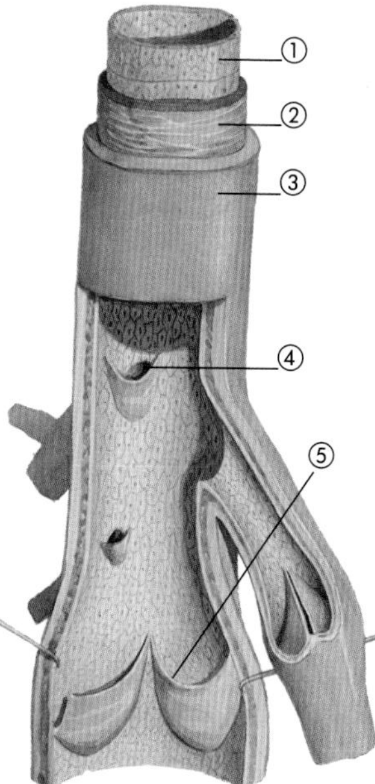

▶ **Venous vessel**
Structure of venous wall:
① intimate tunic
② medium muscular tunic
③ outer or tunica adventitia
④ venous valve
⑤ half-moon valve

THE SPLEEN

The spleen is a lymphoid organ that begins to form during the 5th week of embryonic life and which plays an important role in haematopoietic activities for the first five months of gestation. After birth, it completely loses this function and instead becomes one of the centres of activity for the reticuloendothelial system. It also carries out several other roles in different parts of the body:

- it eliminates any red blood cells that have aged or become damaged;
- as a lymphoid organ it plays an important part in the fight against infections, and having the ability to enhance the action of macrophages, is also one of the places where lymphocyte B cells proliferate.
- in the fight against infections it functions as a gland that produces many beneficial substances that help protect against phagocytes. These include properdin (also called factor P) which is a globulin protein that is involved in suppressing inflammation, along with opsonin which helps antibodies bind to invading microbes. Another agent it produces is tuftsin, a tetrapeptide with a broad spectrum of activities that relate to immune system functions.
- in the accumulation of platelets and red blood cells, which can then be released into the blood stream in response to specific physiological requests.
- in the mechanical filtration of blood: the spleen, in fact, not only clears out any unwanted red blood cells, but also eliminates all other unnecessary and possibly harmful materials.

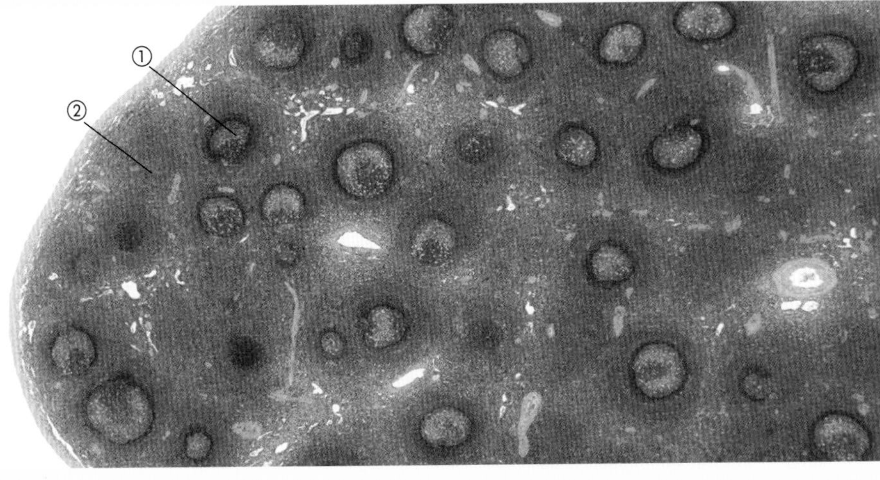

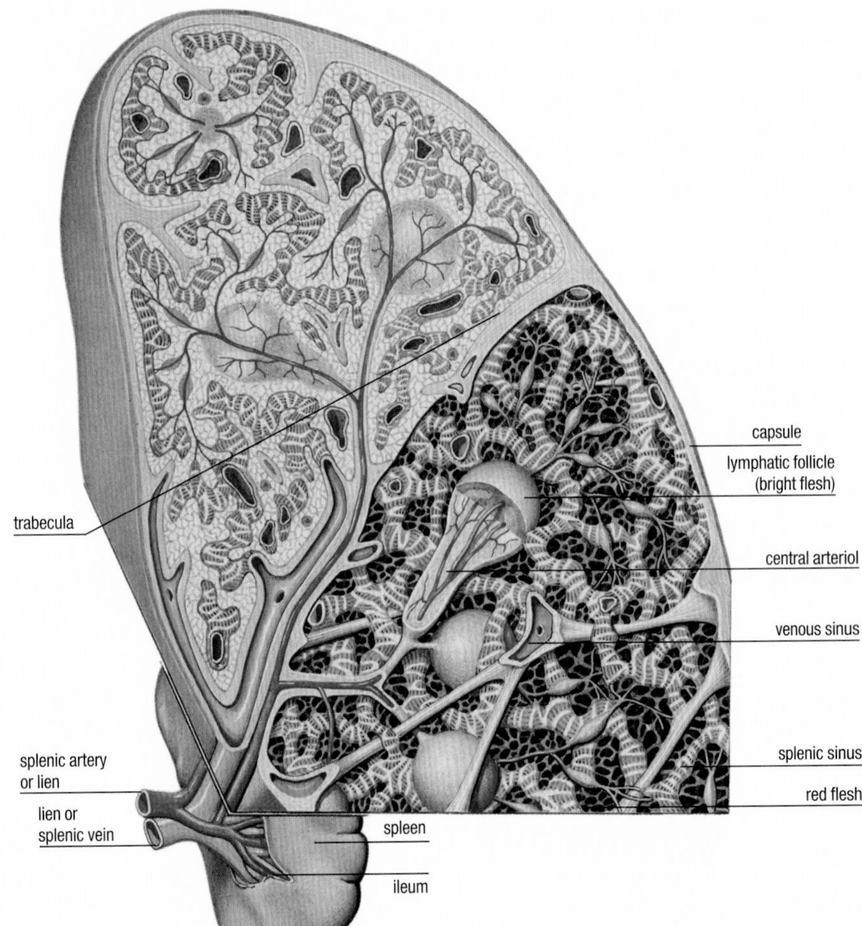

ANATOMY OF THE SPLEEN

The spleen is a gland that is found in the abdominal cavity that consists of approximately 150 grams of lymphoid tissue with a granular appearance. As it is closely linked to the circulatory system, is crossed by a dense network of blood vessels which are connected to one another by modified capillaries. The spleen is contained inside a fibrous layer within which are situated large numbers of fibres called splenic trabeculae. These provide the spleen with an internal support structure.
The spleen itself is elongated and flattened, with two faces (parietal and visceral), two ends (near the dorsal and ventral left kidney) and two margins (cranial and caudal). The outer covering features a depression through which the main blood vessels pass. Approximately 10% of the population also has what is known as an accessory spleens - this is a second splenic structure, which may result from some kind of accidental trauma, or may have been present from birth.
If a section of the spleen is examined, it can be seen that the soft red surface is composed of two types of tissue. These correspond to areas where two main functions are carried out:

- white flesh, which is composed of splenic lymphoid nodules called corpuscles of Malpighi, they contain: follicles that are rich in B lymphocytes and macrophages and form periarterial lymphatic sheaths (PALS).
- red flesh, which is the largest component and consists for the most part of two sections. These are the cords of Billroth and the sinusoids. They contain a number of different elements, including lymphocytes, macrophages and plasma.

The spleen's complex arrangement of blood vessels is vital in supporting its function in separating the red blood cells from plasma. It also accumulates platelets and white blood cells and, if necessary, facilitates their destruction.

- medium veins; these are characterised by an endothelium that rests on a thin layer of collagen fibres, and a tunica media that is composed of smooth muscle cells and connective tissue which is contained in a tunica adventitia that is rich in elastic fibres;
- large veins; these are characterised by an endothelium with a thick sub-epithelial layer, a tunica media that is rich in smooth muscle cells and connective tissue as well as a tunica adventitia that is full of thick elastic fibres. The superficial layer of the larger veins also contains numerous smaller vessels (the vasa vasorum).

PROPERTY & FUNCTIONS

The properties of the veins are organised in a way that allows them to perform the physiological functions for they are intended. The most important ones are:

1. stretchability and high capacity: the remarkable stretchability allows the veins to carry a high-capacity, as it allows them to accept large amounts of blood, exceeding the flows achieved by the arteries and capillaries. Around 70% of the blood that circulates in the body, in fact, lies in venous flow. In the case of veins, however, the stretchability of walls decreases over time due to the increased proportion of collagen fibres in the tunica media. This leads to their deformation under blood pressure, and the development of problems such as varicose veins;

2. total sectional area and pressure: while the total area of section in the veins is lower than that of the capillaries, it is nevertheless higher than that of the arteries, which guarantees that the pressure remains lower than that of arterial blood;

3. flow speed: although it is lower than that measured in the arteries, is still high, so as to ensure the flow of blood to the heart.

THE PHYSICS OF BLOOD

The circulation within the blood vessels does not escape the physical laws that govern the dynamics of fluids. In particular, according to Poiseuille's laws which govern the passage of a fluid in a cylindrical tube, the flow is directly proportional to pressure difference (Δp). This is measured to its peak value, is directly proportional to its radius (r), and raised to the 4th power, while it is inversely proportional to its length (l) and the viscosity (μ)

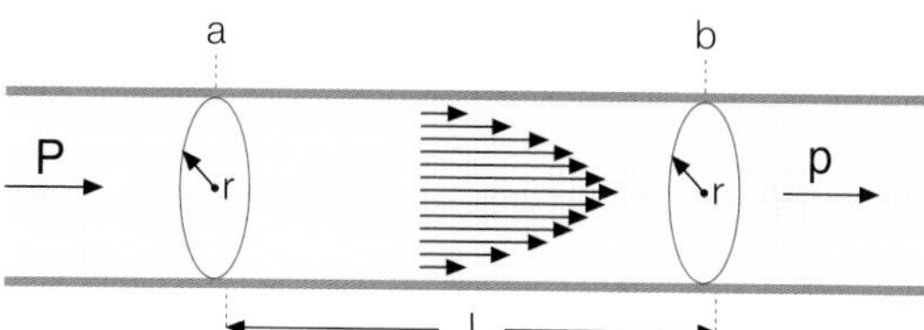

of fluid. This is given by the formula:

$$\text{flow} = \text{constant}\ \frac{\Delta p \cdot r4}{l \cdot \mu}$$

The blood that is pumped from the heart around the body is distributed in a network of vessels which respect this law. The diameter of the vessels in which the blood flows is the most important factor and is variable in order to change the flow of blood. This is why there is a network of nerve fibres that monitor the conditions of the muscle contraction in the vessels, particularly the arterioles. These can stimulate the contraction or relaxation of the pre-capillary sphincters and, by varying the diameter of the vessels, can adjust the influx of blood in the regions of the body where it is needed. The amount of flow depends on the pressure that the blood exerts on the walls of vessels. This is also regulated by a physical law: the pressure (p) is directly proportional to the flow and the resistance to flow caused by friction (a = friction) from the walls, as in the formula:

$$p = \text{flow} \cdot a$$

In turn, in the case of blood vessels, the friction is directly proportional to the length of the vessel (l) and the viscosity (μ) of the blood, and is inversely proportional to the diameter (2r) of the vessel. This is shown by the following formula:

$$a = K\frac{l \cdot \mu}{2r}$$

This means that the blood moves with increasing speed as it nears the axis of the vessel and, as the path becomes longer, the lateral pressure gradually decreases. According to Bernoulli's law, however, the pressure and speed are linked: the pressure in a fluid grows by the square of the velocity of the fluid. This means that while the pressure on the outskirts of a vessel may be high, that in the centre will be much lower.

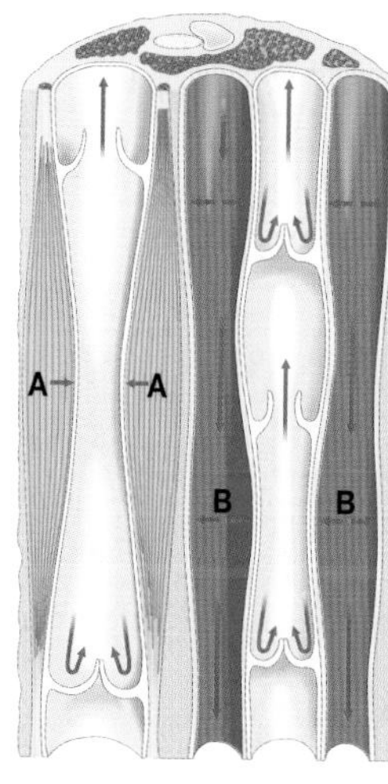

▲◀ **Physical laws**
Schematization of a physical interpretation of the flow in a blood vessel: **a** *and* **b** *are any two points across a length (l) in a vessel, both have a diameter of equal radius (r). At either end of the vessel there is a difference in pressure of the Δp constant, and the vessels flowing blood viscosity and constant density. Of course, in reality things are more variable.*

▲ **Flowing venous blood**
*The flow of blood in the veins, in addition to the movement of smooth muscle in the tunica media of the venous wall, there are also the movements of the surrounding muscles (***A***) and, in the deep veins, the pumping action exerted by neighboring arteries (***B***).*

◀ **Main veins**
Major vein branches in the body.

BLOOD PRESSURE: FEATURES

What we have just seen, however, refers to ideal conditions: a constant blood density and viscosity, a vessel with uniform friction, a constant vessel diameter, and constant pressure. In reality, however, things are quite different, particularly if you look at the arteries or veins, which perform directly opposite functions. Let us briefly examine the main differences.

– Arterial pressure. Every heart contraction pumps blood into the main arteries in proportion to the force of the systolic contraction. The pressure generated by this causes the arteries to expand, but during the diastolic phase their elastic walls allow them to return to their original diameter.

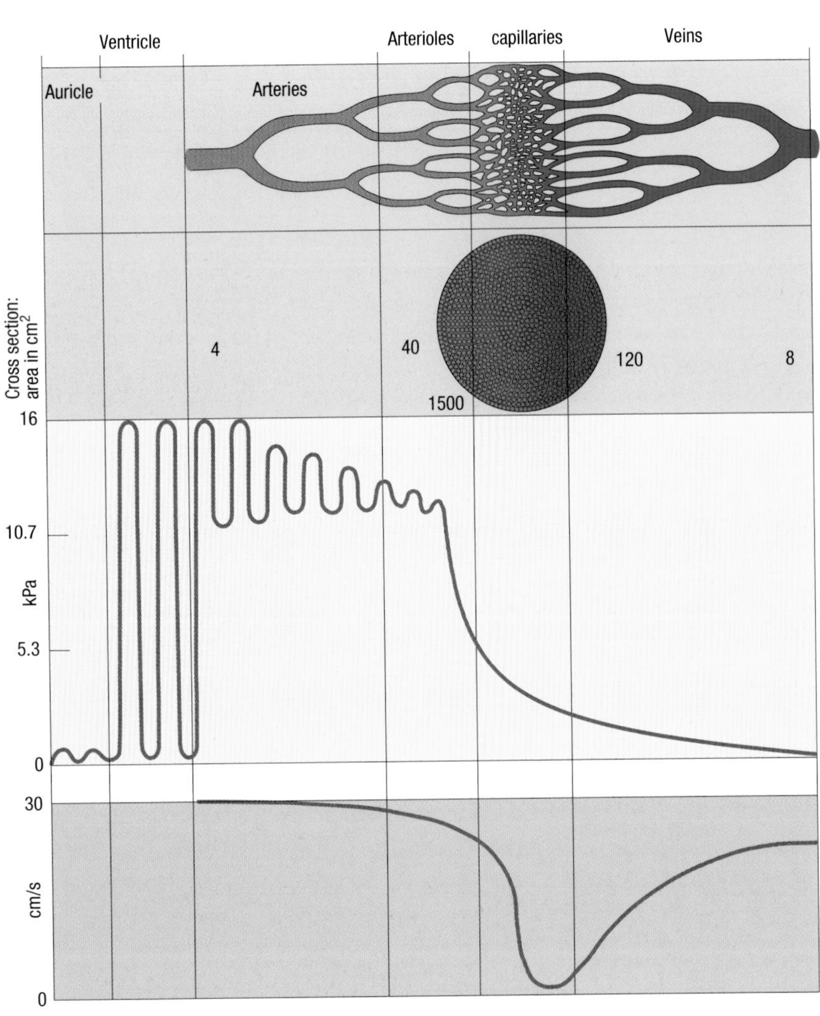

▲ **Vascular system**
We can represent the vascular system as above. The volume of blood that is found in every region of the circulatory apparatus is equal to the transverse sectional area of total vessels multiplied by their average length. For the principle of conservation of mass (Bernoulli), flow through the vessels placed in series (cm3 / s) must be constant, and the blood velocity (cm / s) is inversely proportional to the transverse cross-sectional area. It follows that, as noted, the velocity of blood in the capillaries is minimal.

In the arteriosum system the pressure therefore regularly fluctuates between the maximum and minimum values. As the blood moves away from the heart the pressure falls due to the constrictive nature of the vessels. The actual pressures can be measured with two instant and two mathematical values - these are:

– the systolic pressure; this is the highest pressure reached during the heart's pumping cycle and is achieved towards the end of the ventricle's contractile phase. The actual value achieved depends on a number of factors, but is directly influenced by arterial elasticity, which in turn is determined by such things as age and the individual's overall emotional state. The average in a healthy adult varies between 12-17 kPa (90-130 mmHg), with 115 mmHg being a typical value at rest.

– the diastolic pressure; this is the minimum pressure reached during the heart's pumping cycle and is achieved towards the start of the heart's pumping cycle when both the ventricles are filled with blood. Again, the actual value is determined by such things as arterial elasticity and heart rate. The higher they are, the greater diastolic pressure. The average in a healthy adult varies between 8-11 kPa (60-85 mmHg), with 75 mmHg being a typical value at rest.

– the pulse pressure; this is the difference between the systolic and diastolic pressures, and is mainly determined by the amount of blood flow in the aorta. The average in a healthy adult is 4-6 kPa (30-45 mmHg).

– the mean arterial pressure; this value corresponds to the average pressure generated through an entire Cardiac cycle, and is obtained by integrating the pressure curve. The average in a healthy adult is 10-13 kPa (80-100 mmHg).

The actual pressure values are therefore influenced by a number of factors. These include the amount of arterial elasticity, the heart rate, the individual's general stress condition, their age, level of fitness, and underlying state of health. These parameters in turn depend on other variables: for example, the blood's viscosity can "vary according to the amount of water drunk, the ambient temperature, and the kidneys' filtration capability ▸148 and so on. The location of the measurement is also important - for example, although the average resting blood pressure may be 115 mmHg in a healthy individual, the value in the pulmonary artery might only be 15 mmHg. Other less obvious considerations include the amount of sleep that the person concerned has had, the amount of food they have consumed and even whether the measurements were taken during the morning or evening. Young people tend to have lower than average blood pressures, with the reverse being true for older individuals.

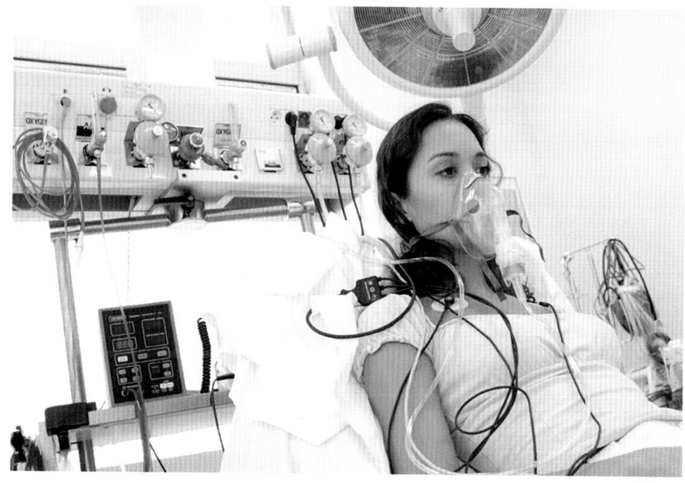

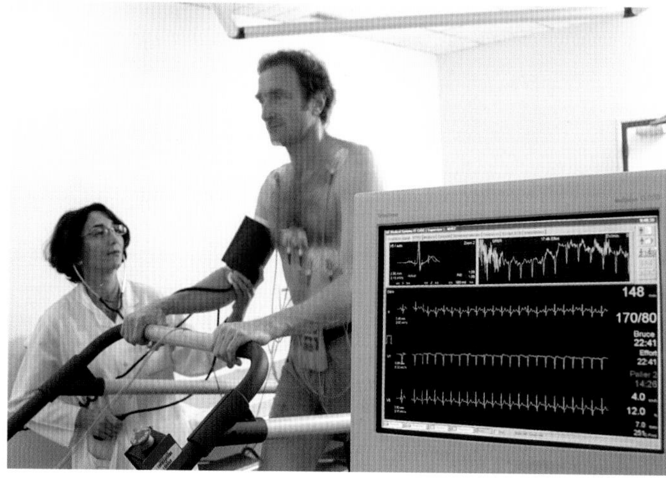

BLOOD PRESSURE CONTROL

The maintenance of blood pressure - and, accordingly, the speed and flow of the blood in the various parts of the body - is under the control of many factors which work together to ensure that an optimal balance is achieved. The autonomic nervous system, for example, regulates the amount of blood that reaches certain parts of the body by varying the diameter of the relevant arteries and veins. It is achieved by contracting or relaxing the muscles in the arterial walls ▸176 through processes known as respectively as vasoconstriction and vasodilation. This flow control mechanism is an important part of the body's temperature regulation system.

The activities of the sympathetic neurons cause the diameters of the blood vessels to adapt to the body's needs. This process is governed by neurons which are located in the medulla of the brain stem ▸200 and is related to the cardiac regulation centre. If the blood pressure increases, specific receptors (baroreceptors) in key regions of the vascular system, send signals to the cardiac regulation centre and the medulla. In this way, it causes a simultaneous decrease in the heart rate and an increase in the diameter of the arteriole, together these tend to lower the blood pressure. If instead the peripheral pressure decreases, signals from the baroreceptors cause an increase in frequency of the heart rate and a reduction in the diameter of the arterioles. In particular, the contraction of the arterioles is the factor that is directly responsible for increases in arterial pressure and decreases in the flow of blood through the capillary network.

The arterioles are very sensitive to substances that are produced locally by the cells of the body. For example, those in the skin are sensitive to vasodilator products from some sensitive neurons which come into action when they are stimulated. Other locally released mediators can include histamine, bradykinin, nitric oxide, etc. The arterioles are also extremely sensitive to the concentration of dioxide carbon produced from cellular metabolism. Its presence leads to a rapid vasoconstriction of the area concerned, and a dramatic vasoconstriction in other parts of the body.

▲ **Controls**
The electrocardiogram (ECG) gives a large amount of information on the health of the heart. Here we see two individuals subjected to ECG at rest (left) and stress (right).

▼ **Atherosclerosis**
Section of an artery with a thick atherosclerosis deposit: the presence of these formations significantly alter blood pressure.

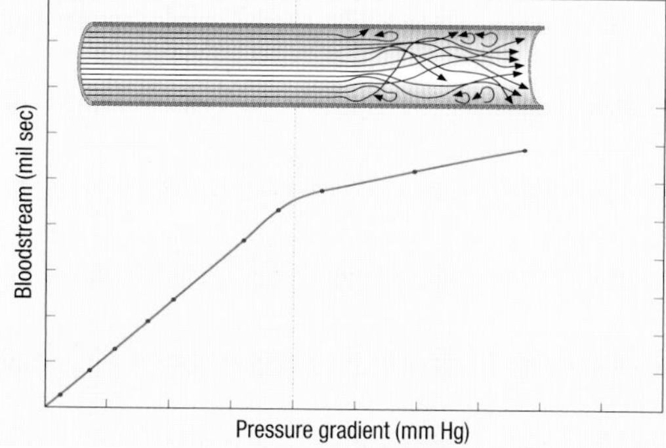

▲ **Turbulent flow**
The maximum speed reached by the blood flow is in laminar flow situations. When a vessel develops internal roughness (due, for example, to the formation of atheromatosis plaques), the flow becomes turbulent, and the speed decreases. At the same time, however, the pressure continues to grow.

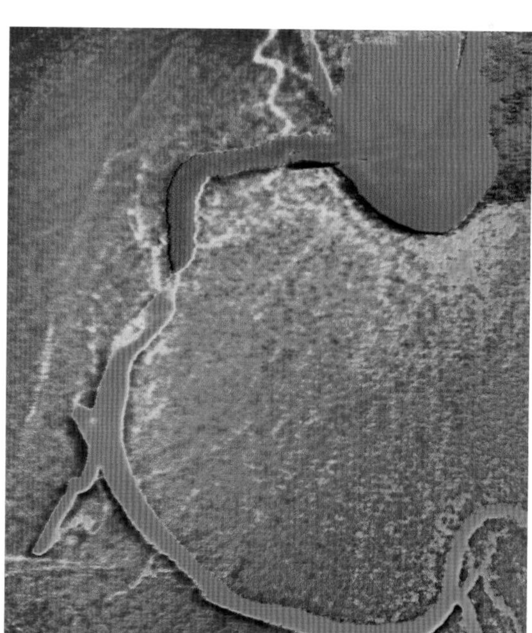

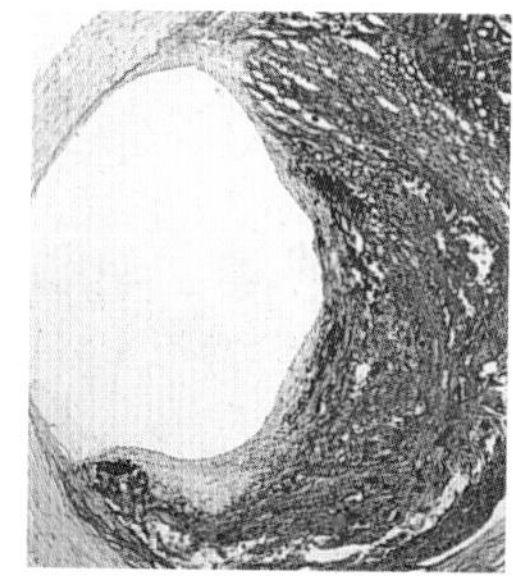

◀ **Angiogram**
Shows a coronary artery blockage in the blood stream, which can lead to heart attack.

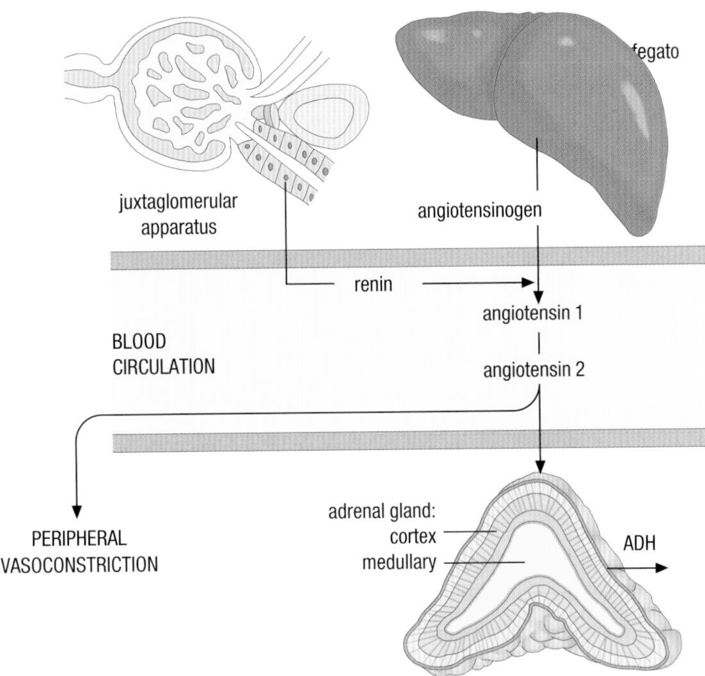

▲ **RAAS SYSTEM**
Schematic of the renin-angiotensin-aldosterone system, which responds to a drastic decrease of Volem. It involves the renal glomeruli (which produce renin), liver (which produces angiotensinogen, the inactive precursor of angiotensin) and the lungs, which concentrates the ACE, the enzyme necessary to activate the angiotensin I. It is the angiotensin II, in fact, that carries out the reactions that increase blood pressure and the Volem.

The arterial pressure depends on the volume of blood in circulation which must remain within precise limits. A regulatory mechanism which is particularly important and is triggered by changes in volume is the Renin-Angiotensin-Aldosterone System (RAAS). These are three closely related renal activity hormones.

If the volume decreases (low volume = Na+ < 135 meq/l), the arterial pressure is also reduced. In addition to this, other stimuli cause reductions in the diameters of the arterioles. This condition also enables the production of renin in some cells of the renal glomerulus ►149.

This glycoprotein enzyme activity transforms the angiotensinogen in the liver to angiotensin I, which in turn is triggered by the enzyme ACE (Angiotensin Converting Enzyme). This is mainly concentrated in the lungs and is transformed into angiotensin II, which has powerful vasoconstriction properties. It has a direct action on the vessels and causes a general increase in arterial pressure and glomerular filtration ►148. It also stimulates the adrenal cortex ►209 to produce catecholamines and aldosterone - a hormone that causes a sharp increase in the absorption of sodium and water in the seminiferous distal of the kidney. In addition, the active adrenal bone marrow produces adrenaline ►210 noradrenaline ►210 and dopamine ►210. These hormones modulate cellular metabolism and the glycidic free fatty acids. They also bind to the α receptors of the vessels membranes causing vasoconstriction. The increase in the blood pressure that follows, in turn, stimulates the carotid and aortic baroreceptors leading to a decrease in frequency of the heart rate.

In addition to binding to the α receptors which cause vasoconstriction in the kidneys, the arteriole gastrointestinal tract and of the skin, adrenaline can also bind to the β receptors of the striated myocardium and liver. In doing this, it acts as a vasodilator and influences the key control centres, causing a decrease in the heart rate. In the case, for example, of serious bleeding, activation of angiotensin II and of the cascade of adrenal hormones provides an immediate vasoconstriction and a rapid decrease in the excretion of sodium and water, thereby increasing the volume. The next action of the adrenaline brings everything slowly back to its initial levels, while increasing sodium in the blood and blood pressure. It also blocks the production of renin, quickly preventing the further production of angiotensin II.

THE IMPORTANCE OF THE ENDOTHELIUM

In addition to the substances that are produced in various organs of the body to modulate overall blood pressure, some molecules that act as vasodilators or vasoconstrictors are constantly produced in the endothelial cells. The endothelium, which is the film of flattened cells that separates the lumen of each vessel from its wall, plays a key role in the control of the arteries, especially at the level of micro-circulation. Endothelial cells, in fact, are sensitive to mechanical signals that are generated by the bloodstream and to the relevant hormones. It reacts by producing substances that act directly on the vascular muscle fibres. The adjustment factor is

► **ALDOSTERONE**
Diagram in 3D, reproduced with a computer.

►► **NORADRENALINE**
Diagram in 3D, reproduced with a computer.

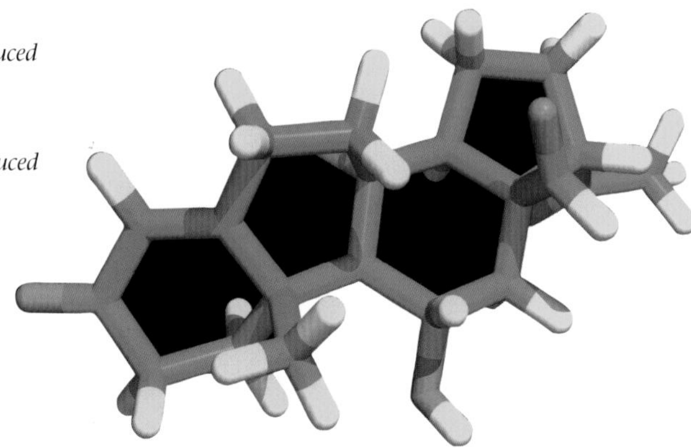

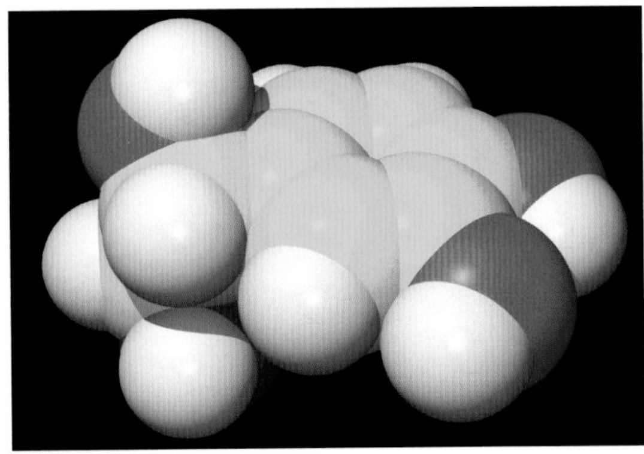

MEASURING BLOOD PRESSURE

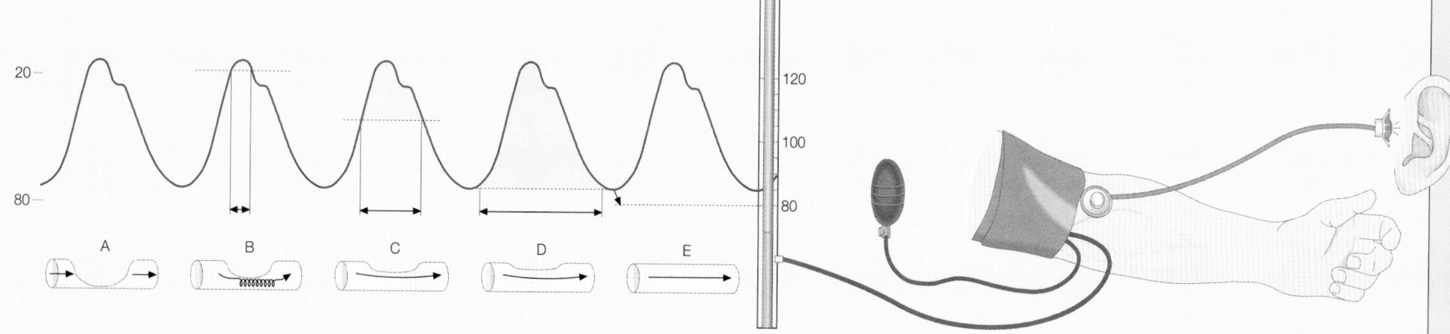

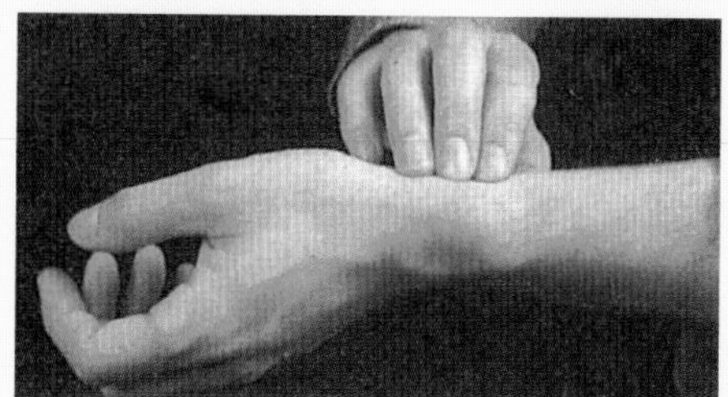

Measuring the blood pressure is a valuable diagnostic tool, since it is directly influenced by the heart's contractile activities as well as by the behaviour and conditions of the blood vessels. The instrument that is used to measure it is called a sphygmomanometer, and consists of a mercury gauge which is connected to an inflatable rubber sleeve.

A measurement can be taken by fitting the pressure sleeve around the arm - this is then inflated until its pressure exceeds that of the systolic phase. This prevents the flow of blood and the stethoscope is then placed on the brachial artery at the elbow and the pulse monitored A. The sleeve is deflated slowly until the sound of the blood flow can be heard again B. The pressure recording taken by the tool is the maximum systolic pressure. The sleeve is then allowed to continue deflating C, D until no noise is heard E: The measured value is the minimum diastolic pressure.

FACTORS THAT AFFECT BLOOD PRESSURE

- **Muscular activity**: physical activity can raise the systolic pressure to around the 180-200 mmHg mark; the diastolic pressure increases less (up to 90-100 mmHg): the pulse pressure increases with heart rate.
- **Digestion**: eating can cause the systolic pressure to rise for approximately 1 hour; after the meal, diastolic pressure may also decrease.
- **Excitement, anger, fear**: emotional changes can stimulate the heart to speed up, raising the blood pressure. In extreme cases, this can cause significant health problems.
- **Age**: this decreases the arterial elasticity - the more rigid the vessels become, the more the variations created during the cardiac cycle are felt throughout the body.
- **Human group**: blood pressure can vary with racial group.
- **Hormones**: hormonal imbalances can have a significant impact on blood pressure control.
- **Diseases**: there are many diseases that have a direct influence on blood pressure. In particular, hypertension is an indicator of alterations in the thicknesses of the arterial walls (atherosclerosis) and hormonal imbalances. Hypotension on the other hand can be an indication of various acute or debilitating diseases and cardiac problems.
- **Position**: the pressure reading will vary depending on the point at which the measurement is taken. For example, when it is performed on the feet, compensation must be made for the effects of gravity - the diastolic pressure increases, however, variations in the systolic increase are less noticeable. This therefore has a direct influence on the pulse pressure value.
- **Sex**: average values always refer to an adult male; women have values that are slightly lower, with those for children being the lowest.
- **Sleep**: a period of quality sleep can reduce the systolic pressure by 10-20 mmHg.

STANDARD PRESSURE VALUES

The World Health Organisation (WHO) has established reference values for arterial pressure:

- in a healthy adult between 20 and 60 years of age: below **140 / 90**
- best values in a healthy adult aged between 20 and 60: lower than **120 / 80**
- hypotension: lower than **120/80** less than 100 maximum arterial pressure values
- slight hypertension: from **140/90** to **159/99**
- hypertension (moderate): from **160/100** to **179/109**
- hypertension (severe): more than **180/110**

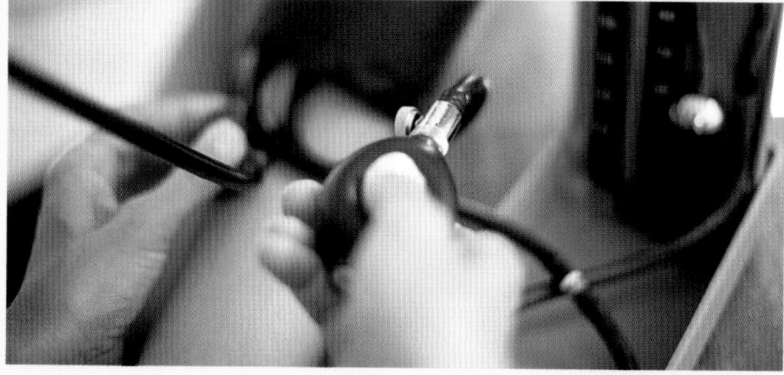

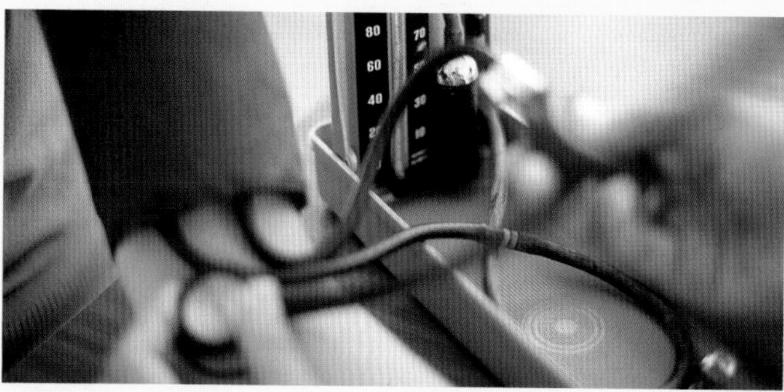

the primary blood pressure: in the absence of other chemical or nervous stimuli, with a constant blood flow, its increase produces a reaction that leads to endothelial vasoconstriction, while its decrease leads to vasodilatation. Moreover, there are two other forces that act on the vessel walls due to blood flow:

- The so-called stress or friction shear stress which is produced by the laminar flow of blood that passes close to the endothelia and activates the cells that release vasodilator mediators;
- The so-called tension stress that is produced by hydrostatic pressure in the vessel. This not only exercises the endothelia, but also puts stresses into the wall of the vessel. It then directly stimulates the smooth muscle cells, making them to shrink, while at the same time causing the stretching of the endothelial cells.

Vascular tone, therefore, is determined by the sum of the effects of blood pressure, stress and frictional stress, which can have mixed results. The endothelial cells also produce numerous mediators that act on vascular muscle, in amounts that are adjusted by numerous stimuli. This includes nitric oxide (NO), which a major endothelial mediator that regulates the arterial tone. Others, like prostacyclin or platelet activating factor, however, are secreted only in response to specific signals such as the presence of bradykinin, histamine, substance P and especially of acetylcholine in the circulation.

The action of nitric oxide has been identified as an agonist of acetylcholine, a neurotransmitter ►162 that, in isolated arteries with intact endothelia, causes vasodilatation. On the other hand, where the endothelium is absent, it causes vasoconstriction by directly stimulating the myocellular wall. Initially called EDRF (Endothelium Derived Releasing Factor), the substance interacting with the acetylcholine was identified as nitric oxide, whose action can be blocked in haemoglobin. It was observed that acetylcholine activates endothelial cells to produce NO by interacting with a membrane receptor and causing dilatation of the vessel. If instead the endothelium is damaged, it causes direct stimulation of muscle cells and vasoconstriction results. The endothelium can be damaged by many pathological conditions, such as atherosclerosis and hypercholesterolemia, diabetes and smoking. These may alter its function in the control of vascular tone and cause a reduction in the fine tuning of the peripheral circulation.

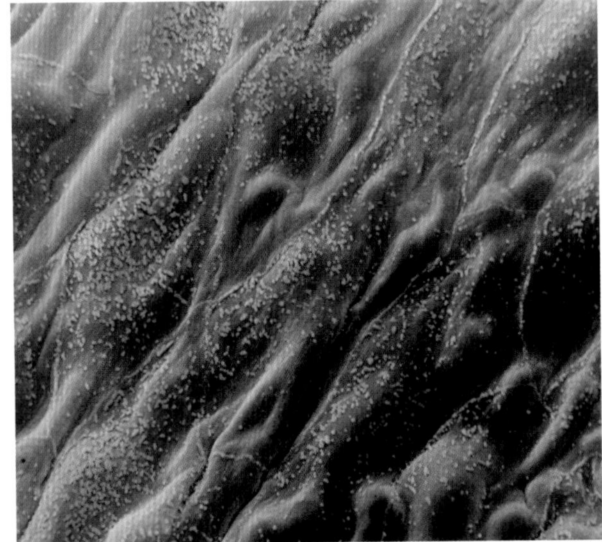

▲ **Endothelial cells** *Endothelium under a scanning electron microscope (SEM) in false colors: endothelial cells (purple) form the stratified tunica intima of the blood vessel. The endothelium consists of a single layer of epithelial cells supported by an underlying basal membrane and connective tissue. Each cell has a large number of microvilli (white dots) that facilitate the passage of nutrients from the bloodstream to tissues. The swelling seen in the photograph correspond to cell nuclei.*

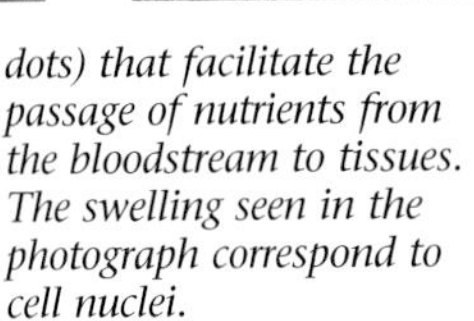

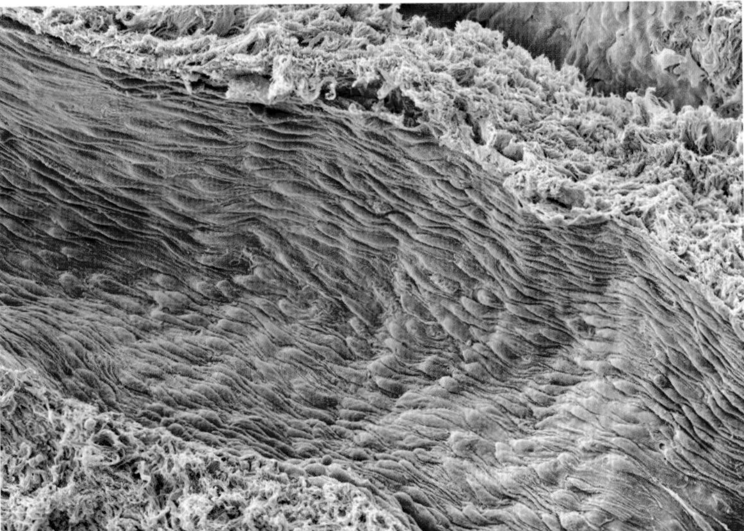

▲ **Blood Vessel** *Longitudinal section of a blood vessel under a scanning electron microscope (SEM) in false colors. The endothelium is pink.*

THE CONTINUOUS REPLACEMENT OF FLUIDS IN THE BODY IS BEING EXPLOITED BY THE SYSTEM TO EJECT EXCRETORY METABOLIC WASTE AND TO CONTROL BOTH THE CONCENTRATIONS OF SALTS, AND BODY TEMPERATURE.

SALT-WATER BALANCE AND EXCRETION

The liquids present in the body are of fundamental importance because they form the environment in which all the body's cells are immersed. Therefore, their composition and their characteristics should remain as far as possible as constants. In particular, their physical features should only vary within narrow limits, regardless of the external conditions. Internal stability is called homeostasis, and is controlled by nervous mechanisms that are auto-regulated and process all the systems and organs of the body. All the components interact in order to monitor the conditions within the environment - the first stage in this is to recognise the various changes that occur. This task is entrusted to a wide array of receptors, which collect information about body position and movement ►216, as well as nerve structures that are sensitive to changes in temperature, pH, pressure and many other factors. They report any changes to the control centres or the spinal cord, where the signals are processed and compared with stored data on the best conditions. The output signals are then produced to ensure the right responses take place. These may be made up of nervous impulses or a hormonal secretions - either way, they cause specifics effect within the homeostatic control system. There are many other physiological processes that are also linked to the conditions of homeostatic balance. These typically have feedback controls - that is, they stimulate the production of substances that help to return the system to a condition of balance.

Between all the elements that contribute to forming the environment within the body, there is one that is subject to more sudden variations than any other - this is water. Any changes have to be attended to very quickly, or there can be lethal consequences. Although the adult body is formed of about 65% water by weight, it has no form of storage for dry periods. As a result, water has to be taken in from the external environment much more often than nutritional substances such as fat, sugar or proteins. Water has to be constantly reinstated to keep the total quantity of organic liquids constant. This is because they are continually lost through metabolic activity. This includes evaporation from the lungs, transpiration through the skin, and especially from the production of urine.

INTERIOR LIQUIDS

Water is the main solvent for many bodily substances, and is divided into:

- intracellular liquids - that is, the water that is held inside the cells; this represents 41 % of the body weight of an adult, and has a characteristic and relatively constant chemical composition, this is due to membrane phenomena and metabolic processes;
- extracellular liquids - that is, the water that is held outside the cells; this is made up of around 17 litres in the average adult. The chemical composition can vary significantly - especially in the protein content, depending on the location. Thus, in accordance with its features, the extracellular water can be distinguished as the liquid in the

intracellular pores and that in the wet tissues. The former comprises around 14 of the 17 litres, and is used to fill the spaces separating the cells. The latter make up the remaining 3 litres, and this is divided between the plasma, lymph circulation, the fluids in the vertebral column and skull, as well as the liquids in the sinovial joints, eye, ear, etc.

The overall amount of water in the body remains constant, which means that there are mechanisms which have to constantly control the balance between liquid that has been lost and liquid that has been ingested. This delicate mechanism, as well as the immediate needs of the body, also takes into account other factors, such as, for example, the climate, the type of activity and the status of health. The recruitment water is stimulated by the feeling of thirst - this is governed by the nerve centres in the frontal area of the hypothalamus ▸179. The elimination of water, on the other hand, is undertaken by the renal system, and is governed by the activities of the pituitary gland through the production of the hormone ADH.

THE SKIN & SWEAT

The regular activity of a multicellular organism depends on the maintenance of stability of the chemical and physical conditions of the fluids that irrigate its cells. Achieving the stability of these internal conditions requires that the volume of water in the internal liquids is continually adjusted, together with the concentrations of several substances that are dissolved in it. In this sense the skin plays an essential role. Although it has to be impermeable and have thermal insulating properties, at the same time it also has to be able to produce sweat and perspire. These characteristics are essential, as they limit the losses of water and help in the thermal regulation of the body.

Sweat is a liquid that is secreted from the sweat glands of the skin, and is composed of about 70% by volume of water. The remaining fraction consists of sugars, ions (Na+, K+, Cl-), urea, immunoglobulins, fatty acids, cholesterol and, if there have been considerable physical efforts, lactic acid. There are about 3 million sweat glands scattered across the surface of the skin - they are subsidiary excretory bodies and can be categorised in two groups:

– apocrine glands, these are generally associated with hair follicles, and are helical tubular glomerular cells whose action is often linked to that of sex hormones. They develop in puberty and atrophy in old age;
– eccrine sweat glands - these are also known as merocrine glands, and are not linked to hairs. They are simple tubular glands that are found over more or less the whole surface of the body.

The process of the secretion of the sweat is called sweating - it has various functions:

• the excretion of waste metabolites;
• the lowering of the body temperature;
• unspoken communication (body odour). This function is actively combated by civilisation, which prefers to conceal sexual availability information or that of health through the use of substances like deodorants and perfumes.

▲ **Subdivision**
Segregation of water in different body compartments: within the closed cells is about half the liquid (63% intracellular fluid), while most of the extracellular fluid (81%, 30% of total) that is located outside the cell is made up of the intercellular fluid, namely those that constitute the tissue fluids.

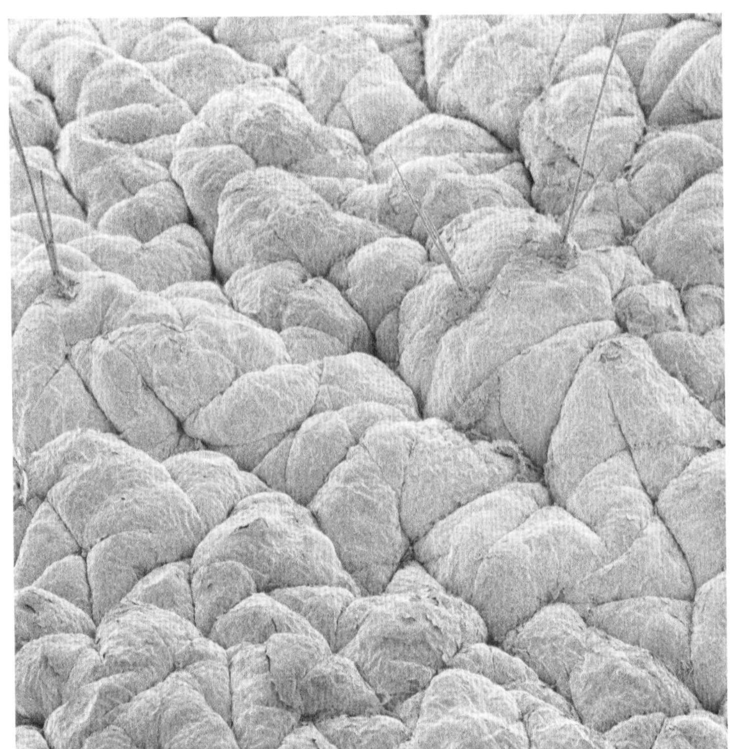

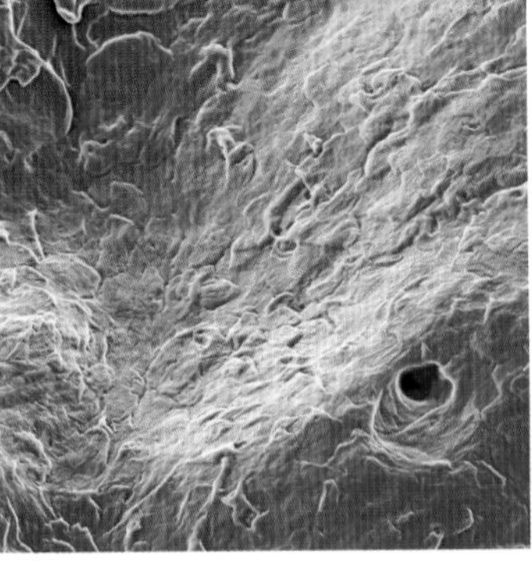

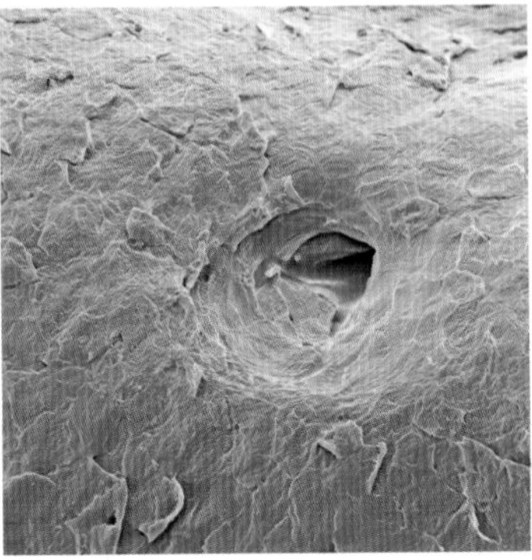

▶ **Excretory organ**
The skin, with its sweat glands, is a huge excretory organ, although much less efficient than the kidneys. In these pictures you can see a stretch of skin and, in more detail (scanning electron microscope photos), the opening of a sweat gland pore.

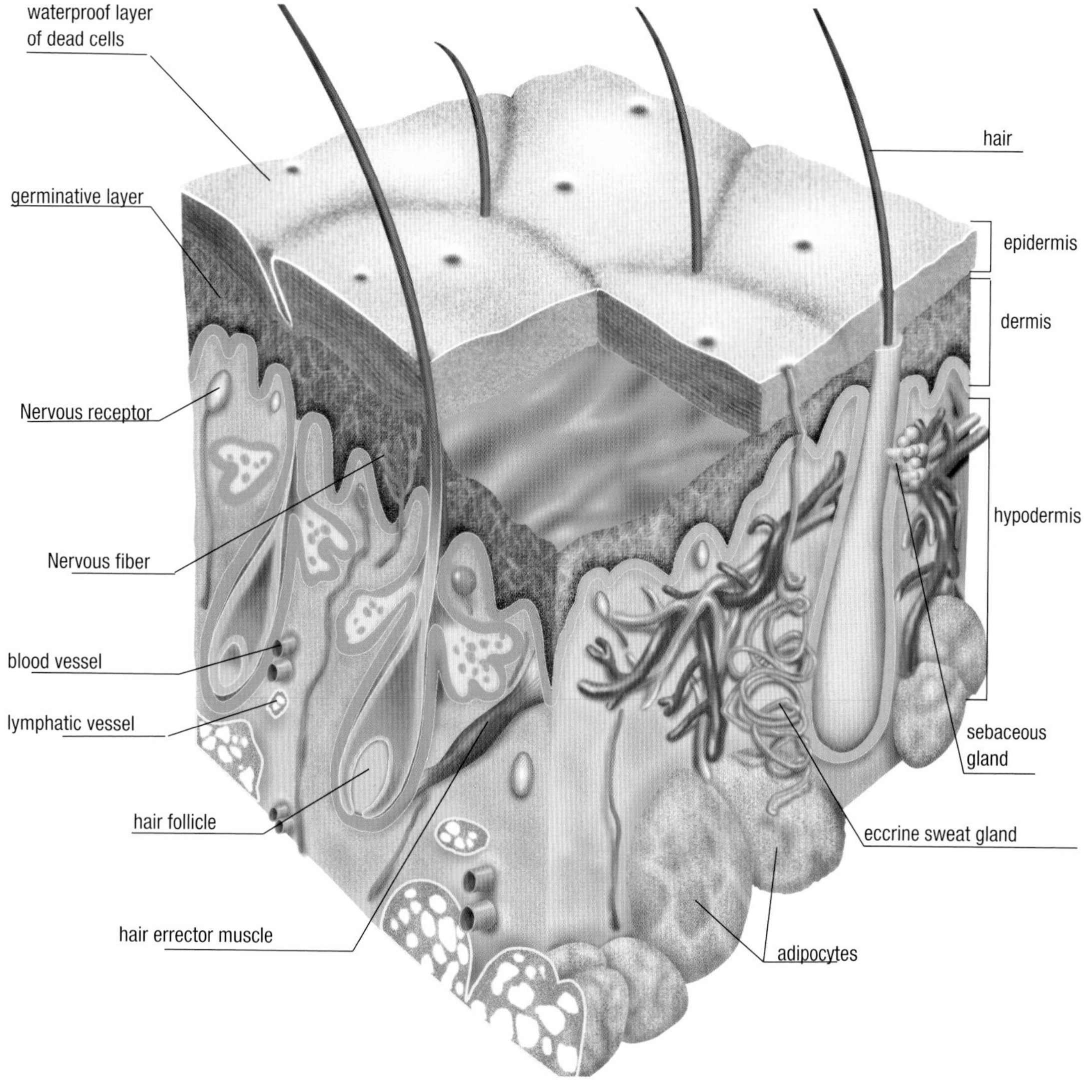

waterproof layer of dead cells
germinative layer
Nervous receptor
Nervous fiber
blood vessel
lymphatic vessel
hair follicle
hair errector muscle
hair
epidermis
dermis
hypodermis
sebaceous gland
eccrine sweat gland
adipocytes

◀ **The skin**
Layers and the main features of the skin.

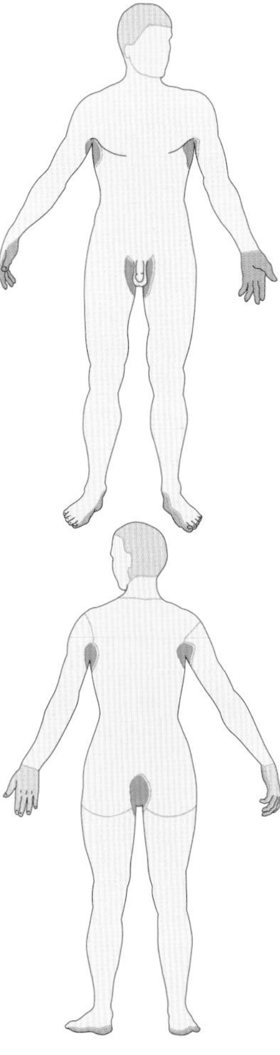

▲ **Sweat glands**
Distribution of eccrine sweat glands compared with that of the apocrine glands (blue):
- *> 300/cm2*
- *> 200/cm2*
- *> 150/cm2*
- *< 150/cm2*

The production of sweat by the eccrine sweat glands is under the direct control of the cholinergic neurons of the parasympathetic nervous system which are in the frontal portion of the hypothalamus, as well as the extended spinal and neuronal columns of the spinal cord. Sweating is triggered primarily as reaction to a change in body temperature, such as that which happens during hard physical work or in an attack of fever, but it can also increase for other reasons, as a rise in the ambient temperature or humidity, which prevents the dispersion of heat. Sweating can also happen as a result of particular emotional or mental states, such as fear or excitement. These stimulate nerve centres that can trigger sweating, but are not linked to temperature control.

blood plasma
intercellular liquid
intracellular liquid
190
180
170
160
150
140
130
120
110
100
90
80
70
60
50
40
30
20
10
0

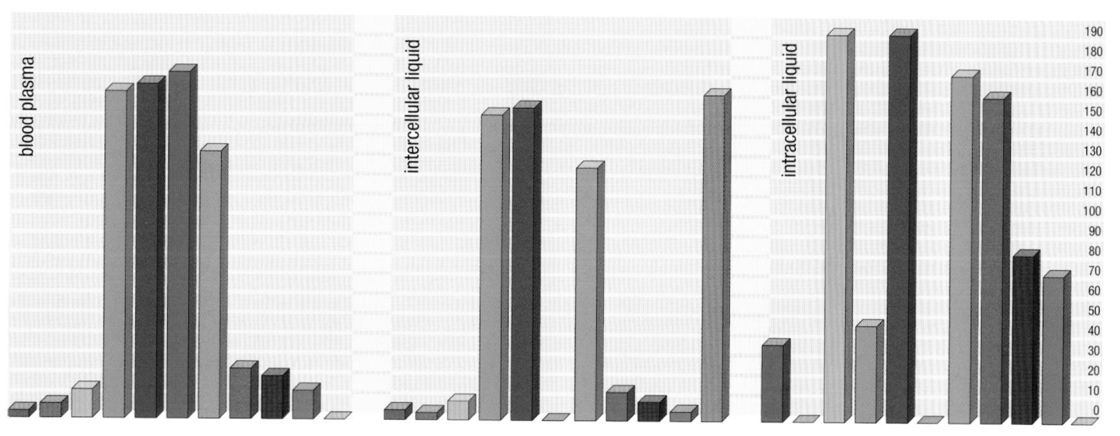

◀ **Comparison**
Composition of plasma, interstitial fluid and intercellular fluid compared.
- *Mg (magnesium)*
- *Ca (calcium)*
- *K (potassium)*
- *Na (sodium)*
- *HCO3 (bicarbonate)*
- *NO (nitric oxide)*
- *Cl (chlorine)*
- *HPO4 (phosphate ion)*
- *SO4 (sulfate ion)*
- *protein*
- *electrolytes*

Thermoregulation and Water-Salt Balance

Life is only made possible by the myriads of chemical reactions that take place within the body. Without the right environmental conditions - as defined by the laws of physics and chemistry, however, these do not happen in the required manner, and disorder or death may result. One of the most important reaction parameters is temperature, and it is vital that this is regulated within precise limits, no matter whether it is freezing cold or very hot outside the body.

The thermoregulatory body is effectively a thermostat that is located in the hypothalamus. Within the frontal region is a group of neurons that are particularly sensitive to increases in temperature. Conversely, in the rear hypothalamus there is a different group of neurons that are very sensitive to reductions in temperature. An external temperature increase or decrease of 1-2 °C stimulates these neurons to respond, activating the protective mechanisms that either lead to the required production or loss of heat

Decrease In Temperature

A decrease in body temperature is usually caused by environmental influences which cause a loss of heat from radiation and conduction. Secondary losses can be due to evaporation and loss of water (through sweating, breathing, intestinal losses and urinary processes). Apart from behaviour and subconscious actions such as the generation of goosebumps, the body fights temperature loss by the production of endogenous heat derived from muscle activity (such as movement or shivering), from nutrition and oxidative metabolic processes. One method is for the hypothalamus to stimulate the endocrine system. This causes the adrenal glands to release catecholamines, as well as inducing vasoconstriction in the skin. This increases blood pressure, making reserves of lipids and carbohydrates available. At the same time, the thyroid gland produces hormones that stimulate heat-generating cellular metabolic activity.

Increase In Temperature

An increase in body temperature is usually generated by environmental influences, but can also be caused by pathological processes. When temperature reduction is necessary, the body activates certain physiological processes. These are typically the reverse of those employed for increasing the amount of heat produced. For example, the hypothalamic pathways reduce the amount of thyroid stimulation and the adrenal glands induce vasodilation, thus speeding up all the factors which lead to the dispersion of heat through evaporation. The breathing rate is increased in order to lose heat via lung ventilation, and at the same time more sweat is produced to cause skin cooling. While this is going on, the stimuli to eat and move are also lowered.

The Sweat

Water is a vital component in the body's temperature control system. It has the maximum possible conductivity and heat capacity of any fluid, and this property is used to full effect to ensure that the correct thermal balance is maintained. While water helps to maintain a constant temperature in the body by allowing chemical reactions to occur, it also makes it possible to cool down very quickly when necessary. The mechanism used for this is sweating - the evaporation of even small quantities of water can bring about a rapid loss in temperature.

The amount of sweat produced by an adult is variable

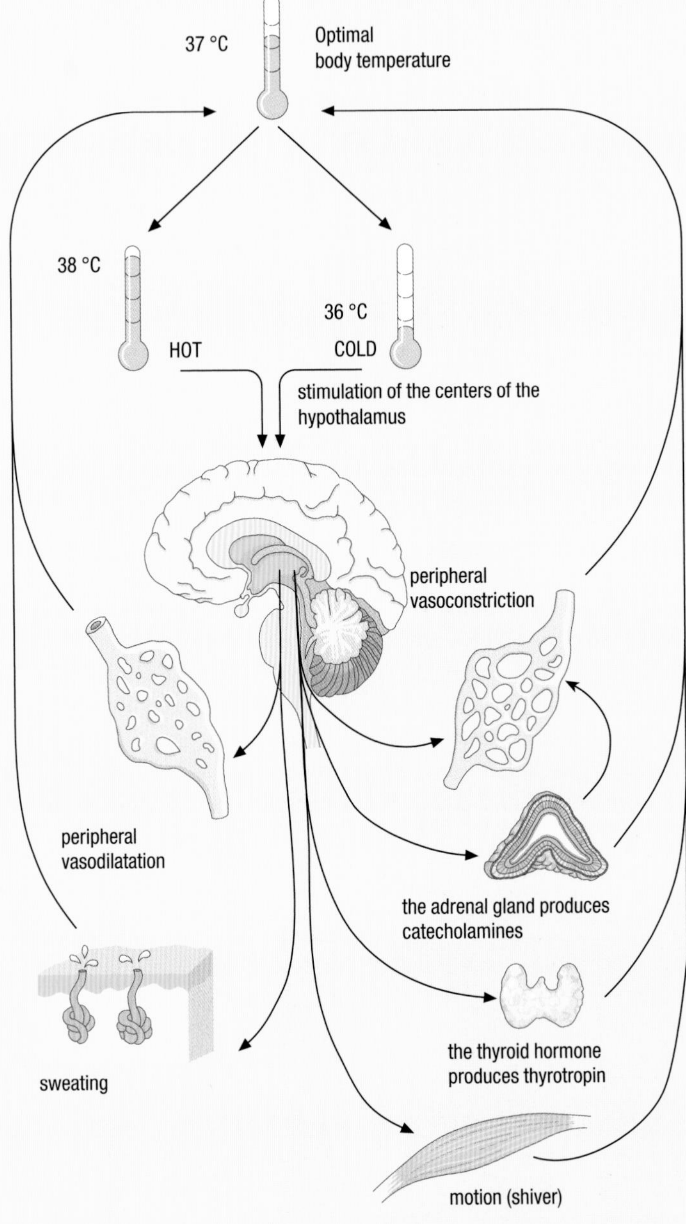

depending on individual needs - it can vary from a minimum of 0.5 litres/day, up to a maximum of 10 litres/day. The amount of sweat produced increases with rises in environmental temperature and the rate of muscular work. If the temperature is not regulated properly and starts to rise beyond to the upper limit, various parts of the body start to suffer, and in doing so fail to carry out their functions correctly. The sweat glands usually work very well, however, they can only do so as long as there is sufficient excess water in the body. If not, heat-stroke is the next stage, and if this is not ameliorated quickly, the situation is likely to be lethal.

The effectiveness of the perspiration apparatus in keeping the body's temperature under control also depends on other factors that are extraneous to the physiology of the body. Since the process is determined by the physical laws of evaporation, its efficiency is dependent on the prevailing weather conditions. If the air is very wet, for example, evaporation is significantly reduced and the body temperature may not decrease fast enough. When the body sweats, it not only releases water but also mineral salts - if too much sweating takes pace and these are not replaced, other health problems may result. If too much water is lost, arterial pressure can fall below the safe limit. Likewise, a similar result can be caused by an excessive loss of salts - in particular that of potassium, which is essential for the maintenance of correct muscle activity. In certain circumstances, the body will increase its temperature as a direct response to the release of toxins by invading microbes. Under extreme circumstances, this can get out of control, with lethal effects.

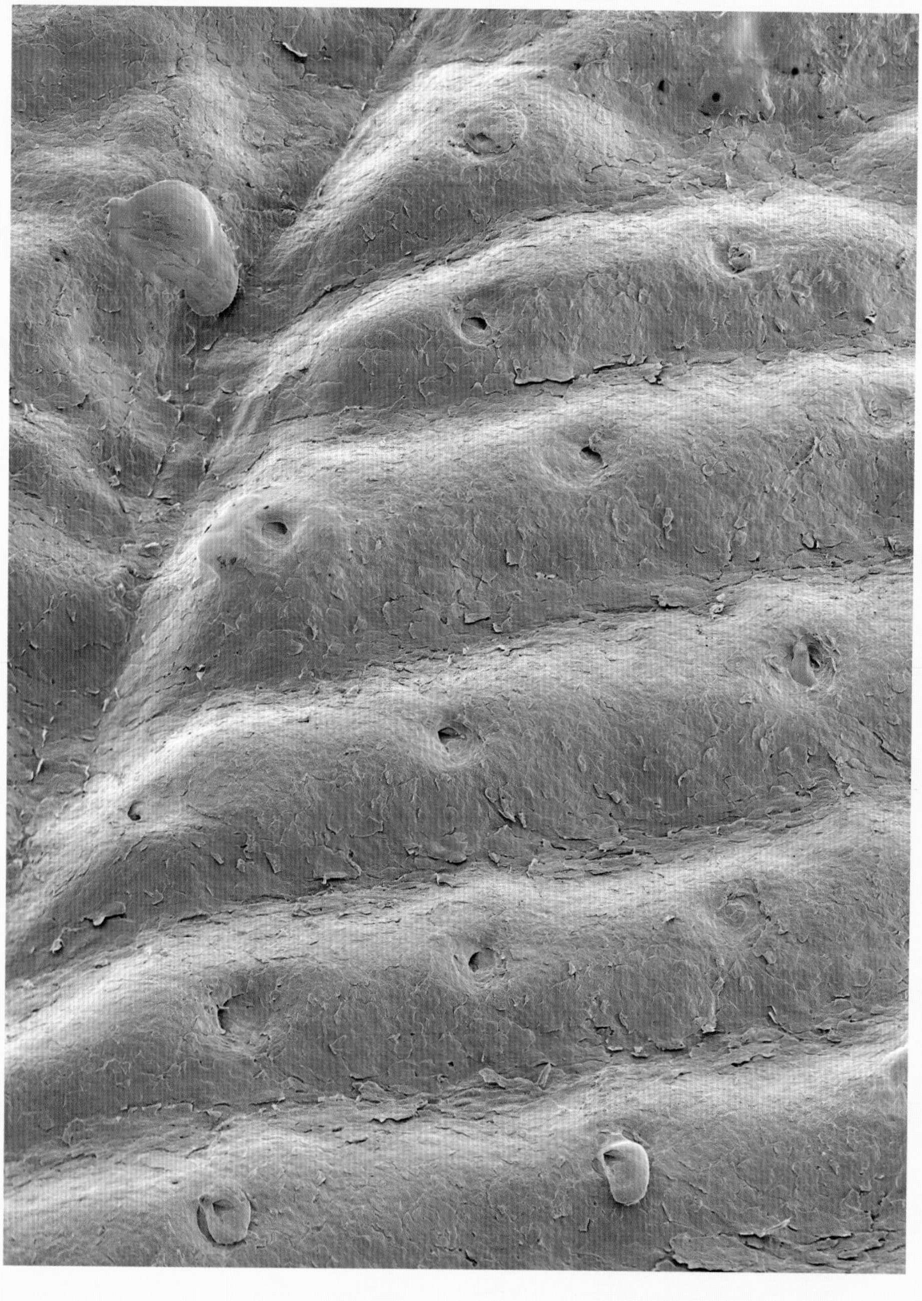

▲ **SWEAT**
SEM microphotography of a stretch of skin surface where a few drops of sweat have just been expelled from the pores.

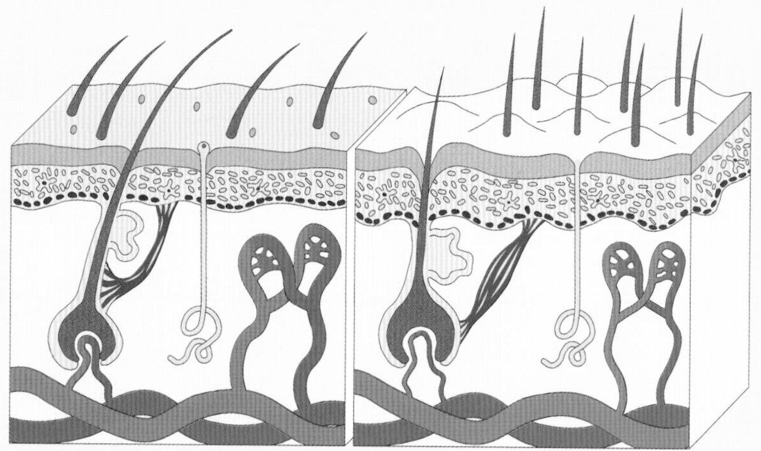

◀ **SKIN REACTIONS**
Effect of temperature on the skin. On the left, hot, on the right, cold. When the temperature rises on the layers of skin above, the blood vessels dilate, and the increased blood flow heats the surface. This stimulates the activity of sweat glands and the production of sweat that is excreted for cooling the skin. When the temperature drops the blood vessels shrink, and the blood flow is lower, the activity of sweat glands stops. The cutaneous muscles are contracted (goose bumps) and erect and straighten the hair in an attempt to increase the layer of air (thermal insulation) found in contact with skin.

THE KIDNEYS: THE PRODUCTION OF URINE & RENAL FUNCTIONS

The skin, lungs, and to a less extent, the intestines, all perform undertake the excretion of metabolic wastes in addition to the functions to which they are primarily dedicated. The most efficient excretory bodies are the kidneys: their activity is essential, in fact, their main role is to produce urine, ensuring the continued disposal of substances that are useless, harmful or in excess in the bloodstream. They also control homeostasis, as well as the blood's pH and its ion concentration.

THE RENAL SYSTEM

Anywhere between a fifth and a third of the blood that leaves the heart with each beat passes through the kidneys. On average, this adds up to around one litre of blood per minute. It is delivered there directly from the abdominal aorta and then into the renal artery, which has a diameter of 5-7 mm; this ensures that there is a sufficient influx of blood. Just before it reaches the hilum, the renal artery is divided into several branches ensuring good distribution. These are referred to as the segmental arteries, which then further divide into the interlobular arteries before splitting into tiny capillaries. These contribute to the formation of the renal clusters, which is where the blood corpuscles are actually separated from waste and excess water. After undergoing ultrafiltration, the blood continues to its destination via the efferent arterioles, forming a peritubular network. This plays an essential role in the control of urine concentration. All the blood from the peritubular capillaries ends up in the venous capillaries, where it continues to make its way out of the kidneys. To do this it travels through the arcuate vein followed by the interlobular veins and then eventually out via the renal vein near the renal hilum. In its entirety, the renal blood network measures a total of about 100 miles (160 km) in length.

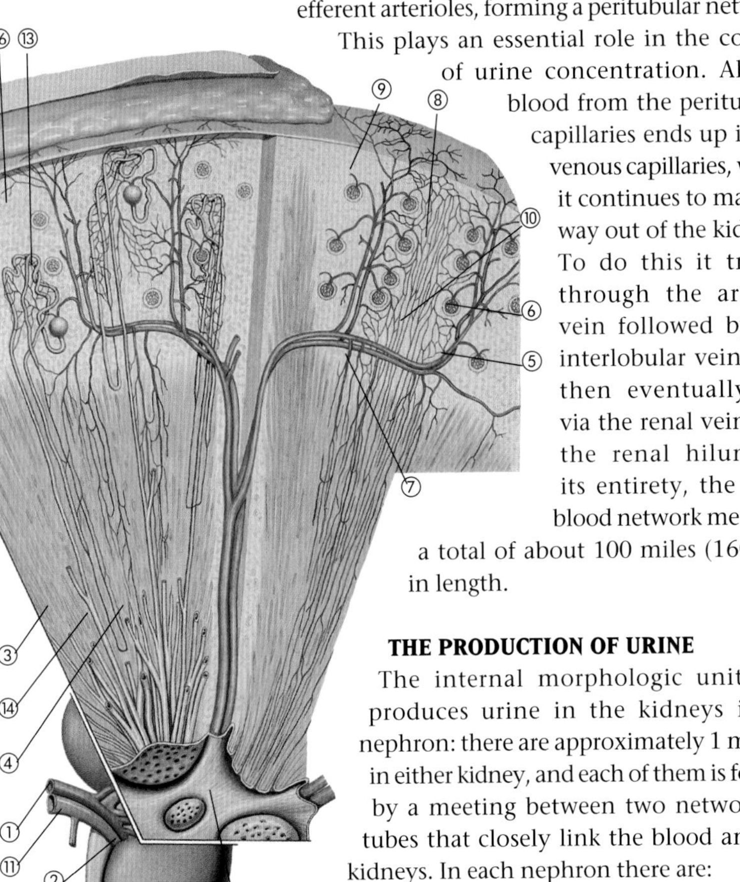

▼ **Structure of the kidney**
Principal elements of a section of the kidney:
① *renal artery*
② *renale illeum*
③ *medullary substance*
④ *pyramid*
⑤ *interlobular artery*
⑥ *renal glomeruli*
⑦ *real artery line*
⑧ *peritubulare network*
⑨ *efferent arterioles*
⑩ *Spurious artery line*
⑪ *renal vein*
⑫ *renal calyx*
⑬ *contorted tubule*
⑭ *papillary duct*
⑮ *ureter*
⑯ *cortex*

THE PRODUCTION OF URINE

The internal morphologic unit that produces urine in the kidneys is the nephron: there are approximately 1 million in either kidney, and each of them is formed by a meeting between two networks of tubes that closely link the blood and the kidneys. In each nephron there are:

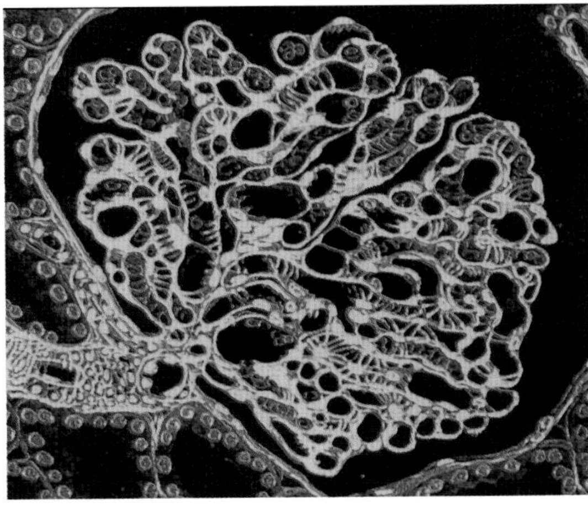

▲ **Renal corpuscle**
Graphic reconstruction of a renal corpuscle, the filtering unit of a frog. We can distinguish the clusters (center, yellow), the space in which liquid waste is filtered and the Bowman capsule (dark blue), which delimits. This space (upper left) is the area of the renal tubule.

▶ **Renal tubule**
MET Microphotography in false colors of a section of the proximal contorted tubule where the reabsorption of water, glucose and other molecules occur. Around the lumen (white) cubic epithelial cells (green, brown nuclei) have numerous microvilli (red) which increase the surface area of resorption.

- The renal corpuscles (previously known as the Malpighian corpuscles) - these have a diameter of 150-300 μm, and are located in the renal cortex, where they produce the first stages of urine:
  – The glomerulus: In this structure, 3-5 afferent arterioles are coiled into a roughly spherical form - this is where the ultrafiltration takes place. The high pressures that are built up as the result of the narrowing of the blood vessels force fluids and dissolved substances out into the Bowman's capsule. The bloods then drains into the efferent arterioles and into the peritubular capillaries.
  – The Bowman's capsule: this is a kind of goblet-shaped structure, the outer or parietal layer of which is composed of simple squamous epithelium tissue. It contains a large number of podocytes, which are the main filtration components. These feature narrow slits through which prevent the passage of unwanted substances and debris.

The production of urine begins with an ultra-filtration process. This is performed by pumping blood into the glomerulus at a high pressure - approximately 9.3 kPa. The internal pressure of the Bowman's capsule, however, is only approximately 2 kPa. This steep gradient causes various substances to pass through the semi-permeable membrane. These include water, inorganic salts, glucose, urea and also small organic molecules, as well as both red and white blood cells, platelets and large protein molecules from the blood such as fibrinogen,

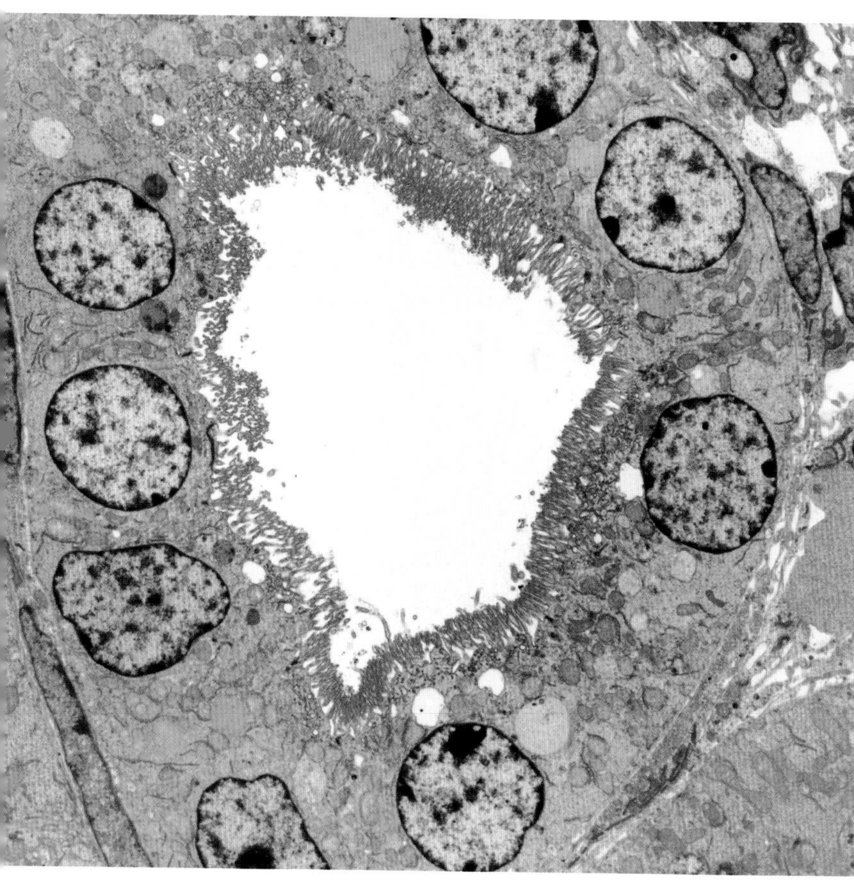

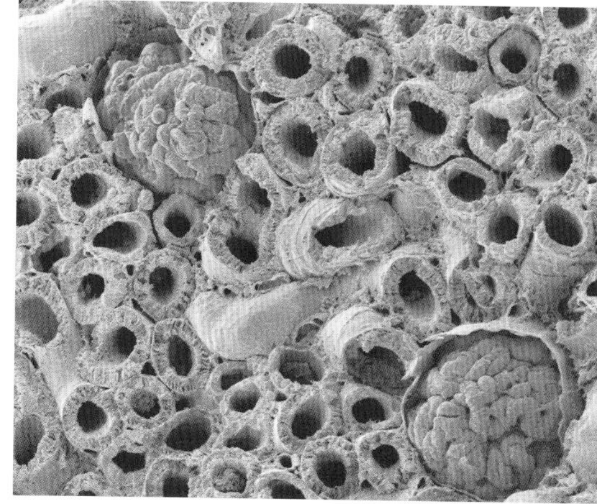

▲ **Glomeruli**
SEM photograph in false color of capillaries (in red) that help to filter the blood in the kidneys. In blue (center), renal tubules and capillaries.

▼ **Functional unit**
Structure of a nefrone:
① interlobular artery
② renal glomeruli
③ Bowman capsule
④ podocyte
⑤ lumen of the capsule
⑥ afferent arterioles
⑦ efferent arterioles
⑧ contorted proximal tubule
⑨ loop of Henle
⑩ collagen tubule
⑪ peritubular network

albumin and globulin.
This results in an effective and selective absorption of water (more than 85 % by volume) together with the excretion of other substances such as sodium chloride, glucose, amino acids, ascorbic acid and creatinine. The glomerulus filters a total of more than 150 litres every day and reduces this to an average of around 1.5 litres of urine. The substances that are filtered in the Bowman's capsule are classified according to their renal thresholds:

- substances with a high renal threshold are completely reabsorbed and are present in the urine only if there is an abnormally high concentration in the blood. This category includes calcium, glucose, chlorine, sodium, vitamin C, various amino acids, etc.;
- substances with a low renal threshold are only partially reabsorbed and are commonly found in the urine. This includes, for example: uric acid, iodine, potassium, phosphates and bicarbonates;
- substances with no renal threshold - these are not reabsorbed and they always appear in large quantities in the urine, as is the case with creatinine and urea.

The proximal tubules absorb around 80-90% of the water that passes through them, as well as around two-thirds of the sodium and chlorine. Further to this, all of the glucose, most of calcium, magnesium, vitamin C and some of the phosphates are reabsorbed. While the water is absorbed due to the concentration gradient, the sodium is reabsorbed actively, this being balanced by the excretion of potassium ion, hydrogen and ammonia, causing an increase in osmotic pressure. This part of the absorption process is regulated in the distal convoluted tubule.

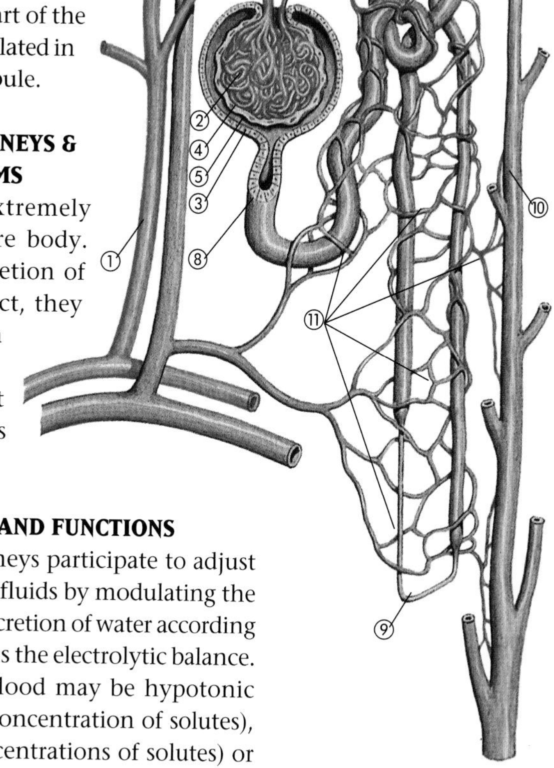

FUNCTIONS OF THE KIDNEYS & THEIR CONTROL SYSTEMS

The renal tasks are extremely important for the entire body. By modulating the excretion of solutes and water, in fact, they do not only undertake a cleaning function, but keep many important environmental parameters under control.

ONE PROCESS, A THOUSAND FUNCTIONS

In the first place the kidneys participate to adjust the volume of the body's fluids by modulating the rates of absorption and excretion of water according to its needs. It also controls the electrolytic balance. Urine, therefore, with blood may be hypotonic (where there is minor a concentration of solutes), isotonic (with equal concentrations of solutes) or hypertonic (where there is major a concentration

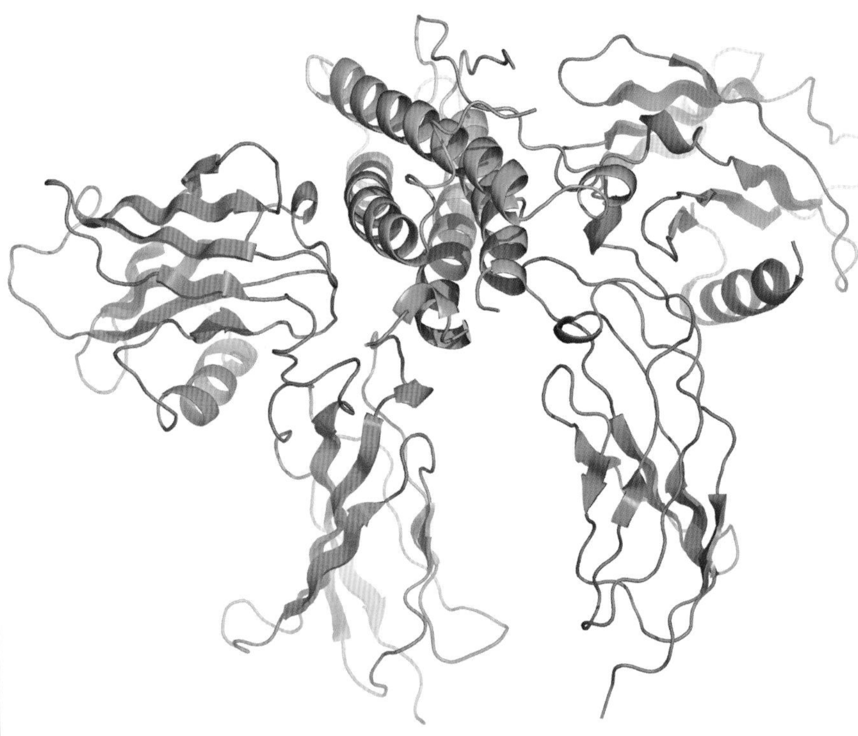

▲ **Erythropoietin**
Computer created structure of a erythropoietin molecule (orange) bound to two molecules of extracellular receptor (pink and purple). The Erythropoietin is a glycoprotein produced by the kidneys in response to low oxygen partial pressure in the blood. It stimulates the maturation of precursors of red blood cells in the bone marrow, the increased production of red blood cells, in fact, is designed to increase the presence of oxygen available.

of solutes). The extracellular concentration of sodium also influences the absorption of water. The absorption of this ion, therefore, alters the volume of body fluids that are necessary. Further to this, the various processes of filtration, absorption, secretion and excretion of glucose, amino acids, uric acid and urea also influence the composition of body fluids. By controlling and regulating these balances, the kidneys ensure that the concentrations of the substances that are essential to health remain within very precise limits.

In particular, the kidneys play a key role in the control of blood concentration of electrolytes: Cl-HCO3–, PO43–, Ca 2+ above all, however, they regulate the electrolytes that are essential to the balance of the cellular membranes - these are sodium (Na+), and potassium (K+). These must be present in specific quantities and proportions to prevent problems that could be especially harmful to the excitable cells in the heart, muscles and nerves. At the same time, however, the kidneys also control and regulate the blood's homeostasis and acid balance thanks to the absorption of bicarbonates and the secretion of hydrogen ions (H+). This is not all they do, however. They also undertake important endocrine functions by producing various substances - these include renin, which plays an important role in the control of blood pressure and erythropoietin. This is indispensable for the formation and the maturation of red blood cells and the prostaglandins ▸145. Calcitriol (1, 25-dihydroergocalciferol) - the active form of vitamin D3 is also metabolised in the kidneys from vitamin D, and is a very important metabolic hormone regulator and a key component in the transport of calcium.

REGULATORY SYSTEMS

Since the impacts of the excretion carried out by the kidneys are so diverse, it is not surprising that the control systems which govern this are numerous and involve different aspects of the renal process:

A. Glomerular filtration. The glomerular basement membrane is the structure that is responsible for the actual filtration of blood, and is made up of both endothelial cells and basal podocyte layers. The Bowman's capsules are permeable to almost all substances with a molecular weight that is less than 65,000 units. The filtration effect depends almost exclusively on the algebraic sum of the pressure values. The arterial blood has a positive pressure of approximately 9.3 kPa, the osmotic pressure that is exerted by the plasma proteins is negative at approximately 3.3 kPa, and the liquid already filtered but still present in the

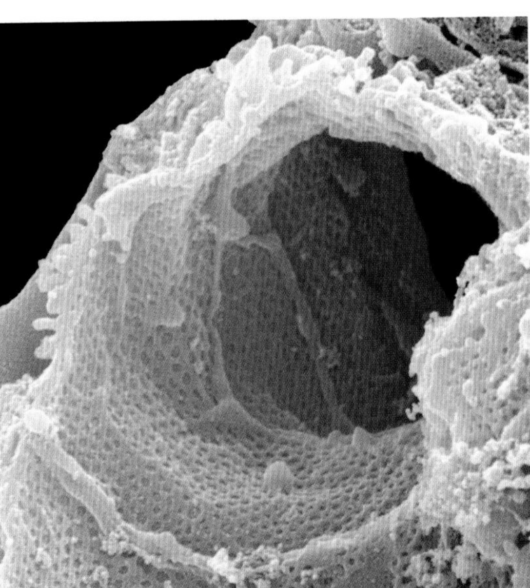

▶ **Blood capillary**
Scanning electron microscope (SEM) photograph in false colors of a capillary inside the arterial part of a renal glomeruli. There are pores which interrupt the wall, from which "oozes" the glomerular filtrate, or preurina.

CHEMICAL COMPOSTITION

SUBSTANCE	concentration in ‰ PLASMA	URINE
WATER	900-930	950
PROTEIN, FAT	70-90	0
GLUCOSE	1	0
UREA	0.3	20
URIC ACID	0.03	0.5
CREATINE	< 0.01	1
SODIUM	3.2	3.5
POTASSIUM	0.2	1.5
CALCIUM	0.08	0.15
MAGNESIUM	0.025	0.06
CHLORINE	3.7	6
PHOSPATE ION (PO_4)	0.09	2.7
SULPHATE ION (SO_4)	0.04	1.6

capsule is negative at approximately 2 kPa.

The nephrons - the kidneys basic filtration units, are regulated by the juxtaglomerular apparatus which increases or decreases the filtration speed as required. It consists of a set of specialised cells that produce renin, these are grouped together in various points in the nephron.

- The vascular pole, this is an enlargement of the relevant arteriole that is located immediately before the glomerulus. The endothelia is discontinuous and the muscle fibres are in part replaced by cells similar to those of an epithelia;
- The extraglomerular mesangial cells, which are known as lacis cells or Goormaghtigh cells, are smooth, granules of myofibril that are made mainly of renin. They are found in small columns between the efferent arteries, and are localised outside the glomerulus close to the vascular pole and macula densa.
- The macula densa; this consists of thin cylindrical cells with pronounced cores, and is found lining the internal walls of the distal tubule. It has close associations with both with the glomerular vascular pole and the extraglomerular mesangial cells. The macula densa is also located in the angle between the two arterioles. Its role is to produce substances that are connected with regulating the blood pressure and volume.

B. Absorption in the proximal tubule. The absorption of the glomerular filtrate is performed by two mechanisms:

- passive transport, which follows the diffusion and osmosis laws. This depends entirely on the gradients of hydrostatic and osmotic pressure between the blood in the capillaries and the tubules. This is the mechanism for the absorption of water along with certain electrolytes;
- active transport, this is undertaken by cells in the proximal convoluted tubule that exploit metabolic energy to extract the glucose, amino acids, proteins and most of the electrolytes. Specific for each group of substances, it seems that this mechanism is mediated by the presence of special carrier molecules on the membranes

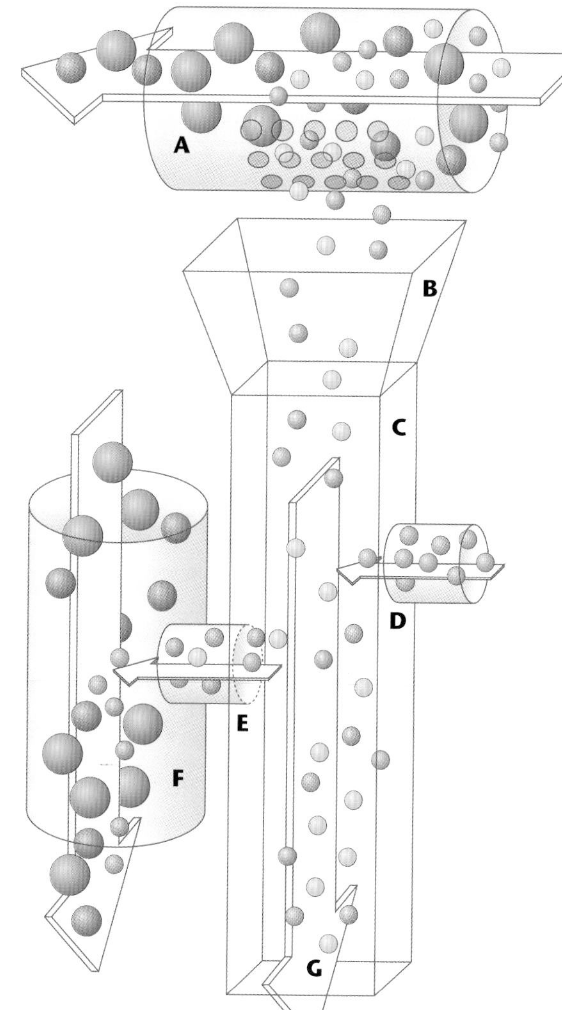

◀ **Formation of urine**
*Diagram summarizing the mechanism that leads to the formation of urine: the capillaries of the glomeruli (**A**) lose water and solutes ending at the Bowman capsule (**B**) which is connected with the renal tubule (**C**). More waste comes from the surrounding tissues (**D**) and tubule cells, selectively absorb certain substances (**E**) which passes back into the bloodstream through the capillaries adjacent to the tubule (**F**). In the end, what remains is urine (**G**), a highly concentrated solution and completely different composition than the glomerular filtrate.*

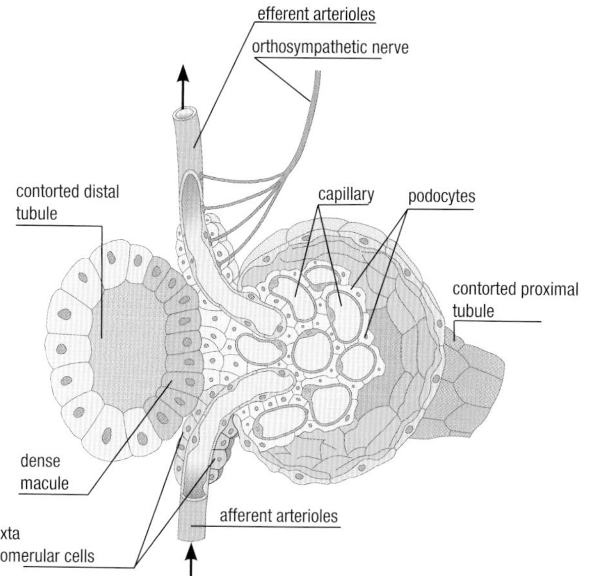

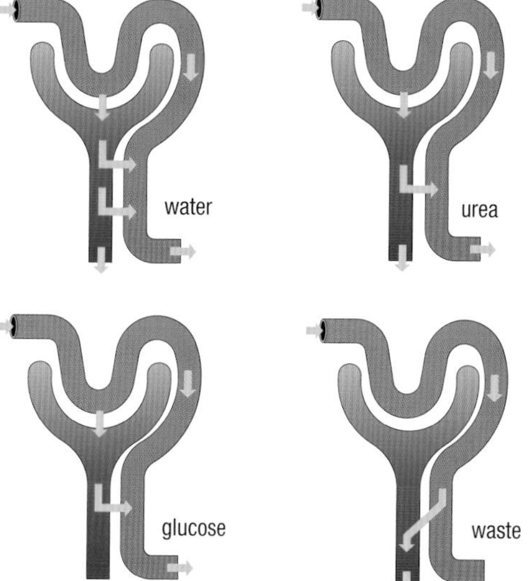

◀◀ **Juxta glomerular complex**
Diagram showing the placement of groups of specialized cells in the kidney hormone production.

◀ **Renal action on various substances**
Diagram showing the action of nefrons on water, glucose, urea and waste substances. You can see that while the water is absorbed continuously, this is not the case with urea and, even moreso, with substances of waste.

THE BIOCHEMICAL EXAMINATION OF URINE

The medical assessment of urine has certain standard procedures - these include chemical analysis and a physical microscopic examination of the sediment. Typically, a sample of only around 10 ml is needed. This is more than sufficient for the most obvious clinical indications to be found and identified - the primary features of the test include:

• **Albumin** - this is the main protein in the serum, and links calcium, hormones and other substances to prevent filtration impairment.. Under normal conditions albumin is absent from the urine, so if it is found to be present, it indicates some form of malfunction in the filtration process.

• **Bilirubin** - this is the main pigment in the bile - it is normally absent from the urine, but if it is present it gives a dark colour to faeces and urine rule. This is a primary indicator for a variety of medical problems. These include anaemia, gallstones and malaria as well as poisoning from arsenic, phosphorus or lead.

• **Calcium** - this is an essential mineral, and is excreted from the body in large quantities - typically about 100-250 mg per day - this is known as the 'normal value' or 'NV'. Larger values may indicate various problems including hyperparathyroidism, osteoporosis, multiple myeloma, Fanconi's syndrome, Cushing's syndrome or Paget's syndrome. Alternatively, it may also be due to a diet that is rich in calcium, such as that obtained by eating lots of tomatoes or spinach. Smaller values can be caused by a lack of vitamin D, hyperparathyroidism, acute pancreatitis, or pregnancy.

• **Color** - this normally varies between straw yellow and amber, but can also be anywhere from red to blue, depending on what has been ingested. A dark yellow colour can indicate dehydration, blood inflammation or jaundice. Green is indicative of jaundice, whereas a pink or red colour may be due to inflammation or a diet rich in red cabbage, cranberries, or artificial colours. An orange coloration can be caused by jaundice or eating beetroot. A dark colour is usually generated by bile pigments being excreted, and is a sign of ongoing liver disease.

• **Creatinine** - this is a primary waste product, and analysis can determine its speed of clearance. Typical values are in the range of NV 0.7 - 2.0 g per day. Any significant decreases from this may be caused by dermatomyositis, diabetes, chronic renal insufficiency, tetanus, but also by trauma, burns or muscular dystrophy.

• **Pregnancy** - this is an immunological test that is performed on the first urine collected in the day and checks for chorionic gonadotropin, a hormone produced by the tissue that gives rise to the placenta.

• **Odour** – this is usually is not very strong, but its intensity can vary diet - especially when things like asparagus are eaten, or when drugs are taken. If a bad odour persists, it can indicate infection.

• **Specific Weight** - this is a good index of renal function, and is determined by the amount of urea, proteins, glucose, urobilin and bile pigments that are present. The NV is typically 1030 units; anything higher may indicate anaemia, cirrhosis, diabetes, pulmonary oedema or nephrosis. Lower values may be caused by renal impairment or hyperthyroidism.

• **Potassium** - this is an essential mineral; urine usually passes a NV of 30-110 meq per day, and any increases over this can result from diabetes, hypercalcemia, Fanconi's syndrome or uremia. Decrease can also arise - among other things, from glomerulonephritis or Addison's disease.

• **Proteins** - these are normally absent or present in very low quantities, with the figures always less than 150 mg per day. Increases can be caused by - among other things, anaemia, cystitis, diabetes, glomerulonephritis, gout, pyelonephritis and nephrotic syndrome, as well as bismuth, arsenic or mercury poisoning. It can, however, also be due to pregnancy. It causes a decrease in the osmotic pressure and greater water loss in the surrounding tissues (oedema).

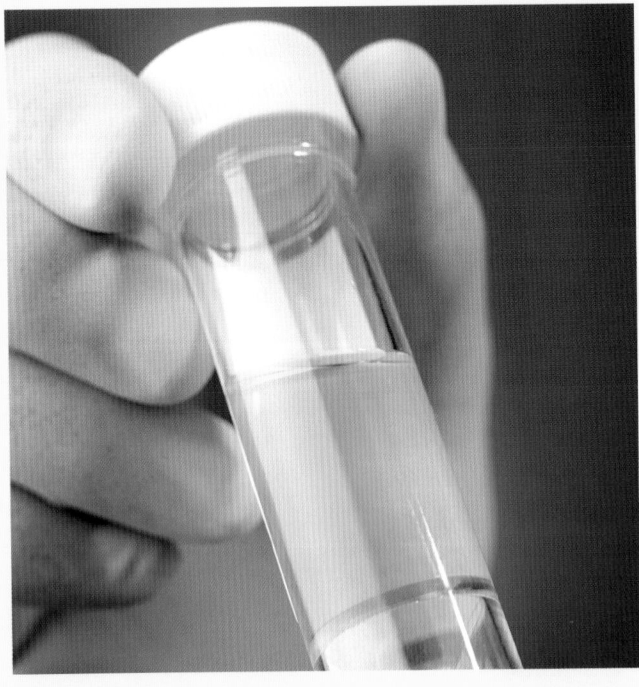

◀ **Aspect**
The normal urine is clear, if it is very clear and almost transparent, it may indicate an excessive dilution and if it is cloudy can indicate an infection (presence of pus or bacteria), an inflammation (mucus) or the growth of crystals (phosphates, as the photo below, or urate).

▼ **pH**
Measure the acidity: the VN range from 5 to 7. More than 7 may indicate metabolic alkalosis or respiratory, urinary sepsis and other syndromes, or a diet rich in fruits, use of antacids or vomiting. Under 5 indicate acidosis from diabetes mellitus, chronic renal failure, or a diet hypoglycemia or fasting.

• **Sediment** - this is normally absent, with any presence being due to fine debris which collects at the bottom of urine containers. Under the microscope it may be seen that there are red or white blood cells, renal tubes, crystals, bacteria or parasites.

• **Sodium** - this is an essential mineral that is excreted at a rate of around NV 50-200 meq per day. Higher values may be due - among other things, to diabetes, Addison's disease, nephritis, chronic renal failure, lack of aldosterone or hypothyroidism. Lower values may be caused by liver cirrhosis, acute pancreatitis, burns, or nephrotic syndrome.

• **Urea** - this is the main component in urine, and has a typical NV of 10-35g per day. Figures higher than this may indicate, amongst other things, hyperpyrexia, hyperthyroidism, leukaemia or burns, as well as poisoning by phosphorus. Lower values may derive from diabetes, liver disease, chronic renal insufficiency, hypothyroidism, or pregnancy.

• **Volume** - this usually is produced at a rate of NV -1500 ml per day. Values above this may indicate alcoholism, diabetes, hyperparathyroidism or hypertension. Lower values may indicate renal blockage, hypotension or traumas.

of these cells. The active absorption leads to an increase in osmotic pressure difference between the interstitial liquids and the liquids in the tubules: this leads to a further water absorption through osmosis.

There are few substances which are not reabsorbed - even urea, will return to the blood spreading slowly through the walls of the tubules. Among others, the anti-diuretic hormone ADH affects the absorption of water and aldosterone affects the absorption of sodium. All are activated by the quality of blood: when the concentration of one particular substance in the blood alters compared to the ideal balance, the endocrine gland that produces the active hormones for the transport of the substance concerned accelerates in order to restore the balance.

To give an example: When a body gets very hot and sweaty, the pituitary gland identifies a water deficit and produces ADH. This is released into the bloodstream, and when it reaches the renal tubes in the kidneys it stimulates the absorption of water from the urine. Until the blood concentration is back to normal, the rear lobe of the pituitary gland continues to produce ADH, and so reduces as far as possible any losses of water in the urine. Conversely, if an individual drinks too much water, the blood becomes diluted and the pituitary gland then identifies a water surplus, and slows or blocks the production of ADH. In a short time, the renal tubes stop absorbing water causing it to be passed into the urine until the water balance is restored. The same type of mechanism adjusts the volume: in this case is the renin-angiotensin system that influences the active absorption of water.

URINATION

Although there is a continuous flow of urine out of the renal tubes, from there to the bladder, however, the flow is intermittent, dependent on the peristaltic movements of the ureter. The waves of contraction happen at a rate of 3 - 6 per minute, and pass through the ureter in less than one minute. The smooth muscles of the bladder are able to expand as urine accumulates. At the same time, however, the pressure inside grows, and when it contains around half a litre of urine the baroreceptors in the wall are stimulated. Their nerve impulses reach:

- The sacral region of the spinal cord and stimulate the parasympathetic neurons that innervate the bladder and the internal sphincter. This causes the contraction of the wall of the bladder and simultaneously the relaxation of the sphincter;
- The higher centres of the nervous system determine the conscious desire to urinate. Because the external sphincter is innervated by voluntary nerves, urination may not occur until a voluntary signal triggers the relaxation of the external sphincter.

When the voluntarily urinary reflexes are deliberately ignored, the desire to urinate can be made to disappear for a certain time, but when it returns, it does so with a greater intensity.

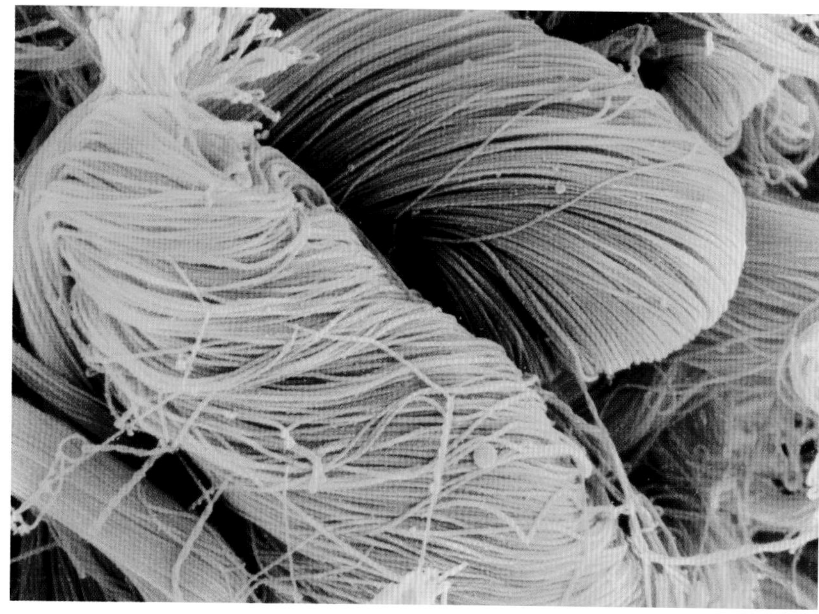

▲ **Elastic fiber**
Bundles of collagen fibers in the interior of the bladder, photographed with a scanning electron microscope in false colors. The thin collagen fibrils (pink), have relatively little elastic but are resistant to tension. They are in narrow beams of spiral coils that are placed in the submucosa of the bladder wall when the bladder fills the beams are held until the fibers reach the full relaxation.

◀ **Urinary apparatus**
Besides the kidney, which plays the role in excretion, there is the bladder, which expels waste with urination.

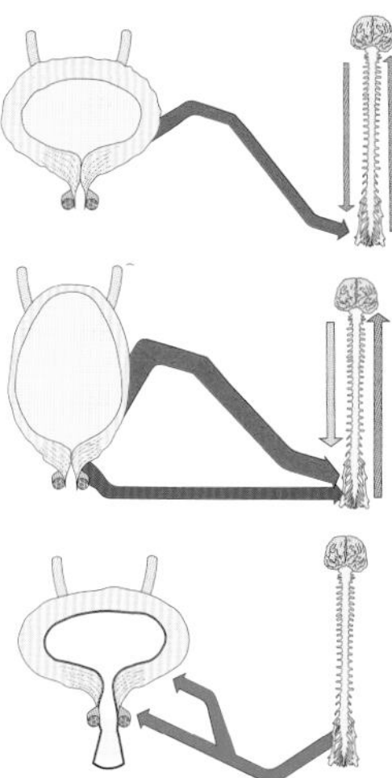

▼ **Control**
The control of bladder contraction and the release of the sphincter:
- *stimuli from the bladder*
- *stimuli from the sphincter*
- *stimuli to the brain*
- *inhibitory stimuli*
- *reflex stimuli*

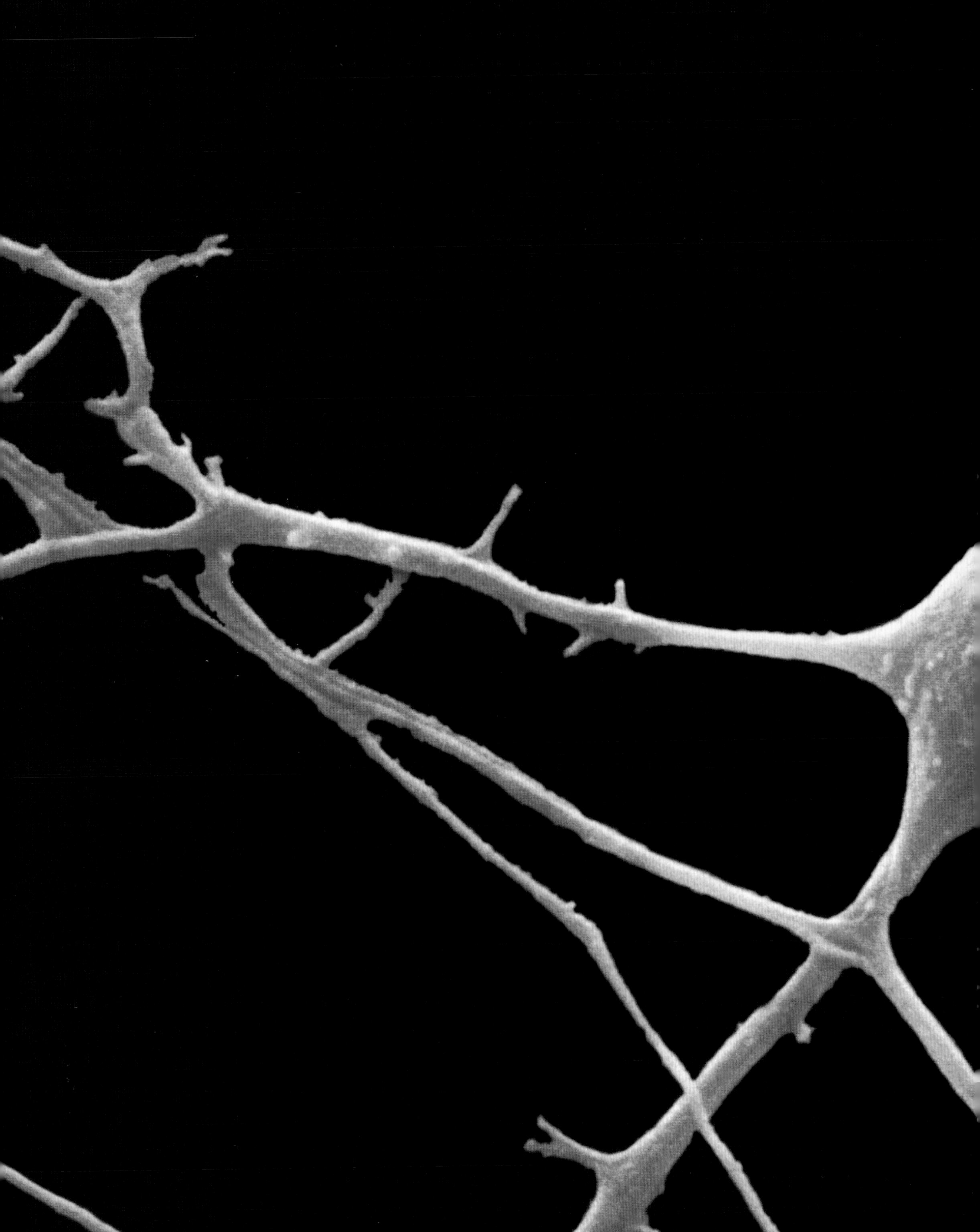

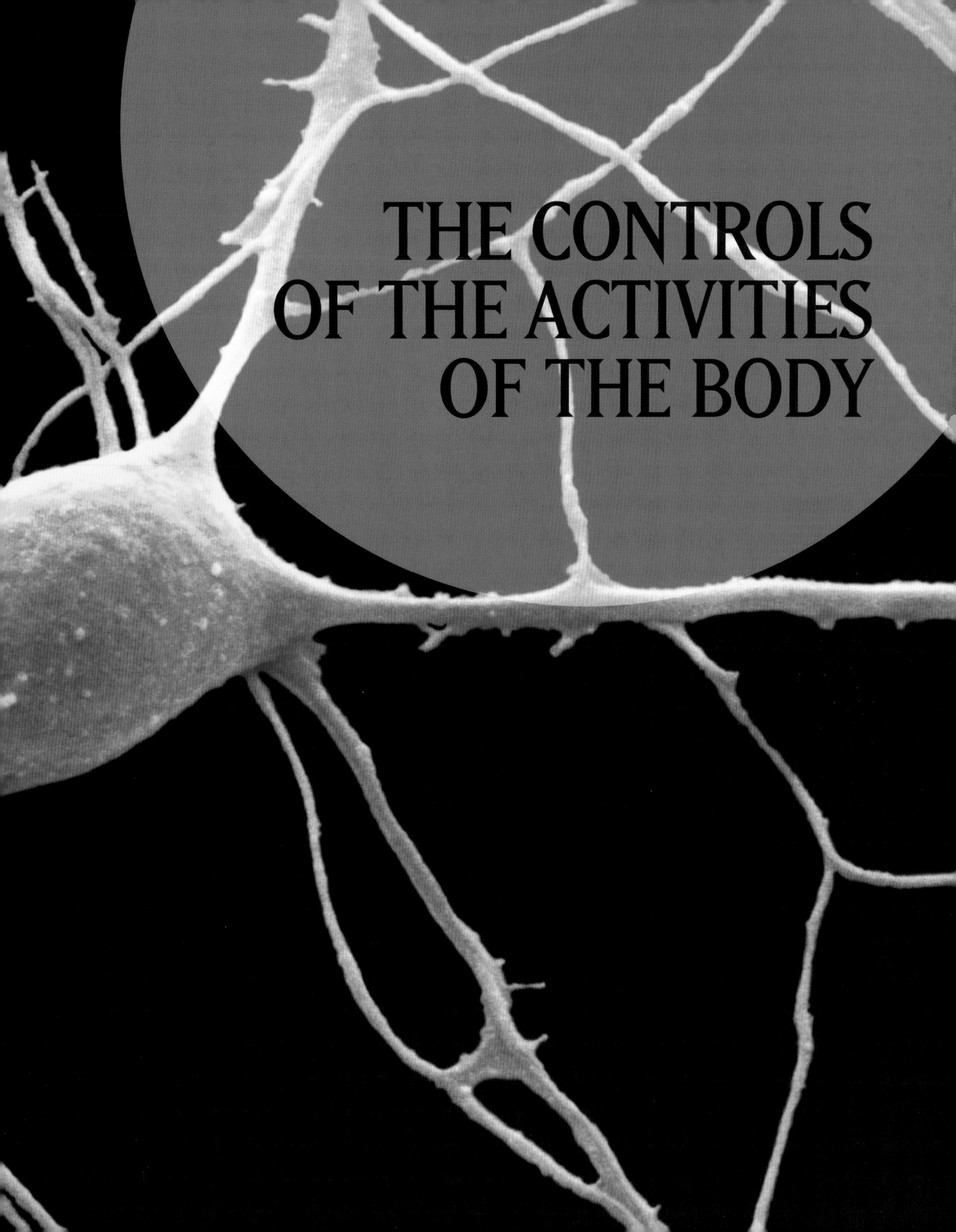

THE CONTROLS OF THE ACTIVITIES OF THE BODY

THE CONTROLS THAT REGULATE WITH PRECISION THE EXACT ACTIVITIES OF THE COORDINATING BODY BETWEEN THEM ARE PERFORMED BY ELECTRICAL IMPULSES AND HORMONES. IN BOTH CASES, IT IS THE INTERACTION OF SMALL MOLECULES WITH THE MEMBRANE OF THE CELLS.

ELECTRICAL IMPULSES AND CONTROL MOLECULES

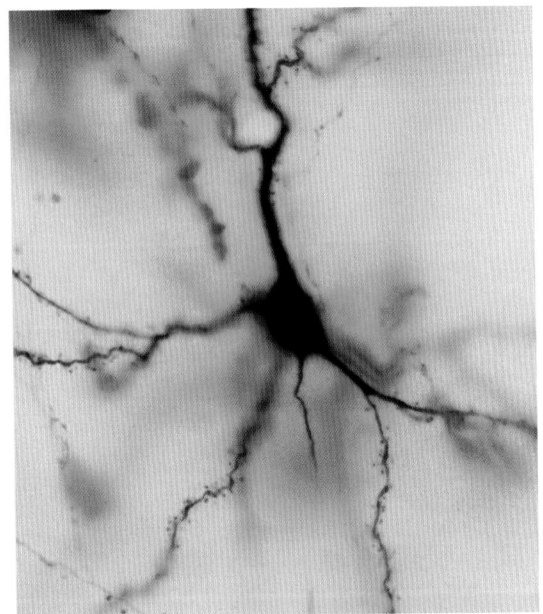

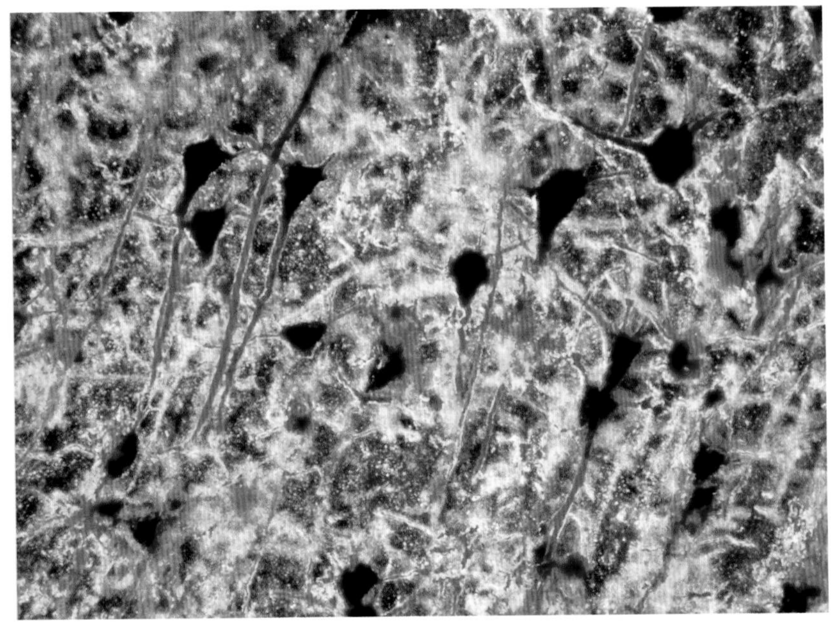

▲ **ELECTRICITY NETWORK**
A neuron (above) from the internal structure of the brain, and (above right) an image of the neural network.

The body's functions have to be very carefully co-ordinated because when necessary, all of its cells can be called upon to take part in specific processes. This needs very precise control and timing, and so information must be passed back and forth both reliably and quickly. This is achieved by a central control system that directs all the activities, initiating or speeding up some processes, and slowing down or stopping others. This is an immensely complex task which requires a dense communication network as well as a core that is capable of rapidly processing data. It has to be able to take account of the vast array of information that is continually arriving and drawing up the appropriate response signals. Finally, there has to be a sufficiently comprehensive reporting system that does not lose track of even a single data element, and is able to send clear orders to the relevant places.

The most direct communication network is made up of nerve fibres, but the blood circulation also actively carries important information to nerve centres distributed around the body. The core of data processing system is the brain, and this, in addition to storing all the necessary reference information and memories, is divided into areas that are specialised for different functions. The brain is not only the core of the reporting system, but it is also at the centre of the network of nervous fibres that carry and distribute the control commands to all areas of the body. It also initiates the chemical signals that regulate, check, and mediate the hormones. These tasks are undertaken by the hypothalamus and pituitary gland, which are not only neuronal encephalic structures but also secretory ones that govern the whole endocrine system. To simplify the analysis of any data that arrives and the preparation of appropriate responses, the main function of this complex control system is to quickly find and restore any disturbances in the interior balances of the body.

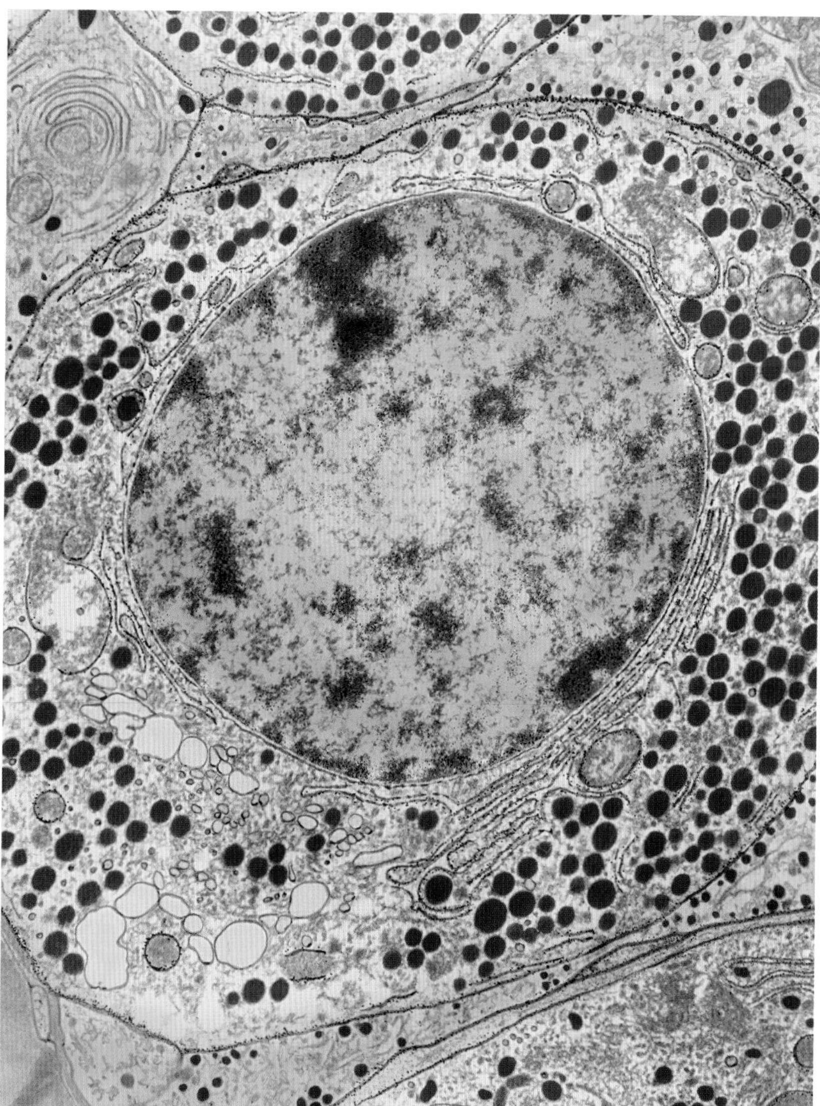

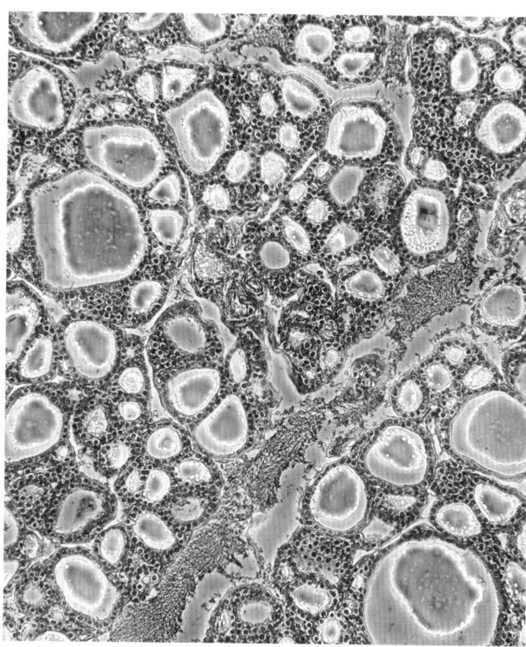

◀ **CONTROL CHEMICALS**
A picture of glandular cells in a section of the thyroid (left) a cell produces hormones to internal adenohypophysis.

STRUCTURAL & FUNCTIONAL DIFFERENCES

The activities of the nervous system, the brain and the endocrine system are very different from one another. However, their cells are all characterised by a common structural element of fundamental importance - that is, the particular sensitivity of their membranes. In the case of neuronal cells, this is an electrical sensitivity where there is the capacity to polarise and depolarise quickly. In addition to allowing the spread of electrical signals, these cells also react to certain stimuli with the production of special molecules.

These cells form a bridge between the body's chemical and physical domains - including those of temperature, pressure, molecular concentrations, light, tastes, smells and pain, with those of the arena of electrical control. They also do the reverse - converting electrical signals into chemical and physical ones. The membranes of the endocrine cells are particularly sensitive to electrical impulses as well as specific chemical signals. These cells respond specifically to any of these signals, producing and releasing into blood circulation - or ceasing to produce - one or more particular substances that are intended to modulate the activity of other groups of cells.

The sensitivity of these membranes - including those in neuronal cells as well as the endocrinal ones is due to the presence of special structures that react to the stimuli by changing the membrane potential. These are the ionic channels and ionic pumps together with their receptors. They are capable of promoting changes in the concentrations of some ions on both sides of the membranes. In other words, these common structures posses similar phenomena which, according to the type of cell involved, lead to various desirable effects.

MILES OF NERVE FIBERS, A TANGLE OF NEURONS, MILLIONS OF CELLS "SUPPORTIVE" ... DISCOVER THE FUNCTIONING OF THE NERVOUS SYSTEM AND MECHANISMS THAT REGULATE IT IS REALLY DIFFICULT, NOT YET ACCOMPLISHED.

ELECTRIC CONTROL

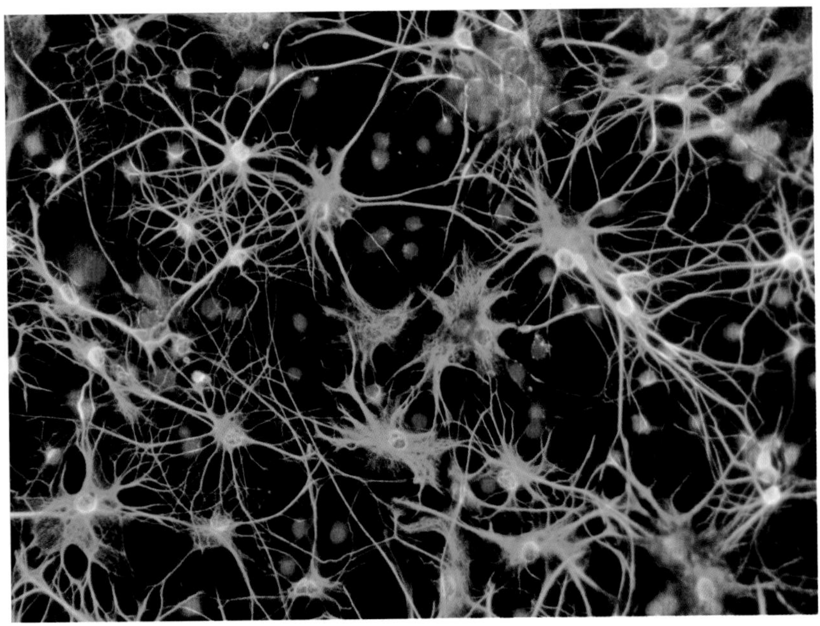

▲ **Astrocytes**
These cells provide both physical and nutritional support for neurons which are star like shape, which gives them their (blue cells with green cytoplasm). They have many branches that form a connective tissue that receive the neurons. It is likely to play some role in storage of information.

The role of control and organisation of the entire body is done by the nervous system, a complex apparatus that continuously collects information from the body and surrounding environment. It then delicately modulates the body's vital functions to maintain optimal performance.

THE ORGANISATION OF THE NERVOUS SYSTEM

The nervous system consists of two types of cells:

- The nerve fibre cells or neurons - these are characterised by differentiated and excitable membranes;
- The glial cells or neuroglia - also referred to as glia, these include oligodendrocites, astrocytes and Schwann cells. In addition to driving neuronal growth during development, they undertake the roles of functional support and provide nutrition for the neurons. They also produce the myelin that accelerates the transmission of nervous signals, and are involved in the elimination of metabolic wastes. Other important roles include the maintenance of a constant concentration of potassium ions (K. +) in the environment as well as the production of neurotransmitters and the removal of various substances from the blood ▶221.

Excitable cells are often combined together according to their functions. In turn, these structures are organised into two major nervous system components:

- Central Nervous System, or SNC - this is comprised of the brain and the spinal cord;
- Peripheral Nervous System, or PNS - this consists of a large network of nerves that connect the central nervous system to the rest of the body. It is further divided into the somatic nervous system and the sensory system.

NEURONS

The neurons are made up of about 100 billion specialised cells. They play different roles according to their location:

- the collection of information from both the internal and external environments and their conversion of this into electrical impulses - these are the neuronal receptors;
- the transmission of electrical impulses to the processing centres - these structures are called afferent neurons;
- the processing of information and consequent production of coherent responses in the form of various electrical pulses: these are the interneurons which link to other neurons forming complex data processing networks. They represent around 97% of the total number of nerve cells: these complex interactions make it possible for higher

mental activities to take place - these include such functions as memory, thinking and emotions;
- the transport of response signals from the processing centres that are located in various parts of the body. These are known as motor neurons or efferent neurons.

Contrary to what happens in other parts of the body, neurons retain an individual behaviour: each has a specific reaction to a stimulus, independent from that of other neurons and neuronal centres which then react to the sum of the inputs from all the connected neurons.

Structure - neurons are comprised of:
- the soma, which contains the nucleus
- the dendrites, which are branched in a manner similar to that of branches on trees (from the Greek, dendron = tree); they are extremely numerous, thin, and have features that allow them to perform intercellular communication. They collect information from other cells or transmit signals from neuron to neuron;
- the axons or nerve fibres, which are long, thin structures that are characterised by an almost constant diameter. They have extremely variable lengths, ranging from 0.1 mm to 2 metres long. The axons conduct signals from the soma to other parts of the body. The action potential of these impulses is in the order of approximately 100 mV and has a duration of around 1 ms. The speed at which the signals are transmitted varies according to the type of neuron, however. In those which have a myelin sheath coating ▸68 the figure can reach 100 m/s.

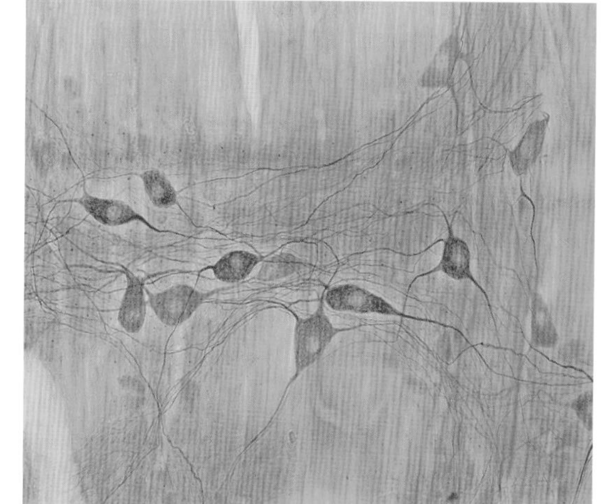

◀ **Neurons**
In this optical microscope photograph of a section of intestine are some neurons in the Auerbach plexus which regulates the local movements of the intestinal wall. Clearly shown are some cellular bodies with long dendrites and axons isolated in the opposite cell pole.

Axons are always present in neuronal cells, but their shapes can be many and varied. Each neuron, however, sends the same type of electrical signal, as defined by the action potential. The signal takes shape in the brain and the path it takes depends on whether it is for a function of particular importance. Urgent messages are transmitted more quickly than those of lesser importance. The fastest method is through the dendrites, which can, when necessary send signals more or less instantly to thousands, tens of thousands or even hundreds of thousands of other neurons.

▼ **Different forms, the same operating principle**
Neurons going about their functions in the same way, despite having some very different aspects: here we see a bipolar neuron, in which the body cell divides the ramifications of the dendritic axons, and two multipolar neurons: one with short axons and clearly visible, the others with a similar axons in all the other dendrites. The contacts that these cells may develop with other cells are on average 10,000, but in the cortex (cerebral and cerebellar) may reach around 150,000.

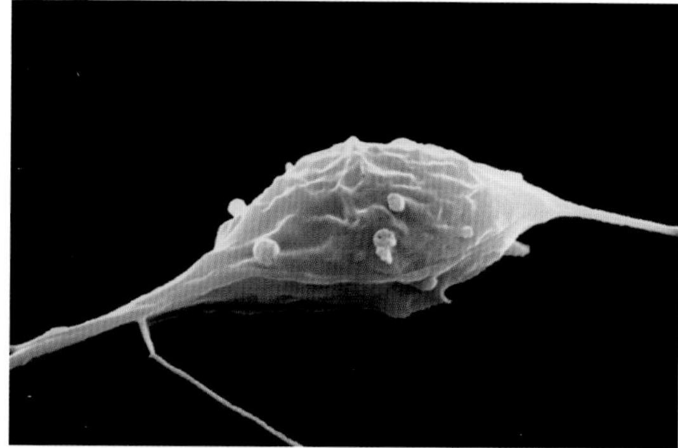

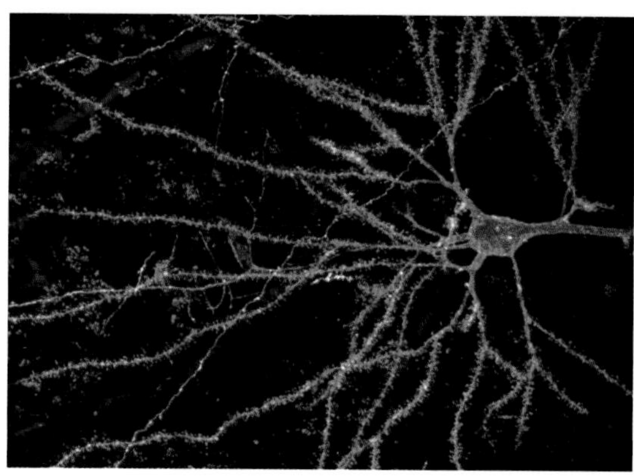

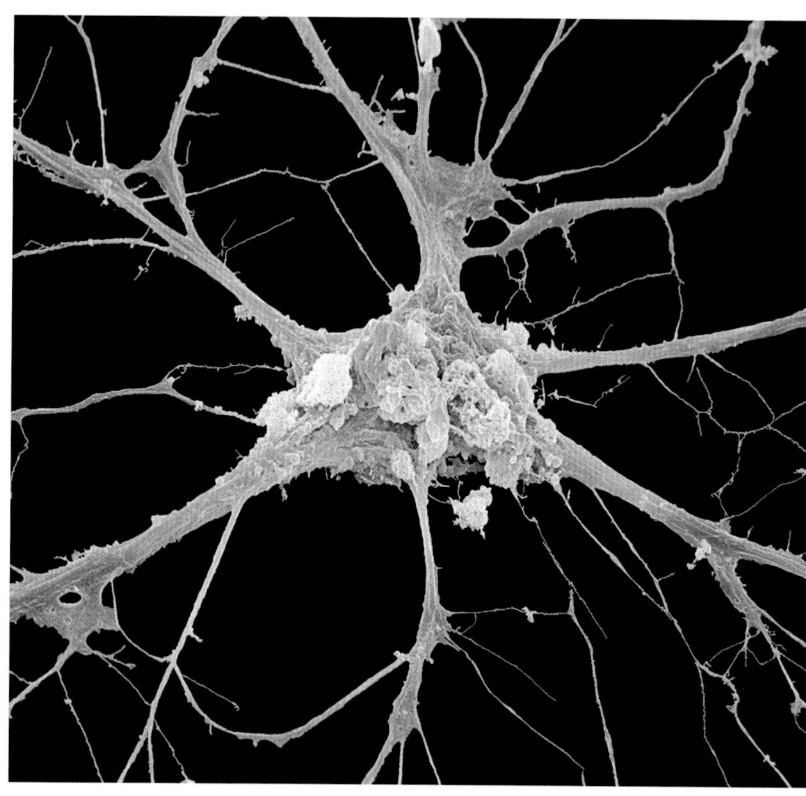

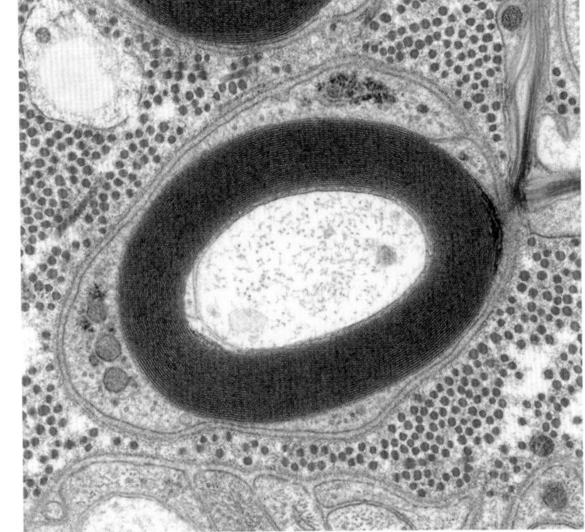

▶ **Myelin fiber**
MET microphotography of a nerve fiber (axons in white) surrounded by Schwann cells (green), producing myelin (brown).

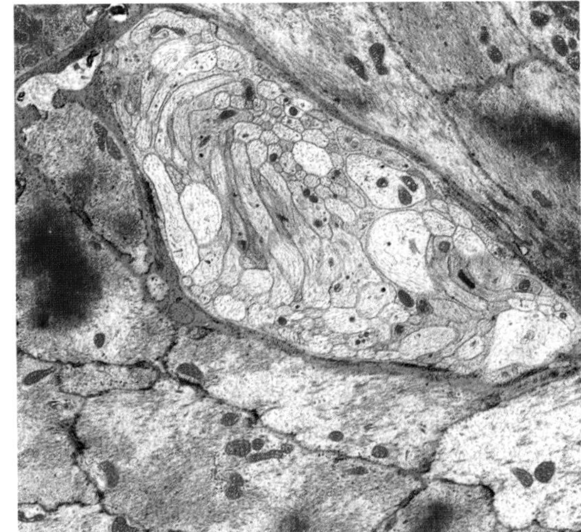

▶▶ **Amyelinic fibers**
Transmission electron microscope (TEM) photograph of a section of nerves (center) surrounded by muscle cells (green), internal the nerve fibers are amyelinic.

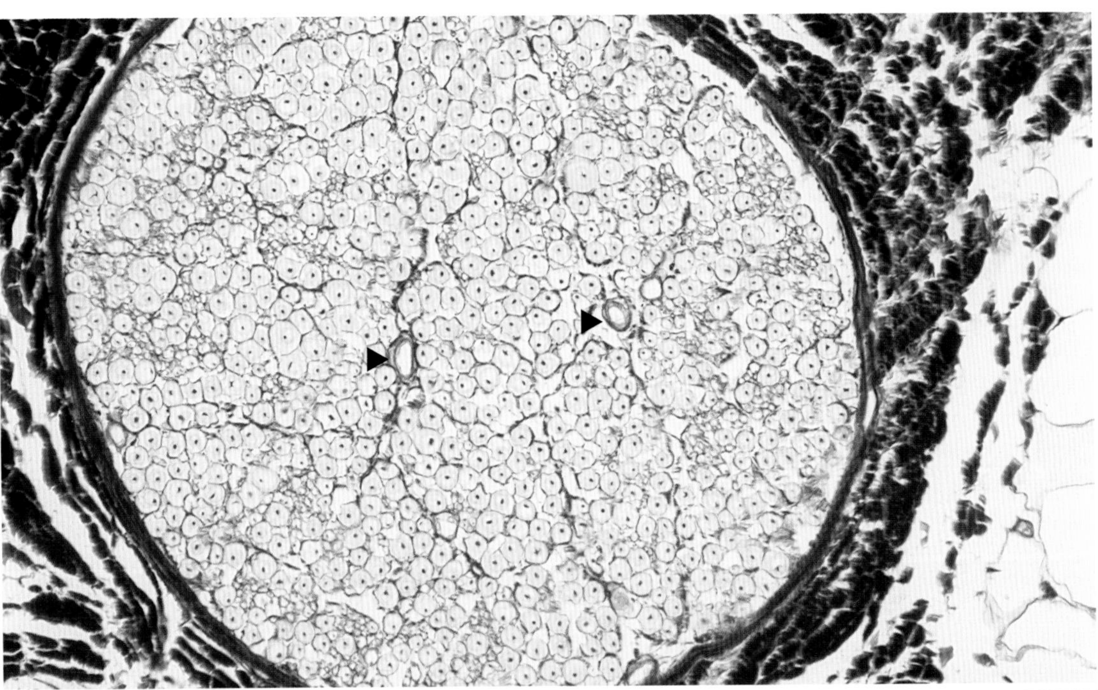

▼ **Sciatic nerve**
Section of the largest nerve of the body. You can see the individual bundles of the nerve fibers myelin and the axons which are the small clear points at the center, made of myelin. The epinervous connective tissue is linked by the perinervos that is is colored purple, which wraps around the nerve and is connective tissue. In the middle of the nerve bundles are (also in section), some blood vessels (▶).

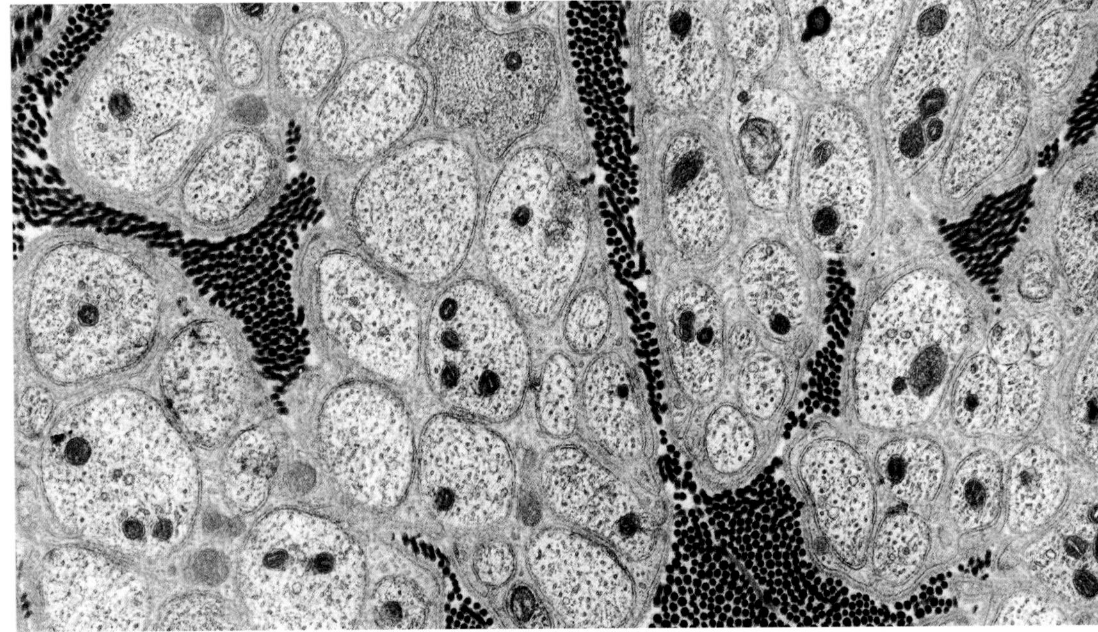

▶ **Amyelinic fibers**
TEM Microphotograph of a section of amyelinic nerve fibers (blue-white) surrounded by glial cell cytoplasm (yellow-green) which are separated into bundles of collagen fibers (brown).

AXONS

There are two basic categories of axons:

- myelinic fibres - these are nerve fibres that are wrapped in myelin ▸32, a substance that is formed from lipoproteins. This acts as a dielectric - that is, an electrical insulator. The presence of this sheathing makes it possible for nerve signals to be transmitted at great speed.
- amyelinic fibres - these are nerve fibres that have no outer myelin sheath. The speed of transmission is lower than that of myelinic fibres, and is influenced by temperature. This is because of the effect on their electrical conductivity due to the presence of surrounding substances.

THE NERVES

The nerves are found in the peripheral nervous system, and are comprised of associations of axons of different types and diameter: They are aligned longitudinally, and intersperse with connective fibres. There are three different types - the afferent, efferent and mixed nerves:

Afferent nerves - these conduct signals from receptors to the central nervous system.

Efferent nerves - these conduct signals from the central nervous system to muscles and glands.

Mixed nerves - these are bundles of fibres that are composed of both afferent and efferent nerves.

The Nervous Impulse - Inside The Neurons

We have already seen ▸26 how nerve cells react, including the changes in the permeability of their membranes to some ions when triggered by a stimulus that arises from a different cell or the environment. Such triggering can have more than one specific threshold though ▸28. In neurons, this variation spreads, section after section across the

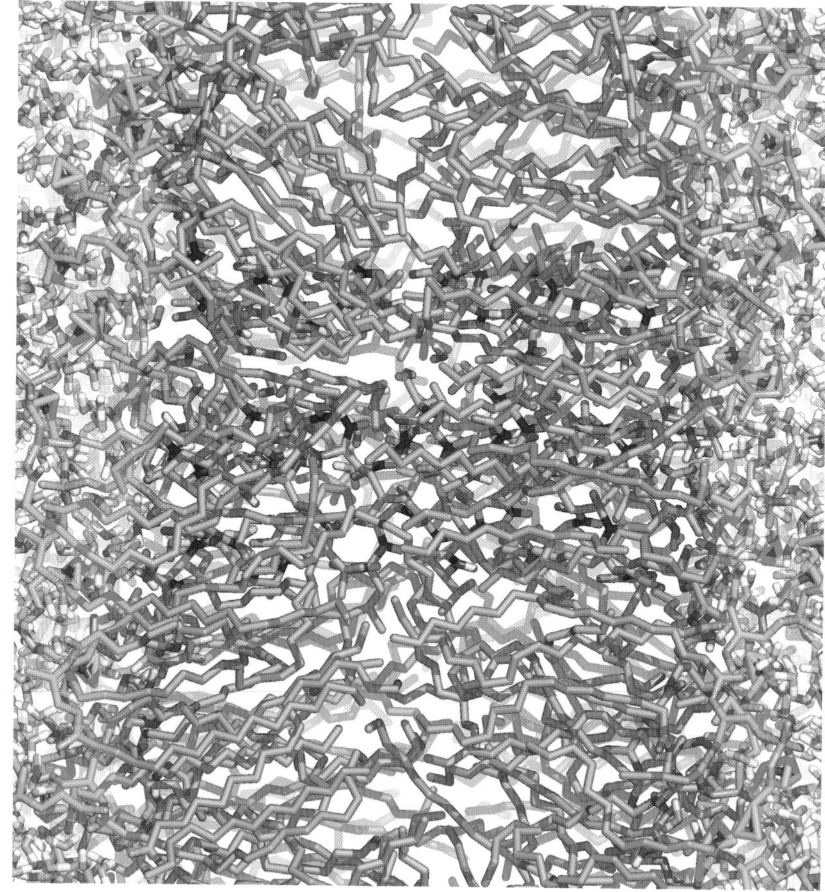

▲ **Ionic canal**
Molecular model of an ion channel formed by a tangle of five molecules of water alamethicin this peptide can form helical structures which fit naturally into biological membranes allowing the passage of ions in both directions.

The atoms in the form of a pipe, are nitrogen (blue), carbon (blue), oxygen (red) and hydrogen (white).

Nervous conduction

The depolarisation of part of a neuron's membrane triggers the opening of localised Na+ channels producing a limited action potential. When this happens, the potential in the membrane switches from around -70 mV to about +35 mV, and the current is directed towards the cell, flowing passively along the adjacent axon depolarisation zones. This leads to the opening of other Na+ channels and the initiation of new potential actions, according to a process that continues until the end of the neurons. The Na+ channels then remain temporarily inactivated:

This causes the membrane to temporarily ignore further stimuli. The repolarisation of the membrane then re-sensitises the neuron to new stimuli. These changes are carried out extremely quickly - within a few milliseconds, and so if they need to be monitored it is necessary to use very sensitive instruments, such as an oscilloscope.

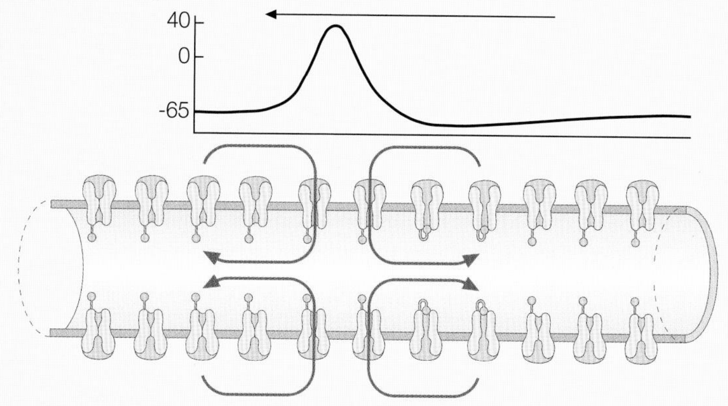

This is done by placing two sensor electrodes either side of a neuron - the nervous impulse that is generated can then be seen on the oscilloscope as a change in electrical potential. The signal curve shows the stage of depolarisation (peak) followed by the slower repolarisation.

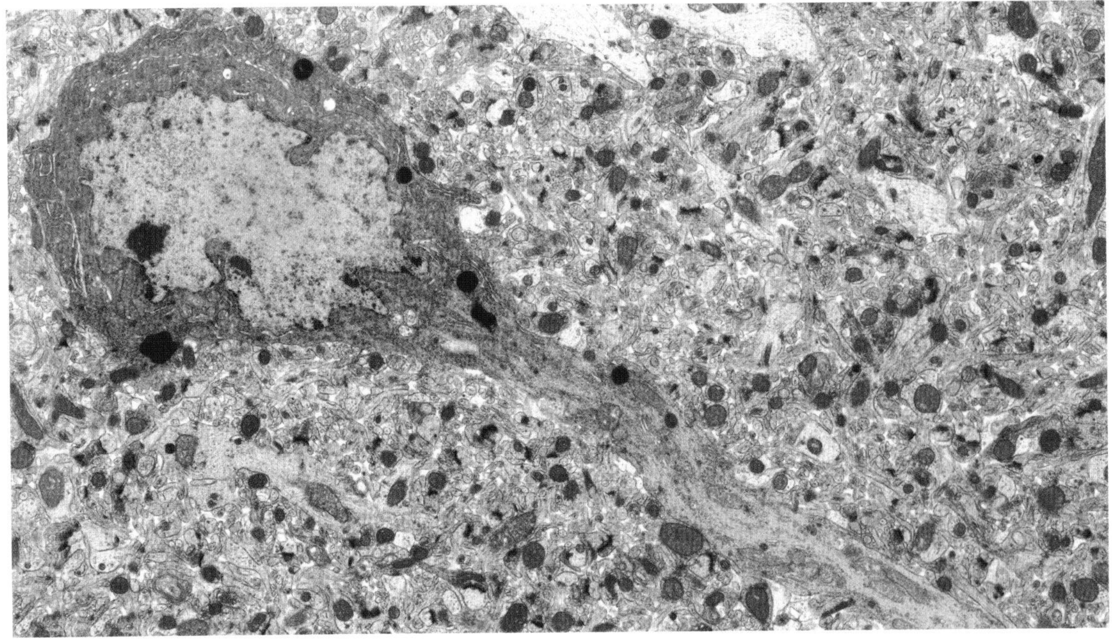

▶ **Neuron**
This neuron, photographed in a transmission electron microscope (TEM), is characterized by a large yellow core at the center of the body cell, and large axons. Inside, you notice that the fibrils allow the flow of energy molecules synthesized in the central body.

surface of the cell, and can be transmitted to other excitable cells. While the initial impetus can due to any one of many kinds, the signal that propagates from it is always electrical. A nerve cell has the ability to alter its electrical balance within a short time (in the order of the millisecond) In neurons in particular this is referred to as potential rest ▸28, and is approximately -70 mV - the sign indicates that the cell is negative relative to its exterior.

The action potential ▸26 is the term used for the capability of a response based on an 'all or nothing' principle. The amplitude of the action potential is not changed by a stimulus that exceeds the threshold; and the signal spreads along the membrane using energy from the metabolic activities of the cell itself.

This ability to propagate the potential action through conductive fibres is determined by the physical-chemical features of the membrane, and in particular from its permeability. Amyelinic fibres, for example, generate impulses that are slower (from 2 m/s) than those produced by myelinic fibres. This is because of the presence of the myelin sheathing which moves the depolarisation to the nodes of Ranvier. Discontinuous propagation of the action potential in the myelinic fibre 68 enables the neuron to save energy. The potential action regenerates point for point along the membrane, and may spread for long distances without diminishing. In addition to this the conductivity - that is, the speed of propagation, of the potential action depends on the diameter of the neuron (the bigger it is, the greater the speed of transmission) and the electrical resistance of the intracellular and extracellular fluids.

Some neurons produce action potential spontaneously - that is, due to the presence of external stimuli. Others are excited by specific stimuli that have specialised internal receptors, whereas other types are initiated by changes in the environment. Some are stimulated by nerve impulses that have travelled along the axons of other neurons with which they are in contact. In all cases, the stimulated neuron does not produce a single nervous impulse, but a series of equal pulses, whose number depends on the intensity of the stimulus that triggered it and the functional status of the cell in which it resides. The information transmitted in the nervous system is of a binary nature: it is linked to the presence or absence of potential action, and is a data unit that has equal characteristics in all neurons. The information itself is graded by two properties of nerve signals: the rate of discharge, i.e. the number of potential actions per unit of time, and the download pattern, that is, the distribution of potential action on a nerve fibre. The information will be of a sensory or motor nature based on the type of neuron that produced the nervous impulse.

SYNAPSES & CIRCUITS

The neuron is the anatomical and functional unit of the nervous system. While acting independently of each other, neurons collaborate continuously. The axons, the dendrites and allied structures form a network that interfaces neurons and connects them to different cells.

The area of contact between two neurons, or between one neuron and a target cell (such as a muscle cell or an endocrine cell), is called a synapse ▸28. In electrical synapses, wherever the two membranes are in contact, depolarisation events can pass from one to the other without requiring any extra brokers. In chemical synapses, however, the membranes are more distant to one another, being separated by a synaptic space of 15-50 nm. In this case the presynaptic cells need chemical mediators in order to bind to the membrane of the postsynaptic cells. Here they bind to an ion channel receptor, and this induces a new action potential. For each type of ion channel that is governed by the same transmitter there are alternative forms that are encrypted by separate genes.

The intercellular communication system that is formed between neurons, or between neurons and other cells, is what allows the neurons to co-operate together to organise the body's various functions. Overall, the neurons are all directly or indirectly connected with one another. The nervous system is therefore an integrated set of cells in which a single neuron can generate a request for action that may be received at the same time by thousands of other neurons. In other words, each neuron has an impressive convergence of information that can also be used to contradict earlier messages (excitatory stimuli or inhibitory stimuli). Each neuron therefore has a wide range of sensitive receptors on the membrane so that the signals from different neurotransmitters can all be received.

NEURONAL CIRCUITS

When a neuron triggers, the signal can - in theory, reach any innervated body area. However, the passage of the signals through the synapses not only slows transmission due to electrical resistance, but they may take different paths depending on which ones offer the least resistance. The preferential directions are established by the level of activation of the various parts of the system, as well as the

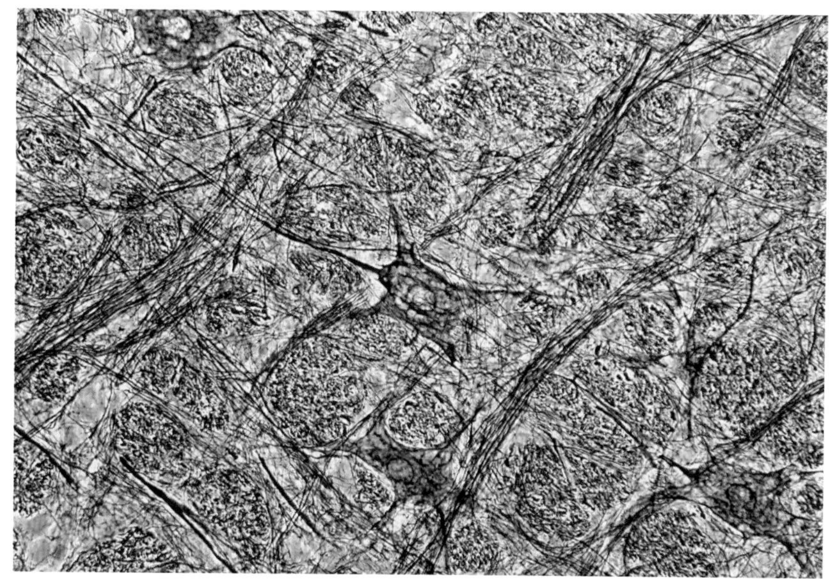

▼ **Interneuronal synapses**
Transmission electron microscopy (TEM) microphotograph of a chemical interneuronal synapse: it determines the passage-way of the signal from one neuron to another (yellow). The synaptic bud is recognizable by the numerous vesicles (red) filled with neurotransmitters and the large mitochondria (pink).

▲ **Network of neurons**
Group of neurons (axons in black) and glia cells (orange) in a section of the brain. The interconnections between these neurons are numbering in the thousands.

▼ **Neuromuscular synapse**
TEM photograph of a synapse of the diaphragm. The red bud in synapse is full of vesicles (blue) containing neurotransmitters. With the arrival of a nerve impulse, the vesicles move toward the membrane and open into the synaptic space by releasing molecules. These receptors bind to the membrane of the postsynaptic cell (a muscle cell), which causes the emergence of a new impetus and the passage of information.

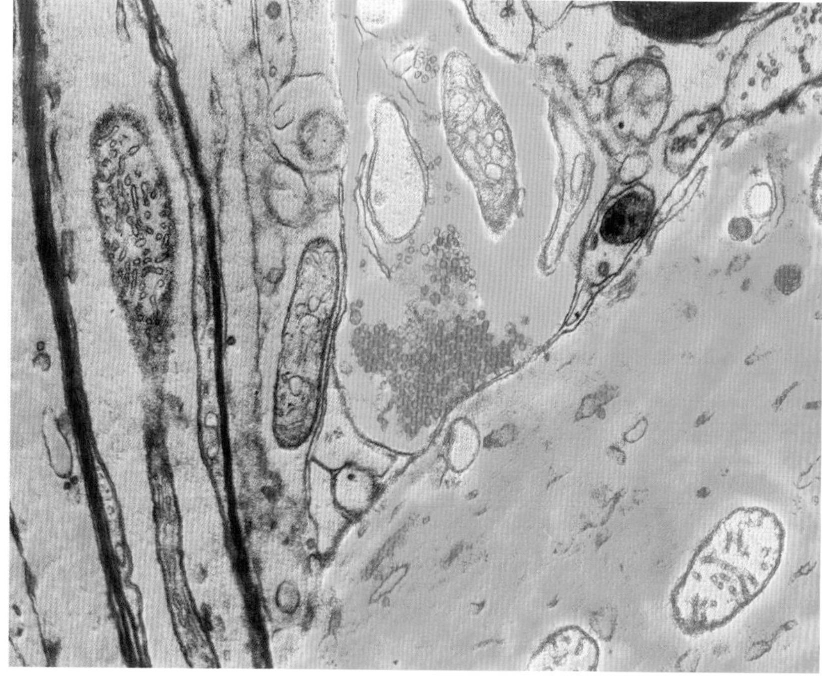

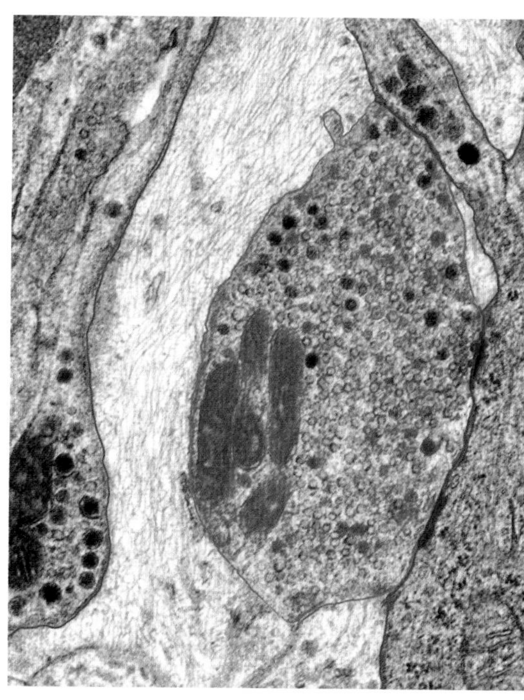

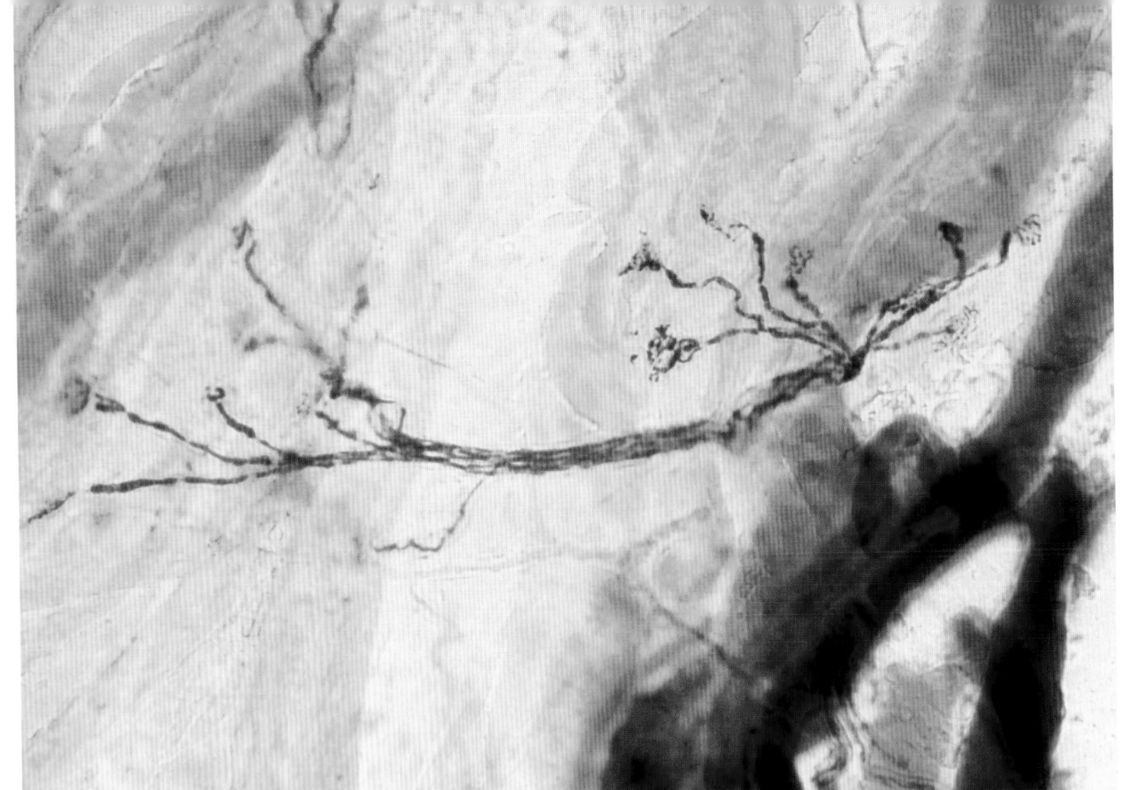

▶ **NEUROMUSCULAR SYNAPSE**
This microscopy of a synapse shows the points of connection between the branched axons of a motor neuron (center) and some muscle fibers (clear bands). Each branch ends in a fiber with a different movement which can trigger muscle activity.

network's general architecture. In particular, in the central nervous system the neurons are organised around plexus centres - these are distinct anatomical structures where neurons join together and form nerve networks. In the spinal cord, for example, the neuronal networks are relatively simple. The stimulus points are distinct, and form sections where collected information is integrated with signals from other neurons that are connected to different parts of the system.

The different types of elementary neuronal circuits can be distinguished according to the action that they have on the outgoing message:

A. The divergent circuit amplifier can produce a wide area response to localised stimuli. It consists, for example, of several branches of the same axon which is in contact with more neurons, each of which, in turn, establishes contacts with other neurons and so forth;

B. The convergent circuit can produce similar responses to very different stimuli, and are formed from several neurons that are in contact with another, single neuron;

C. The recurring resonating circuit has many functions, often aimed at stabilising the transmission frequency. It is composed of chains of neurons with reciprocal connections and also establishes a contact, directly or indirectly, such that exit signals are connected back into the input forming a feedback loop;

D. The parallel circuit repeats the same exit response many times as a result of a single stimulus.

As well as the above, there are other parts of the nervous system with extremely complex neuronal circuits that have only been fully described in a few cases. One of these is located in the spinal cord: there are large motor neurons that have mobile bodies in the ventral horns of the grey spinal substance. There the axons branch out via ventral roots in the spinal nerves and reach directly into the skeletal muscle fibres. These motor neurons, however, receive signals from primary sensory neurons. The information collected from skin and muscle receptors and neurons is then fed to the central nervous system distinct from the motor control function. The spinal cord also has relatively simple neuronal networks, these have similar characteristics to the elementary neuronal circuits that are also found in other centres of the nervous system, albeit with a higher degree of complexity. This is centred in the cerebral cortex, where the neurons are organised into six layers that are linked together. The granular neurons take information from the outer and lower parts of the nervous system and process them. The details are then transmitted to the pyramid neurons which produce output signals intended for other areas of the nervous system.

▼ **SYNAPTIC INTEGRATION**
The postsynaptic neuron reacts to the algebraic sum of the potential action induced by synapses. In this case, an inhibitory synapse is the sum of the stimuli and will be less than the excitatory stimulus alone.

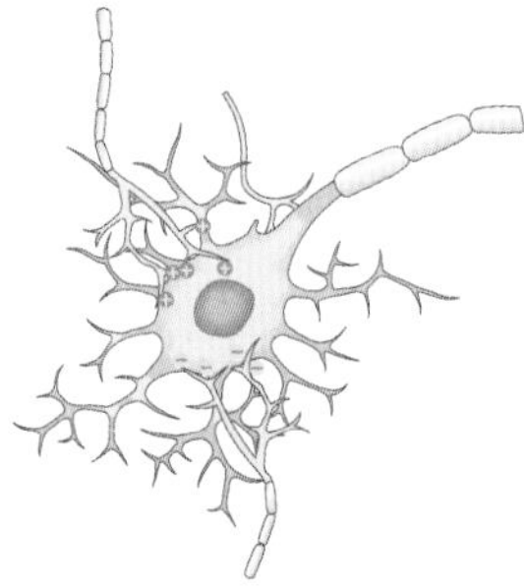

▼ **ELECTRIC FLUX**
Lines of force of the flow of electric current in a postsynaptic neuron, during a discharge of the synapses that stimulates a specific area of the body cell.

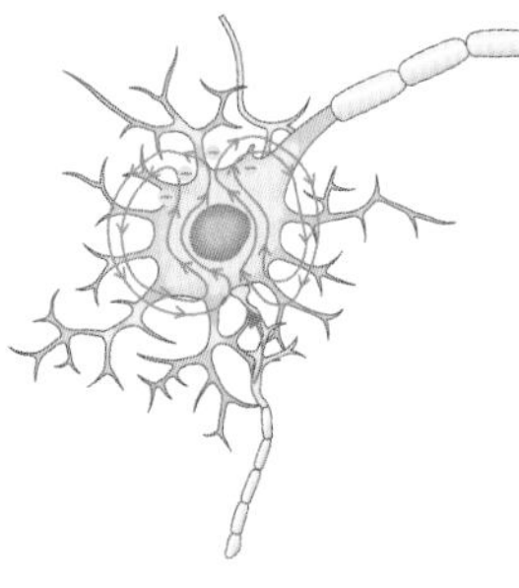

IONIC CONCENTRATION IN NEURONS

ION	concentration in mM	
	INTRACELLULAR	EXTRACELLULAR
POTASSIUM	140	5
SODIUM	5-15	145
CHLORINE	4-30	110
CALCIUM	0.0001	1-2

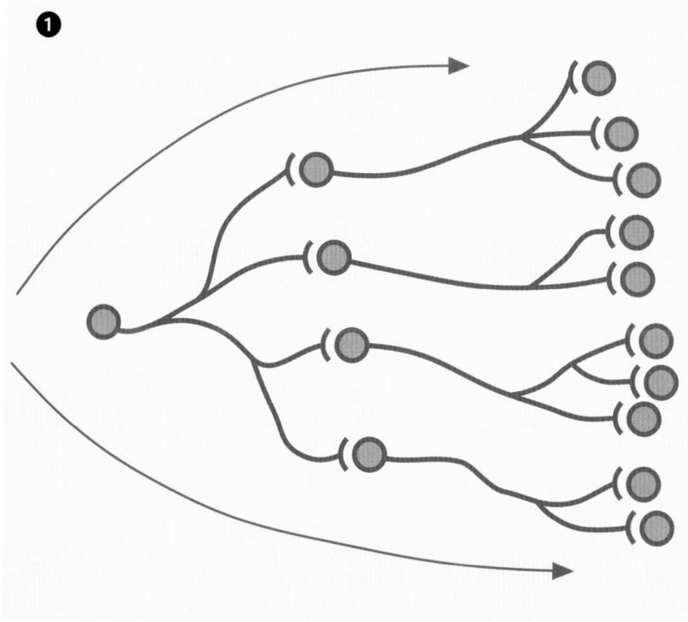

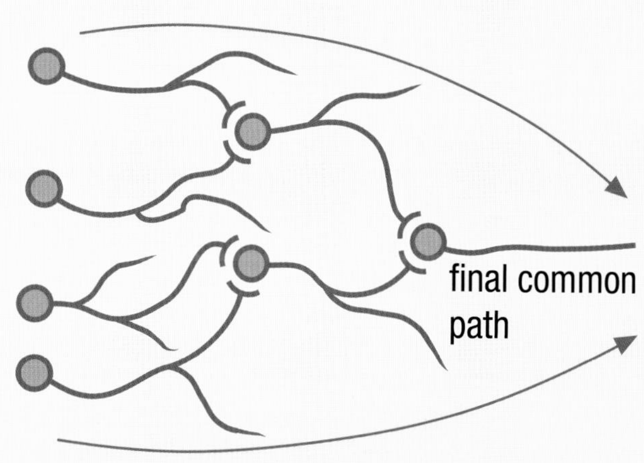

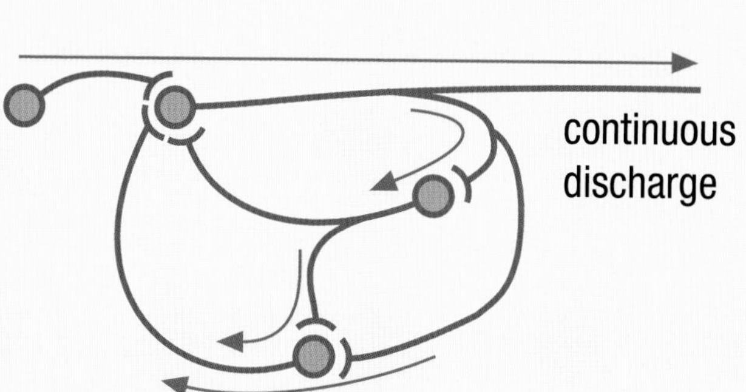

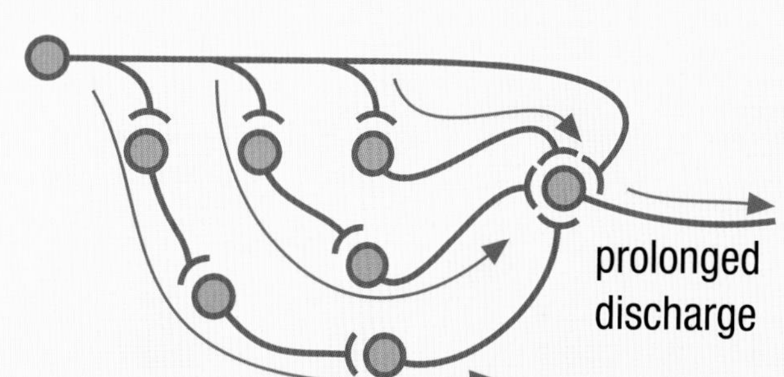

▲ **Elementary circuits**
Schematization showing path of the nerve impulse in a circuit or difference amplifier ❶, a convergent circuit ❷, an recurring circuit ❸, and in a parallel circuit ❹.

NEUROTRANSMITTERS	
NAME	**where it occurs**
ACETYLCHOLINE	drive plates (cholinergic synapses) synapses parasympathetic
AMINO ACIDS: GLYCINE, ACID 1-GLUTAMIC, GABA OR ACID γ-AMINOBUTYRIC	in many different synapses
DOPAMINE	encephalic centers of synapses
GLUTAMATE	central nervous system
NORADRENALINE	orthosympathetic peripheral synapses
NEUROPEPTIDES, INCLUDING OPIOID, ENDORPHINS, ENCEFALINE	sympathetic synapse
AMINE OR SEROTONIN DIPHENOL	encephalic centers

▼ **Nervous system**
From vertebral bodies beyond the ramifications of the peripheral nerve (❶, mainly motor) and those which go to form the ganglia (❷) orthosympathetic nervous system. These are then innervated in the abdominal organs. The posterior nerve roots are formed from sensitive fibers, from the posterior motor fibers (or effectors).

REFLEXES

A reflex is an automatic stereotyped reaction to a specific sensory stimulus that takes place within a very short time of the activation trigger. It has the same 'all or nothing' characteristics typical of a neuronal response. Examples of reflexes include:

Achilles or **ankle jerk reflex** - this is an automatic response that is triggered when the Achilles tendon is tapped. It is sometimes used to check for correct functioning of the sciatic nerve.

Patellary or **knee jerk reflex** - this reflex is triggered when the patellar ligament is tapped. The correct response is for the lower leg to jump involuntarily. Its correct functioning can be used as a test for certain medical conditions.

Biceps reflex - this reflex can be seen when the biceps brachii tendon is tapped. Diminished responses can be indicative of neurological disorders.

Triceps reflex - triggering this reflex causes the triceps brachii muscle to contract involuntarily. Missing or weak responses can be indicative of nerve damage through injury or sever medical conditions.

Pupillary light reflex - this is a reflex in the eye in response to the intensity of light that falls on it. Increases in the amount of light cause the pupil to contract, and decreases result in pupil dilation. Its purpose is to control the amount of light that reaches the retina.

Corneal or **blink reflex** - this is where the eyes blink in response to sudden flashes of light or the presence of debris. It is an involuntary protective mechanism for the eyes.

Pharyngeal or **gag reflex** - this reflex is triggered when an object comes into contact with the soft palate. Its purpose is to prevent items that enter the mouth from causing choking.

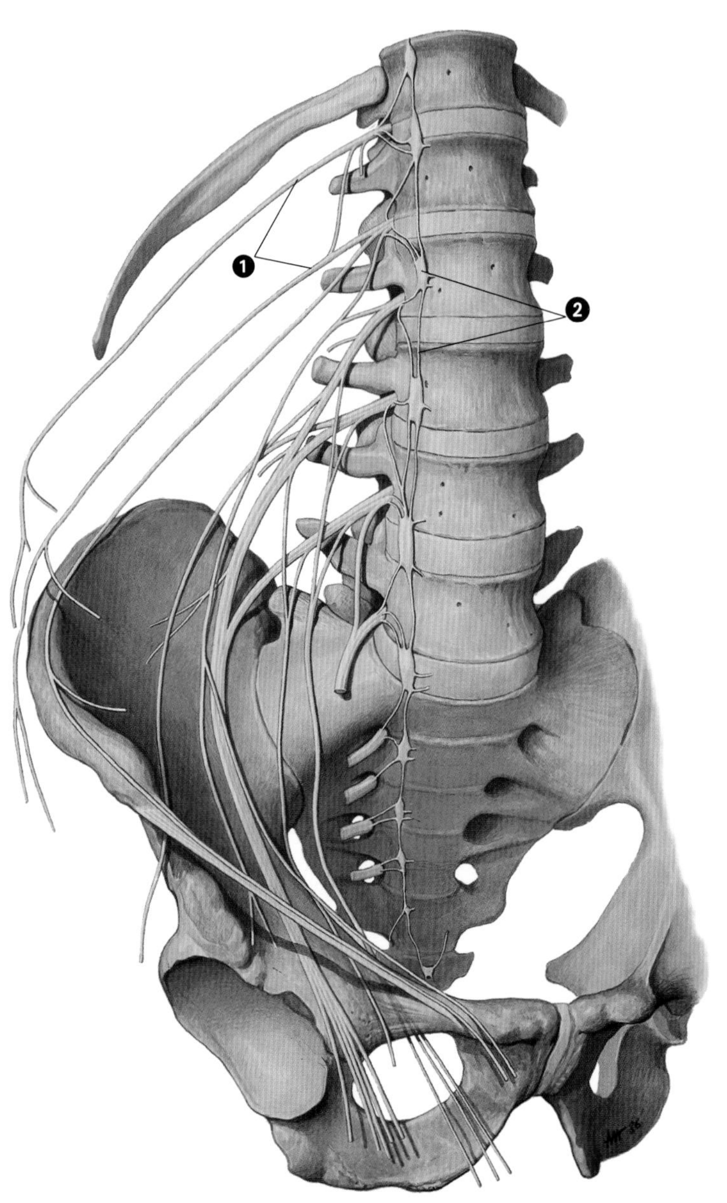

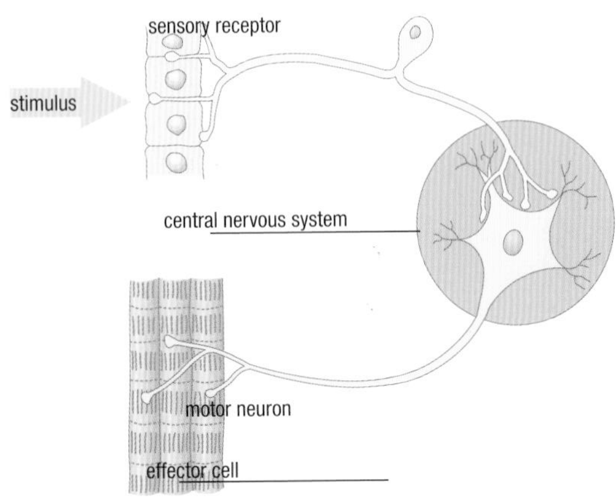

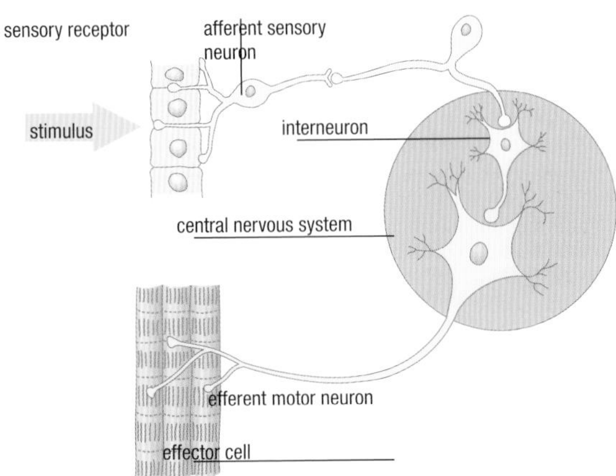

▲▲ **Monosynaptic reflex arc**
The sensory neuron and the effector are connected directly through a single synapse.

▲ **Plurisynaptic reflex arc**
The sensory neuron and the effector are interposed from one or more neurons of the central system.

▼ ANATOMY
Interaction between the bone of a vertebra and the roots of the corresponding peripheral nerves. It is here that the neural processes that determine the actions are reflected.

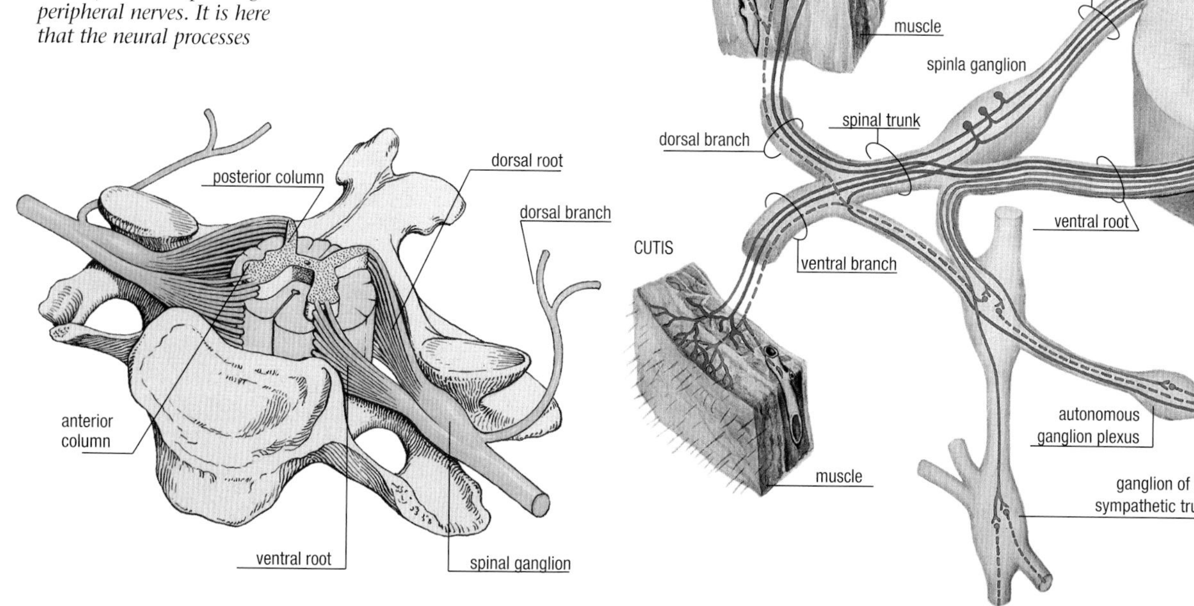

▲ REFLEX ARC "TYPE"
Receptor (skin, mucosa, tendons ...) develops the centripetal sensory neuron that reaches the posterior horn of the gray substance of the spinal cord through the spinal ganglion of the posterior root. For each reflex there is a reflex of the spinal cord or brainstem, where the neuron is connected to the centripetal centrifugal neuron. This develops from cells of the anterior horn, reaching the effector cell (muscle or glandular).

afferent neural fibers (or somatic sensitive)
neural efferent fibers (motor)
afferent neural fibers (or somatic sensitive)
ortosimpatiche neural fibers.

Mammalian diving reflex - this is a response that is present in humans, but more prominent in mammals that spend long periods of time underwater, such as otters, whales, etc. A number of different involuntary reflexes result - these include the heart slowing down, the circulatory system shutting down certain areas, and adjustments in the blood pressure in various parts of the body.
Scratch reflex - this is a reflex reaction to itches on the skin. The main purpose of this reaction is to minimise the chances of insect bites or the attachment of parasites.
Startle reflex - this is where a sudden and unexpected event can cause a person or animal to move involuntarily, as in the expression 'jump with fright'. It may be a response to a sharp sound, a flash of light, a touch, or an object moving near the eyes.
Withdrawal reflex - this where the body makes a sudden involuntary movement away from a painful object or event. It is a spinal reflex that is intended to minimise injury. A good illustration is the example of a person pulling their hand away after accidentally touching something that is very hot.
The basic characteristics of a reflex are the high speed of the reaction that is typically perceived as being more or less immediate, and the fact that it is involuntary. It is not necessary for the brain to think about activating a reflex - indeed, it is only informed after the event has happened.

INVOLUNTARY REFLEXES & THE REFLEX ARC
The best known and most studied form are the unconditional reflexes - these are innate and represent a kind of primitive defence. They follow an elementary neuronal circuit known as the reflex arc. In its simplest and efficient form, it calls into action only two neurons: one that receives the stimulus and one that conveys the reflex command back again. If there are other neurons between them, it lengthens the chain of transmission and the reflex arc becomes more complicated. The immediacy of the reflected reaction is determined by the capacity of this circuit to transmit impulses. This duration of this event is referred to as the 'reaction time' or 'latent time'.
An example of a monosynaptic reflex reaction that is known to everyone is the patellary reflex. This is the automatic jerk of the lower leg that is caused by hitting a specific point just below the knee. In this case the primary sensory neuron comes from the knee, and the motor neurone that innervates the same muscle are in direct contact, separated only by a single synapse.
Other reflex circuits are more complex, and run from a specific part of the body where there are sensory reflex receptors that are connected through several neurons to the spinal cord.
For each reflex, indeed, there is a reflex centre in the spinal cord where the centripetal neuron connects - either directly or through an interneuron. This neuron develops from the horn cells before arriving at the efferent, muscle or glandular cells, which

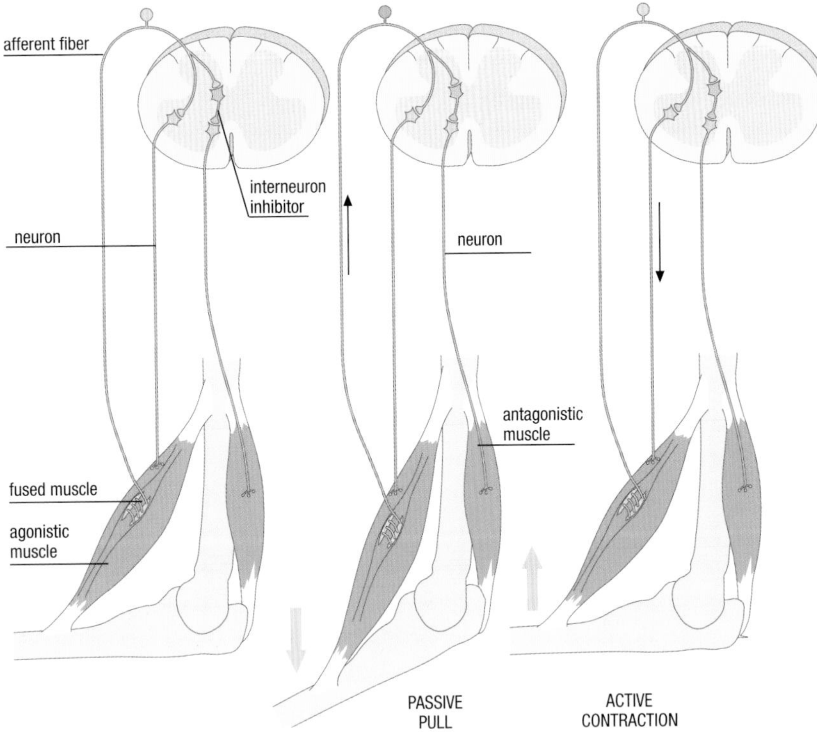

▲ **Gamma circuit**
The stretching of the muscles stimulates the alpha neurons resulting in the contraction (myotatic reflex). If the stimulus is too high, you have the opposite effect (reflection myotatic reverse).

then implement the reflex. As with all neuronal reactions, the stimuli that are collected from the receptors in the area that produces a reflex must reach a certain minimum intensity before they can trigger. The level of the threshold depends on the number of synapses located in the reflex centre. Moreover, different stimuli may produce different reflexes even if collected by receptors in the same area.

Reflex responses can also occur through a phenomenon known as irradiation. This is where the growing intensity and duration of a stimulus that is initially limited to a few effectors will begin to involve more and more receptors until they reach the point where a reflex is triggered. This is due to the fact that when a receptor is first stimulated, activity initially begins in a group of neurons with a lower threshold (zone of discharge) before the neurons around them are stimulated. At this stage the stimulation is said to be subliminal - that is, it is still too weak to be felt.

Another characteristic of neuronal circuits is that articulated convergence may occur - this is where multiple stimuli trigger reflex arcs through divergence. That is, the activation of a single receptor can stimulate more effectors causing multiple reflexes. Alternatively, it can cause an inhibition - this is when an inter-neurone reflex centre blocks the activity of the efferent neuron. The reflex arcs inhibitory functions are also the result of excitatory signals, but since they must always at least include an inter-neurone inhibitor, they are characterised by a relatively high central reflex time.

REFLEXES - CONDITIONED & LEARNED

If a reflex is unintentional, it is considered automatic, even though it may be one that has been learned. It may be thought that a reaction that is not innate cannot possibly be truly automatic. Neuronal research, however, has discovered that when we learn something, we develop new neuronal connections, so learned responses really can become innate. This mechanism allows new circuits to be established, that is, existing networks can be expanded to transmit new impulses.

The first scientist to discover the existence of conditioned reflexes was Russian scientist called Pavlov. His findings were made while conducting experiments on the physiology of digestion. He noticed that the dogs he used in his experiments would immediately react physiologically to the arrival of food by producing large quantities of saliva. To demonstrate that these reflex reactions could be taught, he connected the delivery of food to the sound of a bell. The dogs soon began to associate the sound of the bell with the arrival of food, and, after some training, he found that when they heard the sound, it would stimulate the salivation response.

The innate reflex was therefore reproduced even without the original sensory stimulus - that is, the smell of food, that would normally be found in nature. It was therefore a reflex induced by an artificial event. Ivan Pavlov was convinced that

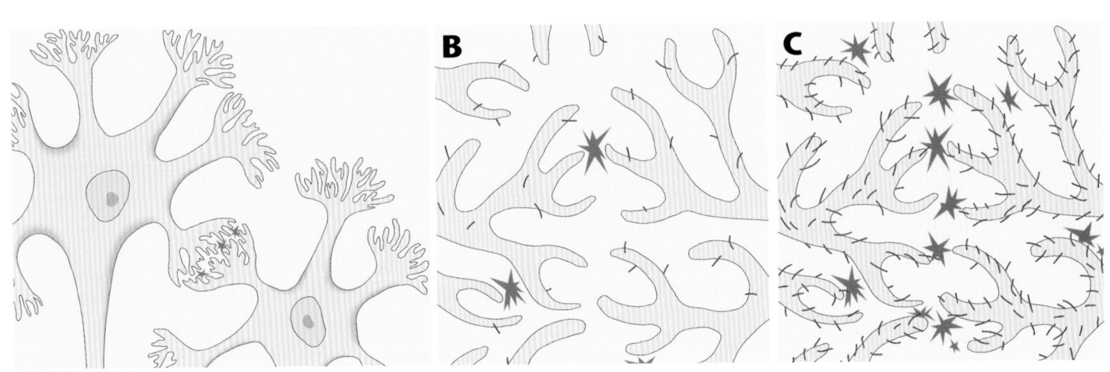

▶ **Learning**
*The dendrites of adjacent nerve cells (**a**) are connected by synapses that transmit a pulse (red). In (**b**) we see a detail of the condition that precedes learning. During learning (**c**) new terminals develop and new synapses: the transmission of certain impulses can therefore firmly impress on the new circuits that are formed.*

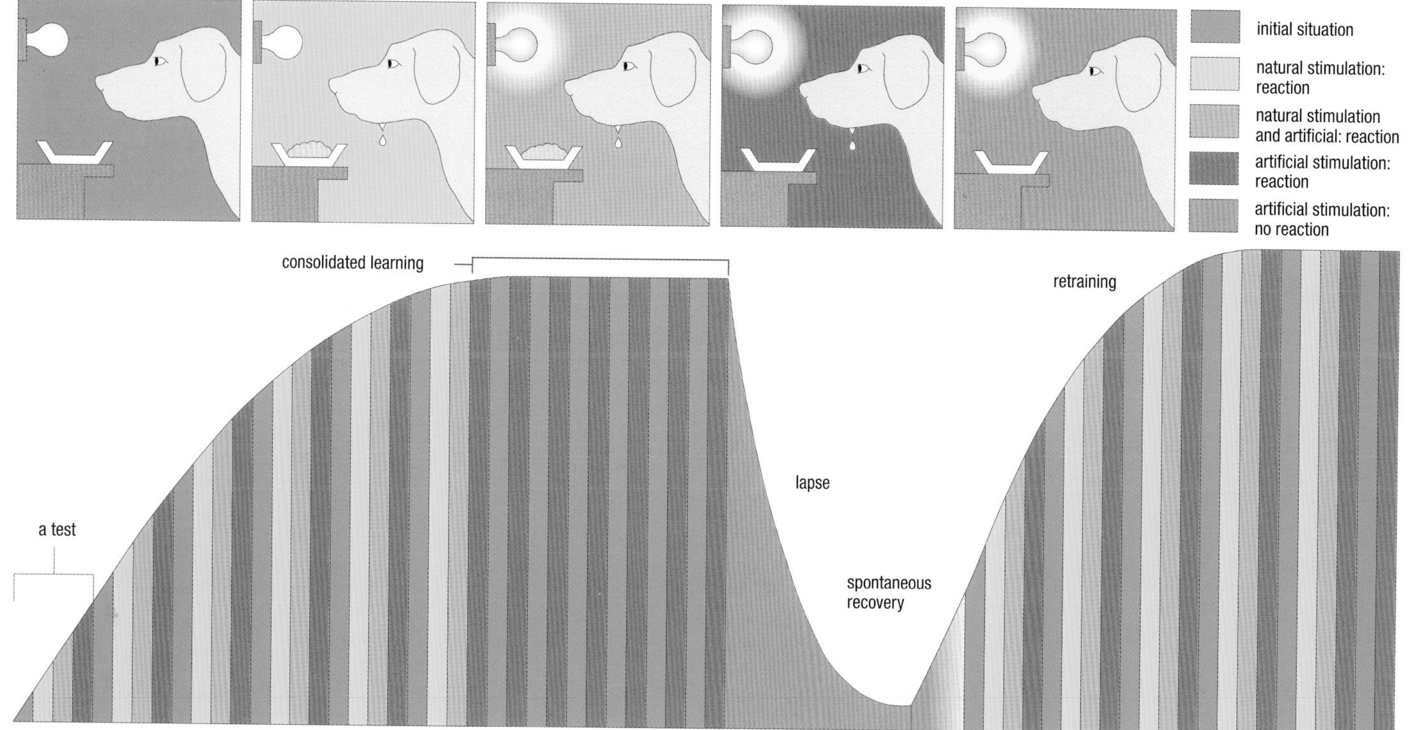

▲ Conditioning
Because the learning takes place, the dog is subjected to a series of tests: **1**. *it starts in a trial situation,* **2**. *is the food (natural stimulus) that results in an unconditional reaction* **3**. *the food is presented with an artificial stimulus (light): you get a response, and then repeating the sequence, it becomes a stereotypical reaction,* **4**. *artificial stimulus alone is now able to induce a response (conditioned response). If you continue to urge the dog with artificial stimuli, not followed by a real "compensation", there is an end to the conditioning (***5***). A subsequent retraining occurs more rapidly than the primary trainer.*

all learning was built on an elementary unit of conditioned reflexes. Subsequent studies have shown, however, that conditioned responses are only one type of learned reflexes. In other words: If you establish a model of behaviour that gives a reward, the subject will continue to choose that behaviour, making it more likely that the response will acquire the characteristics of a reflex.
Conversely, if a given behaviour does not lead to anything positive, it is quickly forgotten. Often, conditioning by aversion therapy is used in psychiatric treatment to treat unwanted behaviour. For example, doctors who administered an emetic medicine to an alcoholic drink found that a subject who tasted it later suffered unpleasant memories whenever he tasted alcohol. In the long term he associates nausea with any alcohol flavours, inducing him to voluntarily renounce any alcohol.
While this may go against the natural reflexes, conditioned reflexes are linked to the superior functions of the brain's cortex ▶187. In humans, things are much more complex than in animals, and the involvement of emotions means that it is very difficult to separate out primary needs like hunger. A specific brain structure called the Hippocampus plays a key role in reflex learning.
The Hippocampus also plays a key role in the selection of information and its storage. It constantly compares sensory data with

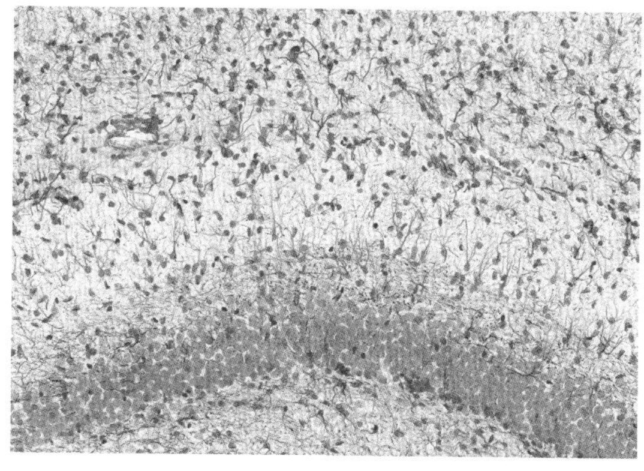

its stored model. In fact, the Hippocampus plays an inhibitory action on the structures in the brain that are responsible for learning. It does this in order to avoid memory overload through saturation - until the conditions in question start changing, the learning areas remain inactive. If the environment changes, or a situation differs considerably from the stored model, the inhibitory action ceases and the learning centres are encouraged to pay attention to the situational changes.
With this mechanism, therefore, it is possible to get used to a background noise without it being considered important, and, at the same time, remain vigilant in order to respond to an unusual noise. In this way the mind can pick out the

◀ Cerebral hemisphere
In each hemisphere there is the limbic system (red, pink and brown) which includes the hippocampus ❶. *The photo above shows a text section.*

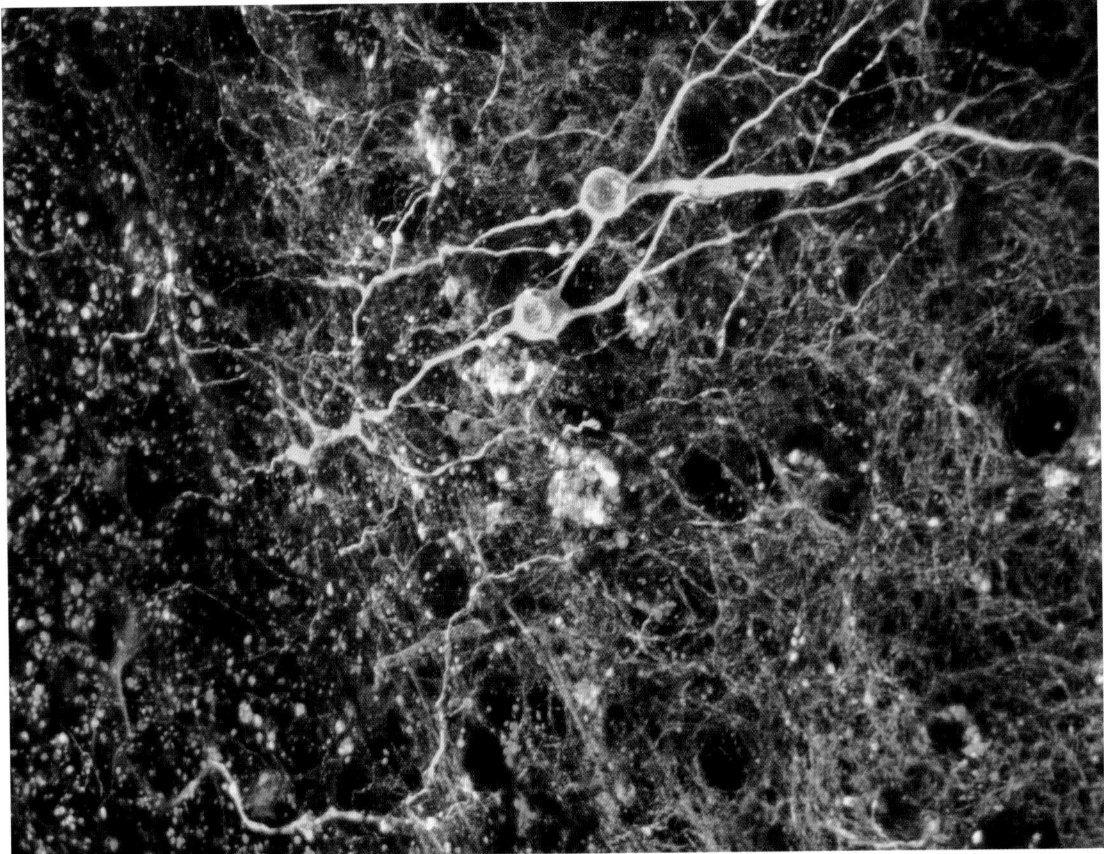

▶ **Conditioning**
Confocal microscope photograph of a hippocampus tissue in which neurons are indicated by a immunofluorescent color. These neurons are responsible for the distribution of information to the interior of the central nervous system and from there to the rest of the body. Recognizable in the photo are ion channels (gold) that allow the exchange of sodium and calcium ions through the membranes that propagate the nerve impulse. As well as in learning, the hippocampus is involved in memory and spatial perception.

important elements from the huge mass of stimuli that continually bombard our nervous system. The ability to selectively focus on the environment and local events, and then compare the information with an archive of past experiences in the long term memory is an essential part of learning. Beyond the Hippocampus, there is a more complicated process of learning that involves other parts of the limbic system.

These take part, for example, in a form of learning that BF Skinner named 'operant conditioning'. Unlike the Pavlov hypothesis, it rewards voluntary responses and not the reflexes. These were based on the observed effects of punishments and rewards of so-called reinforcement. A rat which learns that if it depresses a lever when a light turns on, it gets a reward will continue to do so even if the reward ceases. The situation in humans is, of course, much more complex. Intelligence and the use of language makes learning something much more comprehensive and not a simple reaction to rewards and punishments. The amygdala is also involved in storing lessons, whether they are pleasant or not, of experience and actions. When this part of the brain is damaged, learning on the basis of rewards and punishments is almost impossible. Thus, in a manner parallel to that of the Hippocampus - which allows us to discern between relevant stimuli, the amygdala reminds us of the consequences of our actions.

These deep brain structures therefore transform the world of objective sensory data and reason into the elements of experience and memory. They superimpose on reality a variety of different perspectives, prejudices and learned actions on the basis of expectations and prior experience.

MEMORY & FORGETFULNESS

Although the Hippocampus is an essential component in the fixing of an experience as a memory, it is not the part of the brain that stores it. The processing of a memory is a complicated process that is not yet fully understood.

Different areas of the brain carry out different phases in the storage of a memory:

- the encoding, i.e. the preparation of the gathered information, is dealt with by the Hippocampus.
- the transmission of the encoded information to the storage centres; the mammillary bodies of the limbic system are particularly important for this activity.
- the storage, i.e. the registration of the encoded information; it has been discovered that there are no specific parts of the brain where preferential individual data are stored. If some areas of the brain are destroyed, in fact, it has been found that none of the specific information that is stored is lost. Although memories are stored in the brain, they are not hard encoded in any kind of register - instead the information is spread throughout the entire array of complex memory cells. Data is not stored like a photograph, but through a series of associations. The most effective way of using memory recall is to use some kind of small association. This can then trigger the remembrance of the missing parts of the information.
- the retrieval; that is, the identification of the right pieces of the stored information: this process is done by many different areas within the brain, including the limbic system.

SENSORY MEMORY, SHORT-TERM & LONG-TERM MEMORY

Memory can be classified according to its duration into three types - these are sensory memory, short-term memory, and long-term memory:

- sensory memory: this retains information that has just been perceived by the sense organs - typically it discards around 75 % of this, and in the majority of the cases, it only lasts a few seconds. This leaves 25 % remaining, of which less than 1% of the information is properly encoded and passed to the to the short-term memory.
- short-term or primary memory: this retains information for a period which may vary from a few seconds to several minutes, depending on whether the mind is ignoring the event or devoting attention to it. When it is being ignored, the

▼ Limbic system
The hippocampus is part of the limbic system, the area of the brain closely linked to the hypothalamus, which regulates behaviors related to survival: eating, drinking, gathering food and reproduction. Furthermore, in humans it interprets the signals coming from the environment and other sources: managing emotions, feelings, and thus also our perception of reality. In the limbic system, as well as the hippocampus ❶, the mamillari bodies ❷, the pellucida septum ❸ round parahippocampal ❹, the amygdala ❺, the tube ❻, the serrated turn ❼.

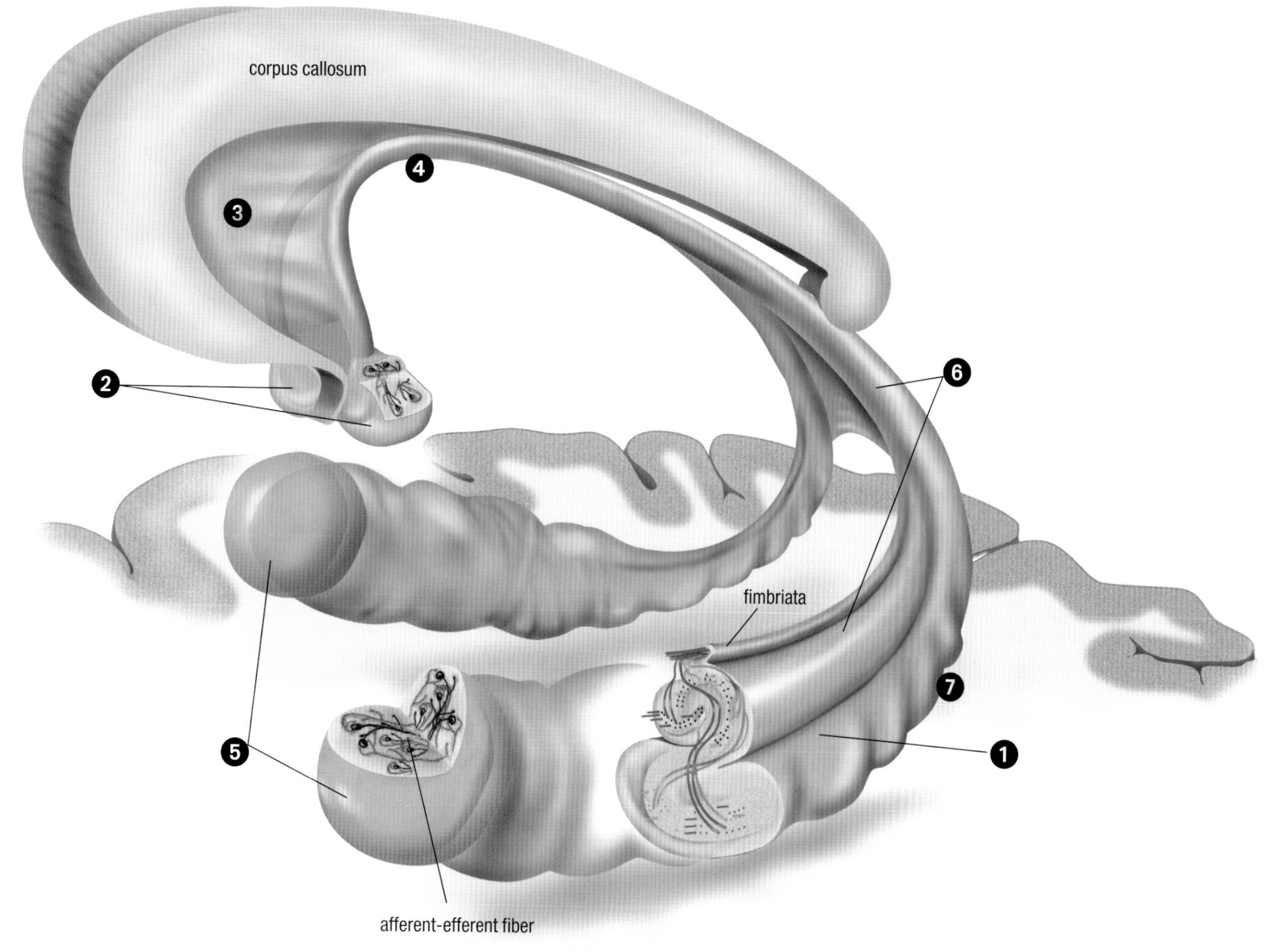

information is more or less immediately cleared, although if the event is repeated, the memory can be restored. If is not repeated often enough, however, his memory will be permanently lost. The data that may still be invoked in short-term memory term constitutes the so-called repeat bearing: it remains archived there until it is replaced by new data or is promoted to the long-term memory.

- long-term or secondary memory: whereas there is a rapid deterioration in the short-term memory, the long-term memory can store the information in a stable manner for extended periods of time that may last from a few days to life. Long-term memory is considered to be virtually unlimited, but recall may be inefficient, depending on what other competition there is for the memory retrieval system. The more associations there are to help with the recall, the better the chances of the memory being brought back.

On the other hand, memory is expressed in the synapses that tie neurons together: recent research has shown the importance of certain neuronal proteins in the preservation of memories. In particular that of a protein called ARC, which would have a key role in regular production of the substances that are involved in the consolidation of the synapses.

Long-term memory can be divided into two types:

- declarative or explicit memory: this is primarily controlled by the cerebral cortex, and is where specific information is stored. This includes experiences, facts, ideas, concepts, emotions and feelings.
- procedural or implicit memory: this concerns the information that is required in order to carry out automatic or involuntary behaviours. Examples include the mechanical skills that are used in learned reflexes. These may be specific activities that have been repeated over and over again for years, and have therefore become unconscious actions.

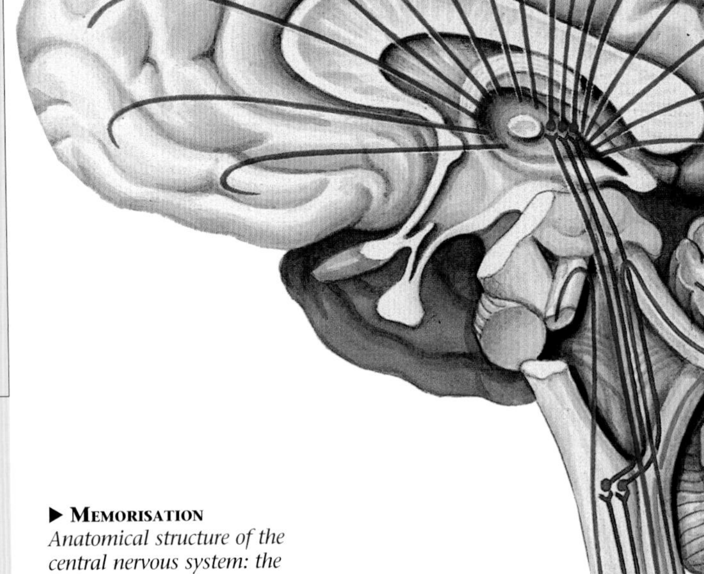

▶ **Memorisation**
Anatomical structure of the central nervous system: the sensitive fibers, which come from the body through the spinal cord, carrying all sorts of information that pass from the brainstem to reach the limbic system. From this information, suitably coded, to reach various parts of the cortex which may be used, stored or destroyed. The different colors indicate different nerve pathways (motor and sensitive).

TO REMEMBER OR FORGET?

One issue that the brain has to sort out is that of where a memory should be stored - would it be better placed in the short-term or long-term memory? The encoding and transfer of mnemonic data is a complicated and delicate process, and needs to be done correctly, or the mind would quickly become very confused. The Hippocampus is the body that is responsible for selecting the sensory data and deciding what information should be remembered and deserves to go to a longer lasting memory bank, and which should be forgotten. The selection process is heavily influenced by the state of mind. Normally, pleasant memories are much more likely to be remembered than unpleasant ones, however, those bad experiences which may influence future survival tend to be securely stored.

It is difficult to learn a subject that we do not like, or in which we have had poor results: recent research has confirmed that a low self-esteem undermines mnemonic capabilities. For the same reason, learning new surroundings has good results: it stimulates the Hippocampus to transfer information to the longer-term secondary memory. Having good self-esteem, a strong motivation, or simply a positive attitude, therefore, can make learning much easier. Recent research in this field has opened new avenues of inquiry. For instance, studies have shown that part of the brain may well be pre-prepared to store new information even before the stimuli are collected and coded. These results were obtained from volunteers by examining the electrical signals in their brains using an electroencephalogram ▸172. Firstly, their brain activity was monitored under quiet conditions, and then the output was recorded when they were asked to memorise new words. The two sets of data were then compared. This showed that the main differences were in the preparatory phase of storing new memories.

It has also been shown that there is a clear link between the brain's electrical activity for preliminary storage and the capacity for mnemonic recall. If the electrical activity is high while a new fact is being memorised, it is much more likely that it will be remembered later. Conversely, if the brain's electrical activity is lower in the first phase, the ability to remember the fact later is much reduced.

Sometimes, however, there are memories that disappear from the active memory. As a result, the immediate recall may fail because the facts have not yet been transmitted to the long-term memory. This means that there are not enough associations in place to rebuild the memory. It is likely that this is the explanation for what psychiatrists call 'removed memories'. These are unconsciously made inaccessible due to the consequences that their presence could have. In this case the brain subconsciously avoids making the necessary associations - if, however, therapy is used to help reconstruct these associations, the memories can be made to resurface again.

▼ **Cerebral cortex**
Optical microscope photo of the human cerebral cortex. ❶ *The axons of this deeper layer, identified as the long dark lines, are woven horizontally and vertically by transferring the information in all directions* ❷ *These neurons (black) are the upper layer: the gray matter is the part of the brain responsible for conscious thought, memory and explicit language.*

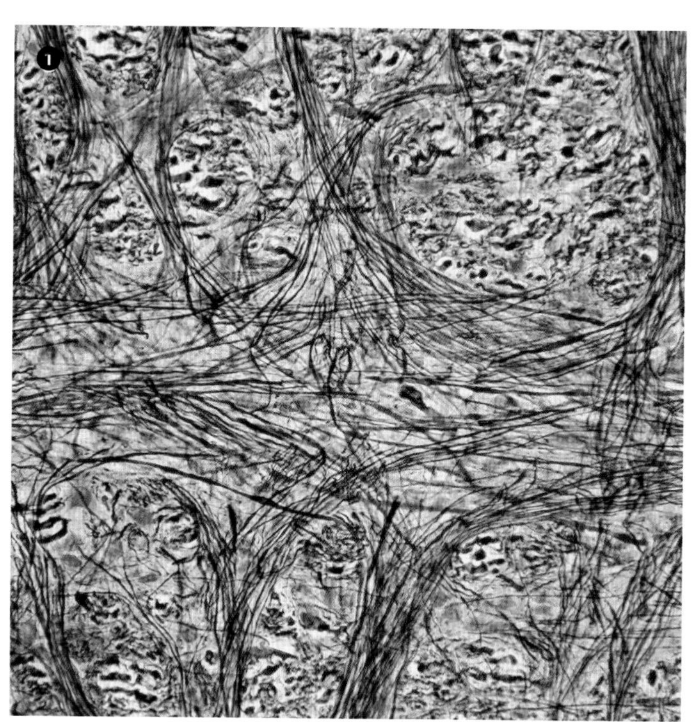

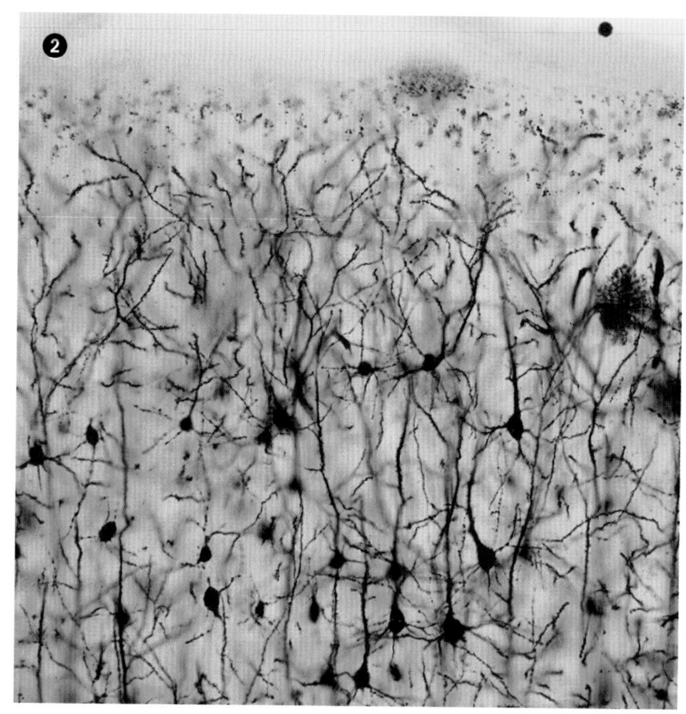

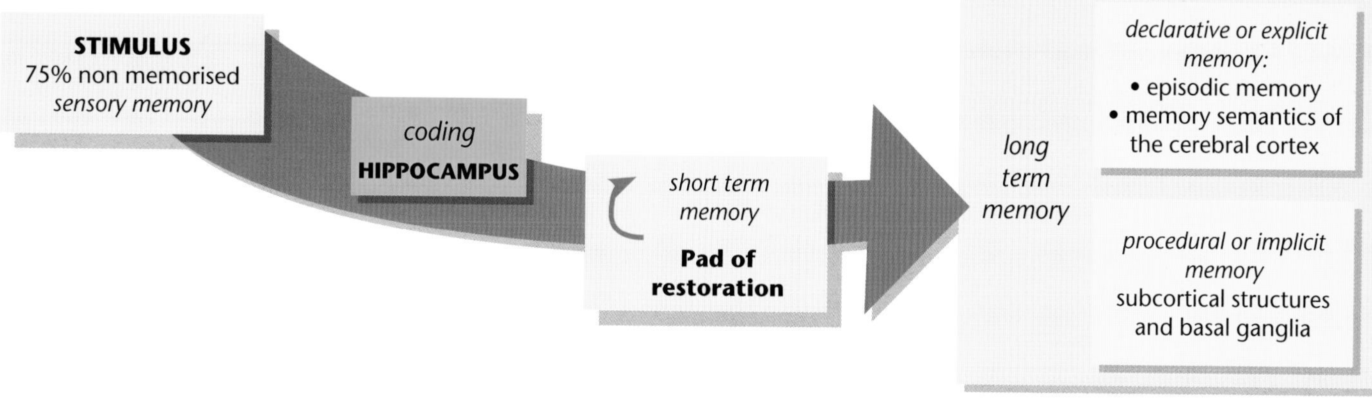

Sleep & Dreams

Sleep is a fundamental biological necessity. It is a nervous process that involves the brain and takes place at regular intervals in accordance with circadian rhythms and certain genetic factors. During sleep there is an almost total break with the sensory contacts and motors that connect the brain to the environment. This leaves it free to act independently, and the result of this are the events we refer to as dreams. The study of these strange and mostly unexplained brain functions has developed significantly in recent years with the use of the electroencephalograph (EEG). This has the ability to make recordings of the electrical signals that result from neuronal activity - these are then displayed on a chart that shows the changes in the spontaneous electrical activity of the brain.

State Of Waking

When an individual is at rest and with closed eyes, the brain's EEG plot shows large peaks that take place relatively slowly - at approximately 10 cycles per second. This is referred to as the Alpha rhythm. If the eyes are then opened, the plot changes and is characterised by a rapid sequence of peaks with smaller amplitudes that are often irregular - this is known as the Beta type.

Synchronised Sleep Or REM Not

When a patient is monitored as they go from relaxation through drowsiness and finally to sleep, it can be seen that the plot changes gradually. The transition from wakefulness to sleep corresponds with the establishment of the Delta phase, which is made up of very large and slow peaks with a frequency of 3-5 cycles per second. It marks neuronal synchronisation, where the neurons of the cerebral cortex are synchronising their activity.

As sleep becomes deeper, it is distinguished by four phases which are referred to as 'NREM', which stands for Non-Rapid Eye Movement. During these phases there are few direct signal orders given out by the brain, such as those to change position, for example. During NREM sleep, in fact, the brain rests but does not sleep completely. While it is in this state it uses a minimum amount of energy, but continues to develop all manner of fragmented mental processes that are not actually dreams. Instead, they tend to be wide-ranging conceptual thoughts, that may be extremely vague, and generally without emotional involvement.

In the early stages of sleep recent thoughts and experiences are transferred to the long term memory. Large areas of the brain that would normally be used to process sensory information are switched over to this task, especially those areas which are involved in learning and the processing of the information that is invoked by memories. Any information that has been gathered during the day is analysed, and then depending on its perceived relevance, is catalogued, discarded or stored. In the absence of dreams, the brain often goes through past memories and refreshes them.

In the analysis of brainwave patterns it can be seen that in this phase of deep sleep the brain triggers action in the areas that are normally involved in learning about new things, or while experiencing new situations. This observation is based on the results of tests that have been carried out using functional magnetic resonance equipment. These showed that a similar mechanism is active while the patient is awake. This demonstrates that the brain accumulates new information and then waits for a period of sleep to reinforce it.

It has been discovered that each area of the brain falls into a level of sleep that is in direct proportion to how hard it worked that day. Furthermore, the better the sleep it experiences, the better that region of the brain will perform the next day.

The quality of sleep cannot be compensated by quantity, however. If an individual spends too long asleep, their brain capacity decreases. This is defined as the "inertia of the sleep" - the longer one sleeps, the more difficult it is to re-emerge from the torpor. As regards the optimal efficiency of the brain - it is has been demonstrated that best performance results from less than eight hours sleep.

In tests that were conducted after three minutes of awakening, it was found that volunteers who had slept for long periods had mental capacities that were much lower than those who had been subjected to sleep deprivation. The cerebral cortex is where the higher intellectual functions - such as mathematical processing, are focused. In fact, it takes much longer to come up to full wakefulness than the other areas of the brain.

Not having enough sleep has similar consequences. It has been demonstrated that the energy consumption of the brain - which is quantified by its rate of glucose consumption, goes down significantly in those people who stay awake for more than 24 hours. In other words, the amount of work it does falls drastically compared to its normal levels. This is especially marked in the cortex, and leads to much lower complex cognitive efficiency.

The early stages of sleep are essential for the recovery of basic metabolic activities. During this period, the brain often switches between wakefulness - where it is aware of the world around it, to one of sleep, where it

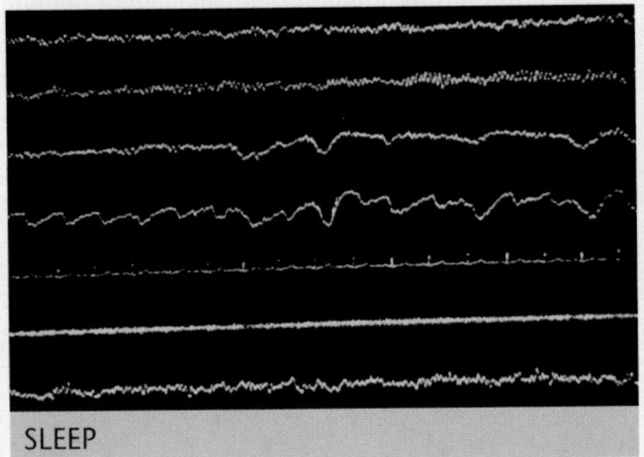

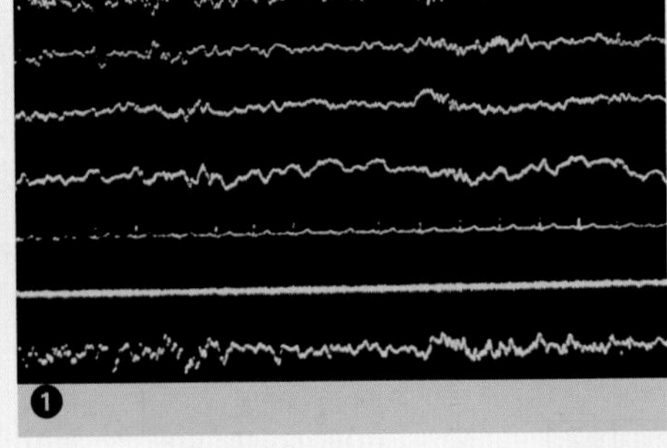

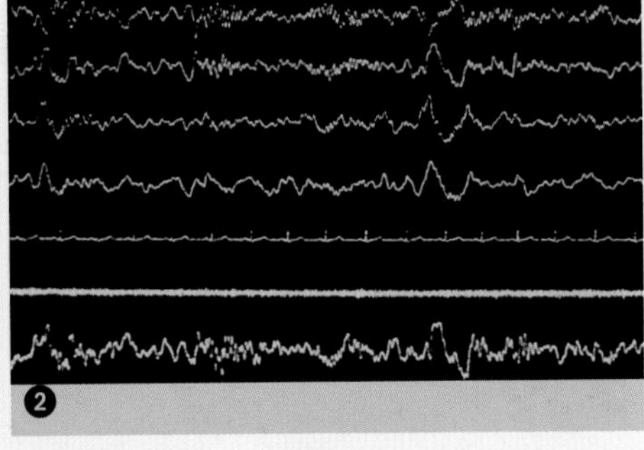

▲ **Sleep**
*Series of photographs that show in false colors in the activity of the brain and muscles during sleep. **1** and **2** are traces of electroencephalogram (EEG), which shows the electrical activity of the brain, followed by the electrooculogram (EOG), which indicate the movement of the right eye (**3**) and left (**4**), **5** is an electrocardiogram (ECG), which reproduces the cardiac activity, followed by the electromiogram (EMG) showing the activity of the muscles of the larynx (**6**) and neck (**7**).*

1 First stage of non-REM sleep
As we move to the next stage, the sleep becomes deeper, although the electrical activity shows no obvious changes.

2 Second stage of non-REM sleep

focuses on internal activities. This gradually isolates the mind from the solidity of the outer environment and lays down a sort of preparatory path towards sleep. It thus manages to eliminate unnecessary information and memorise the beneficial facts, storing them away for future use. In this way, the mind is better prepared to deal with the world when it next wakes up.

- **The first stage of sleep** - this includes the initial sleepiness and the first light sleep. It represents around 7% of the total sleep time. In each cycle, the first stage lasts only a few minutes and during this period the individual concerned is easily awoken by external stimuli.
- **The second stage of sleep** - this stage is characterised by isolated thoughts that are interspersed by confused memories. It lasts for about half of the total sleep time, and each cycle lasts for between five and fifteen minutes.
- **The third and fourth stages** - these are the stages in which sleep is much deeper. There is a sharp decrease in the muscle tone in the third stage and there are few or no movements of the eyes or body. The EEG plot shows a further slowdown (delta rhythm) that is characterised by large waves with low frequency. The fourth stage is where the deepest sleep is experienced, and this is shown by the EEG recording the lowest electrical activity.

These two stages typically occupy 20% of the total sleep time, with the fourth stage lasting between twenty and forty minutes in the first cycle, and then varying greatly thereafter.

Before the beginning of the first phase of REM sleep occurs, the other stages are revisited many times. After the REM phase of the first cycle, the sequencing of the stages of NREM and REM changes. While the REM stages last longer, there are always other stages, with at least thirty minutes of different types of sleep or wakefulness.

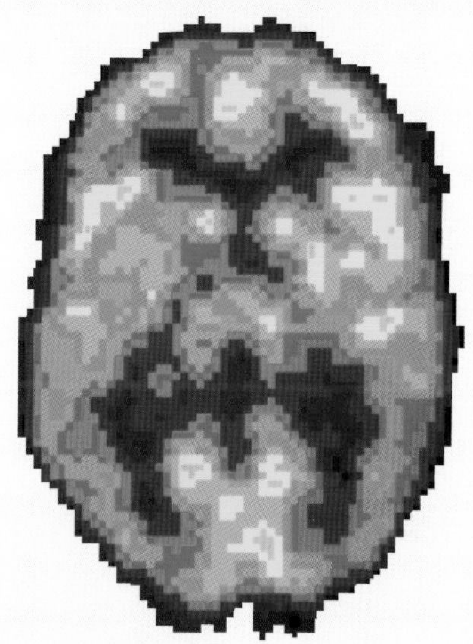

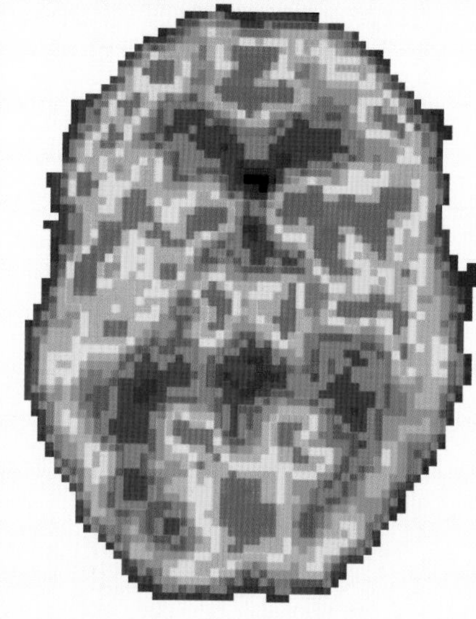

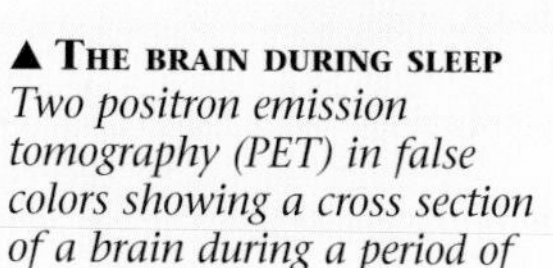

▲ THE BRAIN DURING SLEEP
Two positron emission tomography (PET) in false colors showing a cross section of a brain during a period of NREM sleep (left) and REM sleep on the right. The brain areas are active in red, and inactive in blue.

REM Stage

After about ninety minutes from the onset of drowsiness, and having crossed the four stages of NREM, the brain enters a stage that is similar to that of waking. The waves become irregular, they have low voltage, and occur in short bursts that are characterised by an intensity that denotes a frenetic amount of neuronal work. In particular, this denotes the activation of neurons in the brainstem, which normally transmit information to the cortex and the areas that govern the memory.

The REM stage of sleep is characterised by rapid eye movements and other physiological events that indicate intense brain activity. There is, for example, an additional requirement for oxygen - it has been calculated that the brain consumes more oxygen during REM sleep than during the solution of the most difficult mathematical tasks. To ensure that there is the necessary amount of oxygen, the heart beat accelerates, the blood flow to the brain hemispheres increases and, at the same time, the respiratory pace speeds up.

All this energy is used by the brain - which is more or less completely diverted away from use by the body, to process information. These activities are linked to the higher brain faculties, and REM sleep is therefore indicative of the subconscious actions of the neural mechanisms that are related to the processes of information selection and processing. The decrease in the muscle tone remains throughout the period of sleep except for the muscles of the inner ear and eyes. This is because the motor neurons inhibits their activation, although occasional muscle contractions or spasms occur commonly.

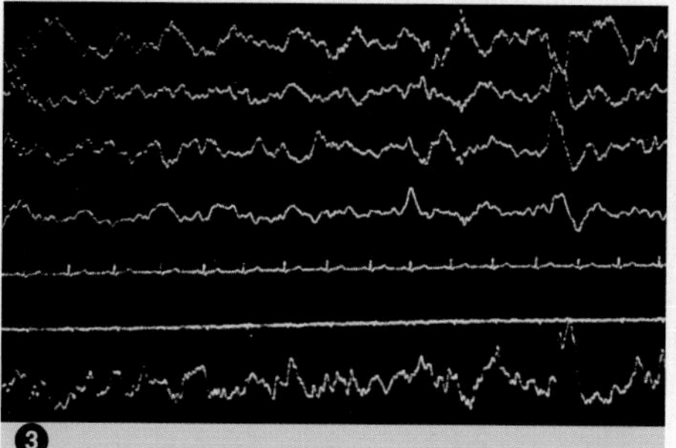

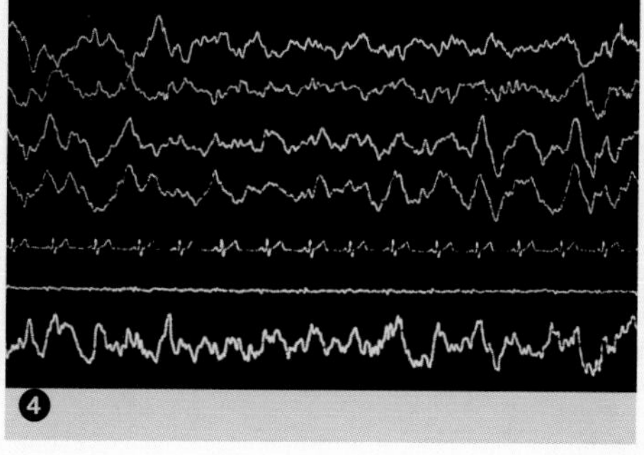

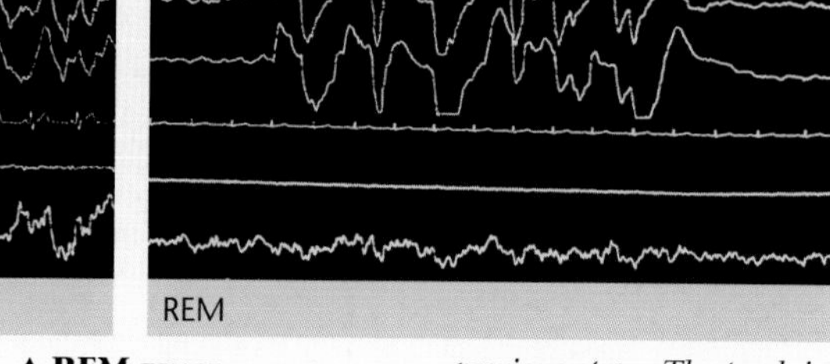

3 THIRD STAGE OF NON-REM SLEEP

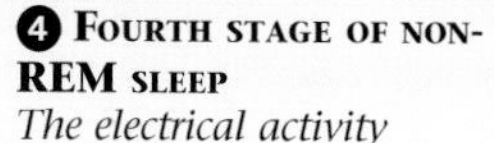

4 FOURTH STAGE OF NON-REM SLEEP
The electrical activity reaches its lowest level.

▲ REM PHASE
As is clearly visible in the tracks, during this phase, characterized by rapid eye movements, the brain electrical activity has slowed compared to the tracks shown in the previous steps. The track is in fact much more similar to that of waking sleep.

BILLIONS OF NERVE CELLS STORED IN THE SKULL ARE THE DELICATE CONTROL CENTER OF ALL ACTIVITIES AND FUNCTIONS OF THE BODY, FROM THE MOST BASIC - LIKE EATING OR BREATHING - TO THE MORE COMPLEX, LIKE THE IMAGINATION, A CHARACTERISTIC OF OUR SPECIES.

A THOUSAND OPERATIONS OF THE BRAIN

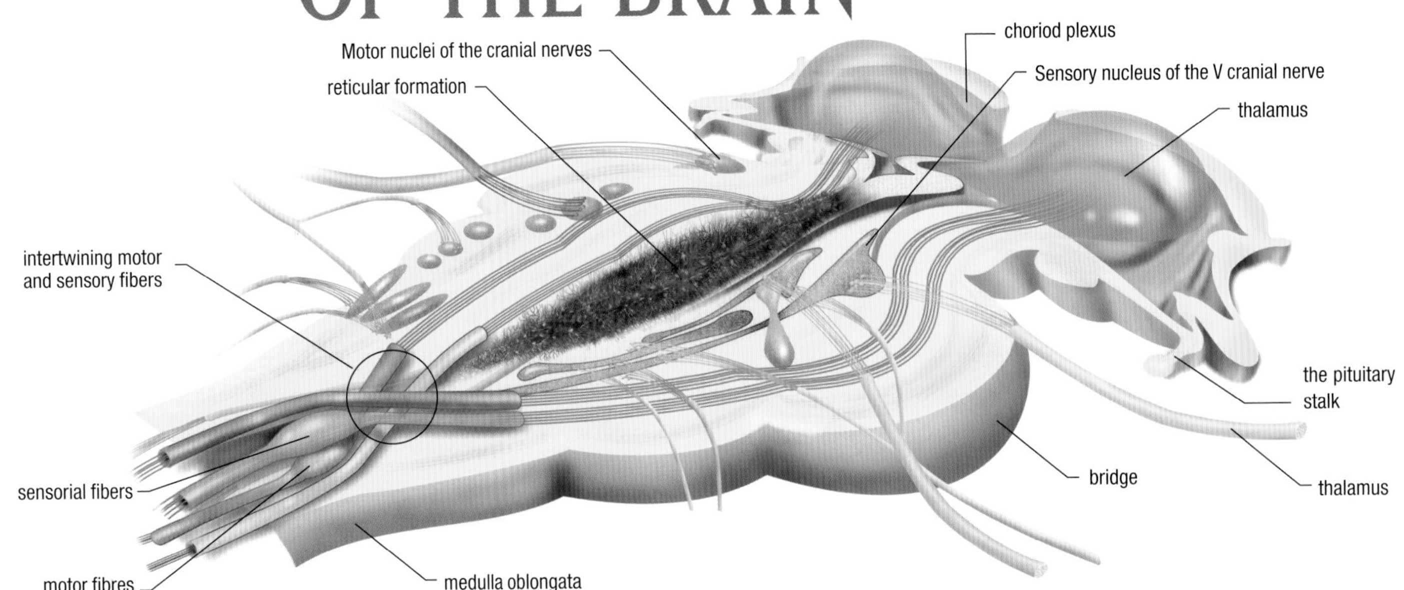

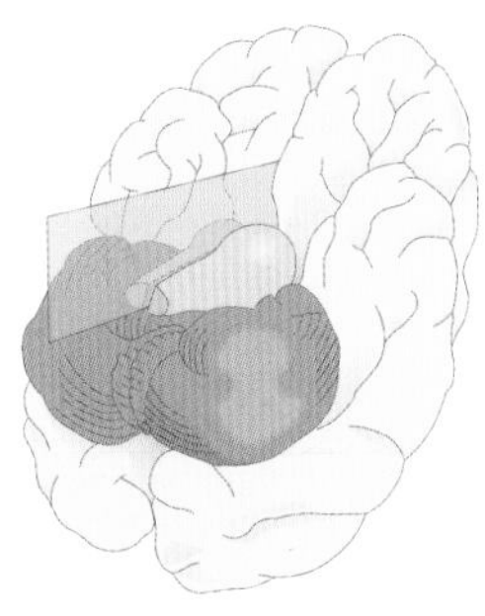

▲ **ANATOMY OF THE BRAINSTEM**
On average only 6 cm long, the brainstem is cut ventral, lengthwise and opened like a book. Illustrated here are all the major nerve pathways that lead from the brain to the body and vice versa.

With an average weight in the adult human of between 1200, and 1300 g, the brain is the control centre of the body. Consisting of about 100 billion neurons, more than half of which is focused in the brain hemispheres 225, it undertakes a huge number of functions that are often independent from one another. For a start, it has to process all the information that it receives from both inside and outside the body, as well as producing the most suitable responses. These may involve anything from movements to specific chemical or physical reactions. They may also be behavioural, or be a combination of several of these features at the same time. In addition to this, the brain governs such complex functions as attention, memory 205, 220, learning 202, conscience, thought, reasoning, imagination and creativity. It also checks whether all the lesser body functions are being carried out correctly. Indeed, to regulate every vital aspect of the body there are structures within the encephalic areas that remain active all the time and yet almost always work independently of the others. This does not mean, however, that there are no links between these different areas, as mental processes such as emotions or motivation are composed of many different - often conflicting factors. As a result, they need to interface very efficiently in order for the processing to produce the optimal response.

THE CONTROL OF VITAL ACTIVITIES

There are many types of encephalic neurons, and they can be very different from one another. They are defined by their shapes, the types of neural connections they form, their biochemical compositions, and their cellular architectures. They perform different functions according to their locations.

THE BRAIN STEM

The brain stem is the area that deals with the control of the most important vital functions. These include the respiratory rhythm ▸46, cardiac

rate, blood pressure, the hours of waking and sleeping ▶172, and from the state of consciousness to that of unconsciousness. Its particular structure and strategic position make the brain stem a key element in the communications between the brain and the rest of the body. It is linked directly with all parts of the nervous system, which converge on it from the nerve fibres of the spinal cord and other parts of the brain, as well as all the main motor and sensory pathways. The nerves from the left side of the body meet with those from the right in the brain stem, and then continue towards their opposed brain hemispheres.
The nerve fibres form a specialised network that descends along the spinal cord and innervates the striated muscles. This provides a precise and fluid method of control, allowing subtle adjustments in the positions of the muscles, and so making it possible for them to perform intricate movements. Without the involvement of these nerves, the muscles could only work in coarse bursts. It is in the brain stem that the information that is sent by the sensory receptors is received and compared with that from other parts of the brain. It is then modified and finally retransmitted along with data from the memory as well as emotional impulses that are derived from the limbic system ▶169. The cortex then uses all the information to give shape to the world of consciousness. At the same time, other brain stem fibres reach the thalamus: when they are stimulated, they can excite large numbers of cortical cells, launching the processing of detailed information which underlies the reality of consciousness.

The neurons and particular network formation of the brain stem are always active. It is involved in everything the body does, indeed, it continually monitors all the basic functions and ensures that they are adequate for the various physiological demands.

THE HYPOTHALAMUS

The hypothalamus is connected to both the brain and the spinal cord through large numbers of nerves. It serves as a link between the central nervous system and the endocrine system ▶200. It is where, the secretory neurons that govern the pituitary activity ▶197 can be found. This is intended to modulate the functions of all the other endocrine glands and such structures as the kidneys or reproductive organs. In addition, the hypothalamus contains nerve centres that supervise many important bodily functions. These include such things as temperature, hunger and thirst. All of these work automatically, and at the same time they monitor and control the autonomous nervous system. Further to this, they also check the metabolic status of the body and the reactions of the defence and immune systems in emergency situations.
Composed of different specialist areas which are in the control of specific functions, the hypothalamus is an essential element in basic metabolic checks. The rear area control the sexual instincts, with the dorsal area considered to be the pleasure centre. It also governs the endocrine system and so is involved in the synthesis of emotions. The frontal area is the control centre for hunger and thirst, while the osmoreceptors check the internal fluid

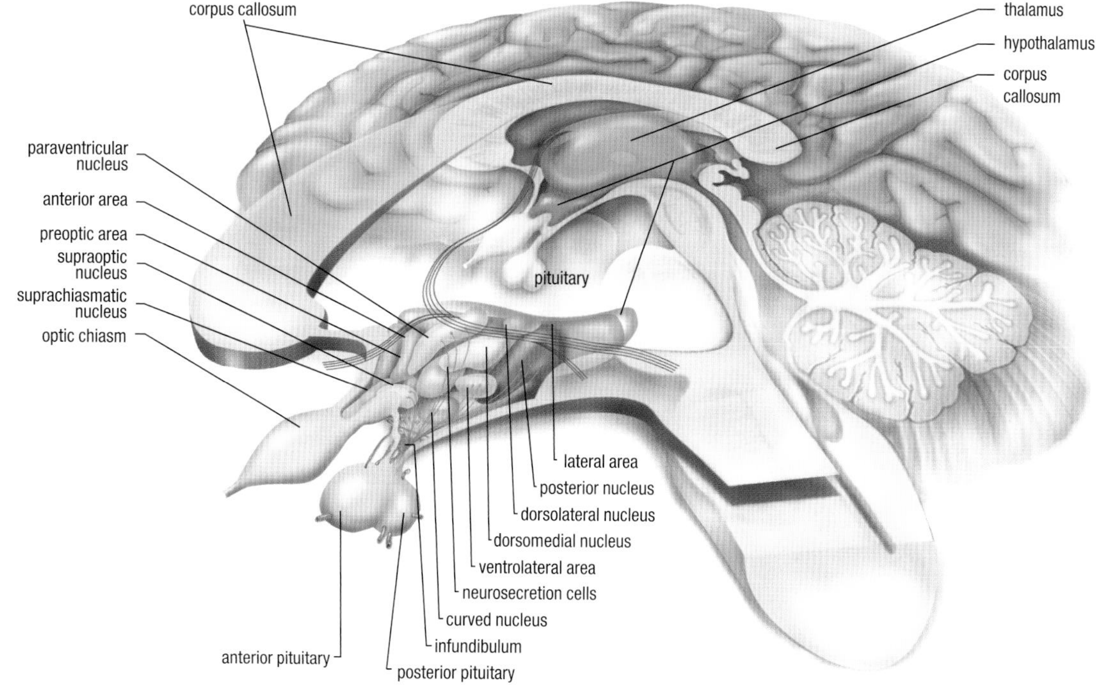

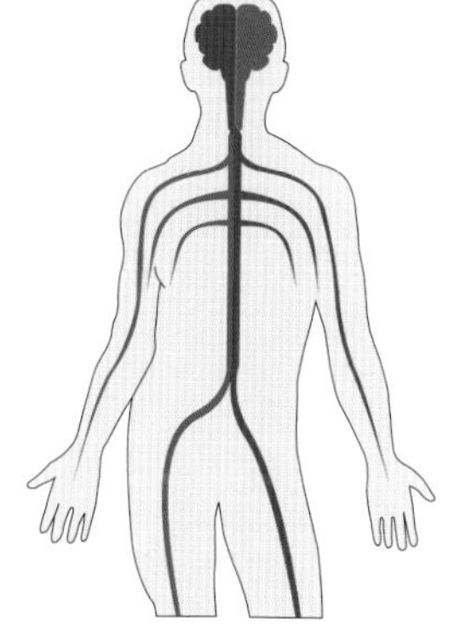

▲ **Path**
The sensitive and motor pathways are intertwined at the level of the brain stem and inverted on the opposite side of the body with relation to the hemisphere.

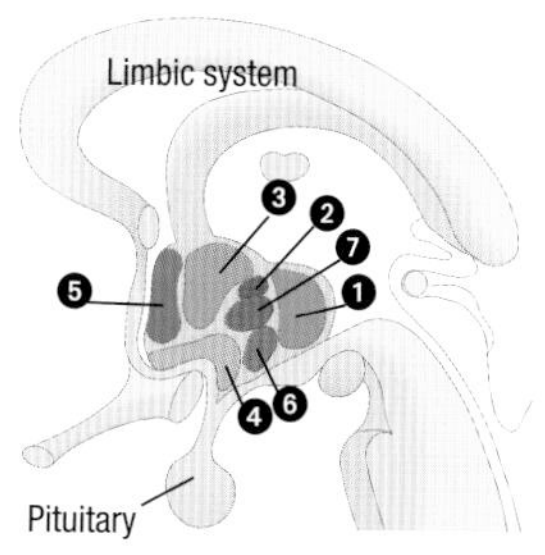

▲ **Hypothalamus**
Main anatomical features of the hypothalamus and, below, its relationship with the pituitary, the brains gland that regulates the endocrine system.
1 posterior area;
2 dorsal area;
3 anterior area;
4 supraoptic nucleus;
5 preoptic nucleus;
6 ventromedial nucleus;
7 dorsomedial nucleus.

The Anatomy Of The Brain

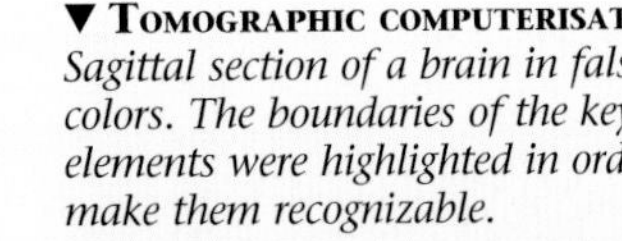

▼ Tomographic computerisation
Sagittal section of a brain in false colors. The boundaries of the key elements were highlighted in order to make them recognizable.

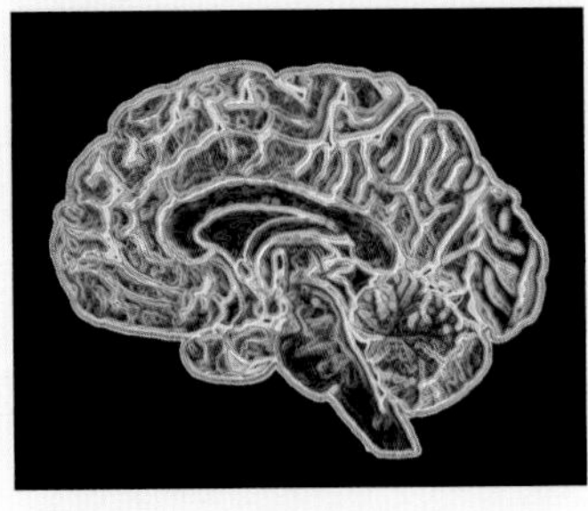

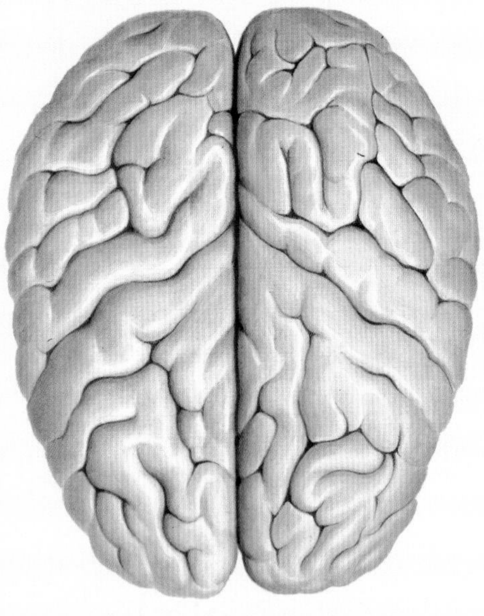

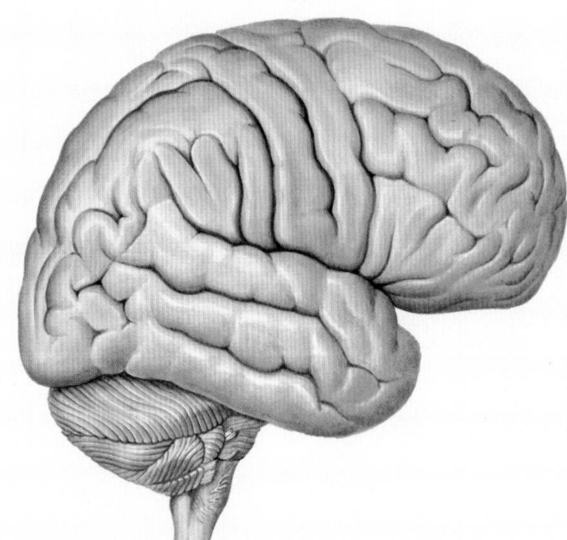

◀ The brain from above and from the right side
In the second image, in addition to the cerebral hemispheres the cerebellum and brainstem are also visible.

The brain - the most important part of the human nervous system, is contained and protected by the cranium which is wrapped in three protective membranes called the meninges. Starting from the outside, these are the dura mater, the arachnoid, and the pia mater. Between the latter two is the subarachnoid space, in which flows a liquid produced by the brain called the liquor. This is responsible for absorbing small movements thus protecting the brain against shock and sudden motions of the head, as well as allowing it to move within the skull.

The brain shows slight differences between the sexes ▸191 - in the male, for example, the average weight is 1320 g, the average length is 17 cm, and the average width is 14 cm. The female brain is significantly smaller, weighing around 1167 g. measuring 16 cm in length and 13.5 cm in width. There are also certain neuronal differences, but from the anatomical point of view the structures can be regarded as essentially similar. Looking down from above, the brain is divided by the longitudinal interhemispheric slot into two hemispheres, each of which is divided into four lobes. These are referred to as the frontal lobe, the parietal lobe, the temporal lobe and the occipital lobe. The central sulcus (which is also known as the fissure of Rolando), separates the frontal parietal lobe from that of the frontal lobe, as well as dividing the primary motor cortex from the primary somatosensory cortex.

If the internal structures of the skull are examined in profile, it can be seen that the majority of the volume is taken up by the brain. This is composed of the cerebellum, which is divided into two cerebellar hemispheres and characterised by a folded surface, as well as the olfactory bulb and brain stem, which extends to the first part of the spinal cord.

If the examination is performed from below, the forms of the olfactory bulb and brain stem become clearer. In order to find out more about the anatomical elements of the brain, however, it is necessary to dissect it. By removing the cerebral cortex, for example, it is possible to uncover the numerous nervous fibres which link the two sections of the brain. These are white in colour, a

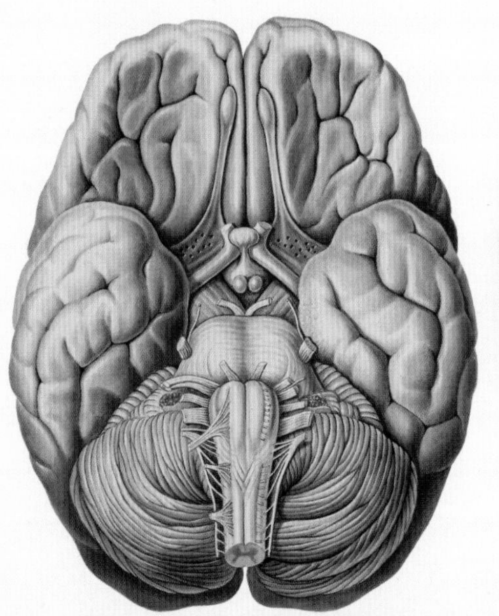

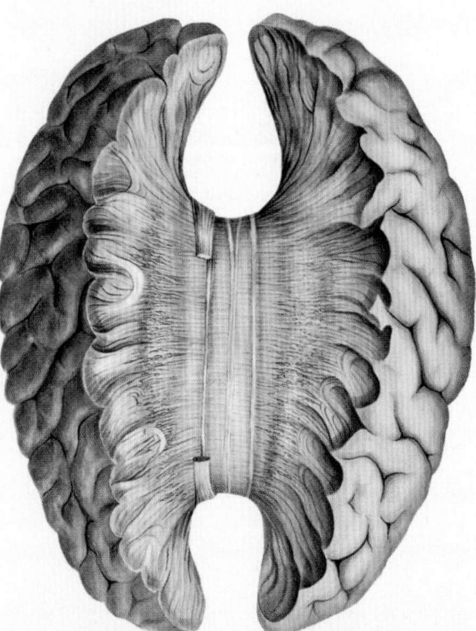

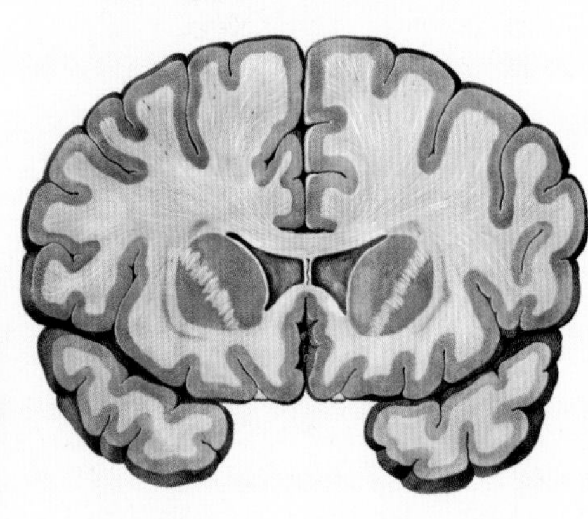

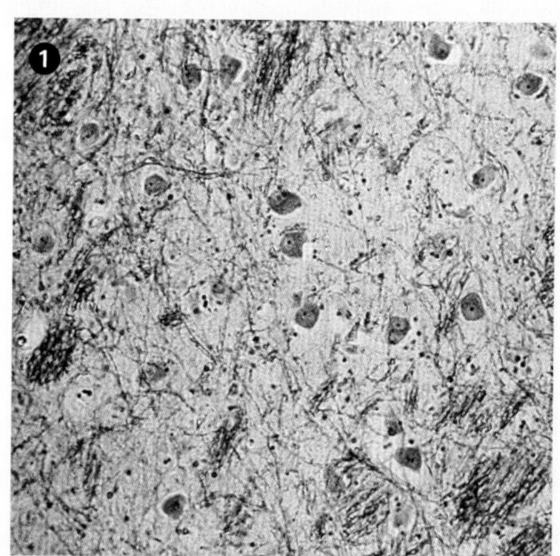

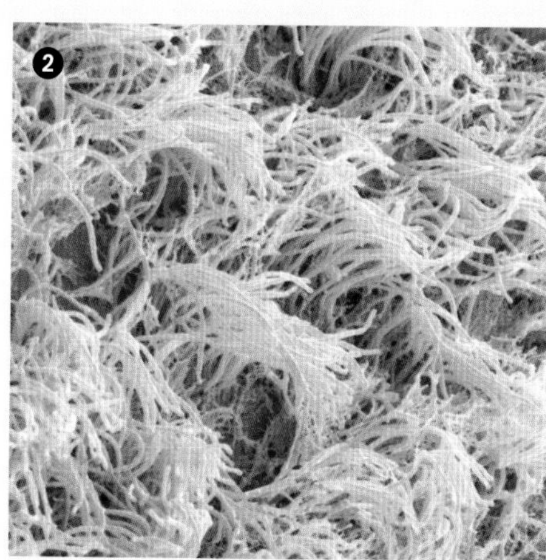

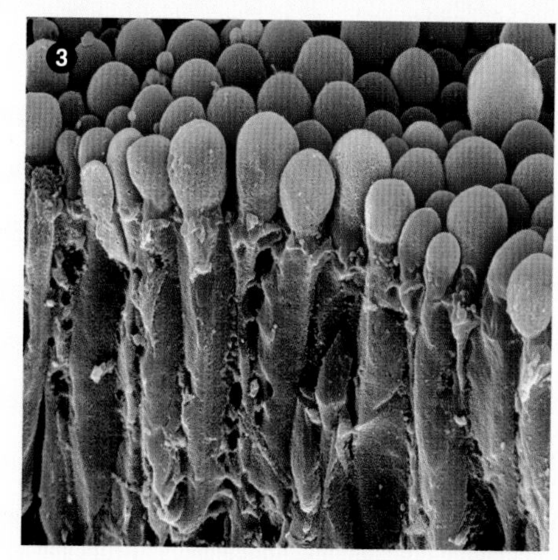

1 Thalamus
Microscopic section of an optic thalamus, two ovoidal elements of the brain governing the vigilant conscience of sensations such as pain and touch. The network of neurons in the thalamus receives signals from all routes except those in the smell senses, and the sorting section in specific regions of the cortex.

2 Cerebral ventricles
The cillia cells that cover the cerebral ventricles push the cerebrospinal fluid to travel from the brain to the spinal cord and vice versa.

3 Choriod plexus
The surface of the choriod plexus, seen here in section by a SEM, is formed by cells with secretory activity (gray) that produce the cerebrospinal fluid (red). The choriod plexus is a network of blood capillaries which is located in each cerebral ventricle.

▼ Cerebellar cortex
Two sections of the cerebellum under an optical microscope with different magnifications. The two cell layers that make up the cerebellar cortex: an outer-called "molecular" (yellow in the photo above) an inner layer called "granular" (brown), separated as in the photo below, a layer which are the cell nuclei. Together, the two layers form the gray matter. At the heart of circonvolution, there is the white matter (orange top, white below), made of compacted nerve fibers.

distinction that is also found in the spinal cord. It is the longitudinal section that allows most of the internals of the brain to be seen. Besides the cerebral cortex, which remains intact in the two separated hemispheres, the following features can be identified:

• The mid-brain - known as the mesencephalon, is located between the forebrain and the hindbrain. Below it are the pons Varolii, and the medulla oblongata, and behind it is the cerebellum. A number of key structures are located in this area - these include the thalamus, hypothalamus, pituitary, the limbic system, and the choroid plexus. This secretes the cerebrospinal fluid that is found in the brain's ventricles, and the central channel of the spinal cord. The ventricles, which are full of cerebrospinal fluid, help to cushion the brain from the shocks and, thanks to the ciliary cells which line their cavities, encourage the fluid to circulate. The cerebrospinal fluid functions as the specific transport system of the nervous system, moving hormones and collecting the metabolic waste materials.

• The brainstem, which forms the lower part of the brain, is divided into:

– The pons Varolii which is also referred to as the pons or pons bridge, is a control structure that passes sensory information back and forth between the cerebellum and cerebrum. It also helps to distribute other various messages around the brain, as well as regulate respiration and sexual arousal.

– The medulla oblongata - this forms the lower part of the brainstem, and is responsible for controlling many of the body's primary functions, including the heart rate, blood pressure and respiration.

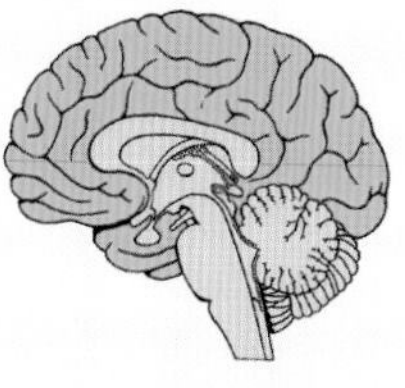

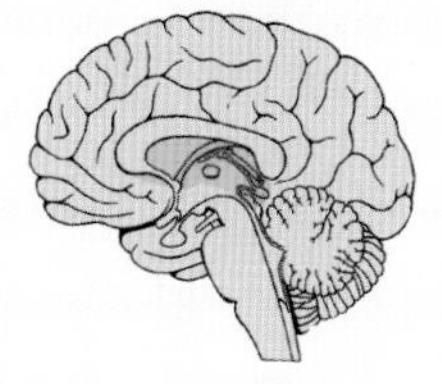

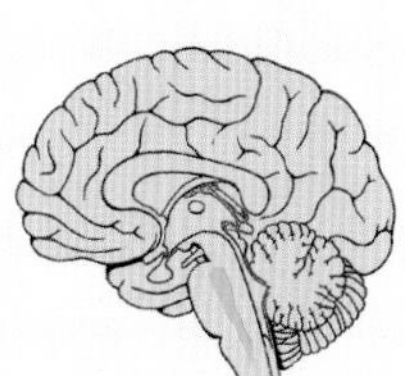

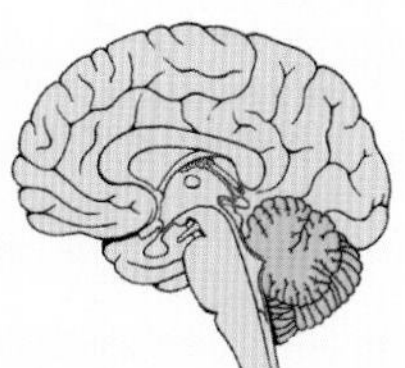

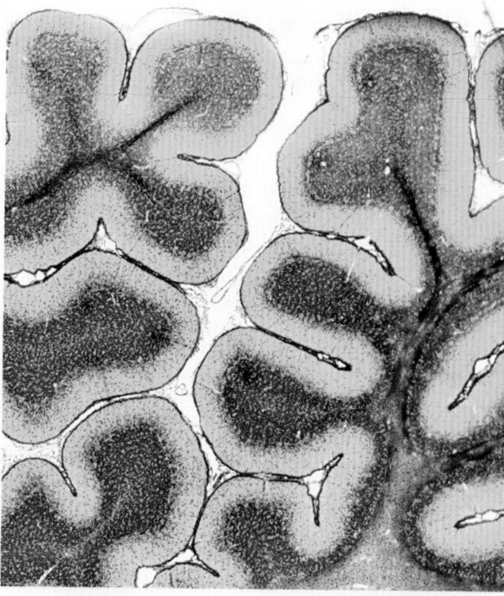

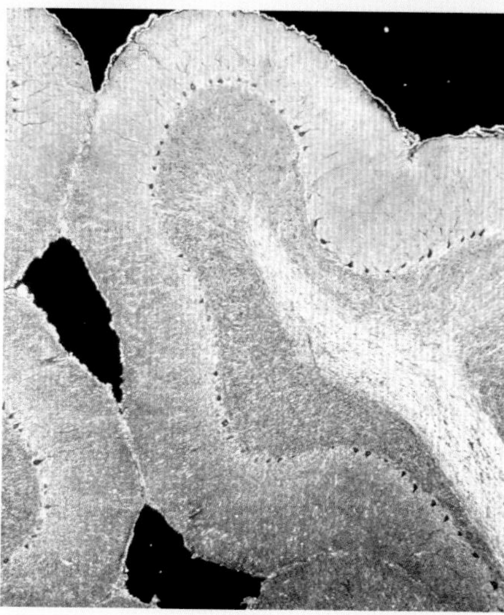

▶ **Cerebellum in ventral view**
In this diagram you can see the big peduncles that connect to the brainstem: the trunk of massive bundles of nerve fibers that connect the cerebellum to the rest of the central nervous system. The colors are arbitrary.

▶ **Cerebellum in dorsal view**
Shows the well-defined lobules of the main fissures. The colors are arbitrary.

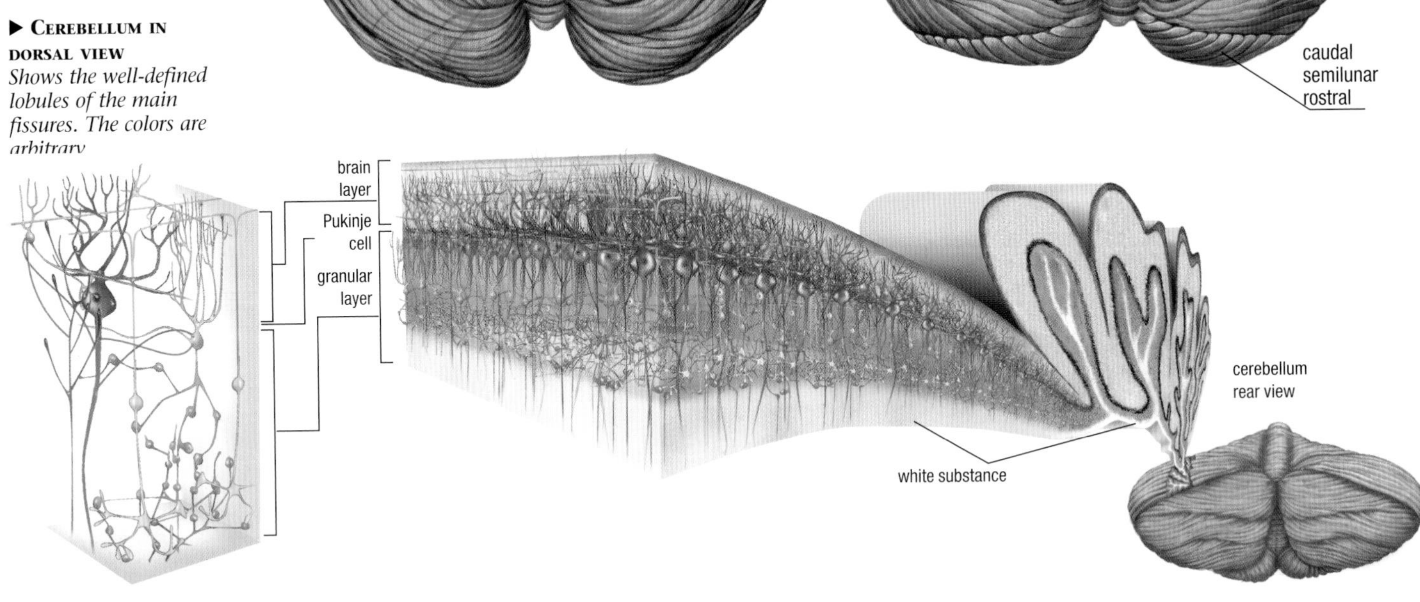

▲ **Anatomy of the cerebellum**
It is a very ancient encephalic element from an evolutionary point of view: it controls the motor coordination and balance, allowing you to always feel the position that the body takes in space. With a rounded shape that resembles a miniature brain, it is separated into two bulbous lobes called cerebellar hemispheres by large central lobules called vermis. As in the brain, the cortex is folded into lamellae and is divided into an outer zone of the gray substance (composed of two distinct layers of neurons - molecular and granular - interspersed by the Purkinje cells) and white matter, composed of nerve ascending and descending fibers.

- *Purkinje cell*
- *Golgi cells*
- *granular cells*
- *stellate cells*
- *basket cells*
- *ascending fibers*
- *parallel fibers*

balance. There are also many other receptors - these are involved such diverse functions as the control of hunger and the drive to eat, and the levels of aggression.

BALANCE, POSTURE & MOTOR SKILLS

There are many other functions that are governed by the brain beyond those we have just seen. These include the basic mobility skills that are acquired whilst growing and that are not lost unless it is as the result of injuries or particular diseases. The part of the brain that governs all of these activities is the cerebellum. From birth it grows much more quickly than the rest of the brain and, within a couple of years, quickly reaches its maximum volume, which is around 11% of the overall encephalic weight. The cerebellum has a very ordered and rigorous cell organisation that has no equal in the otherwise chaotic distribution of brain neurons. It corresponds to a centre of inhibitory actions, which is unique among all the encephalic structures. It never performs stimulating functions, and its cells do not get involved in the exchanges of information. Its role is mainly advisory - within a tenth of a second, the signals that are received by the cerebellum are examined, and if they do not correspond to a correct motor sequence, they are blocked.

The cerebellum actively performs the control of both involuntary and voluntary movements. Information continuously arrives from the cerebral motor cortex - this is derived from the spinal cord, the voluntary muscles and the organs the balance of the inner ear. Depending on the information that is received, the cerebellum modulates the nervous responses, keeping the body in balance in the chosen location or movement, according to stored schemas. Its sole task is the inhibition of signals - it allows certain muscular actions to be performed and blocks others. This produces a modulation effect, with some motor development activities being prioritised over others. Acting continuously on the knife edge of balance, the cerebellum locks or unlocks the muscles, continuously maintaining the control of each tiny movement. In this way, the human body - which is fundamentally imbalanced, manages to stay upright and stable.
It acts the same way on voluntary movements: impulses from the cerebral motor cortex (left cerebral hemisphere ▸189) take a 15th of a second to reach the brain stem. While some continue towards the effector organs (voluntary muscles), others are diverted towards the right hemisphere of the cerebellum. During the time in which muscles begin to act, it quickly compares the motor sequence with the stored database. It determines whether the right action is being performed and alters the

impulses in accordance with the data. This is then sent to the muscles as modulated brain impulses. While this is happening, however, further signals are received from the relevant muscle receptors providing information on the progress of the movement, as well as from the balance sensors. These give sensitive descriptions of the amplitude, speed and direction of the motion, and are quickly returned through the spinal cord to a group of cells in the brain stem. These enable the cerebellum to continue intervening, all the while comparing the information it receives with the stored data bank and making whatever adjustments it deems necessary.

THE HIGHER ACTIVITIES

THE LIMBIC SYSTEM: MOOD AND EMOTIONS

The limbic system is a set of encephalic structures that surrounds the thalamus and forms the inner border of the cortex. It has a key role in the emotional feelings and mood. In addition to this, it also makes a crucial contribution to the mechanisms of learning and memory.

One of the limbic system's most significant structures is the amygdala. This controls such behavioural aspects as 'fight or flight' and the instincts involved in mating. The upper region has a prominent role in expressive behaviour and the emotive states that promote social integration. When the amygdala are stimulated, there may be reactions of anger, agitation, anxiety or excitement, but also sexual interest, as well as rich visions of colour, deep thoughts and relaxation.

These emotions, however, are the result of the interactions between the limbic system, the cerebral cortex, and the bodies that produce specific physical modifications. The relationship between the limbic system and the cerebral cortex is direct, and the emotions can be influenced by reason or memory, likewise, reason and memory can be influenced by emotions.

The limbic system, in addition, filters information arriving from the body before moving it to higher levels of processing. The things that the mind perceives are amended by this part of the brain according to mood and environmental conditions. The emotions can also distort the perception of the world to such an extreme that it can make an individual lose touch with reality. While it is possible to consciously recognise emotions, the reactions to them tend to be completely involuntary. Fear, for example, speeds up the heart rate - this may

▼ Encephalic main elements and their relations

The brain is often divided into three functional parts and basic anatomy, which are covered at three levels of evolutionary development. The brainstem includes ❶ a stretched cord, ❷ bulb ❸ and the cerebellum, it is the most archaic part of the brain, the oldest in evolutionary terms: it regulates the activities of varying complexity. The midbrain, more evolved, is attached to the top of ❹ brainstem, while the prosencephalon is the most advanced of the central nervous system: the cerebral hemispheres ❺, ❻, the thalamus, the hypothalamus ❼ and ❽, the limbic system. The eyes are to represent the great number of endings and sensitive sense organs that collect information to be sent to the brain.

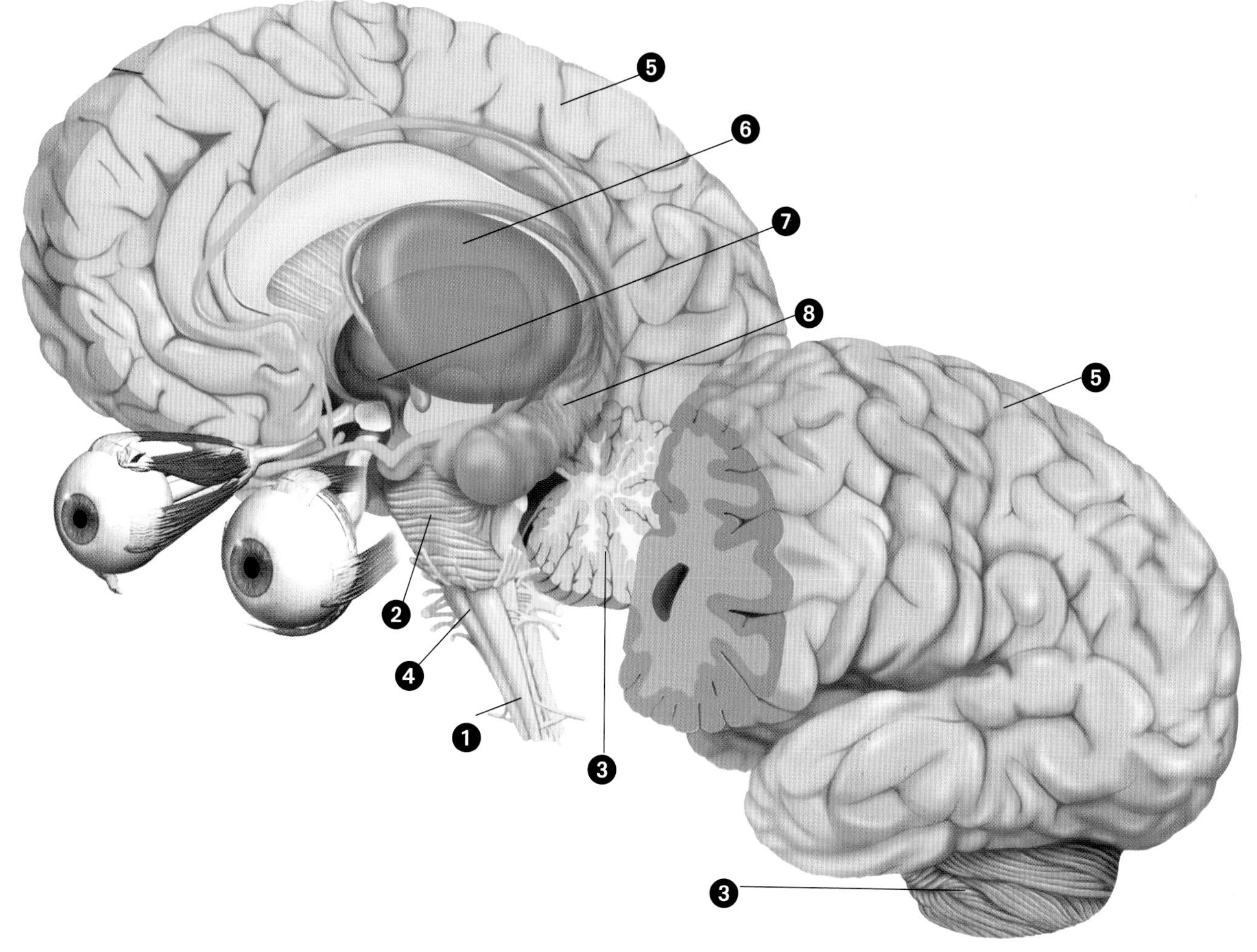

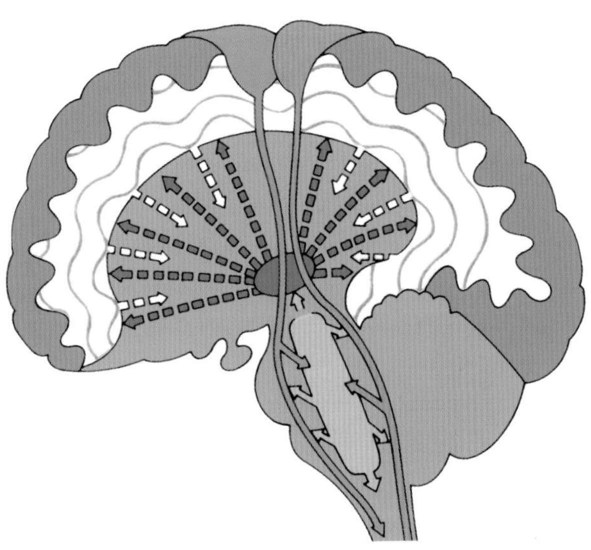

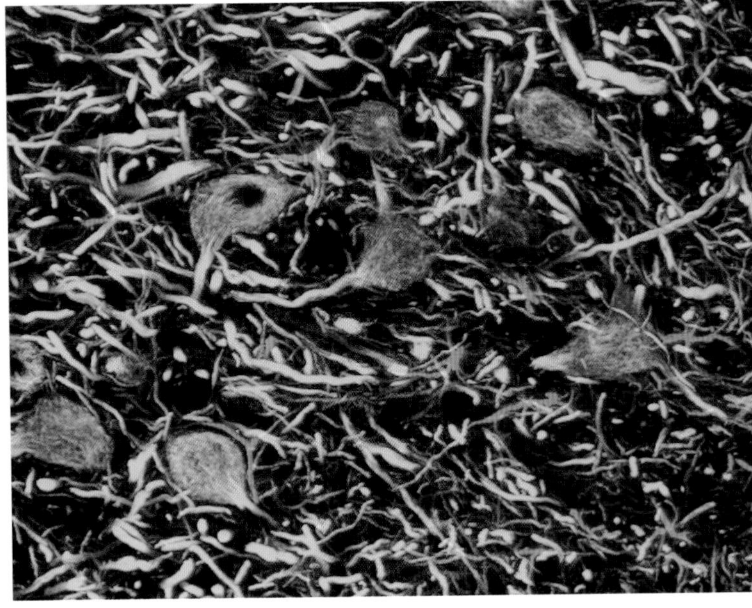

▲ **INTERTWINED PATHS**
The information coming to the brain through the various systems.

The sensory pathways.
The reticular activating system: the heart of the brainstem, which corresponds to the reticular formation, it stimulates the activity and monitors for the entire cerebral cortex.
The cerebral cortex in which sensory messages arrive, and from where they are parsed.
The motor output pathways are derivations in the reticular system which actively interact with the incoming information before moving on to the spinal cord.
The limbic system integrates media and messages to and from the reticular activating system, as well as parts of the cerebral cortex.
Parts of the cerebral cortex which are not directly affected by the stimuli.

▲▶ **CELLS IN THE BRAINSTEM**
Confocal microscopy photograph of some neurons (the cytoskeleton is green) and glial cells (red) brainstem.

be because of enjoyment, a sudden surprise, or as a strong fear. It is no coincidence that when psychologists measure the emotions, they take into consideration quantifiable somatic parameters such as the heart rate and pace of breathing as well as the electrical resistance of the skin.

THE BRAIN: PROCESSING THE DATA MEMORY & HIGHER ACTIVITIES

The brain represents the primary processing centre, and is the point of collection and analysis of all the information from both inside and outside the body. It performs many functions, with the main ones being the processing, analysis and comparison of information. Fundamental to this is the involvement of the memory and the transformation of feelings. The outcome from this is the development of thoughts and decisions as well as the physical or chemical reactions that co-ordinate each vital event and establish overall mental health. This activity is always happening, even while the person concerned is asleep. While it only comprises 2% of the body weight, the brain consumes 20% of the oxygen in circulation, thanks to a dense network of blood that maintains its high metabolic activity.
The brain is divided into two hemispheres ▸225, each of which controls the other side of the body. That is, the right side of the brain processes the information from the left side of the body, and vice versa. In each hemisphere, however, there are several areas that perform similar functions as well as areas that are intended to supervise different roles. In both the right and left sides, for example, there are areas of the cerebral cortex that handle the dexterity responses (the motor cortex), while the control of language is situated almost exclusively in the left side. In addition, the way in which the information is processed varies according to the brain region involved; in the cortex for example, there are:

– primary processing areas: this is where the initial analysis of information from body receptors occurs. Each stimulus collected by a sense organ is processed in this specific primary area. This is often organised according to a precise topography ▸188. The information, therefore, is processed in an orderly manner. In the case of sounds, for example, sensory inputs are processed according to the tone of the sound perceived in a tonal map. Similarly, two adjacent neurons will process the information from two positions that are adjacent in the body or in space;
– secondary processing areas: this is where the information is subjected to a more complex and multi-faceted analysis; it takes inputs and compares them with data that is present in the memory;
– associative areas ▸191: this is where information that arrives from different brain areas is associated in a way that helps develop an overall interpretation of the perceived stimuli. This is needed in order to produce an appropriate response.

THE CEREBRAL CORTEX

The cerebral cortex is the most complex part of the brain. It consists of approximately 8 billion neurons packed into a layer that is only a few centimetres thick, and is folded in many convolutions. It is not homogeneous functionally, but it is possible to distinguish between neuronal centres performing different tasks. It is divided into areas that undertake functions for specific anatomical locations, although

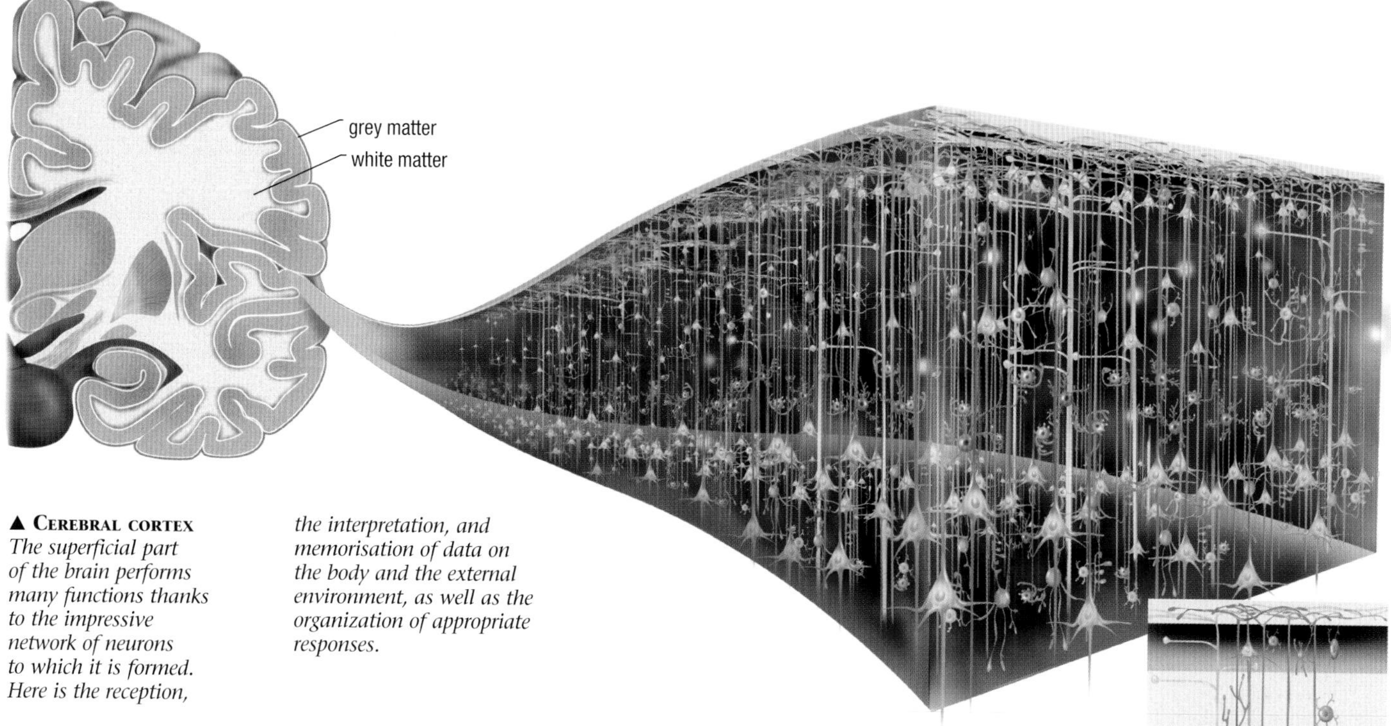

▲ **Cerebral cortex** *The superficial part of the brain performs many functions thanks to the impressive network of neurons to which it is formed. Here is the reception, the interpretation, and memorisation of data on the body and the external environment, as well as the organization of appropriate responses.*

there is still dispute among researchers as to exactly what roles some of them play.

THE FRONTAL LOBES: PERSONALITY AND VOLUNTARY MOVEMENTS

It is thought that the frontal lobes control most of the personality and voluntary movements. They form the part of the brain that deals with the higher mental activities. While the cerebral cortex defines the various aspects that together make each person a unique individual, the frontal lobes constitute the wider area of the brain. They are particularly well developed in the human species, and is where the neuronal centres that govern the activities of judgement and programming are found. These make it possible to develop concepts and edit them on the basis of information that is stored in the memory as well as that which comes from other areas of the brain. The frontal lobes are therefore the specialised centres of organisation and the control of movements. The primary motor cortex includes cells that are organised along topographical lines. This is the part of the brain that develops and sends the signals that are intended to produce the voluntary movements of the different muscle groups.

THE PARIETAL LOBES: BASIC INFORMATION & FEELINGS

The parietal lobes are where the processing centres of the primary somatic and sensory information are found. That is the signals from the skin, muscles, joints and internal organs. They are part of the cortex, that is the part of the brain that collects the stimuli coming from the periphery body, and organises them according to a precise topography. Once it has been properly interpreted, this information is then transmitted to the processing centres for the drafting of an appropriate response.

THE TEMPORAL LOBES: HEARING, LANGUAGE & CLASSIFICATION

The temporal lobes organise the signals that have been collected by the organs of hearing and sent to the brain through the auditory nerves. These are composed of 30,000 different fibres, each of which carries its own sound message. It is where the centres which process the primary aural information are found. These are in cortical layers, and they take the various frequencies and separate them into different categories. Those sounds which cannot be attributed to an encoded reference scheme are deemed to be of no value and are discarded. To give a meaning to the huge mass of sounds as they arrive,

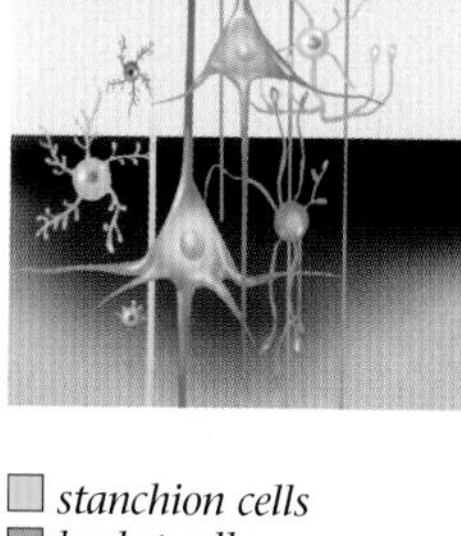

stanchion cells
basket cells
large basket cells
stellate cells
pyramidal neurons

FEATURES OF THE CEREBRAL CORTEX

AREA	FUNCTIONS
Prefrontal	Problem solving, emotions, complex thoughts
Associative motor	Coordinating complex movements
Primary motor	Initiation of voluntary movements
Primary somatosensation	Reception of tactile information from the body
Associative sensory	Multi-information processing
Associative visual	Processing of complex visual information
Visual	Detection of simple visual stimuli
Wernicke	Understanding of language
Associative auditory	Processing of complex auditory information
Auditory	Detection of sound quality (intensity, tone)
Broca or center of language	Production and articulation of words

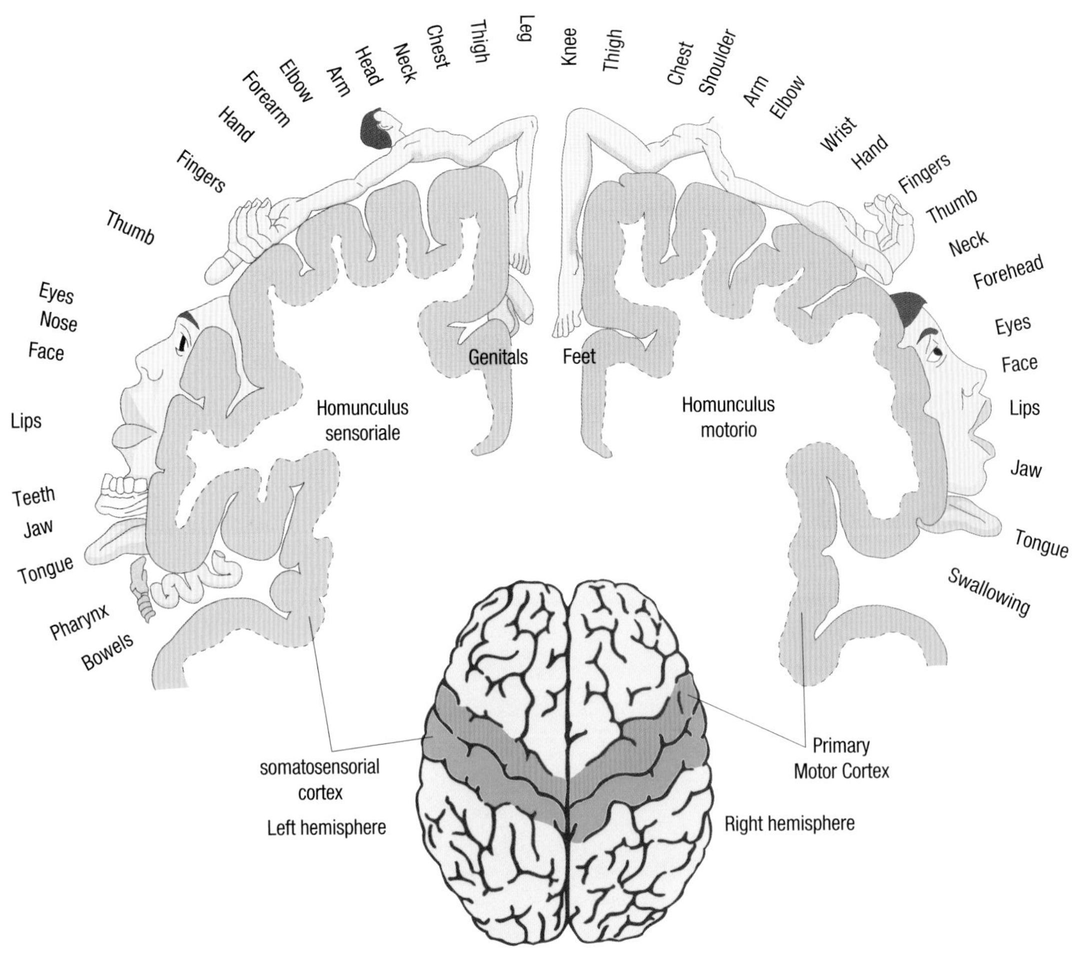

▶ **Functional differences**
Primary motor cortex (right), somatosensorial trunk (left) and topographic location of the main bodies supervised by these areas of the two cerebral hemispheres.

the brain stores information in millions of nerve circuits. This information is not only composed of noise, but also in visual, tactile and olfactory form. It accumulates in the auditory memory from birth, and by adulthood, the average person can identify nearly half a million different signals.

THE OCCIPITAL LOBES: THE VIEW

The occipital lobes are where the centres that handle the primary visual information are found. This arrives from the eyes through bundles of nerves which meet on the lower part of the brain (the optical intersection). Each signal is produced by photosensitive areas of the retina which is then sent to the occipital lobes where it is interpreted and codified. After this, they are sent to the parietal and temporal lobes for secondary processing. Here the images are interpreted on the basis of comparison with stored information. It is where optical illusions are created. If the images are ambiguous or conflicting, the brain can alter them so that they are perceived in a manner that is completely different from the actual reality. Some pictures, for example, appear to be moving when they are not. Others appear to deform as the result of the brain trying to impose a non-existent perspective on them. Yet others appear to be three-dimensional when in reality they are not, and so on. The occipital lobes not only undertake cerebral reprocessing but are also involved in the interpretation of colours, nuances, contrasts, grey areas and brightness. They adapt visual information to match that which has been stored and tested. Viewing an object is not like making a photograph. It is recognised it on the basis of previous experiences that may not be exclusively visual, but can also involve many other aspects of the brain and sensory signals.

THE INTERIOR OF THE BRAIN

In addition to the structures that have already been discussed - that is, the ones that are involved in the control of vital automatic functions, other internal areas co-operate with the brain to process information and form the most appropriate responses:

- the geniculate ganglions are a group of sensory neurons that send visual stimuli to the primary areas of the occipital lobes;
- the structures of the mesencephalic nucleus are part of the visual and auditory systems and are involved mainly in the reflexes and quick responses produced by the stimulation of movement;

A

B

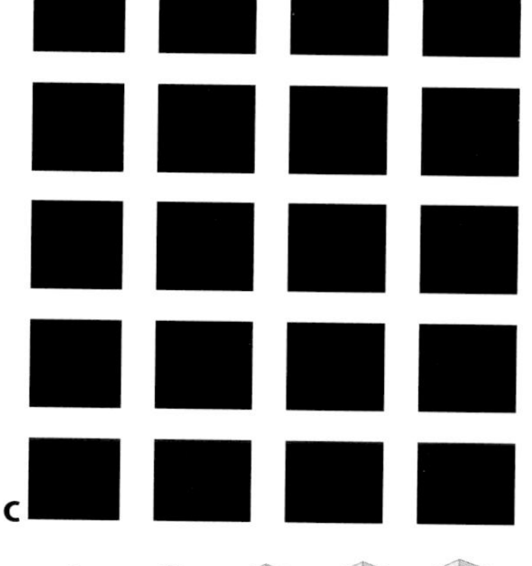
C

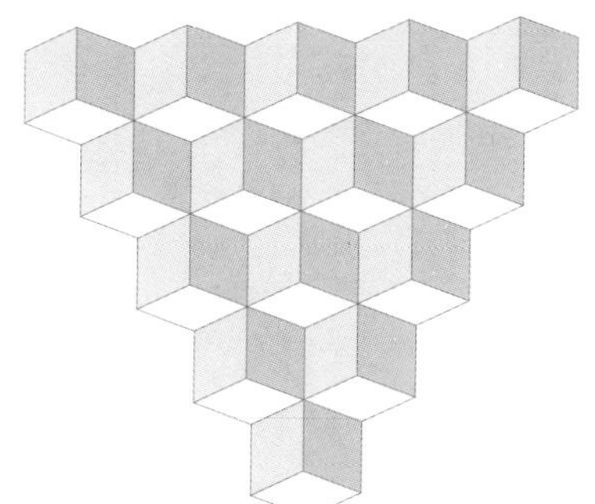
D

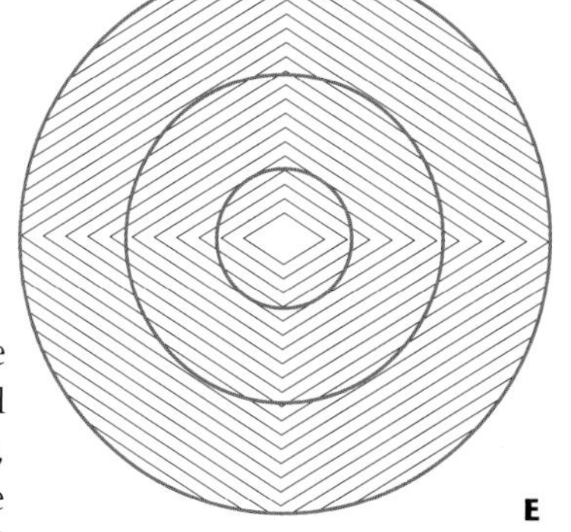
E

► **Optical illusion**
A. *The circular area in the center is made up of bars that are perpendicular to the background and seem to move in relation to what surrounds it, especially if you move. It is believed that the circular contour sends an ambiguous signal to the brain when it meets the vertical bars: the brain fails to integrate the image as if it were something unique. The movements of the eye, therefore, do not lead to a single image, but are interpreted as the successive images of an object in motion.*
B. *The green squares appear brighter if they are in contrast with the yellow (left) rather than the blue (right): in reality there is no difference. In this case the perception of color is affected by the information coming from the surrounding areas. It is likely that this is caused by development of neuronal activity in the retina.*
C. *The intersections between the white lines appear gray where they are not: the effect is related to peripheral vision of the retina that has a priority to recognize shapes and edges of a figure: at a crossroads, the extended space provokes an effect of lateral inhibition that reduces the brightness.*
D. *The Necker cubes are a "conceptual" optical illusion: the figure can be seen as if it "exits" from the page or sinks in the opposite direction. Wrestling with two equivalent interpretations, often the brain switches from one to the other without knowing which to choose.*
E. *Although they appear deformed, the concentric circles are perfect from a geometrical point of view and the lines are straight. In this case, the brain tries to reconstruct a perspective that is not there, interpreting the image as having depth.*

- the grey matter surrounding the aqueduct is involved in the perception of pain;
– the substantia nigra is a substance that is located in the midbrain and involved in the monitoring of muscle movements as well as playing an important role in reward and addiction.

LEFT & RIGHT HEMISPHERES

The two hemispheres of the brain do not play identical functions and, according to the type of function, predominate on one side over the other. For example, the left hemisphere is dominant over the right – that is, it works harder. This is in regard to language, the analysis of details, and the sequences of symbolic reasoning. the right hemisphere, however, is dominant over the left as regards the analysis of spatial patterns, the performance of geometric designs, the recognition of the faces, or the analysis of music. In addition, each of these supervise the activities of the opposite side of the body. Schematically, the left hemisphere is the logical part of the brain, while the right is the creative side. As ever though, things are not that simple. The studies of the consequences of brain injuries have made it possible to allocate to each cortical area a specific function, but also to identify some unilateral areas (i.e. present in only one hemisphere) whose lesion determines a total loss of function. At the same time, however, the same studies have shown that some functions can be redistributed to uninjured parts of the brain with no loss of capacity.
A clear example of brain dominance is shown in the example of the use of the hands: About 90% of humans prefer to use the right hand over the left for handling purposes as well as for writing. This is found in every human group and in every culture, this feature is connected to the area of the brain that manages the drafting of language and that, in almost all cases, is situated in left side.
From the point of view of locomotor activation, putting the control in the left hemisphere allows the movements of the right hand to be more immediate than those of the left. However, people who have suffered an injury to the left hemisphere are able, with time, to refine the mobility of the left hand until it fully replaces the right.

DOMINANT FUNCTIONS IN THE LEFT HEMISPHERE

In addition to the brain's language centres in the left hemisphere, there are the centres that govern the recognition of visual images and conceptual words, groups of words, phrases and numbers. It is also where logical capacity and mathematical aptitude are based, in addition to the ability to develop the mass of information in specific words and actions as well as the thoughts that flow to the brain. Tests that examine vocabulary, verbal understanding or calculation are resolved mainly by the cortical centres in the left hemisphere, and are assisted by the centres of memory. Those individuals who are injured in these brain areas often lose the ability to speak, to write with the right hand, and to recognise words.

DOMINANT FUNCTIONS IN THE RIGHT HEMISPHERE

At one time, it was thought that the right hemisphere had functions which were less relevant and numerous than those of the left. Studies have since shown that this is not true, even if the operation of these brain areas is quite different from that typical of the left hemisphere. In fact, while the information that reaches the left hemisphere is processed in an analytical way and uses schematic-conceptual logical, that which arrives in the right side are addressed in different manner. This involves global processing using perceptive-space, and then integrated, so as to make sense of them as a coherent whole. This process is particularly suited to background information such as that which comes from visual sources. This includes shapes, colours, sizes, geometries and spatial orientation. With contributions from the memory, the right brain centres allow us to remember the way home, recognise a face, draw objects or learn a musical melody.

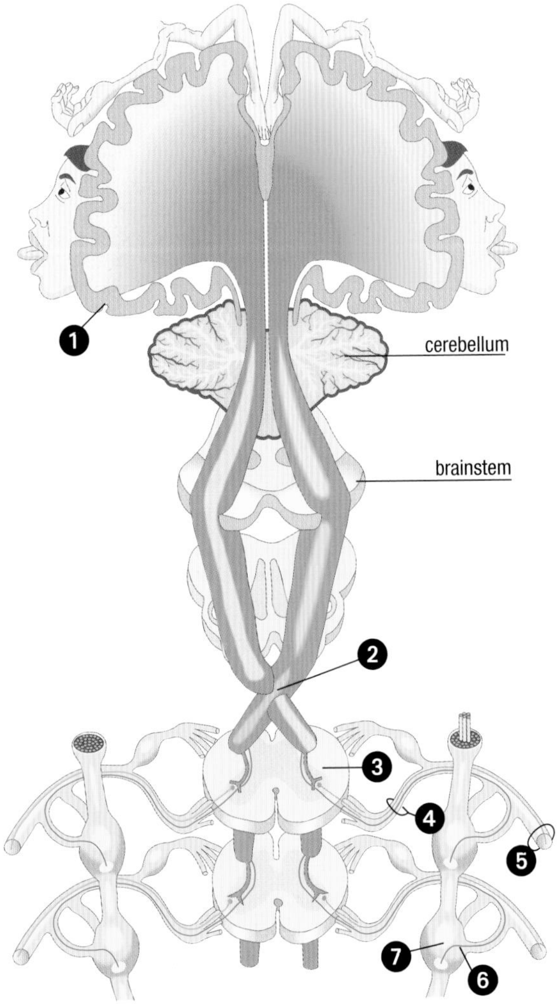

▶ **Intertwined**
The motor cortex ❶ produces pulses that pass through the brainstem along bundles of nerve fibers that cross in the Medulla Oblongata ❷ into the spinal cord ❸. Here, the motor spinal roots make up ❹ and the spinal nerves ❺ that transmit impulses to the muscles. The involuntary movements are controlled by the fibers of the autonomous system ❻, which passes from the spinal ganglia ❼.

1
cerebellum
brainstem
2
3
4
5
7
6

A PERFECT BALANCE

An example of how the two hemispheres co-operate by continuously integrating with each other comes from those patients where the neuronal bridge linking the two halves of the brain has been severed. In these conditions, the unilateral specialised functions remain isolated and the person shows two separate mental structures. Logic, words and analytical matters dominate the left side, whereas the right shows perceptual and spatial capacity, as well as artistic ability.

Simple requests such as "bend the knee" can only be performed on the right side of the body, as it is managed by the left side which is the only one able to recognise the sentence. And vice-versa, if the person is shown a coloured light, only the right hemisphere is able to recognise the colour. The result is that although they are unable to indicate verbally what the colour is, they can point to an object of the same colour and so clearly recognise it. When asked for the name of the colour, the left hemisphere does not recognise it correctly, however, the right hemisphere spots the mistaken response and gives negative mimic signals, such as shaking the head. It does this until the left hemisphere tries again with a new colour. Despite the two sides being separate, the hemispheres therefore continue to interact by sending signals that refine the global responses.

At the same time, not all the faculties are confined to a specific area: the memory, for example. Although some circuits of the limbic system ▸169 will preside over the processes of formation of memories, it is not located in any specific area of the brain. Likewise, many of the other higher functions such as intelligence or creativity are not localised in specific neuronal centres either.

THE ASSOCIATION AREAS

Within a close proximity of the cortical areas where the nerves of conscious perception end are neuronal centres that are linked to primary sensory areas by a dense network of inter-cortical neurons. These analyse messages in the primary area, reworking them and comparing them with stored sensory experiences. It is where the impulses from other cortical areas arrive, including the thalamus, the limbic system and the nervous system.

DIFFERENT BRAINS

That the brains of men and women are slightly different anatomically is not a new idea, even though each time it is discussed it causes controversy. Too often, in fact, these evaluations were exploited in a clearly sexist manner to give a supposed scientific justification for prejudice and discrimination. Ever since the time of Adam and Eve, society has been encouraged to give women the role of domestic assistants. This is according to a dynamic similar to that which today is still used to justify the supremacy of one race over another, by highlighting the clear morphological differences between different groups of humans.

For example, if one examines the differences in the weight of the brain: on average, that of men is higher by 10-15% when compared to that of the female; this is the scientific data. Assuming that a lighter brain is also less intelligent has no proven basis in science. As an illustration of this, the brain of the great Russian writer Ivan Turgenev weighed more than 2kg, while that of the famous French writer Anatole France was only just over one kilo. Intelligence - namely the ability to learn, think, and resolve problems, understand the ideas and the language is linked to innate brain capacity.

Creativity is the ability to combine known elements through new connections to build something original. Expressing it requires more than just brain capacity, however. The brain's innate anatomical structure has to be combined with social interactions, learning, the use of abstract concepts and so on. Typically human, creativity depends on the possession of the ability to make subtle discriminations. These may be composed of words, but also of numbers, colours, of musical notes, geometric balances or physical structures. The higher features of the brain are a therefore a consequence of individual history and the environment in which the person concerned lives.

GENDER DIFFERENCES

Three major categories can be identified:

- genetic differences: These are evident in every cell: the double chromosome X is typical of the female, whereas males have an XY pair.
- structural or anatomical differences: there are differences in brain architecture that have direct consequences on the functioning and development of the brain throughout life.

In general, it may be said that the male brain is heavier, occupies a larger volume and contains a greater amount of brain fluid, something that, with ageing, brings to about a faster shrinking. Furthermore, the percentage of grey matter is smaller and that of the white matter is greater than those of women, which show more developed frontal lobes, and more blood supply. This part of brain oversees behaviour, the mnemonic processes in the short term, and the planning and critical evaluation of the procedures and decisions needed to achieve a goal. The female brain is therefore more closely linked with the areas of emotion 205. This influences the decision-making process, with the logical reasoning between possible solutions often being overridden by emotions that produce less advantageous results.

Therefore, it is more likely that a male's reasoning is sequential, with a close assessment of risks, and any rejection of a solution is arrived at only because the logic does not recommend the choice. A female on the other hand may take account of variables that are only quantifiable emotionally, and so reach an unexpected winning solution. The female brain has a larger number of fibres which bind the hemispheres together. This may be the cause of the differences in the ways that the genders think. If hemispheres are more closely connected, the mental processing of logic (typical of the left hemisphere) and creativity (more linked with the activity of the right) will be altered. At the same time, the ability to reason in parallel (typical of the right hemisphere) will have a greater influence on the development of decisions (activity linked to the left side).

▲ **Brain pathways**
Three-dimensional magnetic resonance image of white matter of the brain seen in left profile. The white matter is composed of myelin nerve fibers carrying information to and from the brain (corresponding to the upper half of image) through the spinal cord (center bottom). The blue shows the neural pathways that go from top to bottom, the green ones that go from the front (left) to the back (right), the red connect the two cerebral hemispheres.

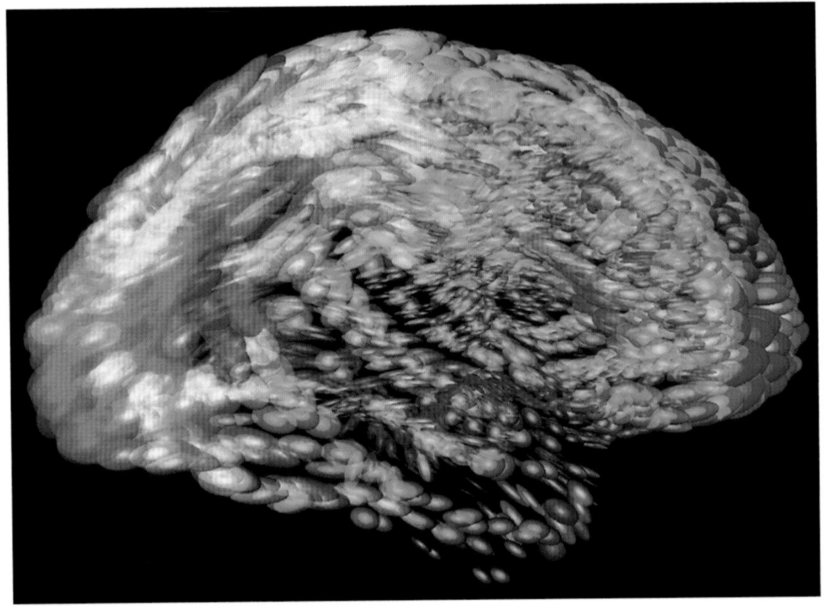

▲ **Variations**
Three-dimensional image composed of 20 overlapping magnetic resonance images in false colors of a healthy brain to highlight areas difference. On the front left, are the centers of the personality that show the greatest degree of variability. The spectrum of variability shows, from pink (high values) to green (average values) to blue (zero). The areas that control the basic functions show the lowest values of variability.

Females might therefore be more intuitive than males, due to the parallel reasoning of the right brain influencing the sequential logic of the left hemisphere. Faced with complex situations, the search for solutions would have an advantage from the less rigid functioning of the brain, leading to women analysing a broader spectrum of variables. For the same reason, the processing of the male brain would be on average more logical, as well as less complex and creative. It follows standard schemas that are proven and reliable, and as well as simplifying situations, males would reach solutions that were less innovative, but faster;

- hormonal and biological differences: the hypothalamus ▸179 and pituitary glands ▸233 regulate general endocrine activity. These differences underlie the physiological ones: the oestrogens, for example, help in the fight against cardiovascular diseases, ensuring that veins and arteries in the female start to harden more quickly than those of males. This allows a better and more lasting oxygenation of the brain and prevents premature ageing. Sex hormones also act on the brain, creating functional and behavioural differences.

COMPLEMENTARY BRAINS

Although the brain differences in the genders affect the strategies of problem solving, organisation of thought and operational creativity, they do not prevent males and females from reaching equal levels of intelligence. Moreover it is likely that the different capacities have evolved to be complementary. For example, having better skills in dealing with more activities at the same time - as found in the typical female brain, would favour the multi-tasking required during child rearing. At the same time the logical brain of the male would be better suited to the requirements of defence and hunting. Often research that highlights the differences is rejected as having poor conclusions and unreliable results. For example: the widespread belief that females have better verbal ability to males is rebutted by hundreds of vocabulary, understanding and reading tests. Likewise, contrary to what is often believed, males and females are equally good in orientation, but follow different paths. Females are generally better at remembering the points of reference, but the males score on their geometric capacity to assess directions and distances. The prejudices therefore continue, and there is still much to discover.

Mirror neurons

Our minds interpret sensations we receive from other individuals and we react to them, in doing so, our brains act as a bridge between ourselves and the people around us. Exactly how this happens though is still not fully understood. Recent advances in the study of neurology, however, have led to the discovery of a particular type of neuron that could be the basis of such innate behaviour.

The initial discoveries were made by researchers at the University of Parma, in Italy. These concerned investigations into the brain of the macaque monkey, and centred around small cells called mirror neurons. These have since also been found in humans, but gaining a full understanding of their functioning is still a long way off. It is thought that they are distributed throughout the brain, and that they are particularly prevalent in the areas that deal with linguistics and other forms of communication ▸230.

Although the primary role of these neurons appears to be to interpret and understand the actions of others, emotional behaviour is so complex that it requires more than just the recognition of a biophysical event. In monkeys, for example, it appears that the activation of mirror neurons leads to an immediate understanding of the intention behind the observed action. This has yet to be fully proven, however. The activation of mirror neurons, therefore, seems to be the neuronal basis that allows further developments of the understanding of observed behaviour, and the intentions that produced it.

The accumulation of experience therefore allows individuals to understand the actions of others without the need for an explicit or conscious communication. This helps people to develop the ability to imitate what they see around them, and is the biological basis of much of human culture. The facility to characterise many animals and, in particular, children represents a primary form of learning, and is an important component in social aggregation.

The key areas within the brain that deal with language feature enormous numbers of mirror neurons. It is thought that the process of learning a language is assisted by these cells. The recognition of spoken words, the comprehension of their full meaning, the understanding of the intentions with which they are used, and their emotion significance may well be based on this mechanism. Mirror neurons therefore use the mechanisms of spoken language and / or simple observation to create a link between a person and those that surround them, whether or not any emotional content is merely a nuance or at the heart of the action.

It is in this manner that other people are able to be accepted into wider social circles. The closest unit is that of the family. Beyond this are streets, villages, cities and nations. Humans can often also empathise well with different species - many pet owners, for instance, are able to interpret the behaviour of their dogs and cats. According to some authors, the link between our actions and those of the other individuals around us may be the basis of altruistic actions, and would therefore represent the biological basis of all ethical behaviour. Individual selfishness, therefore, would be considered unnatural, and against many of the currently accepted psychological and economic theories. According to the physiology of mirror neurons, the happiness of others gives happiness to the observer, and likewise, unhappiness generates further unhappiness. The hypothesis is that such reciprocity therefore connects individuals to those around them, and that the desire for communal happiness is a prevailing natural condition. Not all scientists agree with this optimistic interpretation, however, and much work remains to be done to find the correct answer.

Most people find it possible to empathise with someone who is suffering, but this does not necessarily mean that they want to impose any mirror suffering on themselves. The activity of mirror neurons means that individuals can try to understand what a person is experiencing, however, the next stage is to then try and interpret the information using a combination of conscious thought and past experience. Empathy and sympathy are two distinct processes and while the first is physiological, the second is mental.

The Case Of Autistic Patients

It was then discovered that in autistic patients - especially in children, that mirror neurons do not work equally well in the healthy. It is not yet clear whether this is the physiological basis of the disease, or one of many disorders it is related to, but this would explain why these patients fail to understand the world and people that surround them. Without the brokering of mirror neurons, indeed, you may imagine that the actions of others might appear totally incomprehensible. Crying, laughter, dancing - everything appears alien. If mirror neurons are proven to be the cause of autism, it would open up new avenues for treatment and therefore raise hopes for a cure.

LANGUAGE

From an anatomical point of view there are two language centres in the brain:

- Broca's area, which is located in the left frontal lobe, and presides over the functions of language, including controlling the muscles of the mouth, tongue and pharynx 92. It is involved in the preparation of syntactical processes: it processes the sounds of words regardless of their meaning. Distinctions between the sound of a word and its meaning are, in fact, purely conventional, and symbolic.
- Wernicke's area, which is located in the left cerebral hemisphere, integrates visual forms of information flows, as well as sounds, body sensations and spatial relationships. Wernicke's area stores links between words and the shape or geometry which characterises it.. It represents the language processing centre. It organises phrases and speeches on the basis of stored information, and identifies the meaning of words and their correct use in grammar and syntax. The signals produced are sent through the area of Broca which then transforms them into impulses that lead to the production of articulated sounds.

It is thought that the development of the links between the areas of Broca and Wernicke could be the basis of the development of concepts related to words. These anatomical elements, however, are not the only brain areas involved in language. Others, for example, include the Sylvian fissure (which is in the region prior to the central sulcus or Rolandic fissure), as well as the left sector of the rear cerebral cortex. These and the temporal lobe act as nerve centres which, in close association with cerebellum, work together to control the pace and the grammar of spoken language. The cerebellum and other areas involved in the use of language receive stimuli from many sensory regions of the cortex, and these are processed and the results returned to different dexterity areas. Speech, in fact, requires the co-operation of many different cortical areas with different skills. If a person hears a word for example, their primary auditory cortex is enabled, and this receives the sensory information from the ear. On its own, however, this is not useful - there is no understanding of the meaning of the word without Wernicke area's being activated.

Conversely, if the person wants to say a word, Wernicke's area has to activate and then prepare the first representative impulses of the desired word and transmit them then to Broca's area. Here the signals initiate a detailed locomotor programme that, in turn, produces all the necessary signals to activate the muscles of the facial region (lips, tongue, palate, larynx...) that are required to articulate the word. When a word is read from, for example, a book, the information initially comes from the primary visual cortex, and this is then processed in the gyrus, before being passed to Wernicke area's where it is treated in a similar manner to auditory information.

Language processing then depends on a wide range of connections between the temporal cortex, and the front parietal region, within the framework of the organisation of behaviour and motor sequence, as well as the co-ordination of the short-term memory that is involved in the processing of immediate knowledge.

The Origins Of Language

The evidence of palaeontological and recent genetic discoveries about brain elements and the anatomy necessary for language suggests that human brains have had Broca's and Wernicke's areas for less than 2 million years. Further to this, it seems that the apparatus required for modern speech 92 only evolved some 300,000 years ago and that some genes involved in the articulation of language have only existed for around 200,000 years. These features are required because the brain needs a constant and rich bloodstream to be able to perform the functions of linguistic articulation. Without them, speech is not possible. It is also known that many nerve centres must be activated in order for the necessary speech processing to take place. In particular, the voice, namely the issue of sounds with predetermined tone, frequency and duration, is generated by stimulating and controlling the positions of the lips, tongue and jaw. As this system is only present in humans, it can therefore be said that complex language is a recent development that is exclusive to the species.

According to some scholars, however, a pre-linguistic condition and precognitive independent thought must

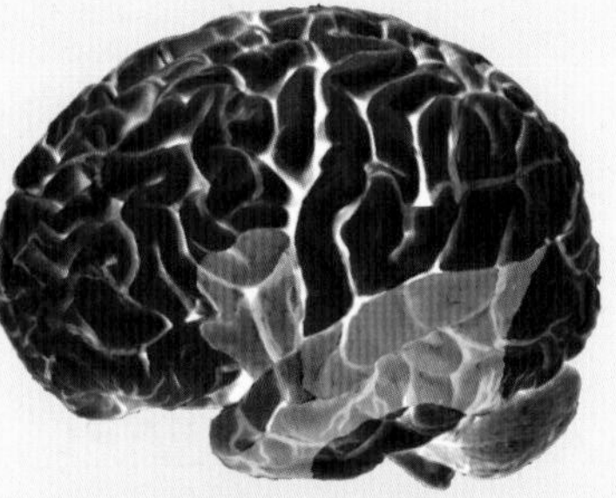

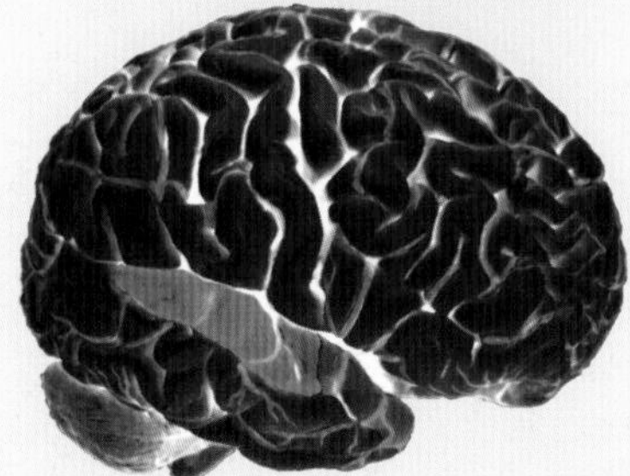

◀ **Known language**
Positron emission tomography (PET) superimposed on an MRI showing areas of the brain that are active while listening to known speech. Above is shown the left hemisphere, which is under the right eye. The red and green areas of the temporal lobe are hearing, and the yellow area in the left is the temporal lobe tah operates on well-known words, the pink area in the frontal lobe is the Broca area, which manages the production of language.

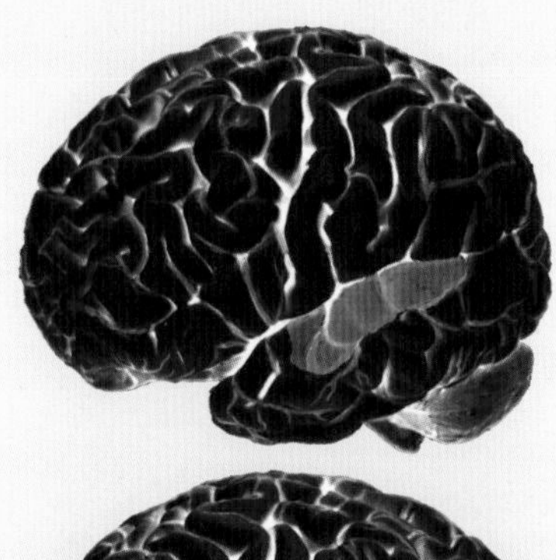

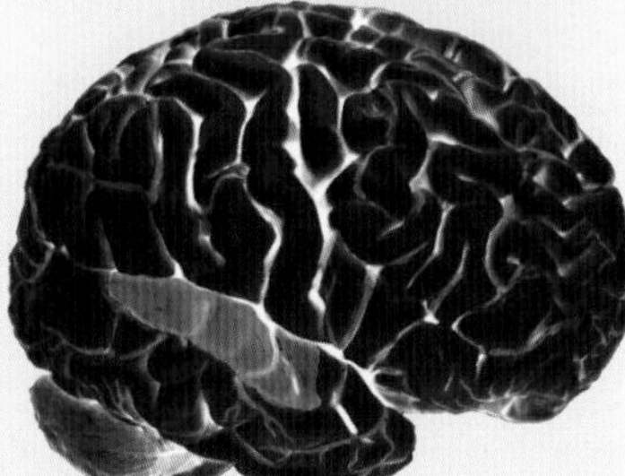

◀ **Unknown language**
Positron emission tomography (PET) superimposed on an MRI showing areas of the brain that are active while listening to an unknown spoken language (the left hemisphere is above, and the right is below). The red area in the temporal lobe is the auditory areas, which the brain does not use for understanding and producing language.

◀ Left profile of the brain
Divided into lobes (frontal = red, blue = temporal, parietal = orange; occipital = green) this shows a computer reconstruction of the two white cerebral centers of language, reading or areas involved in the recognition of an auditory message, to the understanding and composition of sentences. The most frontal is the area of Broca, the other is the area of Wernicke. Yellow in the cerebellum and the brainstem red.

▶ Production of language
Positron emission tomography (PET) in false colors of brain activity during language production. The words are produced from thoughts of sounds: this in the right hemisphere where the active parts (in red/orange) of the frontal cortex have stimulated the involvement of the temporal cortex in the bottom right, the area of memory storage.

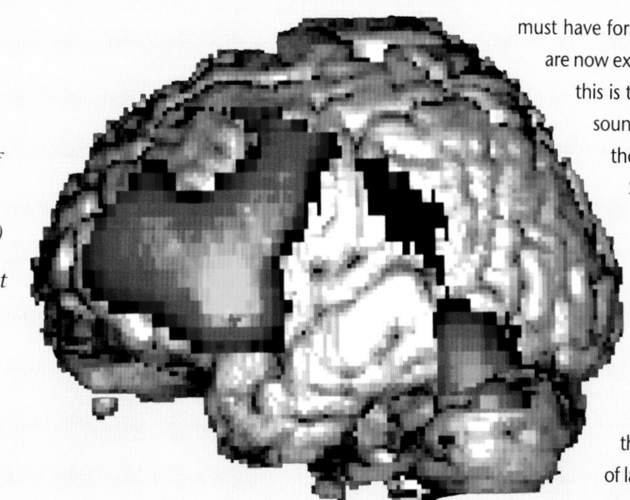

have been present in early hominids. Before they were able to speak, they had to have developed the capacity to conceptualise and co-ordinate their brain activity in the necessary manner. An anatomically important step was the establishment of close connections between the internal pre-Rolandic cortex regions, and then for these to be linked to other cortical areas. It is thought that the Wernicke area arose from an associative area where some sensory information sourced a phonetic correlation. Evolution then led to these stimuli being passed to Broca's area, and gradually the ability to organise phonetic data triggered the development of an operational circuit that could process information. This later grew to include combining memories with a precise and complex vocalisation store. In this way a sophisticated mnemonic system developed that was capable of processing complex pre-syntactic phonemes. The recent discovery of mirror neurons that are active in Broca's area seems to validate the idea of the presence of a true precursor to language. Mirror neurons 229 could therefore be the first neuronal requirement for communication between multiple individuals and the development of a coherent language.

According to this hypothesis, the specialisation of Broca's area would result from an ancient mechanism that was linked to the generation and understanding of actions that were mediated by the mirror neurons. The ability to perform and interpret automatically without mediated movements of the mouth and hands for communication, could have provided the necessary impetus for the development of language between the first men.

Sounds, Language, Thought

Many sounds are present in the language of all peoples: according to a recent survey, children learn to use them by natural predisposition, not for imitation. Sounds like DA-DA , TA-TA , NA-NA , MA-MA , PA-PA... ARE the same everywhere, and many scholars believe that the linguistic structure of child's speech is similar to what must have formed the proto-languages that are now extinct. A good demonstration of this is the fact that the most frequent sounds in the present languages are those that children can say easily. Some children are especially good at learning languages, and can assimilate any language in very short time.

It is thought that the evolution of the linkages between the areas of the brain that are required for the purposes of language have also allowed the emergence of deeper intellectual capabilities such as abstract thought. Indeed, for communication to work properly, it is first necessary to be able to form judgements, to classify the comments in categories, and to extend concepts from experience. For this, language is crucial, and it makes it easier to categorise and manage knowledge in a logical manner.

1A 1B 2A 2B

▲ Use of hands and language
These four positron emission tomography (PET) images show areas of the brain that are active during recognition of words in a right-handed (1A, left hemisphere, and 1B, right hemisphere) and a left-handed (2A, left hemisphere, and 2B, right hemisphere) person. In both cases, the brain activity is shown by the colors red/yellow. The person has to think of a verb associated with the name they heard: in the right-handed brain, activity is widely distributed in the frontal and temporal and parietal areas, in the left-handed, the areas are approximately corresponding to the right hemisphere.

THE BRAIN NOT ONLY PLAYS A "POWER" ON THE ACTIONS OF THE BODY. IT IS ALSO THE MAIN INTERNAL GLAND, AND THROUGH THE PRODUCTION OF HORMONES, REGULATES THE BALANCE OF THE ENTIRE ENDOCRINE SYSTEM.

NEUROCHEMICAL CONTROL

In addition to producing the neurotransmitters necessary for the nervous system, the central nervous system also produces some of the hormones ▸200 that regulate the activity of the main endocrine glands ▸202. In this way, it helps keep the body's chemical systems under control. The encephalic structures that process the nervous impulses and chemical messages are the hypothalamus and the pituitary gland - these are located deep within the centre of the brain, and the latter is positioned in a bony structure called the sella turcica. There are two distinct parts, each with a different embryonic origin and function. These are the neuro pituitary glands and the transfer pituitary glands. The region between them is known as the intermediate lobe. The transfer pituitary glands are very small, and tend to disappear after puberty.

▼ ANATOMY OF THE PITUITARY
In the central image: the location of the pituitary gland in the "turkish saddle".
Below: view of the bottom of the brain from which hangs the pituitary. Immediately above the pituitary recognized the optic chiasm.

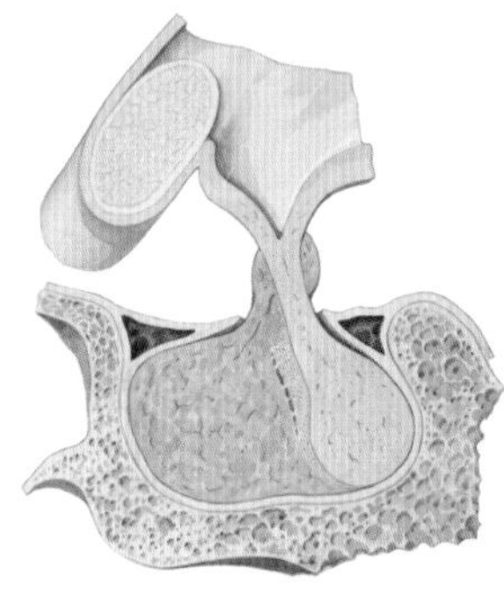

THE HYPOTHALAMUS

The hypothalamus is an encephalic structure that plays an important part in the control over many aspects of physiological activity. It adjusts the biorhythm and the temperature balance ▸142, as well as the basal metabolism and improves the synthesis and catabolism of proteins. It also stimulates the uptake of food and water via the feelings of hunger and thirst, and balances out the water budget ▸139. On top of all this, it responds to situations of stress, emergency and reproductive activity. These processes are regulated electrically, some through the central nervous system, others through the limbic system ▸169 or the cerebral cortex ▸187, by modulating the behaviour. General endocrine functions, however, are regulated through direct nervous control, or through the production of hormones ▸200, via the activities of the transfer pituitary glands or the neuro pituitary glands. In particular, the bodies of the neurons that form the supraoptic nucleus and paraventricular nucleus of the hypothalamus synthesise the anti-diuretic hormone ADH (also known as Arginine vasopressin or AVP), and oxytocin. Here, according to a process of exocytosis, they are released in the vicinity of blood vessels into which they are then absorbed. The key features are:

- The pituitary anti-diuretic hormone (ADH) or vasopressin is a modest vasoconstrictor that has an action that is produced mainly by neurons of the supraoptic core. It causes an increase in arterial pressure, and helps with the absorption of water in the distal tubes as well as in the collector ducts of the kidneys, thereby increasing body's the water content and reducing the concentration of urine ▸144. When the body loses control of the water balance, a condition called Diabetes insipidus can develop. This is characterised by an unquenchable thirst and the body eliminating large amounts of very diluted urine. The action of this hormone on the target cells is to make their membranes more permeable. This is closely linked with specific receptors, and the ADH then triggers a cascade of biochemical events that end with a merger between vesicles containing endocellular channels of acquaporin (a protein that facilitates the transfer of water) and the plasma membrane. The production of ADH is modulated by the supraoptic nucleus of the hypothalamus which is very sensitive to variations in the body's osmotic pressure .

- Oxytocin, this is mainly produced by the paraventricular nuclei, and stimulates activity in the uterine contractile muscles ▸249 as well as myoepithelial components in the cells of the mammary glands ▸249 with the onset of pregnancy, producing an increasing number of specific receptors for this hormone. At the time of the birth, oxytocin has reached its maximum level. At this stage, it facilitates expulsion of the newborn baby and of the placenta and promotes lactation ▸249.

A further increase in the production of this hormone is induced by the neuroendocrine reflexes which are linked to the suction of milk by the baby ▸249.

Other neurons that are part of the paraventricular nuclei of the hypothalamus produce neurohormones that are released into the bloodstream from the upper pituitary artery. These neurohormones specifically govern the secretory tasks of the hormonal cells of the transfer pituitary glands. Some stimulate hormone release, and are so-called releasing hormones, or release factors. Conversely, many of these hormones are inhibitors that are involved in the synthesis and release of transfer pituitary gland hormones. They are therefore known as the inhibiting hormones or inhibiting factors. It is the balance between the production of these neurohormones and inhibiting them that modulates pituitary activity.

THE POSTERIOR PITUITARY GLAND

The posterior pituitary gland or neurohypophysis is, as the name would suggest, located at the rear of the pituitary, although as it is largely composed of axons and pituicytes, it is not really a true gland. It does, however, have a secretory function releasing peptide hormones into the bloodstream via the hypophyseal capillaries - these include ADH and oxytocin. It is derived from the same embryonic source ▸248 as the central nervous system, and remains linked to the diencephalon through the pituitary stalk.

THE ANTERIOR PITUITARY GLANDS

The anterior pituitary gland - which is also known as the adenohypophysis or front pituitary lobe, is the portion of the pituitary gland to glandular activities genuine. It is one of the most important endocrine organs, and controls many vital processes, including growth, reproduction and the management of stress. It is derived from ectodermic cells ▸248, and originates from a structure in the roof of the

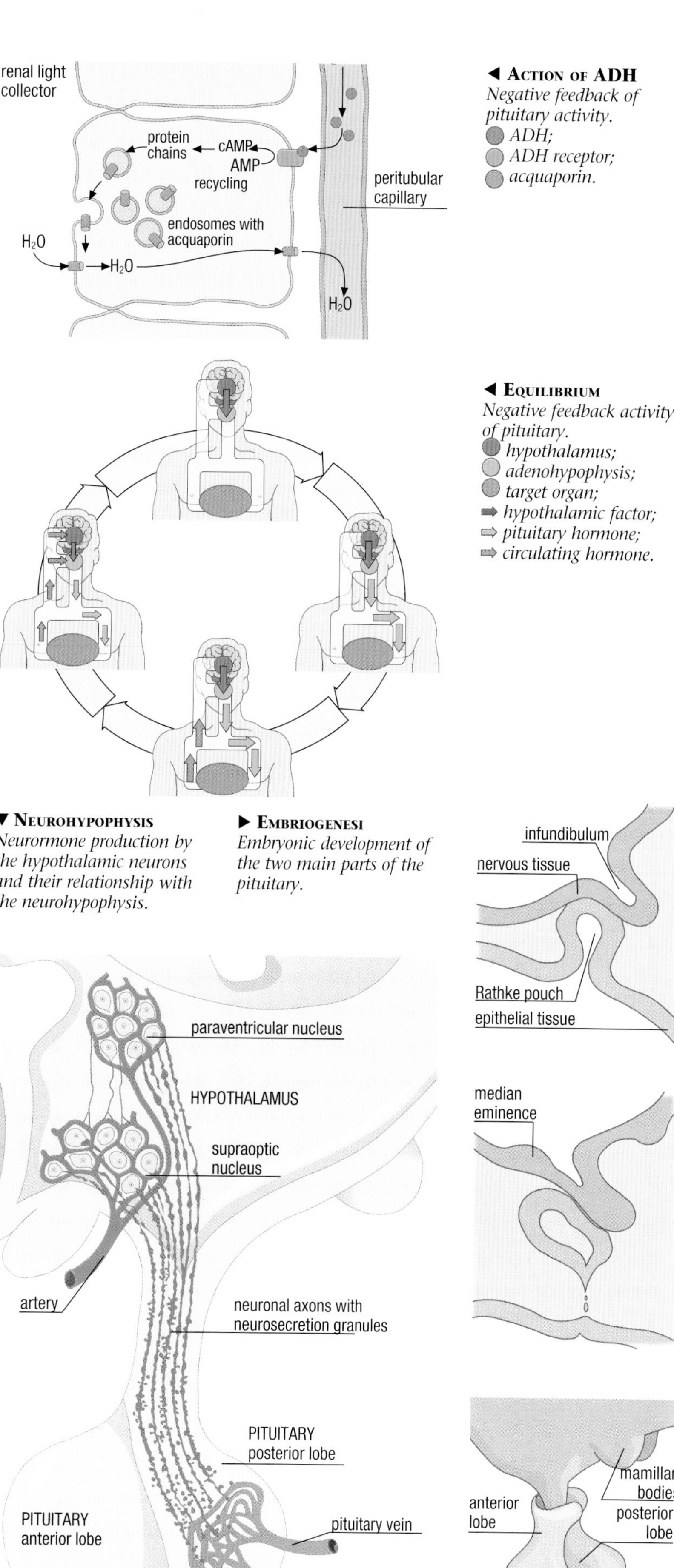

◀ **Action of ADH**
Negative feedback of pituitary activity.
ADH;
ADH receptor;
acquaporin.

◀ **Equilibrium**
Negative feedback activity of pituitary.
hypothalamus;
adenohypophysis;
target organ;
hypothalamic factor;
pituitary hormone;
circulating hormone.

▼ **Neurohypophysis**
Neurormone production by the hypothalamic neurons and their relationship with the neurohypophysis.

▶ **Embriogenesi**
Embryonic development of the two main parts of the pituitary.

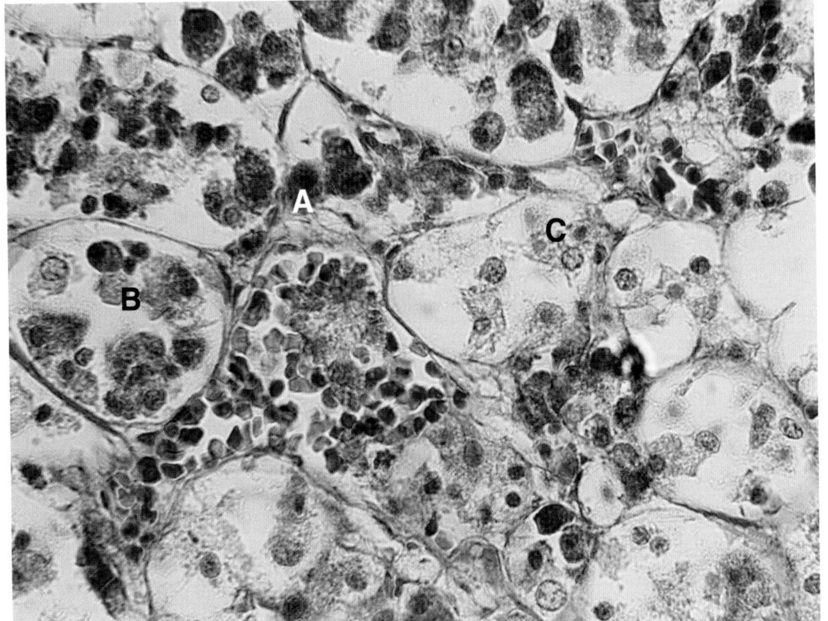

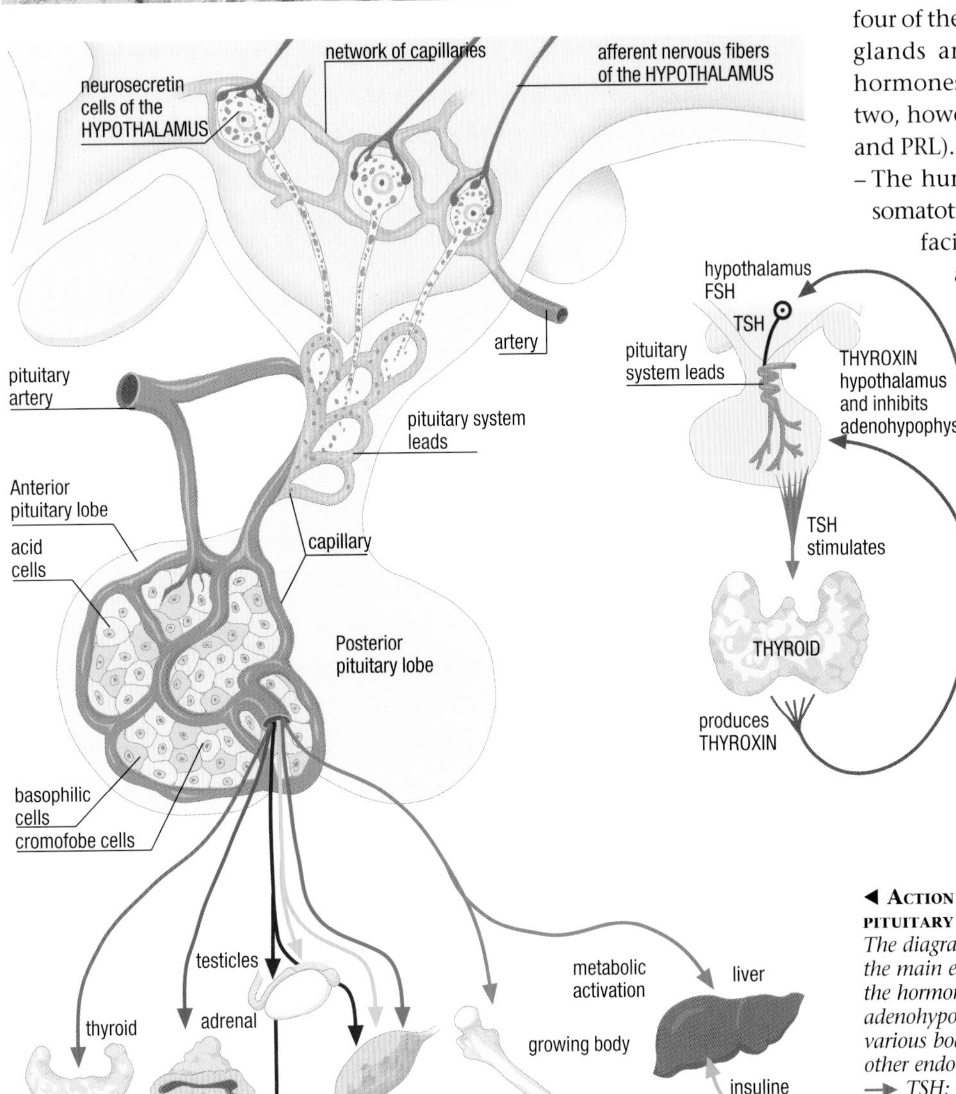

primitive oral cavity of the embryo. The cells that form the transfer pituitary glands are therefore of a different type to those from which the anterior and posterior pituitary glands are derived.

Furthermore, from the histological point of view, the cells can be divided into three types based on how well they take microscopic stains. These are termed acidophile, basophile and chromophobe. Each type of cell produces different hormones, in particular the acidophile cells produce growth hormone (GH or somatotropin) and prolactin (or PRL). The growth hormone stimulates protein synthesis by favouring the transport in the cells of the amino acids and reducing the catabolism of proteins. The basophile cells produce the follicle-stimulant hormone (or FSH); the luteinising hormone (or LH), the hormone luteotropin (or LTH), the hormone thyrotropin (or TSH) and the adrenocorticotropic hormone (also known as corticotrophin or ACHT).

These hormones are all of a protein-based nature, four of them affect the activities of other endocrine glands and, for this reason, are called tropic hormones (TSH, ACTH, LH and FSH). The other two, however, do not act on endocrine tissue (GH and PRL).

– The human growth hormone GH somatropin/ somatotropin STH, stimulates the protein synthesis facilitating transport in the cells of amino acids and reducing protein catabolism. It promotes the mobilisation of fats and their cell catabolism and hinders the use of glucose by the cells (with an opposite action to insulin ▸206) favouring its accumulation in liver in the form of glycogen. It is mainly involved in improving the body by stimulating the hepatic synthesis of somatomedin, a very active growth factor. If the production of GH is insufficient during the early years of life, the result is pituitary dwarfism. If the production is excessive, then the outcome is gigantism. In the adult stage, an excess secretion of GH only occurs in the terminal bones of

◀ **Action of pituitary hormones**
The diagram illustrates the main effects which the hormone secretions of adenohypophysis have on various body parts and other endocrine glands.
→ *TSH;*
→ *ACTH;*
→ *FSH;*
→ *LH;*
→ *LTH;*
→ *STH.*

▲▲◀ **Cells of the pituitary**
Section under the optical microscope of adenohypophysis showing the hormone-producing cells: **A**. *acid;* **B**. *basophils;* **C**. *cromofobe.*

▲◀ **Negative feedback**
The thyroxine produced by the thyroid stimulating adenohypophysis inhibits hypothalamic and pituitary activity, slowing the thyroid.

hands and feet or in the jaw, with an accretion disproportionate to the various parts of the body. This causes acromegalia, an abnormal condition where the bones are unnaturally enlarged. This hormone production is stimulated by the growth hormone releasing factor, GHRF which is secreted by the hypothalamus.

- The thyroid-stimulating hormone TSH controls thyroid activity ▸203 and causing increases in the size and the number of the thyroid follicles. If there is a lack of TSH, the thyroid glands start to atrophy. It is responsible for the uptake of iodine, and the synthesis and the liberation in the blood of the thyroid hormone triiodothyronine (T3) and thyroxin (T4) which in turn, affect general metabolic processes. The production of TSH also depends on the level in the blood of thyroxine: this mechanism of feedback ensures the maintenance of a suitable hormonal balance for the needs of the body.
- The adrenocorticotropic hormone ACTH is comprised of 39 amino acids and is derived through the division of a larger and complex precursor molecule. Its role is to stimulate the production of androgens and cortisol by the adrenal cortex ▸209. Its effects are regulated by glucocorticoid and aldosterone, and stimulated by release factors from the hypothalamic pathways (CRF, corticotropin-releasing factor CRF). The production of ACTH is also subject to negative feedback: cortisol, in fact, inhibits the secretion of the stimulating factors from the hypothalamic pathways. This mechanism preserves the functional balance that controls the activities of the pituitary and adrenal cortex.
- The follicle-stimulating hormone (FSH) and luteinising hormone (LH) gonadotropin hormones: these act on the gonads and stimulate the secretion of sex hormones ▸210. The FSH stimulates the development of the ovarian follicles in women and the maturation of sperm in men. The LH causes ovulation in the woman ▸213, i.e. the breaking of the mature ovarian follicles from where the free egg is released, and in males the secretion of androgens (testosterone and androsterone) from the testicular pore cells (cells of Leydig). FSH and LH in association stimulate the secretion of oestrogens from the follicle cells of the ovary. Besides these primary effects on reproduction, gonadotropin also acts on the secondary sexual characters. The production of these substances from part of the transfer pituitary glands is stimulated by GnRF (gonadotropin releasing factor) from the hypothalamic pathways, and is subject to a negative concentration-dependent feedback based on the hormones produced by the gonad.
- The luteotropic hormone LTH, helps with the secretion of progesterone in the corpus luteum ▸212, the temporary endocrine organ that generates in the ovary following ovulation.
- Prolactin PRL is a hormone that stimulates milk production by the mammary glands. In these cells it stimulates the synthesis of casein and lactose. No release factor has been identified for the prolactin hypothalamic pathways, but it is known that neurons in the preoptic area produce the prolactin inhibiting factor (PIF) that, as the name would suggest, inhibits its release.

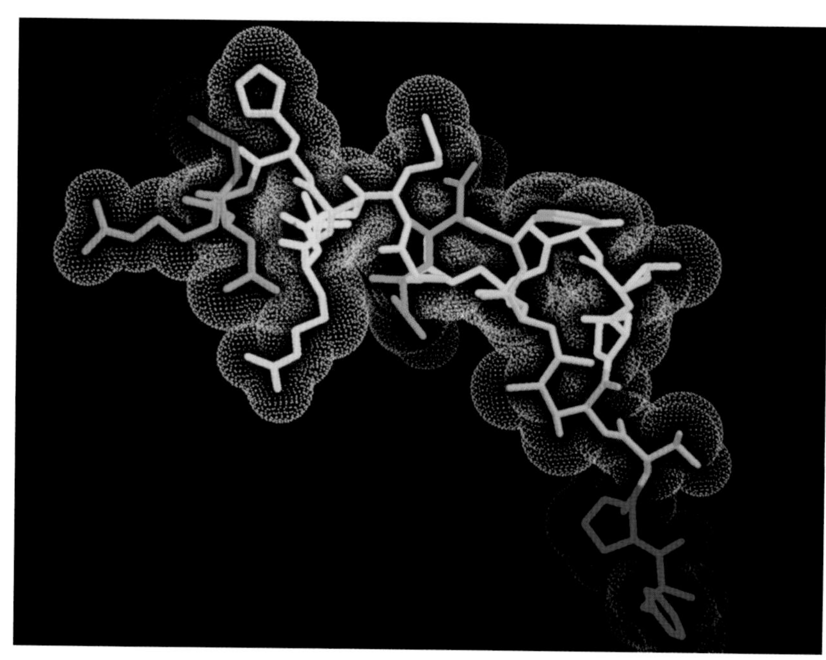

▲ **Somatotropin**
Computer reconstruction of the chemical structure.

THE INTERMEDIATE PITUITARY LOBE OR PARS INTERMEDIATE

The intermediate pituitary lobe, which is also known as the pars intermediate is an important structure in the human foetus, but is of negligible size or completely absent in the adult. It secretes two substances derived from the division of a common precursor to ACTH - this is the hormone called β-lipotropin. In turn, this is a precursor of numerous neuropeptides, including the β-endorphin which has analgesic capacity (endogenous opioid) and melanocyte-stimulating hormones (MSH), which stimulate the melanocytes in the skin to produce melanin. The synthesis of this substance, besides giving colouring to the skin and hair, helps to protect the skin against the UV rays in solar radiation, and is stimulated by dermal exposure to the sun. It is triggered by the melanocortin receptors, and the amounts produced are based on the overall brightness of the environment.

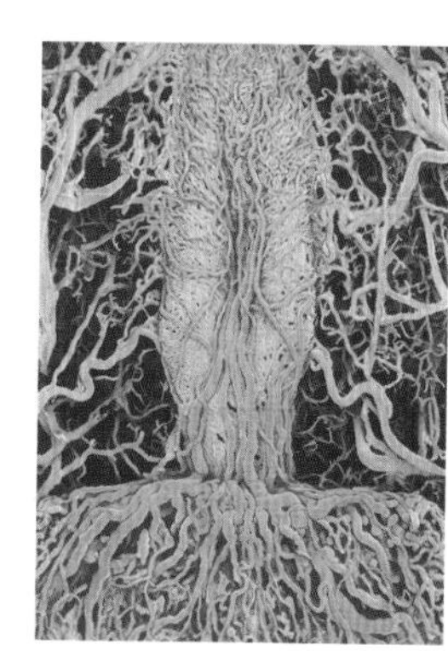

▲ **Pituitary capillaries**
Scanning electron microscope (SEM) photo in false colors of the capillary network that serves the pituitary stalk, the adenohypophysis and neurohypophysis.

In addition to the thousands of chemical messages that cells exchange continuously, there are some that serve as chemical control of the bodies main activities. These molecular signals are produced by special glands, which in turn are under the encephalic control of the glands of the endocrine system.

CHEMICAL CONTROL

▶ **Functioning of hormones**
The figure summarizes the different stages of hormones:
hormone A
hormone B
hormone C
❶ *blood vessel;*
❷ *receptor membrane;*
❸ *non-activated cell;*
❹ *interaction between hormone and* ❺ *receptor cell activated by the hormone-receptor interaction.*

▼ **Major endocrine glands**
The diagram shows the position in the body of the main endocrine glands:
adenohypophysis and epiphysis
thyroid and parathyroid
pancreas
Adrenal medullary
adrenal cortex
gonads

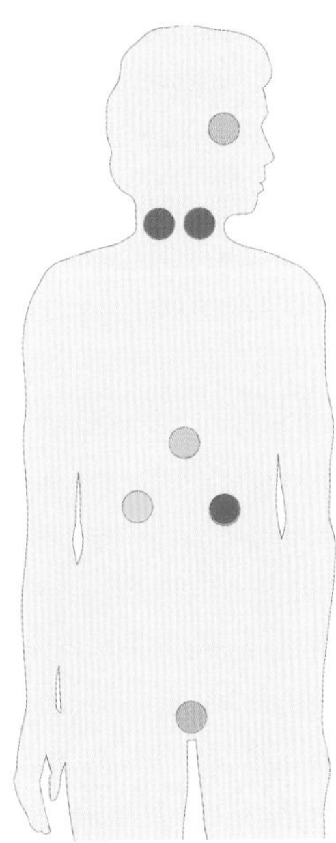

The body uses the central nervous system as a way to monitor the various activities going on in and around it. This information gathering and processing tends to happen very quickly though. This is in stark comparison to the functionings of the endocrine system though, which are slow, spread out and long term. It is composed of a number of heterogeneous and dispersed glandular organs in the body, that produce a variety of chemical messages. These are released into the blood stream, but before they have any effect, they have to reach a certain concentration.

Devoted to stimulating or inhibiting the activity of specific bodies, target hormones produce reactions that may take place anywhere between a few seconds and a few minutes. They last more or less in accordance with their resistance to metabolic inactivation and the excretion. For example, if the typical lifespan of ADH is fifteen minutes, that of the thyroxine is around a week.

These characteristics mean that electrochemical nervous control is best suited to regulating phenomena that take place rapidly and with precision, such as muscle movements or glandular activation. On the other hand, endocrine chemical control is better for controlling more prolonged and general activity such as that which occurs in the metabolic system. In fact, these two types of controls interface continuously, complementing each other in organising the activity of each part of the body.

HORMONES & HOW THEY WORK

Each hormone is selectively produced by a specific gland or type of cell, and undertakes a particular role. Even those which are deployed to the body through blood circulation, can regulate the activity of very specific areas known as target cells, whilst leaving all the others unaffected. This is made possible because they have membranes that contain receptors that are constructed to only bind with the chemical structures of these hormones.

In principle, any substance that mediates in the communication between cells is a hormone. They can be categorised based on the distance over which they operate:

Autocrine hormones - these stimulate the cell in which they were produced

Paracrine hormones - these stimulate the cells in the vicinity of their production

Endocrine hormones - these act over very large distances.

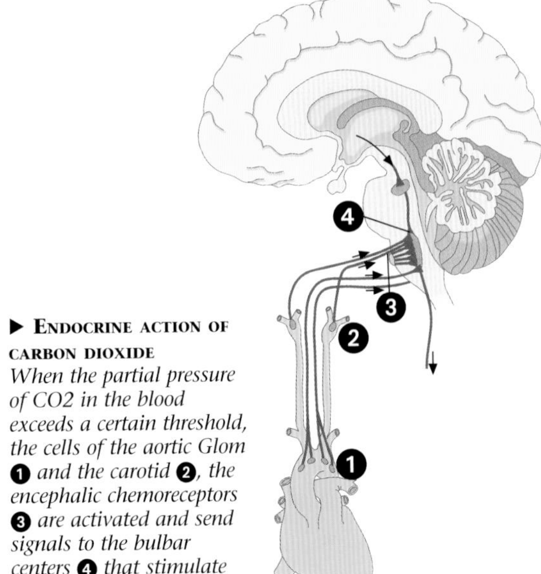

▶ **Endocrine action of carbon dioxide**
When the partial pressure of CO_2 in the blood exceeds a certain threshold, the cells of the aortic Glom ❶ *and the carotid* ❷*, the encephalic chemoreceptors* ❸ *are activated and send signals to the bulbar centers* ❹ *that stimulate the respiratory muscles.*

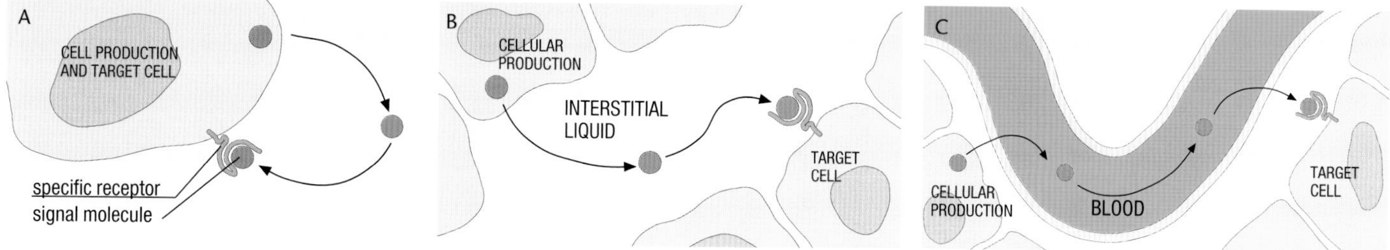

▲ **Distance from action**
*Difference between local hormones (**A**, **B**) and endocrine hormones (**C**)*

Substances that only act at short distances are called local hormones. Included in this group are many substances that are involved in the regulation of carbon dioxide, the control of cell metabolism, those which act on the neurons in the respiratory system, the chemical receptors in the aortic arch, and the smooth muscles in blood vessels. In addition, many cells produce specific physiological substances such as histamine ▸96, that have powerful effects but only in a very localised area close to the point where they have been released. Other local hormones include cytokine and prostaglandin ▸109.

Hormones can also be grouped according to their chemical form:

- amine hormones, these are derived from amino acids. Among their number are serotonin (this is water soluble) which derives from tryptophan, catecholamine (adrenaline noradrenaline dopamine, which is water-soluble) and thyroid hormone (tetraiodothyronine or thyroxine, which is liposoluble) arising from tyrosine;
- peptide hormones, these consist of anywhere between 3 and 200 chains of amino acids, all of which are water-soluble (such as ADH and GH, insulin ▸206 and glucagon ▸206);
- steroid hormones, these derive from cholesterol and are products from the adrenal glands, sexual glands and the placenta. They are all liposoluble and may therefore cross the plasma membrane of the target cells.

Intracellular Receptors – These are protein molecules that are found in cell cytoplasm and that can only be reached by the liposoluble steroids and thyroid hormones that spread in the cell through the membrane.

▼ **Serotonin**
Microphotography of polarized light showing crystals of serotonin. In addition to being a synaptic neurotransmitter, this substance is a powerful vasoconstricting hormone and, in the liver, it activates phosphofructokinase, the enzyme responsible for the transfer of phosphate from ATP to fructose.

Serotonin

Serotonin (5-hydroxytryptamine or 5-HT), is a neurotransmitter as well as a molecule that is involved in hormonal activity. It is formed through a complex modification of tryptophan in which the main stage is carried out by an enzyme - tryptophan hydroxylase (TPH). This occurs in two different forms:

TPH1, this is mainly found in specialised tissues, such as the photoreceptors of the ocular retina, the pineal gland, certain gastrointestinal cells and neuro-epithelial lung cells, the thyroid and the parafollicular cells;

TPH2, this is restricted to the nuclei of Raphe which are found in a restricted area of the brain and a small area of the hypothalamus.

Despite the fact that the total number of these neurons is very low, they develop a broad nervous network which reaches to all the areas of the brain and spinal cord and as far as the muscles.

In addition to the vital role which serotonin plays as a neurotransmitter, it also inhibits other endocrine secretions. These include pancreatic (insulin and glucagon), pituitary (stimulating growth hormone and corticotrophin) and gastroenteric (gastrin, secretin).

In addition to this, serotonin is involved in a large variety of other functions. In one way or another, it controls almost all of the physiological functions, including the cardiovascular, breathing, gastrointestinal and thermoregulation systems. It also contributes to maintaining the circadian rhythm and controls appetite, aggression and mood, and participates in sexual behaviour, learning and influences the memory.

If a person takes antagonistic substances, it is likely that both insomnia and depression will result. It is probable that serotonin, whose release in the blood stream is at a maximum during the hours of wakefulness and decreases with sleep, is responsible for the production of the factors that control the onset of sleep.

At a peripheral level, then, serotonin affects many processes, and so defects in its distribution or production can cause many serious health problems. In addition to this, it affects many aspects of behaviour that may lead to or contribute to aggravating neuro-psychiatric diseases such as schizophrenia, bipolar disorder, anxiety, stress, depression, and may also contribute to disorders such as allergies or migraines.

An excess of serotonin can give rise to exhaustion and nervousness, and reduces hunger stimuli. The production of β-endorphins as well as that of serotonin are strongly influenced by the intake of sugars. This is not only sweet, but has a relaxing and anti-depressive effect; it also reduces the perception of pain and improves self-esteem. The same effect is produced by

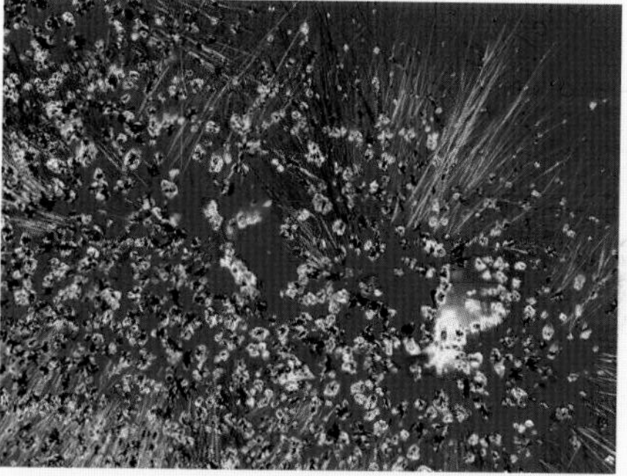

aerobic activity such as running and cycling, especially if it is combined with exposure to sunlight.

Many studies suggest that serotonin acts as a key factor in modular synaptic plasticity and in central nervous system development, as well as in other tissues. It is similar to other neurotransmitters, and works by making adjustments in the signalling processes of embryonic differentiation and morphogenesis, having been identified already in very early stages of development, even before the body has a differentiated nervous system.

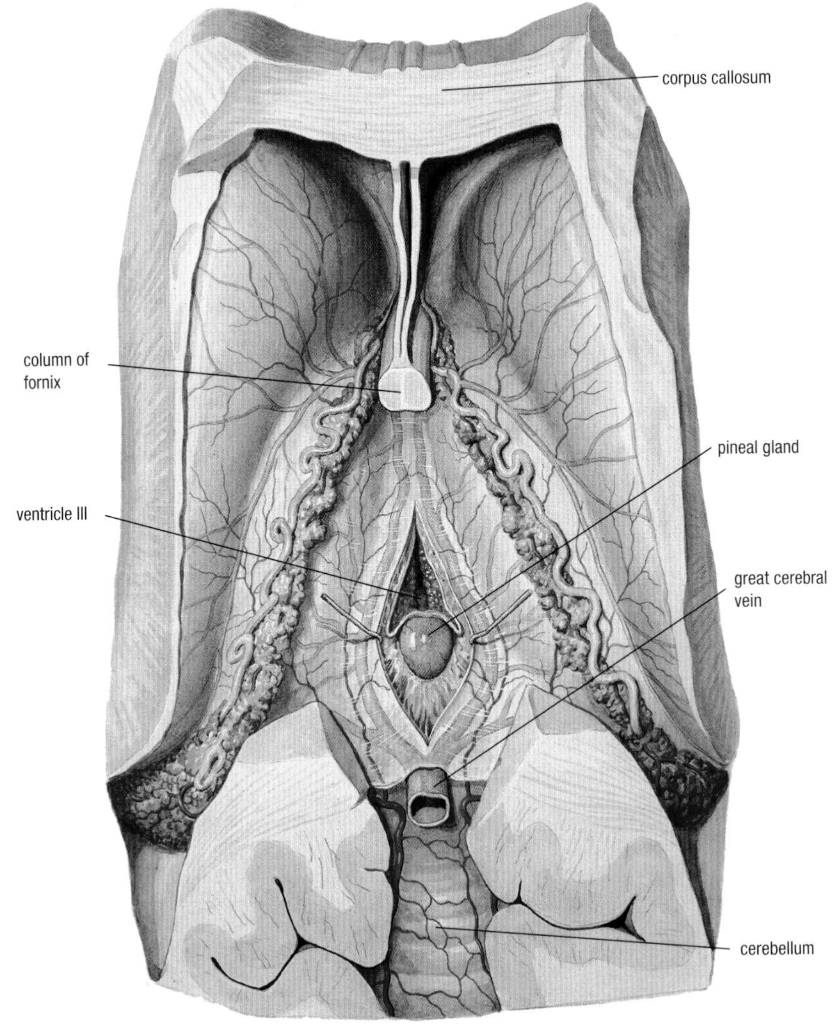

▲ **PINEAL GLAND**
At the heart of this section of the ventral brain, there is the pineal gland.

G protein coupled receptors - these are molecules that bind to the peptide hormones and catecholamine, allowing the transfer of information to the internal cell by turning on an intracellular system which uses G protein as internal signals. This protein group also includes cyclic adenosine monophosphate (cAMP).

GLANDS AND HORMONES

edocrine gland	principal hormones produced	endocrine gland	principal hormone produced
HYPOTHALAMUS	release factors inhibitor factors ADH oxytocin	PANCREAS	glucagon insuline somatostatin
		STOMACH	gastrin
PITUITARY PARS INTERMEDIA	MSH	ADRENAL CORTEX	cortisol cortisone corticosterone aldosterone
ADENOHYPOPHYSIS	ACTH, GH, TSH, LH prolactin	ADRENAL MEDULLARY	adrenaline noradrenaline
EPIPHYSIS	melatonin		
THYROID	triiodothyronine thyroxine calcitonin	GONADS	estradiol estrogen progesterone testosterone androsterone
PARATHYROIDS	parathyroid		

Membrane associated enzyme receptors - these are also molecules that bind to the peptide hormones and with catecholamine; however, their intrinsic enzyme activity is activated when it binds with the hormone. These receptors are very large molecules, and have a specific site outside the membrane to which the hormone binds, and a site within the cell that undertakes the enzymatic function. The change in conformation link with the hormone produced in the molecule determines the activation of the enzyme site and begins the chain of cellular reactions.

FEATURES OF THE MAIN ENDOCRINE GLANDS

In addition to the hypothalamus ▸179, ▸196 and the pituitary gland ▸196 which produce hormones as an integral part of the central nervous system, there are also many other endocrine glands.
Although these also secrete hormones, they do so directly into the blood, rather than through specialised tracts. The permanent ones include the thyroid, parathyroid, pancreas, adrenals, testes and ovaries, but the placenta ▸248 and corpus luteum ▸212 also function as temporary endocrine glands.

THE PINEAL GLAND

The pineal gland is known by several different names, including the pineal body, the epiphysis cerebri, and the epiphysis. It is a small structure – about the size of a pea, that is part of the epithalamus, which is located in the brain near the pituitary gland. It has a reddish-grey colour and the appearance of a pine cone. Coated by a capsule of glial cells, the gland is made up of pinealocytes, and has an important endocrine function.
Arising from the same embryonic cells that gave rise to the photoreceptors of the ocular retina, these cells perform an activity linked to circadian regulation – that is, from the alternating periods of light and darkness. The pineal body is directly connected to the retina by nerve fibres and to the photoreceptors of the hypothalamus.
The productive activity of the pinealocytes is governed directly by nerve impulses from the noradrenaline mediator. In the presence of light, photoreceptors stimulated by the release of noradrenaline send impulses to the pinealocytes, this inhibits the synthesis of melatonin, but stimulates the production of serotonin from tryptophan. Conversely, in darkness, the decrease in noradrenaline unlocks the production of melatonin from serotonin. As soon as it is produced, the melatonin is immediately released into the blood stream.
Discovered and isolated by a researcher called Lerner

in 1958, melatonin is not considered by all scholars to be a true a hormone. This is because during periods of light it is produced by other bodies, and also because by artificially increasing its dosage, did not show and significant effects. Nevertheless, some recent research suggests that it is able to resynchronise the body's biological clock when it has been disturbed by rapid time zone changes.
The pineal gland's production of melatonin follows a precise, independent circadian rhythm that is linked to the daytime or night-time activity of the individual. In the first few hours of the day, its blood concentration increases to a maximum between 2:00 am and 4:00 am. It then decreases as morning approaches and quickly reduces in proportion to the amount of light exposure. In this way, the pineal gland helps to adjust the circadian balance.
Melatonin also has an inhibitory effect on the hormones LH ▸199 and GH ▸198, contributing, among other things, to adjusting the blood sodium levels and affecting the development of the genital organs. The production of melatonin also inhibits corticosteroids and catecholamine, which are often referred to as stress hormones. This explains why sleep disorders are common in people subjected to high levels of stress. When it has performed its tasks, the melatonin is metabolised in the liver and is then excreted in urine.

THYROID

With a weight of approximately 30g, the thyroid gland is structured in two lobes which are connected to the isthmus, and is situated in front of the trachea and under the larynx. It is comprised of cubic epithelial cells and flat thyrocytes, and is arranged in a single layer to form a complex of cavities (follicles) which are full of a fluid known as colloid that includes thyroglobulin, which is an iodised glycoprotein with a high molecular mass that is produced by the thyrocytes from amino acids, tyrosine and iodine. The colloid is used as a sort of storage system for these hormones: both the triiodothyronine t3, and the thyroxin t4, in fact, have their origin in the hydrolysis of thyroglobulin. Iodine in the colloid binds to residues of tyrosine present in the thyroglobulin through iodised enzymes that lead to the formation of two types of molecules: the monoiodothyronine (monoiodinated thyronine or MIT) and the diiodothyronine (DIT). Two molecules of diiodothyronine are used in formation of the thyroxin. These are accompanied by one molecule of monoiodothyronine, and one of diiodothyronine together these form the triiodothyronine. The reaction takes place thanks to the inclusion of hydrogen peroxide (H_2O_2) with the synthesis of triiodothyronine or thyroxin being performed through the removal of a molecule of alanine.

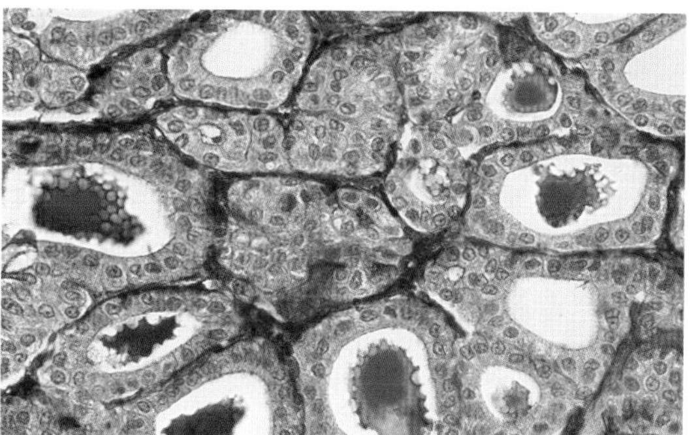

◀ **Follicles**
Optical microphotography of the thyroid showing the follicles contained by a single layer of cells. The follicles have different sizes according to their state of activity (secretory or synthetic). The colloid is colored red.

Once formed, the triiodothyronine and thyroxin remain linked to the thyroglobulin until they are ready to be excreted. Characterised by a fat-soluble structure, and thanks to a high systemic concentration in the cytoplasm, they are released into the blood through the basal membranes in the thyrocytes. In the blood, 99% of these hormones are linked to specific proteins. Since the bond between the thyroxin and the transport proteins is much stronger than it is to that of triiodothyronine (which is the active hormone), at the level of plasma the presence of the two hormones is equivalent. Once these chemicals have reached the target cells, the thyroid hormones enter them through the membrane arriving at the nucleus and specific endocellular receptors. This stimulates the transcription of particular genes, with the production of proteins and metabolic pathway enzymes that are needed for the stimulation of substances such as carbohydrates, lipids or proteins).

▼ **Scintigraphy**
Scintigraphy in false colors of a healthy thyroid: the most active part is in red, the least active in blue. It produces hormones that control the bodies metabolism and energy levels, in addition to the proper mental and physical development of children.

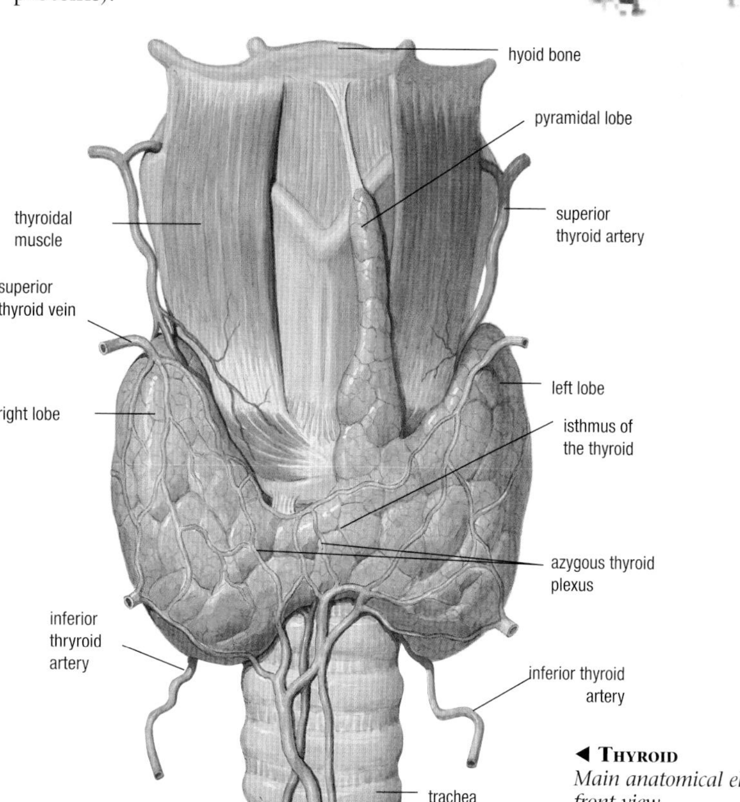

◀ **Thyroid**
Main anatomical elements, front view.

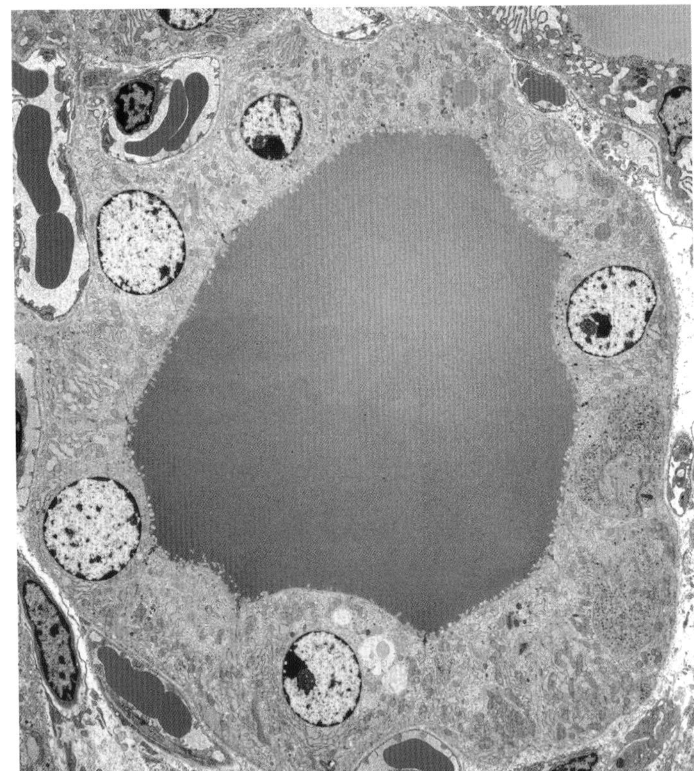

▶ **Follicle**
Transmission electron microscope photography in false colors of a follicle of the thyroid. The layer of thyrocytes (pink) surrounding the follicle are filled with glycoprotein (brown). The follicle is surrounded by blood vessels (red).

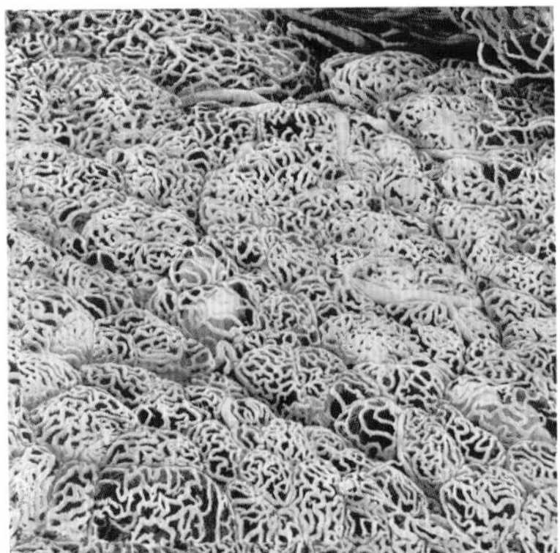

▶▶ **Rete sanguigna**
Scanning electron microscope (SEM) photograph of the network of capillaries through the thyroid.

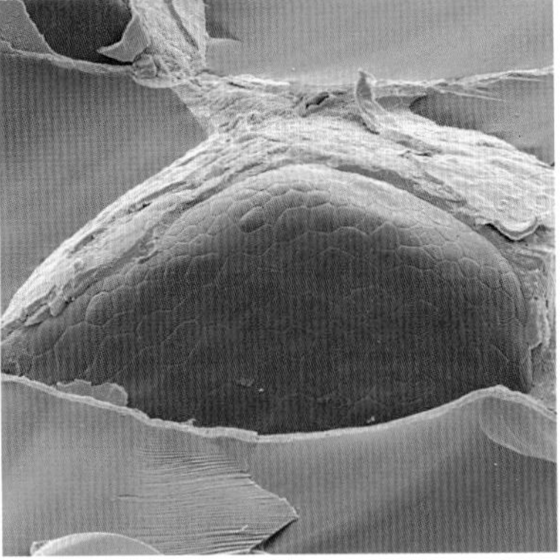

▶▶ **Follicle**
This false color SEM photograph shows a follicle with colloid (purple) that is bounded by cubic epithelium (yellow-brown). On the surface of the colloid is the imprint of the epithelial cells, while the surrounding follicles are seen in section and, therefore, have no structure.

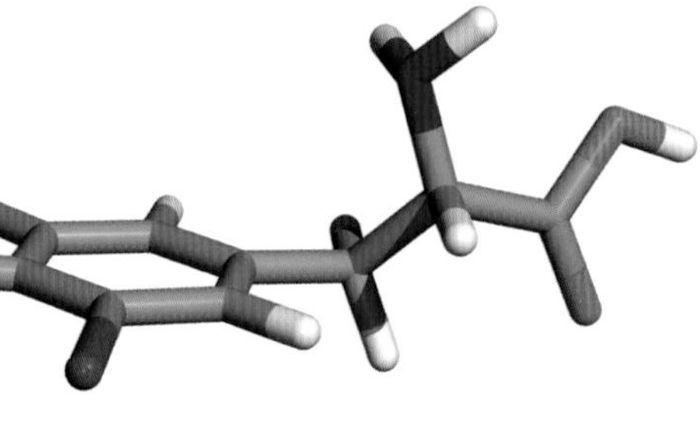

▲ **Synthetic thyroxin**
A computer model of a molecule of levothyroxine (T4 or synthetic) used to prevent the disorder caused by hypothyroidism. The chemical formula is $C_{15}H_{11}I_4NO_4$: C atoms are blue, H in gray, I in purple, N in blue and O in red.

Since the receptors for these hormones can also be found on the membranes of the mitochondria, 48 it is thought that they also function within these organelles by stimulating the synthesis of the enzymes involved in oxidative metabolism. In particular, with the Na-K-ATPases, the enzymes involved in the transport of active carbohydrates and amino acids. This would explain their calorigenic action, which is linked to a global stimulation of metabolic activity within the body. They influence increases in the intestinal absorption of glucose and, therefore, blood glucose levels as well as an increase in the use of lipids at the tissue level and a reduction of lipidemia.

In addition, by stimulating the production of specific cellular receptors, they promote the removal of cholesterol from the blood. In the case of hypothyroidism, they cause a big decrease in the basal metabolism. This is characterised by a number of features. This includes body temperature falls, a lower resistance to cold, decreases in arterial pressure and heart rate, and increases in the sensations of tiredness, torpor and muscular hypotonia.

The most obvious manifestation of hypothyroidism is facial swelling, and above all, of the eyelids. This is due to the accumulation of glycosaminoglycans (GAGs) or mucopolysaccharides in the subcutaneous tissue with the resulting accumulation of liquid (mixedema).

In cases of hyperthyroidism, however, there is instead a strong acceleration in the metabolism. This is characterised by such features as hyperactivity, increased body temperature, and the catabolism of amino acids (especially at the muscular level). This leads to reductions in weight and increases in blood sugar, the heart rate, blood pressure and neuromuscular excitation. Furthermore, it causes significant reductions in the amount of sleep and obvious emotional instability.

The thyroid hormones have a major effect on protein metabolism. These are anabolic, and favour the absorption of cellular amino acids, and therefore, the synthesis of proteins. In this way, they dramatically affect morphogenesis - in the case of hypothyroidism, the body's growth slows down, and may be incomplete or disproportionate. If the thyroid deficit is congenital and not offset by drug treatment within the 4th week from birth, it causes severe and irreversible mental retardation (cretinism).

Thyroid hormone production is controlled by thyrotropin-releasing hormone (TRH) from the pituitary glands, whose secretion is dependent on the release of factor TSH-RF. This is modulated by the

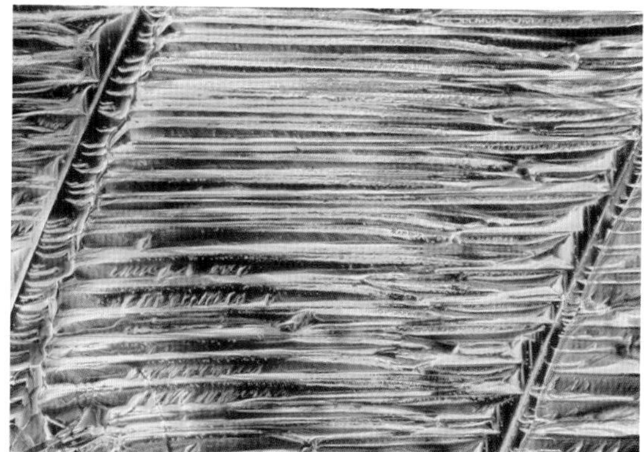

◀◀ Thyroxin
Polarized light microphotograhy showing crystals of thyroxine (T4) above, and calcitonin below.

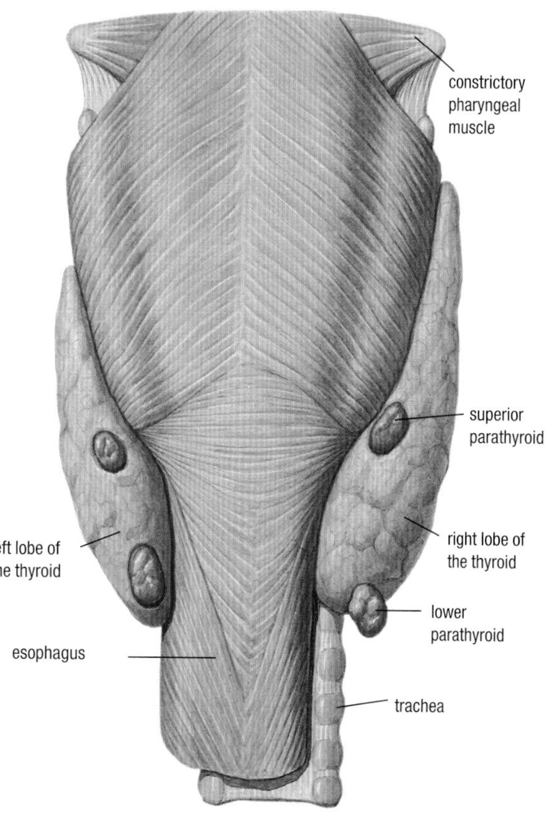

◀ Anatomy of the parathyroid
Anatomical location of the parathyroid and main anatomical features: rear view.

blood concentration of thyroid hormones, which is controlled according to a process of negative feedback. An increase in thyroid hormones reduces the production of the release factor, and conversely a decrease in it increases the production.

Between the follicles, and linked by a network of richly vascularised connective tissues, are the parafollicular or C cells that secrete calcitonin. This is a peptic hormone that lowers the blood concentrations of calcium and phosphate acting on bone tissue. It works in a two-pronged manner. On the one hand it inhibits the activities of the osteoclasts, i.e. the bone cells that produce enzymes and acids that accelerate the demolition of the bone matrix, and encourage the release of calcium and phosphate ions. On the other, it stimulates the excretion of Ca2+ ions by the kidneys.

THE PARATHYROID

The parathyroid glands are four oval structures which are positioned behind the thyroid gland, and consist of a very dense tissue. They secrete the parathormone (PTH) which increases the calcium and reduces the blood-borne concentration of phosphates. Together with the thyroid's parafollicular cells, they regulate mineral replacement within the body. While the calcitonin produced by the thyroid has a hypocalcaemic action, and is secreted if there is excess calcium in the blood, the parathormone has a hypercalcaemic action and is produced every time the calcium lowers. it causes the transfer of calcium from bones to the blood by stimulating osteoclast activity, and it promotes the absorption of calcium from the level digestive tract and of the renal tubules.

The kidneys: these reduce the elimination of calcium and increase the active absorption of Ca2+ ions by raising or lowering the threshold of excretion. They increase the excretion of phosphates by inhibiting their absorption in the proximal seminiferous nephrons. They also stimulate the hydroxylation of vitamin D3, which is synthesised in the skin and processed by the liver. Before it can reach its active form, however, it has to undergo conversion in the kidneys.

The intestine: this increases the absorption of Ca2+ ions in the epithelial duodenal cells, a process that is mediated by vitamin D3. It stimulates the synthesis of proteins for the uptake of Ca2+ ions in the microvilli and to the active transport of the absorbed ions.

The bones: these stimulate the mobilisation of the Ca2+ ions when more calcium is needed. Within a few days of the requirement, the activity levels and division of the osteoclasts is increased significantly. This causes and acceleration in the demolition the bone, which frees large amounts of Ca2+ and phosphate ions.

The removal of the parathyroid or their imperfect functioning causes a drastic reduction in the levels of calcium and the increases in blood phosphates. This causes delays hyperexcitability and tetanic muscle contractions. Conversely, an excess in parathormone levels may lead to extended decalcification of the

▼ Action of the parathyroid
The parathyroids secrete parathyroid (PTH) which helps to regulate the level of blood calcium and phosphate.
A. *The low blood level of calcium ion (Ca2 +), symbolized by the central orange column, causes increased production of PTH (red arrow and orange ball), which mobilizes calcium from bone (blue), it stimulates the intestinal reabsorption (pink) and reduces renal excretion (green).*
B. *A high blood level of calcium ion (Ca2 +) causes the decrease of production of PTH and the subsequent deposition of calcium in bone and the calcium also decreases due to increased renal excretion and decreased intestinal absorption. The process is reversed for the phosphates.*

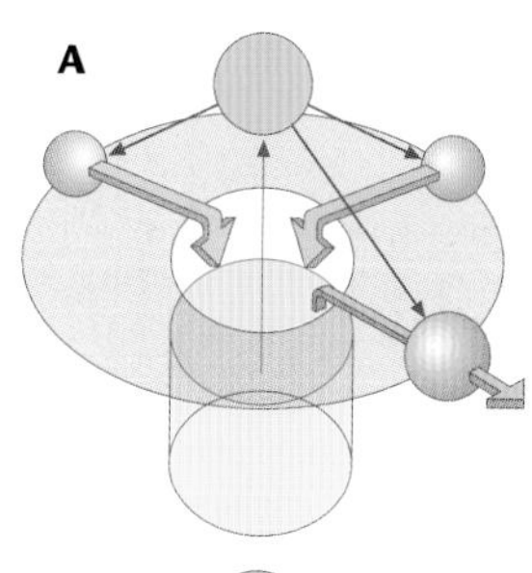

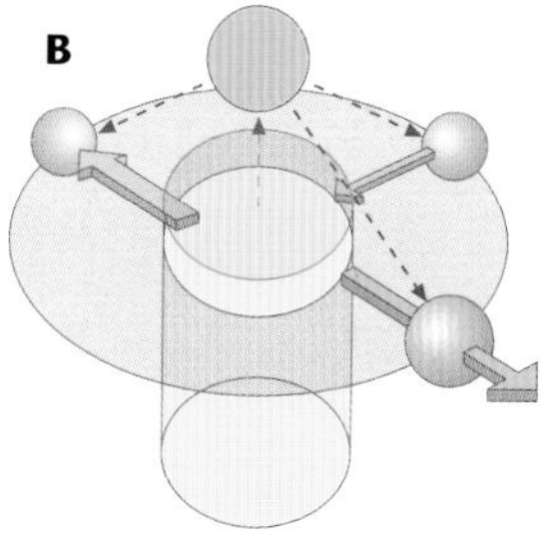

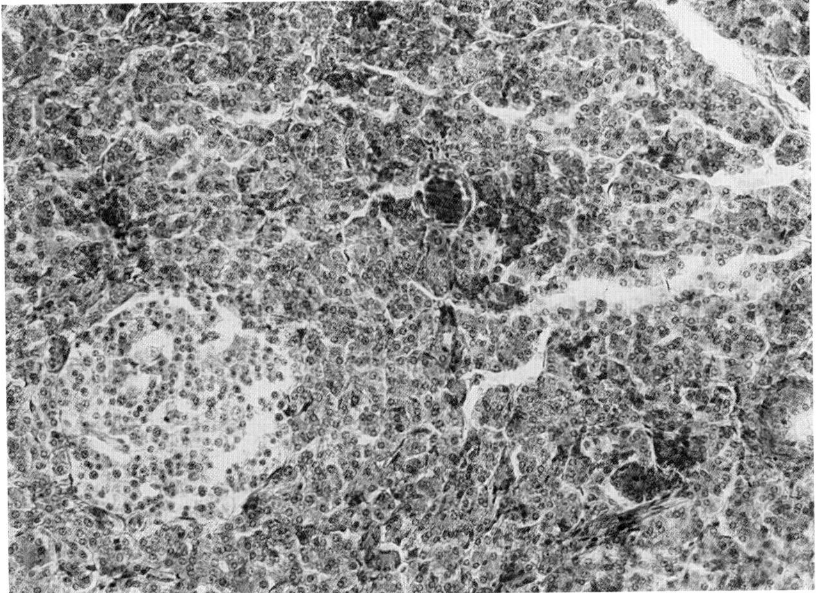

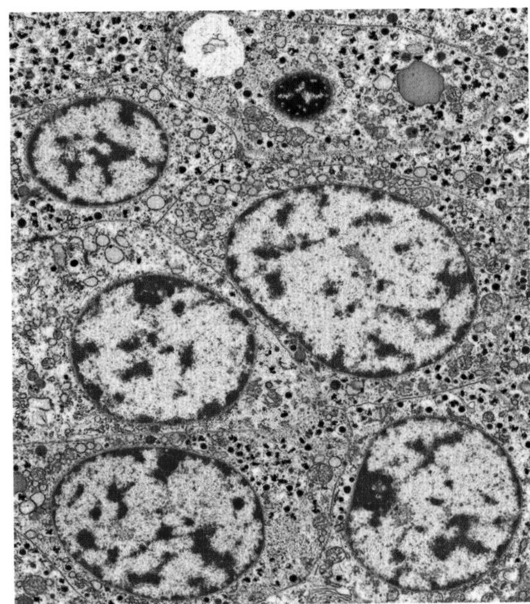

▲ **Sezione di pancreas**
The optical microscope photograph of a section of the pancreas. The clear mass in the lower left consists of cells arranged in cords and islets of Langerhans surrounded by pancreatic more compact exocrine tissue, producing digestive juice.

▲▶ **Insulin**
Transmission electron microscope (TEM) photograph in false color showing the interior of a cell of the endocrine pancreas. The orange granules contain different hormones depending on the type of cell.

▶ **Negative feedback**
Outline showing the chain of processes linking the production of α cells of the pancreas to blood glucose. When the concentration of glucose in the blood falls below a given threshold, α cells release glucagon into the blood, it reaches the liver and activates lysis of glycogen in hepatocytes, releasing glucose into the circulation, raising your blood sugar level. The increase in circulating glucose blocks the production of glucagon.

bone (fibrous osteitis) and the deposition of calcium in various parts of the body.

THE PANCREAS

Distributed between the pancreatic acini that secrete pancreatic juice in the small intestine 103-105, there are irregular groups of endocrine cells which are surrounded by blood capillaries. These are named islets of Langerhans. Apart from a minimum proportion of other types of cells (such as the C cells), the islands of Langerhans are formed by four main types of cells – these are:

- The α cells, (20 %), which produce glucagon;
- The β cells, which are the most numerous (70-76 %) and secrete insulin;
- The δ cells, (3-4 %), which secrete somatostatin;
- The φ cells, (1-2%), which produce the pancreatic polypeptide.

Glucagon, this acts in an opposite manner to that of insulin - it is a hyperglycaemia hormone that causes an increase in blood glucose concentration. It is produced by the pancreas and released when necessary to stimulate the conversion of glucose from glycogen that is stored in the liver. The glucagon is recognised by the liver's hepatocytes which have special glucagon-sensitive receptors that then stimulate the release of the pancreatic hormone. This starts a number of phosphorylation reactions that trigger the release of the glycogen enzymes and the production of glucose. The blood sugar levels then start to rise as significant amounts of it quickly enter the circulatory system. If the deposits of glycogen in the liver become exhausted, glucagon has the sole effect of stimulating the conversion of glucose in a process called lipolysis.

The **insulin** hormone is essential in metabolic homeostasis: it is involved in the metabolism of carbohydrates, lipids and proteins in almost all the

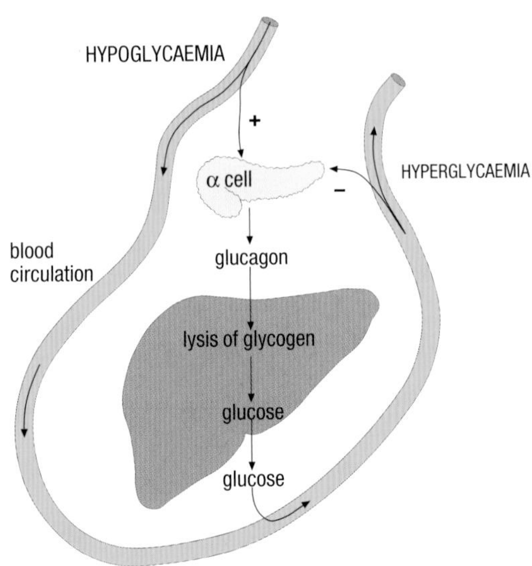

body's tissues, although its action is most apparent in the liver, muscles and adipose tissue. Its action on carbohydrates is triggered when the blood glucose exceeds a threshold level: insulin is then excreted from the β cells and quickly reaches the target cells. Here its strong glucose-lowering action soon takes effect due to various processes that lead to an increased use of glucose in various parts of the cells, and to its accumulation in the form of glycogen.

The insulin accelerates all the processes that cause a reduction in the glycaemia: firstly, it increases the recruitment of glucose by linking to the tyrosine kinase receptor. This enables the muscle membranes to increase the transport of glucose. When the extracellular glucose concentration reduces, any that is left over is stored in the vesicles for another occasion. Furthermore, insulin stimulates the process of glycolysis, and so increases intracellular glucose consumption and facilitates the conversion of glycogen in the liver and muscle, or triglycerides

in the liver and adipose tissues. These processes are also facilitated as the insulin inhibits the degradation of glycogen and the new formation of intracellular glucose. Furthermore, insulin stimulates the metabolism of lipids favouring the passage of free fatty acids from the plasma in the adipocytes and turning them into triglycerides. This reduces the mobilisation of fats and blocks phosphorylation.
Finally, insulin also acts on the metabolism of proteins: it facilitates the transport of amino acids in cells and their transformation into proteins - at the time same, it inhibits the protein catabolism.
The secretion of insulin is governed by blood glucose through a negative feedback mechanism. The β cells are very sensitive to any increases in the blood's glucose, and quickly pass through the membrane, causing a series of biochemical reactions that end with the depolarisation of the cell. By enabling a system of microtubules and microfilaments, the influx of $Ca2+$ ions promote the excretion of insulin. Conversely, If the influx of glucose is low (hypoglycaemia), then the excretion of insulin is inhibited. Continuously excreted from the islands of Langerhans in various doses, insulin contrasts with the effects of glucagon and other hyperglycaemic hormones (such as growth hormone, adrenaline etc.), helping to keep the blood glucose under close control both during the day and night. Peaks of insulin secretion occur in the course of digestion, especially during the absorption of substances, especially that of glucose.
A degeneration or insufficient capacity of the β cells to produce insulin causes a common disease which is known as diabetes mellitus, and is separated into two types:

- Insulin-dependent diabetes mellitus or type I; this is the form which particularly affects young people, and is due to the total absence of β cells. This may be due to genetic causes, or alternatively it may be because of autoimmune problems relating to toxins produced by bacterial or viral infections, or it can be from environmental poisoning by different substances;
- Non insulin-dependent diabetes mellitus or type II; this mostly affects adults, and is due to the growing inability of cells in the pancreas to

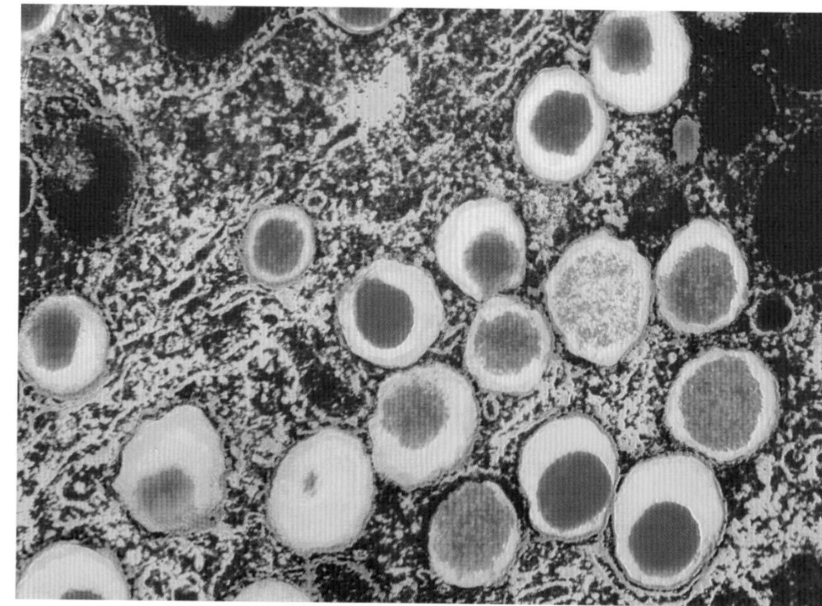

▲ **Negative feedback**
Transmission electron microscope (TEM) photograph in false colors of a pancreatic endocrine cell. The red balls in the pink spaces are secretion granules and are linked to the membrane, they contain a core of densely packed hormone granules, separated from the surrounding membrane.

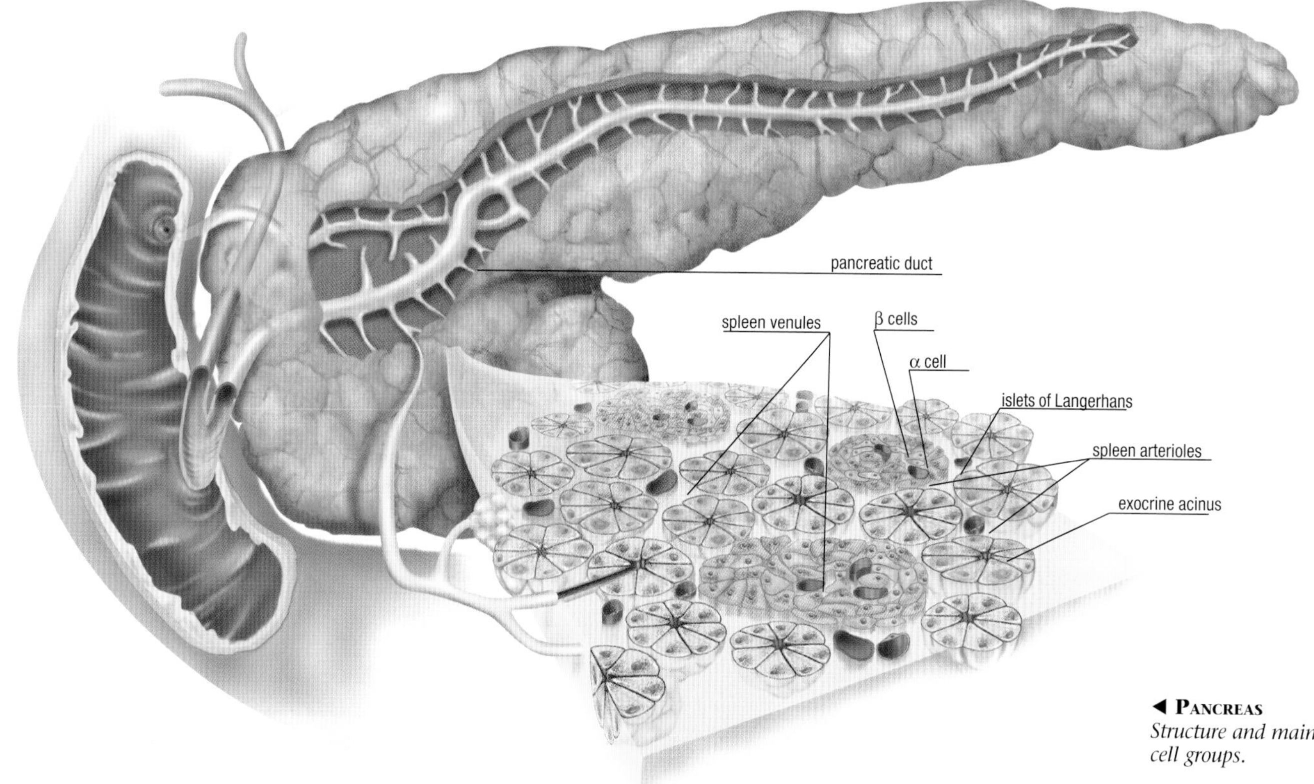

◀ **Pancreas**
Structure and main cell groups.

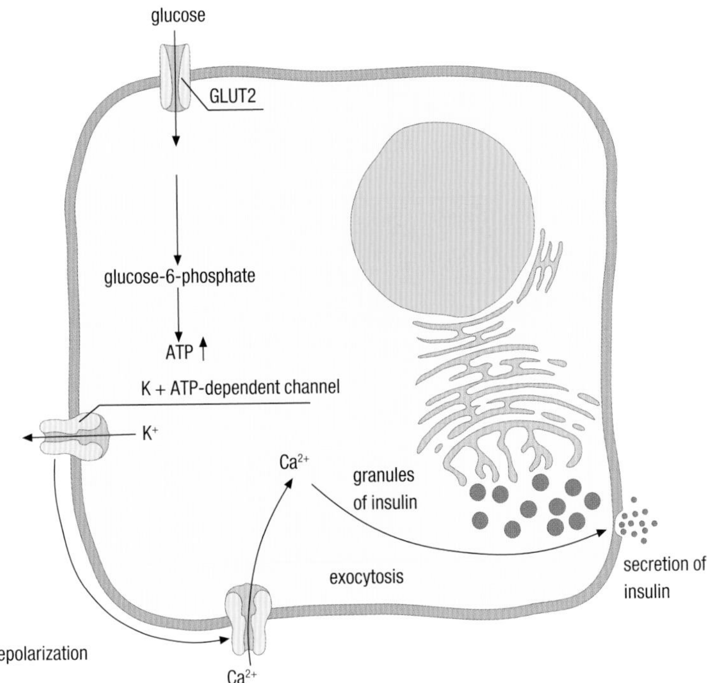

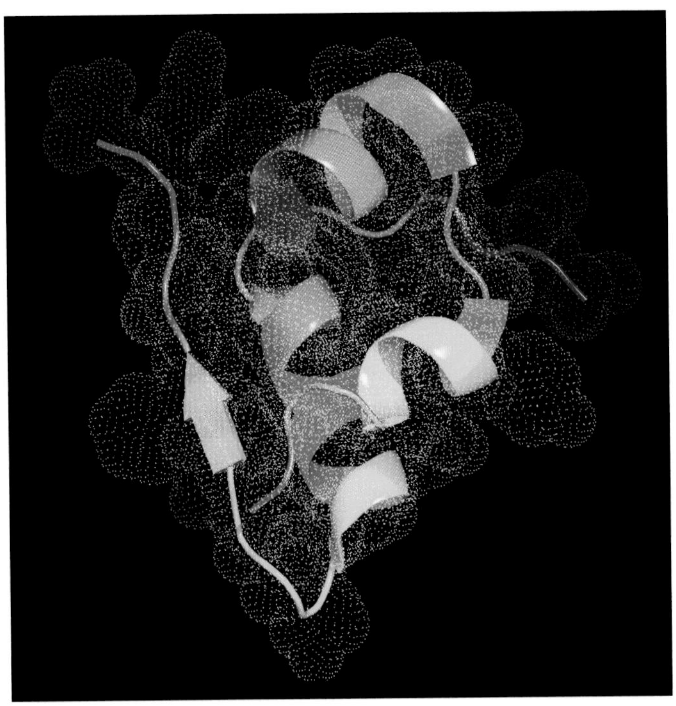

▲ **Production of insulin**

β cells from islets of Langerhans are stimulated by the high glucose concentration outside. The activation of the metabolism of glucose increases the concentration of ATP that determines the closing of K + channels: the resulting membrane depolarization causes the opening of channels of voltage-dependent Ca2 + and the entry of this ion, which triggers the release for exocytosis of insulin.

▲▶ **Insulin**

Computer reconstruction of a molecule of insulin, it consists of two chains (A, center and right, blue to blue wire, B to the left, yellow to red wire) connected by bridges S-S (shown with the ribbons).

produce quantities of insulin that are appropriate to the diet, or to a progressive resistance of body tissues to action of insulin. Here too the dominant causes are genetic as well as acquired or environmental. This includes such factors as old age, poor diet, overweight and obesity, dyslipidaemia, stress, taking drugs, the abuse of alcohol, reduced physical activity, etc. These have a lot more significance if the individual concerned is genetically predisposed to diabetes. The persistence of the acquired and environmental factors causes the occurrence of this form of diabetes in old age. That the number of people suffering from this dysfunction grows in conjunction with economic welfare is a proven fact. It is estimated that up to 3 % of the population in industrialised countries suffer from it.

An inadequate secretion of insulin also characterises other two types of diabetes:

- Gestational diabetes, this is incurred during pregnancy and is caused by the increased demands for insulin due to pregnancy. It is a disorder which tends to disappear entirely with confinement;
- Secondary diabetes, this is caused by any chemical or physical agent that causes pancreatic damage, reducing its endocrine capacity.

In any case, diabetes causes severe alterations in the metabolism of carbohydrates, proteins and fats, with serious consequences for general health.

Somatostatin produced by the pancreas has a powerful inhibitory action on the secretion of insulin and glucagon. Its production in the δ cells is activated escalating the blood glucose levels, the plasma levels of fatty acids and amino acids, and also glucagon intestinal hormones such as secretin and cholecystokinin. At the level of the digestive system it has an inhibitory action on peristalsis and the secretion of gastric juices, and slows the absorption of nutrients. The production of somatostatin in turn, is inhibited by catecholamines and insulin.

The **pancreatic polypeptide** (PP) is secreted by the endocrine pancreas, and is made up of 36 amino acids. It acts to control the secretion of the pancreatic juices and therefore bowel absorption; levels are increased after meals.

THE ADRENAL OR SUPRARENAL GLANDS

The adrenal glands are two small pyramid shaped bodies that are located above the kidneys, a property for which they were named. These glands produce many specific substances that can be categorised according their most obvious physiological actions:

- Glucocorticoids: these are steroid hormones, and include: cortisol, cortisone, corticosterone and hydroxycorticosterone; they are involved in the metabolism of glucose.
- Mineralocorticoids: these are also steroid hormones, and include: desoxycorticosterone, aldosterone and deoxycortisol; they are involved in the control of the body's salt-water balance;
- Androgens: these are also steroid hormones, and include: dehydroepiandrosterone (DHEA) and androstenedione (DHEA), they are involved in the regulation of male sexual characteristics.

It also produces the catecholamines adrenaline and noradrenaline. These act on many tissues and have effects that are either similar to or opposed to those produced by the autosympathetic system.

Each gland consists of two parts with different

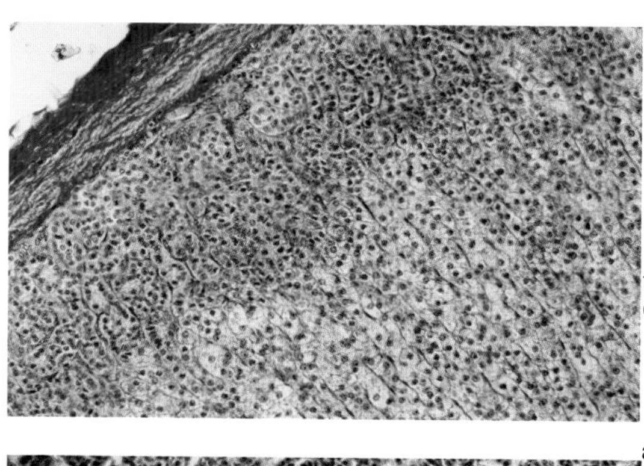

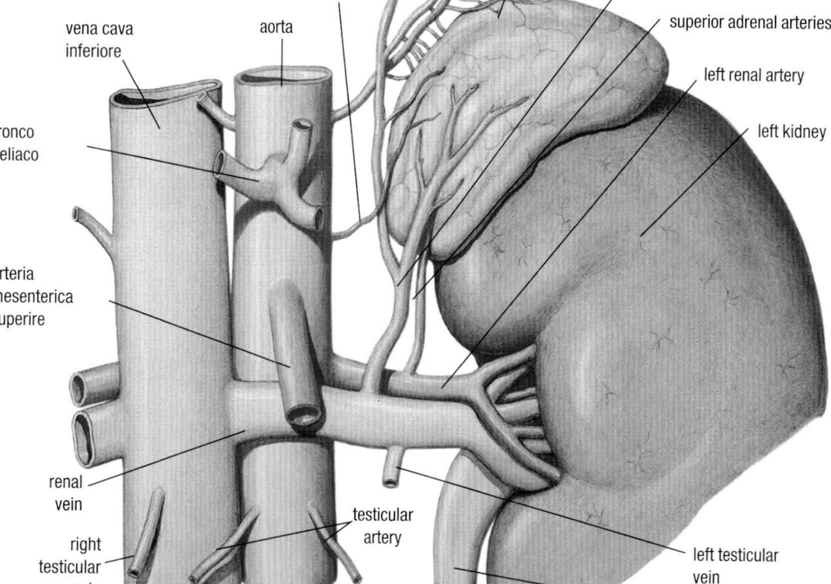

▲▲ **Corteccia**
Optical microphotography of a section of the adrenal cortex. Top left you see the capsule (blue) with area under the glomeruli (dark purple) and the outer zone interior below (clear purple). In purple, cells producing aldosterone are arranged irregularly in ovoid groups separated by connective tissue, the second producing glucocorticoids and are arranged in narrow cords.

▲ **Glands**
Optical microphotography of a section of the adrenal gland showing the difference between the tissue of the reticular zone of the cortex (top, darker, formed by groups of cells that produce small amounts of precursor steroids, dark purple) and the spinal cord (down, made up of compact groups of cells producing adrenaline and noradrenaline).

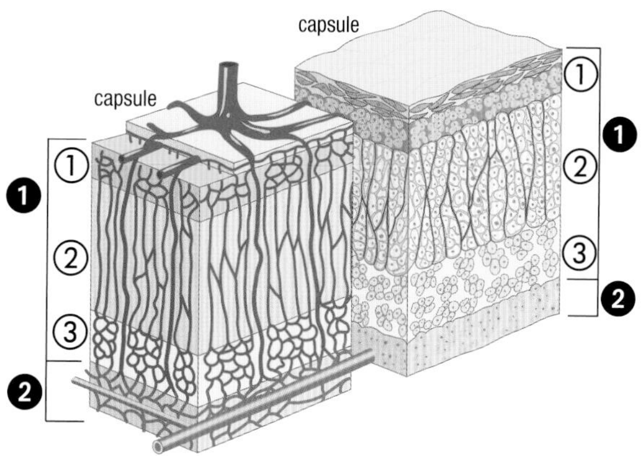

▲ **Male left adrenal capsule**
Available anatomical view of the front, with the main vessels.

◀ **Struttura della ghiandola surrenale**
Richly vascularised adrenal glands innervated by endings of the sympathetic system, there are two excretia areas:
❶ cortex, which responds to stimuli of the pituitary hormone ACTH producing glucocorticoid; consists of three areas:
① glomerular
② fasciolare
③ reticular;
❷ the medullary portion, which produces adrenaline and noradrenaline in a manner entirely independent of the cortex, in response to stimuli of orthosympathetic neurons.

embryonic origins, histological organisations and functions, and they perform entirely independent endocrine activities.

Adrenal cortex - this accounts for 80-90 % of the entire gland, and is derived from the mesoderm ▸248 and is distinguished, in turn, by three concentric layers called zones, these have different macroscopic appearances and structural organisations.

The zona glomerulosa - this is where the corticosteroids are found. In the mitochondrial cortical cells, cholesterol is processed into pregnenolone, the forerunner of all the other cortical hormones. It passes into the endoplasmic reticulum where it becomes progesterone and is then modified further, with the exact manner being different, depending on the type of cell involved. In the cells of the mitochondrial glomerular area it becomes a mineralocorticoid, whereas in the zona fasciculata it becomes a glucocorticoid, and in the zona reticularis it is converted into an androgen.

- The zona glomerulosa is the outer layer immediately under the capsule of connective tissue that surrounds the gland. The cells that it is comprised of secrete mineralocorticoid, the best known and powerful of which is aldosterone. This is involved in the metabolism of sodium and potassium, it stimulates the absorption of Na+ ions in the epithelia and in particular in the distal portion of the seminiferous tubules where it increases at the same time the excretion of K+ ions.

As all the hormones involved are liposoluble, the aldosterone crosses the membrane of the target cells and binds to specific cytoplasmic receptors. Once it has reached the core, it stimulates the expression of specific genes with the formation of RNA for the synthesis of the carrier enzyme Na+ K+ ATPase, which promotes the incorporation into the lateral membrane of the distal seminiferous cells.

This leads to an increase in the transport of Na+ ions

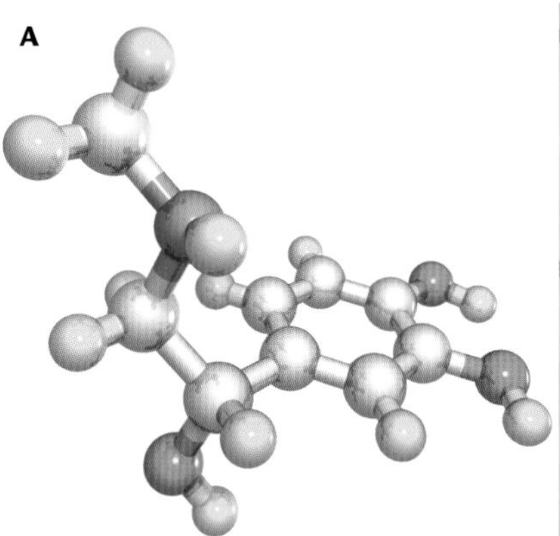

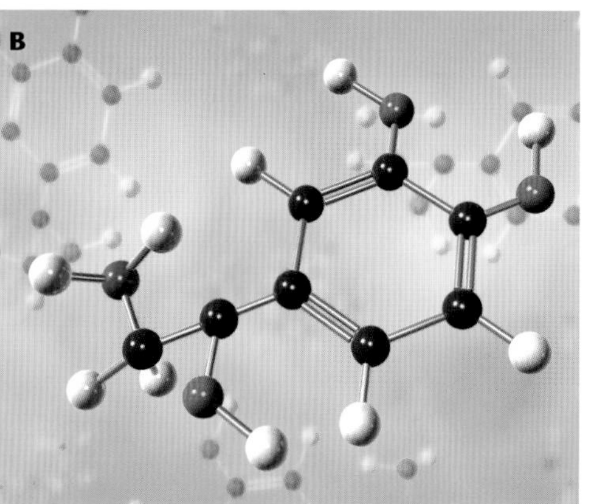

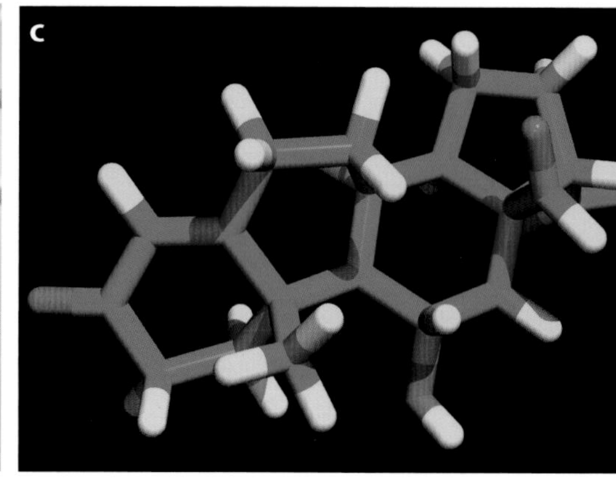

▲ **Chemical structure** *Computer reconstruction of the chemical structure of:* **A**. *a molecule of adrenaline,* **B**. *one molecule of noradrenaline and* **C**. *one molecule of aldosterone.*

▼ **Adrenalina** *Microphotography of polarized light in crystals of adrenaline.*

in the extracellular liquid. The sodium then forms an electric gradient that uses osmotic effects to drag in chlorine ions (Cl -) and 53 also a certain amount of water. This causes an increase in the volume of extracellular liquid and a consequent increase in pressure.

Aldosterone secretion is regulated primarily by the blood-borne concentration of K+ ions. This has direct effects; if there is an increase it stimulates production, whereas a decrease has an inhibitory effect. An increase in blood potassium indirectly encourages the hypothalamus to release the pituitary factor ACTH, which then increases the production of aldosterone. Finally the production of aldosterone is modulated by the renin-angiotensin system ▸148-149.

- The middle region of the adrenal cortex is known as the zona fasciculata. It is located beneath the zona glomerulosa, and is where the glucocorticoids are produced, with the most important one being cortisol. This is one of the better-known stress hormones, and controls the production of many enzymes that influence the metabolism of carbohydrates as well as certain fats and proteins.

One of its main roles is to balance out the effect of insulin. It does this by accelerating hepatic activity so that proteins and lipids (triglycerides) as well as fat deposits are broken down more quickly. This results in raised glucose levels. Cortisol also helps to inhibit inflammatory responses ▸107 by suppressing the body's immune responses. A further significant activity is that it boosts cardiovascular activity and strengthens the action of catecholamine in the production of heat. It also increases the metabolic effects of glucagon, thyroid hormones ▸203 and pituitary somatotropic hormone ▸198.

The production of these hormones is governed by pituitary ACTH according to a negative feedback process involving the hypothalamus. A reduction in the blood concentration of these hormones causes the hypothalamus to produce larger quantities of the release factors that stimulate pituitary transfer activity and vice versa.

- The zona reticularis is made up of cells that form a trabecular system and that produce androgens. These are sex hormones that are associated with male sexual characters. One of the main compounds is dehydroepiandrosterone, or DHEA for short. This is subsequently converted into testosterone that has a chemical structure and functions that are identical to the product made by the testes. When small quantities are produced, they have no effect in the male, but in the female they can contribute to the emergence of some secondary male characters, such as follicle development of the pubis or in the underarm area.

The **adrenal medulla** represents 10 - 20 % by weight of the gland. It is largely formed from chromaffin cells, which are the characteristic cytoplasmic granules. These are derived from the embryonic neural crest cells, and can also be found in parts of the sympathetic nervous system. The adrenal medulla is the main source of the body's catecholamine.

Adrenaline, noradrenaline and dopamine are excreted in response to specific nervous impulses. All of these are derived from tyrosine that is converted

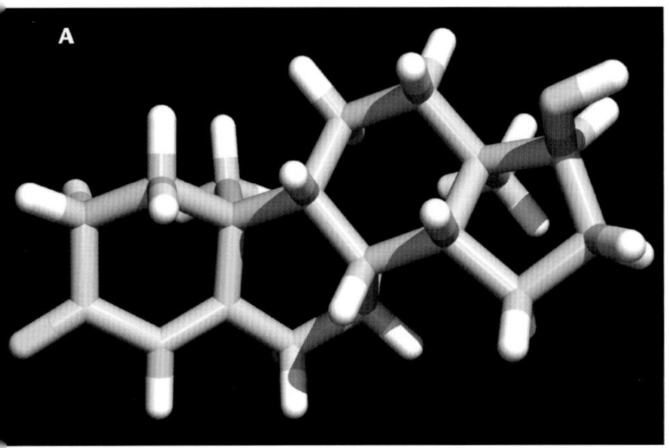

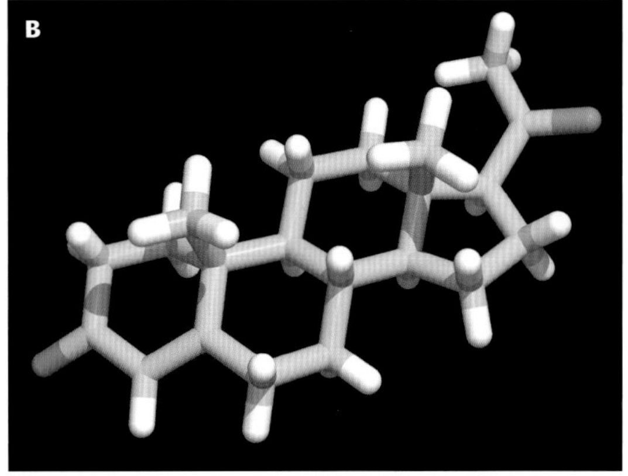

◀ **Chemical structure** *Computer reconstruction of the chemical structure of:* **A.** *one molecule of testosterone,* **B.** *one molecule of progesterone.*

▼ **Blood vessels** *Scanning electron microscope (SEM) photograph of blood vessels that irrigate an ovary (left) and testis (right).*

into dihydroxyphenylalanine (dopa) then to dopamine. Some cells that have the correct enzymes can then further transform the dopamine and noradrenaline into other adrenaline compounds. Once these hormones products have accumulated in the granules they are released into the bloodstream under the control of the nervous system in the manner typical of the synapses. The hormones then bind to specific adrenergic cellular receptors: these are the α receptors, which are mostly involved with excitatory cells, and the β receptors, which are mostly inhibitory. Their action has powerful cardiac effects, raising the systolic blood pressure and altering the metabolism of carbohydrates by stimulating the release of glycogen. Together, glucagon, GH and cortisol are hormones that act to control the presence of insulin. They also affect the operation of the majority of the visceral bodies - they stimulate the heart, inhibit the intestinal movements and relax the bronchial muscles, etc.

THE GONADS & THE OVARIAN CYCLE

The gonads are organs that are intended for sexual reproduction: these are represented by the testicles in males and the ovaries in females. In addition to gametes and the other cells that are required to undertake the reproductive function, there are cells that are specialised in the production of sexual hormones. These have a specific action on the organs that are involved in the development of the reproductive capability, including breeding functionality and determination of the secondary sexual characters. Once excreted in the bloodstream, the sexual hormones bind to serum albumin and β-globulin and, on entering the target cell, are bound to a cytoplasmic receptor. This triggers a specific protein synthesis.

Once they have completed their actions, they are inactivated by the liver, made soluble and then excreted by the bile or with urine. The gonads activity is controlled by the transfer pituitary 235 through the hormone follicle-stimulating hormone (FSH) and the luteinising hormone (LH), this, in turn stimulates the production of specific release factors by the hypothalamus. It is this link between the brain and the hypothalamus that ensures that environmental changes can influence the reproductive cycle.

In males: A number of hormones are produced as the result of activity in the endocrine cells, the cells of Leydig, and the Sertoli cells. The first secrete androgen, including testosterone and androstenedione. A small proportion of these androgens is transformed from the Sertoli cells into oestrogens, this is probably fundamental to their trophic function and for the maturation of spermatozoa.

In females: the cells of the theca folliculi produce small quantities of androgens (testosterone and androstenedione) that the cells in the ovarian follicles transform into oestrogen (oestradiol, oestrone and oestriol). These are intended to stimulate the cells of uterus and vagina and involved in processing secondary sexual characters. They also increase water retention, reduce the formation of hair, affect the deposition of fats and the development of bones. At the tissue level they have an anabolic effect, stimulating the synthesis of proteins. Immediately after ovulation, the cells

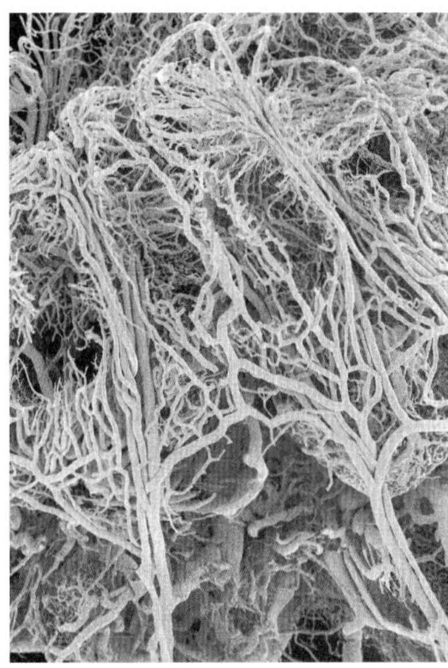

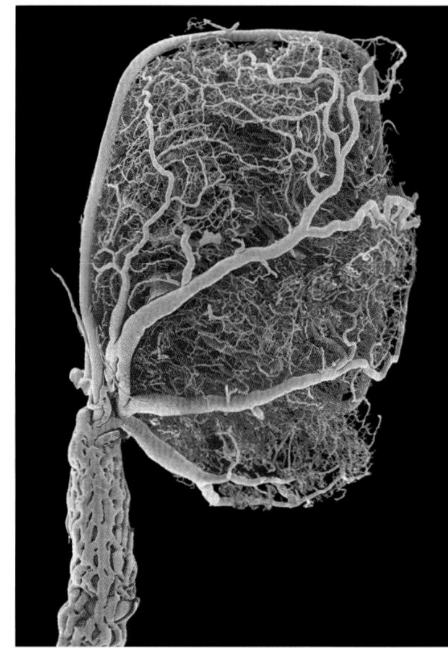

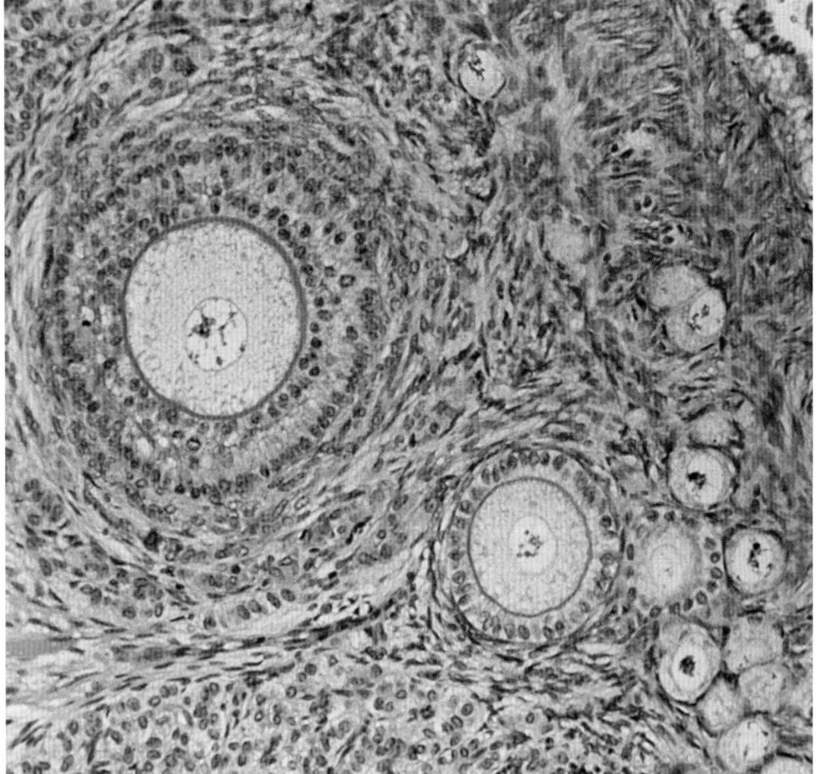

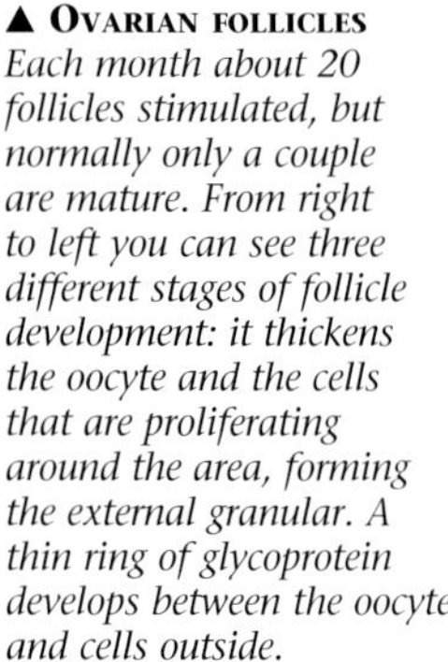

▲ **Ovarian follicles**
Each month about 20 follicles stimulated, but normally only a couple are mature. From right to left you can see three different stages of follicle development: it thickens the oocyte and the cells that are proliferating around the area, forming the external granular. A thin ring of glycoprotein develops between the oocyte and cells outside.

▼ **Hormones**
Changes of hormone concentrations during ovulation in the plasma medium. The pink band indicates the period of menstruation.

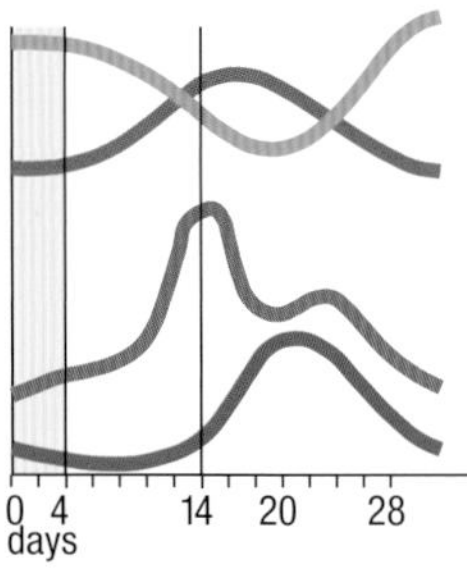

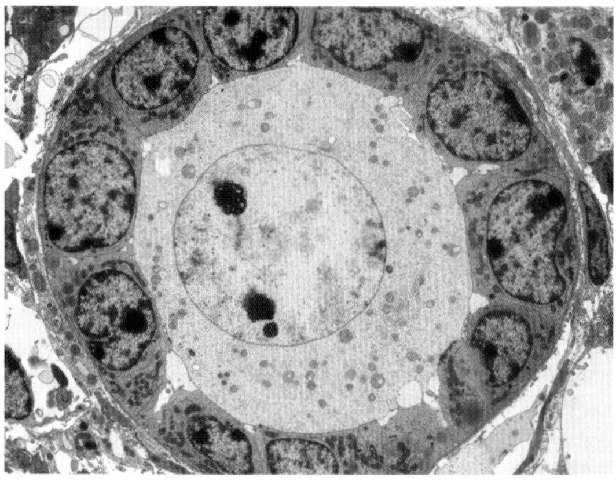

▲▲ **Primary follicle**
Transmission electron microscope (TEM) photograph in false colors of a primary follicle. The oocyte, which is being developed (pink) has a large nucleus (yellow) and is surrounded by cuboidal follicle cells (red).

▲ **Ovule and tube**
An endoscope image of the contact point between an ovary (above) and the fallopian tube (below). The egg is released from the ovaries and captured by fimbriata, the eversion finishes in the tube, and is directed toward the uterus.

that comprised the follicles form the corpus luteum. They then secrete progesterone or lutein and some of its derivatives, actions that oppose those of oestrogen. It is this hormone which stimulates the cells in the ovaries, vagina, mammary glands, and especially the uterus.

It is progesterone that acts on the uterus - which has to accept the fertilised egg, and the structure of the mammary glands to make lactation possible that prepares the female body for gestation ▸249. With the regression of the corpus luteum its production stops. The corpus luteum and placenta also produce relaxin, a hormone that at the time of the confinement, leads the relaxation of the pubic ligaments and the expansion of the neck of the uterus.

The Ovarian Cycle: the control of the female reproductive system is complex and depends on the endocrine activities of the individual cells in the ovary, from the hormone production of both the hypothalamus and pituitary glands. The periodic changes in the levels of pituitary gonadotropins (FSH and LH), of oestrogens and ovarian progesterone determine the menstrual or ovarian cycle that is reflected in a functional cycle which involves morphological variations in the female sexual apparatus. This cycle is classified in four phases

– the follicular phase, the increase in levels of FSH in the plasma stimulates the development of various ovarian follicles, theca folliculi and the granulosa cells. The resulting increase in LH stimulates the theca folliculi to produce androgens. These are processed into oestrogen and released in a cycle, which – according to a positive feedback effect on the hypothalamus and pituitary glands, causes the secretion of LH and FSH to peak which leads the maturation of the follicles;

– the ovulation phase, characterised by the maturation and release of the ovum. The egg is released in the ovulation cavity; in addition, the increase in blood levels of oestrogens leads to the proliferation of uterine mucus. The egg then starts to drop down towards the uterus;

– the luteal phase, the LH stimulates the formation of the corpus luteum that secretes progesterone and certain oestrogens. This causes a negative feedback that inhibits further production by the hypothalamic release factors (FSH and LH). In the endometrium, the progesterone stimulates changes that help prepare the optimum conditions for the acceptance of the fertilised ovum.

– the menstrual phase, takes place if the ovum isn't fertilised: the corpus luteum degenerates,

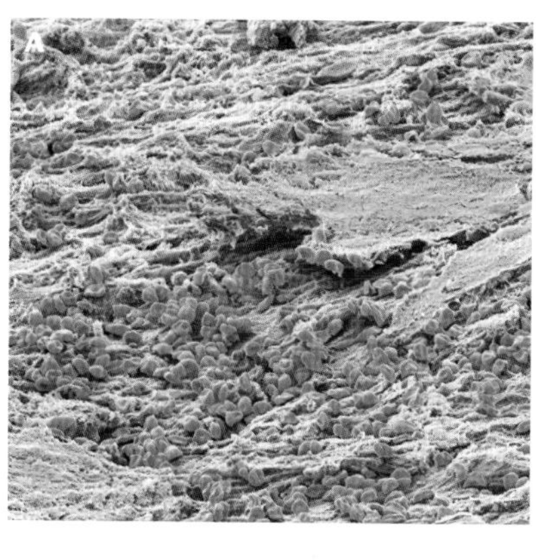

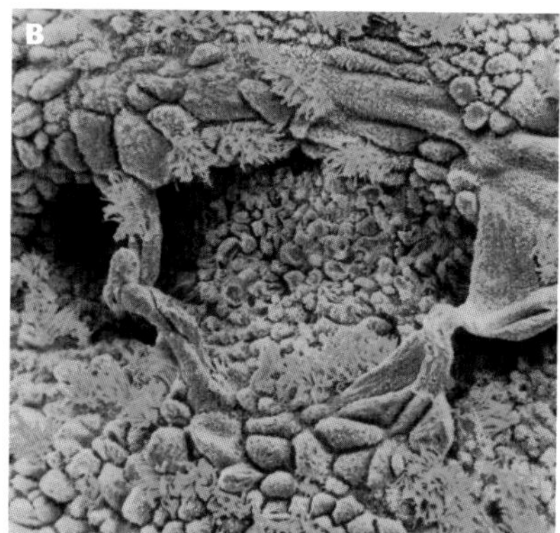

◀ **Aspects of the uterus** *The morphology of the uterine wall changes in the phases of the cycle: in these scanning electron microscope (SEM) photographs you can see:* **A**. *uterus at the end of menstruation;* **B**. *the beginning of the proliferation;* **C**. *in mid-secretory phase;* **D**. *being receptive. In the circle, a detail of the surface being receptive.*

▼ **Menstrual cycle** *The diagram summarizes all the changes - hormonal, morphological, physiological - the different stages which make up the menstrual cycle.*

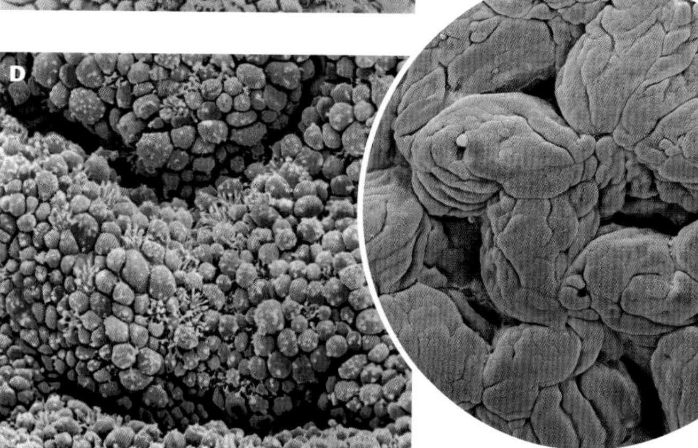

the plasma concentration of progesterone and oestrogen collapses after having reached a peak and, consequently, the uterine mucus is shed. The reduction of hormones unlocks the negative feedback on the production of pituitary FSH and LH, and the cycle begins again.
If the ovum is fertilised, however, pregnancy starts: development of the placental cells begins 8-10 days after fertilisation, together with the production of human chorionic gonadotropin (hCG), a hormone that prevents the regression of the corpus luteum and, therefore, menstruation.

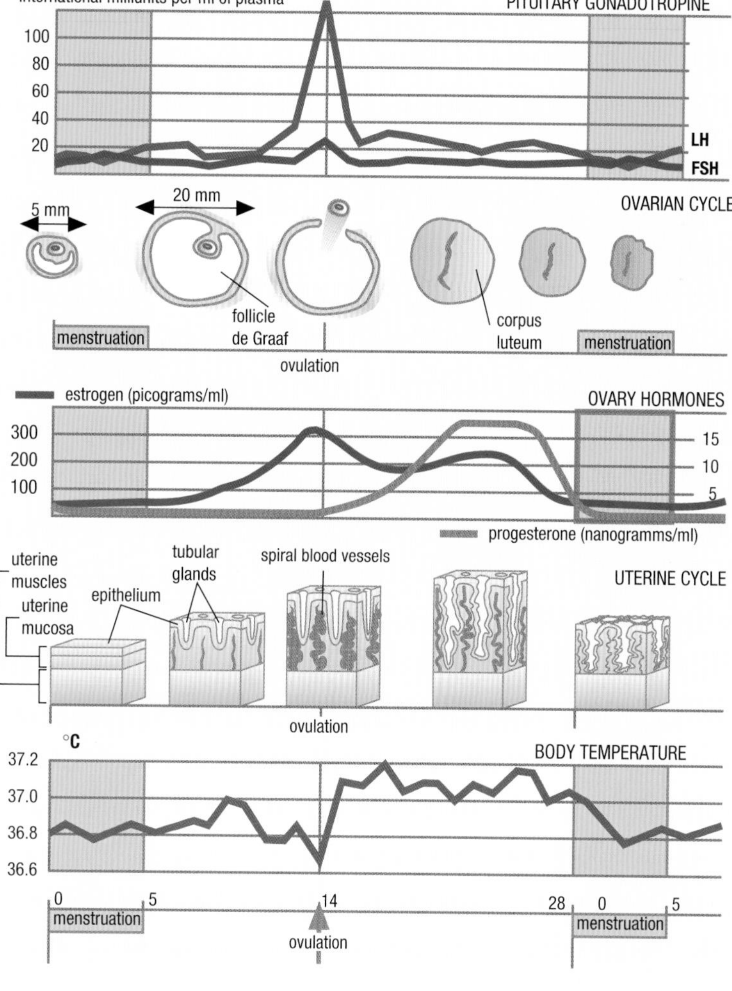

THE INTERACTION BETWEEN BODY AND ENVIRONMENT

THE ABILITY TO PERCEIVE ENVIRONMENTAL CHANGES BOTH INTERNAL AND EXTERNAL, TO KNOW HOW TO MOVE IN THE SURROUNDING TERRITORY, AND BE ABLE TO INTERACT WITH OTHER LIVING BEINGS IS ESSENTIAL TO SURVIVAL.

THESE FUNCTIONS ARE PERFORMED BY SPECIFIC ORGANS OF SENSE AND MOVEMENT.

THE PERCEPTION OF SELF AND THE ENVIRONMENT

In order for a body to thrive it is necessary for there to be a harmonious balance between all its own vital aspects, as well as with the conditions of the environment in which it lives and the interactions that it has with other living beings. In other words, to survive a body - which is in itself delicately balanced, must take into account many external variables. We have seen that the nervous system monitors the internal environment, both from the physical-chemical perspective as well as the metabolic view. It is continuously in contact with the external environment, and takes into account the process commands sent to various parts of the body and ensures that the responses are suitable for the circumstances. It also mediates in real time any disturbance in the body's delicate balance that are cause by exposure to environmental variables.

It is vital that order is maintained in the body's interaction with the environment and that it is able to collect the necessary information about the physical conditions of the local environmental. This task is performed by the sensory receptors - these are sometimes grouped with other auxiliary cells that form real and sensory organs. In other instances, they are dispersed or located in internal organs and tissues.

In addition, there is interaction between the nervous system and the environment (both external and internal). None of the internal balances (breathing, nutritional, circulatory, endocrine...) can be maintained efficiently without the correct muscle function. This is also required for the individual to be able to move around in order to find suitable environments in which to live, as well as to escape any dangers that present, and also to find sexual partners. None of this is possible without a robust locomotive system.

SENSORY RECEPTORS

Sensory receptors are the cells that specialise in reacting to particular environmental stimuli. The signals that are received by the body can be extremely varied in nature. They may be physical, electro-magnetic, mechanical or chemical. The receptors are excitable cells ▸26 that have developed the ability to detect even the smallest modifications to a particular environmental variable. They can then convert the collected information into an electric signal and send it on to the nervous system's central processing areas.

In most cases, information coming from the sensory receptors is transmitted to specific encephalic areas that specialise in processing nerve signals that are perceived as sensations, i.e. as subjective phenomena that are closely associated with each stimulus. The receptors may be at one end of a sensitive nervous fibre that is free from myelinic

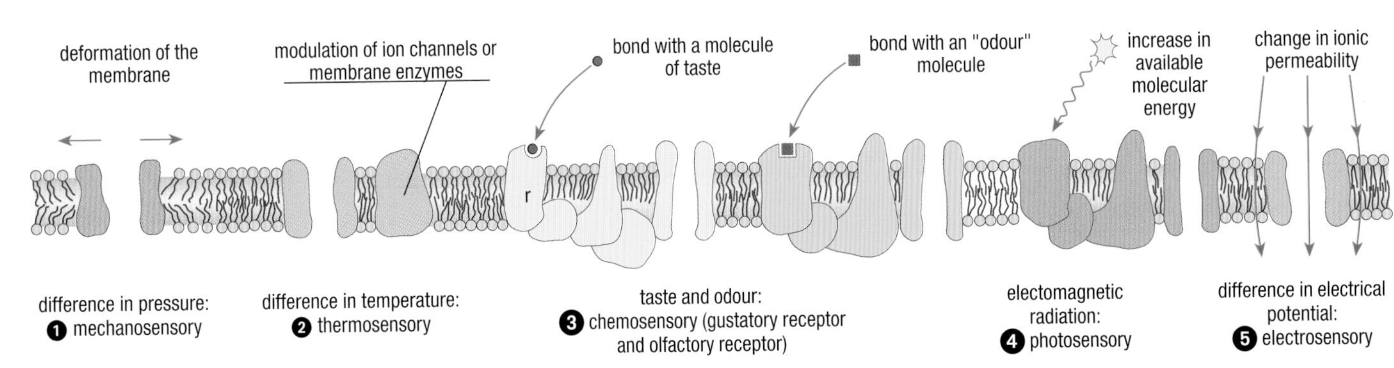

▼ **TRANSDUCTION**
Characteristics of the membranes of various types of sensory receptors. The ionic permeability varies depending on the type of stimulus:
❶ *mechanosensory ion channels that respond to physical deformation of the membrane;*
❷ *thermosensory ion channels or enzymes such as Na +-K +-ATPase which change with temperature;*
❸ *chemosensory membrane receptors that bind to specific molecules (taste or odor) by triggering a chain of reactions that change ion channels;*
❹ *photosensory as the rhodopsin molecules that are activated by radiation triggering a chain of reactions that change ion channels;*
❺ *electrosensory ion channels are directly sensitive to changes in voltage.*

sheathing, or they may come into contact with a nervous fibre's synapse.

Receptors can, however, also be classified by other criteria - they can be distinguished according to the source of the stimulus they receive:

- internal sensors, these are sensitive to changes in the internal environment are found in the organs and tissues of the locomotor system as well as the visceral bodies and the endothelia;
- external sensors, these are sensitive to changes in the external environment, and are located on the surface of the body.

They can also be distinguished according to the type of stimulus they receive:

- photoreceptors; these are sensitive to stimulation from bright light
- mechanoreceptors; these are sensitive to stimulation from mechanical events
- chemoreceptors sensitive; these are sensitive to contact with chemicals
- thermoreceptors; these are sensitive to stimulation from sources of heat
- nociceptors; these are sensitive to stimuli indicating damage to tissue or pain.

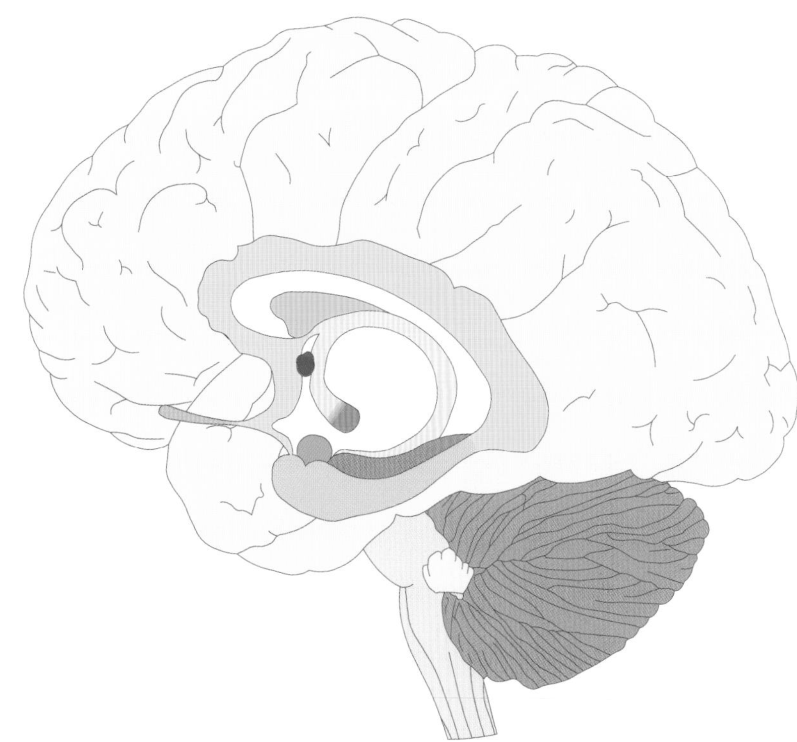

▲ **Integration**
In addition to the cerebral cortex, the limbic system and reticular formation cooperate actively in the production of sensations.

THE COMMON CHARACTERISTICS OF SENSORY RECEPTORS

In order to perform their functions correctly, sensory receptor cells have certain common characteristics. Whatever the nature of the sensory information stimulus that they are specialised in perceiving, be this a rise in temperature, a difference in acidity or a particular wavelength of light, the response is some kind of electrochemical message in the form of an action potential that is sent to the encephalic neurons for interpretation.

The role of the receptors therefore is to transform stimulus from one form of energy to another. This may be thermal, chemical or electromagnetic, and results in changes in the membrane potential. If this is more than the pre-set minimum intensity threshold, it evokes a nervous impulse that is then propagated in the sensory neurons. This potential action generates a message which is sent from the sensor at the body's periphery to the higher processing centres in the spinal cord, encephalic torso and sensory cortex ▸188.

The transformation of a stimulus to a potential difference is called transduction - this a process that involves a significant signal amplification. If information that is received by the nervous system identifies a specific sensation, the stimulus is interpreted as a feeling with a growing intensity. The relationship between the stimulus intensity and intensity of the feeling is mathematically logarithmic.

The intensity of feeling also depends on the number of activated receptors. Each receptor is only sensitive to a specific type of stimulus, and that is usually within a certain range - for example, the receptors of the retina ▸219 are sensitive to electromagnetic radiation that has wavelengths of between 400 and 760 µm.

Quality differences within a given type of feeling are the result of integration at the level of the cerebral cortex ▸191. Some receptors are sensitive to more than one kind of stimulus, but only of the same basic nature. For example, some of the sensors in the skin are able to detect touch, pressure and mechanical vibrations. The frequency of signal generation in receptors tends is often gradually reduced when the stimulus is persistent. If a receptor is continuously stimulated, in may be deactivated. This process is called adaptation, and ensures that the intensity of feeling decreases with time.

SENSORY INTEGRATION

The signals generated by the receptors are sent to specific areas of the cerebral cortex ▸187, the vicinity of which is known as an associative area ▸191. Here, the messages are analysed and processed in the primary sensory area, where they are compared with sensory experiences that are stored in the system's information archive. Associative areas mainly receive impulses from the thalamus and the cortex, but they also get them from by the limbic system ▸169, 214. In addition to processing sensory inputs, they also interpret them - this includes the aspects concerned with instinctive and emotional behaviour, such as joy, fear, pleasure, anger and so on as well as memory.

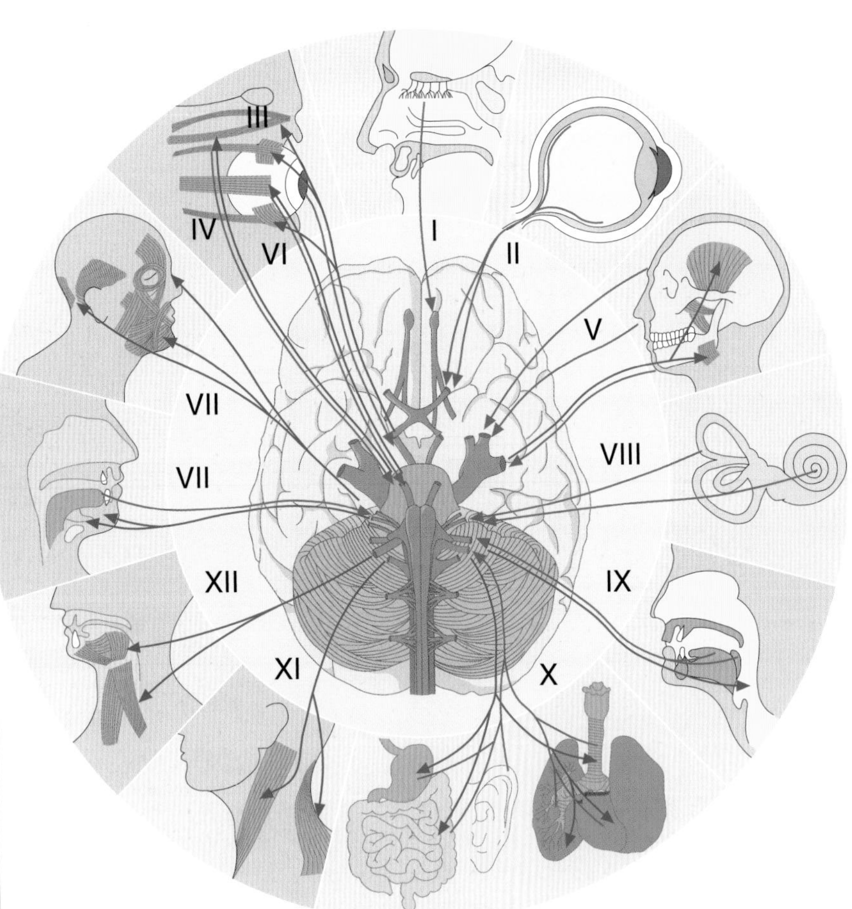

◀ **The cranial nerves**
From the underside of the brain branch off the 12 cranial nerves that send and receive information on the head, neck and most of the internal organs. They are usually marked with a Roman numeral, only three are related, that carry information from sense organs to the brain (A), only two are motors (M) and seven are composed of both motor fibers, and sensory fibers (PM);
I olfactory nerve: (A) transmits sensations from the nose;
II optical nerve: (A) transmits sensations from the eyes;
III oculomotor nerve: AM;
IV troclear nerve: AM;
V trigeminal nerve: AM;
VI abduct nerve: AM;
VII facial nerve: AM, transmits sensations from the taste buds of 2 / 3 of the tongue;
VIII acoustic nerve: A;
IX glossopharyngeal nerve: AM, transmits tactile and gustatory information collected from the back of the tongue and pharynx;
X vagus nerve: AM;
XI accessory nerve: M;
XII hypoglossal nerve: M.

THE SENSE ORGANS

The sense organs are the main source of information from the outside world. It is through the nerve endings that sight, sound ►224, smell ►230, taste ►230,234 and balance ►228 are perceived. The brain receives and processes essential information and then deduces the most appropriate responses to the environmental conditions.

The continuous stream of data stimulates the brain activity. It has been demonstrated that the more information that is received, the better are the brain's intellectual processing capabilities.

This is why some scientists believe that human intelligence is a direct result of the use of hands. The hand is even considered a cortical body, which emphasises the magnitude of the role it plays in the area of representation ►188.

The action potential generated in various anatomical parts by the sensory receptors is transmitted to sensory nerves and then mixed. The two-way sensory system is organised by three neurons - the first neuron sends information to the central nervous system, the second is a door to the thalamus, and the third connects to the primary area of the sensory cerebral cortex.

There are two basic types of receptors. Those that are sensitive to tactile sensations, heat, pain and body position - these are mostly in the skin and are distributed over / throughout the body. The others are the sense organs that are housed in the head, these are protected by the bones of the skull, and are directly linked to the brain through the cranial nerves. This is a strategic situation that is common to all animals: the ability to move the head makes it possible to move the main sensory receptors and so collect more information and guide the consequent response movements.

This leads to a review of the various functions performed by the body's sensory structures.

THE EYE & VISION

The receptors which are responsible for vision are located in the eyes. These are light sensitive, and are connected to other, more complex structures, that make sight possible. There are three functional membranes involved. These are:

- the sclerotic membrane, this is external, tough and resistant, and gives the appropriate form to the ocular globe, keeping it in the desired shape. It is composed of the cornea and the sclera.
- the uveal membrane, this forms the middle layer, and is comprised of the choroid, ciliary body, and iris. It provides the blood vessels which support the blood cells of the eye and the same time, being strongly pigmented, prevents light from reflecting

internally, which helps keep the retinal image clear;
– the retinal membrane, this forms the inner layer and houses the eye's photosensors.

These membranes are arranged so that they form a suitable optical system that concentrate's the rays of light on the retina in the form of images, just as in a camera:

- the sclerotic membrane gives shape to the cornea, it is very convex and approximately 0.5 mm thick. It is the first structure that natural light crosses when it enters the eye. It is not vascularised, and its cells absorb nutrients and oxygen from the veil of liquid products produced by the tear glands as well as from direct contact with air. Moreover, it is the surface of the body that has the greatest density of nerve receptors per square centimetre. It is why even the smallest trauma there causes acute pain;
- the uveal membrane and retina merge forming the ciliary body which is very rich in smooth ciliary muscle fibres. This is where the iris is located - this is effectively a circular cover with an orifice - the pupil, at its centre. Bounded by a muscular sphincter, the pupil is able to vary its diameter, and thus works much like a diaphragm. It therefore adjusts the quantity of light that enters the eye.

The ciliary body also houses the lens and its suspensory ligaments. The lens is a transparent elastic body with a biconvex section and located on average 2 mm behind the cornea. The lens is elastic so that when the ciliary muscles contract, its crystalline microstructure stretches, and when they relax it shortens. This makes it possible for the lens to focus, and therefore obtain clear images.

The space between the cornea and the lens is filled with aqueous humour, a nutritional liquid that is secreted from the ciliary body. The region behind the lens is filled with vitreous humour - this is a transparent gelatinous substance, that is crossed by a delicate network of connective fibres, and is similar to water but is more viscous and also nutritional. Over the passage of time, a number of small opaque objects may become apparent in the sight - these are sometimes referred to as vitreal floating bodies, and are often visible as

▲ **Iris**
Picture of a blue iris: this ring of muscle fibers can contract and relax according to the amount of light, and has different, genetically determined colors. The pupil (the black circle in the center) is the hole through which light enters the vitrous body.

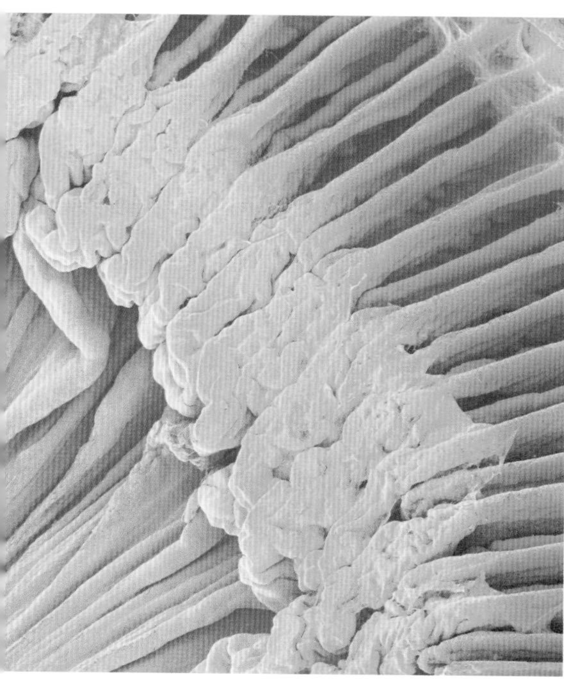

▲ **Cilliary body**
With the lens removed, the scanning electron microscope (SEM) shows a detail of the inner ring of muscle surrounding the iris (in pink lower left). The choroid starts in the upper right. In bright orange are the muscle fibers.

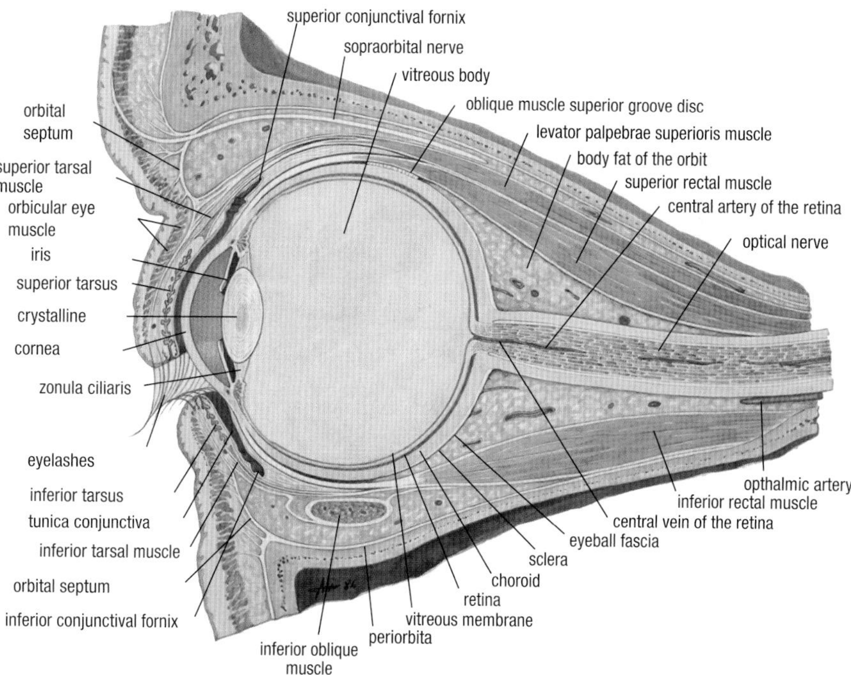

▲ **Anatomy of the eye**
Principal anatomical elements of the eye.

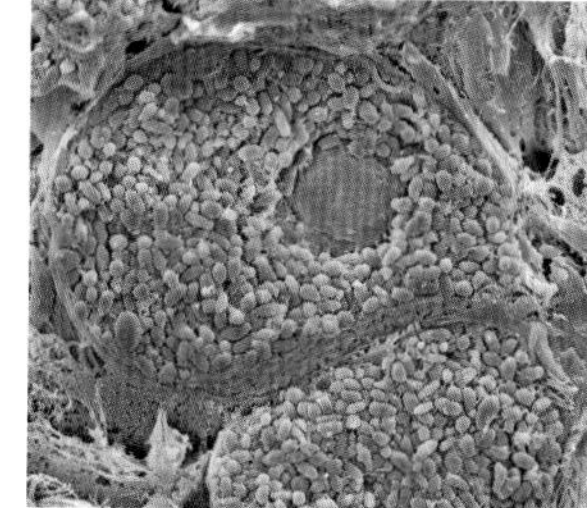

◀ **Choroid**
SEM micrograph of a section of the choroid which distinguishes a pigmented cell (red) which while absorbing light, prevents internal reflection.

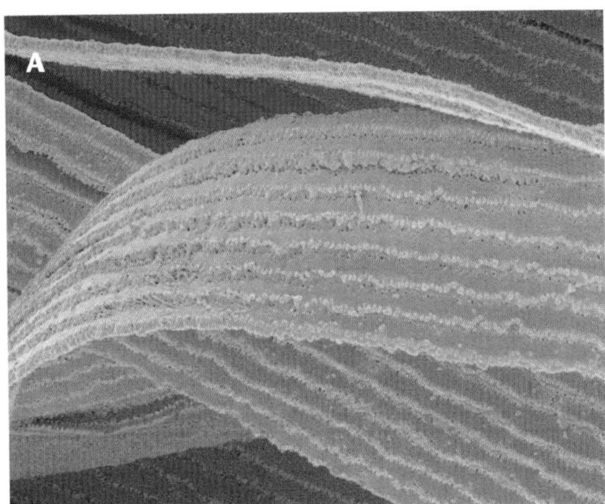

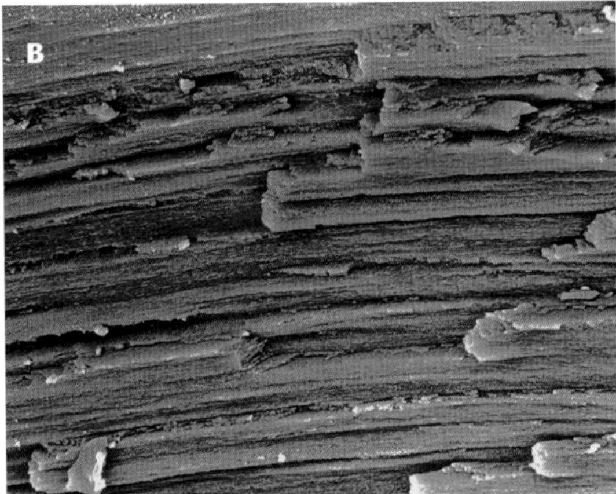

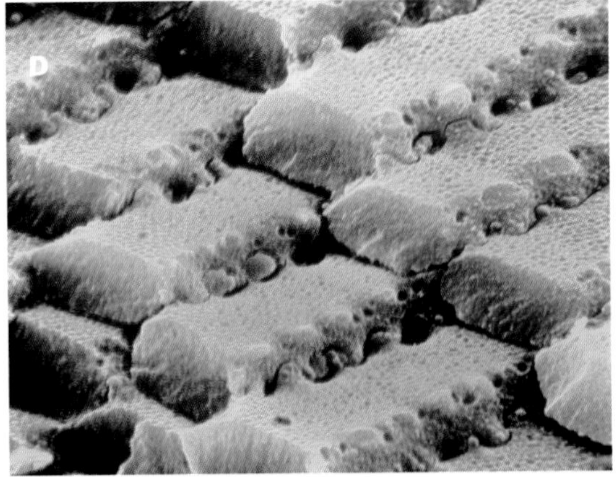

▶ **Microscopic crystal**
False color images of crystalline realized with the scanning electron microscope (SEM) show the structure of the fiber cells.
A. *During development, cells of the lens lose their nucleus and turn into an inert and transparent protein structure. They are not irrigated with blood, but absorb nutrients from the fluids that surround them.*
B. *Adhesive to each other, fibers with their elongated shape and their size proportions: the length of 10 mm is about 2000 times greater than their diameter of only 5 microns.*
C. *The plane of fracture of the frozen sample photographed at a higher resolution, shows the regular layout ("crystalline") not only of cells (gray), but also of the proteins in them (light stripes).*
D. *It is believed that the transparency of the lens and its optical capabilities derive from this very regular arrangement, as well as the lack of nuclei and the number of joints that connect with each other, like a zipper.*

mobile shadows. The front part of the ocular globe is protected by a transparent mucosa membrane called the conjunctiva - this covers the surface of the eye and lines the interior of the eyelids.
In order for vision to be possible, the light taken in by the eye has to stimulate the photosensitive cells which are located in the retina. First, however, it has to pass through the conjunctiva, the cornea, the aqueous humour, the lens, the vitreous humour and then it finally reaches the retina.
Whenever light passes from one medium to another, it is subjected to a specific refraction, that is, it undergoes a deviation from the original direction of propagation. The degree to which the light actually bends is determined by the refractive index of the material it is passing through. The lens is convergent, that is, it is thicker at the centre than at the edges. The result is that it converges the parallel rays of light - in other words, focuses it, onto the photosensitive cells in the retina. The quality of the focus depends on the geometric features of the two opposing surfaces that are altered by the ciliary muscles. When the lens is altered to be more convex, it can focus on close objects, and vice versa when the ciliary muscles relax, it flattens out and allows a better view of distant objects. The ability to change the shape of the lens by contracting or relaxing the ciliary muscles is called accommodation, and the degree to which it occurs depends on how far away the observed object is.
The optical power of the eye is rated at 60 diopter, this is equivalent to a convergent lens that has a focal length of 16.7 mm. The vision of nearby objects - where the light rays are already converging, is made sharper by the automatic accommodation of the lens. Permanent eye deformations or inability of the lens to accommodate sight defines different

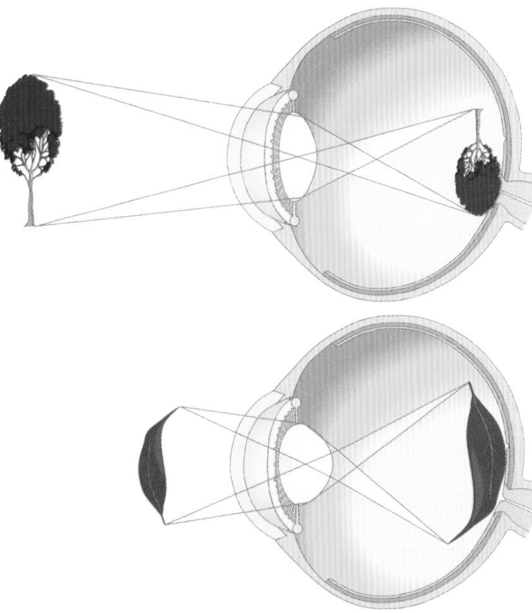

▶ **Focus**
The lens is completely surrounded by the ciliary muscle which is connected by strong ligaments, and can change by varying the thickness and the refracting ability. When the muscles are relaxed, the lens is stretched and its thickness decreased slightly which deflects the light rays in parallel: only distant objects can be seen "in focus". When the muscles contract, its thickness increases making the rays increasingly parallel: this will focus near objects.

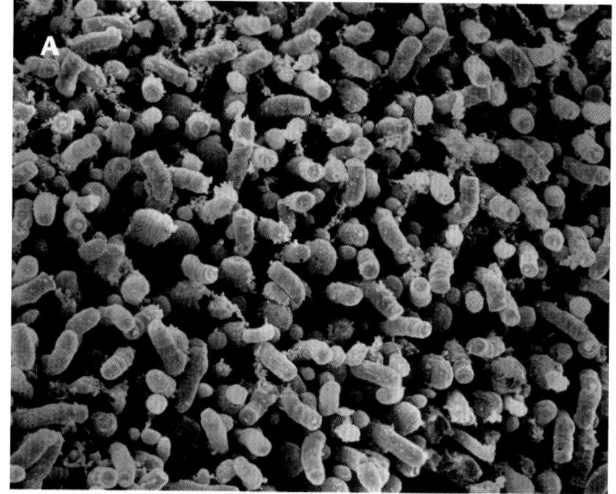

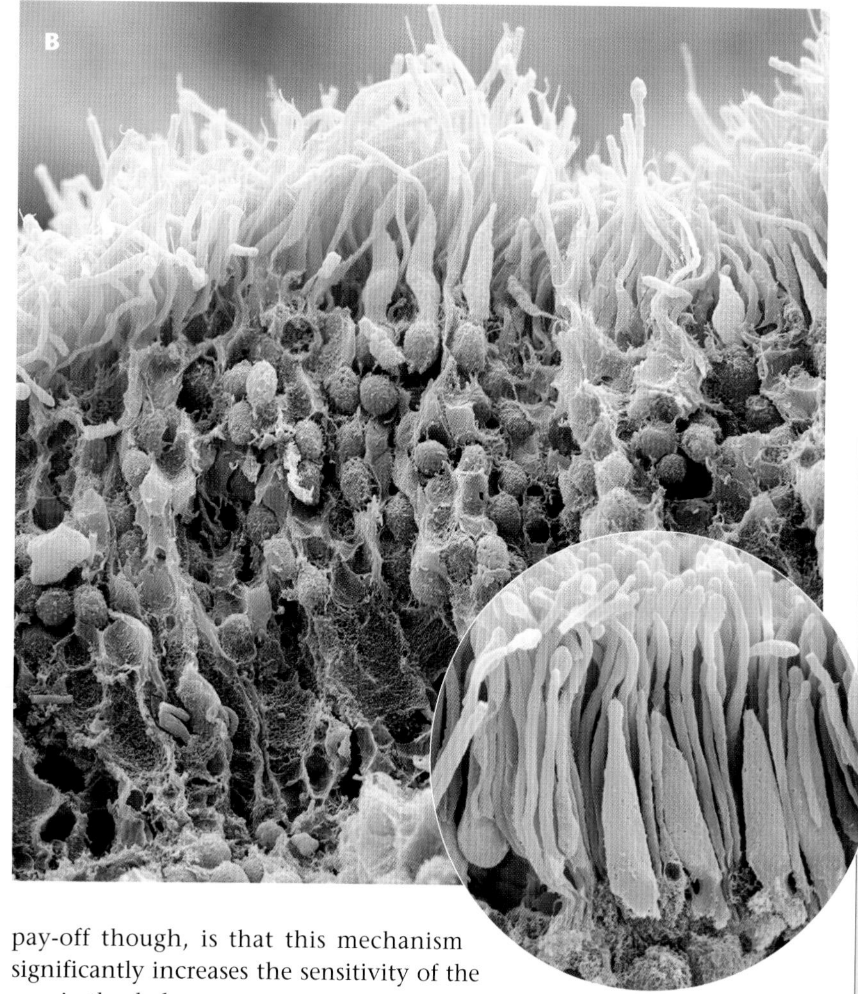

▶▲ Retina under the microscope
False color images of retina from a scanning electron microscope (SEM) show the structure of the various cell types.
A. *Surface of the retina: cones in blue and pink. Rods in purple. There are about 130 million rods in each retina, while there are about 6 and a half million cones.*
B. *Section: from bottom to top: the cell bodies of optical ganglion cells, (light red) that form the optic nerve, the cell bodies of bipolar neurons and receptors (red) and rod receptors to (white) with cone receptors (yellow). In detail, rods (white) and cones (yellow).*

visual disorders (short-sightedness, far-sightedness, etc.). In the retina there are two types of photosensor - both of these are located in the outer layer and are related to bipolar neurons. These, in turn, are in contact with the neural ganglions whose axons are very long - together they combine to form the optical nerve.

The photosensors, which named in keeping with the characteristics of their relative shapes different functions and features:

The rods: these are very abundant, and are distributed across the retina, but especially in the peripheries. They contain only one type of pigment and therefore are not sensitive to colour but simply to variations in brightness. They also work well in conditions of low light intensity - each rod is sufficiently sensitive to react to a single photon. This is made more effective because they are slow to activate - this means that any stimuli arriving within 100 ms of each other will overlap, and even though the energies involved are very weak, it helps to increase sensitivity of photoreception.

There is also another way in which the rods are able to magnify their signals - many are connected to the same inter-neurone, and this combines their action potentials thereby causing an amplified signal. It is, however, not very precise - the images collected by the resolution of converging are of lower quality than they would each be independently. The pay-off though, is that this mechanism significantly increases the sensitivity of the eyes in the dark.

There are far fewer cones than there are rods, and they are concentrated only in the central area of the retina. They contain three different types of pigment, with one type being particularly abundant in every cone. Each cone, therefore, is sensitive to a specific range of wavelengths of light - some are dedicated to short wavelengths, others to medium or long. Those with a peak in the short wavelengths are called S cones (from an English abbreviation for

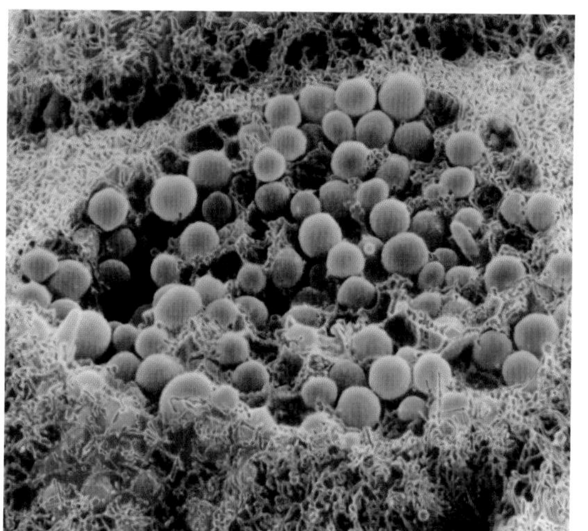

◀ Melanocyte
SEM False color photograph of a retinal melanocyte: membrane partially opened to show the internal granules of melanin pigment which is sensitive to light. Melanin absorbs the light that passes through the retina, preventing reflections and clarify vision. Numerous microvilli (violet) covering the surface of the epithelial pigment cells, the outer layer of the retina, and behind which lies the choroid.

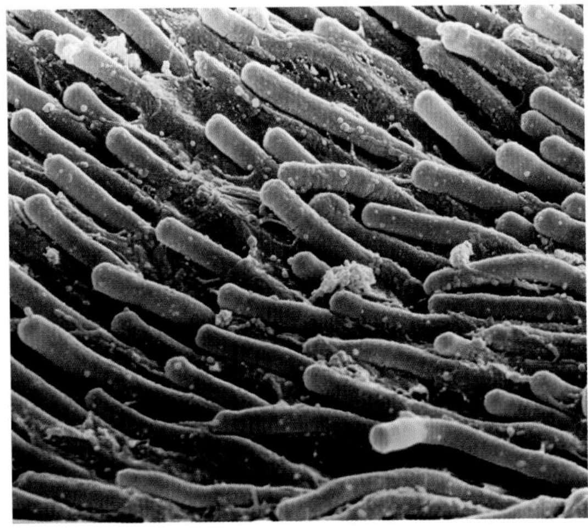

▶ **Peripheral retina**
False color SEM photograph of the peripheral zone of the retina, literally hung from rods.

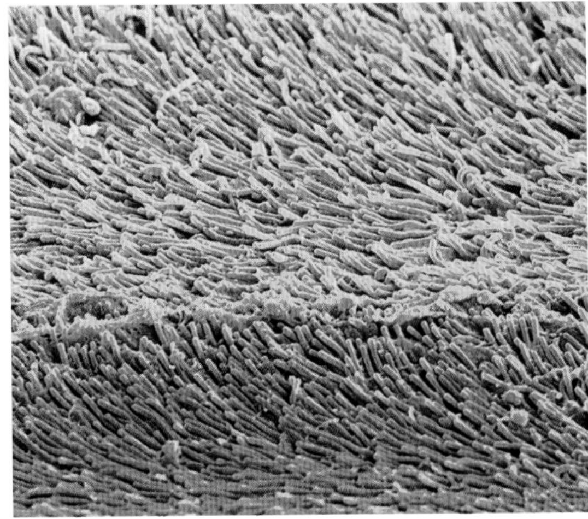

▶ **Rods**
False color SEM photograph of a group of rods: obviously you can only see the outer parts.

short), those with a peak in the medium wavelengths are called M cones, and those with a peak in the long waves are referred to as L cones. The types L and M which are encoded by the genes that are present on the x chromosome are the responsible for hereditary sight diseases such as colour-blindness.

Each of the receptors is stimulated by a particular wavelength of light, but the same wavelength can also stimulate other cones in different ways. For example, the colour yellow has a wavelength of 564 nm - this strongly stimulates the L cones, has an average effect on the M cones and only weakly on the S cones. Once the light has been converted into electrical impulses, the central nervous system then combines the information from each type of photoreceptor to produce the perception of different colours.

Unlike the rods, the cones are not very sensitive to the intensity of light: hundreds of photons are needed to activate a cone. This gives them a slow response speed but provides vision with high detail resolution. When they are stimulated, therefore, rods and cones are depolarised and spontaneously issue the neurotransmitter. The light stimulation blocks this process and causes hyper-polarisation of the membrane. When visual pigments (rhodopsin in the rods, iodopsin in cones) absorb light energy, they change conformation. This causes the activation of transducin, a protein that, in turn activates an enzyme that breaks down the cell.

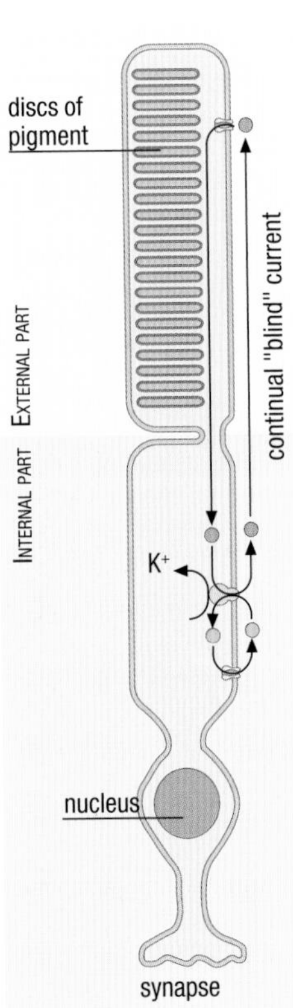

▼ **Rod**
The dark, the sodium channels in the outer membrane of the rod are open: the flow
◯ Na + flowing to the internal part causes a continuous depolarizing current that causes a current in the dark. The continuous output
◯ K + balances the entry of Na + ions and, to maintain constant levels of both intracellular ion intervient the Na +-K +-ATPase membrane of the inner part of the rod, pumping K + from outside.

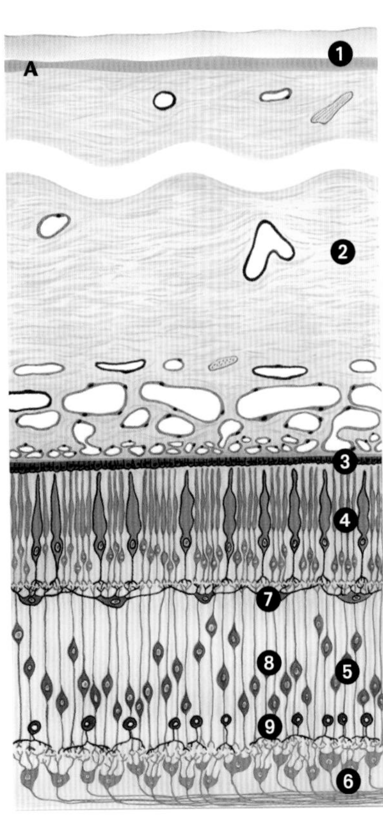

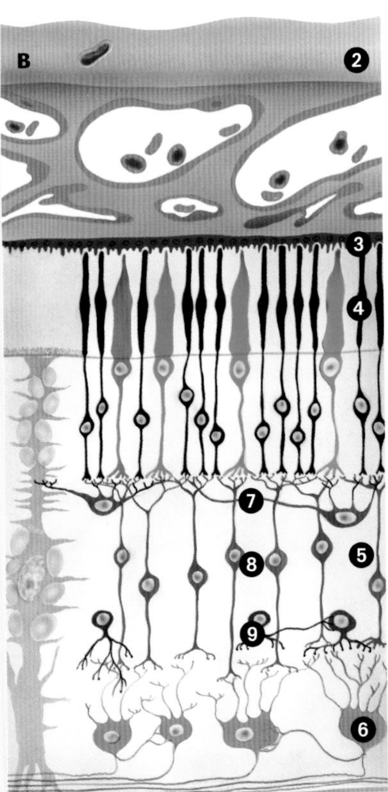

◀ **Light path**
Patterns that reproduce the structure of the eye (A) and retina (B).
Exceeded sclerotic ❶ and choroid ❷, the light reaches the retina, the back of the eye, covering the choroid.
On the surface epithelium is the pigmented cell ❸ followed by a photoreceptive layer ❹: rods (thin) and cones (rounded). Stimuli induce electrical pulses in interneurons ❺ analyzing them to ganglion cells ❻ whose long axons form the optic nerve that reaches the brain. Interneurons are of various types: the horizontal cells ❼, the bipolar cells ❽ and amacrine cells ❾.

Reducing the concentration of these substances closes the ionic channels and the release of the neurotransmitter is paused. This alters the polarity of the inter-neurone the photosensor is linked to. The process is particularly efficient in the rods: activation of a single molecule of rhodopsin can enable hundreds of molecules of transducin, each of which then operates on thousands of molecules per second. It is thanks to this propagation of effects that the rods are also able to react quickly to tiny amounts of light.

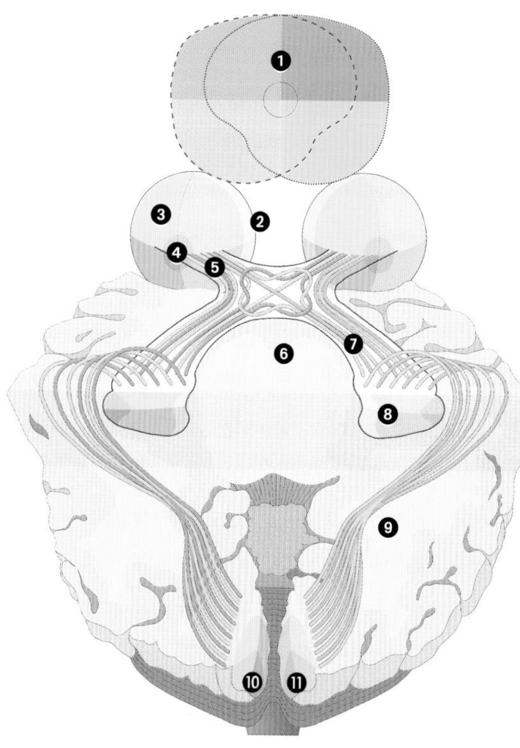

◀ **Visual mechanism**
❶ The combination of the two eyes visual field is divided into four colors to highlight the location of the next image. What is seen in each eye is slightly different, but there is a large overlap.
❷ Periphery of the retina: the images are less sharp.
❸ The retinal image is sharper for the high concentration of cones.
❹ The fovea contains only cone: it has the clearest picture.
❺ The optic nerve carries the information to the chiasm; ❻ in the optic chiasm the internal fibers from of each eye cross, the others continue on the same side. ❼ The optic tract is composed of fibers leaving the chiasm, and divides into branches that terminate in the lateral geniculate body (❽). Hence the optical radiation ❾ continues until the visual cortex: the left occipital lobe ❿ receives information from the left side of both eyes, corresponding to the right half of the visual field, that of the right occipital lobe ⓫ receives information from the right side of both eyes, corresponding to the left half of the visual field.

CONE TYPES

Name of sensitivity	Peak of sensitivity	Scope	Color
S cones	420 nm	from 400 to 500 nm	blue
M cones	534 nm	from 450 to 630 nm	blue-green
L cones	564 nm	from 500 to 700 nm	yellow-green

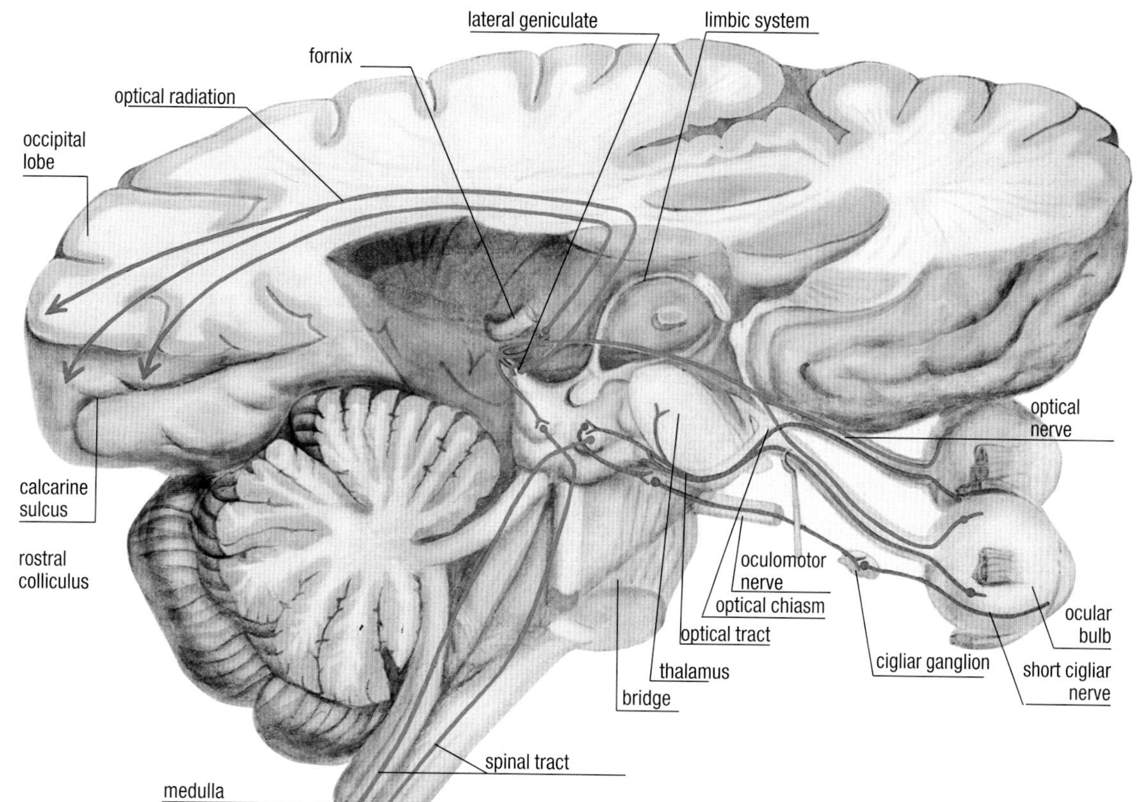

◀ **Location of the optic nerves**
Rear section of the ventral brain showing the location of the visual impulse from the eyes to the occipital lobes of the cerebral cortex.
motor endings
sensory endings.

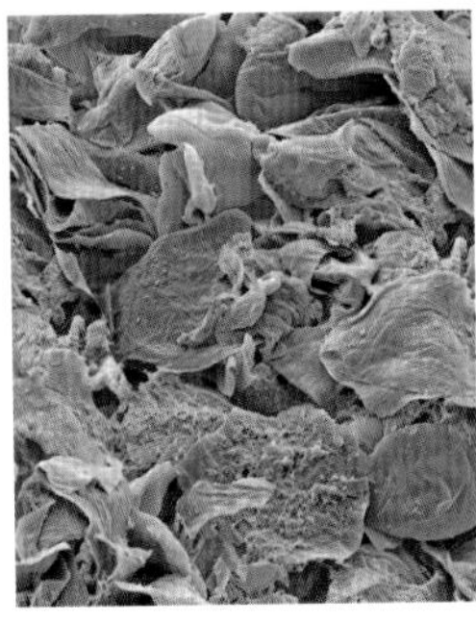

▲ **Auditory canal**
Scanning electron microscope photograph (SEM) in false colors of the inner surface of the external ear canal, lined with wax and dead cells. Produced by glands in the wall, the wax prevents the access of bacteria and objects that could damage the eardrum.

▶ **Ossicular chain**
Malleus, incus and stapes that forward vibration from the eardrum (which supports the arrow) to the oval window of the cochlea.

▼▶ **Anatomy of the ear**
Anatomical elements of the main ear, the bone structure of the cochlea (right, above) and cochlear nerve (right, below).

THE EAR AND HEARING

The ear is the anatomical structure that senses the acoustic waves that arise from the surrounding environment and transforms them into nerve impulses that the brain can interpret. These sounds can convey a huge amount of information at the same time: words, music, noises - they constitute a tangle of waves that must be transformed into intelligible signals.

In order for the brain to be able to receive information in a sufficiently developed manner to be usefully interpreted, the ear needs to be capable of distinguishing the frequency and extent of the various acoustic waves. This means it must be able to distinguish between and recognise the various tones, frequencies and volumes of sounds produced by different sources.

The process of acoustic analysis starts with a progressive transformation of the signal: from waves noise (air), to vibration (bone), to mechanical waves (internal fluids in the ear). This is undertaken by specific parts of the ear:

– the external ear; this consists of the outer fleshy structure known as the pinna or auricle which is specially shaped to conduct sound waves towards the ear canal. This leads to the tympanic membrane or eardrum, and is filled with short, stiff hairs that are used to keep out small creatures and debris.

– the middle ear; this lies behind the tympanic membrane and is comprised of a bone cavity that is filled with air. From it there leads a narrow canal known as the Eustachian tube - this connects to the pharynx, and its purpose is to balance the air pressure on both sides of the membrane. The middle ear contains a chain of bones - the malleus (or hammer), incus (or anvil), and stapes (or bracket). One end of the malleus rests against the eardrum, and the other touches the incus, which in turn touches one end of the stapes. The other end of the stapes pushes up against a membrane that is part of a structure called the oval window. This separates the middle ear from the inner ear. Together, these components take the vibrations produced by sound waves that reach the tympanic membrane and transfer them into the fluid of the cochlea. In so doing, the three bones mechanically amplify the sound waves by around two and a half times. In turn, there is a second amplification due to the difference in sizes of the tympanic and oval window membranes. This produces a significant further magnification.

– the inner ear; this performs two functions - it houses structures that sense both hearing and balance. The former is undertaken by the cochlea, and the latter by the semicircular canals and vestibule. The cochlea is a spiral, shell-shaped structure made of very hard bone that is full of fluid and divided longitudinally by two membranes. It also contains three passages that are filled

incus
stapes
malleus

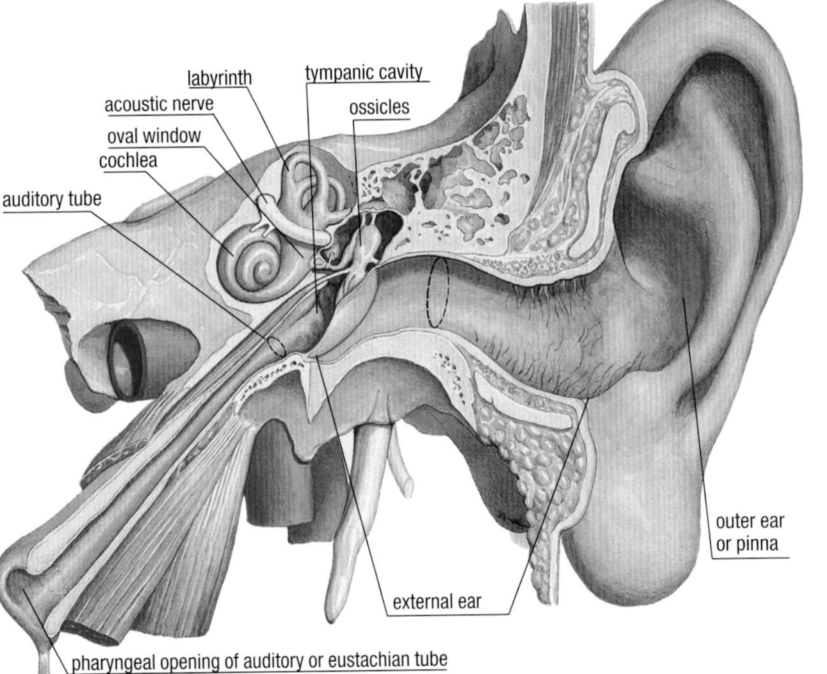

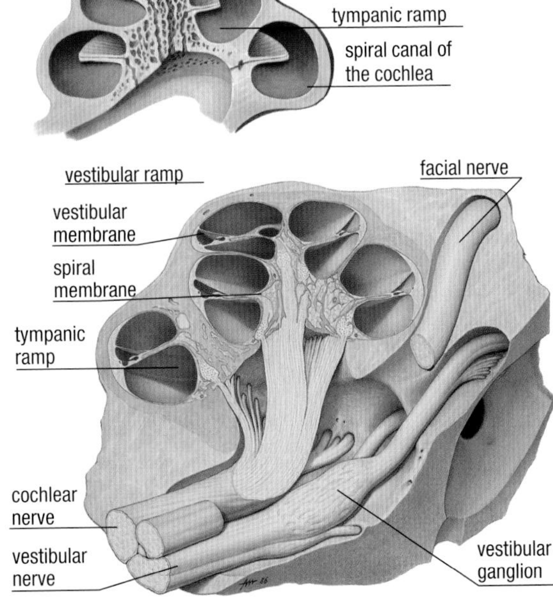

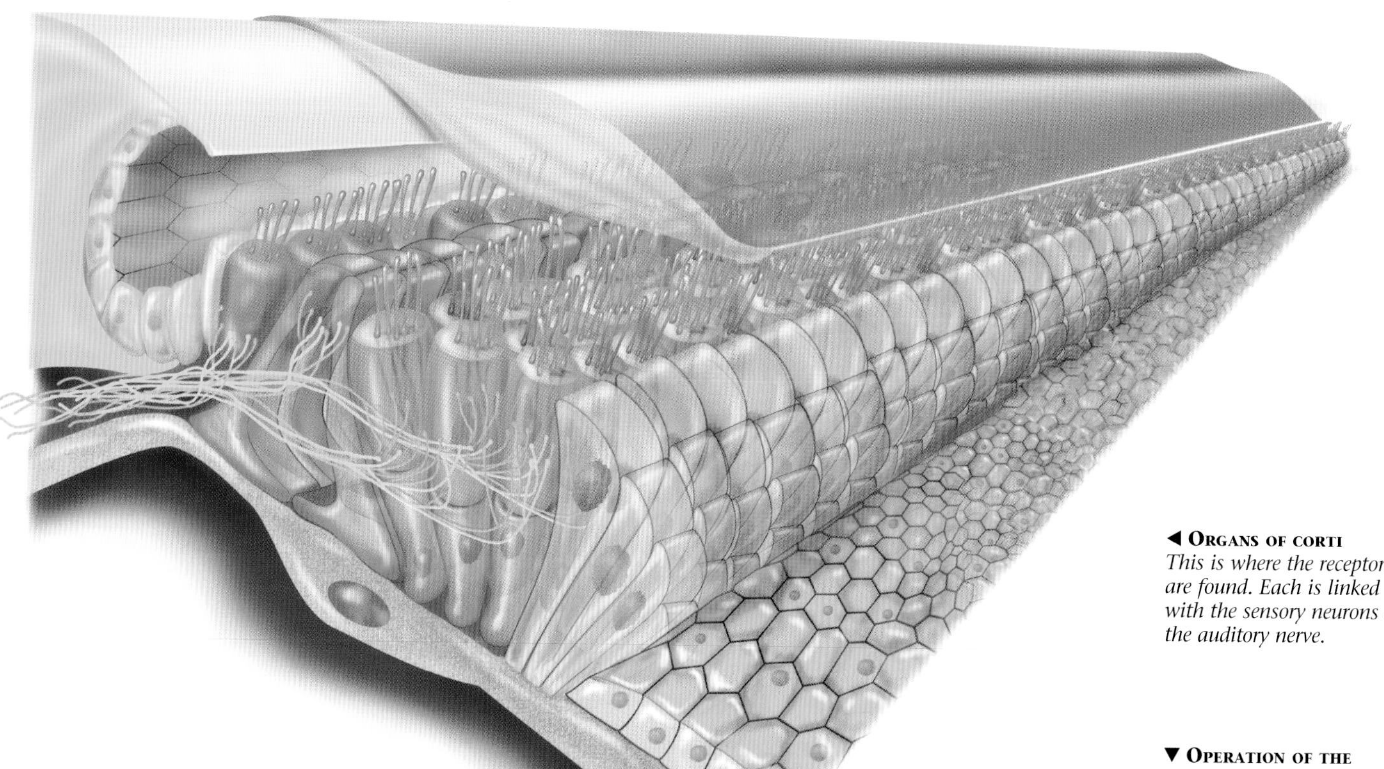

◀ **Organs of Corti**
This is where the receptors are found. Each is linked with the sensory neurons of the auditory nerve.

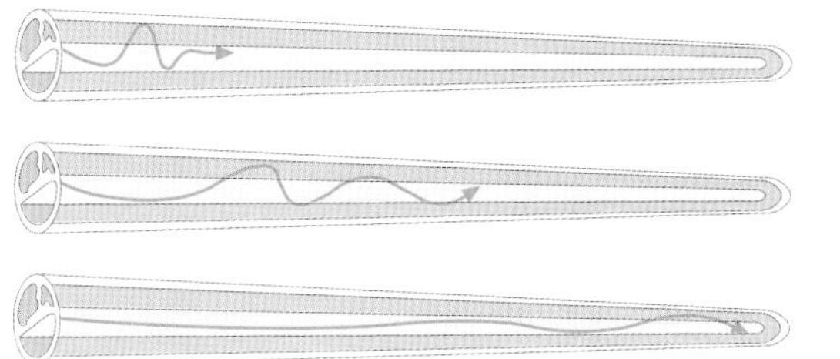

▼ **Operation of the cochlea**
The cochlea is a channel divided into three compartments: the media, cochlear or side ramp, the ramp of the eardrum and the vestibular ramp. The waves transmitted along the ramp reaches the vestibular organ of Corti on the basilar membrane by stimulating receptors on the fixed ciliates tector membrane. Sound waves of different frequencies produce different forms, stimulating different areas of the basilar membrane. In this way, the waves stimulate different receptors, which produce combinations of different sounds.

with fluid - these are the tympanic canal, the vestibular canal, and the middle canal.

- the vestibular membrane (also known as Reissner's membrane); - this is a membranous structure that separates the cochlear duct from a cavity known as the 'scala vestibuli', both of which are filled with liquid perilymph.

The membrane in the oval window is stimulated by vibrations that have travelled up the stapes, and this generates pressure waves in the perilymph of the cochlear duct. In turn, these then stimulate the hair cells of the organ of Corti, which is a specialised structure that contains up to 20,000 sound receptor cells, each of which features a fine hair that is used as a trigger mechanism. These produce neurotransmitters that stimulate the formation of nerve impulses in the sensory neurons with which they are in contact. In this way, in the inner ear fluid turns mechanical energy into nerve impulses that reach the brain. In the cochlea, however, high-frequencies are dissipated before those of lower frequencies. As a consequence of this, high-frequency vibrations enter a smaller number of sound receptors than those of low frequency. This is the basis of the complex frequency analysis

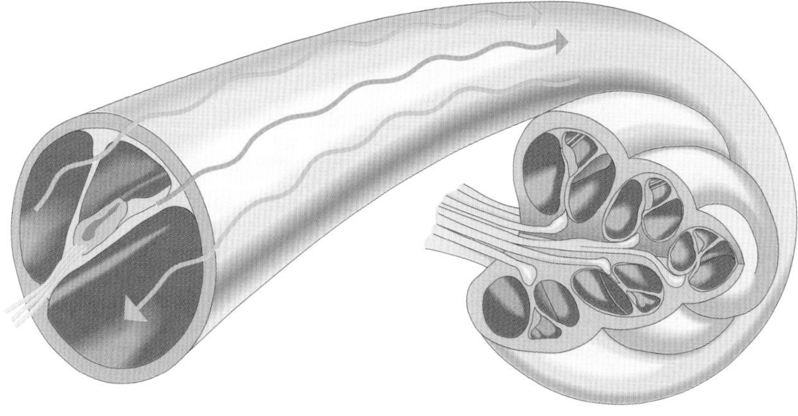

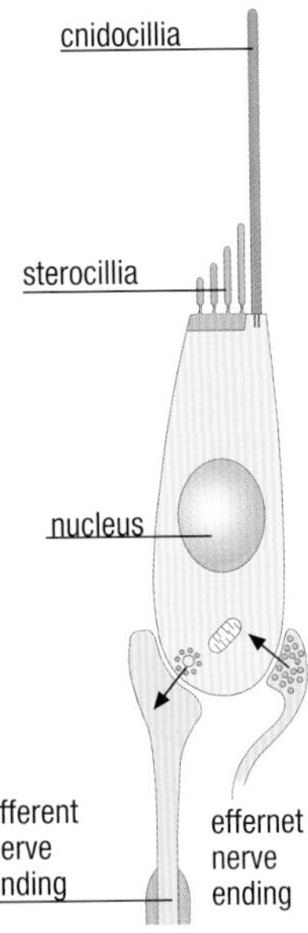

▲ Mechanoreceptors
Diagram illustrating the typical structure of a receptor that is sensitive to movements. The apical pole has many stereocillia that in the absence of stimuli, are still. When the cell is stimulated, they move from a potential action that is transmitted to the nerve cell through the release of a neurotransmitter. Sometimes, the mechanoreceptor is also connected to a synaptically efferent nerve ending, which modulates the excitement.

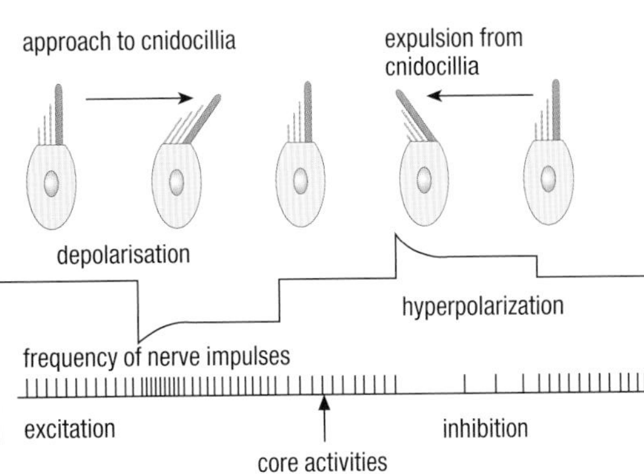

▲ Action of mechanoreceptors
Mechanoreceptors are sensitive to the direction of movement: a shorter movement of stereocillia toward the longer cnidocillia is transduced into a depolarization of the cell and an increase in the frequency of action potentials in the afferent nerve fibers. The opposite movement determines instead a hyperpolarization and a reduction in the frequency of nerve signals.

▼ Organs of Corti
Structure of the cochlea and detail of the organ of Corti in a SEM photograph in false colors: 4 rows of spindly cells, supported by pillar cells. Each cell contains up to 100 stereocillia.

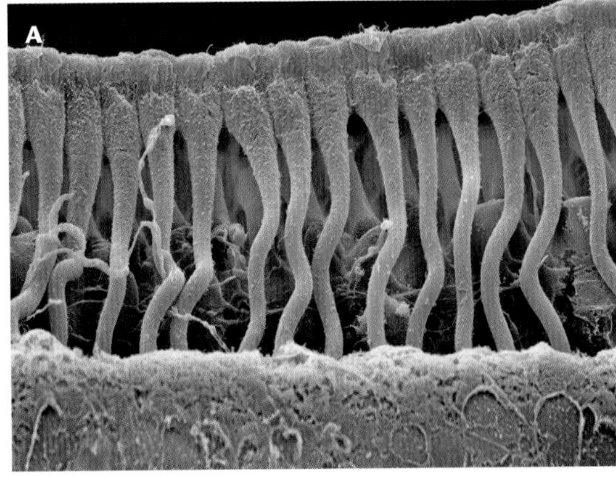

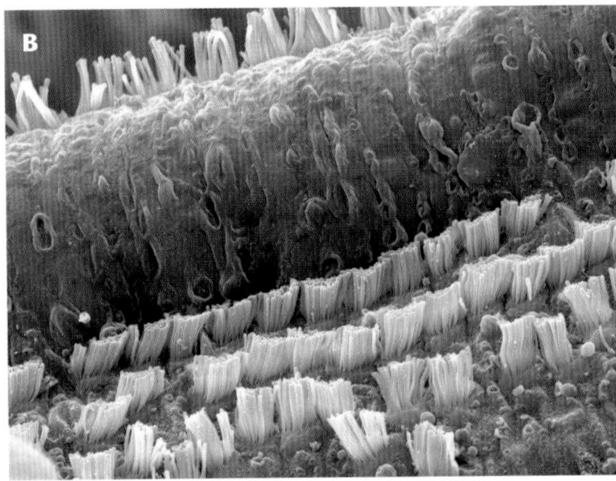

▶ Cochlea microscopic
False color images of cochlea cells from a scanning electron microscope (SEM) in false colors.
A. *Vertical section through the cochlea showing a row of columnar cells, placed along the organ of Corti. They emerge from the basilar membrane (bottom) and their distal surface (top) forms the superficial layer of the organ of Corti.*
B. *Filiform cell: usually found under the tector membrane, here removed. Sound waves deform their cillia activating the nerve impulse.*

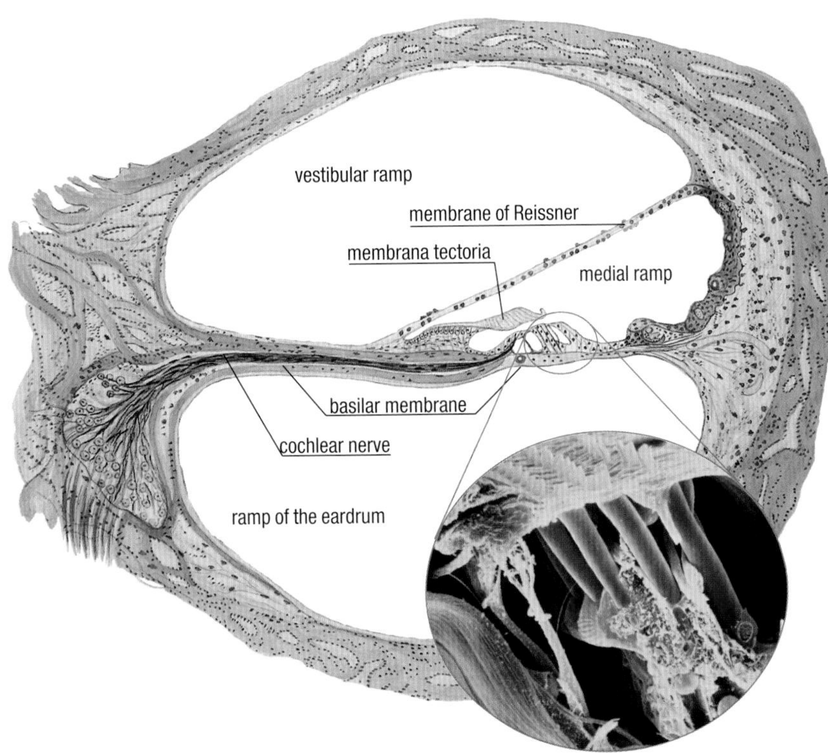

mechanism which allows the brain to discriminate between different sounds.

The analysis of different sounds is further assisted by the fact that the sound receptor cells have different lengths - each varying by a few microns. In addition to this, they are also characterised by having a range of shape recovery abilities. That is, they take different amounts of time to return to their original positions after being subjected to the compressive waves caused by sound transmission. In this way, it is possible for the brain to assess the levels of sound intensity.

In other words, when the frequency of the wave coincides with a point where the receptor is particularly sensitive, it creates a resonance that amplifies the vibration. In this way, some cells are also able to distinguish sounds that are especially weak, and thus still managing produce an electrical impulse. This potential difference is then sent to a bipolar neuron of the spiral ganglions - structures that connect each cell in the organ of Corti, whose central fibres together to form the cochlear branch of the nerve head. They end in the cochlear nuclei of the bulb which terminate in nerve fibres that reach the thalamus. Neurons enable communication between the thalamus and the temporal lobe ▶188 of the cortex, which is capable of decoding the sounds in a process that is still not fully understood. It is able to distinguish pressure variations anywhere between 20 and 18,000 cycles per second.

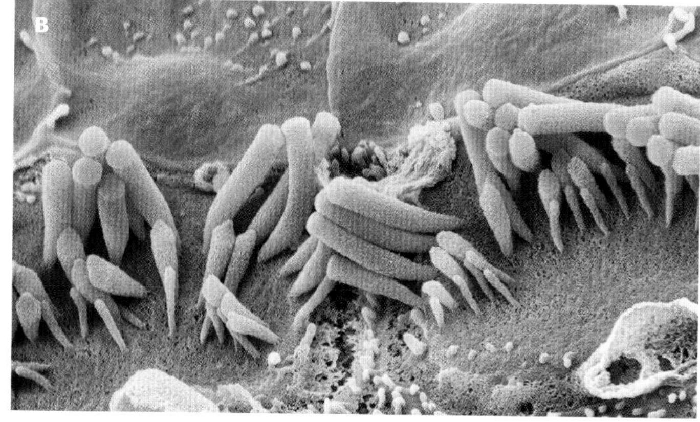

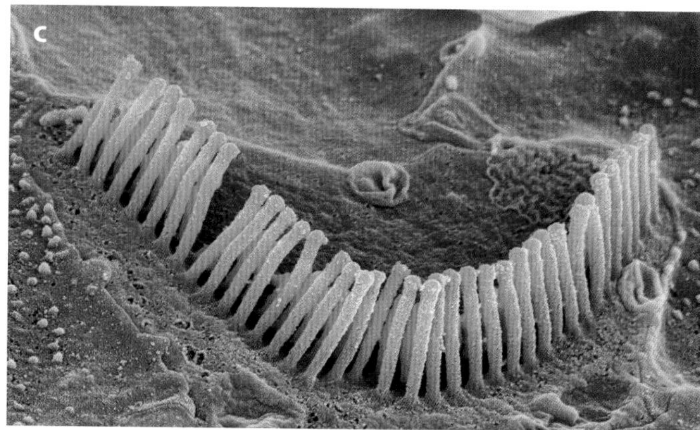

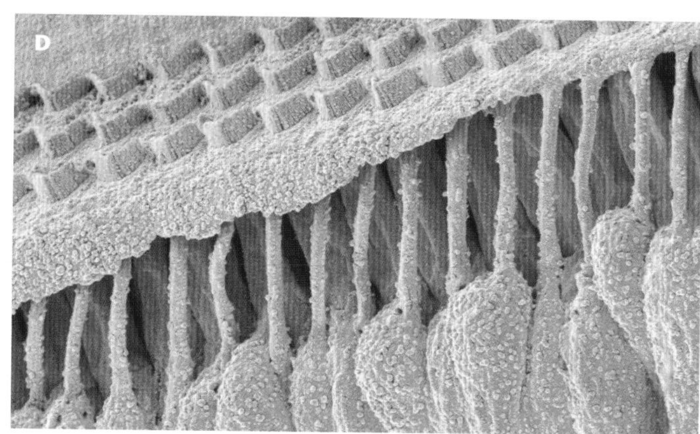

The analysis of sound does not stop there, however, as a huge amount of the information that reaches the brain is unwanted noise. It must therefore be able to identify those sounds that are of interest and exclude the rest. In doing so, it has to recognise the characteristic frequencies, tones and amplitudes of useful sounds, and find their direction of provenance. In addition to pure identification of sounds, therefore, the brain must also integrate an enormous amount of stored information, allowing the recognition and organisation of the features of such things as known languages, unknown languages, music, specific sounds and irrelevant noise.

▲ **Organ of Corti under the microscope**
False color images of details of the organ of Corti seen in false colors from a scanning electron microscope (SEM).
A. *Organ of Corti and filifrom cells on the Interior of stereocillia organized in V-shaped rows (yellow). Usually they are immersed in endolympha. The movements of this fluid trigger a sensitive reaction.*
B. *Magnifying stereocillia at rest.*
C. *Stereocillia moved by sound waves.* **D**. *The three rows of crescent-shaped areas at the top are the stereocillia, and are located on the distal surface of filiform cells. Sound waves that move the fluid causes them to bend, and this triggers the response of the electrochemical cell, which releases the neurotransmitter. This travels through the auditory nerve to the brain with information on the volume and tone of the sound. These structures of the organ of Corti are very fragile and delicate: they cannot withstand the pressure conditions that occur in the ear canal. Even in protected conditions guaranteed by the presence of endolympha, they have a limited lifespan, especially those sensitive to vibrations with higher frequencies. This also explains why with aging you lose noise sensitivity.*

THE EAR & BALANCE

The inner ear also contains other anatomical structures that provide the body with a means of balance. The semicircular canals are special structures that contain three half-circular channels that are arranged 90° to each other. They are interconnected and known respectively as the horizontal, superior and posterior semicircular canals. Their different orientations make it possible for the brain to monitor and assess bodily movements in any of the three axes. The horizontal semicircular canals, for instance, are positioned to sense when the body turns on its vertical axis. The other two canals operate in exactly the same manner, except they detect side to side and up and down movements. The receptors used in the sense of balance are augmented by fine hairs in much the same way as those in the organ of Corti. They are located in the vestibule, and connected to the eighth cranial nerve. The utricle and saccule are both otolith organs that are also found in the vestibule - they are sac-like structures that feature high concentrations of sensitive hair cells and are used to detect movements of the head. The semicircular channels, therefore, are dynamic receptors that respond to movements such as rotation and acceleration.

The information captured by the balance organs is transmitted to the brain - primarily the cerebellum by bipolar neurons ▸182. Much of the information sent by the balance receptors, provokes automatic

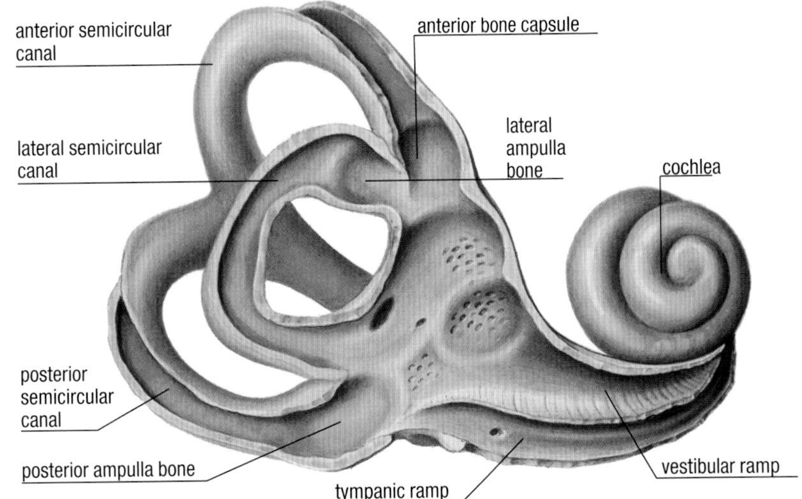

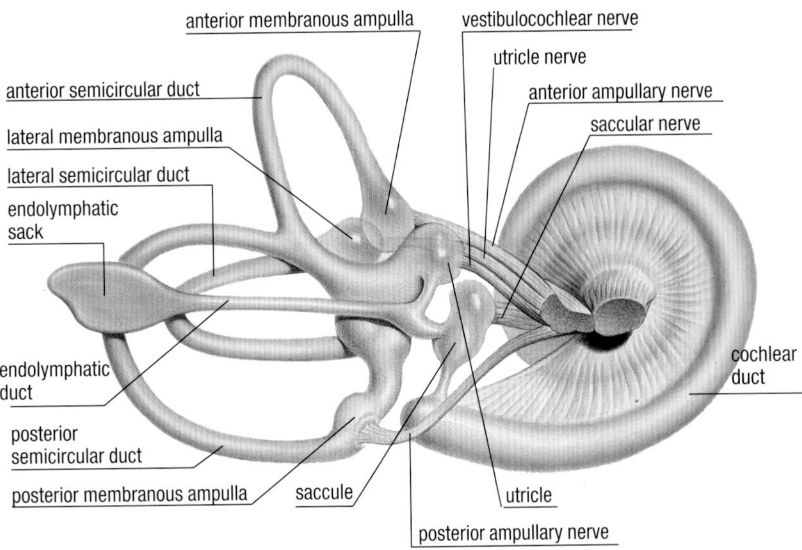

▲ **Anatomy of the labyrinth**
Principal anatomical elements of the labyrinth bone (top) and the membranous labyrinth (bottom).

▼ **Functions of the organ of balance**
At the base of the three channels of each endolympha filled circular maze, are ciliate receptors (red, green, blue). Every movement of the head sets in motion the endolympha that stimulates them, causing the production of an action potential in the nerve terminal where they are connected. The figures below show the movements perceived by receptors with the same color: thanks to the orthogonal circular channels, each type of movement becomes recognizable.

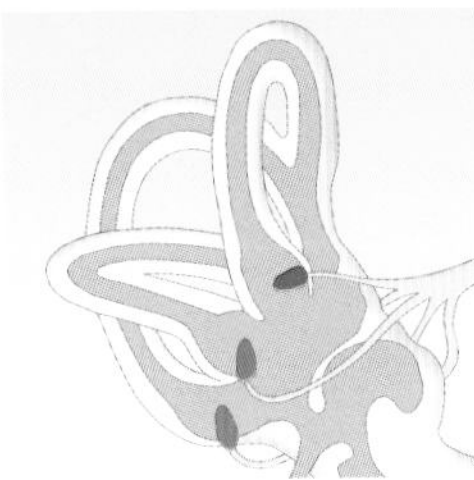

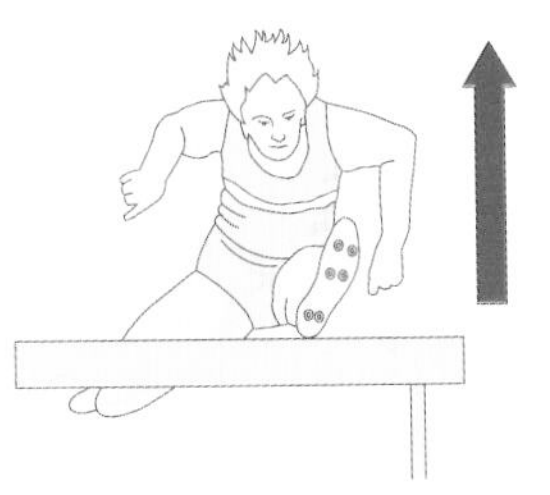

responses in the encephalic zones involved. The data from the inner ear is analysed and continually used to correct the commands that control and regulate the posture, as well as modulate any body movements in both static and dynamic conditions.

The brain also collects information from all the other sensory organs and compares it with that received from the inner ear, it then adapts any reactions either by conscious decisions or - more often - automatically from stored reflex procedures. Sometimes, however, the sensory data conflicts with the signals coming from the inner ear. An example could be the 'giddiness' that is caused if a person rotates vigorously and then stops suddenly. The sudden vertigo is due to the inertia of the otoliths which continue to sense loadings for a few seconds after the endolymph has stopped moving. As a result, the information that is sent to the brain differs from the data that has been collected from the rest of the body, that indicates that the body is standing still. In a similar manners, conditions such as seasickness, carsickness and airsickness are produced by a contrast between the information collected from the inner ear and that from the rest of the body.

CHEMICAL SENSATIONS: NOSE & MOUTH

Receptors capable of distinguishing chemical stimuli are concentrated in two different bodies: the nose, capable of recognising volatile stimuli as olfactory signals, and the mouth, which recognises molecules

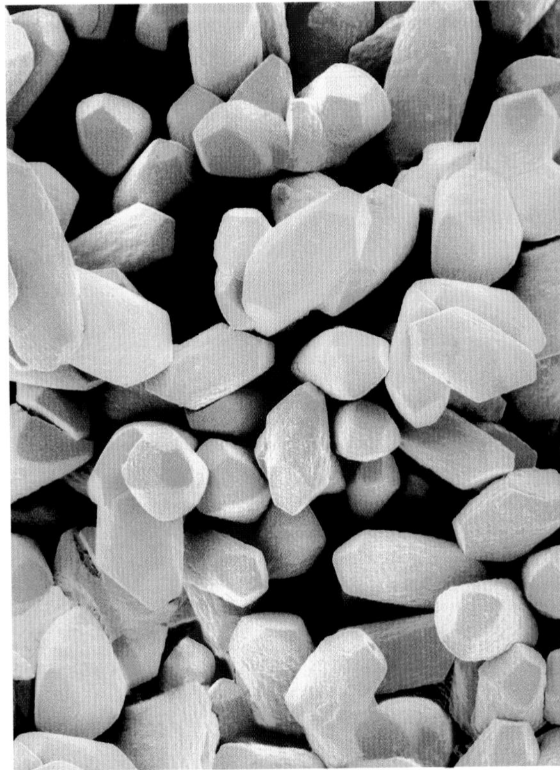

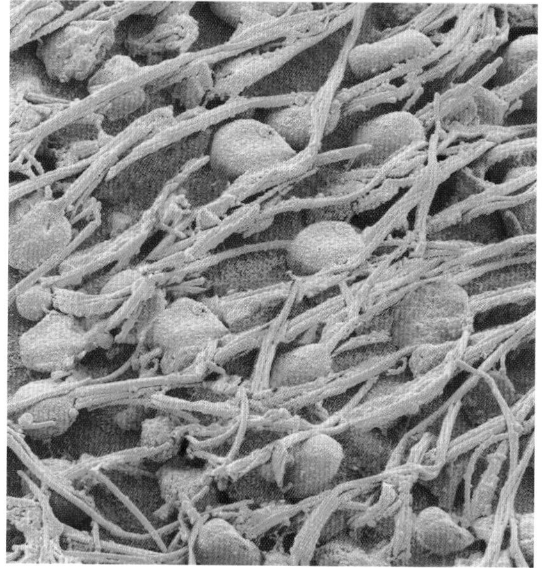

▲ **Cell balance**
Scanning electron microscope photograph (SEM) in false colors of cillia (yellow) of sensitive cells of the labyrinth, and otoliths (round, red). Completely submerged in endolympha, cillia perceive the movements of the otoliths interpreting the direction. The shifts that are induced by the position of the cillia in otoliths and streams of endolympha, trigger the production of a nerve impulse that reaches the brain via the vestibular nerve.

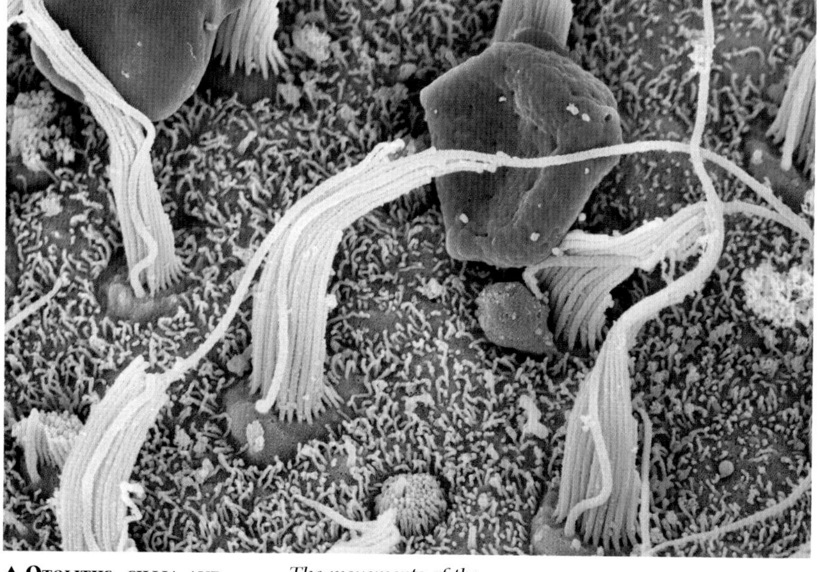

▲ **Otoliths, cilia and microvilli**
Microphotograph (SEM) in false colors of the macula utriculi which is the inside of the labyrinth of the lower part of the ear. The bundles of cilia (blue) are formed by numerous stereocilia and a single longer cnidocilia. The movements of the cilia produced by currents of endolympha give rise to nerve impulses. The supporting cells are covered with microvilli (brownish), while some otoliths are identifiable by the purple crystalline forms.

in solution and turn the consequent signals into taste stimuli.
These have important meanings both for pleasure and for warning of life threatening dangers. The smell of toxic gas as well as the taste of food are both play a role in the defence of the body. The sense of taste is not simply there to help with the enjoyment of eating, but also to help differentiate between food that is fit to eat and that which is not. As a consequence of this, the tongue is very sensitive to the chemical compounds that are related to the processes of biological decomposition. This probably why the cells involved in the senses of taste and smell are the only nervous system components that

◄ **Otoliths**
The utricle and saccule contain numerous and complex crystals of calcium carbonate called otoliths (from an average diameter of 3-30 microns), of which we see here from a scanning electron microscope in false colors. Their movements increase the stimulation of receptive hair cells, facilitating the onset of signs of gravity position.

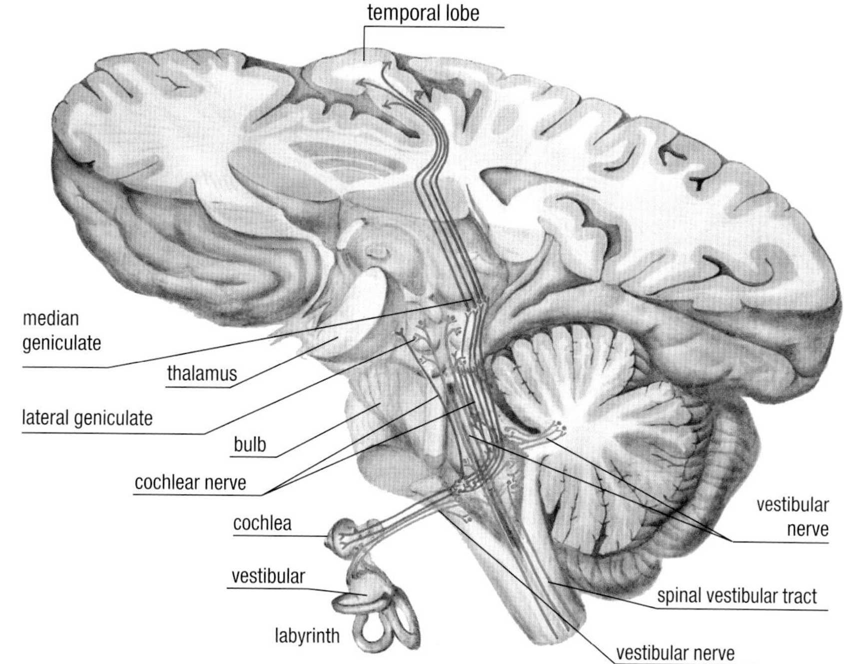

◄ **Auditive and vestibular tract**
Lateroventral section of the brain shows the path followed by the nerve pathways that carry signals to the auditory cortex, primary sensory, and vestibular nerve pathways. They carry information mainly in cerebellum and hypothalamus.
auditive tract
vestibular tract.

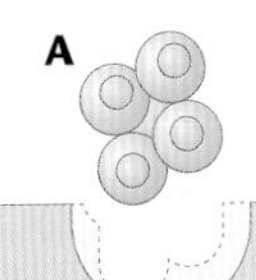

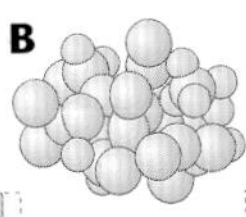

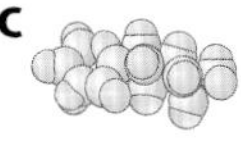

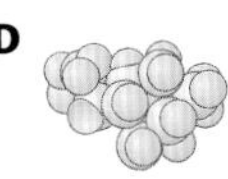

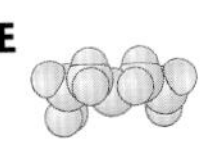

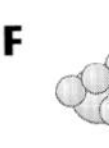

▲ **Odoriferous molecules**
It is believed that there are seven primary odors, from which all others arise. Though, given the extreme difficulty of obtaining objective evaluations, their classification is uncertain;
A. *camphoraceous (eg moth balls);*
B. *mossy (such as angelica root);*
C. *floral (eg rose);*
D. *menthol (eg mint);*
E. *ethereal (eg nail polish);*
F. *pungent (eg lemon);*
G. *putrid (rotten eggs for example).*
The seven substances would have different stereochemical forms, which react with specific molecules or sites of membrane receptors.

are replaced due to ageing or injury.
The functioning of these senses can be seen here: The olfactory receptors have a very high sensitivity: there are at least 40 million of them, and these are surrounded by support cells in an internal area within the nasal mucous membrane that measures just 5 cm2, and located at the ethmoid bone, which is found at the base of the skull.
Volatile substances in the air are drawn into the nose as part of the process of inhalation - the molecules are then caught up in the nasal fluid that covers the olfactory epithelia. At this point they come into contact with the olfactory cells, and this sparks an olfactory nervous reaction. The chemoreceptors have evolved to be extremely sensitive. This is so that they can detect the minute volatile particles which emanate from objects or substances at a distance without physically touching them. Is still unclear what actually causes these receptors to trigger - it may be the shape of the molecules, their size or even their electrical charge.
The complexity of the reception of smell is perhaps best illustrated by comparing the number of different receptors involved with the other senses. Hearing, for instance, uses two different types of receptors, and colour vision on three, whereas smell is based on at least 1000 different kinds of receptors. Each recognises a specific molecule's smell, but the same smell can trigger different types of receptors. On average, it is possible for a human to recognise somewhere between 3000 and 10,000 different smells. This is facilitated by a complex collaboration between the receptors that combine their responses in different ways, and as a result are able to encode a much larger number of signals.
The sense of smell is the one that is most directly

▼ **The smell**
Anatomical elements involved with olfactory sensitivity.
auditory pathways
vestibular pathways.

▶ **The olfactory pathways**
Ventrolateral section of the brain and the nose that shows the anatomical elements of the main olfactory pathways. The first neuron is the receptor, the 2nd is a mitral cell that contributes to the olfactory tract (cranial nerves). Without going through the thalamus, and the surrounding limbic system to reach the primary sensory cortex, the location is uncertain.

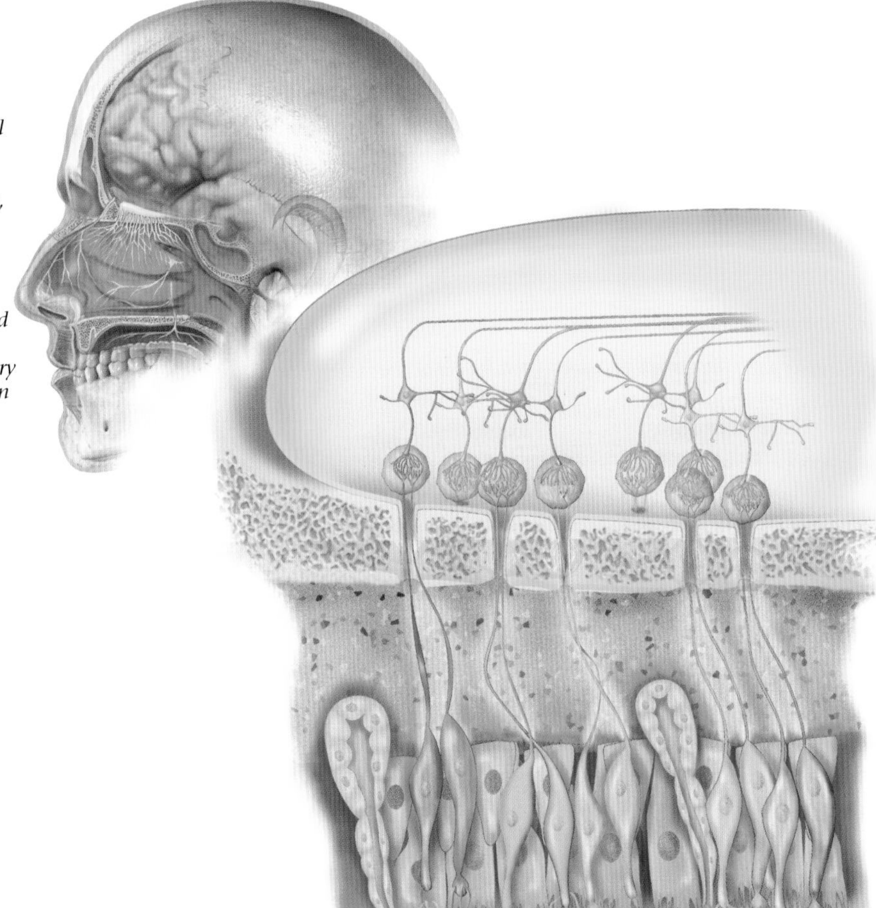

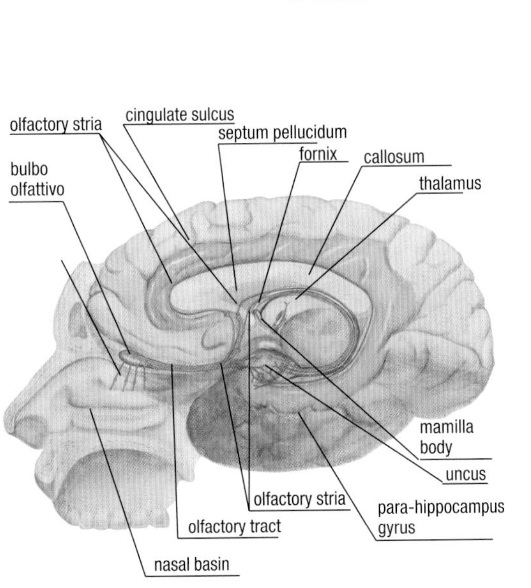

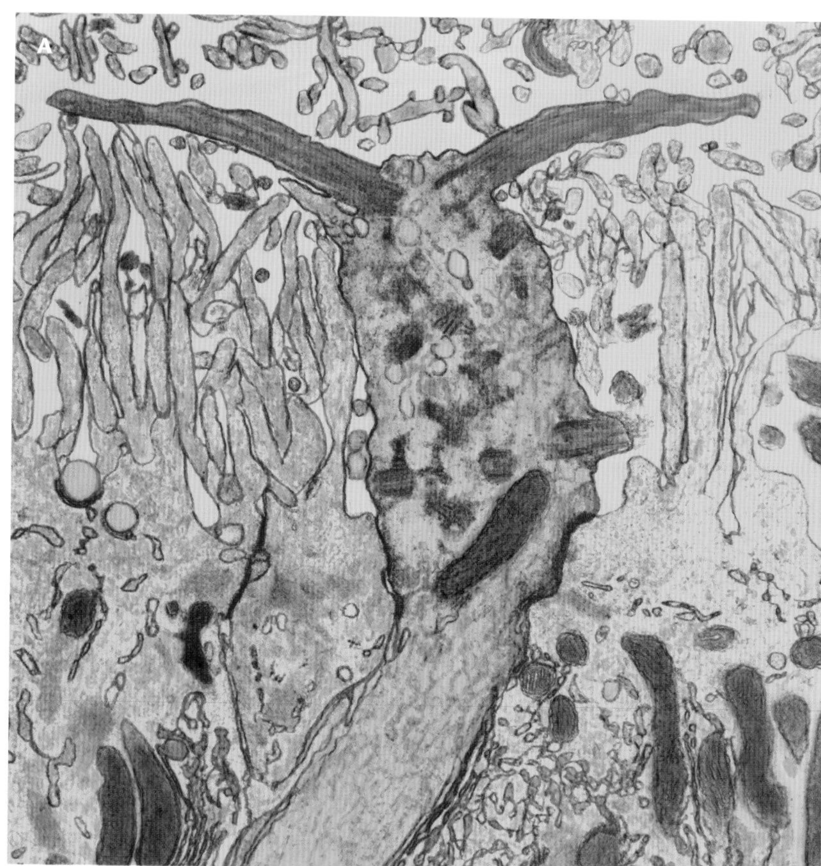

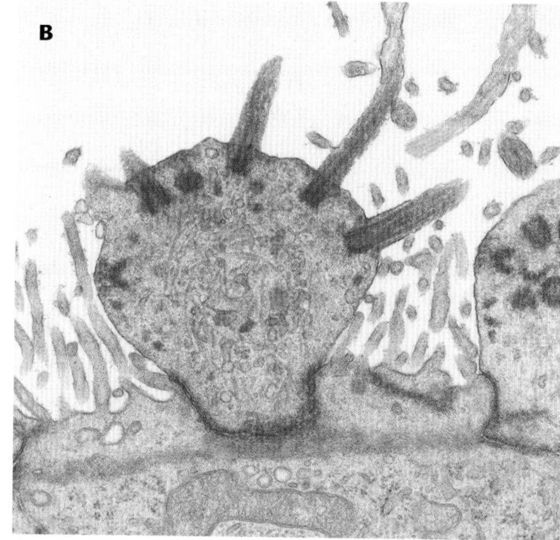

◄▲ **Olfactory receptor**
TEM photograph of a section of olfactory epithelium.
A. *The middle (orange) shows the cell body of a receptor, above, shows two long cilia modified and unable to move but able to "capture", odoriferous substances dissolved in the surrounding fluids. Around the receptor cells are a support of surface microvilli. Mitochondria are visible (purple) and the endoplasmic reticulum (empty vesicles).* **B**. *Receptor (detail) with a greater number of cilia. The round part, is the olfactory vesicle.*

linked to the subconscious states the psyche and memory. The olfactory fibres, indeed, continue from the olfactory bulb through to the various parts of the brain responsible for the reception and interpretation of smell - especially the olfactory cortex. The Hippocampus, amygdala and hypothalamus are all involved, although the exact mechanism is still poorly understood. The sensations of smell can also stimulate emotional reactions - sometimes just a fleeting scent can trigger the recall of an entire scene from the past. As an illustration, take the smell of burning - this is immediately recognised and most people have past connections with this. Sometimes these are positively associated with happy memories, but for others they bring back unpleasant memories. Either way, humans - and many animals, automatically associate the smell of smoke with the presence of flames, even if they are not visible.
In spite of the fact that the process of detecting a smell is very complex, it can take place very rapidly indeed. If just a single molecule reaches a receptor, it is possible for the smell to be perceived less than a second later. The brain has evolved to be able to identify thousands of different smells very quickly - this is not surprising when one considers that such an ability can have a marked effect on survival. When a particular smell is detected in the environment, it is often vital that something is done about it immediately. For example, it would

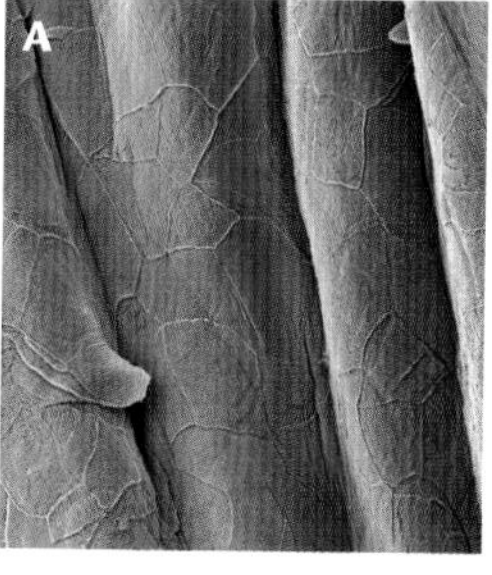

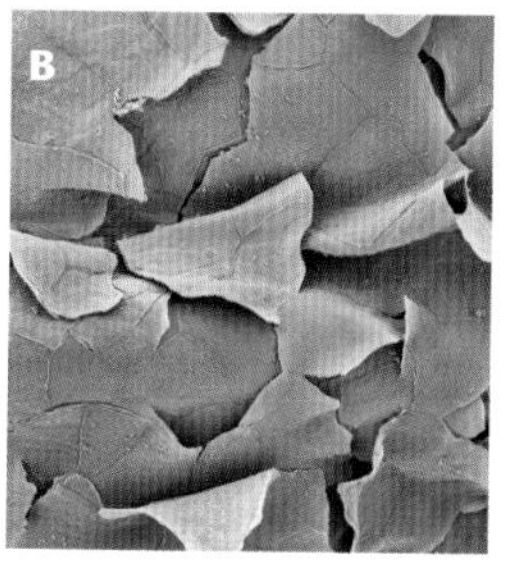

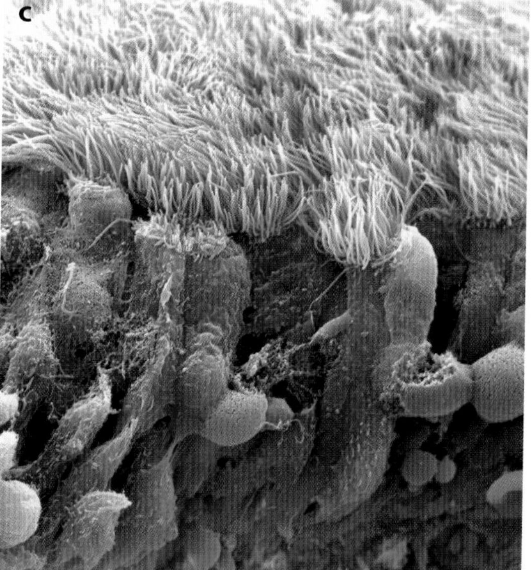

▲ **Nose under the microscope**
False color SEM photograph of the nasal epithelium.
A. *Stratified squamous epithelium folded into the nasal cavity: in addition to olfactory receptors, there are cells that produce fluid and nasal mucus. The folds result in an increase in available surface area to contain the different types of cells.*
B. *Cell surface of the epithelium at a higher magnification: showing the squamous cells that cover the surface.*
C. *Section of the olfactory epithelium: the cylindrical epithelial cells (brown) have the distal end of numerous microscopic cilia (yellowish), which normally covered by mucus (deleted here) move continuously in waves, pushing it toward the back of the nose (larynx), so it can be swallowed.*

have been vital for early humans to be able to detect potential predators - the sooner their presence could be determined, the higher the chances those involved would have in staying alive.

The taste receptors are located in the mucous membrane that covers much of the oral cavity - these are called taste buds. There are at least 10,000 on the tongue alone, but there are also others in the epiglottis, on the palate, in the pharynx and on the tonsils. The number of taste buds is very large in childhood, but this decreases with age. The chemical receptors require direct physical contact with the substances they are detecting. These may either already be in solution, or be quickly soluble in saliva.

Taste receptors are less sophisticated than those of the olfactory system. While each is linked to a nerve fibre, each of these may be attached to multiple receptors. This reduces their sensitivity significantly, and often makes it difficult to develop a specific sense of taste. It is possible to appreciate a huge

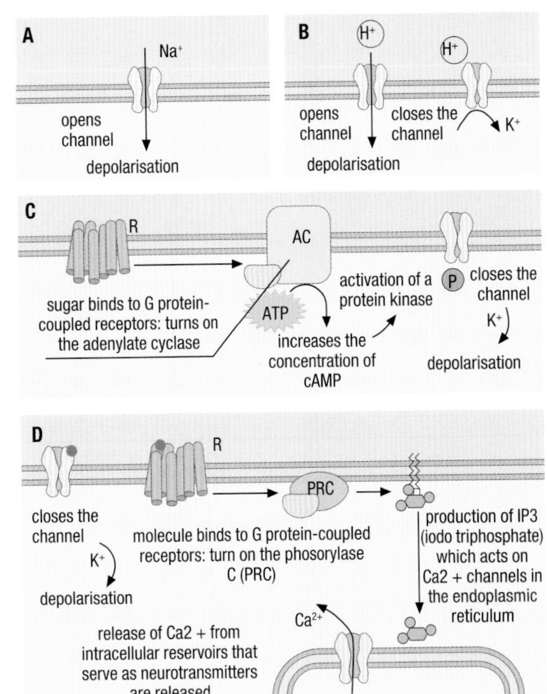

▶ **Physiology of taste**
The membrane of the microvilli of sensory cells contained in gustatory buds. There are specific receptors for various "flavors". The transduction of the stimulus occurs with the interaction between them and the "taste" molecules in solution: a different interaction for: A. salty B. sweet (two locations), C. bitter D. acid (two routes).
outer receptor;
internal receptor.

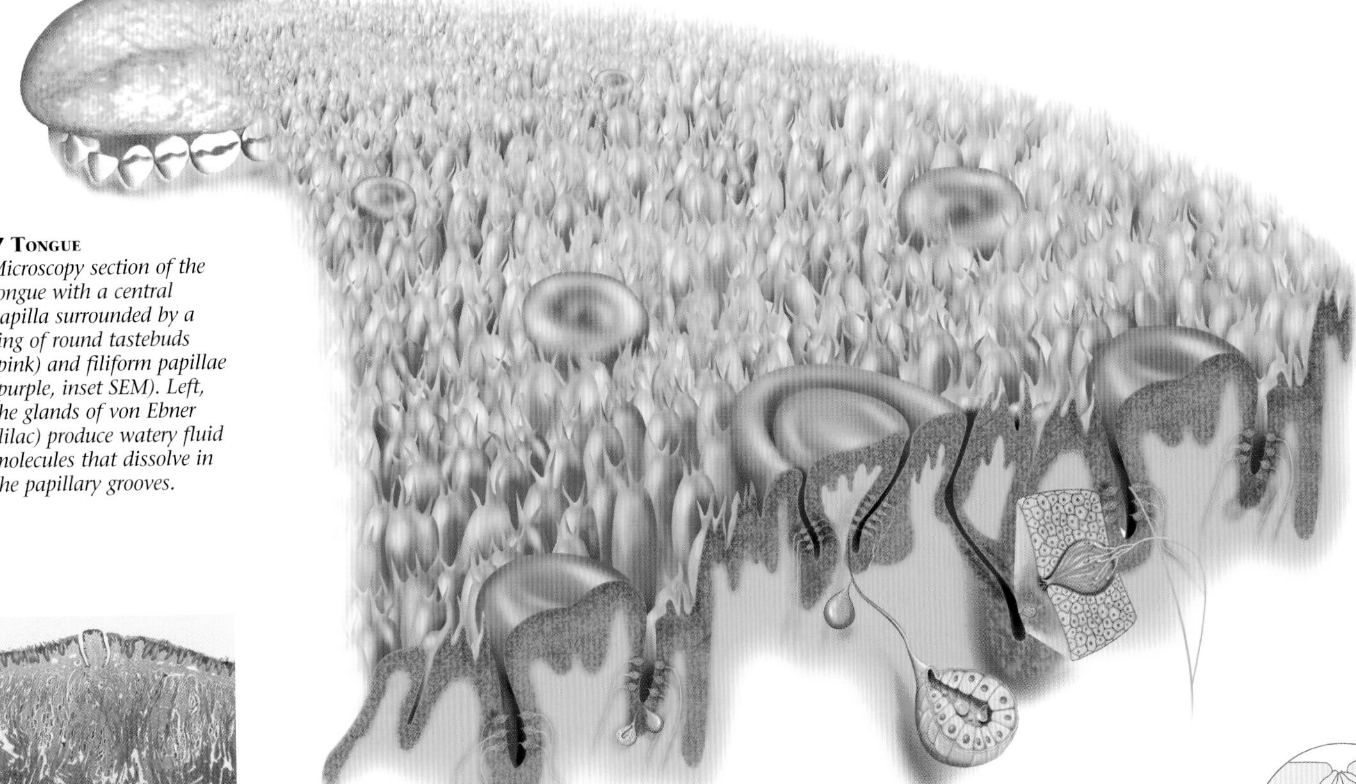

▼ **Papillae**
Reconstruction of the structure of the tongue that shows the different types of papillae involved in the sense of taste.

▼ **Tongue**
Microscopy section of the tongue with a central papilla surrounded by a ring of round tastebuds (pink) and filiform papillae (purple, inset SEM). Left, the glands of von Ebner (lilac) produce watery fluid molecules that dissolve in the papillary grooves.

▶ **Taste buds**
Light microscopy section of foliate papillae showing taste buds (▬). Each papilla is ➡ covered by multilayered squamous epithelium (purple) and reinforced by keratin. The taste buds are groups of spindle-shaped neuroepithelial cells in contact with sensory nerve fibers in specific cranial nerves (II pair). Lateral grooves in the taste buds open into a (▬) taste pore where ➡ the short hairy apical extensions of sensory cells are in contact with the outside world. In the box a diagram of the structure of taste buds.

number of flavours through the sense of taste, but it is not possible to relate all of them to a particular class of receptors.

The sense of taste has similarities with visual perception - just as it is based on primary colours, there are four basic types of taste - these are sweet, salty, bitter and acid. The tongue has specific areas that are tailored to the reception of each of these. In spite of the fact that there are only four basic tastes, a wide variety of flavours can be perceived because of complex interactions with the other senses. These include receptors that can detect pain, temperature and touch/texture. All of their signals reach the brain separately, but these are then processed in an integrated manner, so that - for example - hot milk has taste different from cold, dry bread from wet, and so on. The taste receptors are innervated by the cranial nerves VII, IX and x - these fibres are then connected to the encephalic bulb.

▼ Bud areas
Through the examination of the reactions of the tongue to various chemical solutions, certain areas have been identified to have a predominant reactivity to different flavors:
○ sour,
○ bitter,
○ sweet,
○ salty.

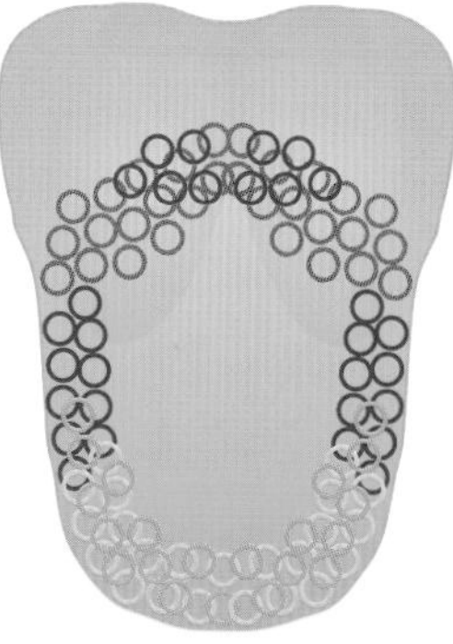

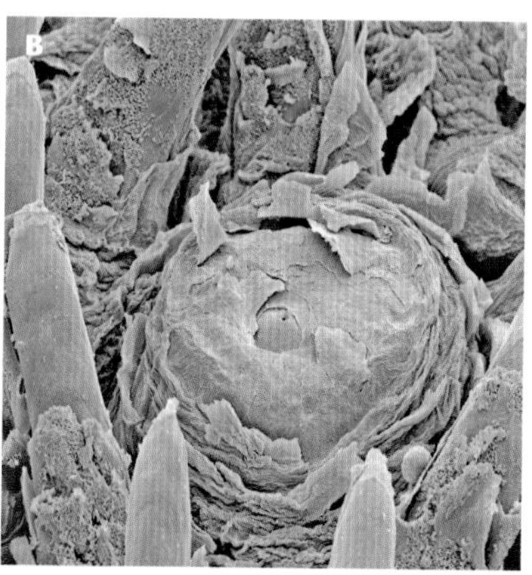

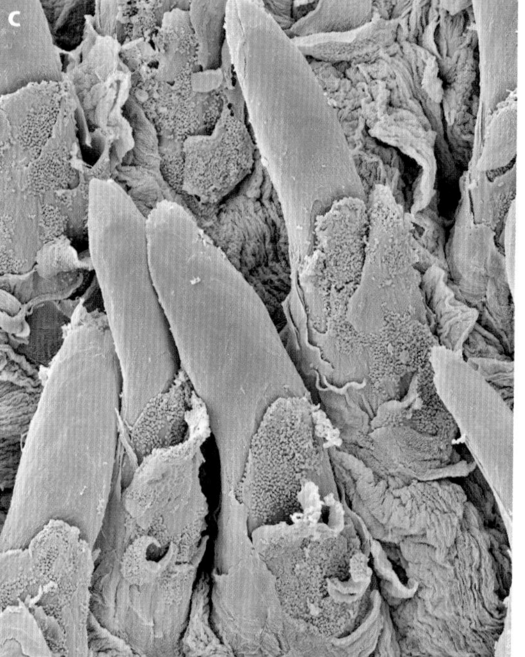

◄ Tongue under the microscope
SEM microphotograph of the epithelium of the tongue.
A. *The surface is formed by squamous epithelial cells (apparently flat) that are constantly renewed.*
B. *Taste buds with an opening in the center of a fungiform papilla. In the two pictures (A and B) are characterized numerous bacteria (yellow-green) of the plaque.*
C. *Filiform papillae (conical): normally covered by the epithelium, do not taste but contain tactile nerve endings: they are much more numerous than the taste buds.*

▼ Gustatory pathways
Dorsolateral section of the brain and tongue, which shows the path of the respiratory buds and the main anatomical elements.
solitary files thalamic;
facial nerve
glossopharyngeal nerve;
vagus nerve;
midbrain tract.

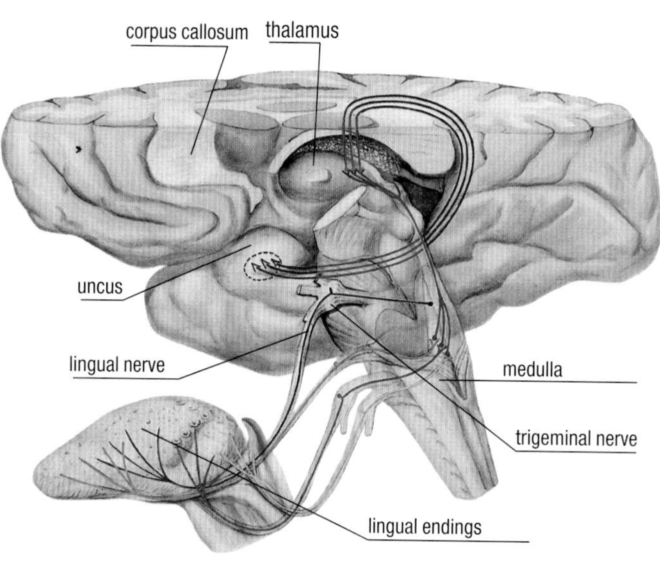

▶ **Stratification**
Anatomical location of the receptors in the skin dermis (deeper) and the epidermis (superficial): ❶ *bulbs of Krause: sensitivity to cold damage;* ❷ *free endings are sensitive to pain stimuli and tactility;* ❸ *Pacini corpuscles, sensitive to deep pressure and to vibrations of 150-300 Hz;* ❹ *Ruffini corpuscles, sensitivity to heat damage;* ❺ *Merkel's disks are sensitive to continuous tactile stimulation;* ❻ *Meissner's corpuscles are sensitive to tactile stimuli, particularly to vibrations of 20-40 Hz;* ❼ *nerve endings of the hair follicles are sensitive to movements of the hair.*

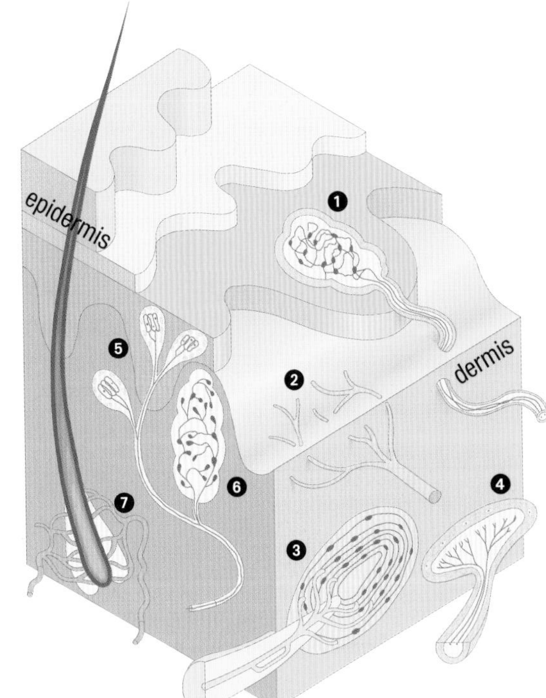

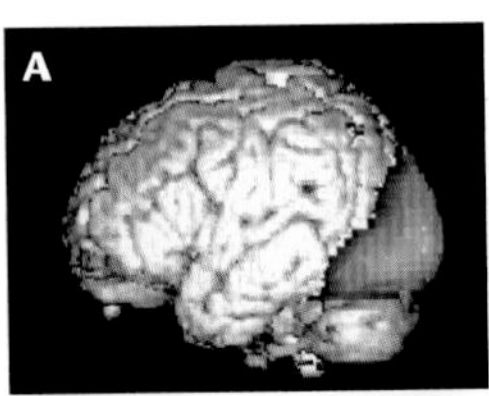

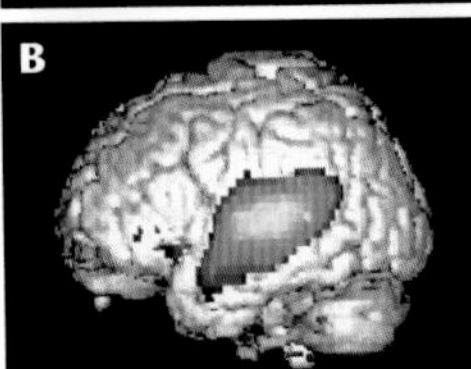

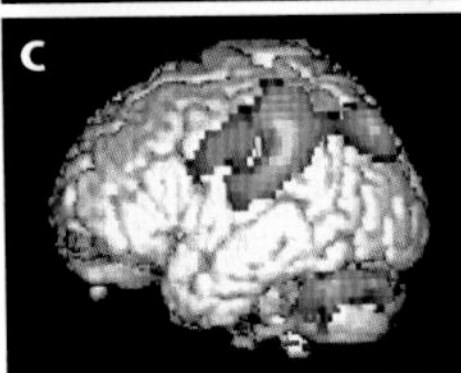

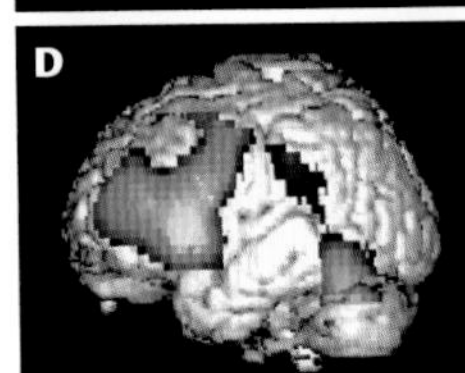

▲ **Cortical zone**
Images of a positron emission tomography (PET) in false color that highlights the cortical areas activated during different activities (the frontal lobes are to the left):
A. *sight,* **B**. *hearing,* **C**. *braille,* **D**. *thought. Reading Braille activates the parietal tactile area well as the cognitive area.*

SKIN & THE PHYSICAL SENSATIONS

The body collects a wide range of tactile sensations from all over the skin's surface, as well as various parts of the body, and from mucous membranes. In addition, it also perceives the changes in pressure that can cause injuries. Skin receptors, for instance, are able to recognise both changes in temperature and pain. The nerve endings gather data from changes in temperature and any cellular injuries. This information is then used by the Hypothalamus ▶179 to monitor the body's state - in doing so, it is able to regulate its overall temperature. Pain and temperature receptors are the most numerous to be found in the skin. There are at least 200/cm2 of skin, whereas there are only 15 pressure receptors, 6 for cold and only one for heat.

Not all the pain stimuli, however, act the same way on the different receptors. The physical pain that occurs when skin, muscles and joints are stimulated, is usually very localised and the limited areas that are stimulated often cause automatic reflex reactions. Visceral pain, on the other hand, that is, the discomfort that occurs when the chest or abdominal organs are stimulated, often causes widespread reactions, and can often be perceived in other parts of the body that are relatively distant. This is because they are innervated by the same nerve roots.

The somatic receptors are very sensitive to potentially injurious sensations, such as heat, cuts, bites and crushing. The visceral sensors, however, are almost insensitive to heat, cold or cuts but they do react very quickly to chemical signals from swelling and inflammation, or mechanical spasms in the smooth muscle.

The most painful stimuli reach the spinal cord through the amyelinic or myelinic nerve fibres; they are then sent to the brain's cerebral cortex for processing. This structure is able to recognise the position, nature, and level of pain intensity, and it is likely that it has a mediation role in the autonomous and emotional reactions to pain. There is also a system modulator for pain that, possibly through the release of endorphins, responds to painful stimuli by blocking impulses within the spinal neurons. The receptors that are located deeper down in the dermis are more complex: the bodies of Meissner and of Pacini are sensitive to changes in pressure and vibrations. Their nerve endings are encapsulated with membranes of connective tissue that enhances their receptive function. The body is especially sensitive to touch in the palms of the hands, soles of the feet, lips, eyelids, external genitalia and nipples.

The nerve fibres that relate to the various receptors in the skin may be of two types. Those that are known as the bodies of Pacini produce a potential difference for as long as the stimulation continues. This is in contrast to the bodies of Ruffini, which react only when a stimulus begins - or, sometimes, when it ends.

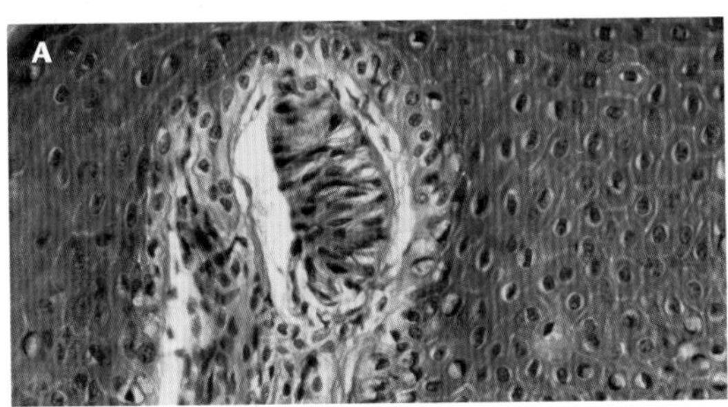

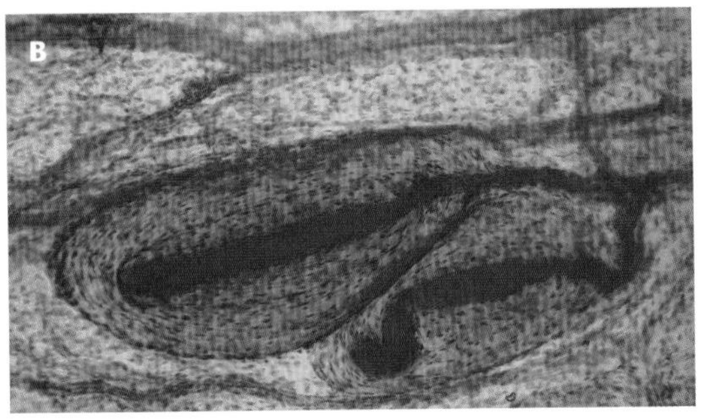

▲ **Dermal receptors**
Optical microscope photographs of different sensory corpuscles of the skin:
A. *Meissner's corpuscle, surrounded by several epidermal cells. Typical of the skin of the finger and pads of the sole of the foot, these particles have a much more subtle sense of touch as they are brought closer together;*
B. *section of a Pacini corpuscle, a receptor sensitive to pressure changes that cause mechanical deformations in the membranes of the capsule that surrounds the layers of nerve endings. These corpuscles are particularly sensitive to vibration.*

It is a feature of life: movement. Both in the environment to find food, water, a climate more suitable for a sexual partner, moving to pump blood into the veins to open and close your eyes, breathe or swallow, movement is an integral part of the activities essential to life.

MOVEMENT

Movement is a vital part of life - in the human body it can take place at the macro level - that is with powerful articulations of the major limbs. It can also occur at lower scales, such as blinking of the eyelashes, however, the really small movements happen at the cellular level such as with the amoeboid crawling of the macrophages ►95. Even when it appears to be still, the human body is always moving. Whether a person is sitting down, lying out, or standing to attention, the muscles are always in action - modulating posture, maintaining the sizes of the blood vessels ►82, adjusting the respiratory tracts, and so on. Despite the variations in function and different kinds of movements involved, all muscles work in the same basic way.

CELLULAR MOVEMENT

At the cellular level, all movements are due to the presence of proteins that change conformation depending on the environmental conditions. They can lengthen or reduce their sizes and bind to surrounding proteins.

FLAGELLA & CILIA

Movement is made possible in the cells of the human body due to tiny structures called microtubules. These are long chains of tubulin (a globular protein) that form hollow cylinder structures with a diameter of around 24 nm, and microfilaments of about 7 nm in diameter that are formed from long coils of a protein called actin. The microfilaments are widespread throughout the cell and form a dense network near the outer membrane. They are very flexible, and may lengthen or shorten by adding or losing monomers of actin. This allows the unit to change shape both reversibly and quickly, and is the basis of all amoeboid movements ►95.

The microtubules ►24 are cellular structures that are formed during the mitotic process in cell replication. They can be permanent features as in the case of the tails in sperm cells, or fixed structural ones such as seen on the inside of neuronal axons where they have no mobility functions at all. In a similar manner to the microfilaments, microtubules may also lengthen or shorten by adding or shedding monomers from their ends. These two molecular structures form the basis of the movements of the cilia hairs that protrude from the free surface of many mucose membranes, as well as for flagella, and also the tails of spermatozoa.

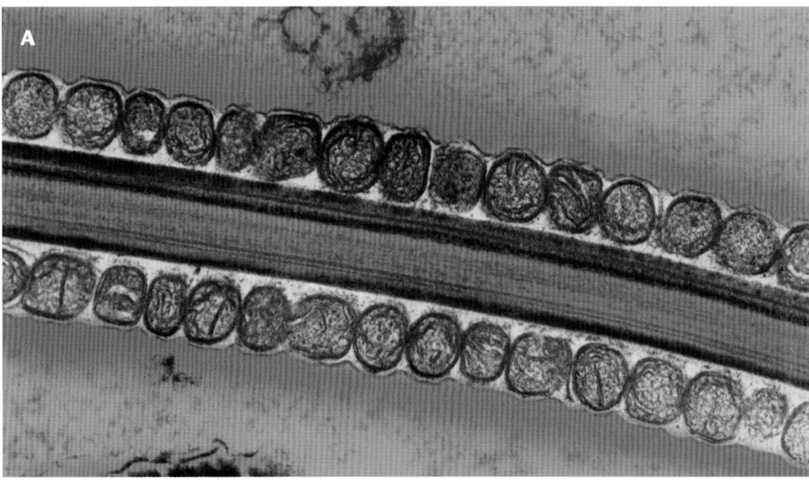

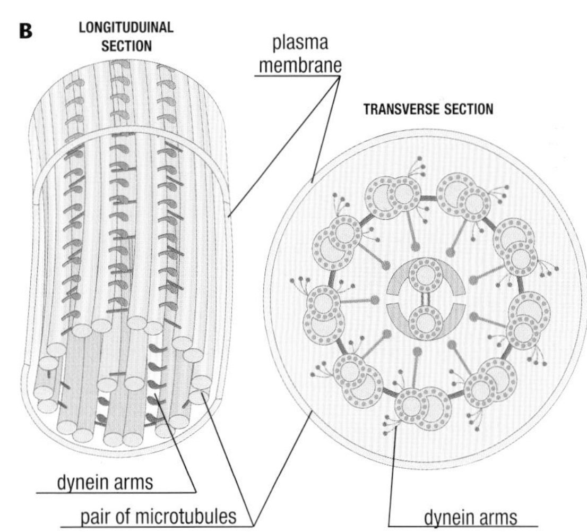

▲◀ **Common structures**
The movement of cilia and flagella is based on processes similar to that of muscle movement.
A. *Longitudinal section in the central area of a sperm tail. The structures are oval Verdine mitochondria, which are responsible for providing the energy needed for stereochemical modifications of microtubules (pink) that create the movement.*
B. *Diagram of the molecular structure of a flagella, but also applies to a cilia, with the characteristic 9 +2 arrangement of pairs of microtubules.*

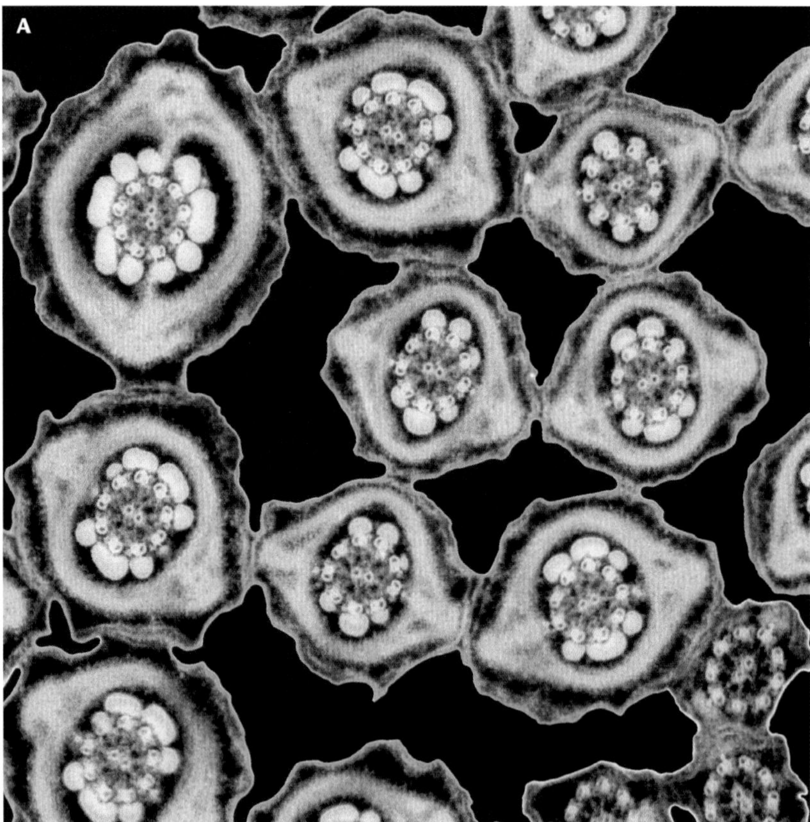

▲ **Details**
TEM electron microscope photo in false colors of the cross sections:
A. *sperm tails;*
B. *cilia: similarity between these structures is evident. Each of them contains two central microtubules (white rings) surrounded by 9 pairs of microtubules. The pairs of parallel microtubules, sliding over one another, create a swinging motion. The microtubules are part of the cytoskeleton of the cell. They are surrounded by more dense fibers that give rigidity and protection to the structure. A protective membrane surrounds the whole.*

Cilia and flagella have structures that are composed of bundles of microtubules divided into 9 + 2 pairs. One of them is in the middle, and the others surround it at regular distances. This beam is surrounded by the plasma membrane and always has a diameter of 0.25 µm. Its length, however, can vary from a few microns to 2 mm.

MUSCLE CONTRACTION

The movements of muscle cells are due to similar mechanisms to those discussed above. The motors which drive these movements are based on two protein components:

- myosin, this is a filamentous motor protein that is characterised by the presence of ATPases, which are special enzymes that are involved in energy production. It consists of two polypeptide chains that are wrapped into double helix that ends in two major heads.
- actin, this is also a filamentous protein, however, it is thinner than myosin, and is formed by monomeric molecules that have been polymerised and arranged in a helical form.

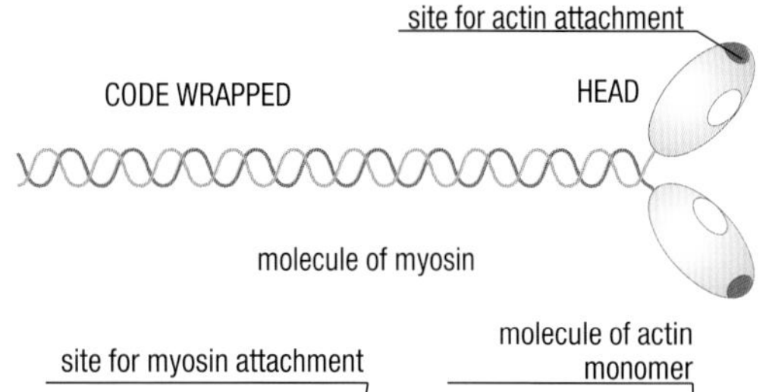

► **Chemical structure**
Diagram of a molecule of myosin (top) and a polymer of actin (below): each molecule (ball) has a site of attachment for a head of myosin (blacks dots).

Muscle fibres are almost entirely formed from actin and myosin, which is organised in multiple myofibrils. They are abundant and work in a synchronised manner so that contraction and relaxation movements involve the whole cell. The filaments that form contractile proteins within the myofibril can be distinguished by the following features:

- thin myofilaments are formed from two long actin polymers in a spiral structure, together with long continuous filaments of tropomyosin wrapped around polymers of actin, and from a complex of troponin that binds to specific sites of the molecules of tropomyosin. The three peptide subunits of which it is composed form a strong affinity for the Ca2+ ions and these then link with the tropomyosin and a regulator. This creates a link between the actin and myosin activity (every molecule of actin monomer has a binding site specific to the head of Myosin);
- thick myofilaments are formed from 200-400 myosin molecules that are arranged in parallel to each other along the entire length of the filament. Half of them are oriented in one direction, the other half in the opposite direction and both have

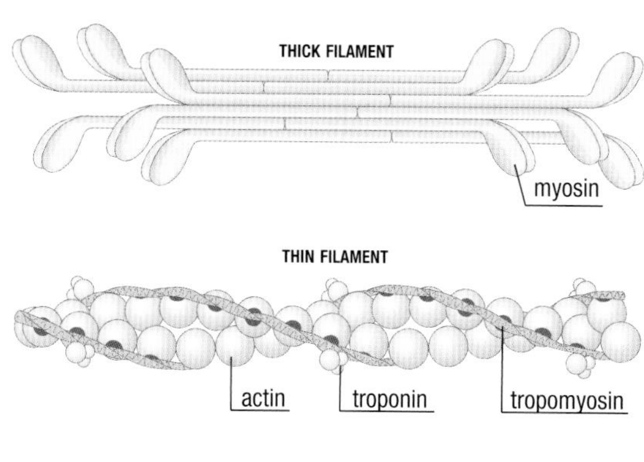

▲ **Myofilament**
Diagram of a myofilament often made of myosin (above) and a fine filament of actin, tropomyosin and troponin (below).

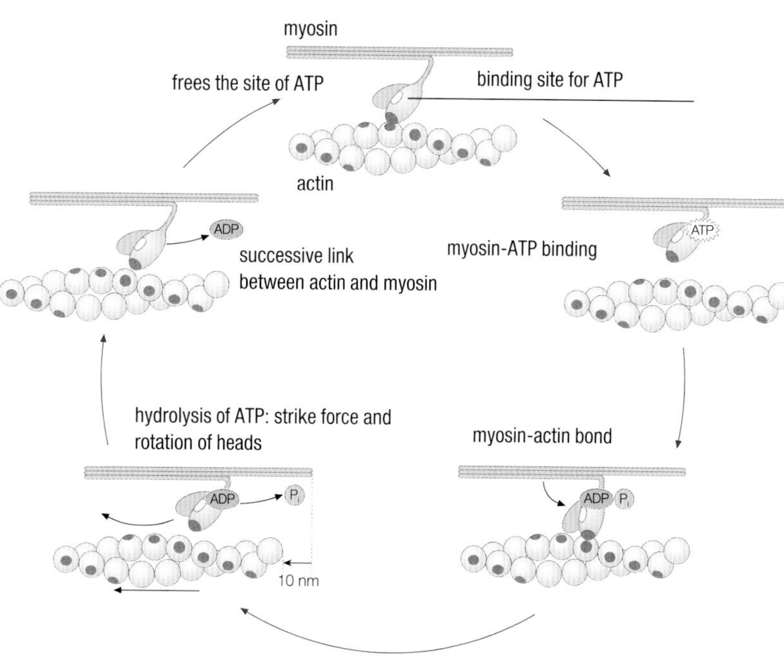

▶ **Cycle of motion**
Diagram of the sequence of reciprocal movements of actin and myosin leading to the contraction of a myofibril.

an overall spiral form. The filaments are immersed in the cytoplasm (sarcoplasma) and are often very small, there is also a thin layer under the sarcolemma, which is the outer reticular membrane that envelops the cell. The sarcoplasma is rich in proteins, glycogen and phosphates, in particular high-energy ATP (adenosine triphosphate) and CP (creatine phosphate). It also contains large numbers of mitochondria that occupy the spaces between the myofibrils.

As in the case of the flagella and cilia, the contraction of muscle fibre is based on a complex molecular mechanism that results from the processing of chemical energy (ATP) into mechanical energy. These cells perform very well when it comes to the process of transforming chemical energy into mechanical energy. The conversion efficiency is very high - around 55% of the energy is transformed into motion, with the rest being released in the form of heat.

ATP – adenosine triphosphoric acid, is the molecule that makes it possible for useful energy to be released in all the processes of cell energy transformation. It is hydrolysed from ADP (adenosine diphosphoric acid) and is needed for such vital processes as the shortening of myosin filament cross-bridges, the basis of cellular movement. The Division of the ATP modifies the myosin conformation and leads to a shift of the proteins in the filaments. This causes the fibre to shorten - at the same time there is an increase in its diameter. Subsequently the ADP is transformed again into ATP by catabolic cellular processes.

In physiological conditions, the contraction of muscle fibres is induced by stimuli that have been transported from nerve fibres which are linked by a number of neuromuscular synaptic joints. In general, every fibre has its own innervation. The action potential 64 for the muscle fibre is generated by the release of neurotransmitters (acetylcholine, choline, nicotine) by the presynaptic neuron. The sequence of events that follows is similar to that of the transmission of the action potential in nerve fibres. Here too, in fact, the action potential spreads from the point of occurrence throughout the muscle fibre thanks to its ability to conduct electrotonic currents. A big difference is the total duration of the action potential - that of the muscle fibres lasts much more, up to 5 MS.

The action potential spreads along the sarcolemma and switches the voltage-dependent channels which then enables specific receptors to release Ca2 + ions. In turn, this activates specific receptors that open the channels in the sarcoplasmic network which allows a massive flow of ions to the myofibril. The acetylcholine, moreover, also directly operates on the membranes that surround the bundles of myofibril, making them permeable to the Ca2+

▼ **Neuromuscular plaque**
A neuromuscular synapse (dark oval) viewed under an optical microscope, connecting the axon of a motor nerve (not visible) in some striated muscle fibers.

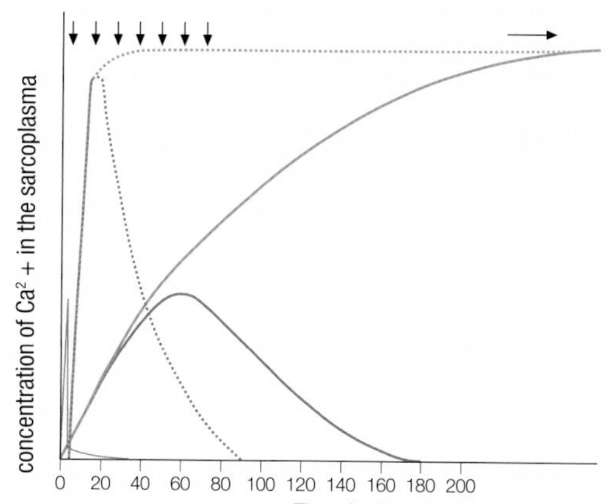

◀ **Diagram**
Relationship between the sarcoplasmic concentration of Ca^2 + and the contraction of a myofibril.
action potential;
tetanus muscle;
Ca^{2+} during tetanus;
Ca^{2+} during the simple shock;
simple muscular shock;
→ *stimulation.*

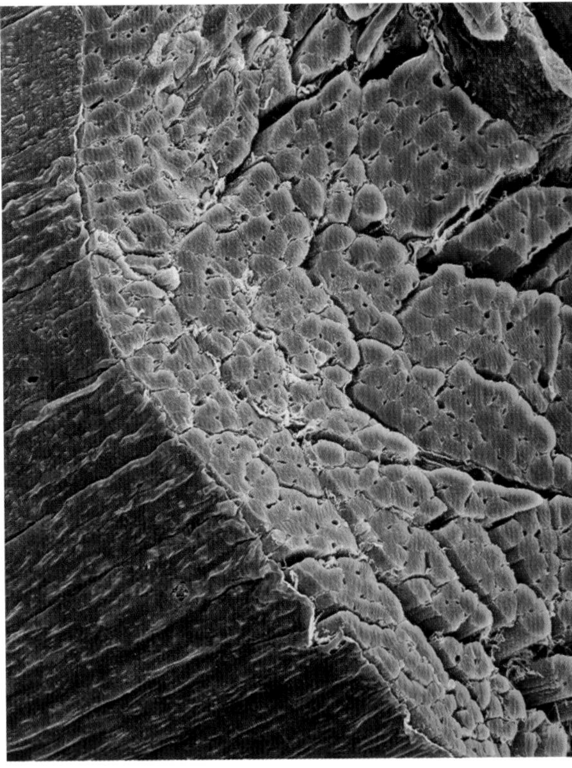

▶ **Striated muscle**
Scanning electron microscope (SEM) image in false colors, showing a cross section of a skeletal muscle. Bundles of fibers (red) are held together by epimysium (purple) a strong sheath of connective tissue. Each bundle is surrounded by an additional sheath (perimysium), as each instalment is delimited by miocellule endomysium.

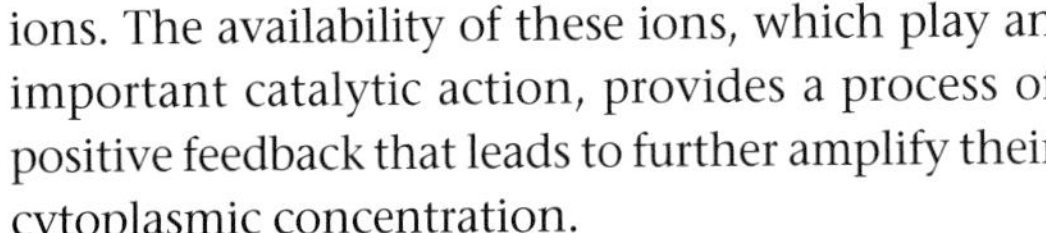

ions. The availability of these ions, which play an important catalytic action, provides a process of positive feedback that leads to further amplify their cytoplasmic concentration.

In particular, troponin is catalysed from the Ca2+ ions and links with the tropomyosin. At the same time, the mitochondria liberate further ATP. This process also leads to activation of myosin phosphatase, an enzyme that is used to dephosphorylate the myosin, causing it to detach from the actin.

Every time a muscle fibre generates an action potential, that is, every time a signal arrives from the motor-neurone - the motor unit to which it belongs, a contraction occurs. This has a variable duration according to the type of muscle, but it always has three distinct phases:

– a brief mechanical latency phase, this is the time between receiving the signal and the contraction actually starting;
– a phase where the fibre shortens;
– a slightly longer, with regard to the stage of latency, resting phase, this allows the fibre to return to its initial conditions.

The trigger for the muscular contraction is a simple 'all or nothing' event. It only arises if the stimulus exceeds the threshold required to generate the action potential, and is not increased in size even if the intensity of the stimulus grows. The contraction then manifests itself as wave that follows the action potential after a short delay. In comparison, however, it lasts much longer.

The force that each muscle fibre can develop depends on the frequency with which it is stimulated. If a second stimulus is received by a fibre muscle that is already contracting, it is added to the first signal and the relaxation phase is delayed. Increasing the frequency of stimulation causes the force to continue to grow to a point where saturation is reached - at this point the developed power remains at the same maximum level (tetanic contraction).

A

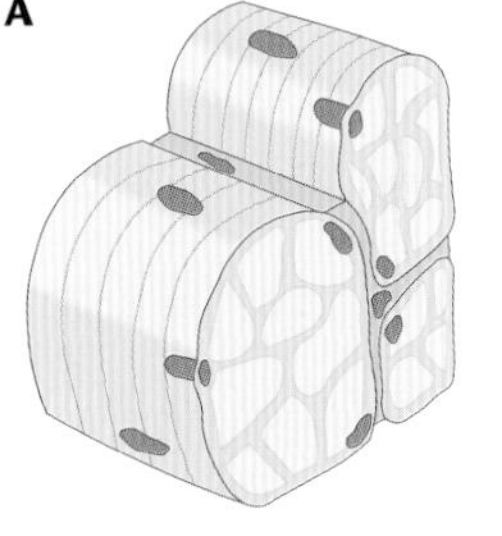

B

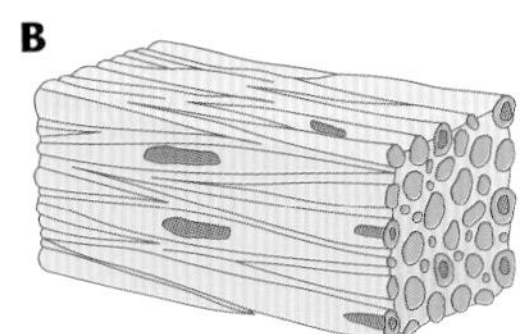

C

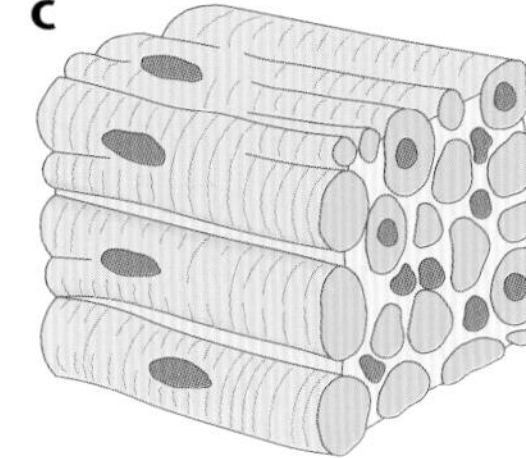

▲ **Muscle Types**
Diagram showing the obvious differences between the three types of muscles:
A. *smooth muscle;*
B. *cardiac muscle;*
C. *skeletal muscle.*

MUSCULAR MOVEMENTS

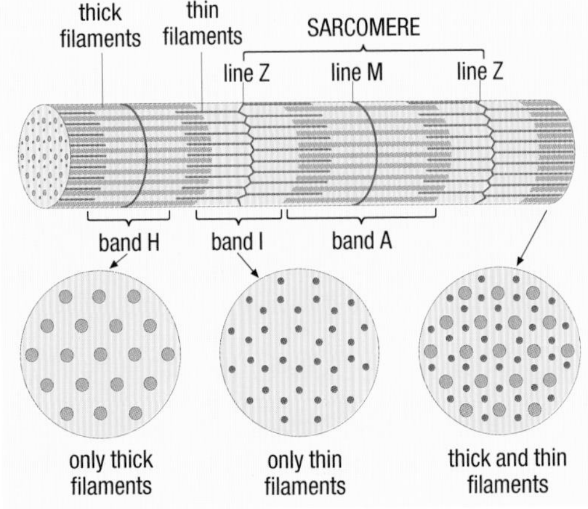

▶ **Sarcomere**
Structure diagram of a sarcomere.

The bodies that have the highest proportion of muscle tissue are the muscles. There are morphological, structural, and functional differences between the various types; these include skeletal, smooth and cardiac muscles. This arises because of different embryonic origins and to a different anatomical distribution.

SKELETAL MUSCLES

The fibres of the skeletal muscles are wrapped in connective tissue and when observed through an optical microscope, appear striped widthways - this is due to the presence of alternating bands of light and dark. This is because some are mono-refringent - that is, they reflect light equally in each direction, whereas others are birefringent, which means that any reflected light is split in two directions. The former are constructed exclusively from isotropic actin and, in the median proportion, show as a dark line called the Z line. The latter are made of anisotropic filaments of myosin, and at the centre have a zone that is less dense optically - this referred to as the H zone. This area disappears when the muscle contracts. When the clear and dark bands correspond, it gives the tissue the characteristic striped aspect. The area between the two Z bands is called the sarcomere, and is the basic functional unit in contraction of the striated muscles.

The myofilaments, are also all oriented parallel to the axis of the myofibrils. Running through the fibrils there is a branching network of intracellular tubules. The sarcoplasmic network communicates with the surrounding areas through a series of pores and with a system of membrane terminals that form expansions called tanks. In this region there large quantities of reserve Ca2+ ions, which are released when an action potential arrives.

Characterised by rapid contractions, the striated muscles are involved in both voluntary and involuntary movements of the skeleton. They are governed by the central nervous system, and are more or less directly related to the bone system. The tendons are formed from tissue rather than elastic connective fibres, and their presence makes it possible for bones to rotate on the joints without failure.

If there is nothing to stop the muscle shortening, the contraction is isotonic and although not much force is developed, the process happens at the maximum possible speed. On the other hand, if there is resistance to the muscle's movement preventing it from shortening, the maximum force is developed, and the contraction is isometric. In each muscle, then, the fibres react to stimuli from nerves that are completely independent of them, and as a result the action potentials that are created to generate contractions are specific to each one. For example, in the same muscle fibre you can find both fast fibres and slow fibres, each having different speeds of contraction and relaxation. In this situation, contrary to what happens in a single muscle fibre, the power developed by a group of muscles that are in a state of contraction increases with any increasing intensity of the stimulus. There is, therefore, proportionately more overall strength developed by the muscle, as the power available is made up of the sum of the forces of all the individual muscle fibres involved. It is when all of a muscle's fibres are activated by high frequency stimuli from the central nervous system and tetanic contractions occur, that the maximum power is developed.

The response mechanics of muscle, therefore, are different to those produced by a single fibre. They do not follow the law of 'all or nothing', and the intensity of the contraction does not depend on

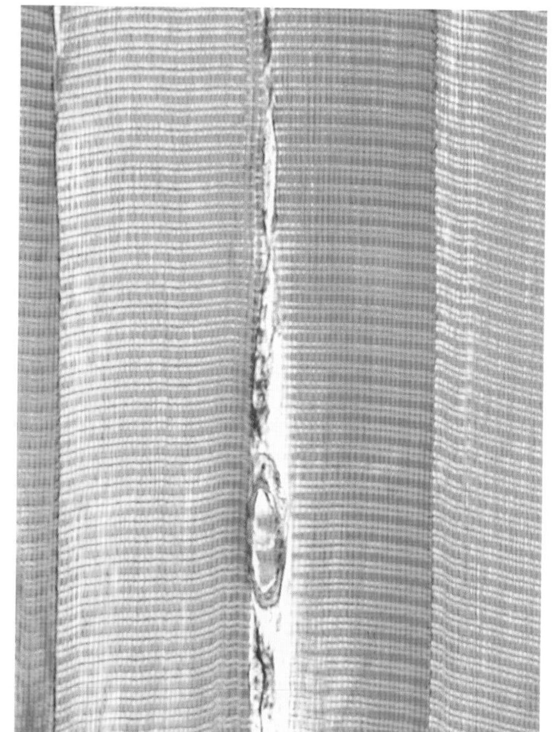

◀ **Striated muscle**
Optical photomicrograph of a longitudinal section of skeletal muscle, showing characteristic striation of the fibers.

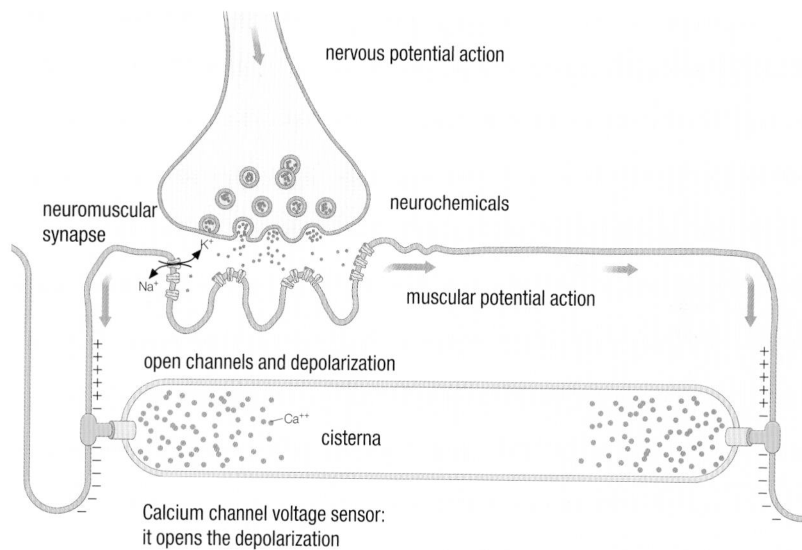

▼ **Contraction**
The arrival of the stimulus to the presynaptic terminal causes the release of neurotransmitters which induce the postsynaptic membrane potential by action. This propagates up to the T-tubules (= transverse) where, by changing the conformation of a protein, opens Ca^2 + channels. Ions accumulated in the sarcoplasmic reticulum, spread out among myofilament, initiating the contraction.

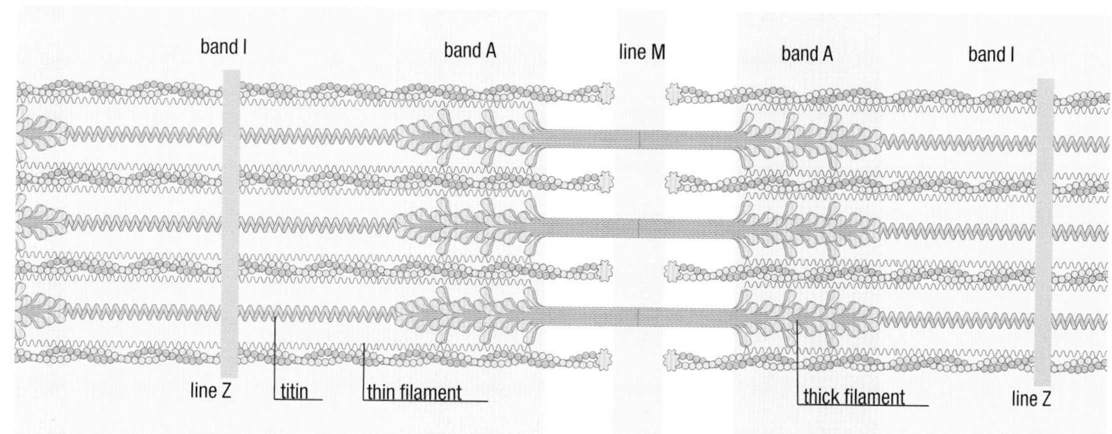

◀ **Filaments**
Diagram of the arrangement of filaments of the sarcomere in a section parallel to the axis of the myofibril. The thin filaments are anchored to Z lines, those are held in place by large molecules of titin in turn connected to lines Z.

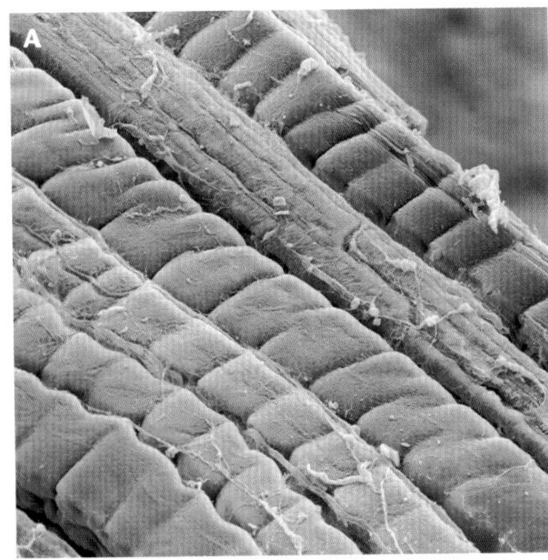

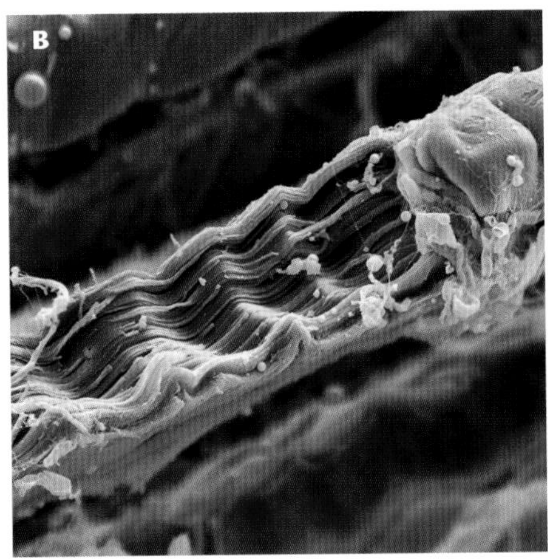

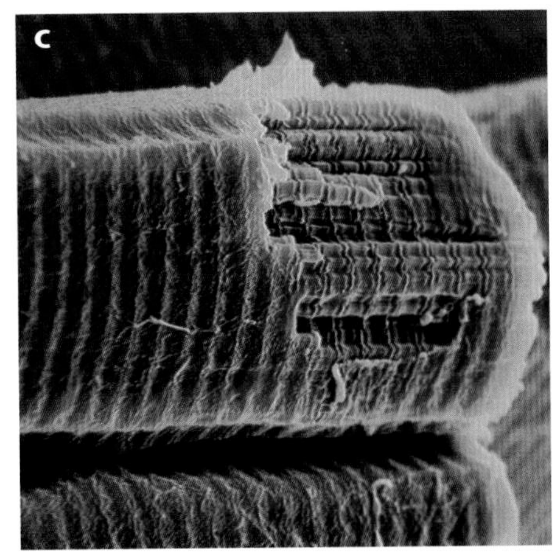

▲ **Muscles under the microscope**
SEM image in false colors, showing the muscles and skeletal muscle fibers at different magnifications: **A.** *skeletal fibers that have the appearance of "stripes" due to the alternating bands of actin and myosin.* **B.** *Skeletal muscle fibers are long and cylindrical: one of them has been opened to show the constituent myofibrils. The fibers of connective tissue (yellow) belong to the endomysium.* **C.** *Striated muscle fibers. Along the length of each fiber are characteristic protein crystallizations in myofibrils: the alternation of different proteins creates light and dark areas.*

the intensity the individual stimuli. Instead, it is the frequency with which they occur. This phenomenon makes it possible for the nervous system to adjust the force of contraction.
The number of muscle fibres that take part in an action also determine the muscle tone. If the muscle must undertake a very delicate task, each nerve will be linked with just few muscle fibres. If, on the other hand, the action requires power but little precision, every nerve is linked to a higher number of muscle fibres. The group of innervations on branches of the same nerve fibre are said to form a motor unit, and usually, the number of motor units for muscle is very high. So, the strength of a muscle contraction can be modulated not only by varying the frequency of stimuli, but also by changing the number of motor drives enabled.
If the stimulation of muscle is prolonged, phenomena can occur that are connected to fatigue. The tetanic voltage decreases, and if the muscles are not relaxed, constriction can set in. Various factors contribute to muscle fatigue - the cellular energy reserves become exhausted, there is an accumulation of acid lactic and other toxic or inorganic phosphate metabolites, and the pH can fall to injurious levels.

SMOOTH MUSCLES

The muscles that are made up of myocellular tissue can be seen under the optic microscope to be homogeneous. That is, they do not have a succession of bands with different optical characteristics; these are referred to as smooth muscles.
Their main features are:

- smooth muscles are found in the visceral cavities (the digestive tract, blood vessels, uterus, etc.). For the most part they are so called because they are organised in clusters that are both electrically and mechanically linked. They are therefore capable of being excited or relaxed as though they were a single cell, even if only one of them is stimulated. This constitutes a form of functional regulation, which is oriented in alternate layers. The end result is that they produce slow muscle contractions that can lasts for long periods of time;
- multiunits muscles are formed by cells that have independent activities, they are contracted only for individual tasks. These muscles are used in places where fast contractions are required. For instance, in the walls of large blood vessels, in the bronchi, to make rapid adjustments in the eye, and so on.

Smooth muscles are smaller than striated muscles: they measure between 100 and 300 μm in length and between 2-5 μm in diameter. They have a single nucleus, little myoglobin, a few mitochondria and little in the way of glycogen stores. Despite the structural differences, the contraction of smooth muscle is initiated in a similar manner to that of striate fibres, being always produced by an increase in intracellular Ca2+ ions. They do, however, have very different mechanical functions to those of the skeletal muscles. If they are stretched (elongated), for example, against a strong resistance and they are able to relax, they can clear the initial tension within a few seconds. As a result, they may even triple their length for repeated elongations. Conversely, they can shorten themselves down to around 70 % of the original length. This property, called plastic adaptability, characterises the walls of such anatomical bodies as the stomach or uterus. Furthermore, the contraction takes place about 20 times more slowly than with striated muscle, even

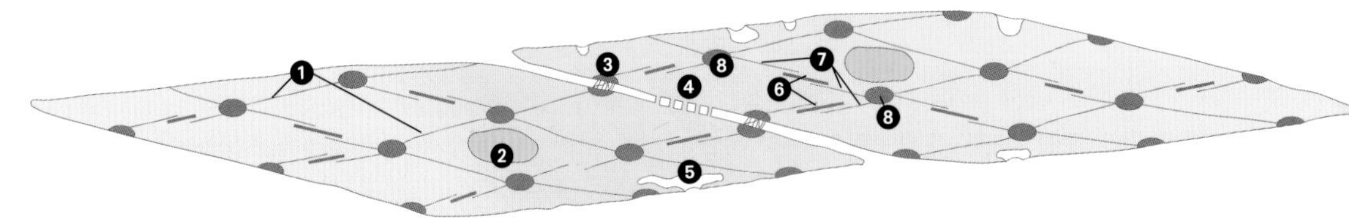

▶ **Smooth myofibers**
Structure of two smooth tissue myocells: ❶ *intermediate filaments;* ❷ *nucleus;* ❸ *Desmosome or attached junction (spatial distance of 20-60 nm);* ❹ *junction gap (junction ion: the space between the plasma membrane is only 2-3 nm);* ❺ *sarcoplasmic reticulum;* ❻ *thick filaments;* ❼ *thin filaments;* ❽ *dense bodies.*

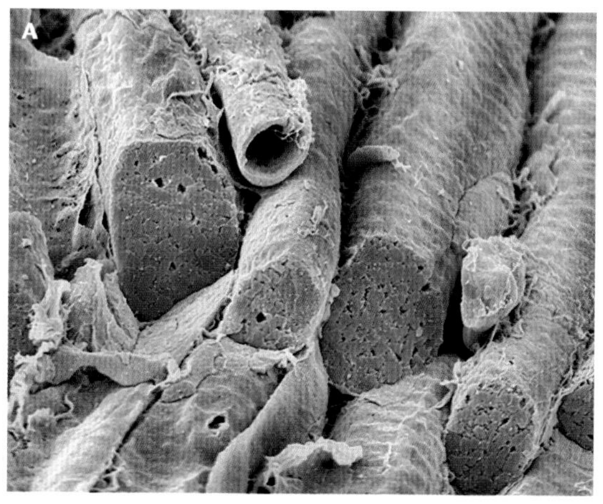

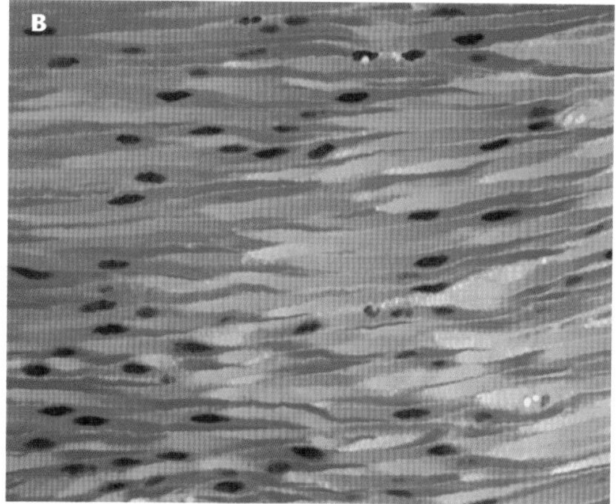

◀ **Smooth muscle**
A. *Scanning Electron Microscope image in false colors of smooth muscle fibers (pink). Top left, a blood vessel (red). The cross section shows smaller fibers surrounded by larger fibers.* **B**. *Images of smooth muscle under an optical microscope. It is composed of fusiform myocells grouped in irregular bundles. The dark spots are the nuclei of each cell.*

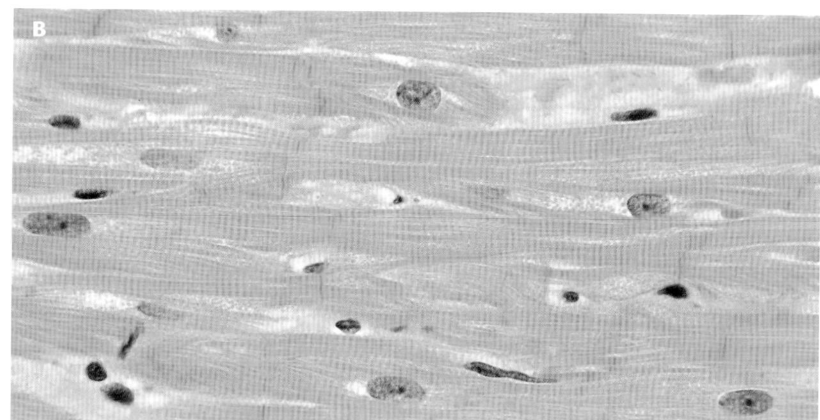

▲ **Cardiac muscle**
A. *SEM image in false colors of fibrils of the heart muscle (blue) surrounded by mitochondria (pink): the vertical T-tubules demarcate the division of sarcomeres. These myofibrils have a diameter of 1-2 microns.* **B**. *Longitudinal section taken with an optical microscope: in each myocell there are 1-2 elongated nuclei and extensive cytoplasmic ramifications (pink). In the interlayer disks (thin pink vertical lines) the electrical resistance is minimal and allows the rapid passage of the stimulus from cell to cell.*

though the developed force is the same. This reduces the energy expenditure, making it very efficient: the consumption of oxygen in the striated muscles is about 30 times higher.

THE LOCOMOTOR NERVOUS CONTROL

Striated muscle. The neurons that innervate the myofibre of the striated muscles are controlled directly and without interruptions from the central nervous system. Each of them innervates a number of muscle fibres through a large number of branches which then divide when they reach the muscle.
The central nervous system modulates the strength of each muscle, varying the number of motor drives that are enabled. This provides fine control over the contracting muscle - and consequently, allows very sensitive movement. The degree to which this happens depends on the number of control units involved in the muscle's movement - the more that are involved, the better the control.
In the eye muscles, for example, each neuron innervates only 6 myofibres, While in the gluteus maximus it innervates 750. On each locomotor neuron, however, it converge with many others:
- The afferent neurons terminate in the same muscle;
- The inter-neurons connect to skin receptors through complex circuits;
- The nerve fibres connect to the neurons in the brain's cortex or the encephalic trunk.

All contribute to modulate the activity of individual motor units. Neurons that innervate the myofibre of striated muscles have cell bodies in the cerebrospinal axis. They are controlled directly and without interruption by the central nervous system. The main motor control routes are:
- The two-way pyramid, this starts in the frontal lobe of the cortex of each cerebral hemisphere, and from there nerve fibres connect to the motor-neurons of the encephalic trunk and the spinal cord;
- The two-way extrapyramidal, these are all motor control routes from the higher centres not included in the pyramid system.

Smooth muscles. The neurons that innervate the myofibre of the smooth muscles have synapses outside the cerebrospinal axis. They start in the central nervous system, with the axon of one neuron located in the spinal cord or encephalic trunk. This then comes into contact with a second neuron whose cell body is located in the autonomous ganglia, in the vicinity of the spinal cord or of the innervated body.
It is this postganglial neural axon that innervates the visceral muscles, even if the contacts between the nerve endings and the myocellular regions do

Standing & Walking

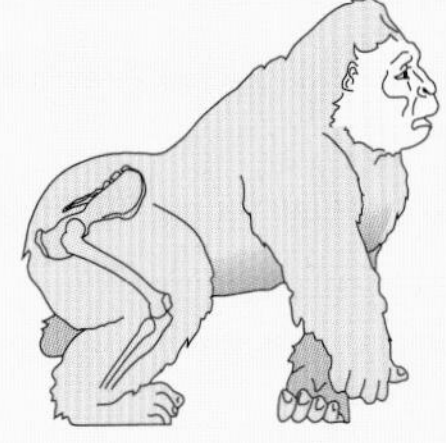

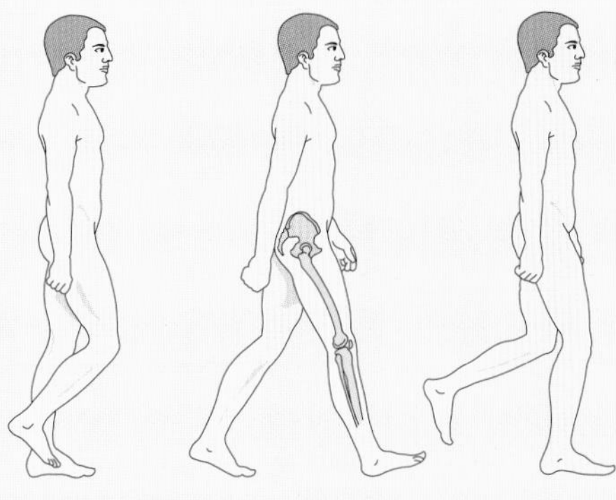

▲ **Walk**
A. *Comparison of the disposition of the bones of the leg in a quadraped and a bipedal human. The angles of the joints are completely different.*

The muscles as a rule, do not act in isolation from one another, in particular the skeletal muscles work closely together. A well studied example of this concerns the maintenance of the standing posture as well as that of walking. In order to achieve this, in addition to special muscular-skeletal structures, there are many muscles with a balanced centralised control system.
It is no coincidence that the way of keeping upright and moving is unique among mammals. The upright stance is not a very efficient solution, considering that just a small push can cause the individual to lose their balance. The centre of gravity of the body is, in fact, situated in a position that guarantees an unstable equilibrium. Walking is therefore results in a continuous "recover from a fall" state.
Metabolic tests, however, have shown that a body consumes more energy whilst sleeping than it does while walking. This is due to a perfect balance of forces that occur in the anatomical structures involved.
The **spine**: The vertebral column has a vital role; the three physiological curves (the cervical, thoracic and lumbar) are disposed in such a manner that they balance each other. The function of mechanical support is guaranteed by the stability of these curves, which are held in place by ligaments and by the continuous vertebral adjustments made by the muscles which compensate for any event that varies the overall balance.
The **lower limbs**: The knee and foot bear the majority of the mechanical stresses. They form an exceptionally sturdy structure that is firmly linked to the vertebral column, and have the fundamental task of maintaining the body as a balanced column. In particular, it is the articulation of hip that solves many of the major static and dynamic problems. Supported and consolidated by strong muscles and ligaments, it allows the femur to move whilst maintaining functional support. It is centred, tilted to 41° above the horizontal, and has the neck inclined at 125°, and the head of the neck inclined at 12°-30°.
The **knee joint**: Co-ordination of the knee is perhaps the heaviest of all the static and dynamic skeletal functions, both supporting and moving the body. Its stability is guaranteed by strong ligaments, while the meniscus increases the area on which the weight of femur bears. Finally, the joint capsule is filled with synovial fluid that acts as an integral shock absorber.
The ANKLE is responsible for a large proportion of the body's stability and co-ordination, and distributes the weight of the body onto the arches and soles of the feet. This reduces the amount of work the muscles have to undertake.
The **foot** provides both a means of support and a mechanism for movement that works as a lever amplification system and is the driving force of the leg. Whilst walking it acts to smooth the overall movement and distribute the body's weight evenly on the ground.
Despite these solutions, the problem of maintaining balance remains and a fall is always possible. The body's sophisticated sensory systems are continuously involved in the maintenance of the relationship between it and the three-dimensional environment.

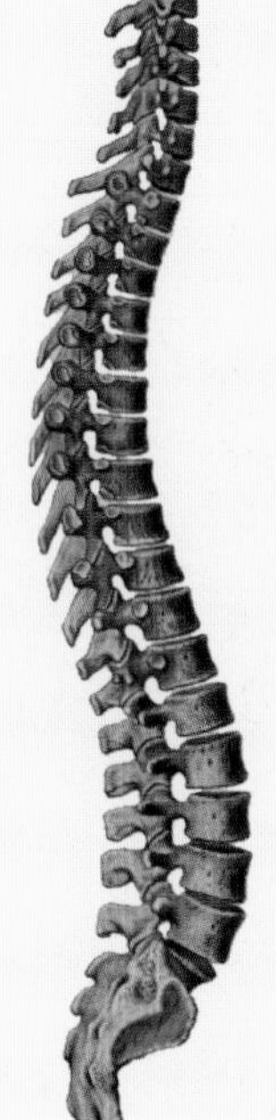

◀ **Curve**
The curves of the human spine help to stabilize the entire bone scaffold and better distribute the weight on the lumbar region, the basin and the lower limbs, when standing still or walking:
cervical lordosis;
dorsal kyphosis;
lumbar lordosis.

◀ **Standing muscles**
The contrasting activities of the muscles keeps the leg set vertically, with the centroid falling into the sole of the foot support.

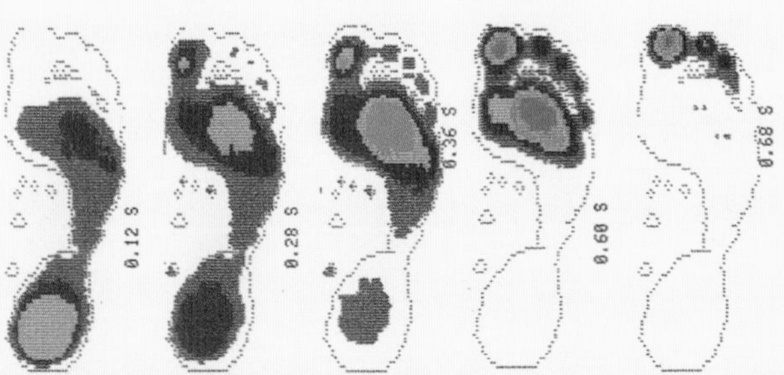

◀ **Pedobarograph**
Changes in pressure on parts of the foot while walking. The colors from white to green areas indicate increased pressure.

not appear to be differentiated. It forms mediated chemical synapses that often participate in the muscular actions. These motor-neurons, indeed, can belong to the central nervous system or the parasympathetic ▶177, and can initiate both excitation actions or inhibitory ones. The central nervous system fibres are generally involved in stimulating activities, whereas those of the parasympathetic nervous system are usually inhibitory. Both, however, always have an antagonist effect when they innervate the same muscle. While the stimulating fibres can cause or increase muscle contraction, the inhibitory fibres raise the threshold of muscle excitability, or reduce the frequency of the contractions.

Motor coordination. At any time, therefore, any motor-neurone produces actions by the sum of exciter stimulation and inhibitors. This defines its level of excitement and its frequency. A body's movements are the result of many muscles that at any one time are either enabled or relaxed. For this to happen reliably, it needs to be very well co-ordinated, and this is successfully achieved by a large number of motor-neurons that overlap their information in complex neuronal circuits. Unfortunately, a great still needs to be learned about exactly how this is done, as our knowledge of the detail is still poor.

◀ **Movement**
To move the body consciously you require more than just a muscular-skeletal system: there is need for accurate and coordinated cooperation of all other functional systems.

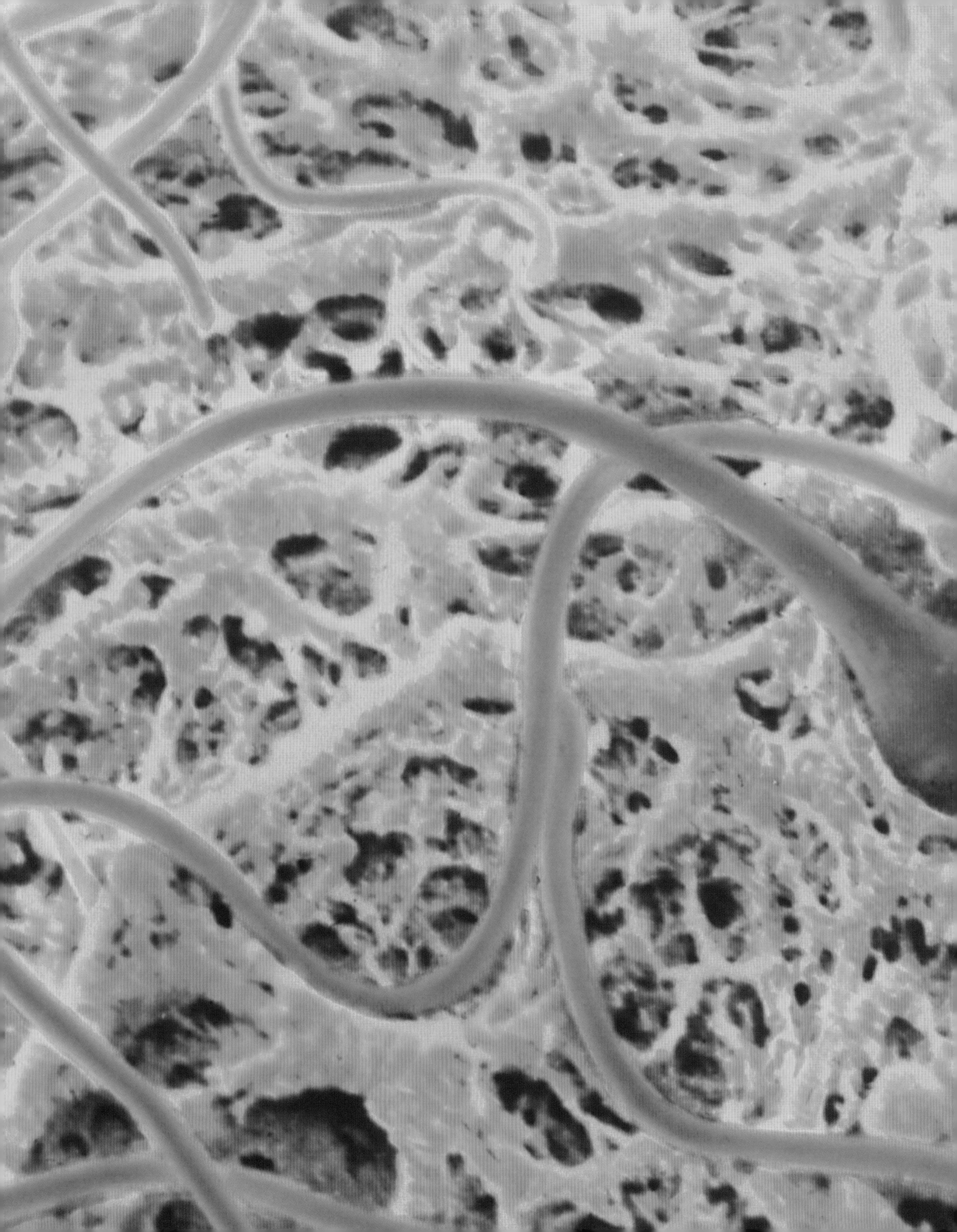

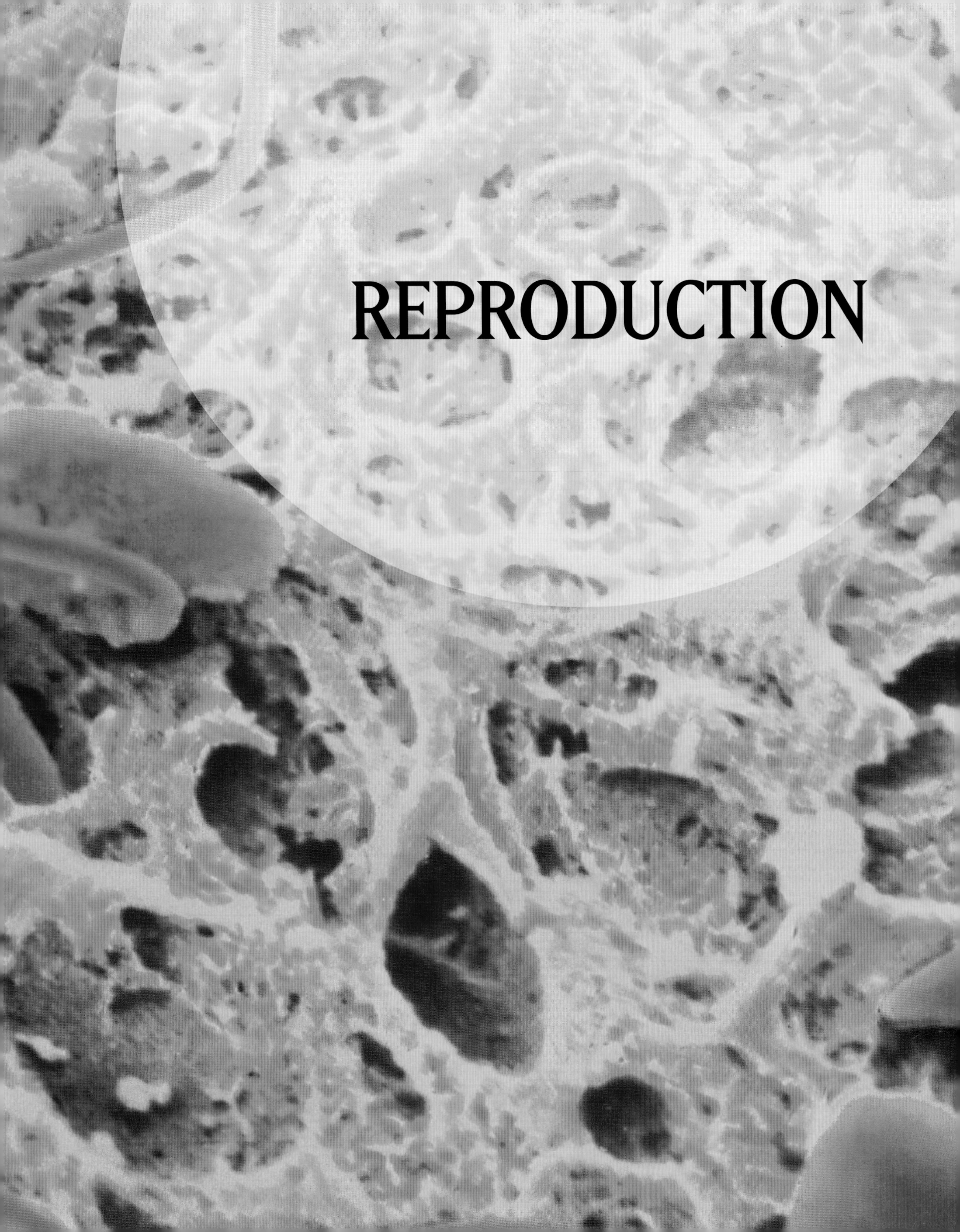

REPRODUCTION

Reproducing is the ultimate goal of every organism, even if not a vital function: it certainly does not require replication to be able to live well, and this is especially true in the case of man, where breeding has become a choice.

THE MAIN EVENTS OF REPRODUCTION

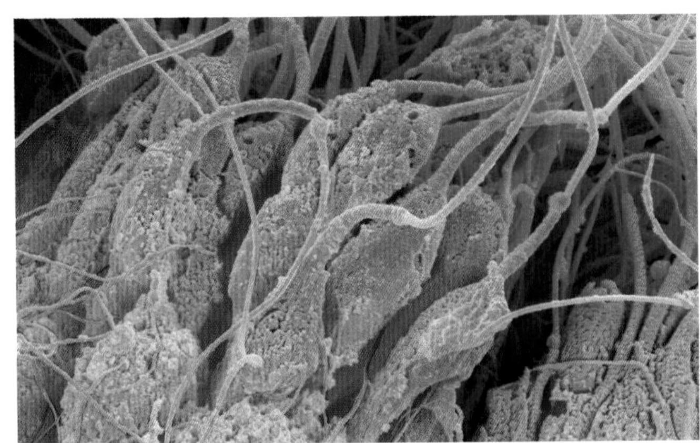

▶ **Seminiferous tubule**
Scanning electron microscope photographs of a section of seminiferous tubule in false colors and in two different magnifications. At the interior, are the blue tails of newly formed sperm, leaning against tailless spermatids.

The breeding systems of the male and female are structurally similar: they both feature two gonads that produce gametes, i.e. cells with a small number of chromosomes intended for breeding, as well as various tubes that link with the outside world and allow the gametes to meet.

The differences are mostly in the actual reproductive organs: the male's penis is erectile in order to make it possible to deposit sperm in the female. The female's vagina and uterus are equipped to accept and nourish an unborn child until birth. The production of gametes, coupling, fertilisation of the embryo, its development, the confinement and lactation, are all phenomena related to reproduction and controlled almost exclusively by the neuro-endocrine system.

THE PRODUCTION OF GAMETES

The first of the various processes that must happen for a reproductive event to occur is the production of gametes in a process called gametogenesis.

The male: from puberty onwards, the pituitary gland secretes the protein hormone gonadotropin - this stimulates the production of testosterone by the Leydig cells which are located in the seminiferous tubules of the testes ▸210. This induces the production of sperm and determines the development of a number of secondary sexual characters. It also ensures the maintenance of the functions that are necessary for sexual activity. Growth and differentiation of sperm takes place under the supervision of the follicle-stimulating hormone (FSH), but their final maturation occurs outside of the seminiferous tubes, and is due to the combined action of gonadotropin and testosterone.

The female: the first stage is initiated by follicle-stimulating hormones (FSH) being secreted by the pituitary gland - these stimulate the ovaries to begin the process of puberty. This causes physiological changes in the skeleton, muscular system, brain, breasts, and reproductive organs. The ovaries do not start producing eggs until after the menarche (the

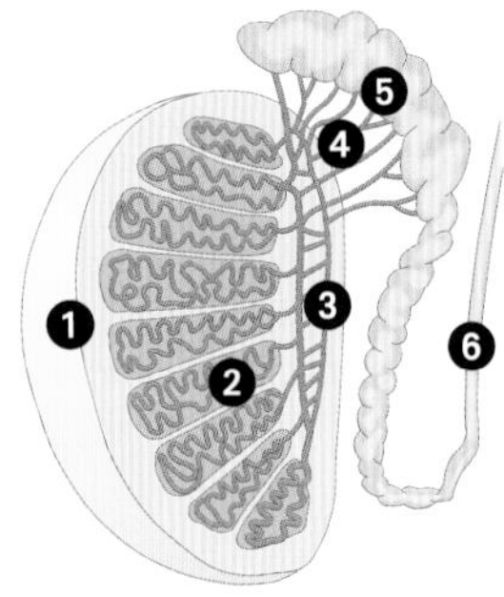

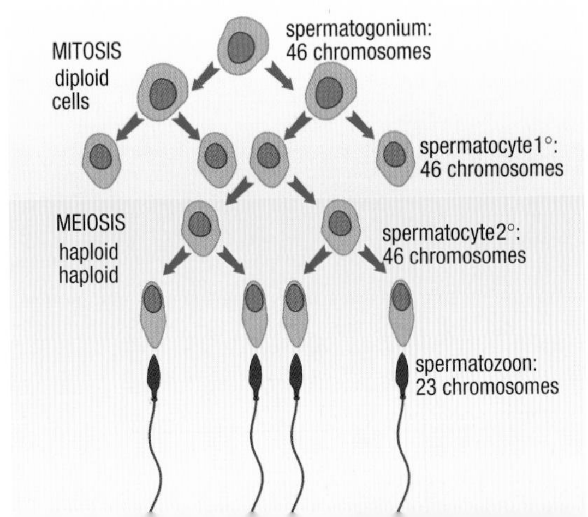

▲▶ **Spermatogenesis**
Structure of a testicle and on the right, the process that leads to the formation of sperm with a half the number of chromosomes. ❶ *Capsule;* ❷ *seminiferous tubules;* ❸ *Network testis;* ❹ *efferent ducts;* ❺ *epididymis;* ❻ *vas deferens.*

first menstruation) has taken place. In stark contrast to the production of vast numbers of male sperm, where many thousands are produced, only small numbers of eggs are involved in each cycle. These are produced by structures known as the ovarian follicles - during each menstrual cycle around 20 to 30 begin maturing, but typically only one reaches ovulation - the others then degenerate into corpus luteum ▸210. Once expelled, the ovum migrates along the Fallopian tube - it is here that the ovum must meet with sperm in order to be fertilised.

COUPLING

For coupling to take place successfully, sexual desire is essential, and this is related to special chemicals that are released by the brain. These include small quantities of dopamine and serotonin. There is also a reduction in the production of endorphins by the hypothalamus while at the same time it increases the production of Growth Hormones ▸198.

Sexual arousal is linked to a series of specific psycho-physical phenomena - these constitute the so-called sexual response cycle. It is distinguished by four phases:

- excitement or arousal phase - this covers the first signs of sexual excitement, and is usually accompanied by such physical activity as petting and genital stimulation. There may also be increases in sweating and pulse rate - one or both participants may also fantasise. The male's penis will begin to swell, followed by full erection. The female's arousal is signified by secretions of vaginal lubricant and certain overt physical factors such as pupil dilation and swollen nipples.
- plateau phase - this is the stage between initial arousal and orgasm; it is accompanied by the act of penetration, where the penis is inserted into the vagina.
- orgasm - this is accompanied by intense feelings of pleasure, although the intensity of this depends on a number of factors, including the level of arousal, the effectiveness of the physical stimulation and the psychological predisposition. The orgasm consists of a series of contractions - in the female it is mainly felt in the vaginal and uterine areas as well as the clitoris; in males it is felt in the penis and prostate regions.
- resolution phase, this is the stage where there is a progressive reduction in sexual tension, although there are profound differences between how it occurs in men and women. If the stimulation continues, the female may experience a fresh orgasm. The male, however, undergoes a refractory period, the duration of which is extremely variable and subjective. It is characterised by a rapid reduction in the swelling of the penis and a raising in the threshold of excitability.

The intensity and duration of each phase varies considerably due to the strong psychological involvement. This may stimulate or even depress the desire for sexual activity.

The male: the most sensitive area of the male reproductive organs is the glans. This forms the head of the penis, and is rich in the specific receptors that transmit sensations through the spinal cord to the brain. Sexual excitement causes the release of the hormone testosterone, which in turn triggers a

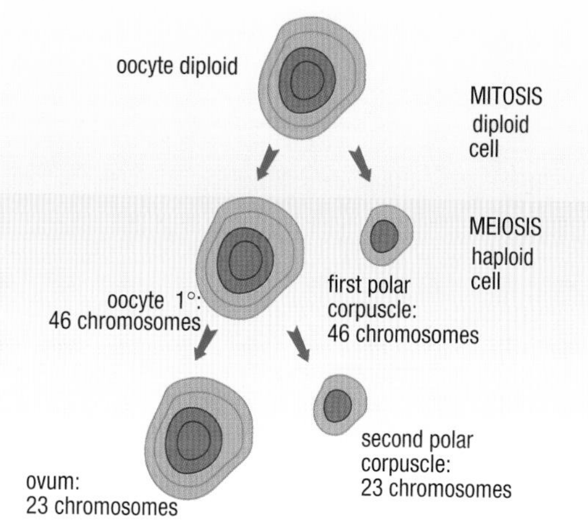

◀ **Oogenesis**
Process that leads to the formation of eggs with half the number of chromosomes.

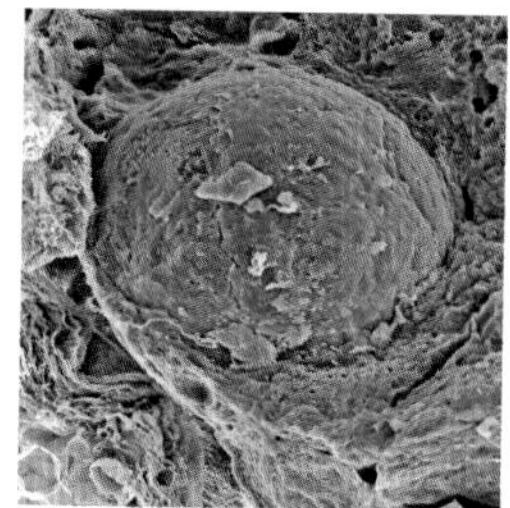

▲ **Ovulation**
Ovum in dehiscence photographed with a scanning electron microscope (SEM) in false colors.

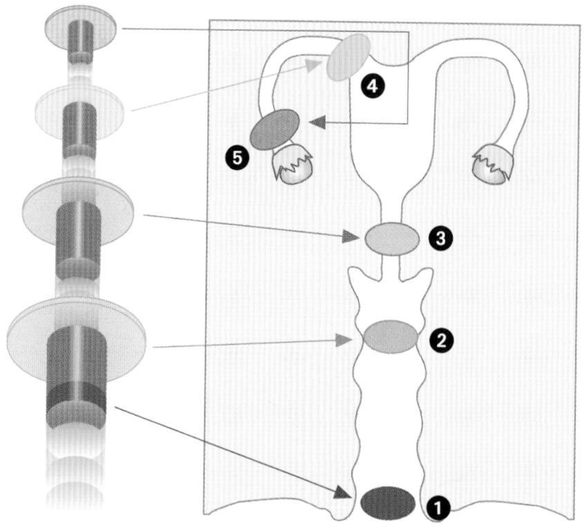

▼◀ **Sperm selection**
The number of sperm that remain viable at all levels of the female reproductive system is dramatically reduced: ❶ up to 1/4 of the 350 million is anomalous and non-competitive; ❷ cervical mucus, many sperm are destroyed by released enzymes that allow others to pass; ❸ only 1 million comes to the cervix; ❹ about 1000 arrive at the fallopian tube; ❺ about 100 reach the ovum.

◀ **Capacitazione**
Spermatozoa on the surface of the uterus seen by scanning electron microscope (SEM) in false colors. Moving through the uterine cilia (yellow), they undergo the process of capacitation, which takes about 7 hours, the layer of glycoproteins and seminal plasma protein that covers the head is removed, allowing those who reach the egg, to release the enzymes needed to fertilize.

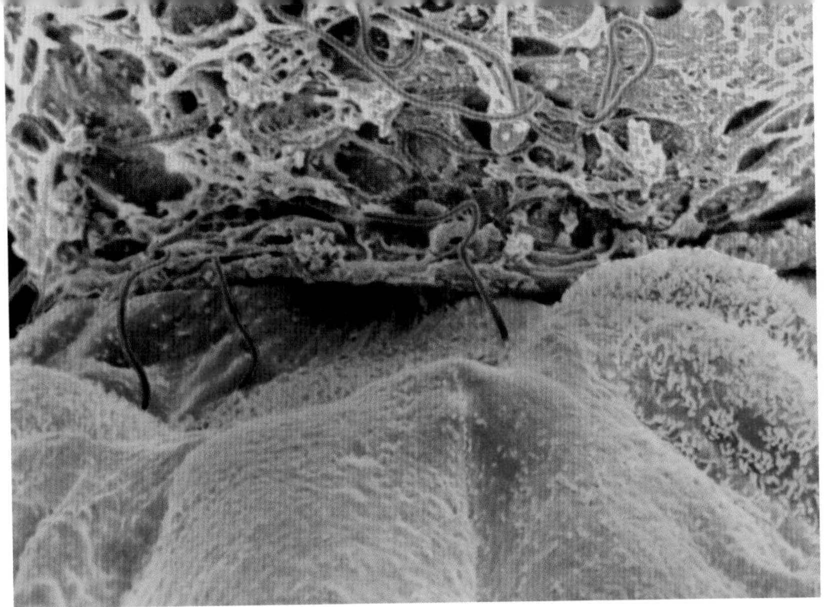

strong blood flow to the penis, which then brings about an erection. The male orgasm is characterised by a series of violent rhythmic contractions followed by ejaculation, which is the release of semen and fluid accessories in the urethra.

The female: the first stage of excitement is vaginal lubrication - this makes the coupling possible. The secretions also contribute to reducing the acidity of the vagina, which helps the motile sperm survive. The centres that control the female's sexual response are located at the medullar level, and are connected to the central nervous system. The stimulation of the clitoris activates thousands of nerve fibres, and triggers a series of cardiovascular and endocrine reactions that lead to congestion of the vaginal area. The outer labia relax and smooth out, while the body of the clitoris increases in size and the

▼ **Formation of the placenta**
Formation of embryonic and attached placenta. **A**. *Transformations of the blastocyst,* **B**. *nested embryo elements:* ❶ *embryo;* ❷ *protective amniotic sac,* ❸ *yolk sac gives nutrition for the first weeks,* ❹ *chorion: embryonic membrane extensions which go to form the placenta,* ❺ *uterine wall,* ❻ *allantoic sack gives rise to blood vessels of the umbilical cord.*

▼ **Embryonic layers**
Before joining the uterine wall, the surface of the blastocyst is made of a single type of cells: the cytotrophoblast. Then, they differ in 3 "packages" of cells that give rise to particular types of tissue. ❶ **mesoderm**: *gives rise to cartilage and bone, muscle and the lining of blood vessels and ureters;* ❷ **endoderm**: *gives rise to the surface of the digestive tract and glands related to the surface of the lungs, bronchial, tracheal and larynx;* ❸ **ectoderm**: *gives rise to the brain, nerves and sense organs, the dermis and dermal appendages as well as coatings of nose, mouth and anus.*

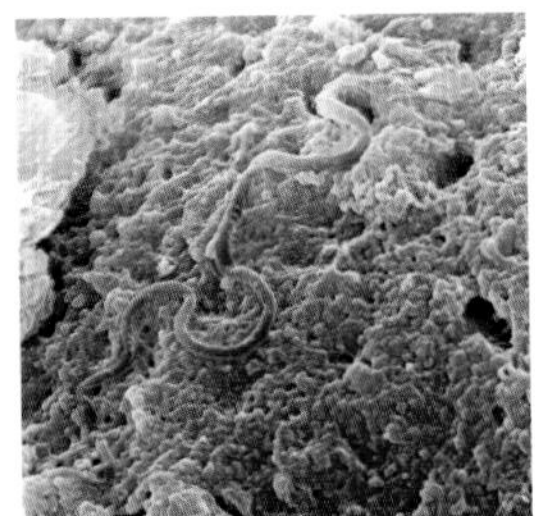

▲ **Fertilization**
SEM photograph in false colors of a human embryo (blue) in the blastocyst stage (5 days after fertilization). The blastocyst is a hollow sphere formed by cells called blastomeres and a center fluid. Most of them will form the placenta and embryonic membranes: only a small group (the inner part) will form the embryo proper. Here, the blastocyst is detaching from the pellucid zone (greenish), the protein shell that surrounded it before fertilization in which were trapped some sperm tails (red). At this stage, the blastocyst is ready to implant.

▲ **Fertilization**
SEM photograph in false colors, showing a sperm fertilizing an egg.

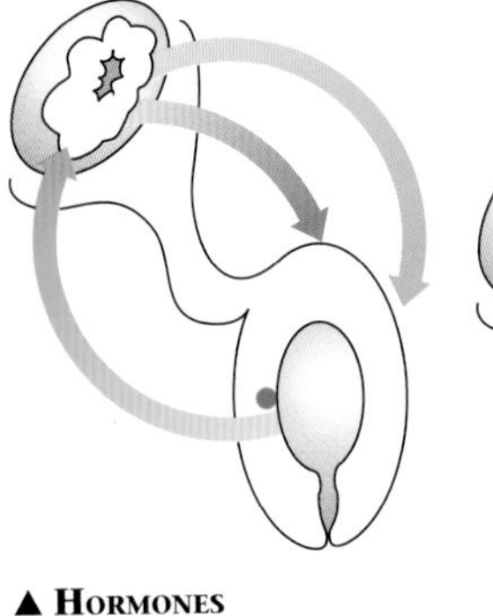

▲ **Hormones**
Chorionic gonadotropin maintains active production
estrogen
progesterone by the corpus luteum. From the third month, the placenta takes over.

▼▶ **Placenta**
False color SEM: villi inside of the placenta with exposed side and, in the box, details of villi.

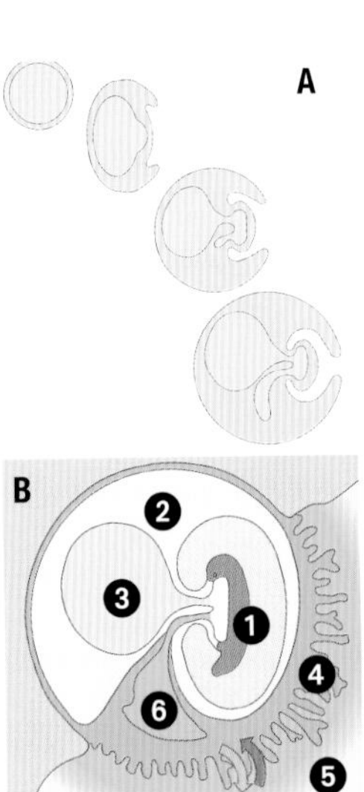

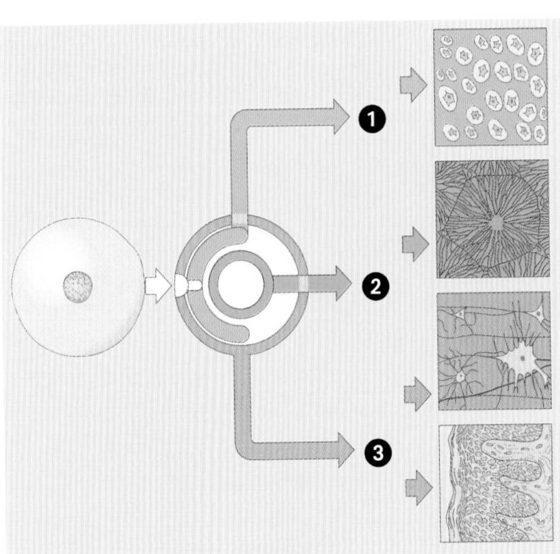

REPRODUCTION

vaginal wall is lubricated throughout. When orgasm is reached, the vagina expands and contracts while the uterus raises the cervical channel making it possible for the semen to be deposited in a favourable position.

THE EMBRYO & PLACENTA

If fertilisation takes place, the corpus luteum persists, whereupon it becomes known as the corpus luteum graviditatis. In this state progesterone continues to be excreted - this prevents the maturation of the ovarian follicles and inhibits the contraction of the uterine muscles. It also helps to thicken the lining of the uterine walls.

Implantation Phase: the lining of the uterus is called the endometrium - during the peak of the menstrual cycle it becomes enriched with blood-filled tissue. If a blastocyst (fertilised embryo) is released into the uterus - typically around the fifth day after fertilisation, it adheres to the endometrium in a process referred to as implantation. This allows nutrients to reach the rapidly growing embryo. A typical human pregnancy lasts 39 weeks.

Decidualisation: this is a process that occurs in the placenta if the womb has adequate support of oestrogens and progesterone. In essence, it involves a series of changes in the uterus that make it possible for an embryo to be implanted.

CONFINEMENT & LACTATION

At the end of pregnancy, childbirth is induced by the release of oxytocin. There are several stages, however, with the first being referred to as the 'latent phase'. This takes place during the last few weeks of pregnancy, and is characterised by initial cervical dilation and the onset of contractions. The next stage is known as the 'dilation phase', and is considered to have begun when the cervix is about 3cm. This is when labour begins, and its duration can vary considerably, with first-time mothers typically taking much longer than those who have previously given birth. After this comes the 'expulsion phase' - this is when the baby is actually delivered. This is followed by the 'placental phase', which is when the afterbirth is expelled.

Confinement is the term given to the period immediately after birth, while the mother and child recover from the consequent stresses. The duration of this varies considerably between different cultures - it may last anywhere between one and one hundred days.

Lactation is also controlled by a combination of nervous and hormonal activity. It begins in the fourth month of gestation, when increased progesterone levels stimulate the growth of cells in the mammary glands.

◄ **Fetus at 8 weeks**
Dimensional relationships between the fetus and placenta.

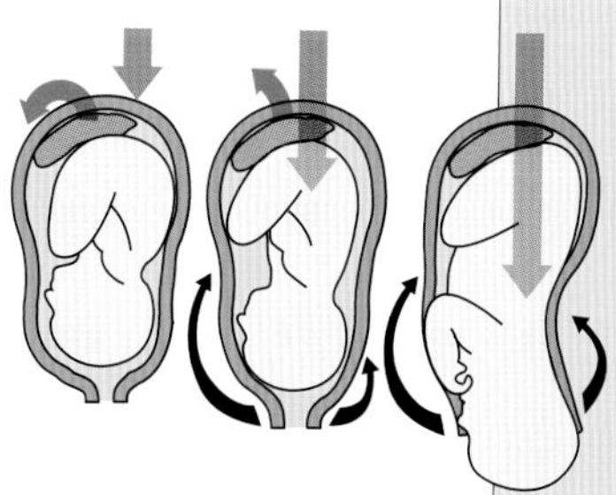

▼ **Childbirth hormones**
The birth is induced by the gradual decrease and production of progesterone, growth of pituitary oxytocin which stimulates muscle contraction of uterus.

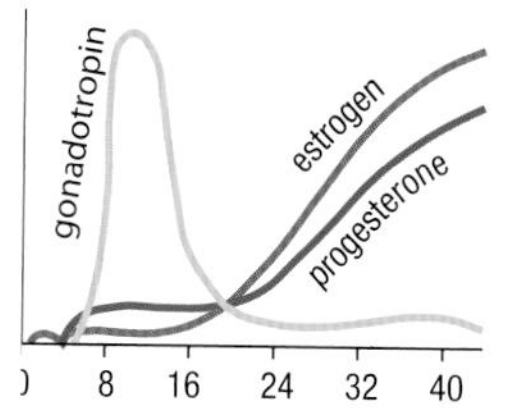

▼ **Maternal hormones**
Changes in plasma hormone concentrations in maternal blood during pregnancy.

▼ **Lactation**
Suckling induces nervous reflex that stimulates the pituitary gland to secrete oxytocin, which stimulates the contraction of muscle fibers by stimulating the removal of the breast milk, and prolactin, which enhances production.

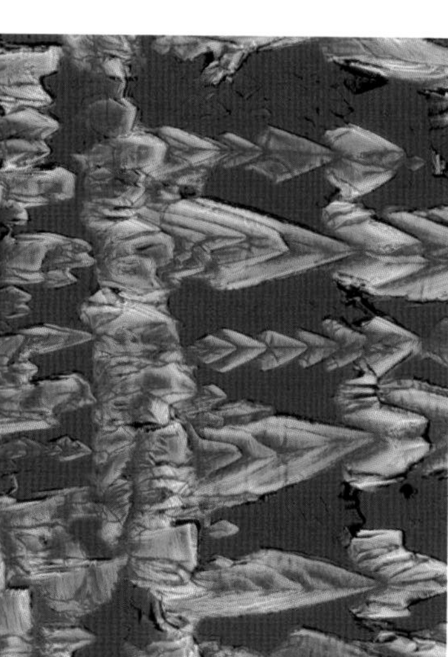

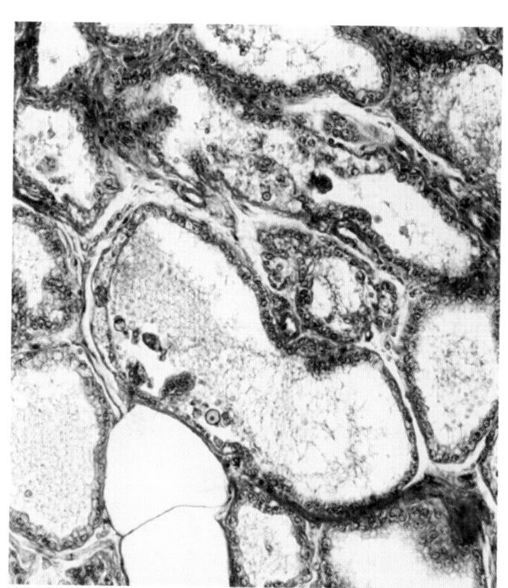

◄◄ **Oxytocin**
Crystals of oxytocin in the electron microscope in polarized light.

◄ **Milky tissue**
Optical microscope section of breast tissue during lactation: the wide spaces surrounded by glandular cells are filled with milk.

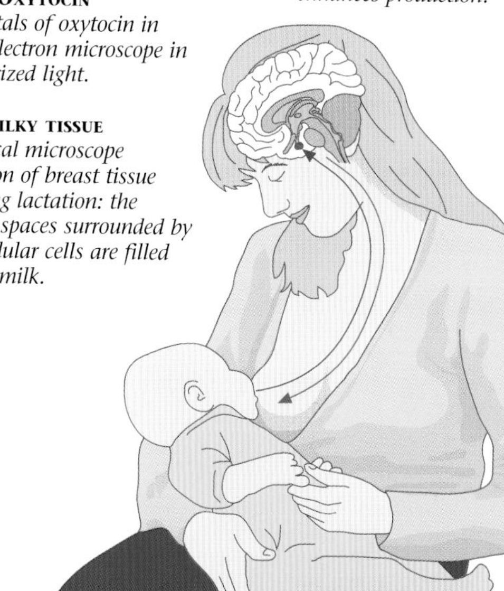

THE BIONIC MAN

Sometimes the complex and functional "human machine", can make mistakes. Modern disciplines such as medicine, surgery, engineering, genetic, embryology have been trying to find a remedy to those problems. While the latest genetic discoveries will hopefully allow us to reproduce "in vitro", and without the risks of rejections (starting from a cell of the patient's body) the necessary tissues for a transplant (from the cerebral tissue to the red blood cells, from the hepatic tissue to that of the pancreas), the attempt to substitute the damaged pieces of the "human machine" have been involving for years other fields such as medicine, engineering and biotechnology. In the recent years we have made much progress in both the development and the use of synthetic materials better fitted for different surgical needs, and in the miniaturization of instruments to assist defective organs, and in the creation of new reconstructive and transplant surgical techniques. For example, we must not forget the recent development of many bioartificial organs: skin, cartilage, bones, semi synthetic ligaments and tendons are already a reality (for those that can afford it) in the US, but also in other advanced institutes.

Genetic engineering is still a big question mark: among thousands of ethical, moral and scientific controversies, research moves on. In the future we will probably have animals cloned with the same characteristics of humans, to be used for xenotransplants; we are already working on the human embryonal tissues, whose cells are still undifferentiated and therefore perfect for the reconstruction of organs perfectly compatible to those of the patients'…

For now, the most popular surgical interventions remain the "traditional" ones: transplants from compatible donors, use of mechanical instruments (such as pacemaker or the artificial articulations), prosthesis that can partially substitute the damaged pieces of our body.

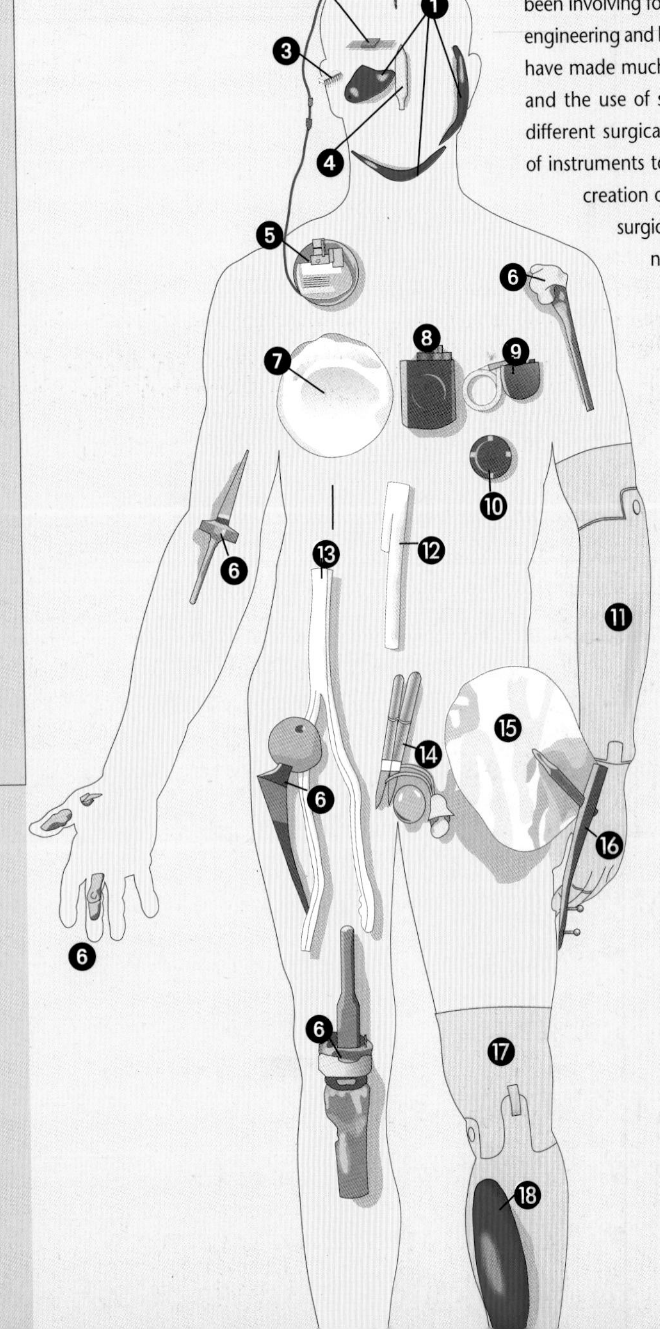

◀ SUBSTITUTIVE PIECES
Here are some popular elements surgically used to substitute organs or missing parts of the body:

1. *different materials prosthesis substitute certain bone structures of the face (zygoma, mandible, maxillary, etc.)*
2. *electronic prosthesis used to increase vision*
3. *electronic prosthesis to increase hearing (hearing aids)*
4. *electronic prosthesis for the reconstruction the nasal septum*
5. *electronic equipment for the regulation of motor impulses, in the cure of Parkinson's disease*
6. *artificial joints: shoulder, elbow, hand, hip, knee*
7. *mammary prosthesis*
8. *cardiac pump*
9. *pacemaker*
10. *titanium cardiac stimulator*
11. *prosthesis of an arm, with electronic hand*
12. *artificial aorta*
13. *artificial veins and arteries*
14. *erectile penile prosthesis*
15. *artificial anus*
16. *articulated femoral prosthesis*
17. *prosthesis of the lower limb, with foot and knee joint*
18. *calf prosthesis*